BOTANICAL ART
TECHNIQUES

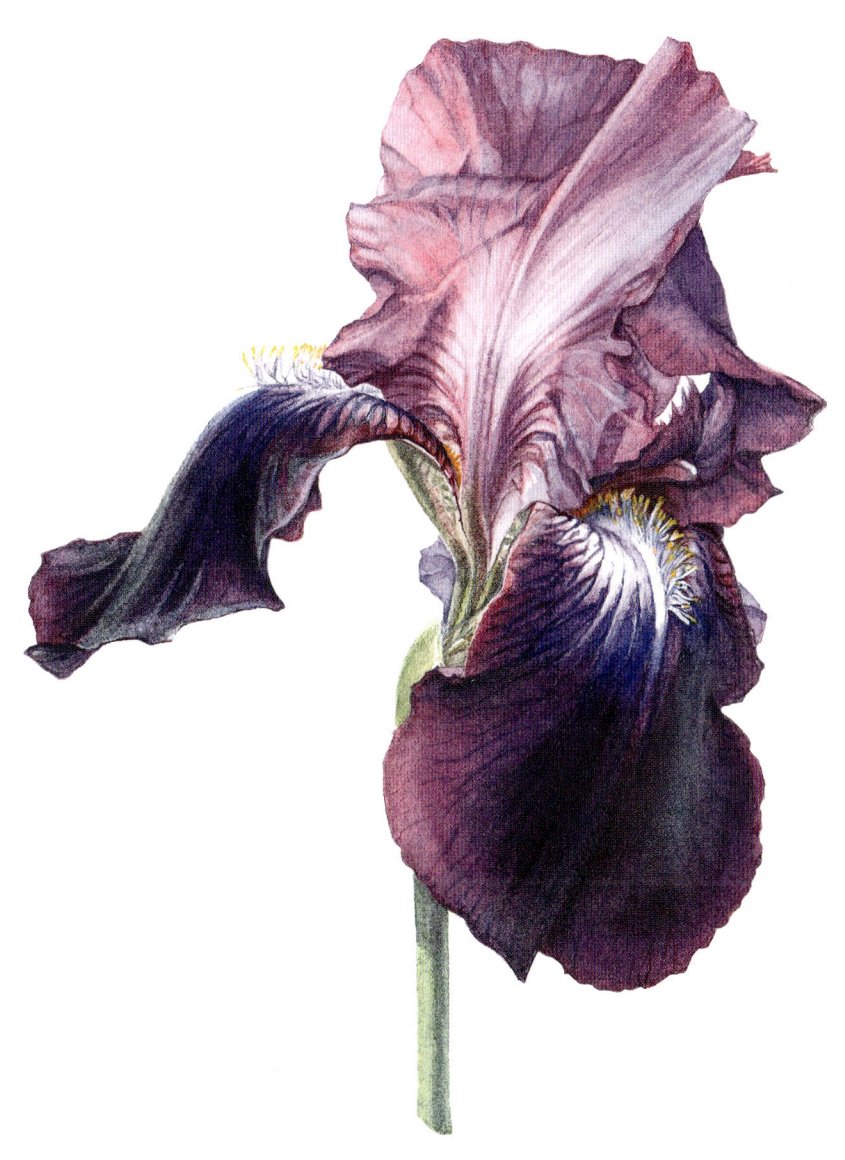

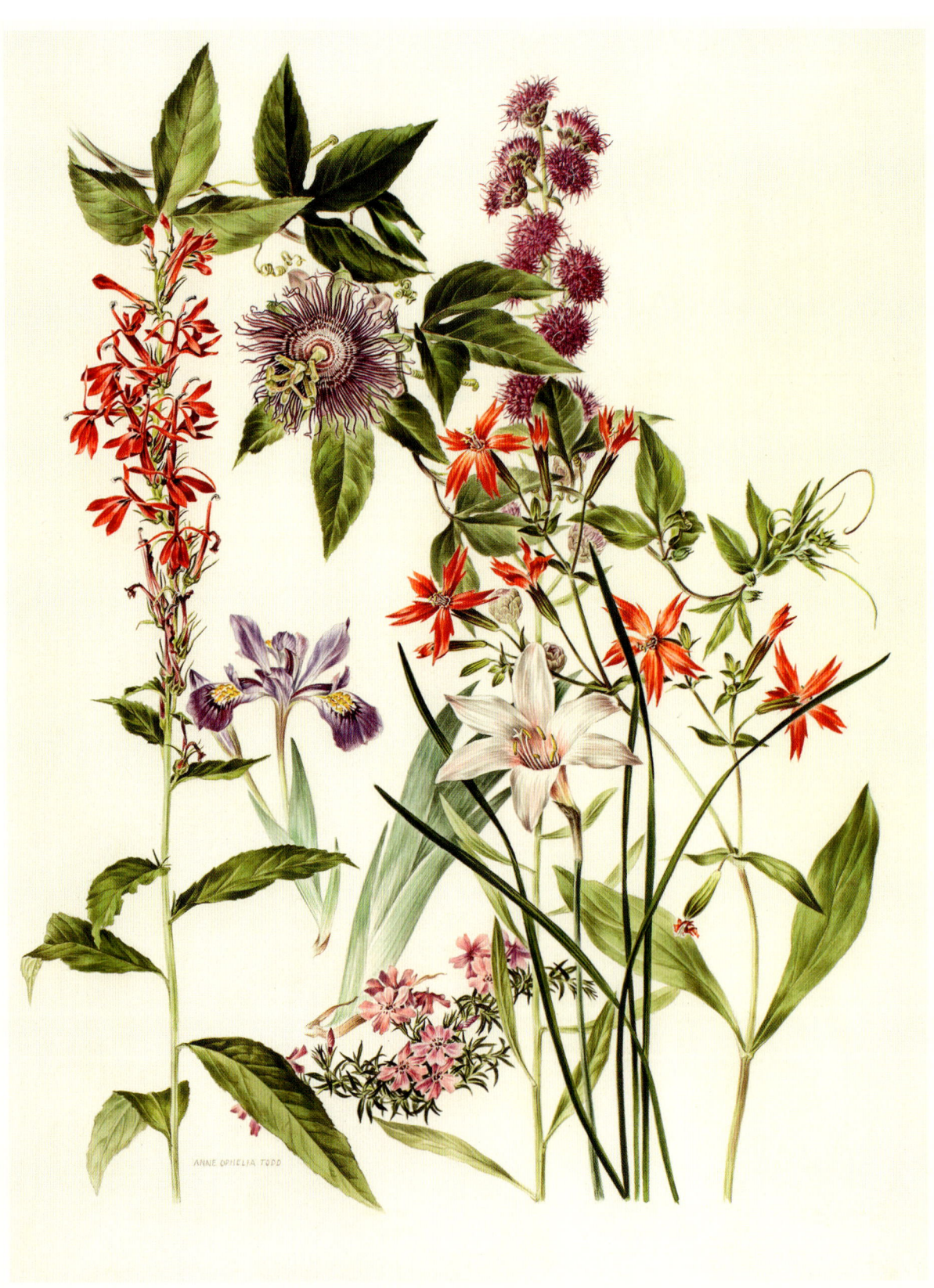

ANNE OPHELIA TODD

BOTANICAL ART
TECHNIQUES

A Comprehensive Guide to

WATERCOLOR, GRAPHITE, COLORED PENCIL,
VELLUM, PEN AND INK, EGG TEMPERA, OILS,
PRINTMAKING, AND MORE

The American Society of Botanical Artists

EDITED BY CAROL WOODIN AND ROBIN A. JESS

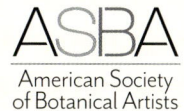

TIMBER PRESS
PORTLAND, OREGON

Page 1: Bearded Iris, Watercolor on paper, 8 × 9 inches [20 × 22.5 cm],
© Constance Sayas

Frontispiece: Southeast: Atamasco lily, *Zephyranthes atamasco*; blazing star,
Liatris aspera; cardinal flower, *Lobelia cardinalis*; crested iris, *Iris cristata*; fire
pink, *Silene virginica*; moss pink, *Phlox subulata*; passion flower, *Passiflora
incarnata*. Watercolor on paper. 22 × 18 ½ inches [55 × 46.25 cm]. From
"Wildflowers for gardens: 50 plants from six U.S. areas are the best to grow
at home," *Life* 42(21): 94, 1957. Anne Ophelia Todd Dowden.
HI Art accession no. 7466.1. Courtesy of Hunt Institute for Botanical
Documentation, Carnegie Mellon University, Pittsburgh, Pennsylvania.

Opposite: B & B, Multiple Circles, Watercolor on paper,
9 ½ × 12 ½ inches [23.75 × 31.25 cm], © Asuka Hishiki

Page 6: Larger Than Life—Two Fading Anemones, *Anemone coronaria*,
Watercolor on paper, 29 × 20 ½ inches [72.5 × 51.25 cm], © Julia Trickey

Page 8: Rhubarb, *Rheum rhabarbarum* 'Glaskins Perpetual', Watercolor on
paper, 25 × 18 ½ inches [62.5 × 46.25 cm], © Elaine Searle

Timber Press
Workman Publishing
Hachette Book Group, Inc.
1290 Avenue of the Americas
New York, New York 10104
timberpress.com

Timber Press is an imprint of Workman Publishing, a division of
Hachette Book Group, Inc. The Timber Press name and logo are
registered trademarks of Hachette Book Group, Inc.

Printed in Shenzhen, China, (APO) on responsibly
sourced paper
Fifth printing 2025

Text design by Adrianna Sutton
Cover design by Isaac Tobin

ISBN 978-1-60469-790-2

A catalog record for this book is available from the
Library of Congress.

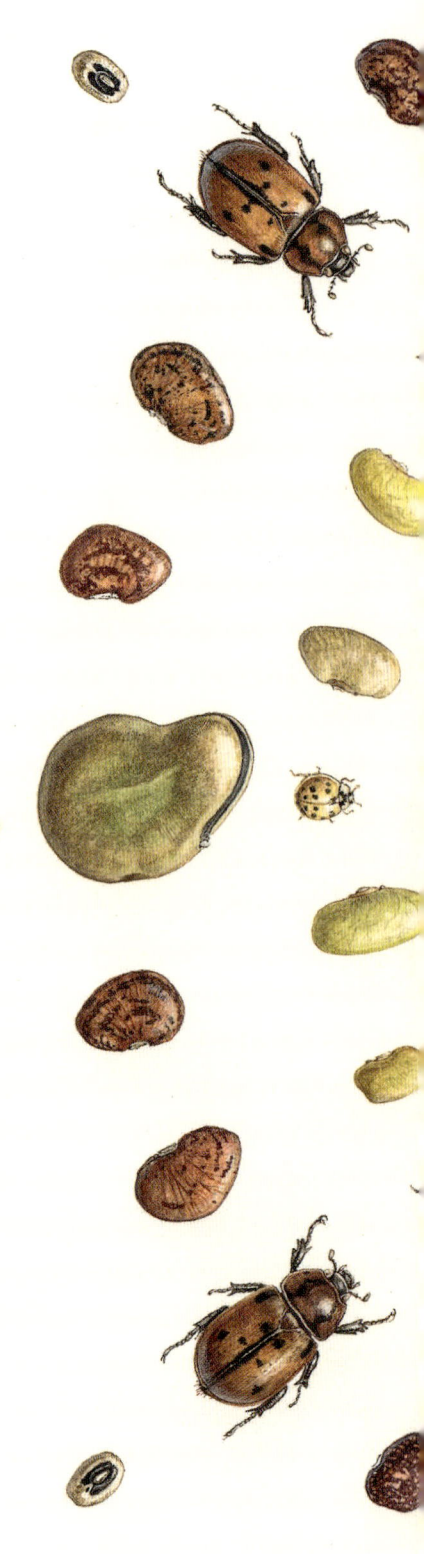

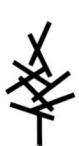

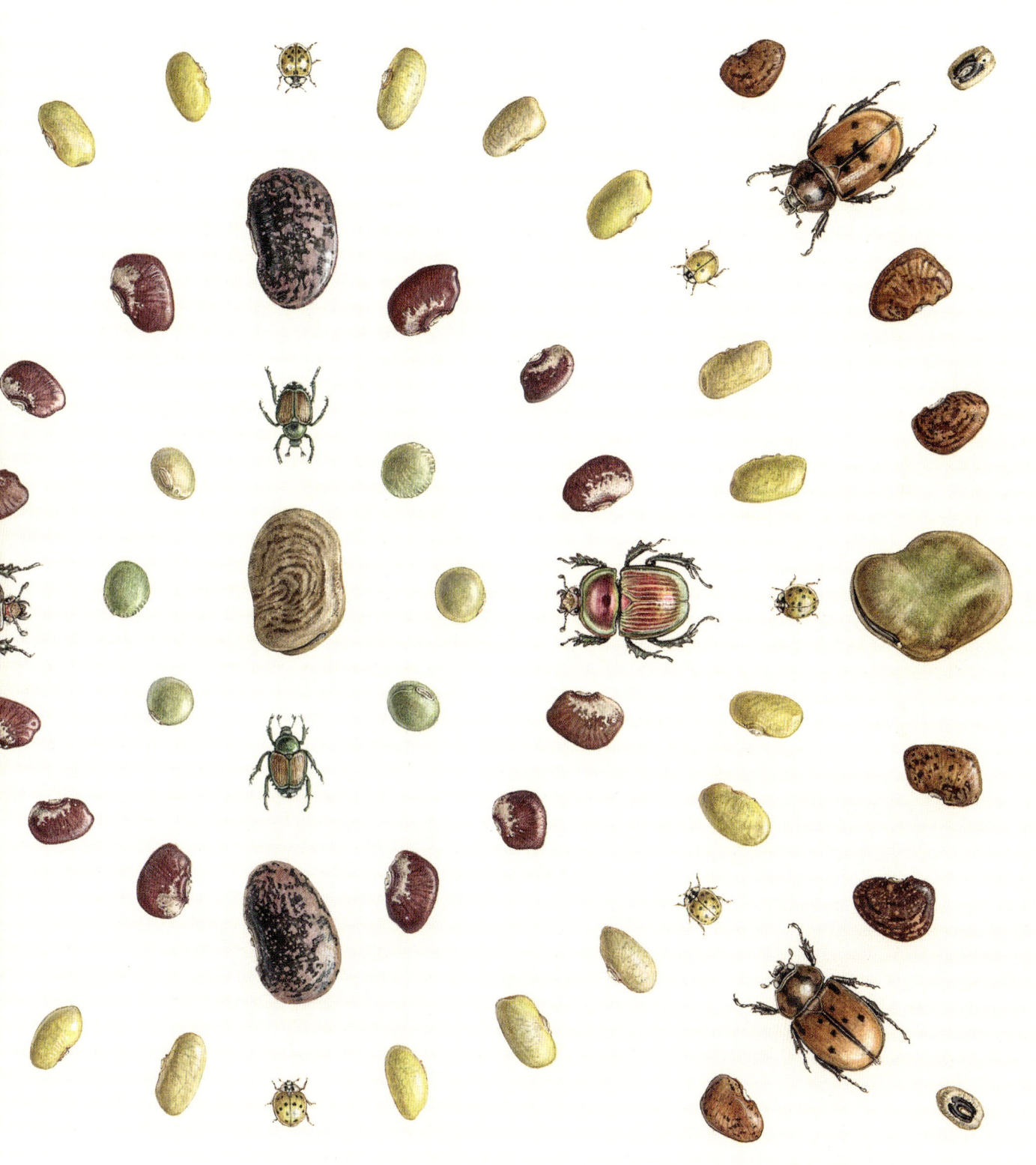

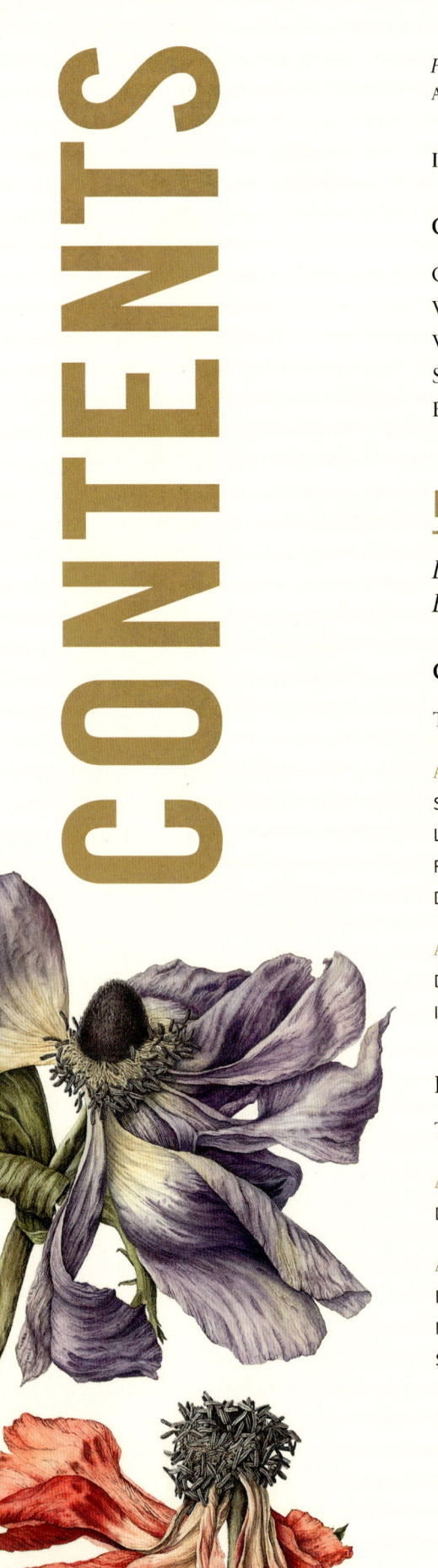

CONTENTS

Foreword, by Diane Bouchier, Founder,
American Society of Botanical Artists   9

Introduction   10

Getting Started   13

Caring for Cut Flowers   13
Wild Plants in the Field   16
Working in a Backcountry Location   20
Setting Up a Studio   22
Basic Botany for Botanical Artists   26

PART 1

*Drawing Botanical Subjects in
Black and White*   35

Graphite Skills   36

The Basics   36

APPLIED TUTORIALS
Shaded Flowers   48
Leaves   56
Fruits, Vegetables, and Branches   63
Drawing Spiral and Diagonal Patterns   77

ADVANCED TUTORIALS
Drawing an Inflorescence with Many Flowers in Graphite   85
Illustrating a Plant Portrait from Roots to Tips   91

Pen and Ink   97

The Basics   98

APPLIED TUTORIAL
Drawing of a Thistle Head in Seed   107

ADVANCED TUTORIALS
Depicting Cactus Spines   111
Making a Scientific Ink Dissection Drawing with Technical Pens   115
Scientific Botanical Illustrations in Pen, Brush, and Ink   125

PART 2

Botanical Subjects in Color 135

Colored Pencil 139

The Basics 140

APPLIED TUTORIALS

Three Flower Types in Colored Pencil 146
Depicting Leaf Texture with Colored Pencil 153
Fruits and Vegetables in Colored Pencil 160

ADVANCED TUTORIALS

Grisaille Techniques on Rose Hips with Colored Pencil
and Watercolor Pencils 167
Kiwi Vine in Colored Pencil and Graphite 175
A Crabapple Branch in Colored Pencil on Film 179

Watercolor on Paper 183

Properties of Watercolor Paints 184
Palette Philosophies 189
Transferring a Drawing onto Paper or
Vellum before Painting Begins 192
Watercolor Wash and Wet Techniques 195

APPLIED TUTORIALS

Drybrush Layering, Glazing, and Detailing 199
Flowers 205
Leaves 212
Stems, Twigs, and Roots 219
Painting a Leaf in Sepiatone 227

ADVANCED TUTORIALS

Painting a Slipper Orchid Using Wet Techniques
and Masking Fluid 231
Painting Gloss, Bloom, and Reflected Light in Grapes 235
Drybrush Watercolor and Color Mixing 241
Creating an In-Situ Painting 249
Painting a Magnolia with Watercolor Washes 251
Drybrush Tomato with Masking Fluid 261

Watercolor on Vellum 267

A Brief Overview of Vellum 268
Techniques of Watercolor on Vellum: The Basics 270

APPLIED TUTORIALS

Drybrush Lines, Washes, and Crosshatching on
Kelmscott Vellum 277
Painting Leaves on Vellum 282
Painting a Dried Leaf on Vellum 289
Painting Bloom on Fruit 294

ADVANCED TUTORIALS

Achieving Deep, Rich Color in Watercolor on
Kelmscott Vellum 299
Using Opaque Watercolors on Dark Vellum 305
Painting a Flowering Cherry Tree Bough 313

PART 3

Specialized Techniques and Composition 319

Field Sketchbook and Journal 321
Graphite and Watercolor on Vellum 325
Egg Tempera, Gouache, and Casein: A Comparison 330
Etching Techniques 339
Painting a Branch with Lichens in Gouache and
Watercolor 349
Gouache on Paper: Spruce Needles and Cones 355
Metalpoint 359
Painting in Acrylics 365
Painting in Oils 368

Composition 373

Composition in Practice 374
Elements and Principles of Composition
in Botanical Art 378
Different Approaches to Botanical
Composition 382

Additional Reading 398
Acknowledgments 398
Contributors 399
Index 404

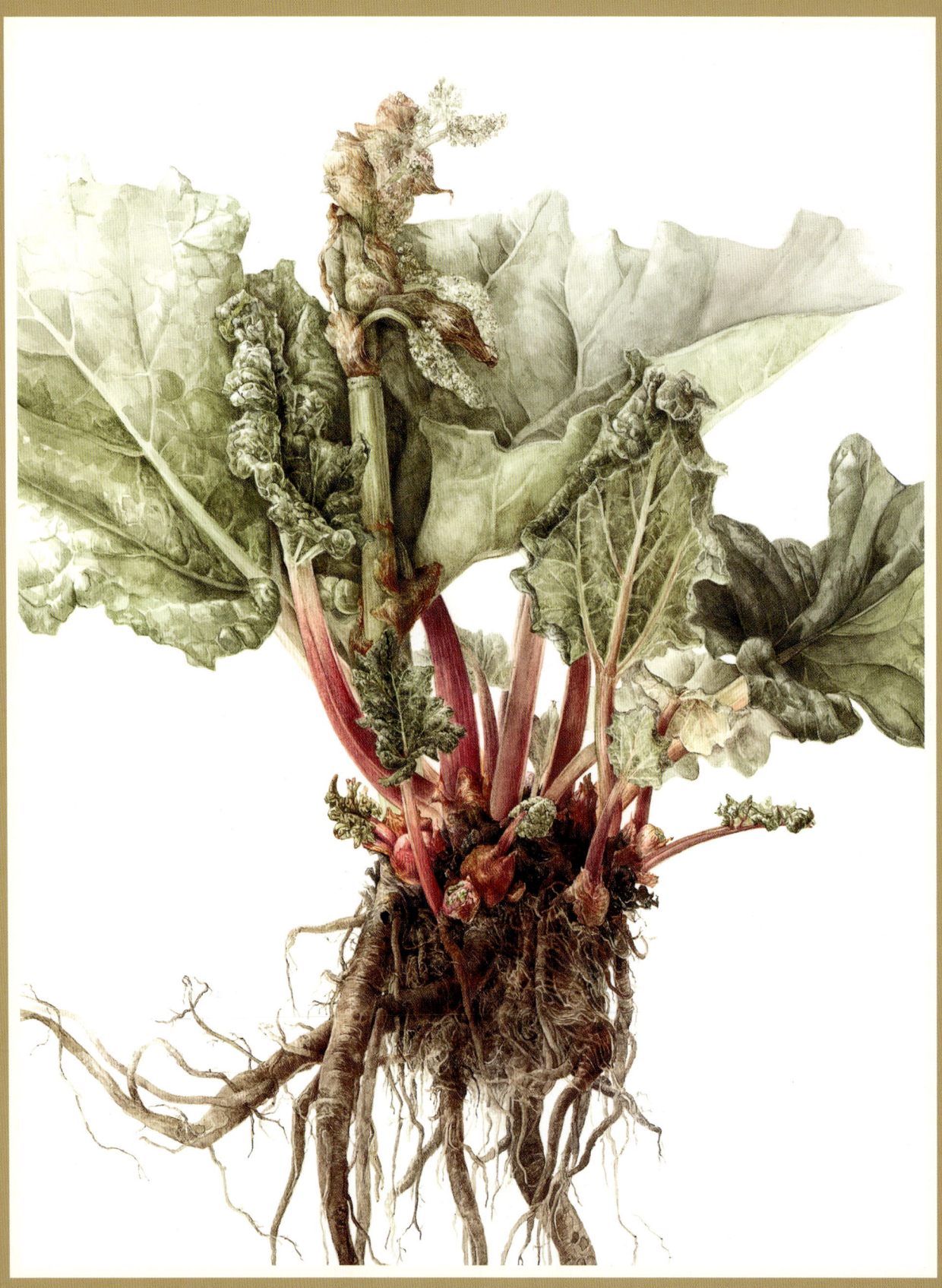

Foreword

The American Society of Botanical Artists (ASBA) started with a serendipitous encounter. In autumn 1994, British botanical art instructor Anne-Marie Evans was teaching her first master class at The New York Botanical Garden, and I was among her students. At some point, Anne-Marie asked, with Britain's Society of Botanical Artists in mind, "Why isn't there an American Society of Botanical Artists?" I was challenged by the possibility of creating a society that would better correspond to the American context: an organization whose membership was open to botanical artists of all skill levels, as well as to non-artists, and would emphasize both education and excellence. With a lot of help from other people and organizations, the ASBA began to take form and attract participants.

From the beginning, we sought to create ties with other organizations. The Hunt Institute for Botanical Documentation at Carnegie Mellon University in Pittsburgh, Pennsylvania, played a critical role in the early years by sharing its lists of botanical artists worldwide, sponsoring our website, and hosting our first annual meeting and many others that followed. Leading botanical and historic gardens quickly joined the ASBA as institutional members. Their number has now grown to more than thirty institutions in the United States and another dozen international institutions. At an important point in our development, The New York Botanical Garden offered us a home for our headquarters, and the ASBA has benefitted greatly from this partnership.

As its name indicates, the ASBA was originally seen as a national organization. But from the beginning we received membership requests from artists living abroad, and so we have welcomed an increasing number of international members. The ASBA's *Annual International* exhibition was hosted by the Horticultural Society of New York for twenty years and marked its twenty-first year at Wave Hill, in the Bronx, in 2018. Other exhibitions, such as

The New York Botanical Garden's Triennial exhibitions, attract international artists who depict a wide diversity of plants. The most impressive example of the international breadth of contemporary botanical art was *Botanical Art Worldwide*, a global effort to document the world's wild flora, and the declaration of May 18, 2018, as the Worldwide Day of Botanical Art. The ASBA mounted an exhibition entitled *America's Flora* at the United States Botanic Garden in Washington, D.C., an exhibition that later traveled to the Missouri Botanical Garden in St. Louis; the Leigh Yawkey Woodson Art Museum in Wausau, Wisconsin; and the Botanical Research Institute of Texas in Fort Worth. Similar exhibitions were held in twenty-four other countries around the globe.

Education figures prominently in the ASBA's mission. Both the website and the society's journal, *The Botanical Artist*, contain articles about the contemporary practice of botanical art and historic collections, as well as listings of certificate programs, courses, and other educational resources. Annual conferences, held in different locations around the U.S., offer workshops, lectures, opportunities to share ideas, and camaraderie. In addition, the ASBA sponsors a program of small grants available to members to encourage public outreach. A recently funded program used botanical art classes to introduce inner-city Chicago teenagers to native and urban plants while another project in Australia sought to raise public awareness of the impact of eucalyptus dieback in a region of New South Wales. These are only a few examples of the impressive list of achievements that the ASBA has compiled since its founding, and we look forward with great anticipation to its ever-growing contribution to public awareness of botanical art and its role in promoting plant diversity.

—*Diane Bouchier, PhD, Founder,*
American Society of Botanical Artists

Introduction

Botanical artists love plants. This is a simple, obvious truth, but one that explains the hours, days, weeks, and often months spent taking the artwork from research sketch to completion. Botanical artists are fascinated by details and relish the exploration and accurate depiction of the intricacies of those details. This passion for detail is primarily what separates botanical artists from floral artists, or artists who depict plants in an impressionistic or expressionistic manner. Understanding a subject's form and function through direct observation gives great delight. Perhaps the desire to share that delight with others is part of the artistic impulse.

In the late twentieth century, some would have written off botanical art as a dying art form. Artists working in the field were isolated and knew at most a handful of other artists. Exhibitions were few and education in the field was uncommon. Much has changed in the ensuing years. Now undeniably in the middle of a renaissance, botanical art has become a vital and thriving field with a worldwide following. Around the world, artists are communicating with one another, working on significant projects documenting today's plant life, and creating ever more accomplished art.

This turn of events is surprising, considering the world in which we live. Botanical art requires large blocks of time for focused concentration, and it nurtures traditional forms of artistic endeavor long out of fashion. It encourages cross-disciplinary connections and communication among artists and asks for close study of the natural world. As we have become more and more accustomed to constant electronic and digital stimulation, people are drawn to practices that don't rely on electronic intermediaries, and find botanical art is a way of looking at the world anew. This is an art form built on observation and technical skill, and a lifetime can be devoted to its study.

Botanical Art Defined

What is botanical art? Even within the field there is lively discussion about the definition. Practitioners agree that its predominant definition is the botanically accurate depiction of one or more plants or fungi, reflecting an intimate knowledge and understanding of the subject based on firsthand observation by the artist. The American Society of Botanical Artists (ASBA), as well as many other botanical art organizations around the world, limits the definition further to works created by hand in traditional media. Botanical artists find the personal relationship that develops between artist and subject central to the final product.

Historically, details such as a plant's reproductive parts were always shown in the artwork. These works were often made to serve a scientific purpose, so species identification was paramount. Today, artists are free to break with this tradition, unless the purpose of the work is scientific or illustrative. Contemporary practitioners are pushing the boundaries and placing the genre firmly in the twenty-first century. Although flowers are still subjects, so are dead leaves, bulbs with roots, seedpods, fruits, and vegetables. Artists sometimes contextualize the main subject by including some of the surrounding plants, placing the subject in situ.

Botanical art contains within it a broad sweep, ranging from images created for scientific illustration to those whose main goal is aesthetic. The gamut is covered in this

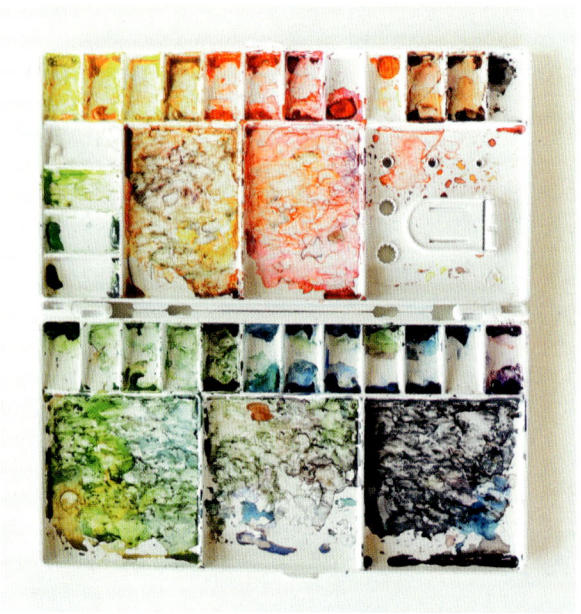

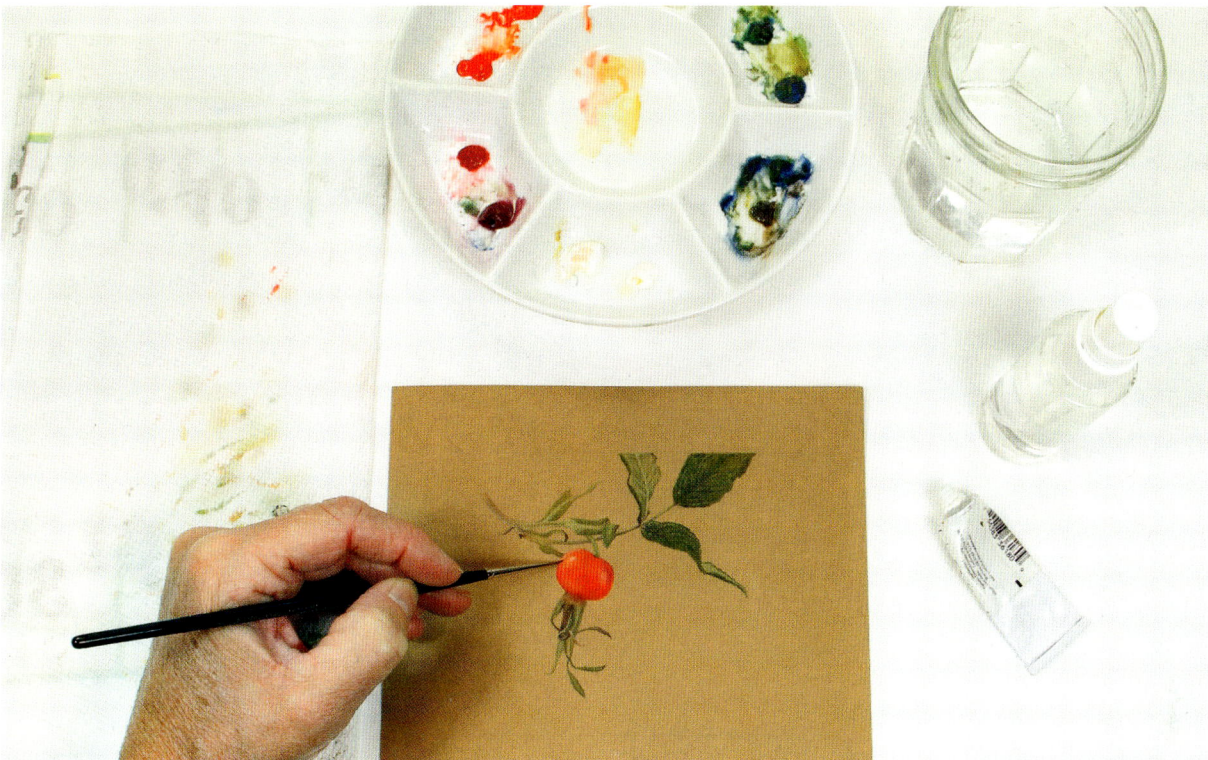

book. On the scientific end, it is recommended that every new plant description include an ink dissection drawing to aid in identification. New plants continue to be discovered and described, so illustrators who make dissection drawings are still actively employed. In the middle range of the gamut, some botanical artists make color illustrations that fit within the tradition of the eighteenth and nineteenth centuries, showing vegetation and flowers, sometimes accompanied by floral dissections. On the fine-art end, artists employ approaches based in modernism, depicting as much or as little of a plant as their artistic vision desires. Bursting buds, overripe fruit, heavily cropped details, and entire plants, roots-to-tips—these can all be subjects of an artist's scrutiny.

Why Is This Renaissance Occurring Now?

While vast numbers of people on the planet seem to be drifting away from the natural world in favor of digitally mediated experience, the botanical artist makes a conscious effort to build and strengthen ties to it. Spending days and weeks observing a single plant is a luxury that botanical artists are fortunate to enjoy. Studying plants in depth allows a focus that is rarely found in other fields.

As one of the few fields of contemporary artistic endeavor based in accurate representation, botanical art provides a haven for those who relish figurative work. The study of botanical art and illustration provides an artist with tools that can be applied to other types of artistic figuration.

Ecological awareness, along with an elevated sense of rapid biological change, contributes to driving artists into the field. Artists can choose from the hundreds of thousands of wild species found around the planet, each evolved to fill a niche and each delightfully unique. Considerations for selecting a subject to depict may revolve around whether the subject is common, rare, or endangered, or whether it is in a certain plant family or geographic location. Artists may choose plants of garden origin, those that have been hybridized for centuries and cultivated for ornamental, food, construction, or medicinal purposes. The possibilities are endless and last a lifetime.

Yet another motivation is that the work contains the potential to affect the way people look at the world. All artists communicate through their art, and a desire to influence the way the public views plants is central for the botanical artist. Some plants found today may no longer exist by the end of our century, let alone in several hundred years. The artwork will last and may be among the few records a future world may have of the plants we know today. Even some of the most common plants make the most beautiful artworks and have the potential to inspire viewers to take a fresh look at the green things around them. Botanical illustrations are not dispassionate records; they are both artistic and documentary. This is what is at once fresh and lasting about botanical art: It communicates the intrinsic value of plants and their centrality to human existence, both contemporaneously and through history.

Last, but not least, the field has grown into a generous and resourceful community of artists, scientists, horticulturists, conservationists, and collectors. Organizations devoted to botanical art can be found on nearly every continent, launching projects, providing educational opportunities, and forming networks of artists. Botanical gardens, arboreta, conservation organizations, art museums, and others are joining with botanical artists to reach new audiences and interpret their collections. Through social media, artists are sharing their techniques and experiences with colleagues. Today's botanical art landscape features thousands of artists working in every corner of the globe.

About This Book

Fine botanical art displays scientific accuracy, mastery of hand-created technique, and a sense of aesthetics. These are its tenets. Contemporary botanical art has often been pigeonholed as a lesser art because it does have certain essentials. However, those principles don't constrain or limit the genre.

Misconceptions exist about botanical art that we hope this book will help dispel. One is that botanical art is simply copying nature, and in its devotion to that goal, it all looks the same—regardless of the artist. The tutorials in this volume show that each artist approaches a subject in an individual way, choosing widely varying subject matter and techniques. Long-standing artistic concepts such as composition, negative space, gesture, space, value, depth, and picture plane are apparent in these pages.

Another misconception is that there is only one way to work, an ideal formula that, once found, will yield success. In reality, each artist brings a unique perspective to creating art, and there are many ways to approach a subject and a variety of techniques to work with, as demonstrated by the range of approaches, preferences, and techniques included here. We hope that this wealth and variety of vision will encourage you to explore new techniques and philosophies. The genre of contemporary botanical art is fluid and constantly evolving as artists push the envelope by exploring and growing their imagery.

With tutorials by more than 50 artists, this book provides an engaging sampling of beginning to advanced methods. Readers can see many artists' preferred ways of working. Rather than presenting a single technique and a single artist, here are numerous vantage points and approaches for each medium. Opportunities for expanding your skills can be found, whether you are a novice or an experienced artist, as well as new modes of handling specific aspects. Much detail is devoted to graphite, pen and ink, colored pencil and watercolor, the most frequently used media, however, other media such as tempera, casein, and gouache are touched upon. We hope to convey the enthusiasm botanical artists feel for their chosen medium and the breadth of possibilities that exist within the genre.

As artists read through this book, they are encouraged to keep an open mind, try something new, and determine what ideas, media, and techniques resonate. Many have had their artistic lives changed by a single suggestion. Enjoy your exploration of the pages ahead!

—*Carol Woodin and Robin A. Jess, Editors*

Getting Started

Caring for Cut Flowers

Today's botanical artists are free to choose any plant at any stage of its growth for their subject matter. Many subjects, from fruits and vegetables to cones and seedpods, remain remarkably stable over time, giving a botanical artist plenty of time to study and draw them. However, the subject that tends to last the shortest amount of time is also the favorite of many artists: flowers. Artists have many sources for cut flowers, including florists, grocery stores, flower markets, and their own gardens. But keeping these flowers in good condition for the time needed to complete a painting is challenging, if not impossible. After initially blocking in the colors and shapes of your composition, then focus on painting the flower that will change the most.

If you are working with a cut flower, you should immediately make multiple sketches of all aspects of the flower and its associated leaves and stem, especially those that will be hard to see once the specimen has faded. You can never make too many sketches, color studies, and color swatches, or take too many photographs for backup. An important fact: for a successful painting, an artist's sketch is much more valuable for recalling the character of the plant than a photograph.

There are many means to extend the life of flowers, including picking them at the best time of day, conditioning and caring for them, and refrigerating them (or not). Following is some general advice for enhancing the longevity of cut flowers, but you can also learn additional methods from flower societies, florists, growers, and from your personal experience.

Water

Placing flowers in deep water is always better—deep water makes it easier for the capillary action to draw the water up the length of the stem to the flower. The water temperature can be varied according to what response is sought from the plant. Warm water will make flowers open more

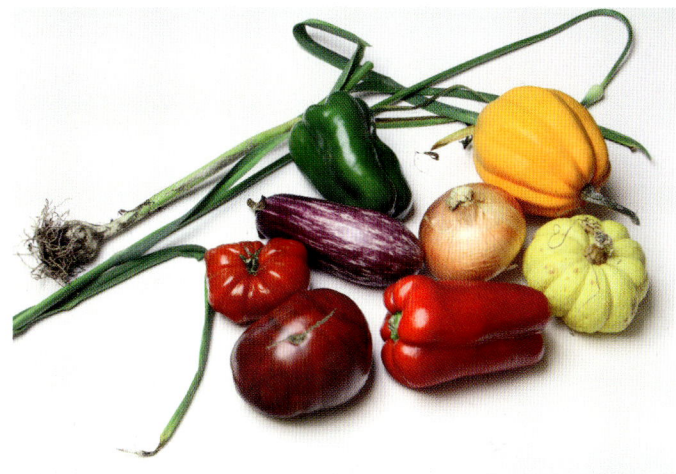

Fruits and vegetables are popular subjects partly because they tend to last longer than flowers.

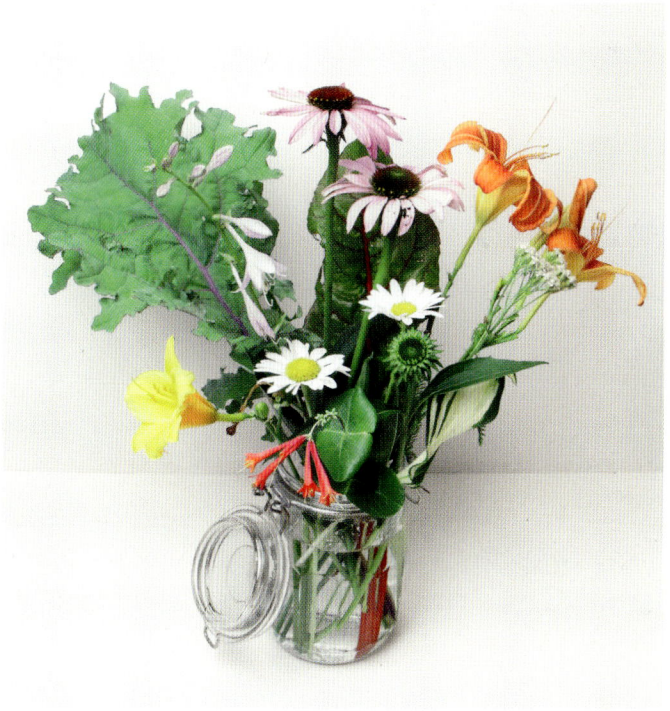

Put flowers and leaves in water to lengthen their lives. While they are working, many artists place their subject against a white backdrop so that there are no visual distractions and the subject's colors can be more clearly read. Here, the leaves have been removed from the stems below the water line, but you should keep the leaves on if you are still working on them.

quickly and cold water will slow the process. Inserting some tougher herbaceous (not woody) stems in a vessel filled with boiling-hot water for a short time (10 minutes or so) before putting them in cold water can help extend a subject's longevity. It's helpful to cut the stem at an angle, then put flowers in warm water for a few hours to facilitate water uptake. If your goal is to keep flowers in bud or to slow their progression, use cool water. Change the water after four or five hours by introducing colder water into the container while keeping the cut submerged.

Preservatives and Additives

There are many commercially prepared water additives that all aim to do the same thing: keep the water in the vessel bacteria-free to lengthen the viability of a cut flower. Crushed aspirin, a drop of bleach, a little vodka—these are all homemade preservatives that will help prolong the freshness of a cut flower. Whichever you use, be sure to supplement it with a fresh change of water daily—that is the most beneficial step you can take. Commercial florist sprays can be used on the underside of flowers to help keep a flower perky and delay wrinkling. Hair spray, the old heavy-duty type, can also work in this way; however, very delicate flowers will not appreciate the weight of a spray.

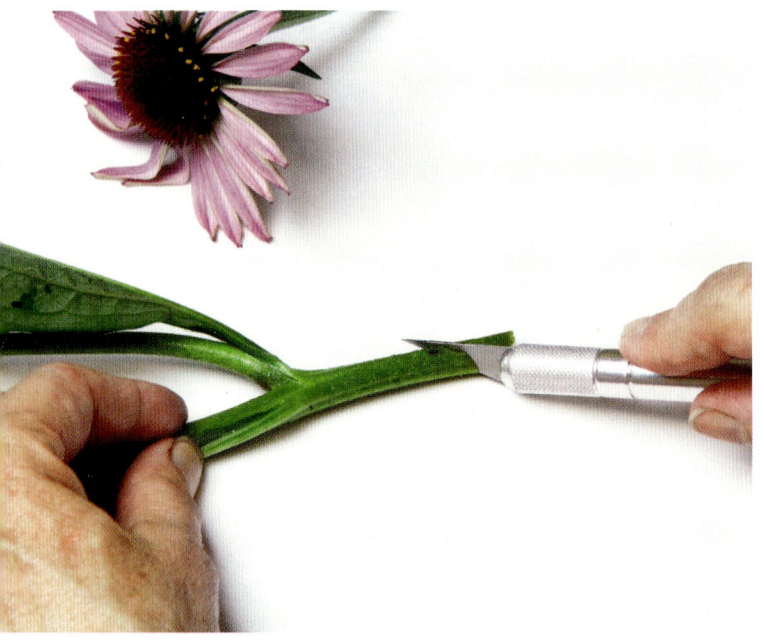

Cutting an *Echinacea* stem at a 45-degree angle with a sharp craft knife. Cutting the stem at an angle results in a larger open surface area, allowing the stem to more readily take up water.

Environment

Heat, light, and humidity affect the rate at which cut flowers open and eventually dry or decay. In general, warmer temperatures and brighter light encourage opening, and cooler temperatures and less light delay it. Refrigeration can stave off the opening of temperate-zone flowers, but it can darken and damage some tropical plants. Keeping flowers in plastic bags to maintain moisture sounds like a good idea, but in warm weather they may develop mold quickly. A small amount of humidity in the room is beneficial, as opposed to very dry conditions. Bowls of fresh water placed near the cut flowers will increase the amount of moisture in the air. Keeping flowers on the cool side, at a temperature similar to the nighttime temperature they would naturally experience outdoors, is a good rule of thumb to maintain stasis.

Cut Flowers

Some common cut flowers readily or seasonally available from a florist benefit from a fresh cut of at least ½ inch [1.25 cm] from the stem, done at a 45-degree angle with a very sharp blade, such as a single-edge razor blade or an art utility knife. Once you've cut the stem, immerse it in deep water. Using the packet of preservatives provided by the florist will retard rotting and deterioration. You can portion out the preservatives so that when you change the water, you can add a bit more of the preservatives. Tulips will absorb water better if the base of the stem is split, but daffodils don't need that. Extra leaves on daisy-type flowers (Gerbera, sunflower, snapdragons, chrysanthemum) should be stripped off, especially those lower on the stem. Make a sketch to record the position and shape of the leaves before they've been removed and note any changes in form farther down the stem. Leave the little tube (often provided by the florist) around the base of sunflowers or Gerberas in place to help support the weight of the flower head. Carnations are the champs of the cut flower world; they can last up to a month with continued fresh water and repeated fresh trims on the stems.

When cutting tulips, daylilies, or daffodils from your own garden, or selecting them from your provider, choose flowers that are just beginning to show color before opening. Siberian iris flowers should be tight, but tall bearded

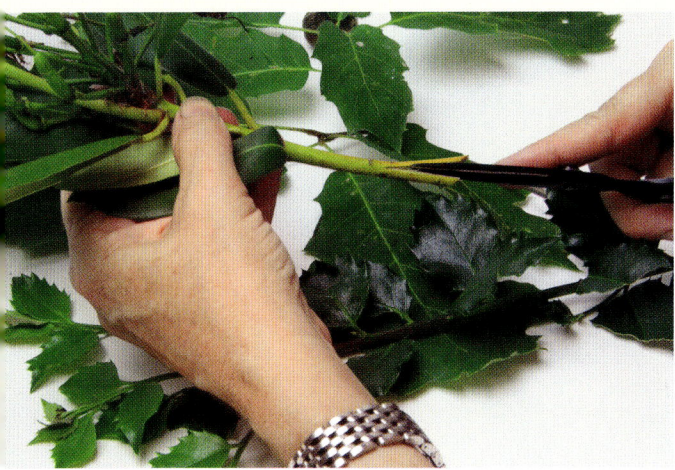

Cutting upward into a stem increases the surface area for absorbing water. This is especially helpful with woody stems of trees.

iris should be a bit more unfurled, so that they will open fully after being cut. Irises usually only last for a day, so try to find stems with additional buds that may open. If iris and daffodils prove slow to open, they will benefit from a deep, warmer soak that may loosen the gel-like fluid they exude. Composite flowers such as daisies and sunflowers will hold their form longer if they are cut or purchased when the ray flowers are open, but the disk flowers are still closed. Gladiolus stalks should be cut when only a few flowers are open, recut daily, and dead flowers removed. While daylilies are true to their name, and each flower lasts only a day, removing the spent flower and cutting the stem will encourage the other buds to open. Removing stamens of an Asiatic lily (after drawing them of course) keeps the flowers longer.

Tropicals or plants with waxy sepals or petals, such as gingers or spathes like anthuriums, last a very long time, but refrigerating them can have a detrimental effect on them. Some types of potted flowering orchids and anthuriums change very little over a few weeks. Flowers with milky sap such as milkweed, poppy, spurge, and Poinsettia can be singed with a match or lighter at the cut to quell the flow. For any subject featuring cut flowers, remove the flowers that have passed if they are not included in your composition.

Woody-stemmed flowers are a greater challenge. Most benefit from being split with pruners and even so, they don't last very long. When cutting inflorescences such as lilacs and wisteria, some of the woody stem should be included, rather than cutting just the green part of the stem. Split the bottom inch [2.5 cm] and then immerse it

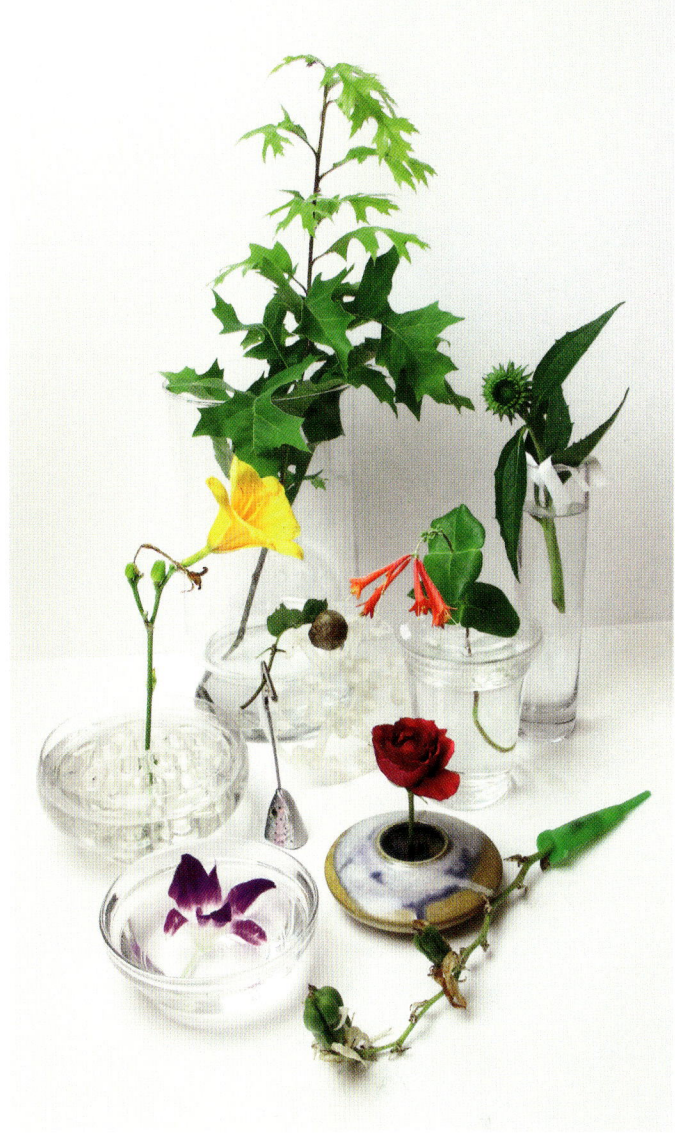

There are a number of ways to hold specimens in position. Individual flowers can be floated in water to keep them upright and hydrated, like the magenta orchid flower (lower left), or placed in a frog in a bowl or vase, like the yellow daylily (left). Florist's water tubes like this pointy green tube (lower right) can be helpful, especially for transporting specimens, and alligator clips (center; this one has a base shaped like a fish head) are indispensable for smaller subjects that don't need water. Artists use all manner of vessels, sometimes improvising to position a subject, like the orange honeysuckle flower (right), which is inserted in the straw hole of a plastic cup's lid.

in very deep water. That inch [2.5 cm] could also be peeled of the very outer bark. Try to pick them when only half of the flowers are open and don't take a long piece of the branch. Make sure the flowers don't have water sitting on them and remove any unnecessary leaves.

Popular and beautiful subjects are forced spring branches, whether flowering quince, forsythia, certain witch hazels and all the lovely cherry, crabapple, apple, peach, and plum flowers. They need to be clipped from the shrub or tree when the buds are tight and brought indoors. Splitting the stems, then steeping them in deep, warm water in a warm and sunny room, will induce the flowers to open. In any case, be prepared to work quickly as the flowers are ephemeral. After bloom, often the leaf buds will open too. Keeping pussy willows out of water will maintain the silvery male catkins, while warm water will cause them to go to pollen, leaves to emerge, and roots to develop.

Certain flowers like camellias or inflorescences like mountain laurel (*Kalmia*) or rhododendrons and azaleas can be floated in a shallow bowl that gently supports the outer petals or flowers.

Roses, while on new growth, have tough stems. They prefer a fresh cut and split to the stem daily, and they last longer in deep water. Keep several leaves on the stem above the water line. Gently inserting a sewing or hat pin through the center of the petals, straight down into the stem an inch or so will help to keep the rose from drooping. A tall, thin but heavy vase with loosely balled chicken wire or tissue paper at the top can be used to help prop up heavy flowers.

Developing relationships with reliable, knowledgeable florists, suppliers, and growers will stand all botanical artists in good stead, as will honing the skills necessary to make accurate drawings quickly. Recording the essential forms, colors, and textures of the subject is the best way to ensure good results.

Wild Plants in the Field

TUTOR: CAROL WOODIN

There is a growing interest among botanical artists in capturing wild flora and working in the field to do so. Given that most botanical artists are concerned about conserving native flora but may have only minimal training in plant conservation, it is important to provide some background to prevent artists from unwittingly damaging wild plant communities. When artists are seeking out wild-plant subjects, there are several aspects to consider that are not factors in depictions of cultivated plants. An artist should be aware of these aspects before venturing into the field to make studies of wild species.

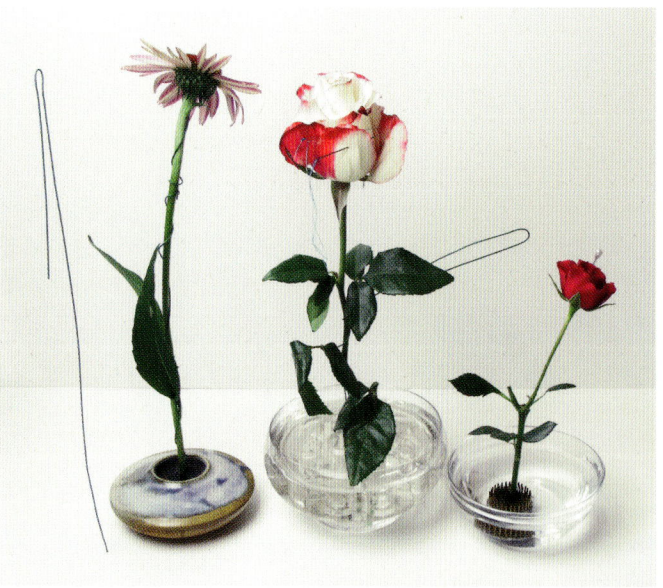

Using pins, wires, and needle and thread, these three flowers have been guided into position. On the left, wire is wound around the stem and up into the flower head to hold this coneflower in the desired position, revealing the underside of the petals and bracts. In the center, wire is used to tilt leaves forward, and the rose petals are sewn to prevent further opening. Rose flowers, once cut, often flop over, and a large hat pin can be inserted through the center of the flower into the stem to prevent this.

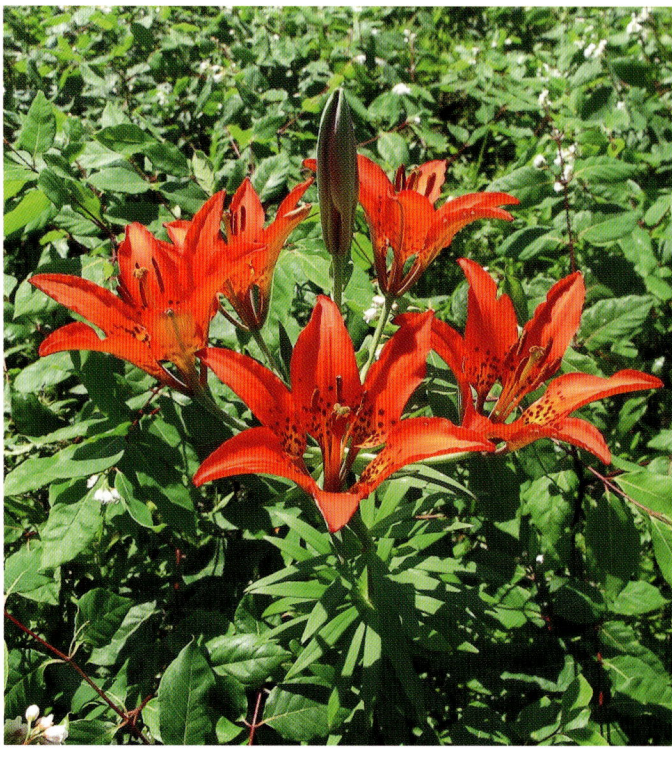

Lilium philadelphicum, wood lily, protected in some states and unprotected in others, in a field in Maine.

Many questions can be answered by working with knowledgeable botanists, conservation scientists, caretakers, and organizations that share a concern for common, rare, and endangered native plant species. A nuanced understanding of wild plants and their habitats, and the best practices to follow when interacting with them, is an educational goal of these partnerships. Greater understanding leads to a lower likelihood of damage to the plants and habitats that are so important to conserve. To learn more about working with wild plants, consult the ASBA's Code of Ethics, found on the organization's website (*asba-art.org*). In addition, the U.S. Forest Service has excellent information about the ethics of interacting with wildflowers that can be found on their website (*www.fs.fed.us/wildflowers/ethics/index.shtml*). Following are some considerations and questions to ask before embarking on a journey to depict a wild plant.

Plant Status

What is the conservation status of the plant you are seeking? Some wild plants are non-native, others are very common indigenous plants, and some are uncommon. Others are legally protected as threatened or endangered by individual states or federal agencies. Your approach will depend on the status of your subject. A good starting point in the United States is the United States Department of Agriculture website (*plants. sc.egov.usda.gov*). Look up your subject plant by its scientific name, then check its status under the Legal Status tab. Most states have their own site devoted to the listing of protected plants within state boundaries. The status of your target plant or location will determine your behavior in seeking it out.

Guidelines

Introduced wild plants: With permission, parts of these plants can be gathered. If the plant is invasive, take care not to spread it to new locations, especially via seeds that may be contained in flowers, capsules, or on your shoes.

Very common native plants: When plants are common, with permission, parts can be gathered.

Uncommon native plants: Follow a "least-impact" philosophy by completing studies on-site and taking photographs for further work.

Rare and protected native plants, sensitive habitats: With permission to visit a sensitive habitat, reduce the disturbance to the location by minimizing the number of people in your group and watching each footstep to avoid trampling small plants not readily visible. Avoid compacting the soil near rare plants. Keep information about the location private and remove no plant parts, leaving site as you found it.

Location Status

What is the ownership or management status of the property where the plant is located? It is important to ask for permission to access many types of land, including private property, and to ask for guidance about how to behave on-site. Land-management philosophies and rules vary widely, so familiarize yourself with your targeted location's policies regarding plant materials on-site. Some locations allow you to pick up detritus (for example, acorns, dropped leaves, and branches), while others allow no removal of plant materials whatsoever. Some private lands are accessible with owner permission and others are off-limits. Venturing off-trail is not allowed in some locations, although exceptions are sometimes made when you are traveling with an employee or caretaker; other locations may have no restrictions. When you arrive on-site in a sensitive habitat, quickly scout the surrounding area. Note the locations of your target plants so that nearby specimens are not inadvertently damaged.

Alternative Sources

Can the plant be found at a botanical garden, arboretum, or nature center? If so, an employee will often provide

A good rule of thumb to follow is: Leave the site as you found it

—

A "least-impact" philosophy is encouraged, regardless of the status of the plant or property. Any impact on wild plant communities should be minimized as much as possible.

plant cuttings or access to growing areas where artists can work. Working with a botanical garden or other institution helps keep traffic in sensitive habitats to a minimum. Developing relationships with botanical gardens and arboreta can advance projects and ensure an enriching experience for artists as well as horticulturists, botanists, and managers. These relationships form part of a botanical artist's wealth.

Go Into the Field Prepared

Before heading into the field, assemble your field kit. It should be lightweight but have high functionality, and it should include an art kit suitable for working in the field, items for your health and safety, and navigation tools. A folding field stool is only useful if your plant is tall enough and the ground is firm enough. Sitting on the ground often provides the best vantage point.

Collecting Information About Your Subject

The three main methods of collecting information about subjects are field studies, gathering specimens, and taking photographs.

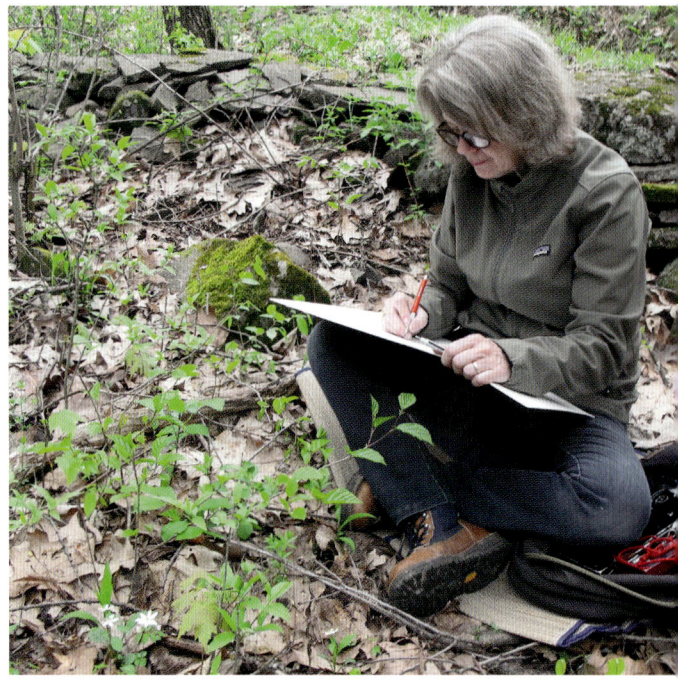

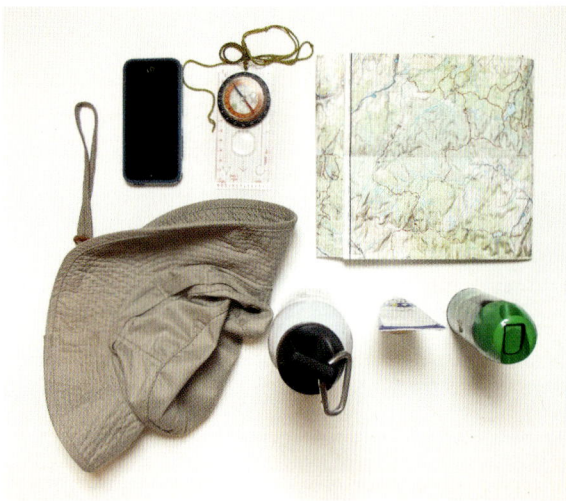

Field kit: Health, safety, and navigation supplies for working in the field include a cell phone, compass (and any additional navigational guidance that would be helpful), ruler, water, map, and water bottle. Be prepared for sun, heat, rain, insects, and cold with a hat, sunscreen, insect repellant, rain gear, and jacket. Bring a plastic bag or sheet to sit on if the ground is wet. Bring a companion. Don't rely on your phone for location information; sometimes there is no signal, or the details about your location are insufficient.

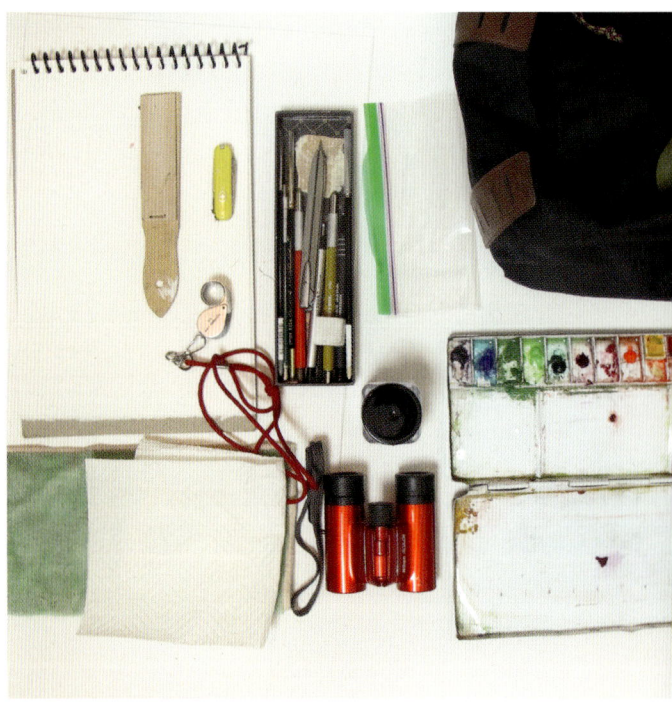

TOP Use a straw mat to stay dry while you are sitting on the ground. Bring lightweight tools, and only the tools you will need to make field sketching quick and simple. Here, the artist is seated away from the plants to avoid compacting the soil and inadvertently damaging these wood anemones.

ABOVE *Art supplies field kit:* Drawing or watercolor paper; a hard surface to place paper on (either matboard or foamboard); sandpaper; jackknife; loupe magnifier; box with pencils, dividers, erasers, and worn brushes; resealable plastic bag; backpack; field watercolor kit; plastic water bottle; binoculars; paper towel; and cloth.

Field studies: Be prepared to spend some time drawing and making color studies while you are working in the wild. The more time you spend capturing the details of your plant, the better the results will be when you are back in the studio. Gestural sketches done in the field can be followed by increasingly detailed graphite drawings. Some artists like to make quick watercolor or colored pencil studies help them understand the colors present and remember exactly what they are later on; others prefer to make color swatches in the margins of the paper.

Gathering specimens: If the plant is not at risk and cuttings and gatherings are allowed, snip representative parts of the plant and protect them inside of resealable plastic bags. Use water vessels to nourish them until you arrive at home. Put leaves, sticks, and acorns in plastic bags to prevent them from drying out.

Field photography: Field photographs can be difficult due to wind, bright light, darkness, deep water, and other conditions that you may find on-site. An artist's goal with photography is to capture the details of subject plants so that if questions arise later the photos can be consulted for answers. Field studies are your most important record from a site visit. While making the studies, you are learning about the plant and answering questions you might have about it. Compositional problems can be resolved during a field visit as well. Photographs should be considered secondary documentation and supplemental to these studies.

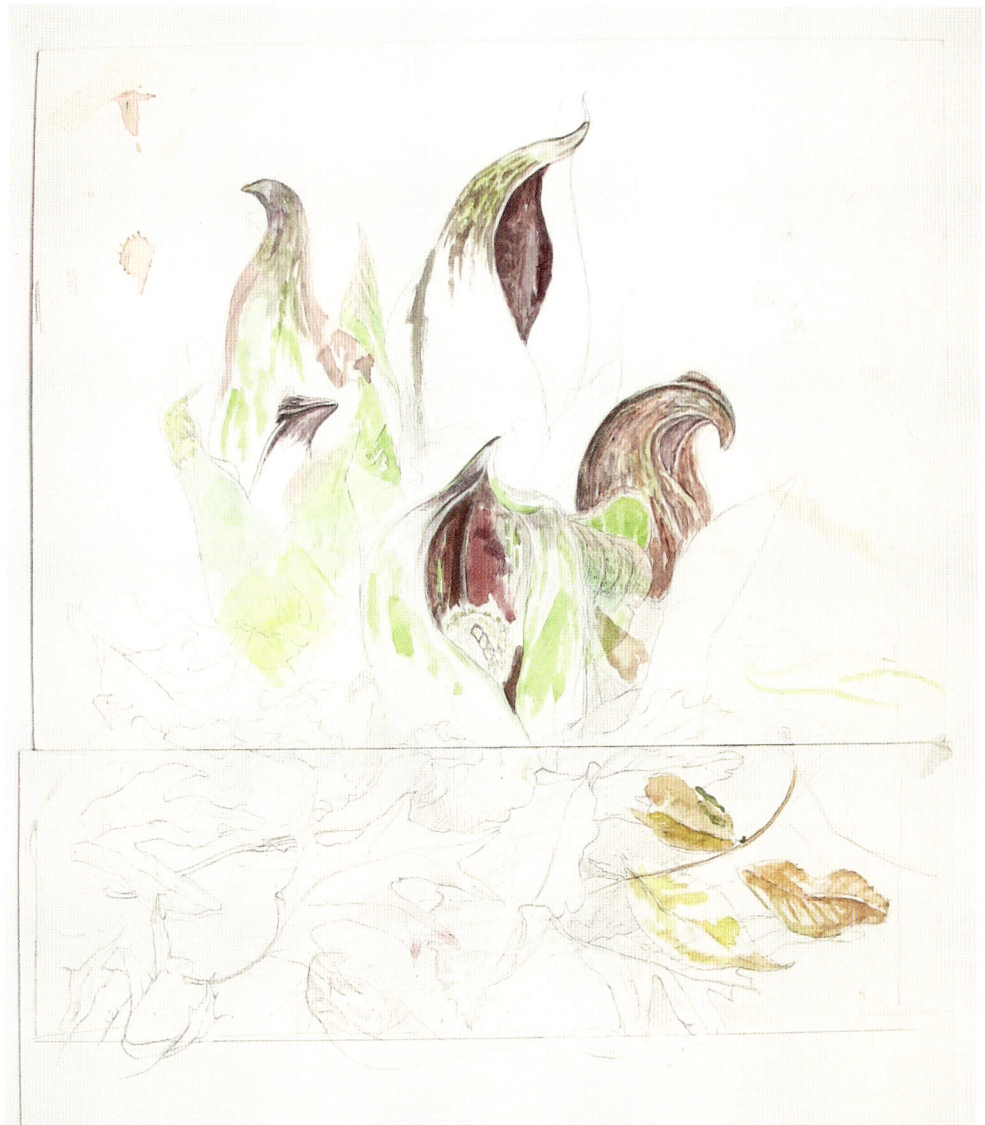

This study of *Symplocarpus foetidus*, skunk cabbage, was done over two field sessions. The first day's work, composing a group of plants in graphite and watercolor notations, was done on the top piece of matboard. Then for further field work, a second piece of matboard was added to extend the picture plane. Dead leaves were then gathered to add more forest floor information in the studio.

WORKING IN A BACKCOUNTRY LOCATION

Fascinated by the massive scale of Borneo's rain forests, botanical artist Mieko Ishikawa first visited the island in 1994. Since then, she has traveled to Borneo's jungles many times to capture rare wild plants that can't be seen any other way, and she has often needed to climb mountains in search of these plants. Her most frequent subjects in Borneo are *Nepenthes* and *Rafflesia*. Before visiting a habitat, Mieko decides what she wants to draw and collects information on the plants and locations. She always travels to Borneo with her husband and hires a guide when she is going into a jungle for the first time.

As *Nepenthes* often grow in Borneo's highlands, trips require tough climbing. This necessitates hiring a guide and a porter, and sometimes a cook and a ranger as well. It is essential to hire a guide with good knowledge of plants. *Rafflesia* is very difficult to see in flower. It does not bloom seasonally, and the flowers, once they bloom, become black in four to five days. Several habitat visits may be required before good luck results in an encounter with the flowers in their best form.

In order to sketch plants in situ, Mieko carries sheets of drawing paper ranging in size from 14 × 20 inches [35 × 50 cm] to 28 × 40 inches [70 × 100 cm] in a large portfolio. Mieko often has to sketch plants in a limited time during climbing or trekking. She begins with rough sketches and takes measurements of all the important details. Since the plants may not be removed from the habitat, she takes many photographs to refer to when she is working at home. Sketching plants in their habitat for later work is a must, as by doing so, she memorizes the habit surrounding the plants as well as plant details. The foam board she is using as a stiff backing for the drawing paper is lightweight and easy to carry.

Weather is fickle in rain forests, so Mieko travels with rain gear. A light-colored umbrella is useful when drawing under a burning sun. Insect repellent and mosquito coils are must-have equipment for protection against mosquito bites in a low-elevation jungle. Her painting kit is lightweight, including a metal palette and small plastic water container. Despite the challenge of working in difficult conditions, Mieko finds drawing plants in rain forests brings her great joy and reward.

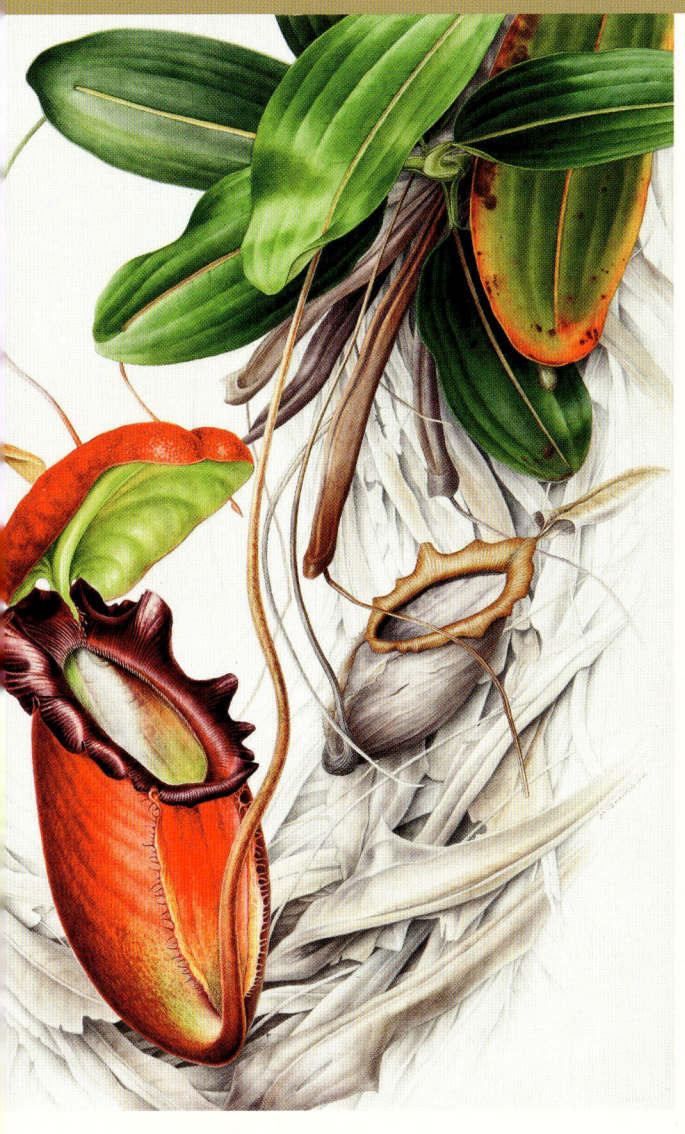

Nepenthes rajah Watercolor on paper 26 × 19 inches [65 × 47.5 cm]
© Mieko Ishikawa

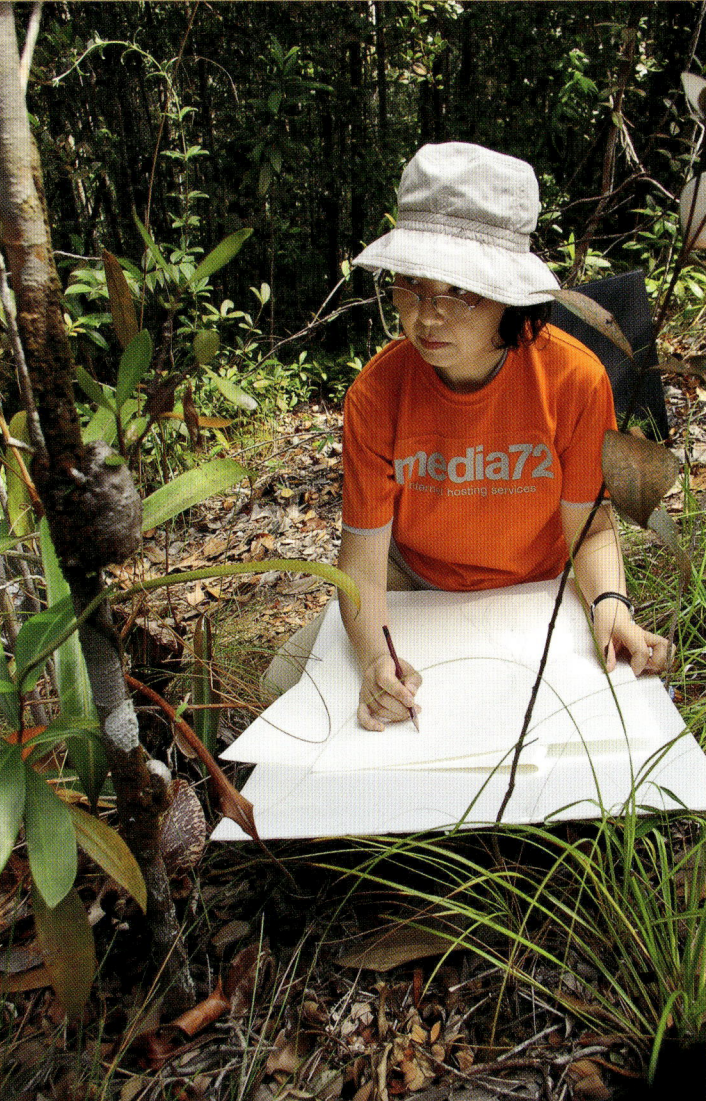

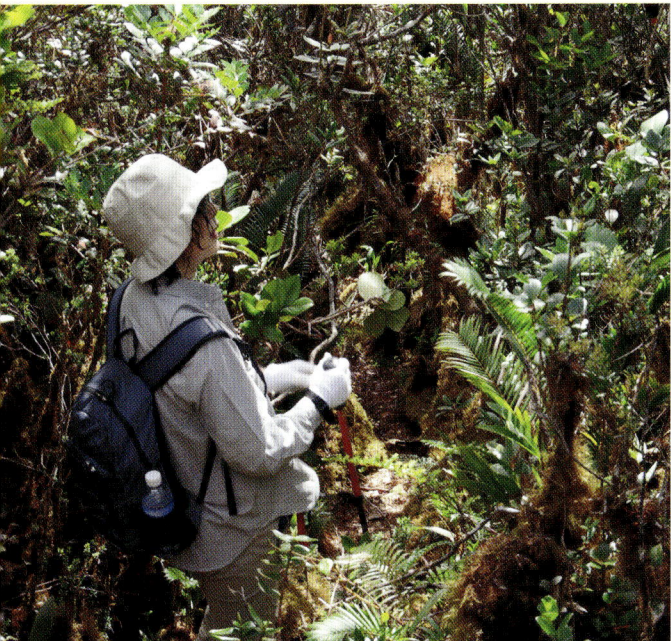

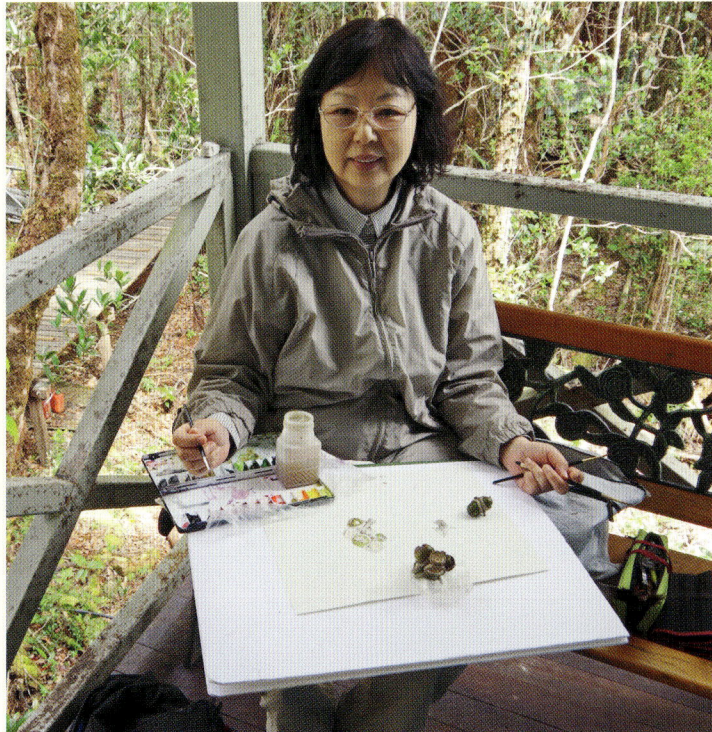

Setting Up a Studio

Some artists plan their studio space, for others it evolves over time. Each finds a set-up that works well for them, depending on the amount of space they have available, the medium in which they're working, and their work habits. Choose lighting, magnification, work surface, seating, and a place for tools and materials according to your needs, comfort, and style. Here is a peek into the studios of four experienced botanical artists working in different media, showing a general overview and then a closer look at each artist's workspace.

Carrie Di Costanzo

The studio in my home was originally a spare bedroom. The room is small, but it is large enough to contain all my painting needs. The desk is large, and it holds a computer, printer, books, and paperwork. Opposite the desk is a long table where I paint. My desktop easel is adjustable and works well in this space. The two windows in the room allow for some wonderful natural light, which I utilize as much as possible. I also use overhead lights and desk lamps when necessary. The work in progress on my easel is of a celosia flower from my garden, which is being painted in gouache and watercolor. My original tracing-paper drawing is taped to the wall in front of the easel for easy reference.

The artwork in progress is sitting on a tilting desktop easel. This allows me to work at an angle, while my materials remain on a flat surface. I use a small handheld magnifying glass to see small details. Close at hand are pencils, brushes, and a couple of round plastic palettes. Near the wall is a pencil sharpener, a cup containing more brushes, and containers for water. More brushes and paints are stored in drawers nearby and are easily accessible. The original flower for this painting has since died, so I cut another flower to refer to for color and texture.

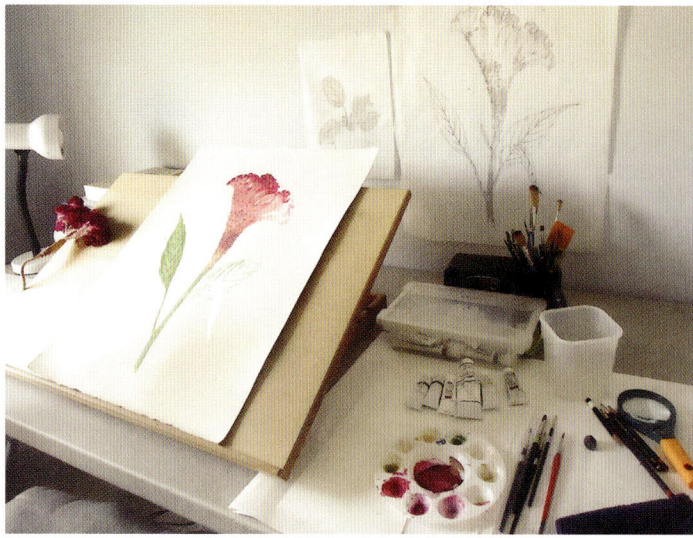

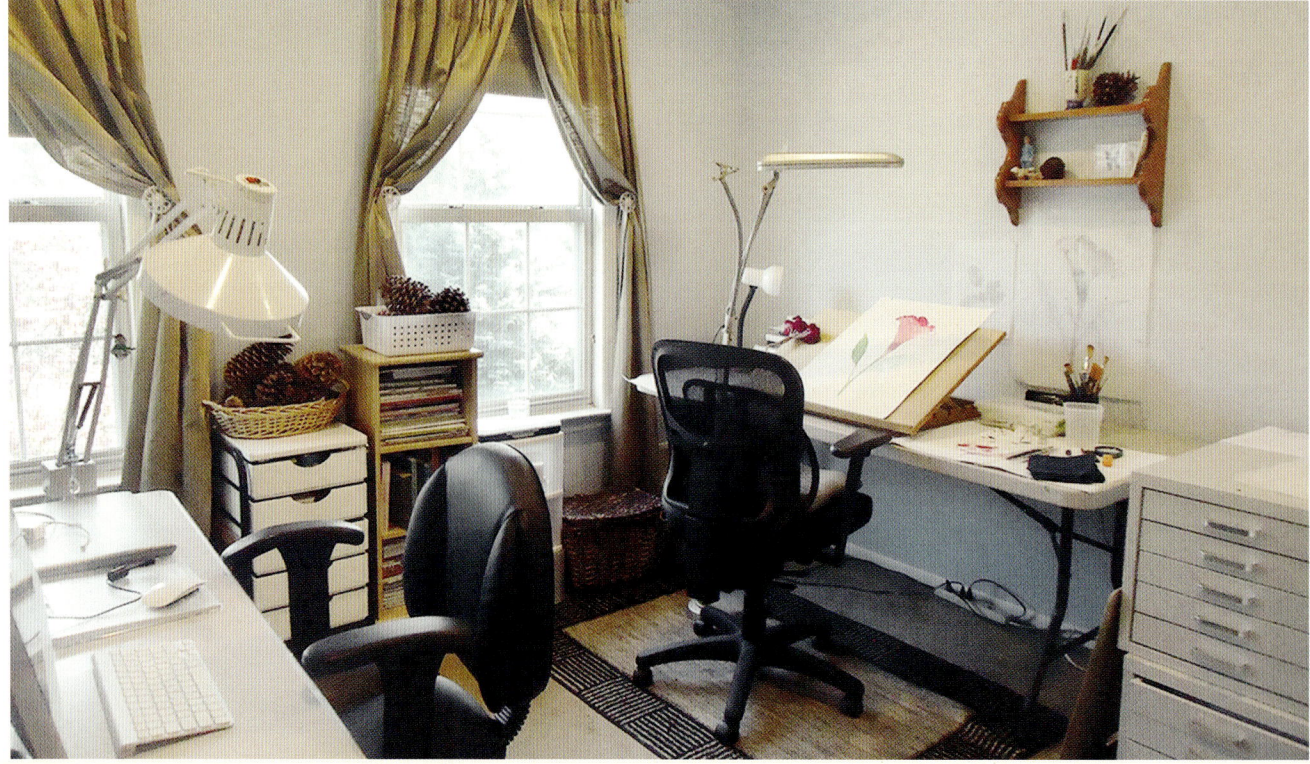

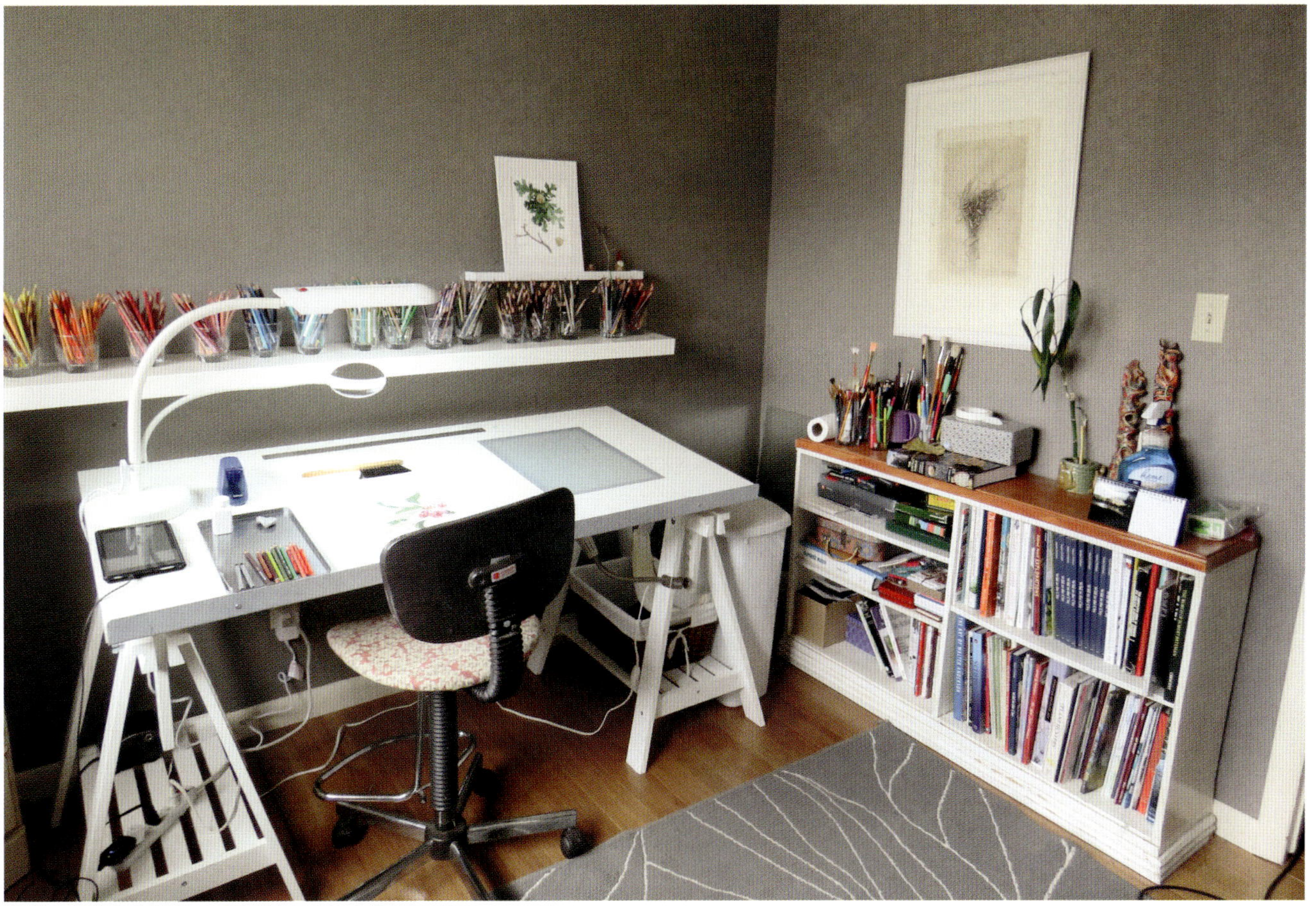

Dorothy DePaulo

My studio is in a spare bedroom in my home. At my drawing table, which has a built-in light box on one side, I do colored-pencil work. I keep my pencils in clear drinking glasses so that I can see them all at once. Once I select the colors to be used, I keep them on a tray beside my work along with erasers. I have good natural sunlight during the day, and use a daylight-spectrum lamp at night. I prefer a snake-neck magnifier because it is always there when I need it, but can be easily pushed out of the way when it's not needed.

A colored-pencil drawing on drafting film is in progress on my desk. The drawing is taped to a piece of foam core, which allows me to turn the piece in any direction. Also on the drawing table is a natural-light snake-neck lamp with a separate magnifier, digital tablet for listening to audio books or music, retractable and kneaded erasers, battery-operated pencil sharpener, brush, 24-inch [60 cm] metal scale, and colored pencils. For removing larger areas of the drawing, I keep a cotton swab and a small bottle filled with a household cleaner nearby.

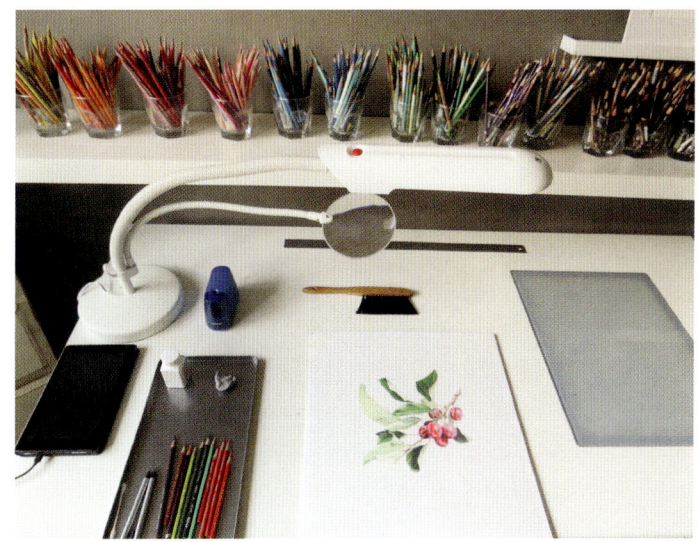

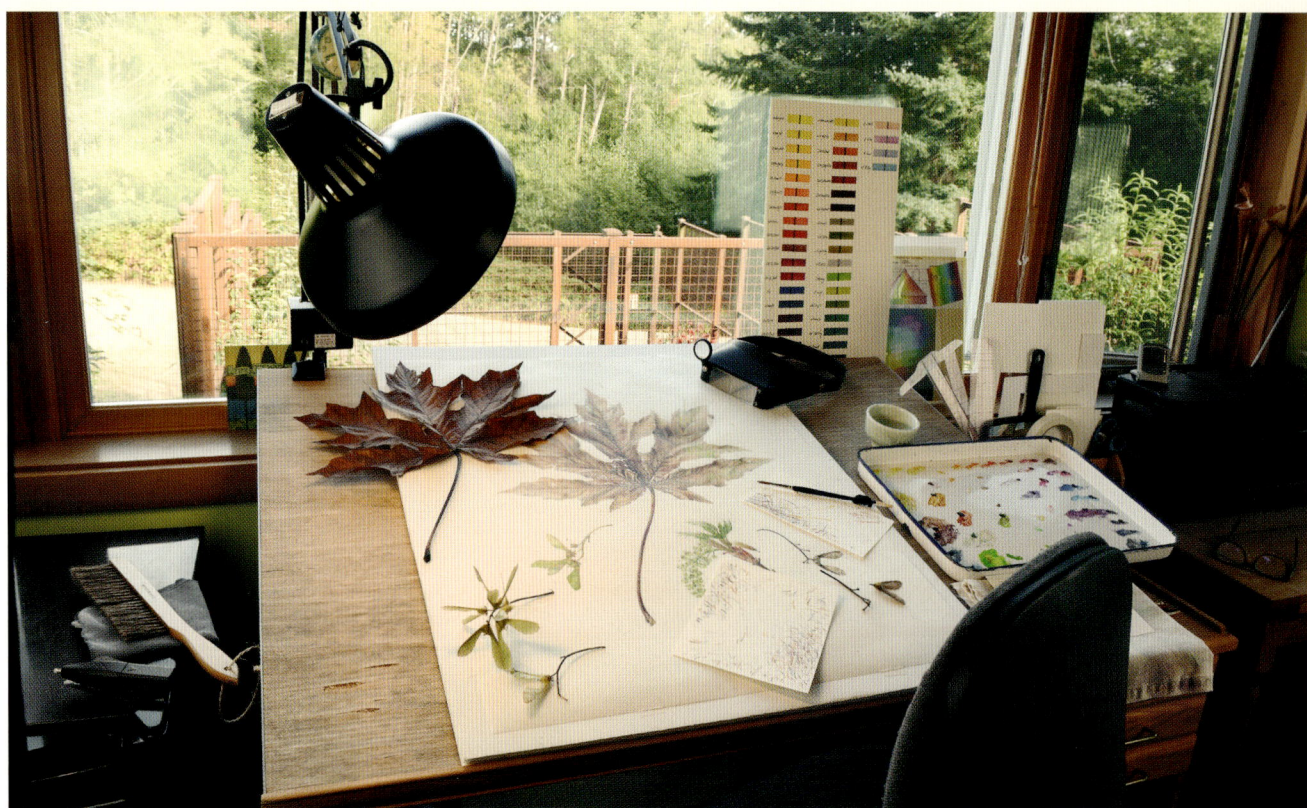

Jean Emmons

Adjustable furnishings, such as this lamp, desk, and chair, open up a lot of possibilities for different ways of working. For small- or medium-size paintings, I like to work with my desk slightly tilted. For large paintings, I prefer to start with the artwork flat in order to paint washes and large areas of drybrush. Sometimes it is better to stand: I can move around the painting, turn the painting, and use more of my whole arm. Then, for the final details, I put on my headband magnifier and raise the angle of my desk. Or, I may switch to a tabletop easel.

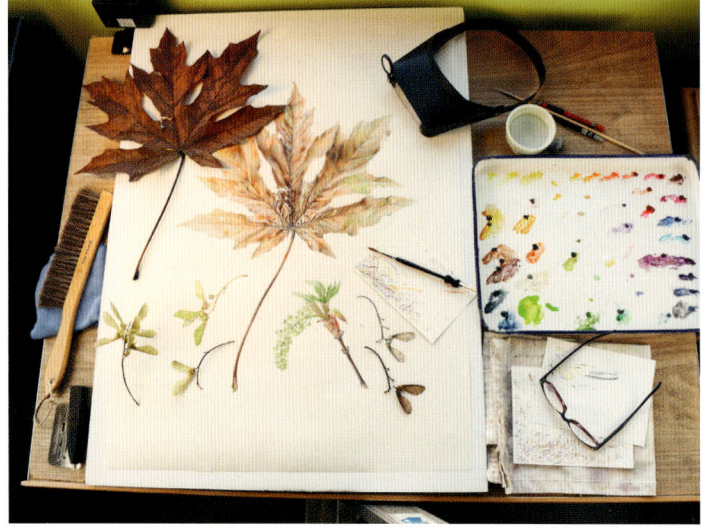

While it's important to have essential art supplies nearby, I try to keep my work area spare. Too much clutter makes me feel constricted, and the paintings can reflect that. Beyond the usual supplies, on hand is a color chart; lots of masking material to protect areas of the painting; scraps of paper for testing; a hand mirror for looking at the work in reverse; a small refrigerator for specimens; and, of course, a view of my garden.

The tools on my desk include an eraser and eraser shield for softening areas; a microfiber cloth; a drafting brush; subject; headband magnifier for detail work; a round no. 1 bristle lifting brush; a small mat knife; a mechanical pencil with a 2H lead; a kneaded eraser; a small container for water; a butcher-tray palette with lots of room for colors; a Kolinsky brush; a scrap piece of paper for testing the amount of water and paint on a brush; a lintless cotton towel for adjusting water and paint on a brush; an in-progress painting on Kelmscott vellum taped to a board with artists' tape.

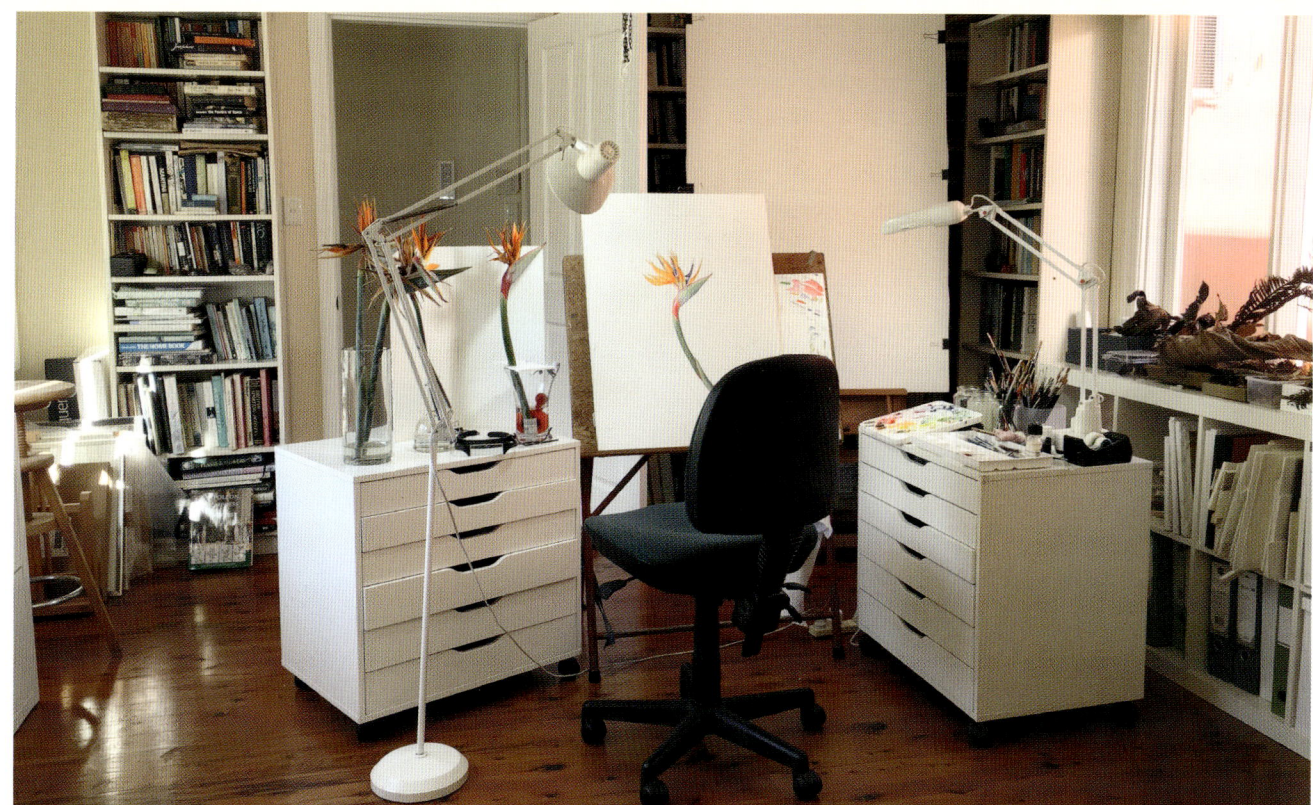

Beverly Allen

My studio is upstairs in my home. It has large north- and south-facing windows fitted with blinds. I use an old, small freestanding drawing board that's about 24 × 32 inches [60 × 80 cm] with a narrow wooden lip at the base. To work on detail, I position the board so that it is nearly vertical and paint standing up. For applying larger washes, I tilt the board back to a flatter position. Paper is taped to foam core so that I can turn the piece around to work on it. For very large paintings, I use an easel. To the right of the easel is a storage cabinet on wheels; this holds my palette, brushes, and other materials, with a studio lamp situated over the palette.

On my left, where my subject is placed, the set-up is more flexible and depends on the subject. If the subject is large, then I place it on the floor securely supported by whatever it takes. Otherwise, I place the subject on another chest of drawers or on a round stool that can be raised or lowered. A hook hangs from the ceiling for hanging a subject, like a branch, or to help keep a subject upright. My main light source for a subject is a floor lamp that can be positioned to suit my needs.

These workstation pieces can be moved around in the room to take advantage of the natural light coming in. A set of metal plan drawers holds works in progress, finished

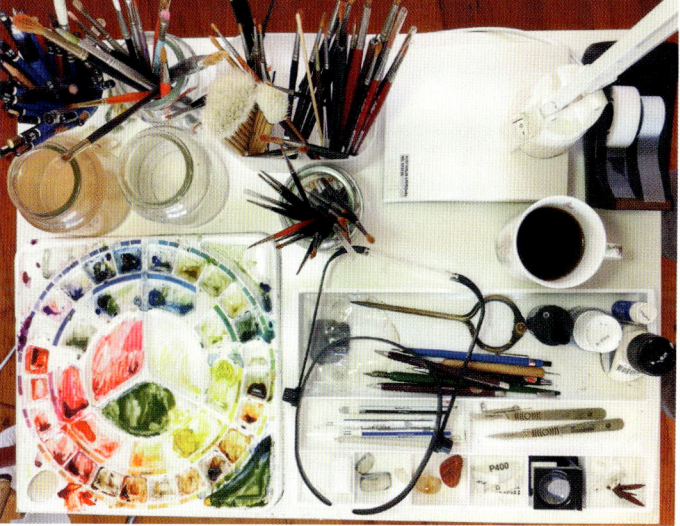

work, and all the paper stocks I have on hand. I have another desk for a computer and files, and a radio.

The items on my work table have been pared down to the essentials that are in constant use (apart from too many blunt brushes); including palette with six basic colors (which I expand with the subject); two jars for water; large brushes for dusting; a supply of tape; a magnifier; and a natural-light lamp over the palette. Also on hand are various erasers; lead holders; burnishing stones; fine knives for scraping; and a headband magnifier.

BASIC BOTANY FOR BOTANICAL ARTISTS

TUTOR: DICK RAUH, PhD

Whether a botanical artist paints fruit, a whole plant or part of one, or only flowers, some knowledge of the science behind their subject informs the work and contributes to its accuracy as well as its beauty. This understanding is a large part of what distinguishes a botanical artist.

Knowledge is power, and knowledge of botanical form and function is exciting and gives confidence to an artist. The more an artist understands what is being drawn, or knows how to evaluate what is being observed in the plant from a morphological standpoint, the more convincing and clear the artwork will be. The image will be all the more compelling because of its accuracy. What follows is a brief guide to plant parts that will, I hope, provide a greater understanding of the marvels of plant anatomy.

Flowering Plants

The plant kingdom's first major division is the presence of flowers (angiosperms) or not (gymnosperms).

The development of two adaptations is among the reasons for the success of flowering plants. One was the flower itself, which became the agent of pollination, the means by which the anchored plant induced outside vectors to move the male reproductive units onto the receptive female organ. The other adaptation was the development of fruit from the ovary, the container of seeds within the body of the flower that serves to distribute the seeds away from the parent plant.

The flower itself is made up of four organs, which are called *series*. Starting from the outside, the first organ in a flower is the *calyx* (series), made up of the *sepals* (parts). Generally, but far from always, the calyx is green and photosynthetic, and its function is to enclose and

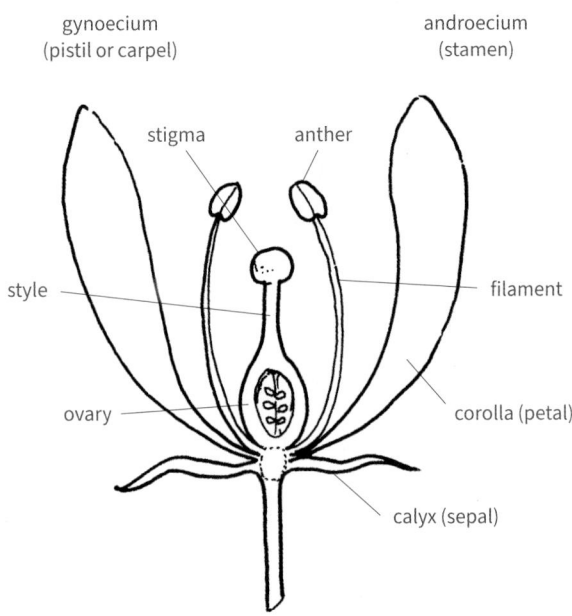

Perfect flower with superior ovary, showing four series.

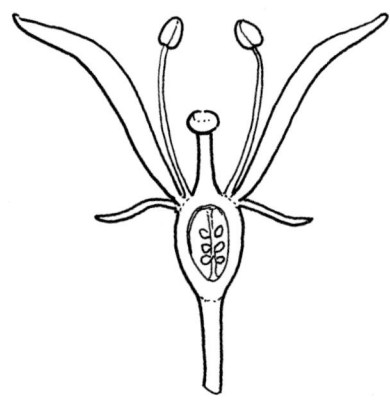

Perfect flower with inferior ovary.

protect the flower bud, and later the seed container. Next comes the *corolla* (series) made up of the *petals* (parts), and here the function is principally one of attraction. The pollen-producing series is next: the *androecium* with its *stamens* (parts). Last, and in the center, is the *gynoecium* (series), made up of the *pistil* or *carpel* (parts), which hold the undeveloped seeds—the *ovules* enclosed in an *ovary*. Sometimes the ovary sits above the other three series, and we say it is *superior*. Sometimes it is buried in stem tissue and sits below the other three series, and it is labeled *inferior*. While the sepals and petals are complete in themselves, the stamens are in turn made up of two parts called the *anther*, which holds the pollen, and the *filament*, which holds up the anther. The pistil or carpel is made up of three parts; the *stigma*, the sticky surface that catches the pollen, the *style* (a necklike structure attaching the stigma to the saclike ovary), and the ovary itself. The order of series is always the same, from outside in: calyx, corolla, androecium, gynoecium. The sepals are alternate to the petals; that means the center of the petal falls exactly between the two sepals, and the stamens are alternate to the petals, positioned between two petals, which make the sepals opposite (directly behind) the stamens. Although flowers can, and do, have fewer than four series, sometimes only having one, they never have more. When a flower has all four series, we say it is "complete." When a flower has the two reproductive series, the androecium and the gynoecium, we call it "perfect."

Inflorescences

The economics of floral production and the responses of mutations have created an alternative for the plant. Instead of a single showy blossom, the plant masses numerous small flowers together to produce the same attractive (meaning attractive to pollinators) effect. Often this occurs with much less expense in energy and with tremendous advantages. For example, more flowers extend the receptive time period of the pistils, or the distribution of pollen. These groupings are called *inflorescences*, and they are categorized by whether the terminal bloom is the first or the last to reach maturity. An inflorescence where the oldest flowers are the lowest down on the stem, and the newest buds are crowded at the apex, is called *racemose*. The most typical of the inflorescences showing this habit is called a *raceme*. The term *habit* refers to the typical way a specific plant, or its inflorescence, appears. Each of the flowers in a raceme (sometimes called *florets* to distinguish them from solitary flowers) is subtended by its own stalk, called a *pedicel*. Generally, but not always,

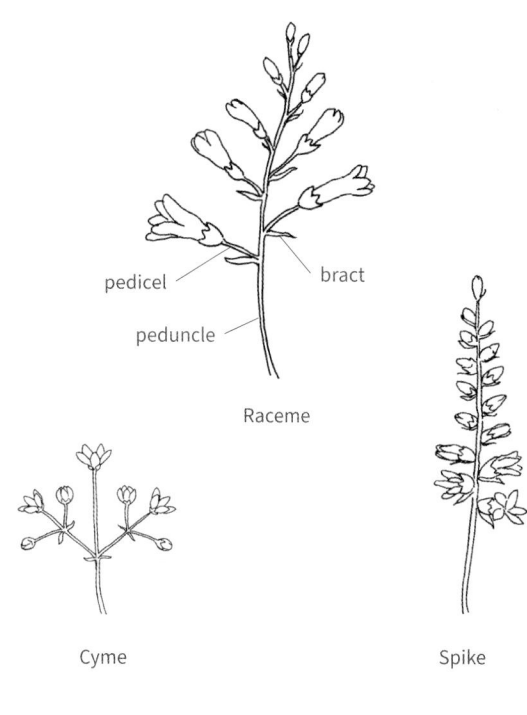

Raceme

Cyme

Spike

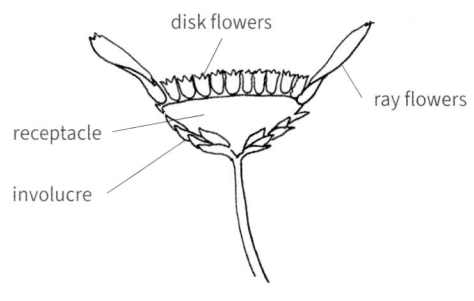

Head (pseudanthium)

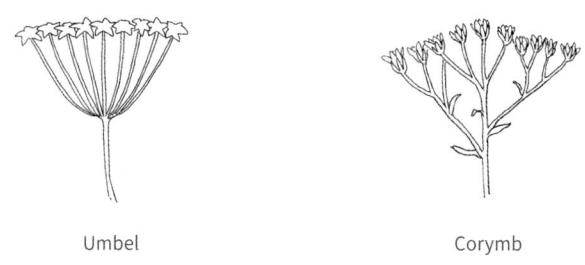

Umbel

Corymb

each of these pedicels arises from the angle of a *bract*, a leafy appendage associated with a flower. On the other hand, an inflorescence where the terminal flower is the first to bloom, and succeeding blossoms appear later lower on the stalk, is called *cymose*, and the inflorescence a *cyme*. A racemose bloom without any pedicels, that is, the individual flowers grow directly from the peduncle (sessile flowers), is called a *spike*.

There are two main types of flat-headed bloomers. The *corymb* is one in which the pedicels of the flowers run spirally up along the axis, arising separately and consisting of different lengths to form the flat top. The other, and more common, flat-topped inflorescence is the *umbel*, and this comes in simple and compound forms. The primary difference is that the pedicels arise as a whorl from a single place. A daisy is an inflorescence called a *head*, which consists of numerous individual flowers grouped together to make a *pseudanthium*, or *false flower*. For the most part the head consists of two distinctively different flower types. The outer, petal-like ring of *ray*, or *ligulate*, flowers is mostly imperfect as well as incomplete, lacking stamens and sepals. Generally, the single petal sits above an inferior ovary and folds at the base to enclose a style and two-parted stigma. The *disk* or *tube* flowers that make up the center are generally perfect. Sometimes a head may have only ray or only disk flowers. These are but a few of many other forms.

Habit

When artists labor assiduously to illustrate blossoms, they can't ignore the stems that support them and the leaves and bracts that surround them. Very often it is vegetative structure that helps distinguish a species or helps to confirm the subject's membership in a particular group. When painting the plant in which flowers are a part, it's necessary to know a bit about the stems, leaves, and even the roots. Habit (the whole plant) breaks down to two basic forms—herbaceous or woody. A plant is woody when it has a phenomenon called secondary growth. In shoots, as in roots, the primary unit of cell division in a growing plant is a group of small cells called *meristems* that exist in the tip (or apex) of the shoot. Woody plants do indeed employ this primary method, but another, secondary, growth distinguishes them: a lateral enlargement, or girth. The layer of cells that encircles the interior of the stem to achieve the lateral enlargement is called the *cambium*; it is a single row of actively dividing meristems. Outside of this is tissue known as bark. It is easy to name the types of woody habit: trees, shrubs, and the woody vines known as lianas. Herbaceous growth on the other hand, is often characterized by the temporal growth habit itself—perennial, biennial, or annual.

Stem

A stem is mainly responsible for the support of the plant, and artists must look closely to note its rigidity or flexibility as well as other characteristics—perhaps it is ribbed or winged. Most stems are *terete* (rounded in cross section). Some families are characterized by stems that are square (the mints) or triangular (the sedges). Stems are also propagative units because they have *nodes*, special areas that give rise to leaves and lateral buds. Thickened stem tissue is adapted to store nutrients and water. *Corms*, the reproductive unit of *Gladiolus* or *Crocus*, are flattened below-ground stems. A horizontal underground fleshy stem is a *rhizome*; above ground this is a *stolon*, and if it's skinny it's a *runner*. The bark-covered stem of a woody tree is a *trunk*, but the primary supporting axis of most plants is a stem.

Leaf

The other primary vegetative unit is a leaf, one that is of particular import to a botanical artist. A typical leaf is made up of two parts: the blade, or *lamina*, and the stalk, called a *petiole*. There are many aspects of leaves: arrangement on the stem (phyllotaxy), how they are attached to the stem, their form and shape, and their texture and margins, each of which has its own set of terms. Some leaves are arranged separately on a spiral, and this is called an *alternate* arrangement. Another plan finds two leaves attached at one node, known as *opposite*. There are plants where the opposite leaves more or less fall in two ranks, a condition known as *opposite distichous*, and the appearance of the branch is rather flat and spreading. Other opposite arrangements have the succeeding opposite leaves at a 90-degree angle from the preceding ones (four ranks) a condition known as *opposite decussate*. Anything missing a stem, whether leaves, flowers, or fruits, is known as *sessile*. Sometimes these sessile leaves don't just meet the stem but wholly or partly surround the stem, called *clasping*. Some leaves carry this further, not only surrounding the stem but with blade tissue that extends all around called *perfoliate*.

Leaves basically come in two forms: simple or compound depending on whether the leaf is an entity on its own or is made of a number of leaflets. Simple leaves are either *entire* (which in this case means unlobed) or *lobed*.

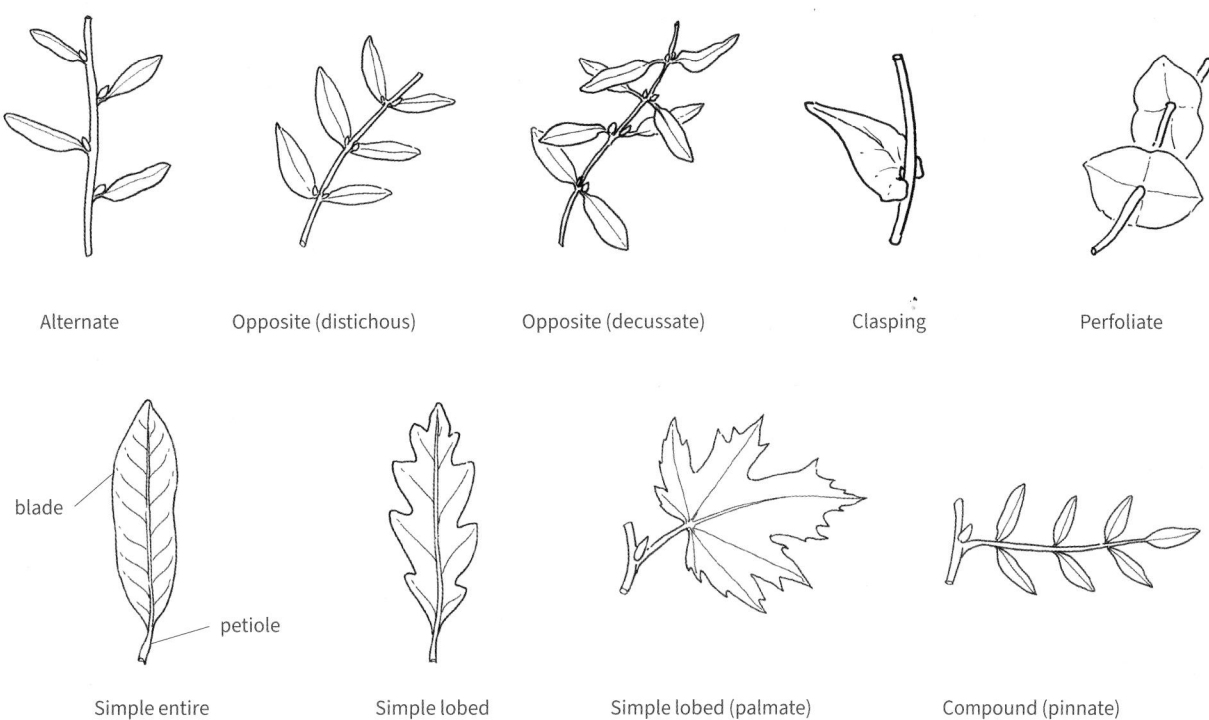

Alternate   Opposite (distichous)   Opposite (decussate)   Clasping   Perfoliate

blade

petiole

Simple entire   Simple lobed   Simple lobed (palmate)   Compound (pinnate)

Lobed simple leaves that have the lobes branching out from a single point where the blade meets the petiole is called *palmate*. A leaf with lobes arranged vertically along the midrib, like a feather, is called *pinnate*. The leaflets of a compound leaf are similarly arranged, arising from a single point at the head of the petiole, or arranged vertically along the axis. The shape of a leaf is another way to distinguish it, along with the shape of its apex and base, margins, and texture. There are countless technical terms to label in infinite detail each aspect, and references, but an artist's own attention and keen observation are the best source for accurately showing these details.

Fruit

The many varieties of fruit pose equally challenging subjects still belonging in the category of botanical art. Biologically the ovary wall is the predecessor of the fruit wall, and is divided into three layers, the endocarp (closest to the seed), the mesocarp in the middle, and the exocarp to the outside, and often fruit types are differentiated by what happens to these layers. When they are mostly succulent the fruit is fleshy. When the endocarp becomes hard or bony enclosing a single seed, it is a drupe, the so-called stone fruits. Another fruit type formed from a superior ovary, but one where all three layers are undifferentiated, is the berry. Similar fruit types, but classed as *false berries,* are from inferior ovaries. Another type of fleshy fruit from inferior ovaries is the fruit of Cucurbitaceae, or gourd family, called the *pepo*, which has a leathery epidermis and a rind. Another fruit derived from an inferior ovary is the *pome* where the endocarp (the core) has become papery surrounding the seeds. The citrus fruit of the family *Rutaceae* is called a *hesperidium*. It is a fruit from a superior ovary, with a thick, leathery skin with essential oils, with much of the insides forming "juice hairs."

Dry fruits generally emphasize the use of wind as the agent of dispersal. The definition of fruit as a maturing of the ovary wall still holds, but now it becomes dry and composed of dead cells; sometimes leathery, sometimes papery, sometimes stony. The dry fruit *achene* is a seed enclosed in an outer shell (what's become of the ovary wall), with the seed only attached to the fruit wall at one point. An achene made up of two carpels and with hairy tufts (called *pappus)* attached to its apex is called a *cypsela*.

A *samara* is an achene with a flat blade or wing that makes use of wind to spiral the seed or seeds within the achene away from its parent. Probably the most important economic food in the world is a variation of the achene that is the fruit of the grass family. Here the seed and fruit wall are fused into a single unit called a *caryopsis*, or grain. When the wall becomes stony, and there are one to three carpels, the fruit is known as a nut or a *glans*. There are fruits termed simple, coming from a single pistil, and fruits that come from many pistils, sometimes from a single flower, and sometimes from the many flowers in an inflorescence. It is again not the technical name that is important here, but the artist's eye.

Roots

Generally hidden from sight are the roots, and rarely are they included in flower paintings, except when there is a desire to include the entire habit or if the roots have an interesting structure. Roots take a number of forms; a primary root grows directly downward, and later forms lateral branches, while a fibrous or adventitious root has masses of hairy, fiberlike extensions of varying degrees of thickness with no single root taking precedence. Epiphytes (air plants, those growing without soil) often have roots that act as their main photosynthetic organs, and others (such as many orchids) have fibrous roots encased in large vacuolated cells that are designed to hold water, called *velamen*. Certain climbing plants (like ivy) grow adventitious roots along the stem that act to attach the vine on tree bark and bricks, or any other likely surface.

Mushrooms

Mushrooms are now understood to be closer to animals than plants, but they are still accepted as subjects for botanical art. Mushrooms are the fruiting, spore-producing bodies of fungi. Fungi get energy from consuming organic substances, as opposed to plants that make their food from sunlight through photosynthesis. Were it not for their large mushrooms, brackets, or puffballs, fungi would be virtually invisible because the rest of their bodies, or *hyphae*, are hidden in whatever they are feeding on, such as fallen trees, decaying wood or leaves, underground roots of dead trees, or mulch—any decomposing plant material.

Artists are attracted by the fascinating forms and colors and variety of mushrooms. Their mysterious lives—appearing suddenly and disappearing nearly as quickly—capture the imagination while their textures provide lots of possibilities for exciting images. Lichens are also popular subjects or components of larger works. A lichen is a partnership of fungus, algae, and cyanobacteria; or a fungus

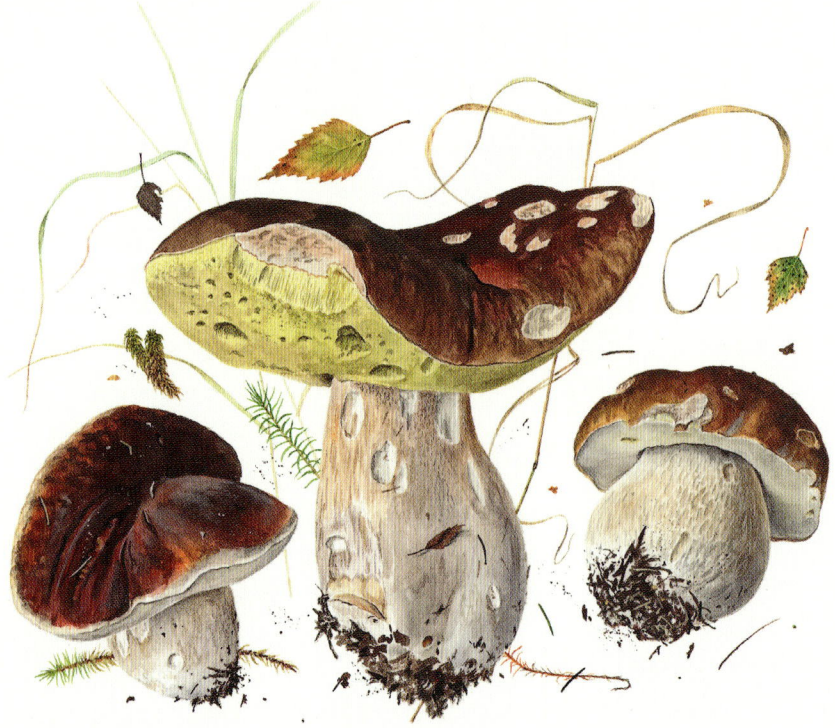

Boletus edulis II
Watercolor on paper
11 × 15 inches [27.5 × 37.5 cm]
© Alexander Viazmensky

and algae; or a fungus and cyanobacteria: fungus providing the structure and algae providing the food through its photosynthetic ability.

Ferns

Ferns are an ancient division of vascular plants. Fossil records show them to predate and exist with the dinosaurs.

Having neither flowers nor seeds, ferns owe their attraction to the fascinating forms of their leaves, commonly called fronds. From tiny grasslike plants to huge tree-form ferns, their diversity is astounding.

Fern fronds can be entire without divisions or divided or dissected into all manner of pinnae. Fern fronds unfurl as they grow from a rhizome and some are quite elegant. On the underside of the fertile fronds are *sori*, or masses of sporangia that produce spores, part of the alternation of generations of the fern reproductive cycle.

This polypody has an unrolled frond on the right called a "fiddlehead" or "crozier." Fiddleheads can be stunningly architectural and captivating to the botanical artist.

Classification

The groupings of flowers, large and small, help to identify salient features, and ultimately, the more secure the artist is in knowing into what category experts have placed a plant, the more securely an accurate and believable rendering can be made. Artists rely on scientists to group plants into a hierarchy based on similarity of characters. The highest and most encompassing group being the most general, proceeding to more and more particular groupings. For artists, one of the most valuable is "family," because it can be used to stress those features in a specific plant which tie it to its nearest relatives. The family name has a suffix ending in "aceae." Below the family category are the two names that identify the plant throughout the world: the Latin binomial. The first part of the binomial is the genus, a grouping where the identifying characters are fairly narrow. Next in this twosome is the specific epithet, or the species, the term that identifies the ultimate reproducing unit—this plant and no other. In print the binomial is italicized, the first letter of the genus is capitalized with the rest in lowercase (even when the specific epithet derives from a proper name). When writing a Latin binomial, or placing it in calligraphy on a painting, it is accepted to underline the phrase, instead of italicizing. Use this Latin phrase to identify the plants being portrayed, whether it is the flower, the habit or the fruit.

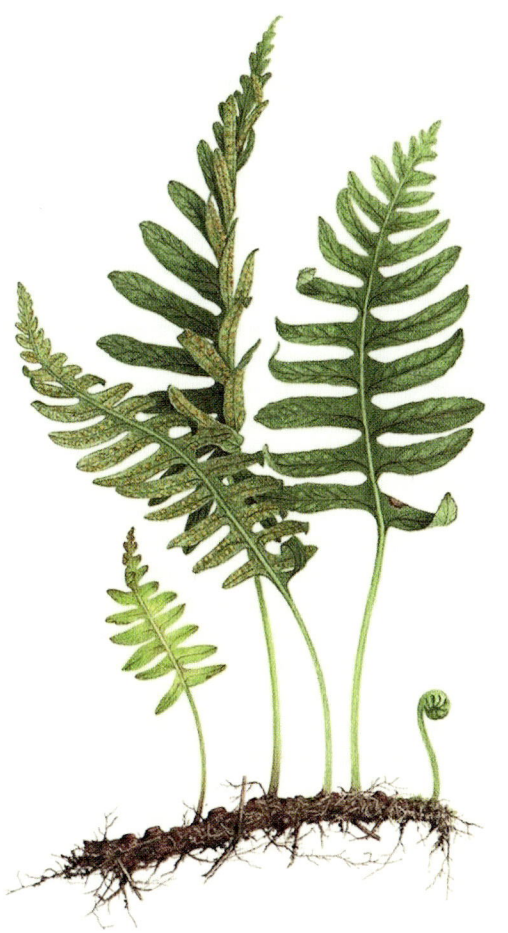

Common Polypody
Polypodium vulgare
11 ¾ × 15 ¾ inches [29.38 × 39.38 cm]
Watercolor on paper
© Vincent Jeannerot

Vincent Jeannerot's common polypody shows the growth habit of this fern.

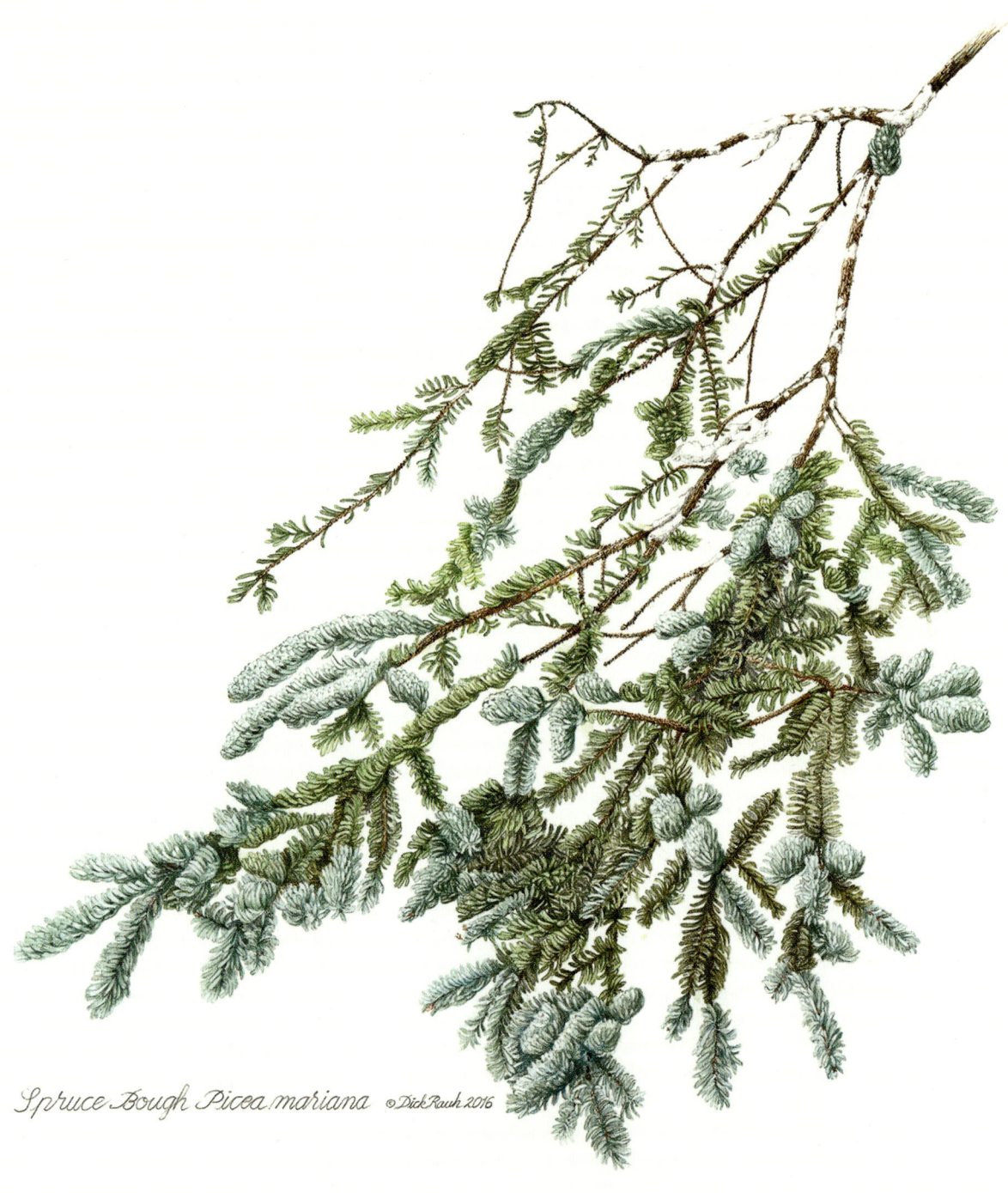

Spruce Bough Picea mariana © Dick Rauh 2016

Spruce Bough
Picea mariana
Watercolor on paper
34 × 26 inches [85 × 65 cm]
© Dick Rauh

Cone-bearing vascular plants are some of the most stunning living things on earth. Although they are not as numerous and diverse a group as angiosperms (flowering plants) or cryptogams (ferns, horsetails and clubmosses), the variety of the group's cones and types of leaves nonetheless provide ample opportunities for botanical artists.

With needle- or scale-like leaves, all conifers are woody, perennial plants, usually evergreen trees or shrubs including majestic redwoods, ancient bristlecone pines and lovely blue spruce. The familiar cone is female and the seeds are loose within its scales yielding the group name Gymnosperm meaning naked seeds. The male cone that produces pollen is usually less conspicuous and breaks down within a few weeks after pollen release. However, some male cones are very brightly colored during their short existence and can make exciting subjects.

The new growth of needles on the branch tips of many conifers can be quite showy, such as the beautiful blue foliage of Dr. Dick Rauh's painting of black spruce.

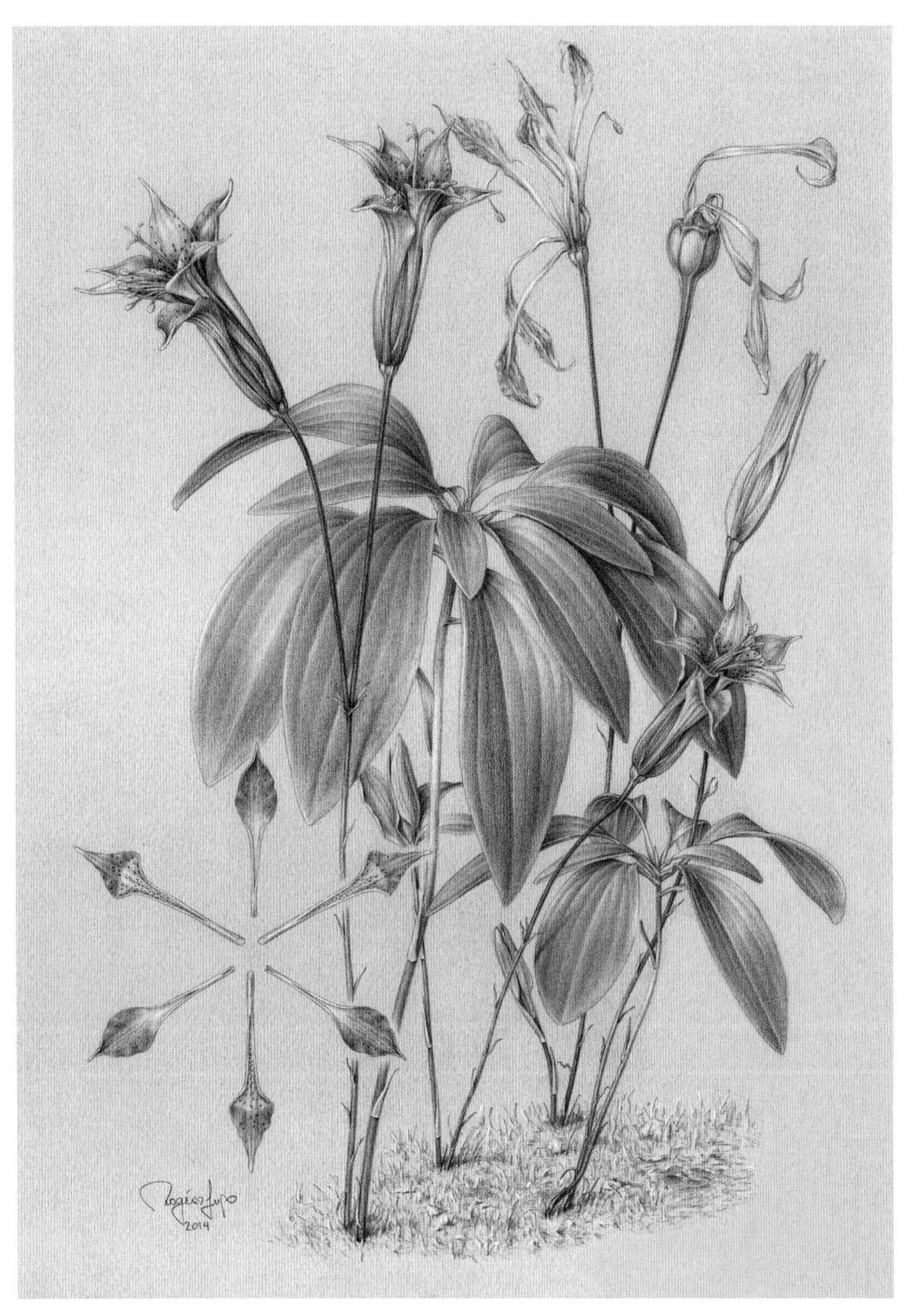

Alstroemeria stramonia Graphite with ivory-colored pencil on paper 14 ⅜ × 11 inches [36.25 × 27.5 cm]
© Rogério Lupo

PART 1

Drawing Botanical Subjects in Black and White

Graphite Skills

The Basics

TUTOR: HEEYOUNG KIM

Strong drawing skills underpin every botanical artwork in any medium. Heeyoung Kim demonstrates basic graphite pencil techniques in detail, then geometric shapes, which contribute to the accurate rendering of botanical subjects, are drawn and shaded. These shaded forms provide guidance in visualizing light and shadow on more complicated subjects.

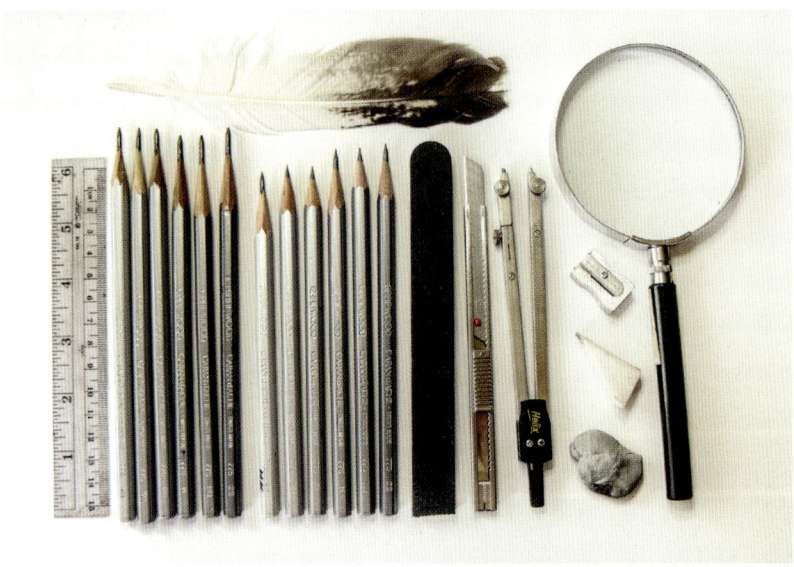

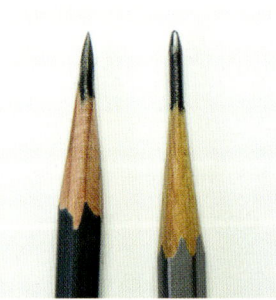

Tools: Feather; magnifying glass; kneaded eraser; white plastic eraser cut into a triangle shape; pencil sharpener; dividers; craft knife; emery board; ruler; sharply pointed pencils (2B, HB, H, 2H, 3H, 4H); a set of long bullet-pointed pencils (2B, HB, H, 2H, 3H, 4H); ruler.

A sharply pointed graphite tip (left) is ideal for drawing fine lines and details, and for making precisely placed marks. A long, bullet-pointed graphite tip (right) makes soft preliminary line drawings, which can be erased without leaving marks behind. The long, smooth side of a dull graphite tip can be used to shade large areas quickly.

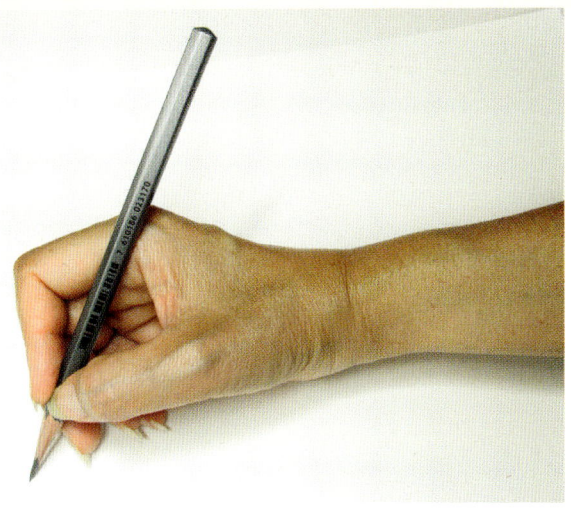

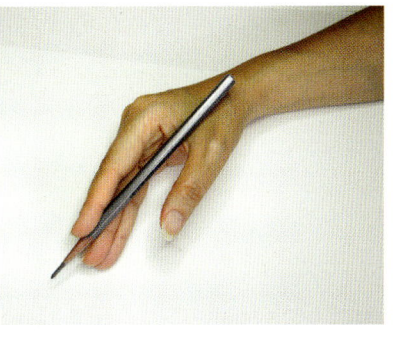

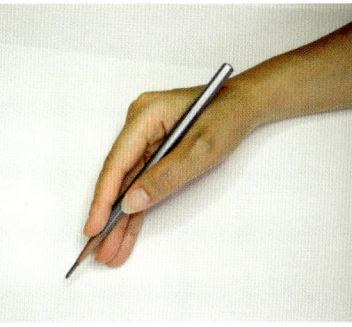

PENCIL CARRIAGE

A "writing grip" refers to holding a pencil approximately 1 inch [2.5 cm] from the tip. A normal writing grip is suitable for making short strokes in drawing.

To create steady, fluid lines, your hand and pencil will need skillful kinetic coordination. Hold the pencil between your index and middle fingers, and gently press the pencil with your thumb with your hand resting comfortably on the drawing surface. Then pivot your hand, moving your fingers as a unit in the intended direction of the drawn lines. A light touch works best.

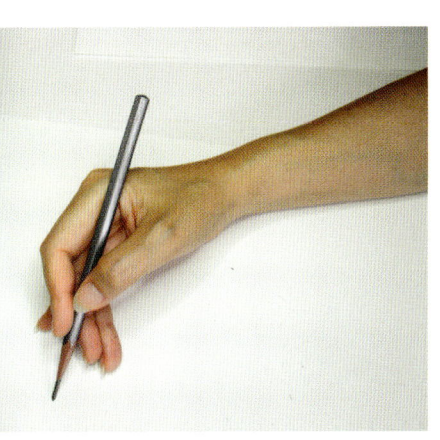

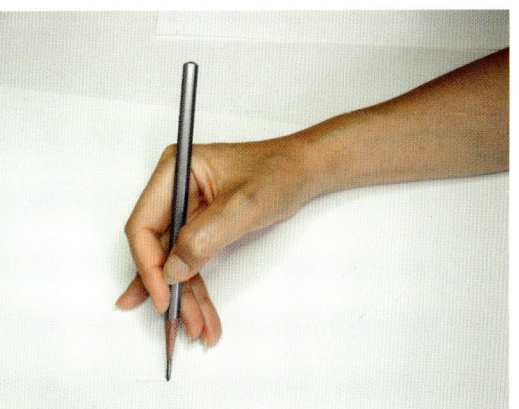

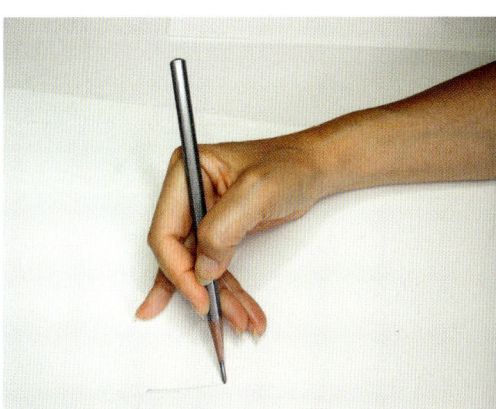

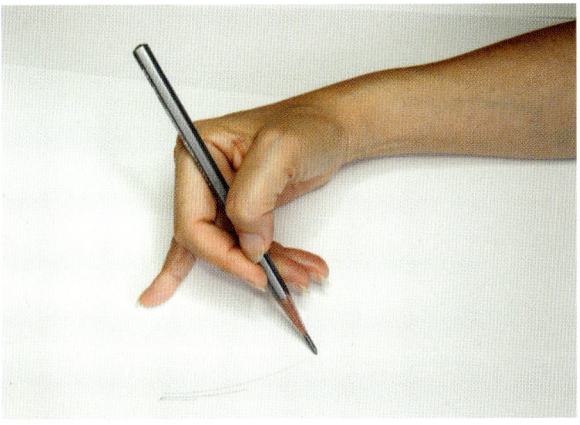

To draw steady lines, firmly position the palm of your hand as an anchoring point to help control the angle of your finger movements and the length of your strokes. Your pinky finger can be used as a pivot and for further control. Changing the pressure of your thumb will vary the line weight. Protect the drawing paper from skin oils and moisture by placing a piece of tracing paper between your hand and the drawing paper.

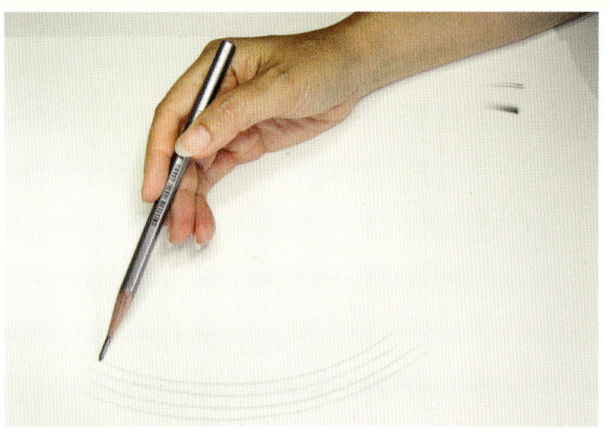
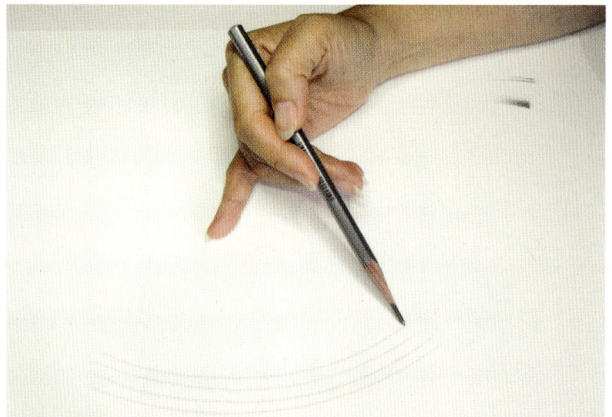

Using the same technique, but gripping the pencil farther from the tip, longer smooth lines can be drawn. For even longer lines, your wrist or elbow can be the anchoring point. After drawing the first line, move your anchoring point and draw the second line, continuing in this manner to make parallel lines, as if using a compass.

LINE CONTROL

The pencil's angle, point, and softness matter for controlling lines. When you are drawing, the side of the pencil tip pointing away from you holds the control. There is not control over the underside away from the tip. This dramatized image of a line shows how the point creates a controlled, straight line, but the underside creates a ragged line. (A)

Either sharpen your pencil on a sanding block, or use a sharpener that grips the pencil to center it. Either of these methods will make a symmetrical point. After you have sharpened the pencil, smooth the graphite on an emery board or a piece of fine sandpaper to make it even more pointed, then wipe off the graphite dust with a soft cloth or paper towel. (B)

When the pencil is very pointed, the lines are more precise because you know exactly where the pencil will contact the paper. To make very fine lines, use hard pencils such as 2H or 3H. Soft pencils tend to break when they are very pointed, splashing graphite powder on the paper, which results in smudges. (C)

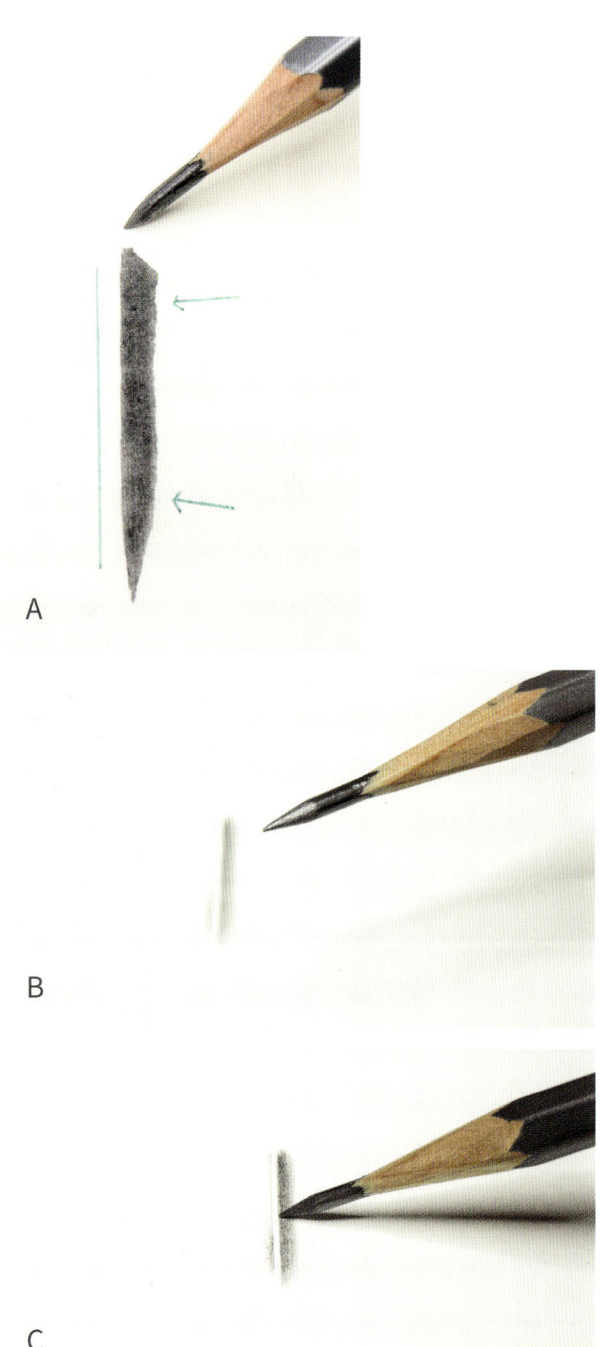

A

B

C

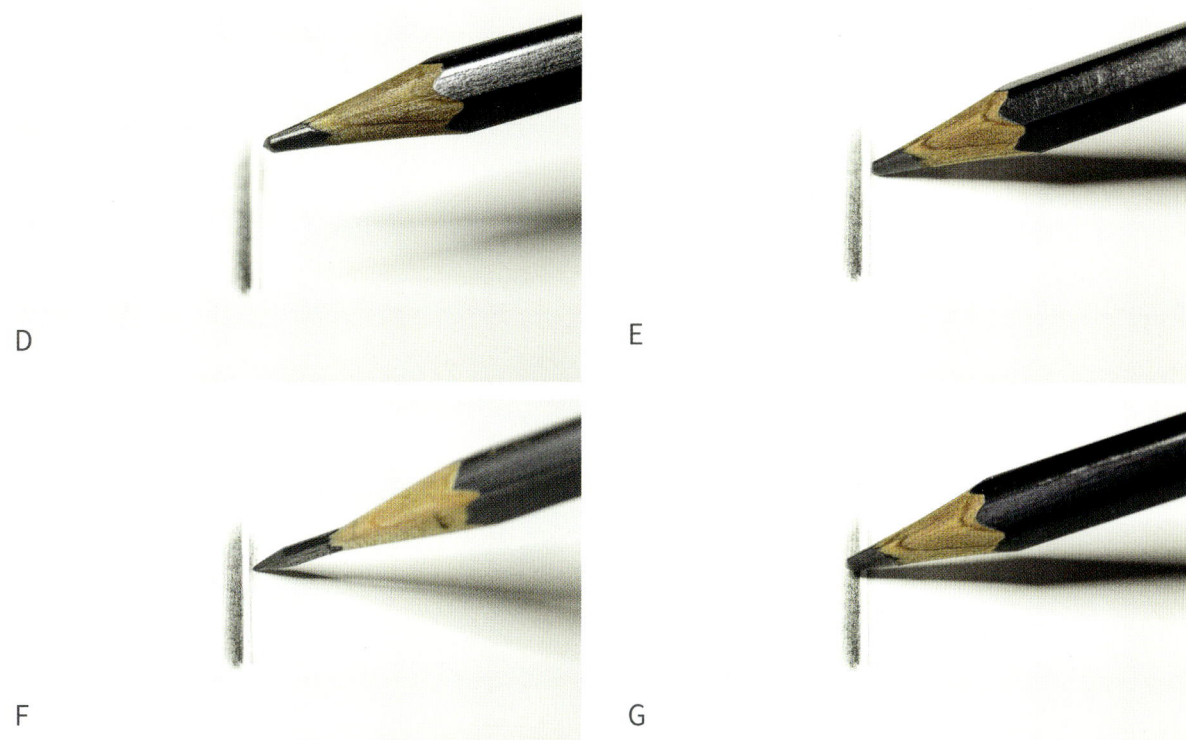

D

E

F

G

To see a comparison, with this not-so-well-defined point it is unclear exactly where the tip will contact the paper. (D)

Without knowing or seeing where the pencil tip will contact the paper, it won't be possible to get a precise result. The graphite might go over the line, or it might be blurry, or there will be lots of small white spots, resulting in a sloppy look. (E)

Turn the paper around to work on the other side. That way, the tip is in the control position and the narrow space is safe from overflowing graphite on the underside of the pencil. (F)

Working on the other side from the same angle, without turning the paper, will result in lines that are not sharp. The small white area will be fuzzy or obliterated. (G)

Compare these drawings, both made with a very pointed pencil. On the left, the paper was not turned around, and the left line covers up about a third of the white line and looks fuzzier. On the right, both sides are crisp and clear by simply turning the paper and working with the tip in control.

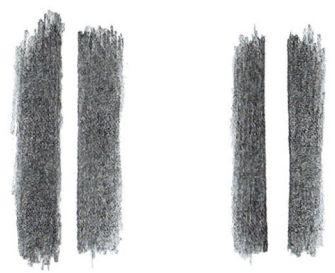

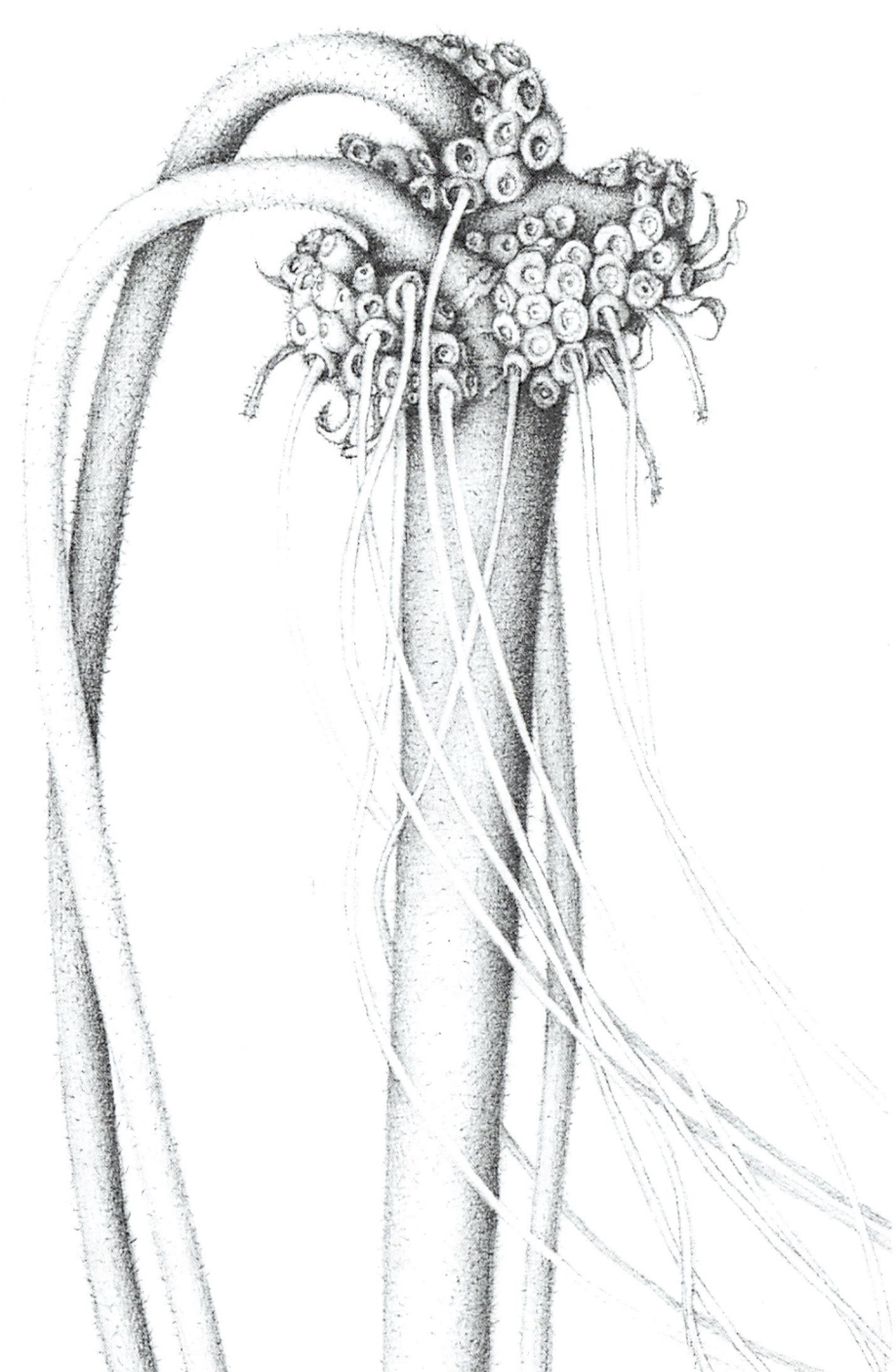

Milkweed Seedpod
Graphite on paper
22 × 17 inches [55 × 42.5 cm]
© Heeyoung Kim

In this drawing of milkweed
seedpods, the round peduncle scars
and the few remaining peduncles
are as narrow as one millimeter.

LINE WEIGHT

Make loose lines for your initial drawings with a lightly carried bullet-pointed pencil. At first, sketch out compositions and plant positions freely without putting much weight in the lines. These preliminary lines can be easily erased later if needed. Use H pencils for your initial drawings, because they smudge less.

To define shapes and details, hold a sharply pointed pencil in a writing grip, apply a consistent and equal amount of pressure, and move the pencil slowly. Weight, speed, and the type of pencil point all affect the quality of the line.

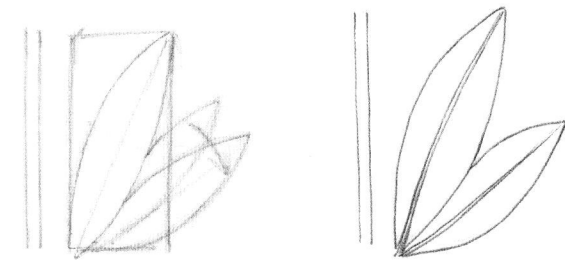

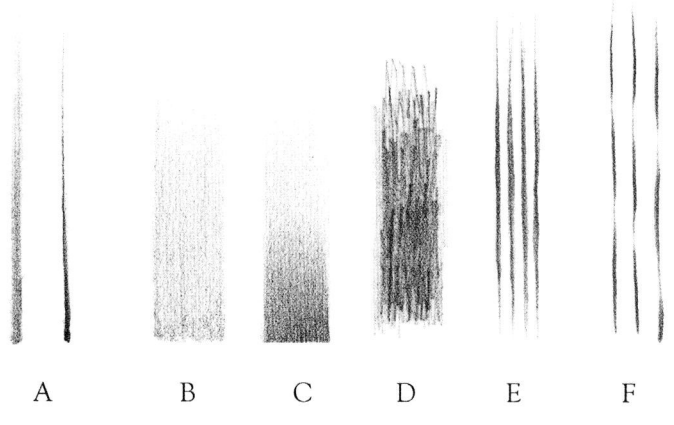

A   B   C   D   E   F

A. To create naturally tapering lines, start with substantial pressure and gradually lift to a lighter pressure. Both bullet-pointed (left) and sharply pointed (right) pencils can be used to obtain different effects.

B. For making a smooth gradation, layer tapering lines. Using a light touch, fill in the desired area with a bullet-pointed pencil (2B here, but any grade can be used).

C. In a dark shadow area, add another layer with short tapering lines made with a sharply pointed pencil (same grade or softer). Add more layers if needed. This works best when all the strokes go in one direction, from the darkest area toward the lightest area.

D. When strokes are made in a continuous line moving up and down, the turning points result in darker blotches, whether your pencil tip is sharp or dull. This technique can be used in dark or textured areas, but it's not ideal for fine gradation.

E. Lines drawn in the manner of an airplane landing and taking off—a feathering stroke—are very graceful and flexible. Start the line with a light touch (the airplane touching down), gradually increase the pressure to normal or heavy (the airplane rolling down the runway), then release the pressure and end lightly (the airplane lifting off). To make a continuous long line, this technique is useful for connecting a few segments without showing where the segments connect. This works with both sharply pointed and dull pencils.

F. When lines are drawn intermittently, you can make veins or patterns flow naturally with highlight and shadow. These lines were drawn with a bullet-pointed pencil; you can achieve more variations in line thickness with a broader pencil point.

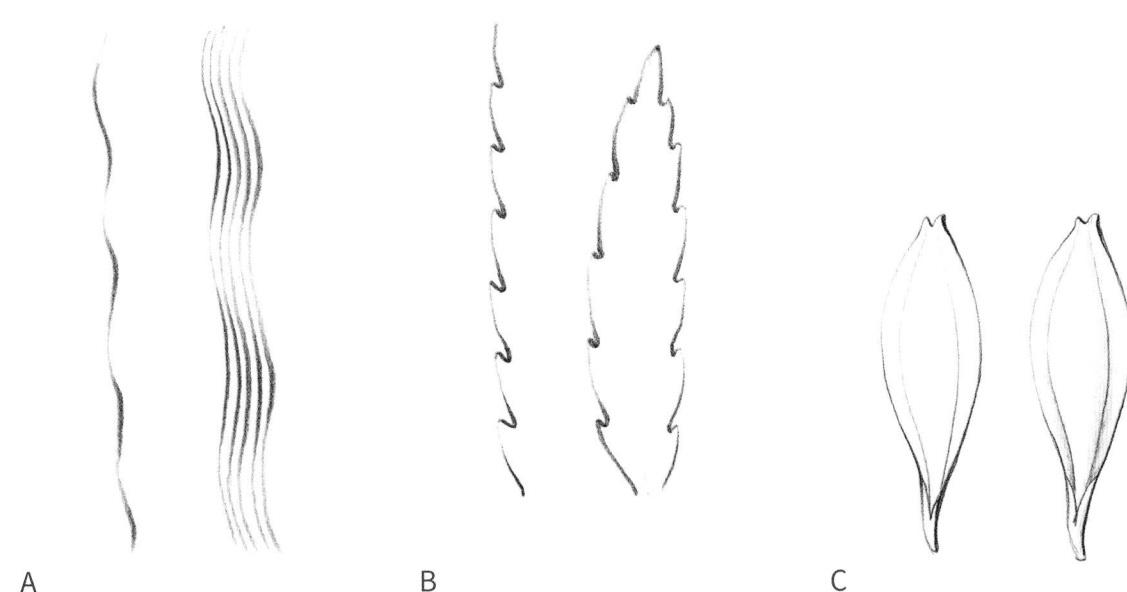

A B C

By fluctuating the pressure along a line, wavy lines can ripple between light and dark. When repeated, the movement dynamically expresses highlight and shadow. (A)

At left, a serrated line with varying weight. By applying light pressure toward the tips of the leaf serrations and heavier pressure in the indentations, a leaf margin can be easily defined. (B)

By applying heavier line weight in the shadow area, and lighter weight in highlighted area, flower petals look light and airy, but have a strong appearance. (C)

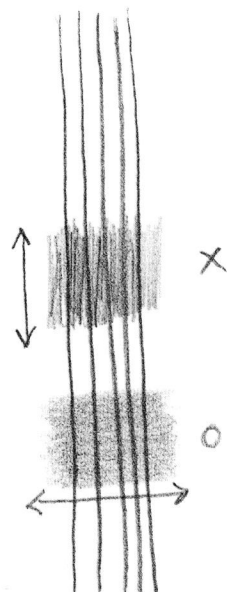

When you need to darken areas or lessen contrast where details are already defined, add strokes perpendicular to the major lines of the underdrawing (O). The details will be preserved. The side of a bullet-pointed pencil will work best. On the contrary, lines added randomly or in the same direction will confuse the underdrawing (X).

VALUE

Successful drawings demonstrate a full range of value from white (the lightest value) to black (the darkest value) and various grays in between. This example shows the range of value that can be achieved with an HB pencil using various line weights—more pressure makes darker lines. Each grade of pencil will have its own range.

Graphite pencils are graded from 9H to 9B (H: higher numbers are harder; B: higher numbers are softer) with HB in the middle. Grade F indicates graphite that sharpens to a fine point and is roughly equivalent to HB. A wide range of grades produces a full value scale.

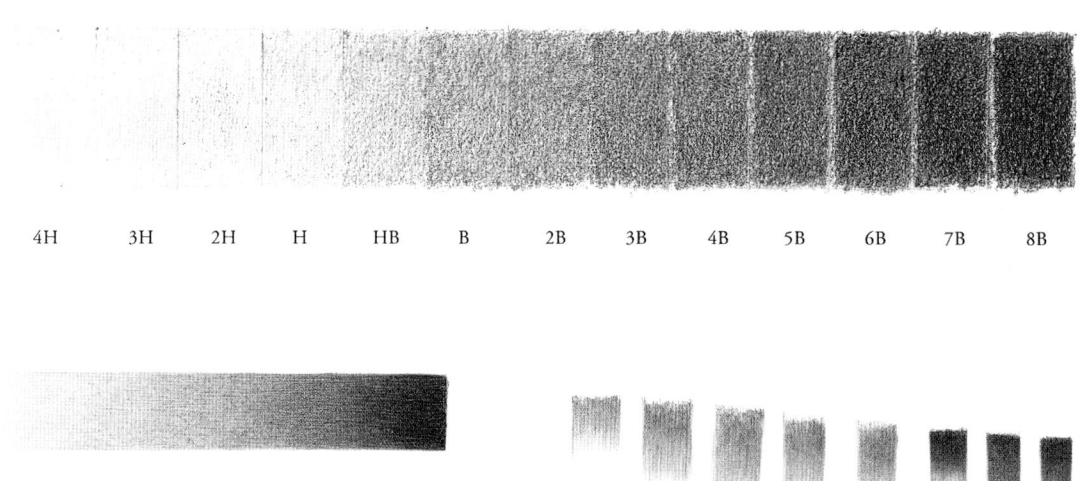

| 4H | 3H | 2H | H | HB | B | 2B | 3B | 4B | 5B | 6B | 7B | 8B |

However, it is not necessary to use the full range of grades to achieve a full range of values. Using 3H, 2H, H, HB, B, and 2B pencils can produce a wide range of values by applying different pressures and pencil points, as shown here. A freshly sharpened pencil, carried with substantial weight, produces darker lines than lightly drawn lines with a dull point. The pressure on the pencil is more important than the pencil grade itself.

With bullet-pointed pencils, fill the darkest area with B, then draw longer strokes with HB, and continue with H, 2H, and 3H to build up value scale. Using harder grades over softer ones minimizes smudging. Repeat the process using sharply pointed pencils. Short tapering strokes in one direction, not zigzag, yield the finest result. Blend the highlight into white paper with 4H. This illustration shows each step described above, from left to right. Keep building layers until a smooth transition is achieved from very dark to white.

Light and Shadow on Basic Shapes

These four basic shapes—sphere, cylinder, cone, and cup—are repeated throughout the plant kingdom. Using these shapes for guidance will help you accurately render any botanical subject.

LIGHT AND SHADOW ON A SPHERE

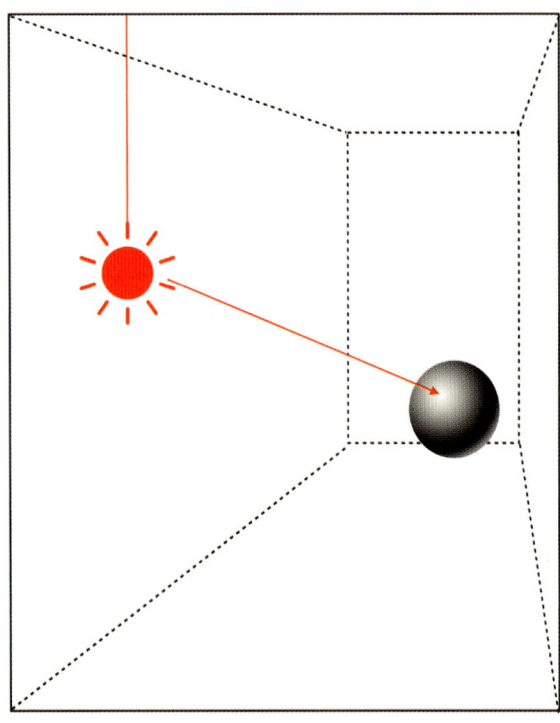

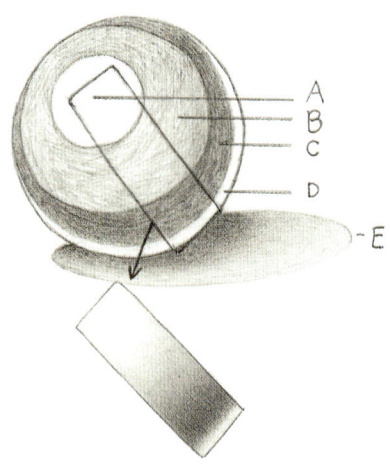

Light and shadow shown on a sphere.

A: Highlight

B: Shadow or medium shadow

C: Core shadow (the darkest shadow on the object)

D: Reflected light (light that comes around from around the back of the round object)

E: Cast shadow

Light source: artists can position the main light source wherever they like. The commonly used light source in botanical art and illustration, shown in this diagram, (light front left side at about 45 degrees) has its merit: the object has a widely spread medium shadow area which will deliver accurate color and details. This light source is used in the following exercises.

When light hits on A, the curved form of the sphere generates shadow that becomes gradually darker toward the edge. There is a subtle reflected light along the sphere's edge.

Shown on slice: Refined gradation from highlight to reflected light. Color and details tend to be washed out in the highlight, hence appear almost white and darken toward cast shadow area. The most accurate color and details can be shown in the medium shadow area. Transition from light to dark should be carefully executed without blotches or coarse borders between A, B, C, and D.

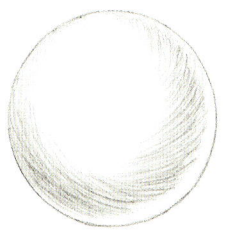 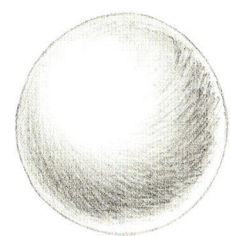

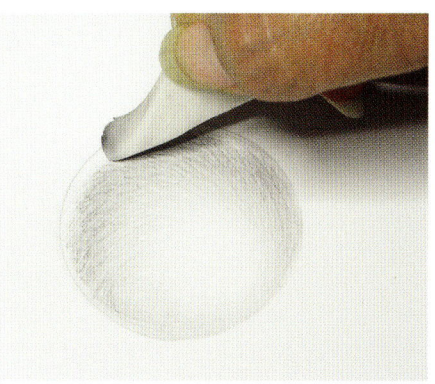

Draw a circle with a diameter of about 4 inches [10 cm]. With bullet-pointed H, start to shade in core shadow area. To represent reflected light, leave the paper white. Make the strokes taper from the core shadow toward medium shadow area. Follow the contour rather than drawing straight lines.

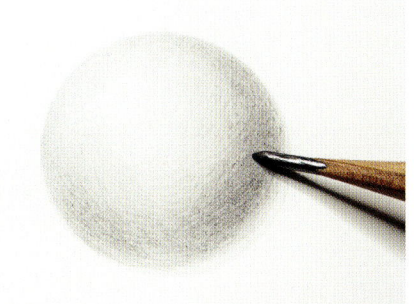

Using a bullet-pointed 2H, continue to draw tapering strokes toward the highlight area. Keep adding strokes in the same manner with 2B in the core shadow, and B, H, 2H, and 3H gradually toward the highlight area. Add layers with hard and soft pencils on top of one another, until they blend smoothly.

Using the flexible end of triangle-shaped eraser, soften the outline and the blunt endings of pencil strokes in the reflected light area to create soft hint of light.

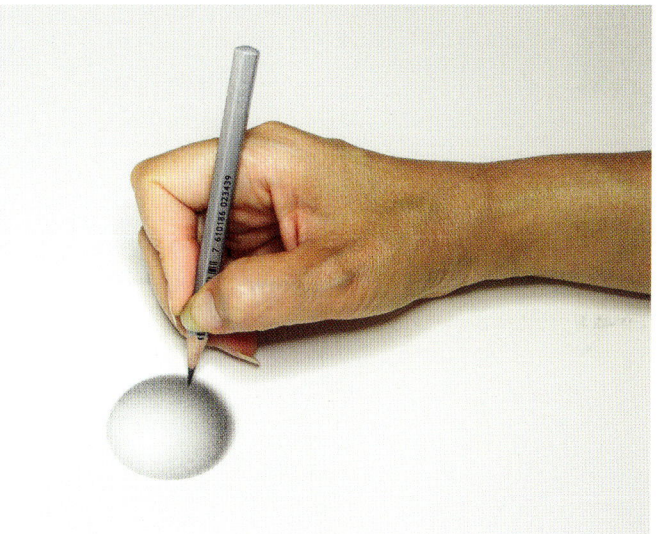

Continue blending and layering until the gradation is satisfactory. Pay close attention to softening the transition between the core shadow and reflected light, so it doesn't look like a line of white around the edge of the sphere.

Using sharply pointed pencils, with a close grip, darken and refine the whole area with short strokes. Use 2B in core shadow, and B, H, 2H, and 3H gradually toward lighter area to create perfect value scale. Refine the reflected area with 4H. If the highlight is lost, recover it by using the soft edge of the cut eraser or kneaded eraser.

Finished sphere showing highlight, medium shadow, core shadow, and reflected light in fine gradation and full range of value from the darkest to the lightest.

Draw a cylinder that is about 4 inches [10 cm] high. With bullet-pointed H, start to add shadow on both sides of the highlight. Note that medium-tone shadow occurs on the left side, too, while the darkest shadow is on the right side. Use tapering strokes and leave some white space for reflected light.

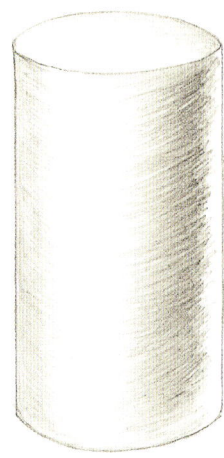

With bullet-pointed pencils from 2B to 3H, build up various tones from the highlight area to the core shadow until a three-dimensional cylindrical form emerges. Remember to follow the contour.

Clean up the reflected-light area with eraser. The edge of core shadow looks very rough at this stage. Dab along the rough area with flexible end of the eraser. It will soften the blotchy edge and lighten the outline. Make the outline on the reflected light area as light as possible.

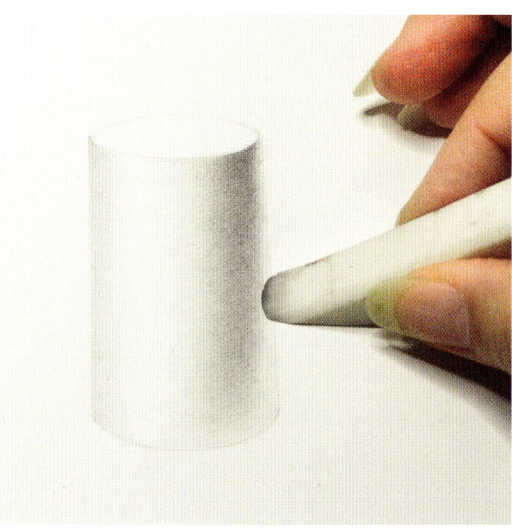

With sharply pointed pencils, ranging from 2B to 4H, darken and refine the surface accordingly to show subtle tone transition from highlight to core shadow.

Finished cylinder. The cylinder form occurs in tree trunks, stems, leaf and flower stalks, and tiny tendrils. Therefore, practice on slightly modified forms of cylinders, for example, curved or twisted, is highly recommended.

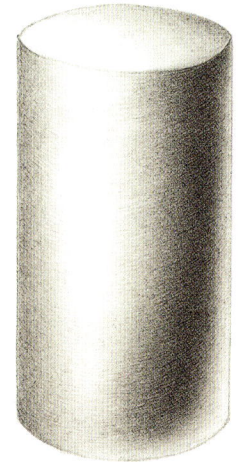

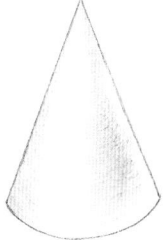 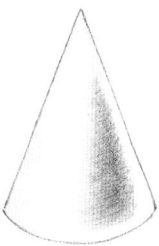 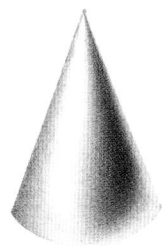

Go through the same drawing process as with cylinder. Pay special attention to the narrow apex where ranges of tone occur in a tiny space. Use a pointed hard pencil such as H in the small area, as soft pencils break easily and get smudgy. These cone shapes occur in many tubular flowers.

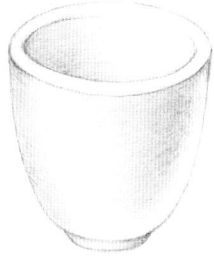 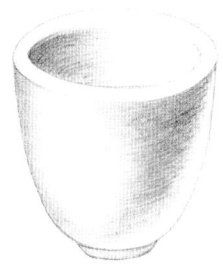 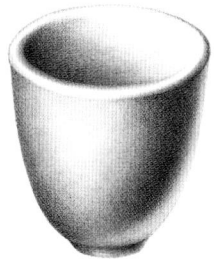

Light and shadow appear on the outer surface (convex) and inside (concave) of the cup opposite to one another. Study the light and shadow carefully, then start to add shadow with H on the inner and outer sides of the cup. Reserve some white space for the highlight, reflected light, and rim.

Build up various tones with bullet-pointed pencils. Follow the curve of the cup shape, especially in the dark area of the concave interior. The pencil strokes will be blended eventually, but their movement enhances the round form of the cup when finished.

A sharply pointed pencil gives clean definition around the edges. Finish up with small strokes. Add details around the rim to show subtle light change. This shape is common in the plant world and can be instructive in adding overall shading to a cup-shaped flower or seedpod.

Heeyoung Kim demonstrates how to use geometric shapes to lay out graphite drawings of a variety of floral shapes. Start with ellipses for a radial flower, a rectangle and triangle for a cup-shaped flower, and a rectangle with a centerline for a bilaterally symmetrical flower. Beginning with these simple shapes, flowers can be accurately and proportionally rendered.

Shaded Flowers

TUTOR: HEEYOUNG KIM

Chrysanthemum

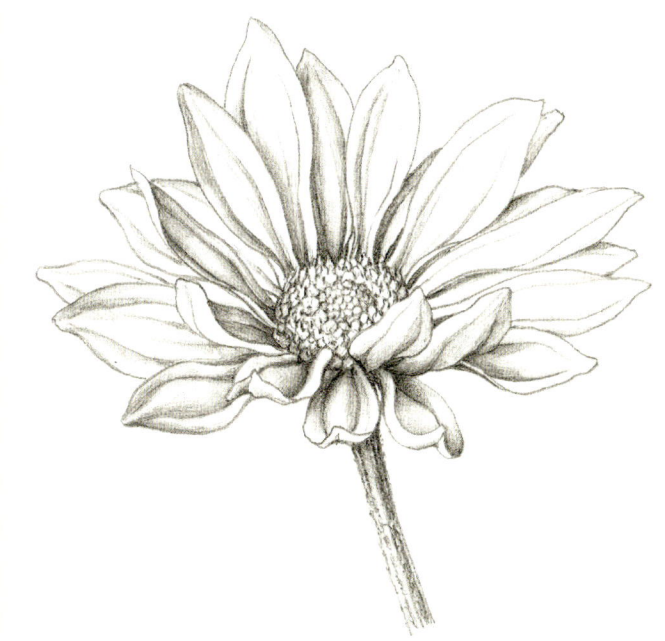

Chrysanthemum Graphite on paper
2 ¾ × 3 inches [7 × 7.5 cm]
© Heeyoung Kim
HOURS TO COMPLETE: 15

MATERIALS: Feather; magnifying glass; kneaded eraser; white plastic eraser cut into a triangle shape; pencil sharpener; dividers; craft knife; emery board; ruler; sharply pointed pencils (2B, HB, H, 2H, 3H, 4H); a set of long bullet-pointed pencils (2B, HB, H, 2H, 3H, 4H); ruler.

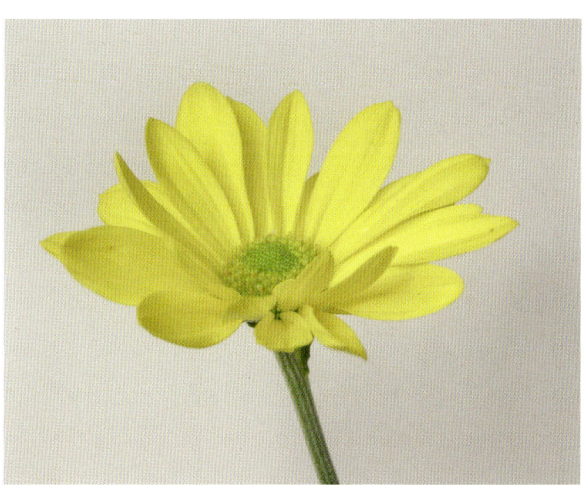

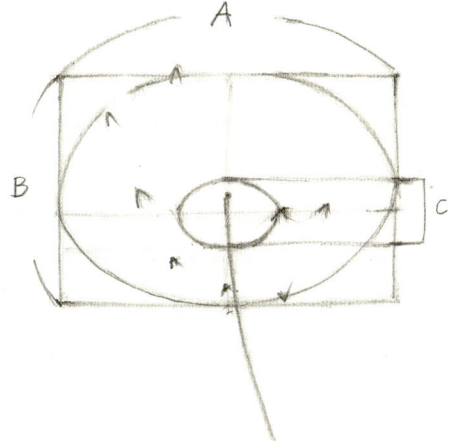

This yellow chrysanthemum is an example of a radially symmetric composite flower. This type of flower looks overwhelming at first glance, because of the number of petals and the complicated form of the disk flower (center structure), but it is not as difficult to draw as it appears, especially if you approach it in a methodical manner. Start by measuring, and making simple lines and shapes. Closing one eye during measuring is helpful.

First, draw a line showing the curve of the stem up to the center of the disk flower. Then, measure width (A), height (B), and the dimensions of the disk (C). Using the measurements for the width and height, draw a rectangle first, then draw ellipses within the rectangle for the perimeter of the flower and for the disk in the center. Then mark the petal tips that deviate from the ellipses, either by extending beyond the ellipses or not reaching the edge the ellipses.

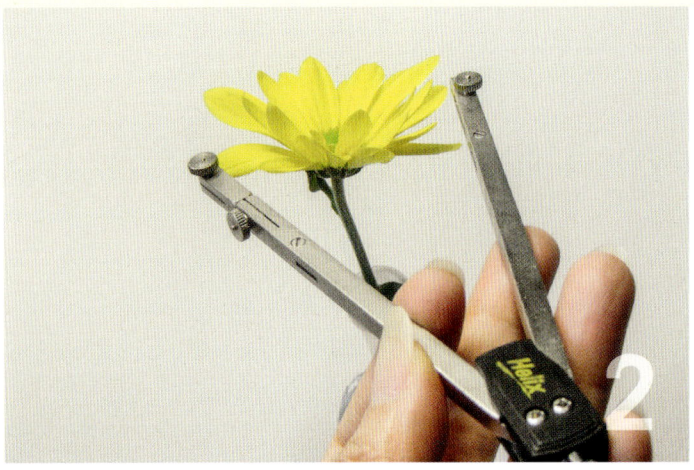

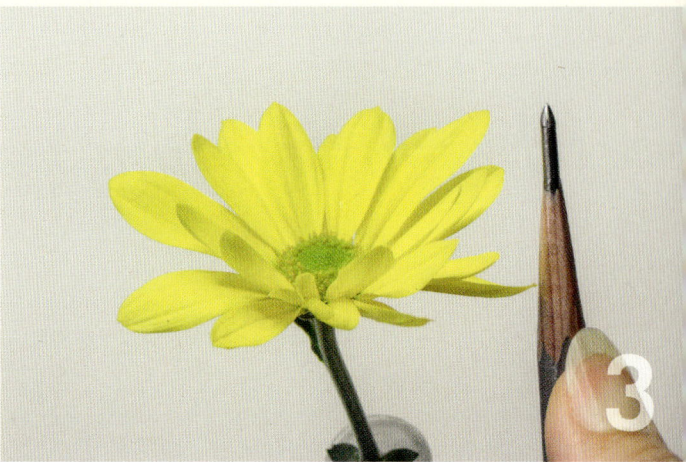

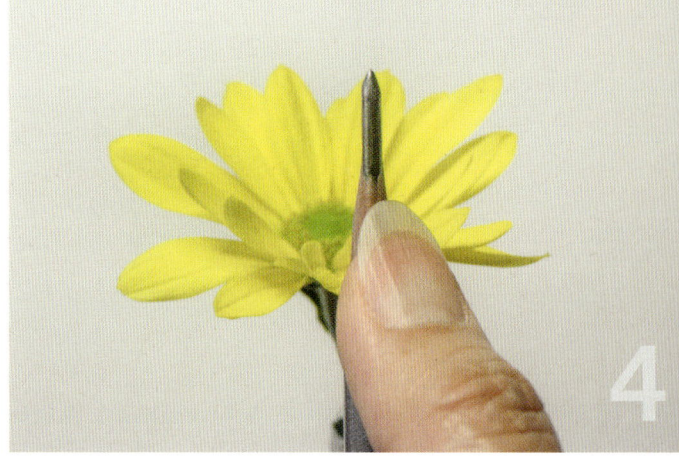

To measure with dividers, measure the full width of the ray flowers from the edge of one side to the other (A). Then measure the height in perspective (the angle at which you are looking at it, not its full height) (B). Take notes of all dimensions for future referral. Imagine a flat vertical plane in front of the flower, and don't tilt the dividers.

To measure with a pencil, mark the flower width on the pencil with a fingernail, holding your arm straight out (A). Transfer that width to the paper. Measure the height in perspective (as in photo) and transfer that height (B). Repeat for the center disk flowers (C).

In the same manner, measure the length of the ray flower petals in perspective and make note of the length. Always remember to hold the pencil straight and close to the flower with your arm extended, elbow locked, keeping the same distance from your eye for each measurement.

With a bullet-pointed 2H pencil, roughly and lightly sketch petals within the ellipses. Make sure all the petals originate at the base of the flower where it joins with the stem; the base is not visible from the top. Pay special attention to the petals marked in step 2; they are mostly foreshortened or curved, and subject to mistakes.

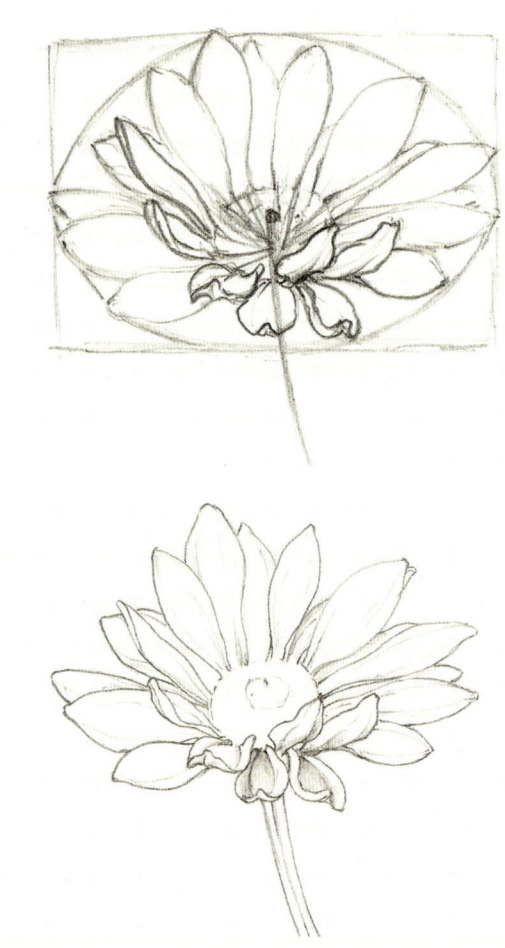

With a sharply pointed H or 2H pencil, and applying substantial pressure, draw individual petals in detail. Draw the stem by adding lines on both sides of the initial stem centerline. Then, with the eraser's soft end gently erase all the initial lines. Due to the eraser's flexibility, the final lines will remain, while the lightly drawn initial lines will be erased.

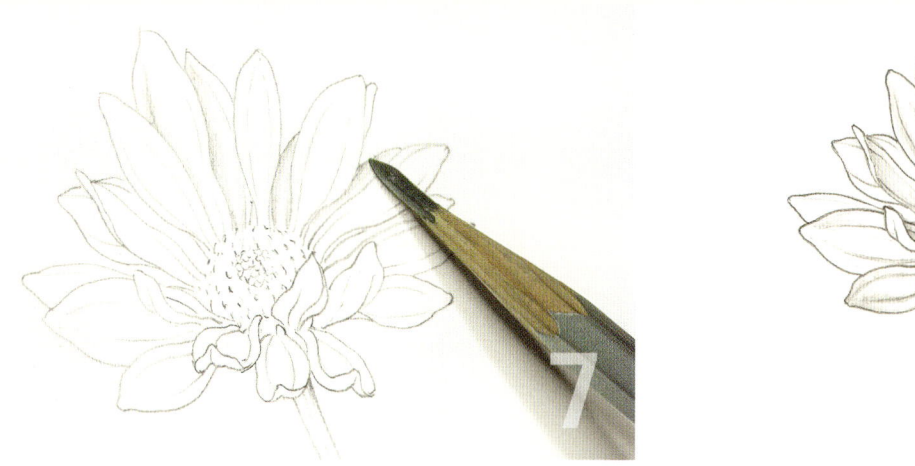

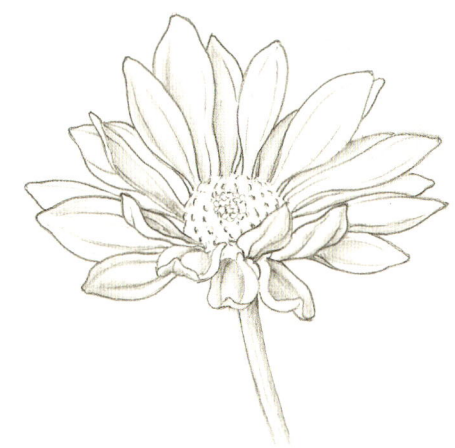

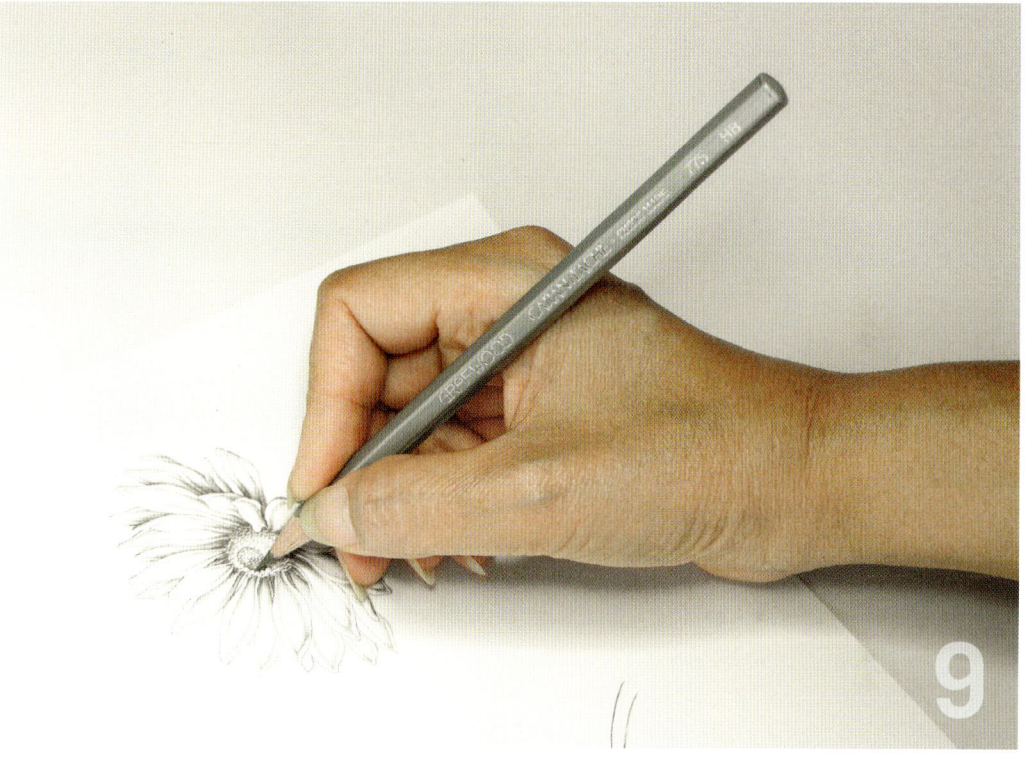

If the paper becomes scuffed, trace and transfer the drawing to a new piece of paper using a light box or tracing paper. With the side of a bullet-pointed 2H, add the first layer of shadow where it appears on the flower. Preserve some white space on small curved edges. Shade the underside where petals overlap.

With a bullet-pointed 2H, add shadow roughly on the whole flower to see its form and depth. Do not use soft pencils such as B or 2B yet, because they smudge and become messy when erased. Mark spiral lines for the center disk flowers.

With sharply pointed pencils, add details, deepen shadows, and finish the center. For the tiny flowers in the center, avoid drawing too many little circles because they will make the whole center dark. Instead, add small strokes in the shadows of each circle, consistently on one side. Then you will see the little flowers emerge. Darken the disk by shading using strokes with the curve of the disk, except in highlight area. Finish up the ray and disk flowers. The challenge in drawing composite flowers is in making the shadows dark, yet clearly separated from each other. Avoid adding too much shadow along the edges of overlapping petals. Keep the tips of petals light as much as possible. Add just enough shadow strategically at dark corners with a sharply pointed B or 2B pencil.

Tulip

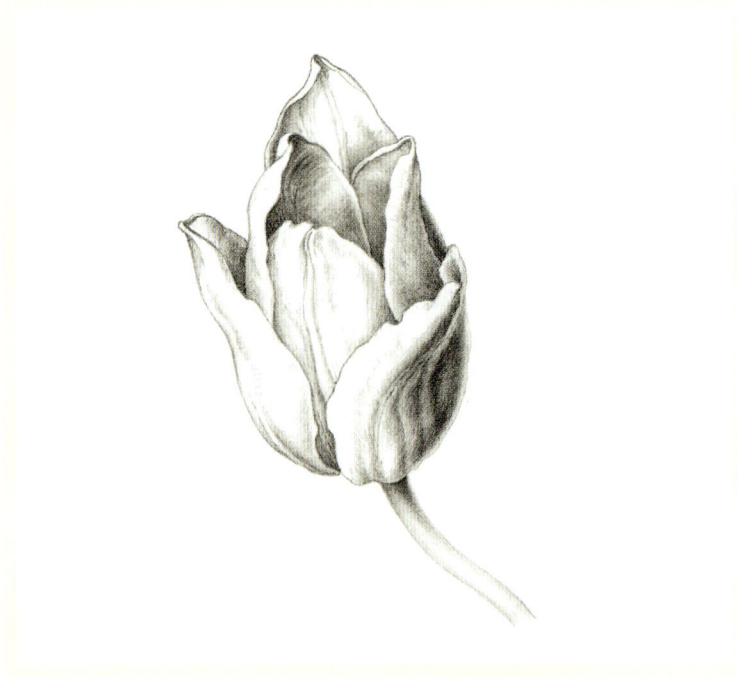

Tulip Graphite on paper
3 ½ × 2 ⅜ inches [9 × 6 cm]
© Heeyoung Kim
HOURS TO COMPLETE: 15

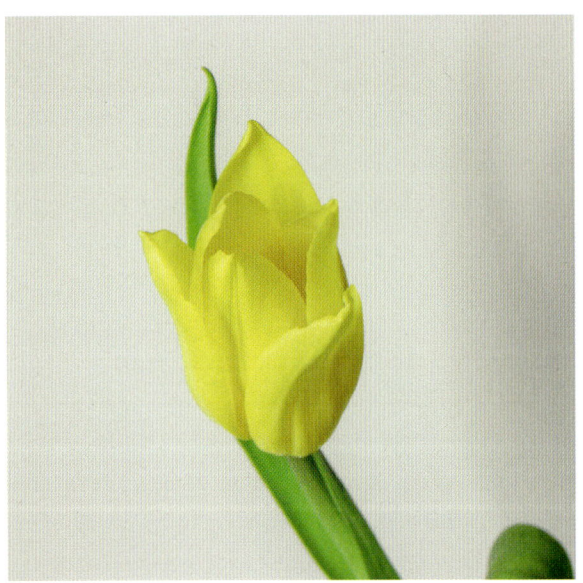

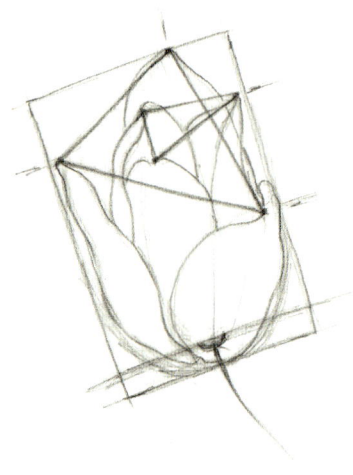

Tulips are cup-shaped flowers. They have six petal-like structures, but only three of the structures are true petals. Tulips are composed of three outer sepals, which were the outer cover of the bud, and three inner petals, which are true petals. Knowing botanical structure helps create scientifically accurate illustration, because the two parts may have slightly different coloration, shape, and texture.

With bullet-pointed 2H or H, measure the outer dimensions of the tulip and draw a rectangle. Then measure the tips of three sepals and connect them in a triangle. Do the same with three inner petals. By examining the angles and crossings of the triangles, confirm whether their placements are correct or not. Now, sketch in the sepals and petals focusing on accurate position and proportion.

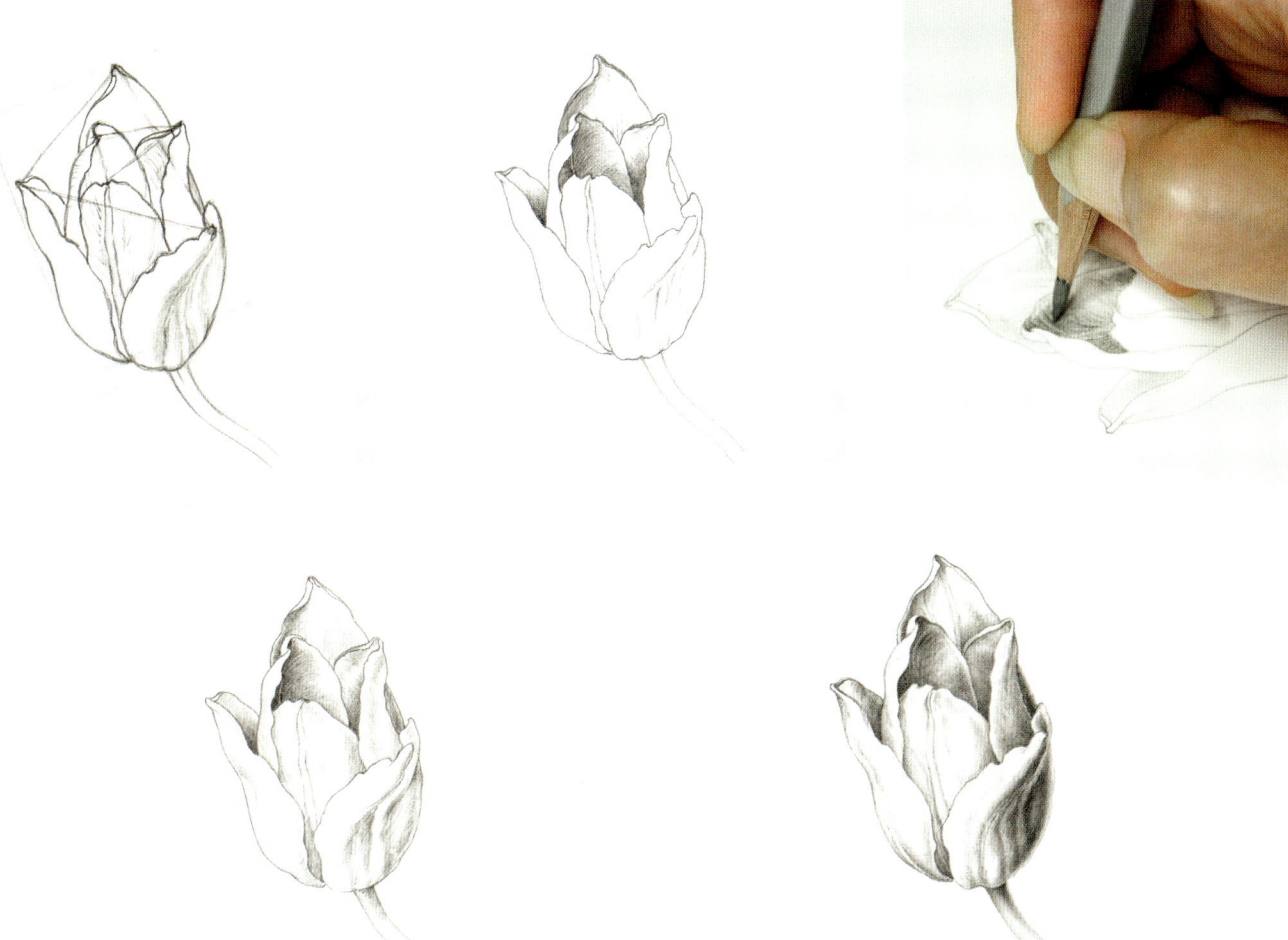

With a pointed 2H, and using substantial pressure, draw a detailed shape of each part. For foreshortened shapes, add some shadow early on, which helps to better show the form. Carefully observe any tiny vein lines and their direction on the petals and sepals and mark them. They will make the curves look organic and realistic. After the final lines are drawn, erase the initial lines.

Trace the drawing onto good-quality paper if necessary. Now, add shadow on the inside (concave side) of the petals and sepals. There are two concave shapes created by the inner petals and outer sepals. Observe carefully where the darkest shadow occurs.

With a pointed pencil, draw vein lines following the curvature. The fine lines might not be very visible when the drawing is finished, but they enhance its formation. By doing so, details and textures can be added as well.

Add shadow on the outside (convex side) of petals and sepals. By separating the shading process on concave and convex parts, it becomes clear how forms affect light and shadow. Hence, the drawing will be more accurate and logical.

Now refine the gradation of the shadows, refine the clean edges, and deepen the dark shadows. Using an eraser and a light touch, recover reflected light, then add any finishing touches. When you are drawing thin and translucent flower petals, you may notice some unexpected bright corners where you would expect very dark shadows (see the front sepal on the right side). This happens when light penetrates the thin petals, instead of being blocked.

Orchid

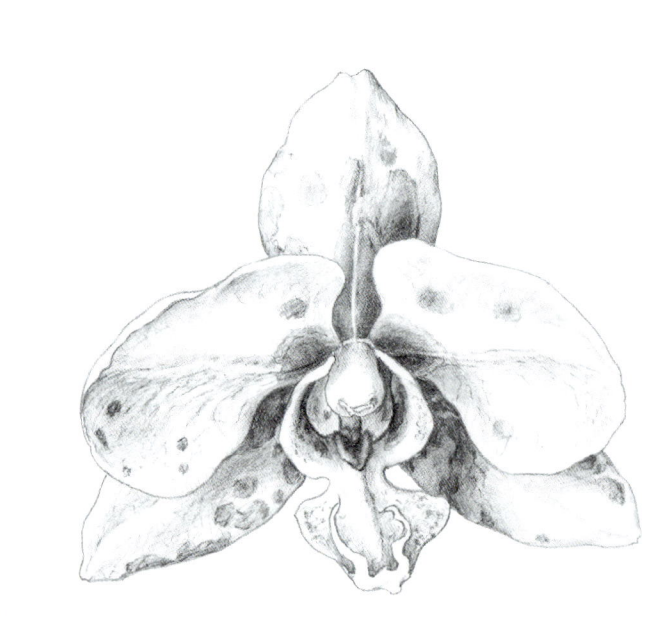

Phalaenopsis orchid
Graphite on paper
2 9/16 × 3 inches [6.5 × 7.5 cm]
© Heeyoung Kim
HOURS TO COMPLETE: 15

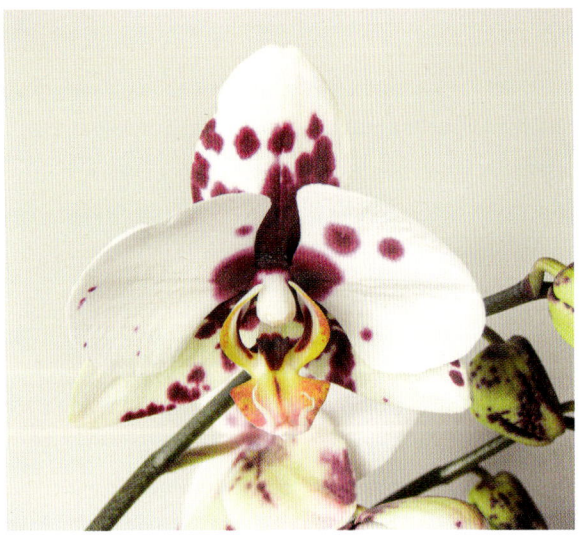

Like all orchids, this *Phalaenopsis* orchid has some aspects that are unique to orchids. First, orchids are bilaterally symmetrical, which means that they can be divided down the middle and the left and right sides will be mirror images of each other. Second, its sepals look similar to petals. When viewed from behind, however, the difference in coloration and texture is usually apparent. And third, one of the petals forms a lip.

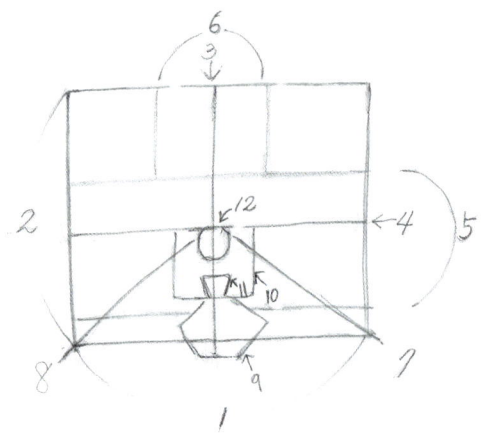

With bullet-pointed 2H or H, measure width and height (1, 2) of the orchid and draw a rectangle using those measurements. From the center (12), draw vertical and horizontal lines (3, 4) to help with the bilateral symmetry. Measure and mark the width of two petals (5), three sepals: dorsal sepal (6) and lateral sepals (7, 8), mid-lobe (9), side-lobe (10), and callus (11).

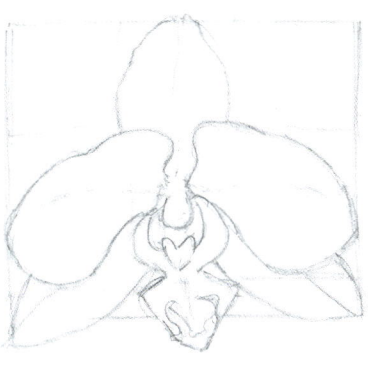
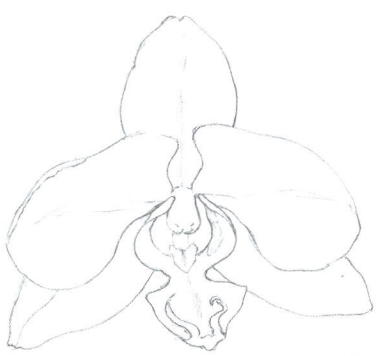
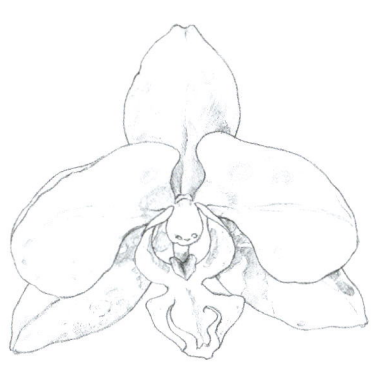

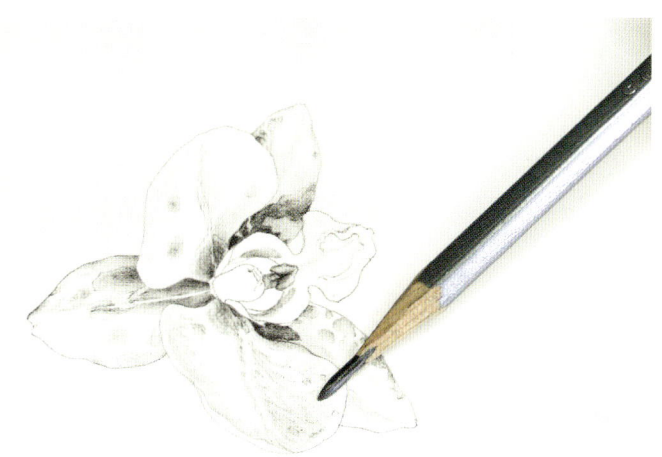
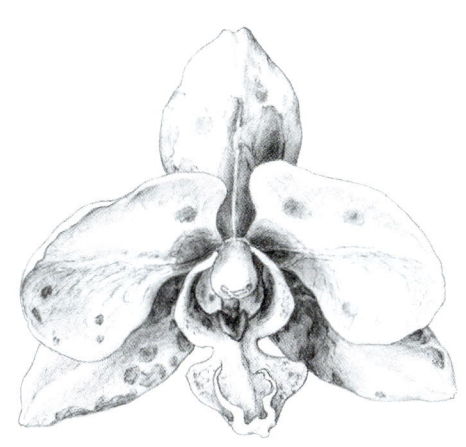

With bullet-pointed 2H or H, draw flower parts within the measured spaces. At this stage, focus on proportion and spacing. By checking crossing points based on the initial lines, keep track of the shapes, sizes, and proportion of the flower parts. Draw these initial lines very lightly, so that they can be easily erased later.

With sharply pointed 2H or H, draw final lines and details. Add two tendrils at the end of the mid lobe. Then, with flexible edge of the eraser, clean off all initial lines. Trace the image onto good-quality paper if needed.

With bullet-pointed 2H, draw patterns lightly. Study the shadows very carefully, as they will determine the value of the patterns, too. The patterns will need to be adjusted, depending on the shading of the form, in order to make the whole flower three-dimensional. Make the patterns lighter in highlight and darker in shadow areas.

Very often it's necessary to darken or tone down an area after adding lots of details. This can be done without losing the details, just by adding strokes perpendicular to the major line direction with the smooth side of bullet-pointed pencil.

With sharply pointed pencils, harder ones on lighter areas and softer ones on darker areas, define edges and darken shadows, especially at the center where many little parts are crowded. Keep edges lighter on petals and small parts in the center.

Ann Hoffenberg demonstrates drawing three different textures of leaves in graphite. Ann uses dividers to measure relative dimensions and placement of leaf components such as lobes and veins.

Leaves

TUTOR: ANN HOFFENBERG

Sweet Gum Leaf

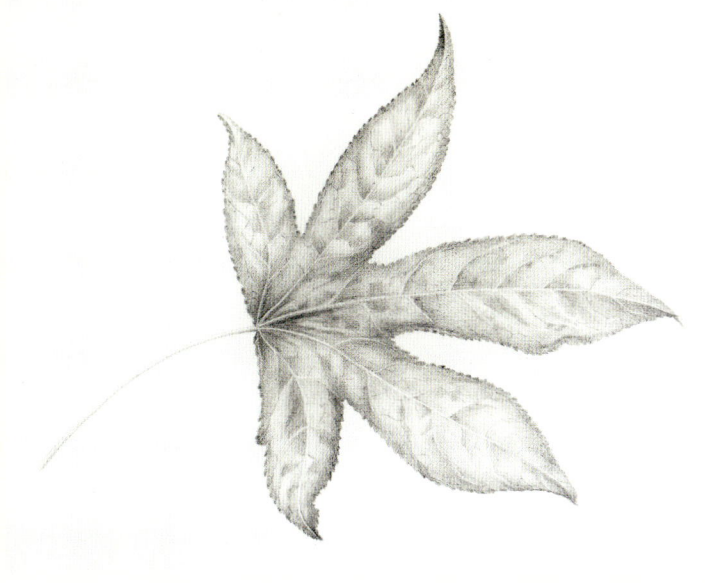

Sweet Gum Leaf
Liquidambar styraciflua
Graphite on paper
6 × 5 ½ inches [15 × 13.75 cm]
© Ann Hoffenberg
HOURS TO COMPLETE: 7

MATERIALS: Manual pencil sharpener; electric pencil sharpener; sandpaper block; heavy lead pointer; portable lead pointer; Styrofoam lead cleaner; white-plastic eraser; kneaded erasers; retractable eraser; eraser shield; soft bristle brush; craft blade; lead holders; lead, HB, 3H, and 2B; dividers; pencils; ruler.

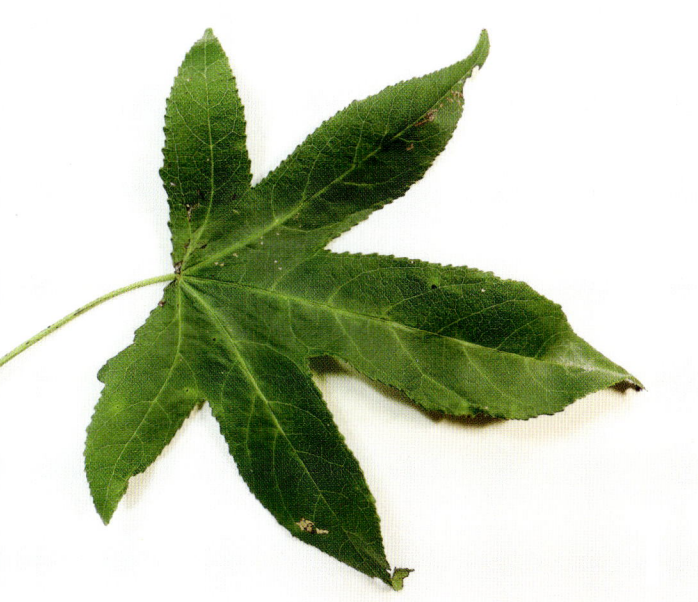

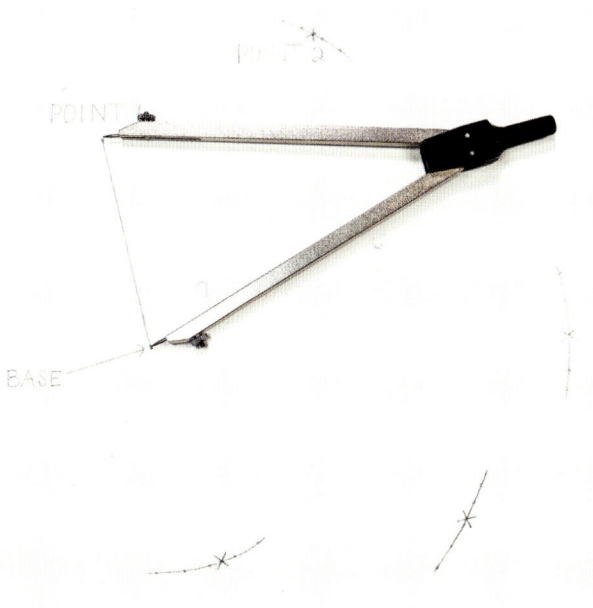

This sweet gum leaf has simple palmate lobes with serrated edges. Use dividers to measure the lobes and sinuses and to determine the placement of the lobes. Begin by holding the dividers against the leaf itself, then placing those dimensions on the paper. This results in a life-size drawing. Do not press the divider's points into the paper.

Mark a base point from which all the lobes radiate. Measure and mark the length of the first lobe (pt.1). Measure and make several adjacent marks for the location of the second lobe tip, sketching an arc for its general placement. Measure the distance between the tips of the first and second lobe tips on the actual leaf. Measuring and drawing arcs can also be done using a compass fitted with a graphite lead.

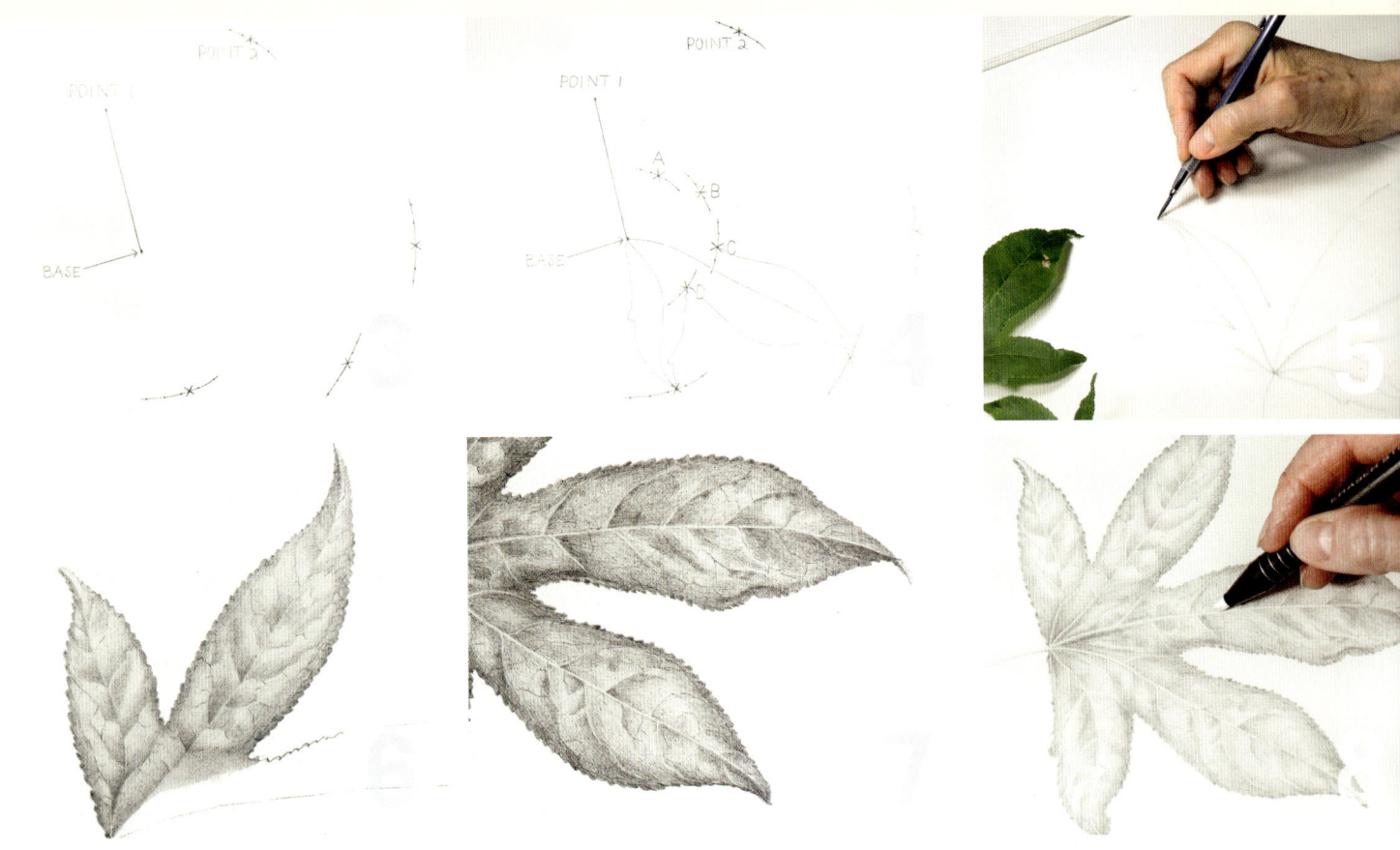

After measuring the distance between the tips of the first and second lobes, place one end of the dividers on point 1. Where the other end of the dividers meets the arc is the exact placement of the tip of the second lobe. Repeat this process for the remaining three lobes, locating the tips of all the lobes.

Similarly, a measurement from the leaf base to the bottom of each "V" (sinus) was made, indicating each with an arc. The distance from the bottom of each sinus to an adjacent lobe tip was measured, then used to find the point of intersection from the lobe tip to the arc on the paper.

Using these reference marks and observing curves and negative spaces, make a basic line drawing. Draw primary veins on each lobe and add the petiole. Trace the drawing and transfer it to high-quality drawing paper, lightening the outline as much as possible with a kneaded eraser.

Add serrations to the leaf edges. Draw the primary, secondary, and some tertiary veins. Using a sharp H lead in a lead holder and holding it nearly horizontally, lightly render the toning by making straight, continuous strokes to show surface contour.

Refine and tone the lobes one at a time, and adjust highlights, using a kneaded eraser where necessary. Darken overall tones to indicate the value of the leaf. Holding the pencil away from the tip, smooth the drawing by making light continuous strokes, layered in all directions.

Using a razor-sharpened retractable eraser, carefully lighten some veins as desired. Examine the drawing in a mirror, which helps to view it anew. This can reveal things that previously went unnoticed and need adjustment. Finally, refine details and clean up edges with a kneaded eraser.

Holly Leaf

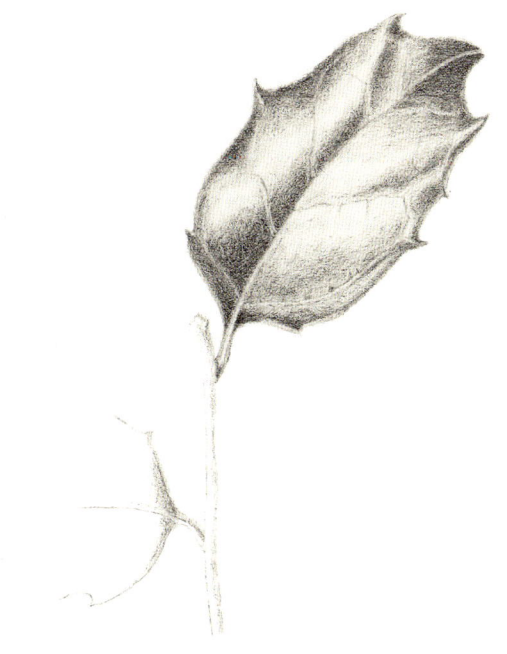

Holly Leaf *Ilex opaca*
Graphite on paper
2 ½ × 1 ½ inches [6.25 × 3.75 cm]
© Ann Hoffenberg
HOURS TO COMPLETE: 4

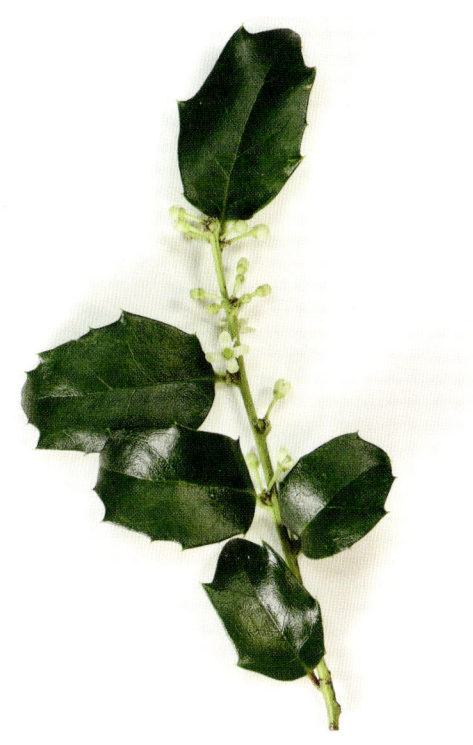

Holly (*Ilex*) has a simple, leathery leaf with spine-tipped teeth on the margins. The dark green, glossy surface exhibits bright, distinct highlights when well lit. High-quality drawing paper with adequate tooth for retaining graphite was chosen and an HB pencil was used to render sufficient darkness.

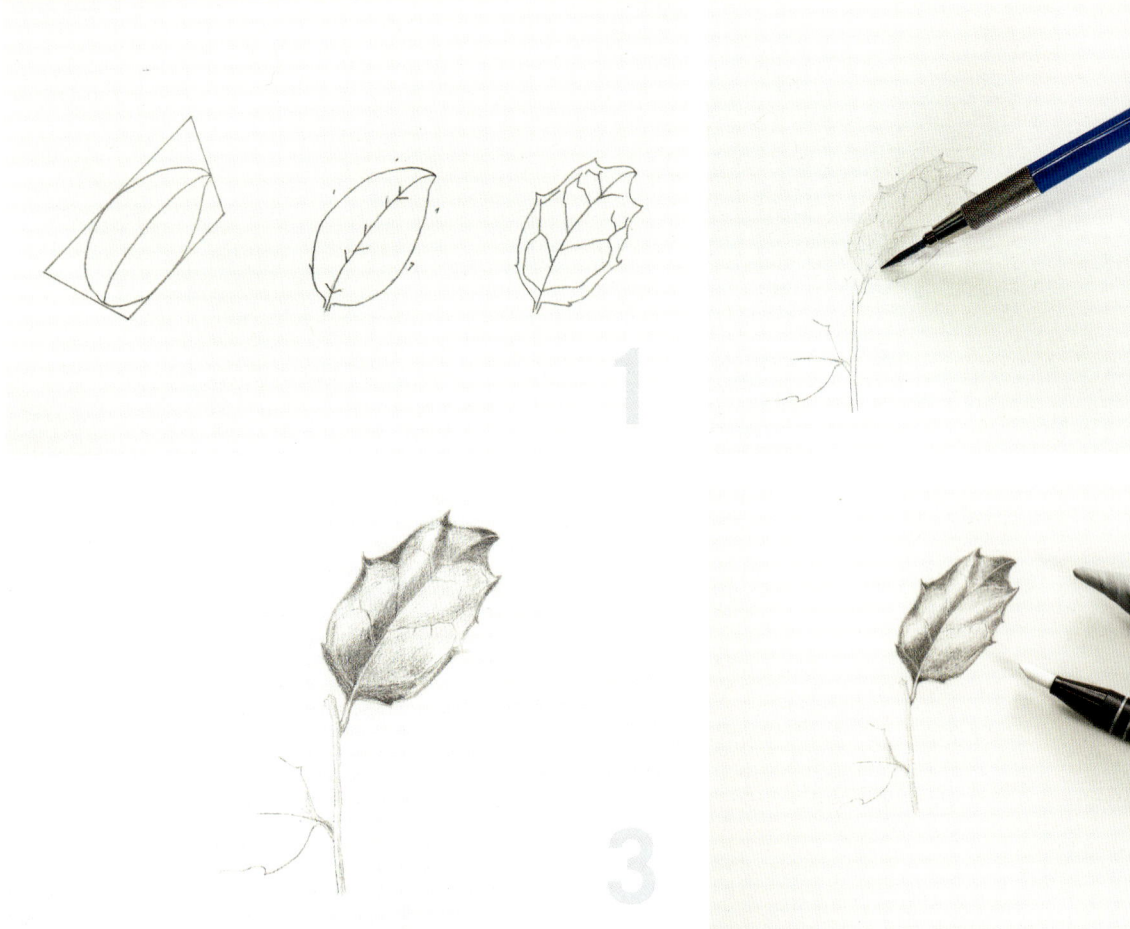

Begin the leaf shape by measuring the leaf's width and length with dividers. Make the shape in which the leaf will be drawn. Use dividers to measure the positions of the spiny teeth and the secondary veins with respect to the central vein, and make corresponding marks. Use these reference marks to create a more complete line drawing.

Trace the line drawing and transfer it to the drawing paper. Hold the pencil very gently at the opposite end from the lead and move it back and forth using your middle finger. Layer strokes in one direction and then in other directions to achieve an even, continuous tone. Using light pressure preserves the paper's tooth.

Use one light source, striking the leaf from 45 degrees above your left shoulder. Place additional layers of tone where the surface contour curves away from the light. Leave highlighted areas, struck with more direct light, untouched so that only the original layer of toning remains. Define veins and the leaf outline further or modify as required.

Intensify some areas of tone, then lighten veins and highlights where needed. Use a retractable eraser tip chiseled into a sharp edge with a razor blade to draw thin bright lines. Where necessary, use a kneaded eraser formed into a slightly pointed end to lighten value. Use an erasing shield to protect surrounding tones if necessary.

Observe the drawing in a mirror. This provides a fresh look and makes any unwanted or unfinished features more noticeable. Deepen toning in the darkest areas to achieve the perception of the holly leaf's dark local color. Finally, clean up edges with a kneaded eraser

Common Mullein Leaf

Common Mullein

Verbascum thapsus

Graphite on paper

4 ½ × 2 inches [11.25 × 5 cm]

© Ann Hoffenberg

HOURS TO COMPLETE: 5

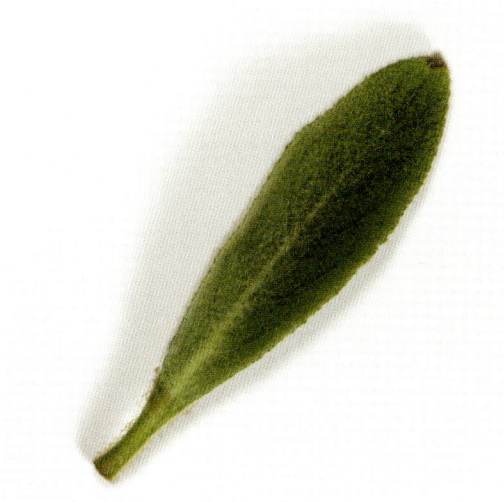

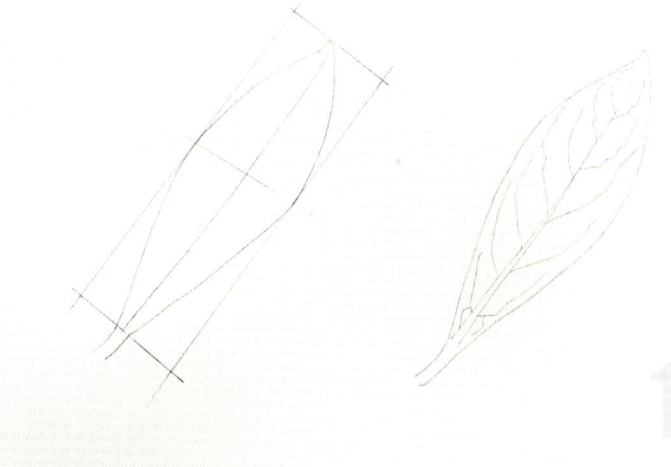

Common mullein (*Verbascum thapsus*) is a hairy biennial plant with a first-year rosette and in the second year, a tall unbranched stem ending in a dense spike of flowers. This relatively small and simple leaf is from a rosette. It is a light-to-medium shade of green and entirely covered with short, thin, branching hairs.

Left: The leaf is lanceolate and symmetrical. Measure its width and length with dividers and make a corresponding rectangle. The middle line here shows that the leaf begins to slightly curve to the left toward the tip. Right: Hold light behind the leaf to see the veins better. Use dividers to indicate where veins come off the midvein (the center vein that extends from base to tip). Draw secondary veins.

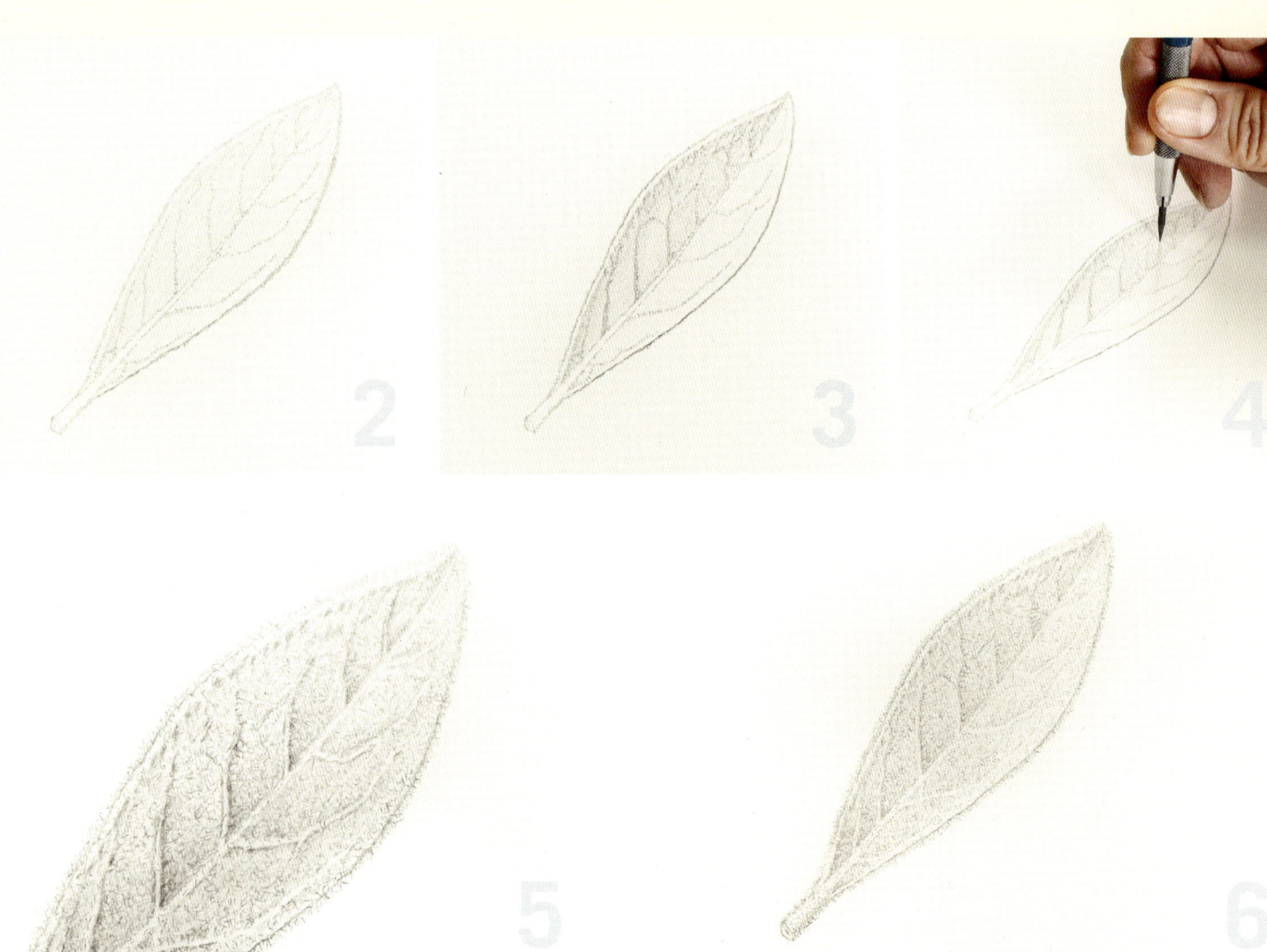

Lighten penciled-in veins with a kneaded eraser and replace with marks for small hairs. Draw the slightly scalloped edge and petiole with hairs. To add tone, use back-and-forth continuous tone lines, holding the pencil lightly at the end. Create pale toning with the left half being darker than the right.

The left edge of the leaf is tilted upward, so this leaf edge is shown in highlight. More details were added to the leaf and toning on the left half was increased. The scallops were made more obvious by increasing their value, and some hairs were added to the leaf surface.

Drawing hairs requires a well-sharpened pencil which should be held perpendicularly to the paper. Hairs were observed and found to be going in all directions. Draw hairs accordingly and cover the entire surface of the leaf, including the petiole (here they appear to be somewhat sparser but slightly longer).

Draw hairs all over the surface of the leaf. They are even present on the light-colored veins on this leaf. Further define the veins by toning. The left side of the leaf was kept darker than the right side.

Observe the leaf in a mirror, and add more hairs and some toning to bring the values closer to the actual leaf. Finally, refine the details and draw denser hairs over the entire leaf surface; less so on the petiole.

As when drawing flowers, fruits, vegetables, and other forms can be simplified into basic shapes such as spheres, cylinders, cones, and cubes. Each of these have predictable tonal patterns when lit with a single source. All of the drawings in this tutorial were made with HB graphite in a holder on hot-pressed watercolor paper. The drawing surface is slightly tilted to avoid distortion in foreshortening (and to relieve pressure on the artist's back and neck). Graphite is kept extremely sharp and only kneaded erasers are used on the watercolor paper (not plastic erasers). Tracing paper layers are used to make corrections and adjustments before transferring.

Fruits, Vegetables, and Branches

TUTOR: ROBIN A. JESS

Granny Smith Apple

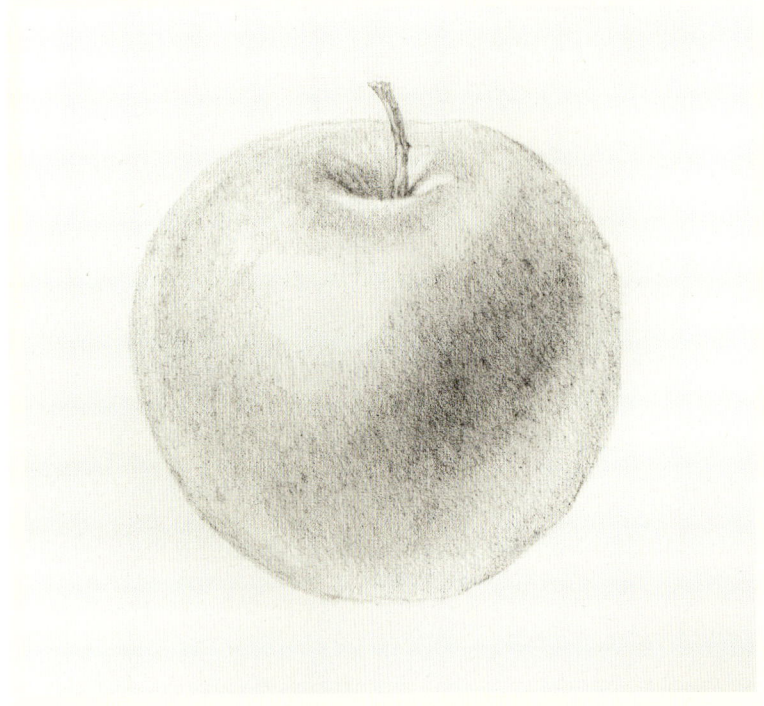

Granny Smith Apple
Graphite on paper
5 × 5 inches [12.5 × 12.5 cm]
© Robin A. Jess
HOURS TO COMPLETE: 3

MATERIALS: Manual pencil sharpener;
electric pencil sharpener; sandpaper block;
heavy lead pointer; portable lead pointer;
Styrofoam lead cleaner; white-plastic eraser;
kneaded erasers; retractable eraser; eraser
shield; soft bristle brush; craft blade; three
packages of graphite lead; lead holders; lead;
dividers; pencils; ruler.

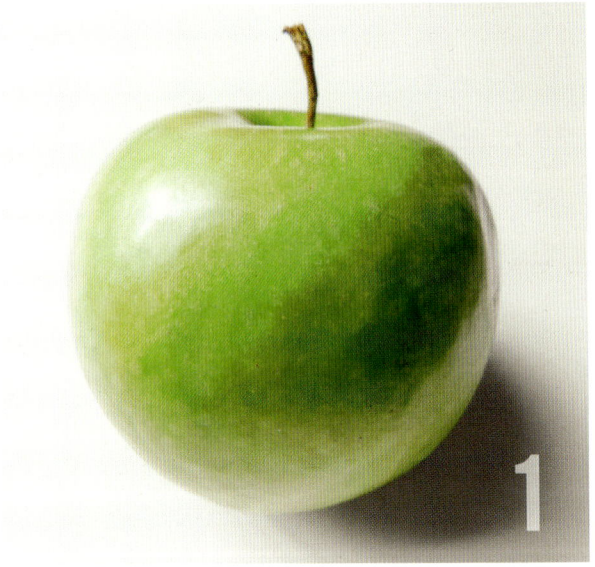

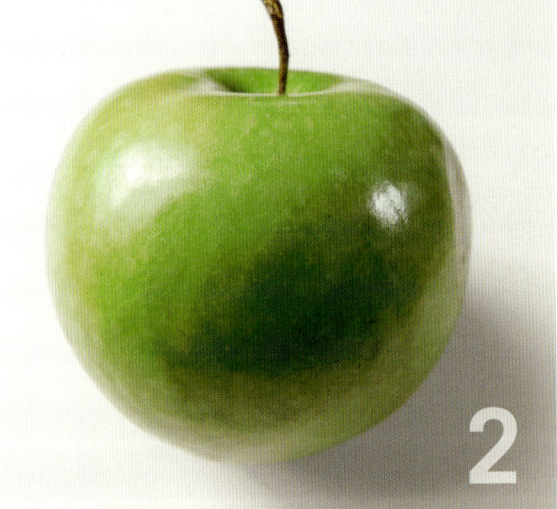

This apple is a simple sphere. Even so, rarely is anything perfectly round, so take care to capture the variations from the geometric shape. The apple is lit with a single source from above left.

This is the same apple, lit the same way, but with a second light source on the right. When illuminating a subject in the studio, avoid using multiple light sources, because they will cause confusing highlights and shadows. Be sure to also avoid extreme contrast between light and dark—aim for a naturalistic appearance.

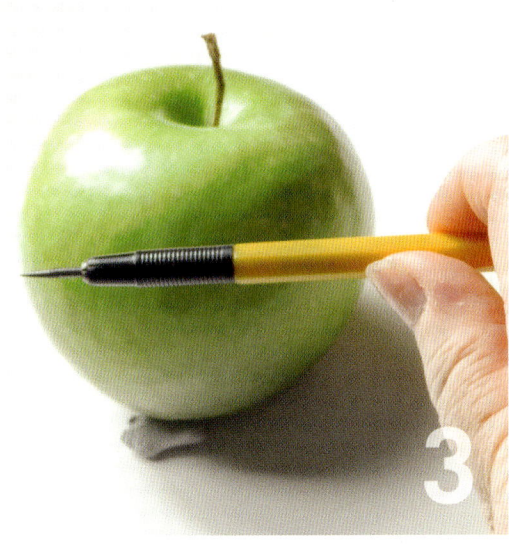
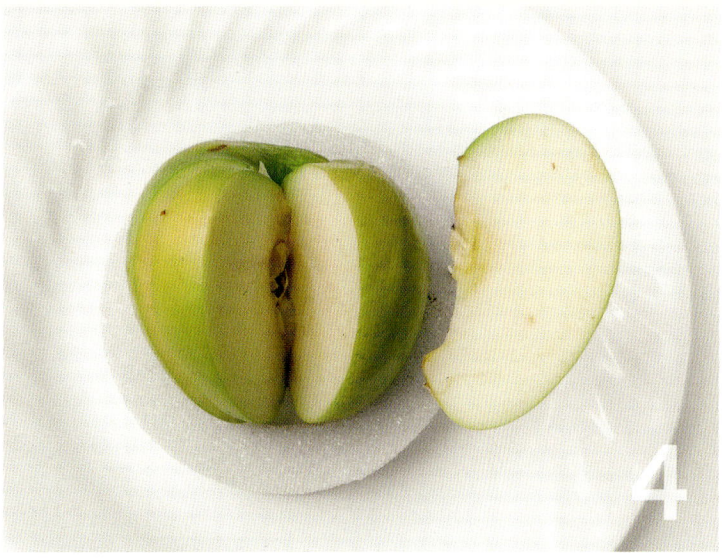

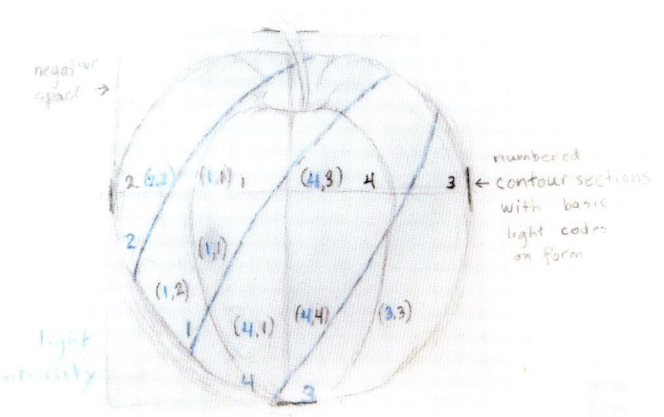
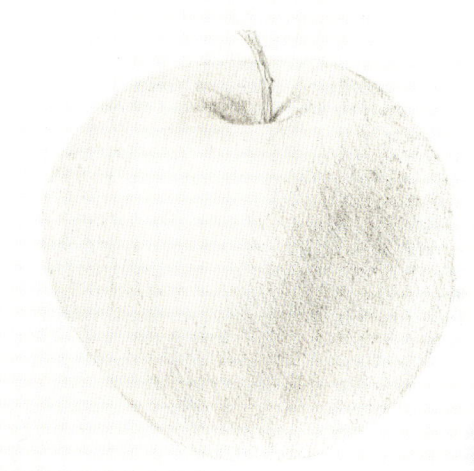

Use a clear ruler, or simply a pencil to determine a proportional measurement. Closing one eye to eliminate volume and flatten the image, align the graphite tip at one edge and the thumbnail at the widest point. Do the same vertically, with the eye and arm the same distance and angle from the subject. Draw those dimensions on tracing paper.

Before beginning to draw, consider the contours of the apple as if it were sliced into wedges. Highlights, lines, or tones to depict the form should follow these contours. In the next image, the contours are indicated in graphite lines.

Draw the outside edge of the apple within the measured square, taking care to convey the way it deviates from a perfect circle. To help visualize values, number the contour sections in graphite: 1 = highlighted, 2 = next darkest, 3 = nearly darkest (reflected), 4=darkest. Light blue lines similarly indicate light from the source falling on the form.

Transfer the image onto very smooth paper such as hot-pressed or Bristol vellum or plate. Tones are applied with HB graphite in a holder and the values follow the previous tonal diagram. The diagram helps keep track of the range of tones. The values are enriched and a highlight on the indentation's edge is lifted with a kneaded eraser. The peduncle's cast shadow is added, darker next to its base, and the edges of the apple are firmed up. This is complete, but a more polished drawing could be further developed and the overall tone deepened as needed to indicate color.

Carrot

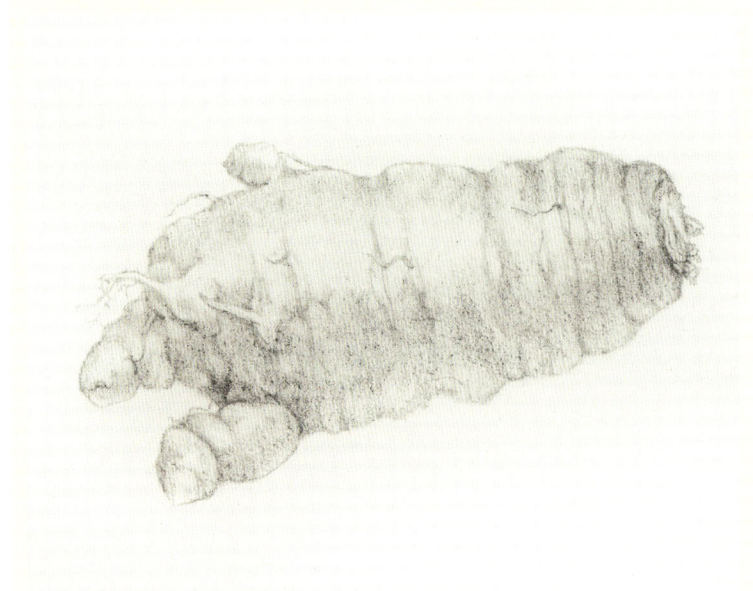

Carrot
Graphite on paper
4 × 6 inches [10 × 15 cm]
© Robin A. Jess
HOURS TO COMPLETE: 5

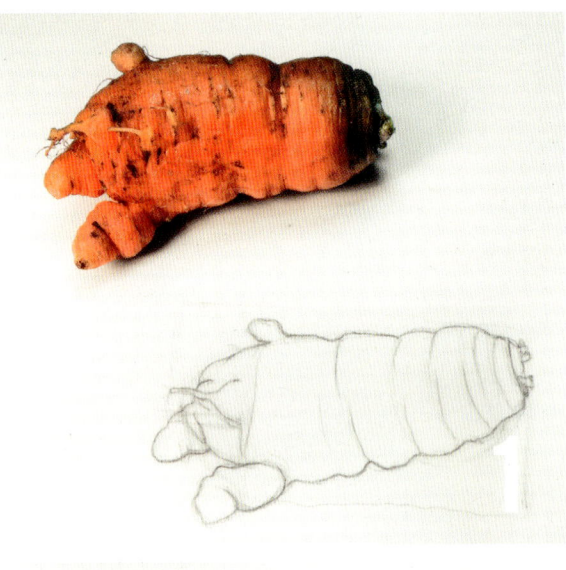

An approach similar to the one used to draw the Granny Smith apple was used to draw this unusually shaped carrot. Proportional measurements were taken to draw a rectangle on tracing paper. Negative shapes are visualized by closing one eye and holding a straight pencil next to the carrot.

The carrot is essentially the same shape as a horizontal cylinder and will follow a tonal diagram of 2, 1, 4, 3. Use that concept to begin the value drawing and establish the basic form.

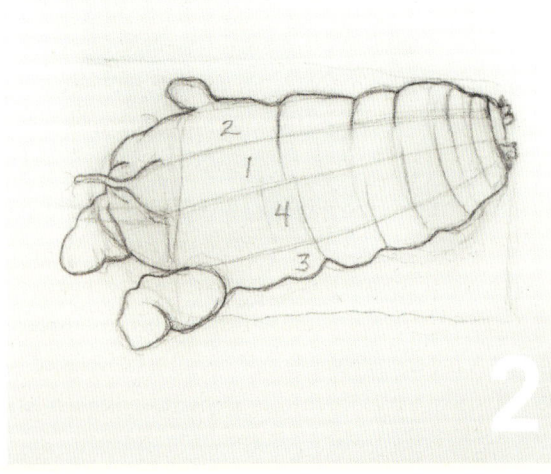

Holding the pencil or lead holder very loosely, long parallel strokes are made over the whole surface, creating a base value. The base value could also be created with oval marks, continuous tone, or whatever line system you prefer. The objective is to establish beginning tone. With a white subject, reserve the paper for the number 1 highlight.

Additional layers of parallel lines build up tones in darker areas. The hand usually has a preferred position to make lines smoothly, so it's easier to turn the paper each time a new direction of lines is added. This loosely held approach is good for broad layers, but once detail is required, the pencil should be held using a writing grip.

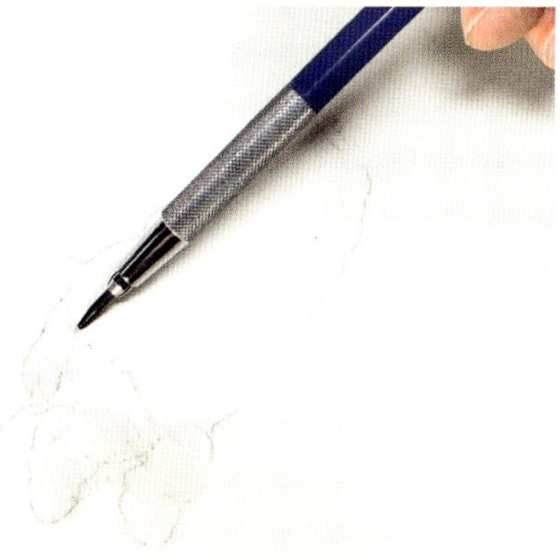

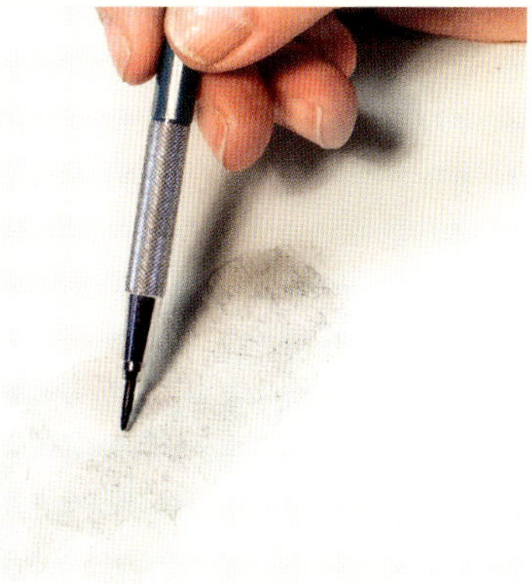

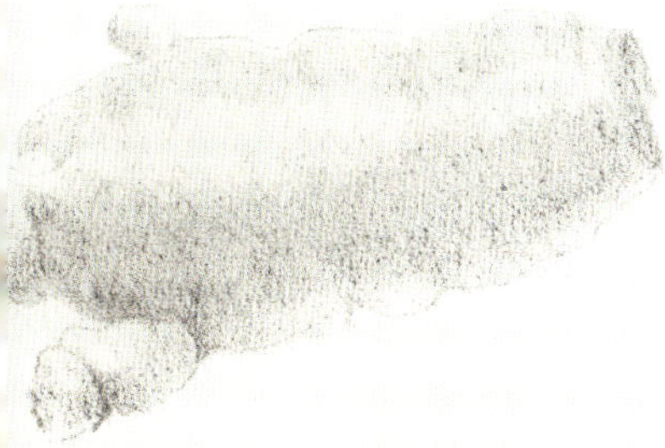

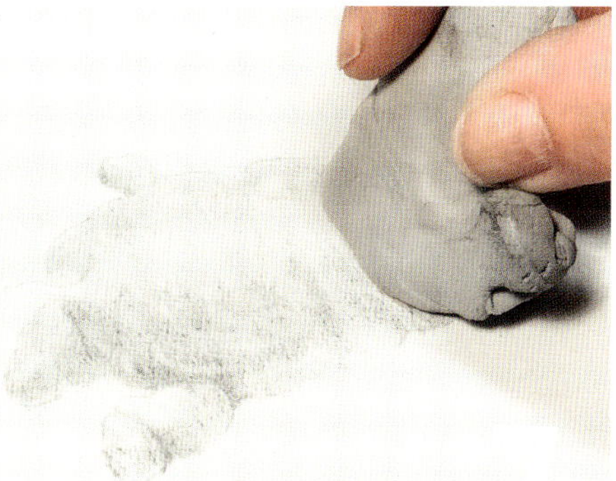

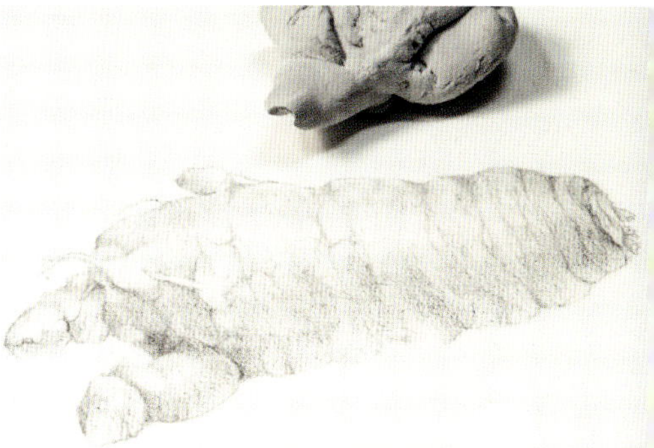

The various directions of the lines are apparent, following a 2, 1, 4, 3 pattern. Many botanical artists don't want to see lines in their tones and prefer a smooth look. If desired, this technique can be made smoother by using a kneaded eraser and a blending stump.

The small appendages on the carrot are also shaped like cylinders; hence each one features the same value diagram.

Dabbing—not rubbing—the lines with a kneaded eraser, tapered to a wedge, will blend the lines. Adding subsequent layers of graphite lines and picking up with the eraser will create a less linear look.

A kneaded eraser can be formed into various shapes, such as the inverted C-shape created in the protrusion on its lower left side. Think of the kneaded eraser as a drawing tool, not merely a cleanup tool. Light lines and small highlights can be lifted or drawn from darker tones with this eraser.

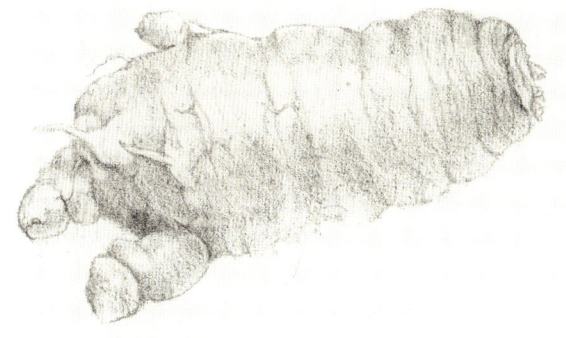

More detail is added in the small roots and the leaf end of the carrot using a sharply pointed graphite pencil and holding it upright in a writing grip. Adding more layers of lines and erasing builds up the form. Using a kneaded eraser, reflected light and highlight are brightened. More details and shading are added. Further detail can be added, but it must be accompanied by alterations to the overall value, or the drawing may appear overworked.

Potato

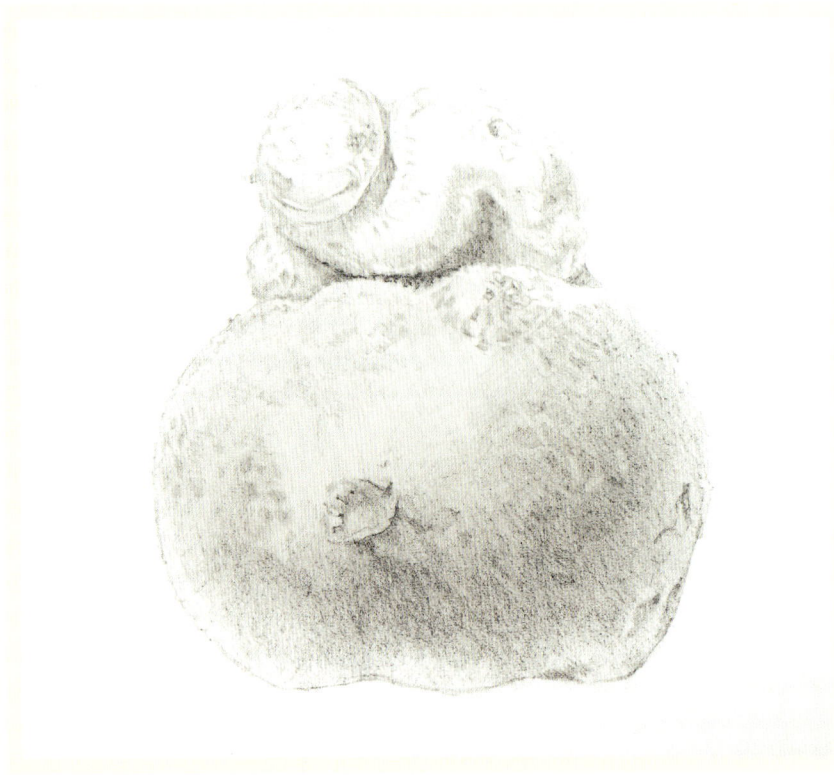

Potato
Graphite on paper
6 × 6 inches [15 × 15 cm]
© Robin A. Jess
HOURS TO COMPLETE: 6

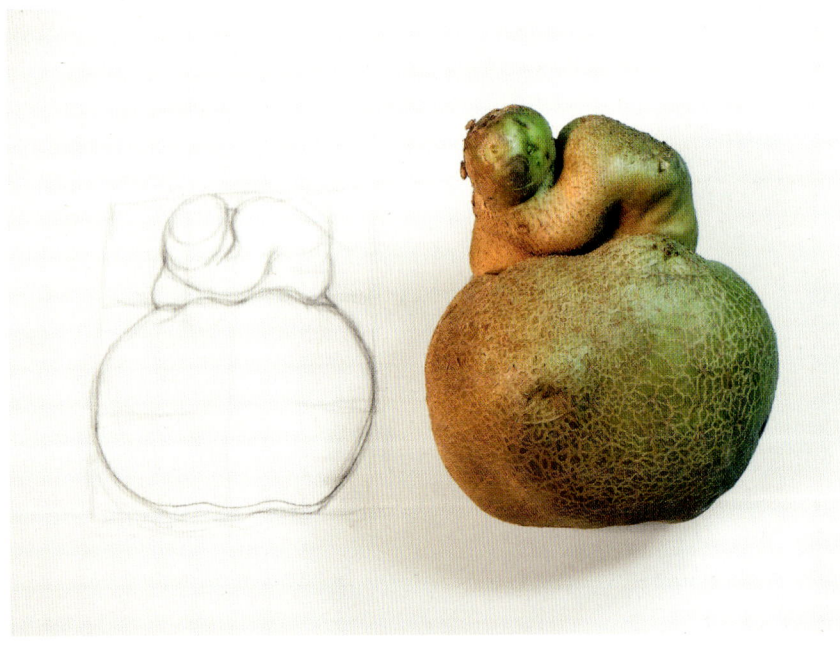

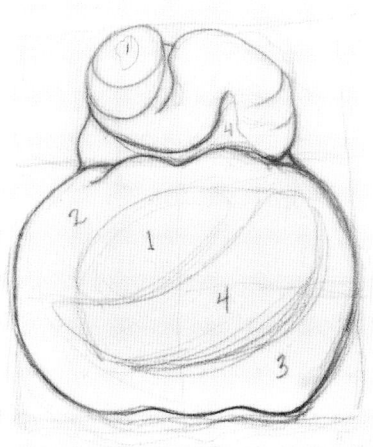

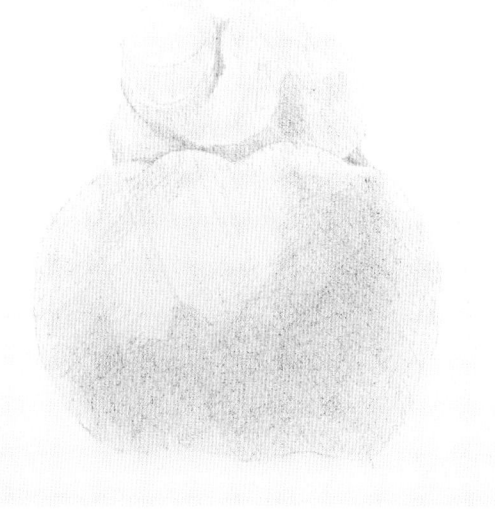

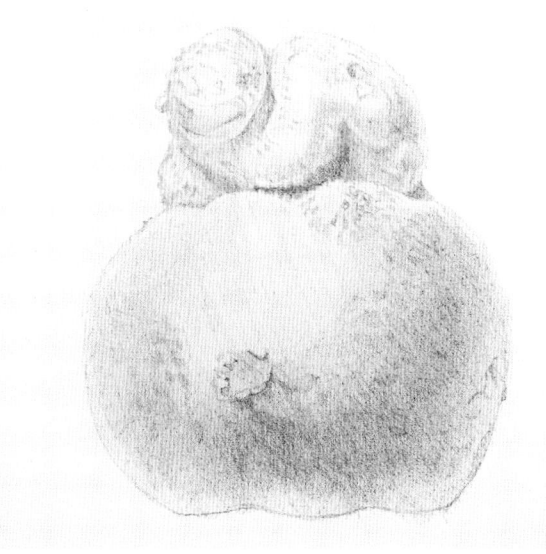

 Unusual subjects can hold your attention through the often-lengthy drawing process. This strangely formed potato is sketched onto tracing paper. Proportional measurements were taken and guidelines were drawn to help place parts accurately.

Tones are indicated as a roadmap for placing the light and dark areas. Then transfer the drawing to the final paper.

Holding the pencil or lead holder very loosely, long parallel strokes are made over the whole surface to begin making the basic tone. Note that the weird shape on top is a twisted cylinder, so it will have its own tonal range. A shadow will be cast from it onto the main part of the potato, as well as reflected light coming up from the potato.

At the bottom of the illustration, an outline anchors the potato, keeping the reflected light from dissipating into the paper. Making an edge fade can be a deliberate artistic decision if desired, but in this case it's not. More textures are made in the shadows. Tapping and drawing with the kneaded eraser evens out some of the line work and integrates tones.

Squash

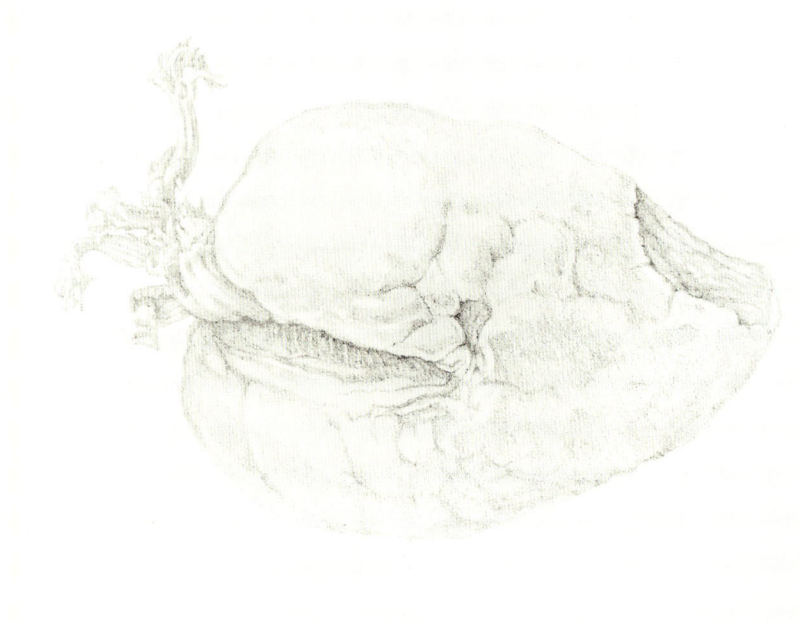

Sprouting Chayote Squash
Graphite on paper
4 × 5 inches [9.8 × 12.5 cm]
© Robin A. Jess
HOURS TO COMPLETE: 6

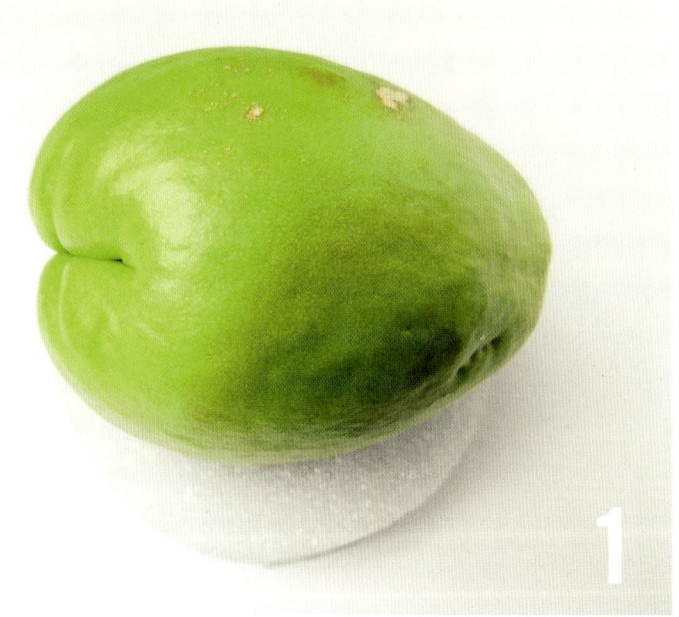

A chayote squash is puckered where it was attached to
the vine, creating an area of interest in an otherwise ovoid
shape. Its smooth skin is softly reflective but does not have
a glossy highlight. The squash is placed on a cut-out piece
of foam to prevent it from rolling.

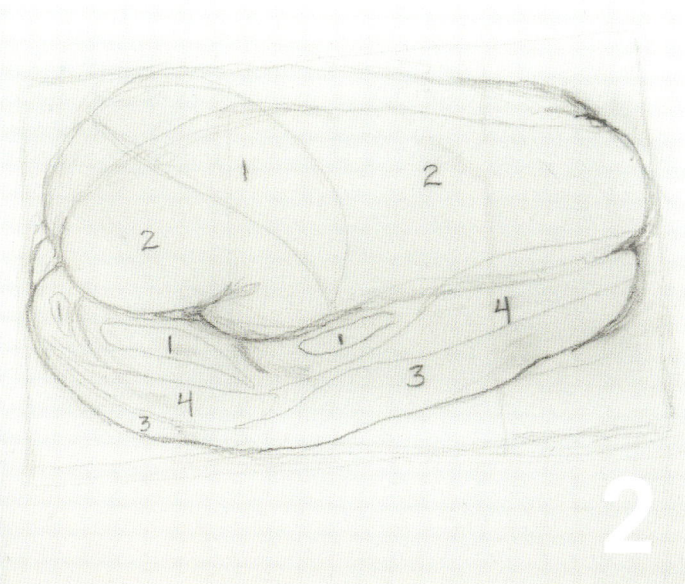

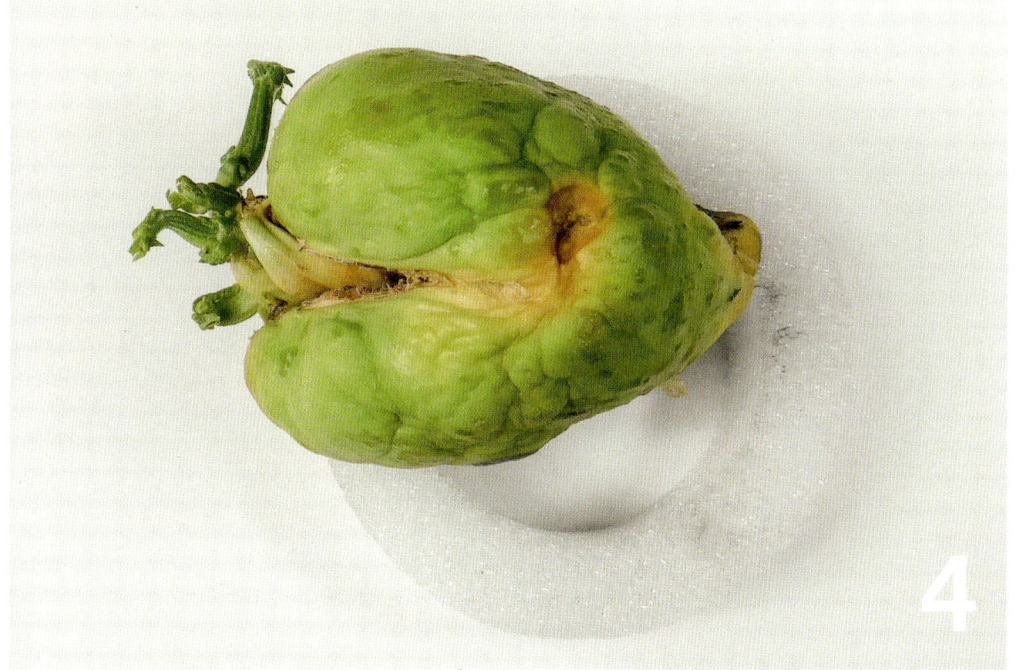

The chayote's shape is almost bisected laterally, so there are two sets of the basic tonal pattern, with multiple areas of reflected light.

The initial tones are hatched with graphite in a holder. Multiple directional hatched areas are still visible.

Time passed before the subject was again addressed and it had transformed. The chayote seed inside the flesh had sprouted, creating a different and more challenging subject. Botanical subjects are always changing, and a single drawing is necessarily one particular stage of this progression. In this case, the new stage of the chayote was embraced.

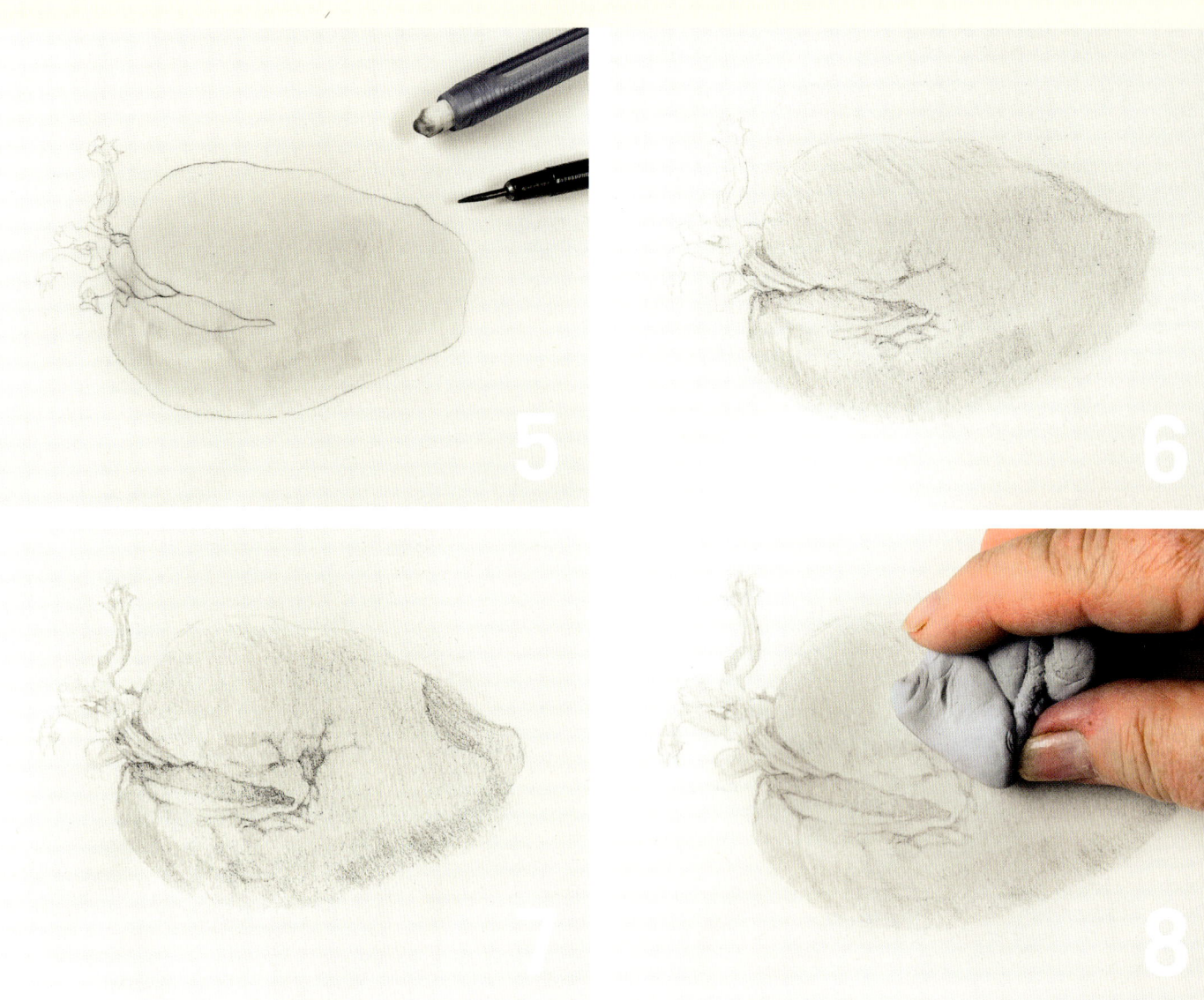

Tracing paper is placed over the initial drawing and the sprouted area is added. As the shoots grew, the puckering was forced open and continued to split. The bottom part of the drawing remained consistent with the changed fruit, but the top part was moved up and a sense of the decay on the right side was suggested.

With a very sharp graphite lead, held in a writing position, membranous shreds are lightly drawn within the opening, and shadows placed under and around the emerging shoot. A personality seems to emerge as spots and abrasions continue to appear.

More decay is shown on the right using a sharp pencil. Reflected light is lifted a bit more with a kneaded eraser.

Apparent lines are softened with a kneaded eraser to build and smooth tone. Wrinkles in the surface are clarified and the two darkest shadow areas are deepened. Details in the leafy sprout are sharpened with a sharply pointed lead.

Twig

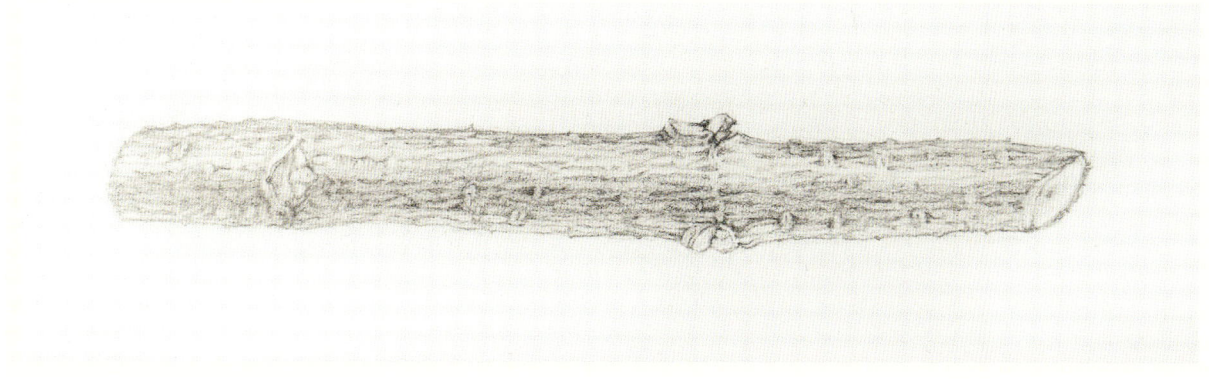

Section of Japanese Lilac Tree Sucker *Syringa reticulata* Graphite on paper © Robin A. Jess 2 × 6 inches [5 × 15 cm]

HOURS TO COMPLETE: 3

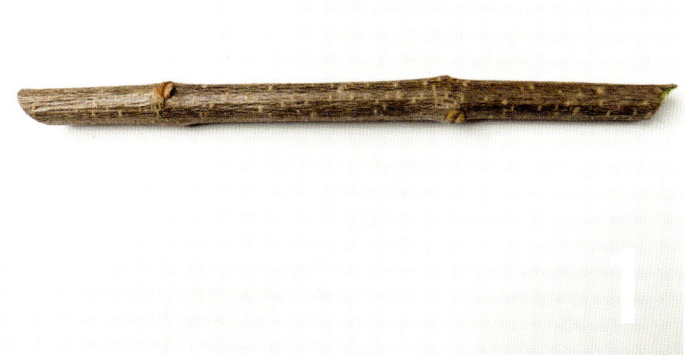

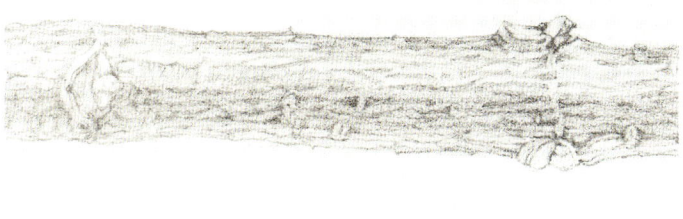

A long, thin cylinder is the basis of this twig, as it is the basis of stems and roots. Note the tones, keeping in mind the basic 2, 1, 4, 3 tone pattern from top to bottom.

To create interest in something as simple as a twig like this one, details are essential. Placement of the leaf scars and speckled aspect of the lenticels are the things that make small subjects like this fascinating. The light and shadows indicating form must be maintained even though there is surface texture.

Magnolia Branch

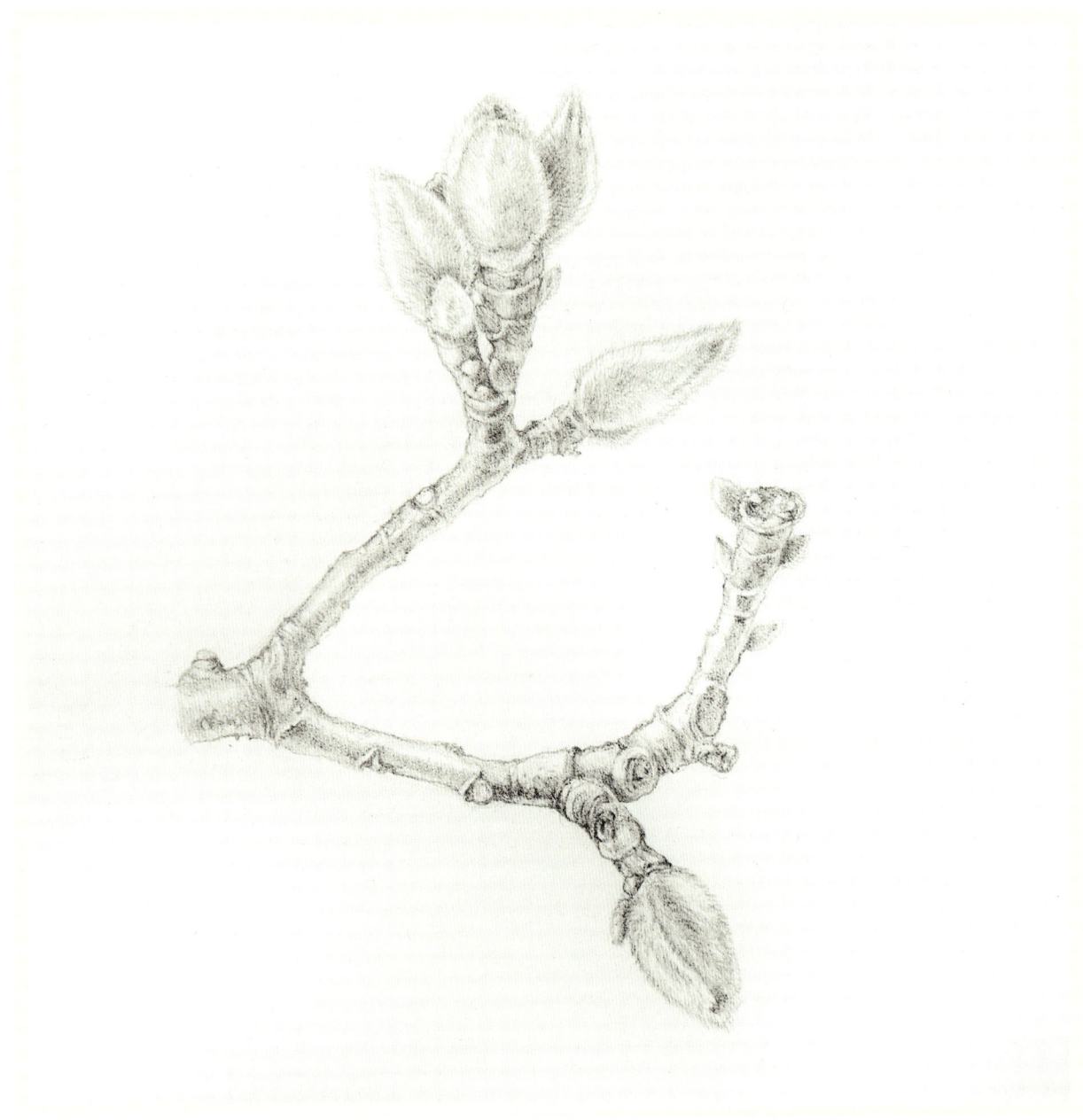

Magnolia ×soulangeana **Branch** Graphite on paper 6 × 6 inches [15 × 15 cm] © Robin A. Jess

HOURS TO COMPLETE: 5

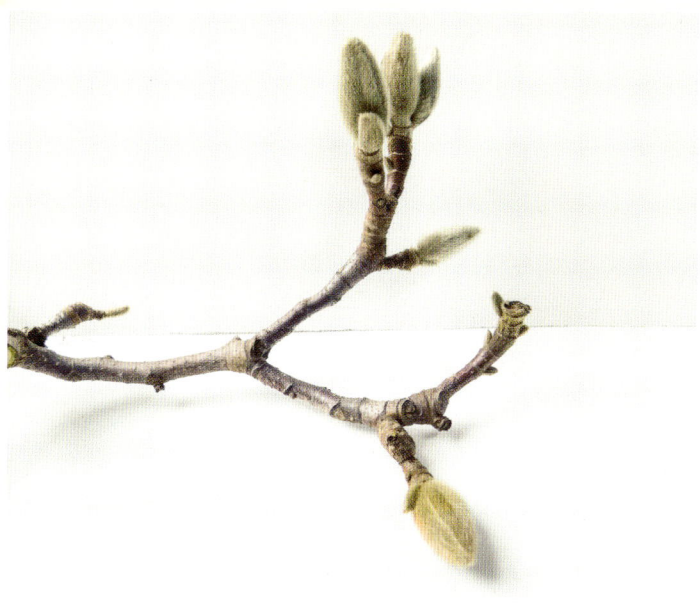

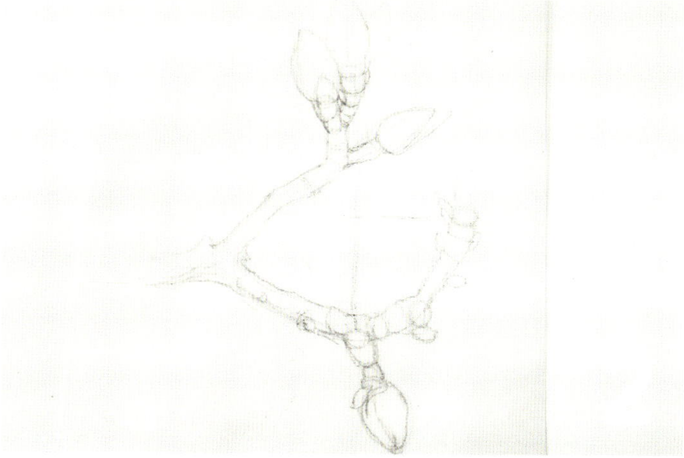

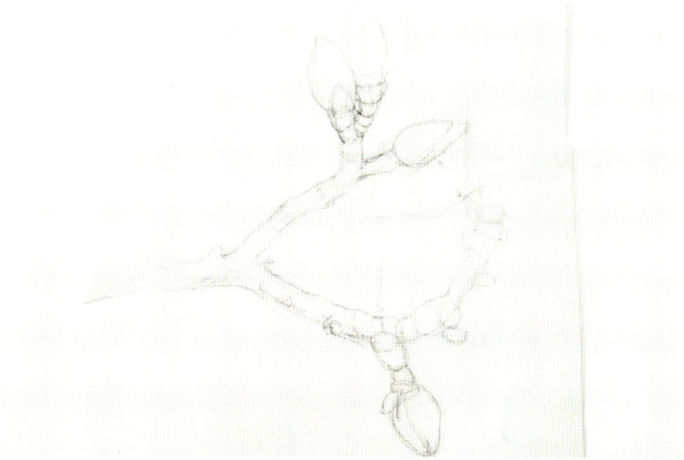

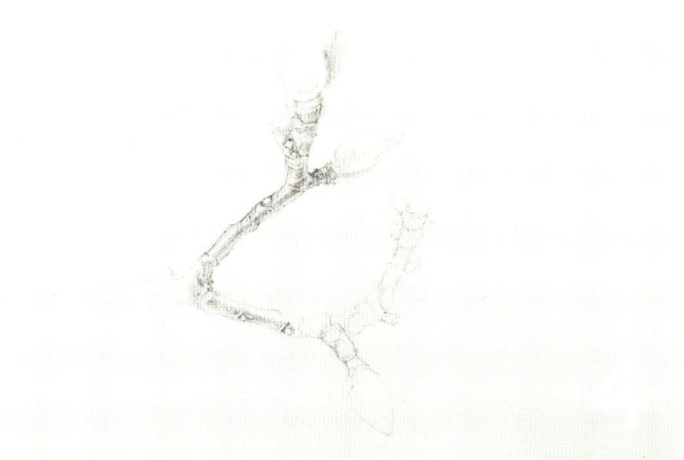

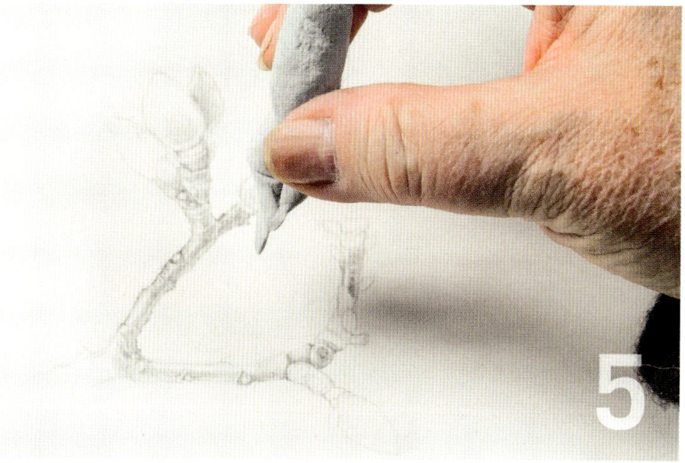

Magnolia sets its buds in the fall for spring blooms. The newly set buds on this fallen branch make it a lovely subject; the branches are gracefully curved cylinders tipped with silky cone-shaped buds.

A drawing on tracing paper is made; the sight lines are used to line up the positioning of various aspects of the branch. It's important to capture the gesture of a branch like this, because it was the initial attraction.

Even so, it was felt that there was too much negative space in the center. The drawing on tracing paper was cut and the lower part repositioned before transferring onto hot-pressed watercolor paper for the final drawing.

Once transferred, the cylinders of branches were toned using an HB lead in a lead holder, taking care to reserve the lighter areas as well as the tone number 1 area. Areas around branch sections and bud scars are darkened.

Pale lines can be drawn and highlights picked out using a kneaded eraser molded into a thin drawing tool. Sharpened graphite adds small details in the bark and short, light lines are used to make the furry bud. Note that the silky hairs look soft because the edges are drawn without hard outlines using very light strokes.

IMPLYING COLOR WITH GRAPHITE

When you are working in black and white, you must consider the values created by the light source on each subject as well as the local color of each subject. Here, Howard Goltz has shown a full tonal range for each pepper while also conveying the impression of each pepper's color.

For this group of peppers, Goltz used lead holders in 4H, 2H, H, and F combined with 2B and 4B pencils. He applied minimal pressure on the tip of the graphite to make a range of strokes, from parallel to oval, building up tones in successive layers applied in different orientations. The peppers were begun with 6H contours, then 2H graphite was used to designate the overall tonal and shaded areas. These areas were gradually developed and blended with H and F graphite. The darkest areas and fine lines were finished using 2B to 4B graphite. Blending stumps were primarily used in cast shadow areas. The primary graphite grade used on the work was F.

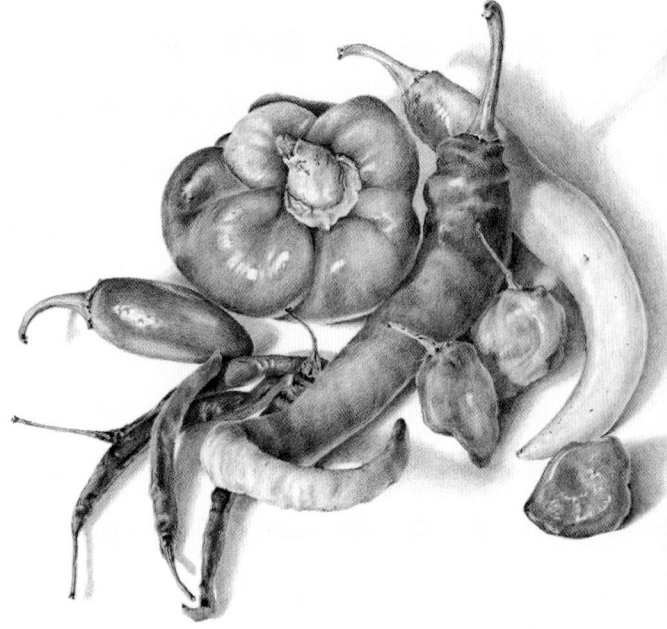

Capsicum annuum and *chinense* Varieties
Graphite on paper
10 ½ × 11 inches [26.25 × 27.5 cm]
© Howard Goltz
HOURS TO COMPLETE: 24

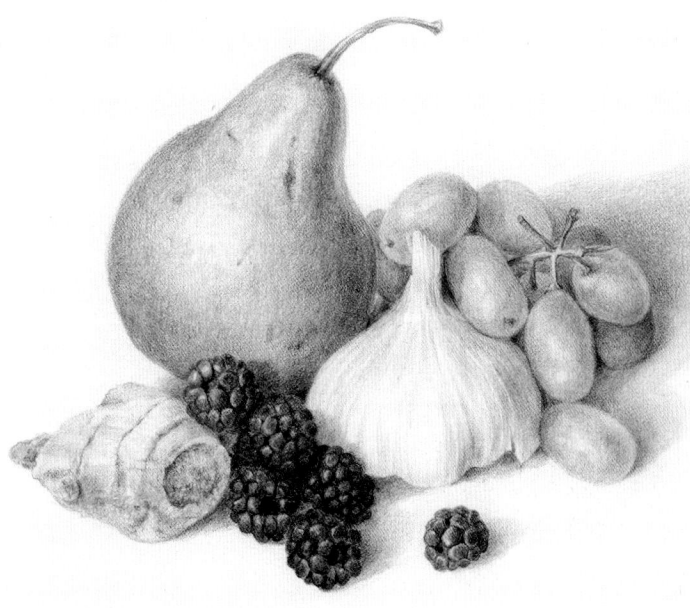

Katy Lyness used only HB and 2B graphite on her drawing. From the pale papery covering on the garlic through the mid-scale values in the grapes, ginger, and pear to the dark raspberries, all the tones were made by changing pressure and building up many layers of graphite in the deepest colors. Trying to darken tone too quickly by using too much pressure can make the graphite shine, which may make it difficult to add more layers on top. However, if value is built up gradually with multiple layers using less pressure, subtle, rich values can be achieved.

Ginger, Pear, Raspberries,
Garlic, and Grapes
Graphite on paper
6 × 9 inches [15 × 22.5 cm]
© Katy Lyness
HOURS TO COMPLETE: 24

Spiral and diagonal patterns exist throughout the plant world. They can be straightforward, like the structure of a conifer cone, or intricately complex, like the multiple spirals in a Romanesco broccoli. The simple steps in the following examples will demonstrate how to observe and record complex patterns to create a clear and concise path to a completed work.

Drawing Spiral and Diagonal Patterns

TUTOR: KELLY LEAHY RADDING

Camellia

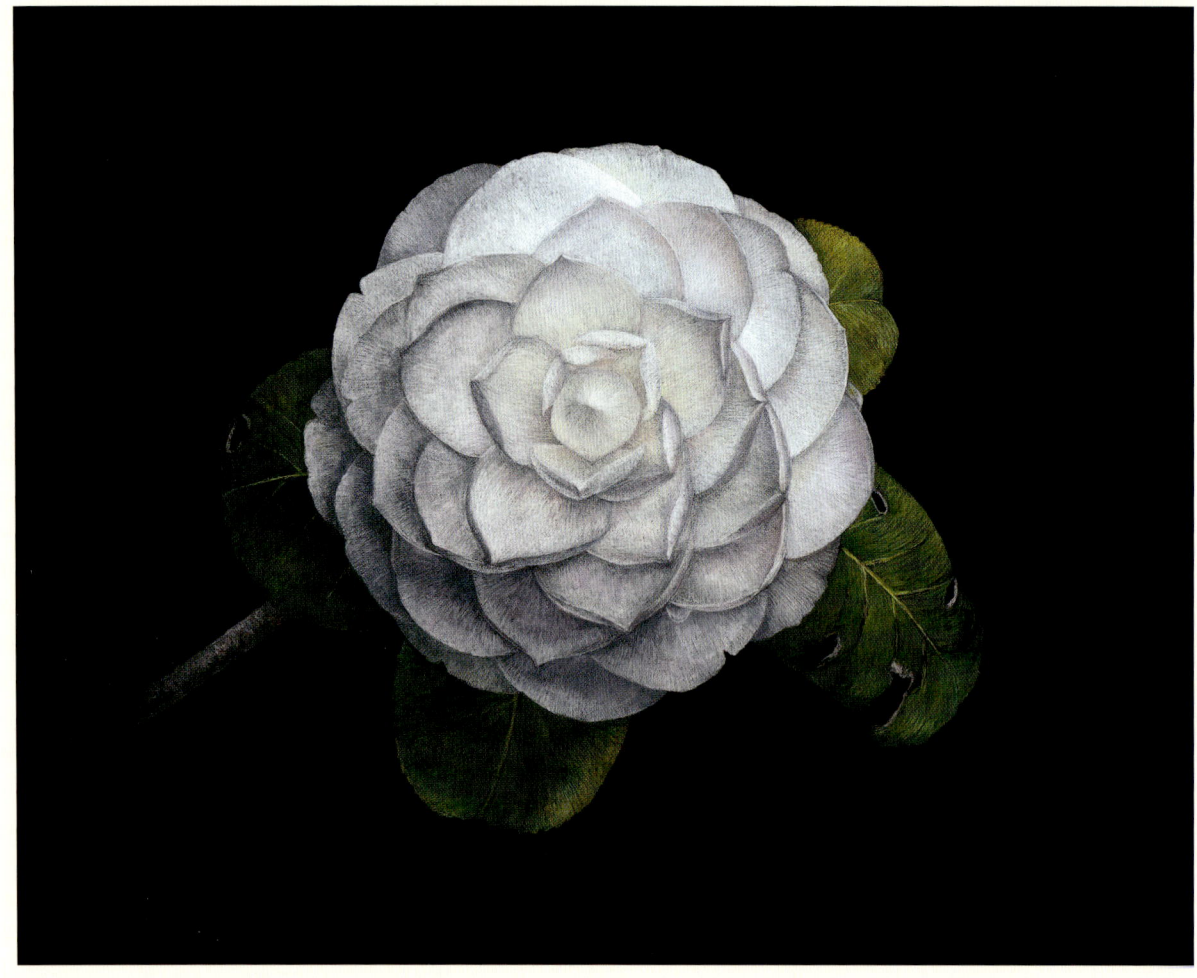

Fibonacci's Camellia Gouache on board 10 ½ × 12 inches [26.25 × 30 cm] © Kelly Leahy Radding

HOURS TO COMPLETE: 40

MATERIALS (for the layout drawings): Tracing paper; sketchbook; lead holder with 2H lead; technical pencil; colored markers; black plastic eraser; white-plastic eraser; ruler; dividers.

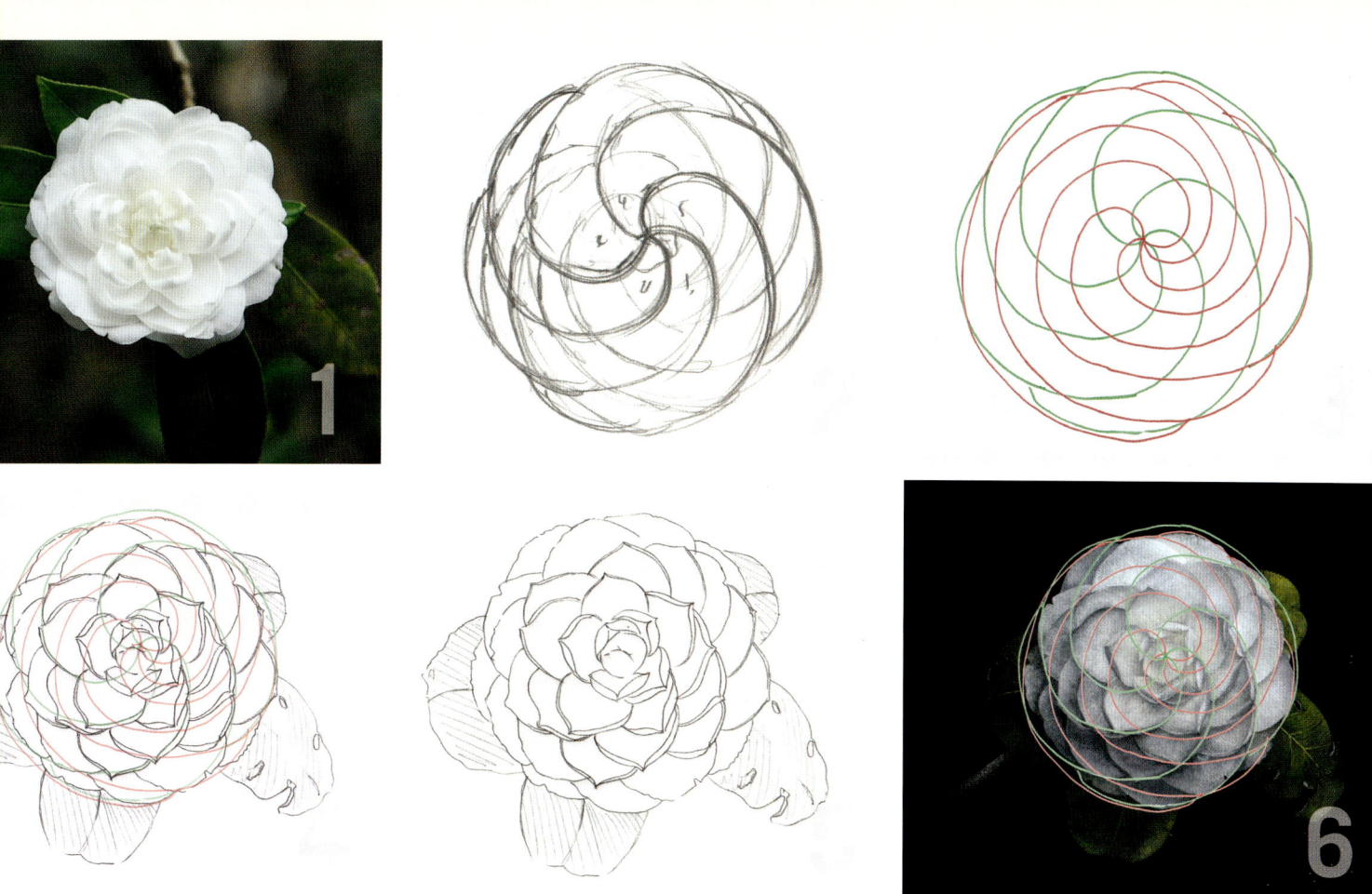

A double camellia has petals arranged in spirals. Begin by mapping out the spirals on a piece of tracing paper after laying out the outside dimensions of the flower. There are five spirals going clockwise and five spirals going counterclockwise.

Sketch a diagram of the spirals. Beginning in the center of the flower, look closely to see the patterns made by the petals in a clockwise direction. Then, using a lighter line, follow the counterclockwise spirals.

Refine the spirals on tracing paper (you may need to use several pieces before you are happy with your drawing). Different color markers delineate between clockwise and counterclockwise.

Using a technical pencil and following the spiral map you made in step 3, start drawing in the petals, carefully observing how they fit into the spiral pattern. Pay attention to how the petals overlap one another, and note where they are not quite within the framework of the map. Adjust the illustration according to your observations.

Continue refining the drawing in consecutive tracing paper overlays until you have a final tracing paper drawing.

This is the completed painting with the spiral map superimposed on top.

Sequoia Cone

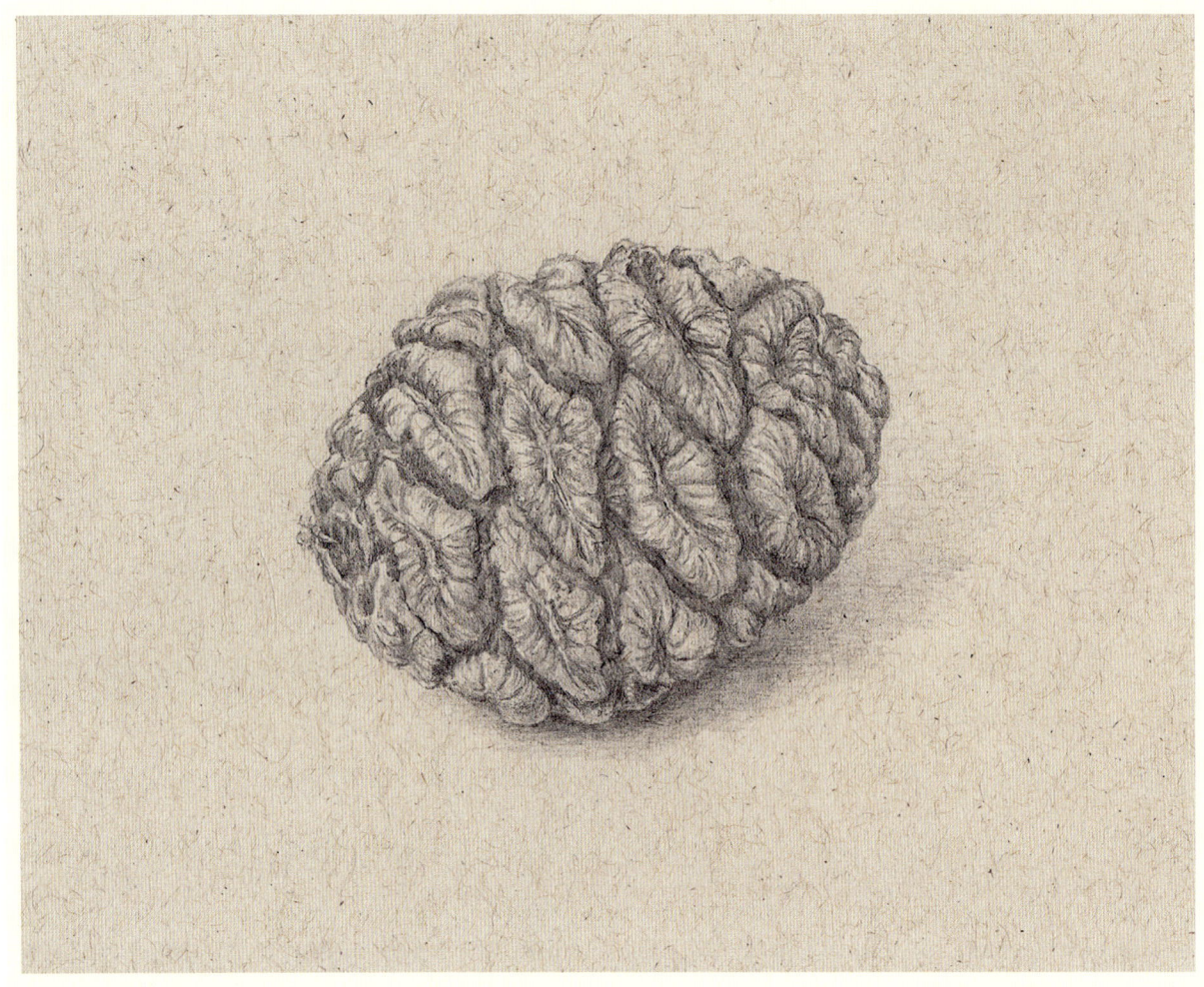

Sequoia Cone Graphite on toned paper © Kelly Leahy Radding

HOURS TO COMPLETE: 6

Graphite drawings on toned paper take advantage of
the tone of the paper as one of the values in the drawing.
A cone with a value range at the darker end of the scale
is a perfect subject for toned drawing papers.

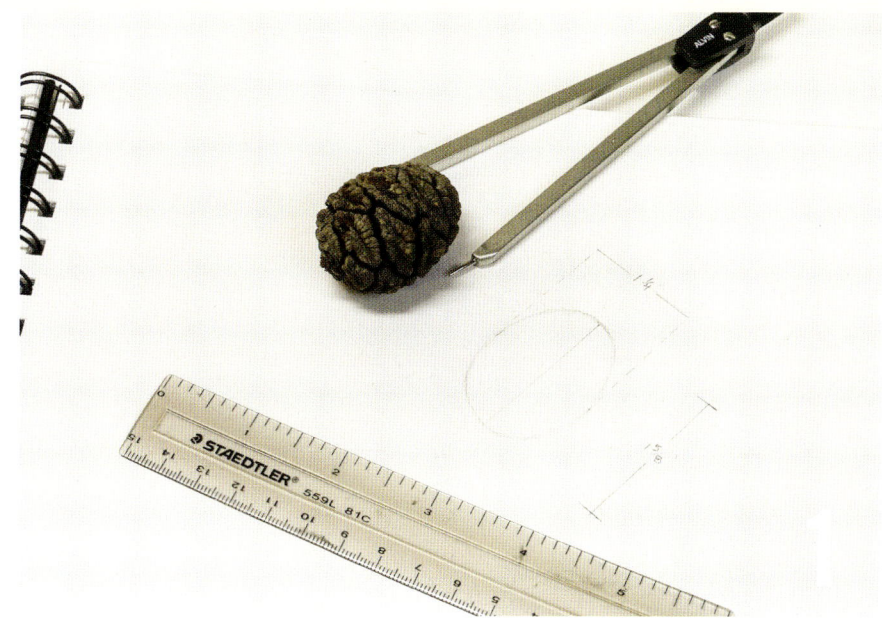

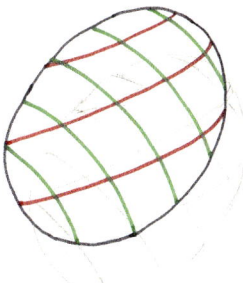 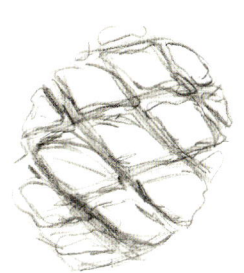 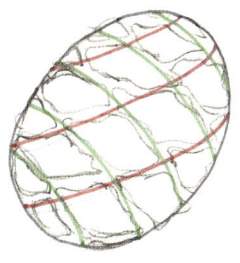 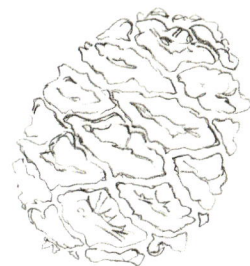

A sequoia cone contains a spiral pattern that can guide a drawing. Cones contain scales that can be closed or open. Map out the shape and size of the cone. To create a life-size drawing, use a ruler or dividers to measure the cone.

Begin by blocking in the shape of the cone and the diagonally intersecting lines, then sketch in the scales. The space between the scales is where the lines intersect.

Make sure that the number of spaces created matches the number of scales on the viewed area of the cone. Using your drawing as a rough guide, carefully observe the cone and refine the drawing in detail.

Artichoke

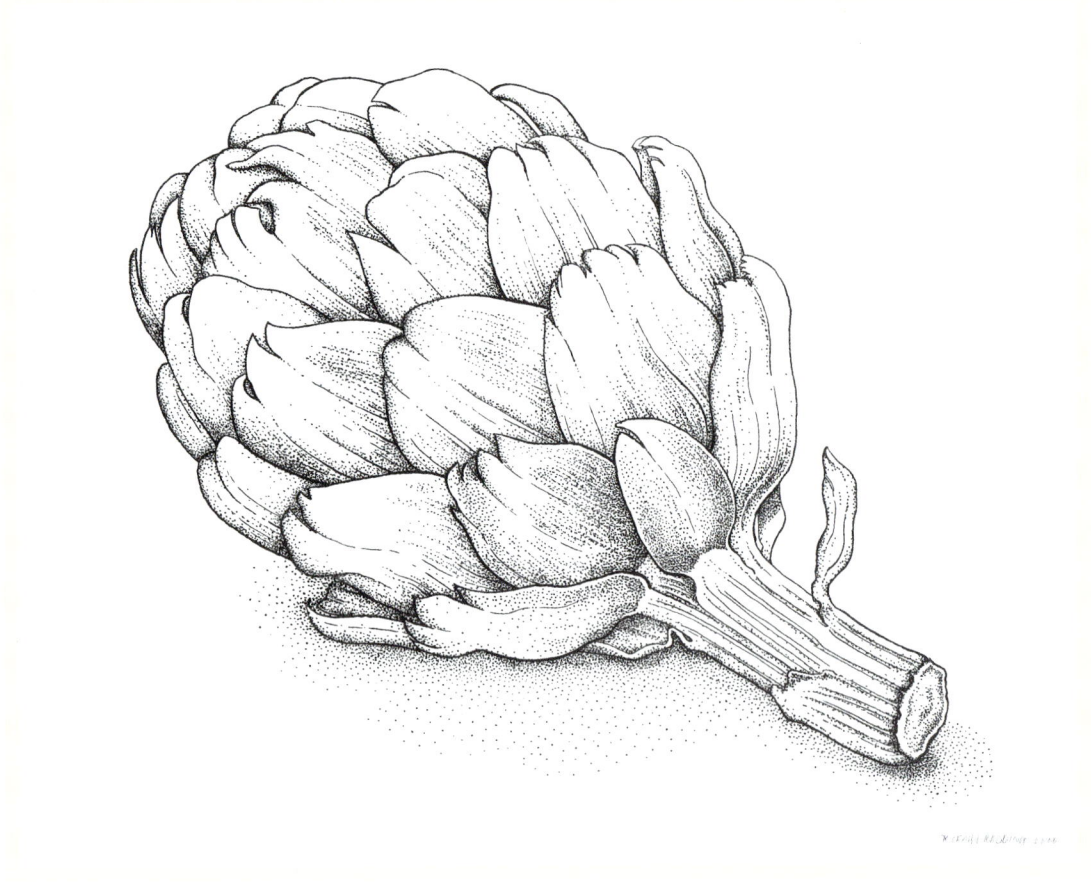

Artichoke Pen and ink on paper 5 × 6 inches [12.5 × 15 cm] © Kelly Leahy Radding

HOURS TO COMPLETE: 20

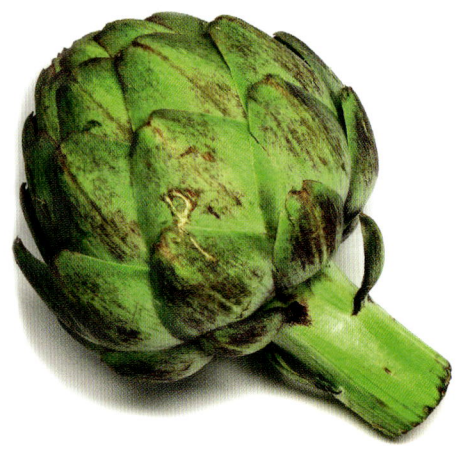

Artichokes also contain
spiraling, intersecting lines.

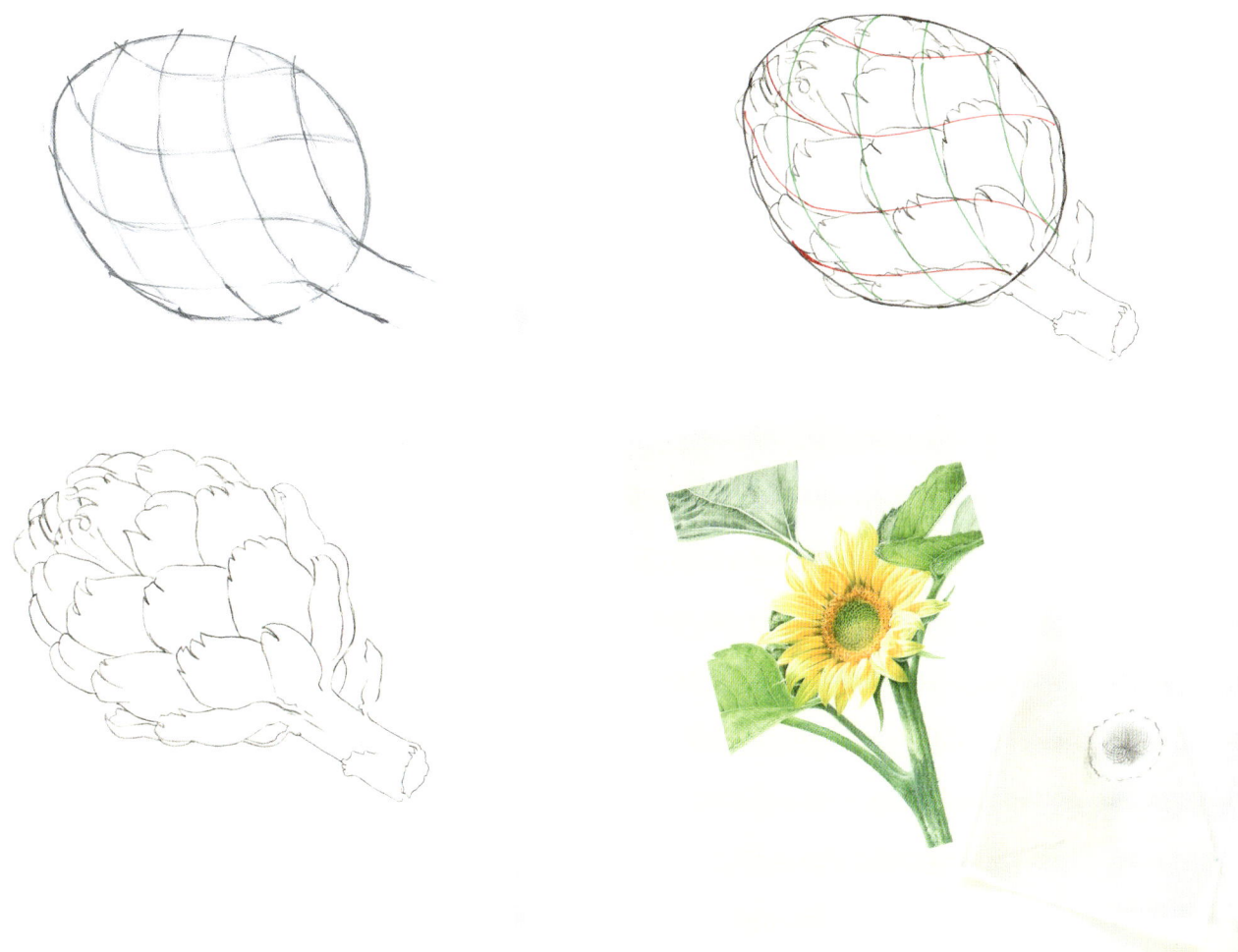

Begin by blocking in the outline contour with a lead holder, then find the diagonal lines to create a map.

Using the map as a guide, key out the clockwise (shown here in green) and counterclockwise (shown here in red) spirals in different colors, then begin to draw the leaves into the spaces between the intersecting lines with a technical pencil.

Continue refining the layout drawing until it is complete. Now the drawing can be used to create a final piece in the medium of choice, in this case, in pen and ink.

This method for finding a subject's pattern can be applied to many subjects that contain spiral and diagonal geometric arrangements of scales and petals, such as pineapples and flowers or seed heads such as sunflowers. Even if the pattern is only suggested in the drawing or painting, it is still helpful to create a sketch of the pattern to follow and refer to.

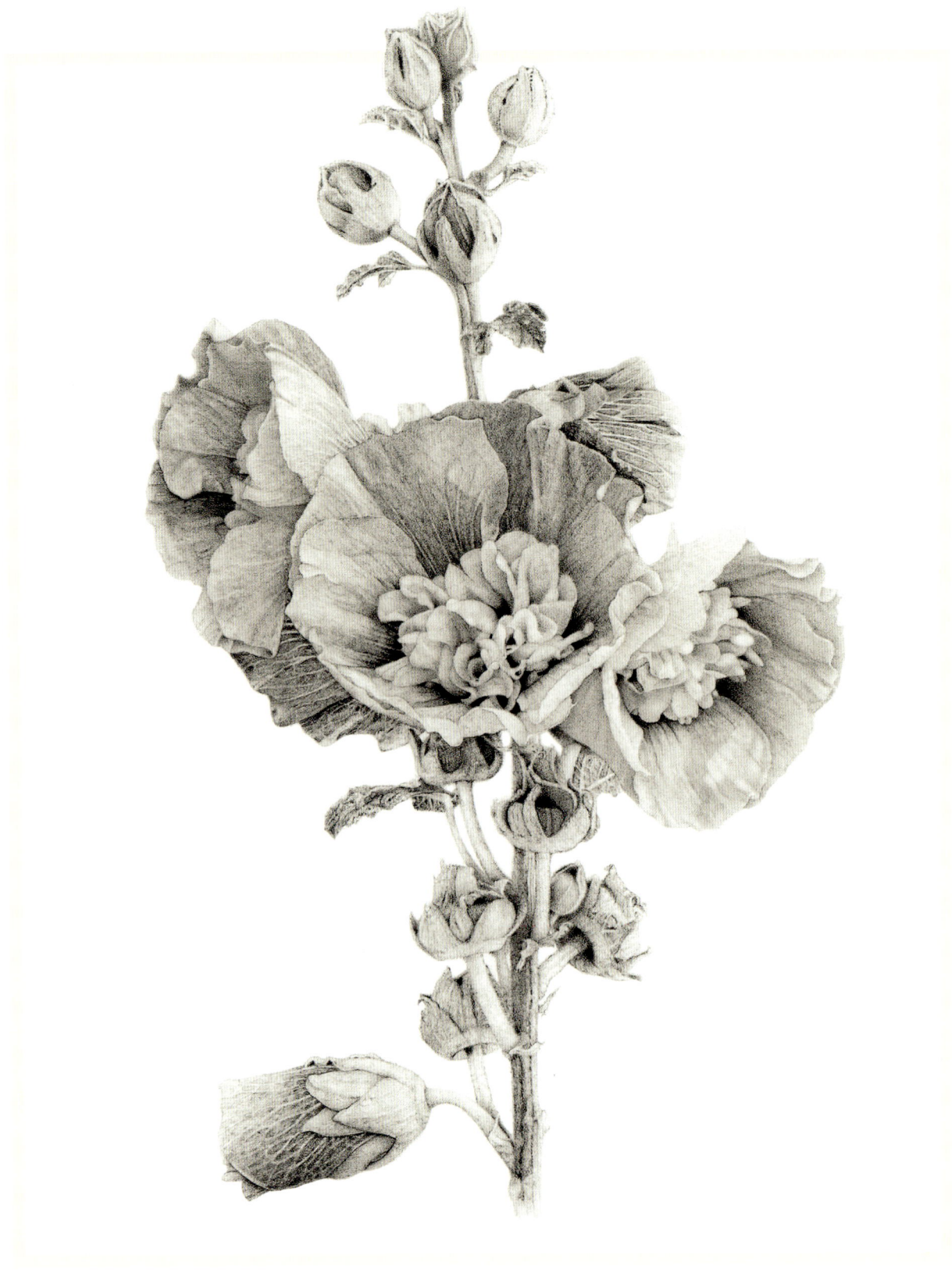

Hollyhock *Alcea rosea* Graphite on watercolor paper 14 × 9 inches [35 × 32.5 cm] © Melissa Toberer

HOURS TO COMPLETE: 200

MATERIALS: Ruler; lead holders with 2B and 4B leads; 4H graphite pencil; kneaded eraser; rotary lead pointer.

Beginning with basic shapes, Melissa Toberer demonstrates drawing a complex inflorescence in graphite. A basic drawing with buds and flowers accurately laid out and placed on the stem serves as the foundation for further graphite work. Successive layers are built one upon the other, increasing value and detail. With simple tools such as pencils and an eraser, a full range of tones is achieved.

Drawing an Inflorescence with Many Flowers in Graphite

TUTOR: MELISSA TOBERER

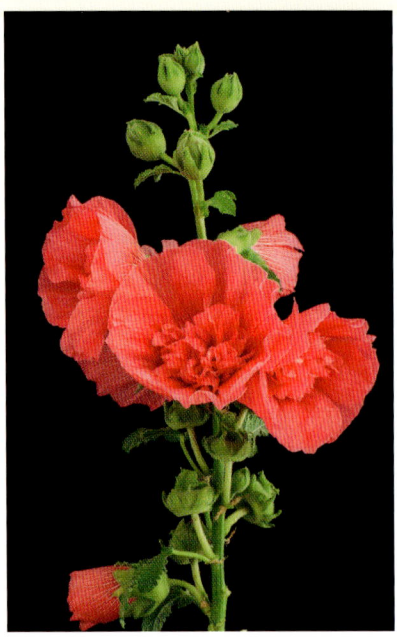

This hollyhock displays interesting movement, and the composition is well-balanced. Its five flowers, grouped together, provide a strong center of interest and cascade slightly downward, bringing the eye to the flower on the lower left. The seedpods and buds, arranged on the vertical stem, provide contrast to the horizontal grouping of flowers.

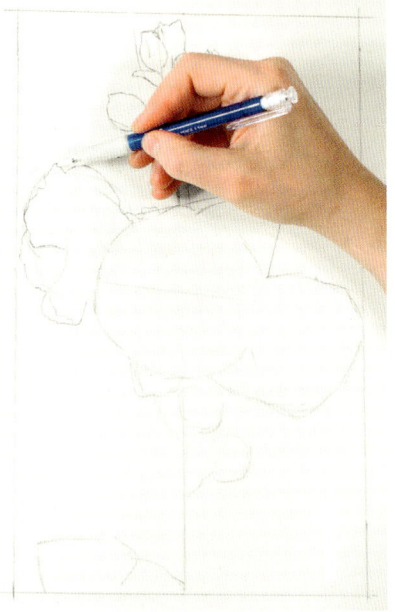

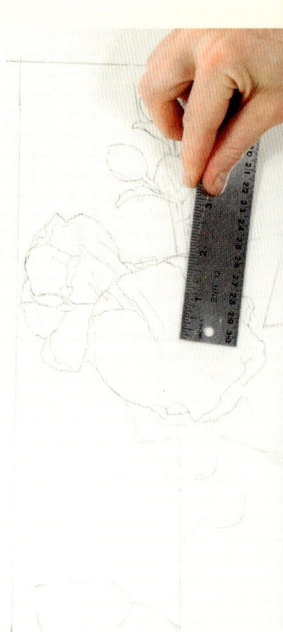

Complete a preliminary drawing on sketch paper. Take measurements from the specimen, and draw the guidelines and boundary box based on the measurements. Lay out the basic shapes and angles with a rough gestural drawing. The flower, stem, and bud outlines will be refined within these shapes.

Use a ruler to check the accuracy of the spatial relationships while you are completing the preliminary drawing.

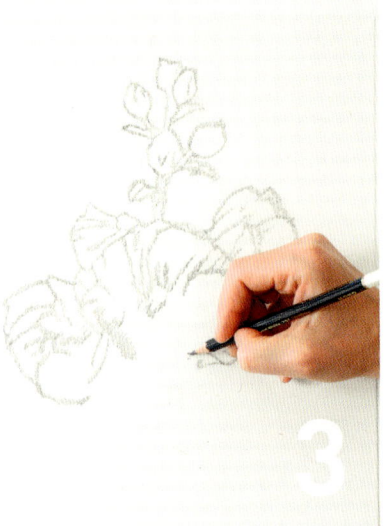

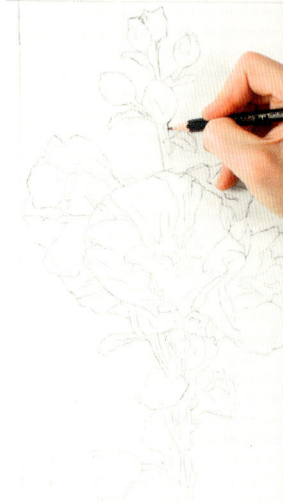

To prepare the preliminary drawing to be transferred, apply 4B graphite to the reverse side of the sketch paper. If needed, place the sketch on a light box, or hold it up to a sunny window, to better see the lines of the drawing.

Transfer the image to hot-pressed watercolor paper with a very sharp 4H lead. Use enough pressure so that the lines are visible when transferred but have not left indentations on the final watercolor paper.

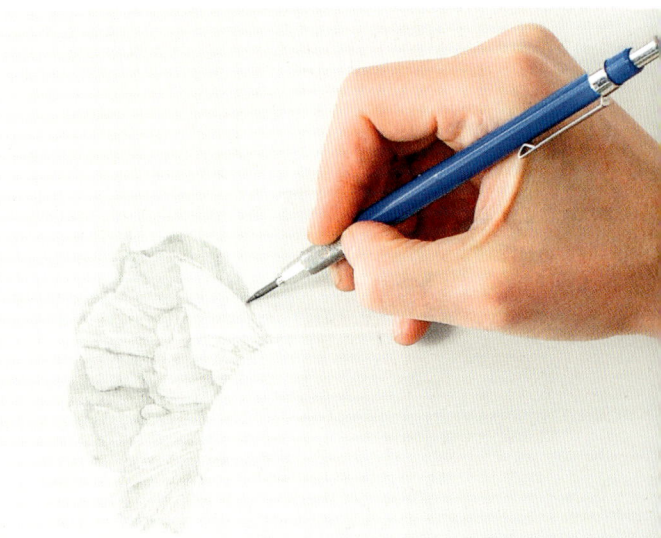

Starting with the flower on the left, use a 2B lead to block in the darks. Roughly 80 percent of the drawing will be completed using 2B lead. Create dark tones by building up numerous layers of graphite applied with a light touch. Do not use heavy pressure, because it can polish the surface and make further layers difficult to apply.

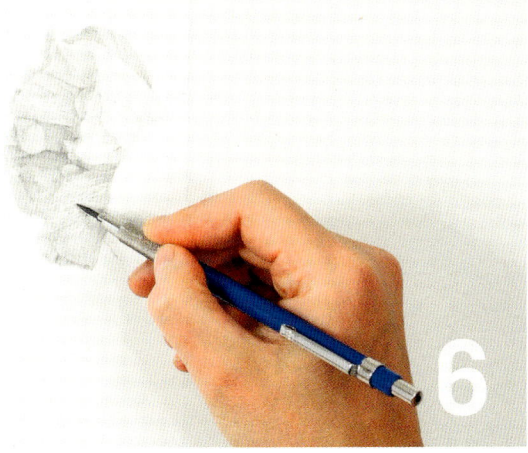

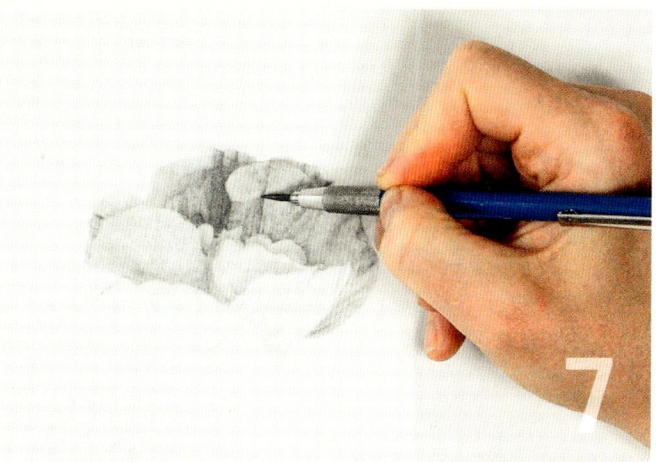

Add details in shading and texture with care to create even and gradual transitions in value. Avoid drawing sharp lines—any marks that appear as lines should be created using tiny hatch marks.

Add graphite layers until the correct values are reached. Rotating the drawing so that it is upside down or sideways helps to spot inaccuracies in shapes and values that you might not have noticed while working in the previous orientation.

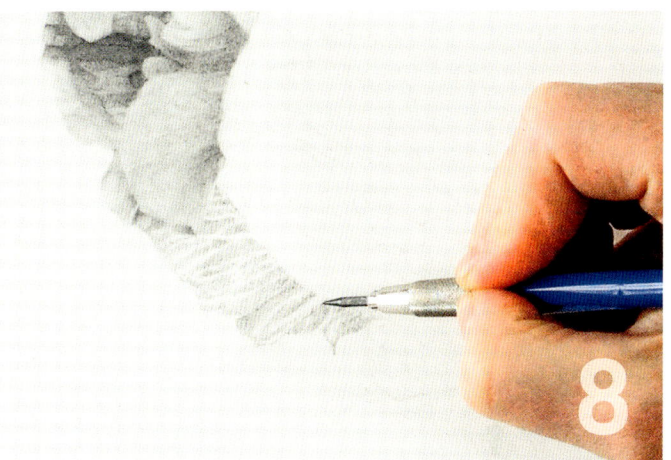

Veins are more prominent on the back of the petals. Focus on the dark shapes that surround the light veins and draw these shaded areas rather than a line where the raised vein would be.

Dab each layer of graphite lightly with a kneaded eraser. This creates variation in texture and value, while also suggesting the transparent quality of flower petals. Dabbing with the kneaded eraser softens any harsh lines and helps to blend the graphite layers.

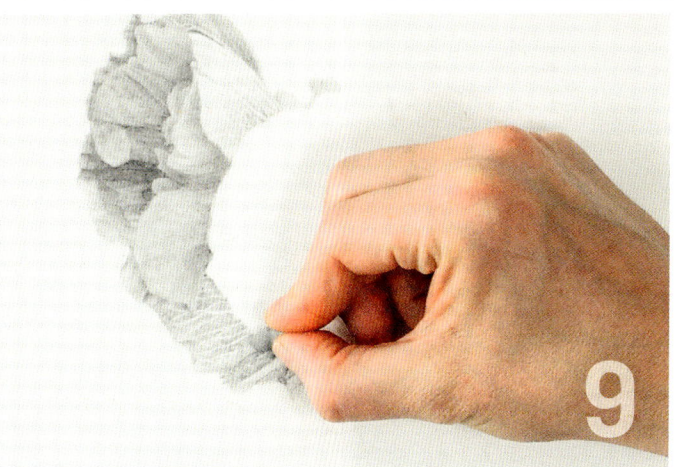

After many layers have been added and a rich texture achieved, redefine the veins and shadows. Emphasize the dark areas surrounding the light veins, creating these shadows using very small stippling or hatch marks.

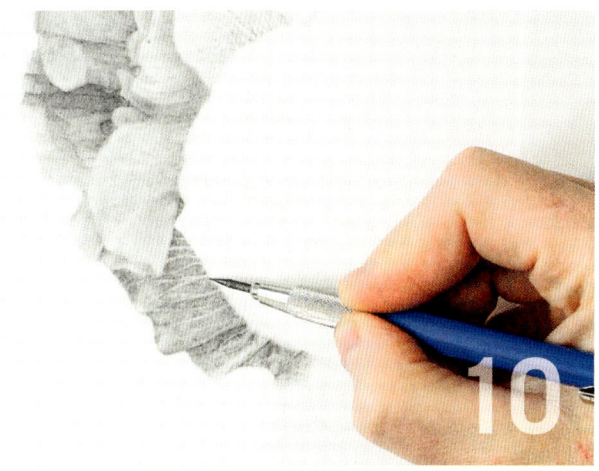

Shadows, highlights, and veins often follow the contours of the folds and creases in the petal, so take care to accurately portray them as they fall on the subject.

Add a light touch of value to even the brightest highlights, then use a kneaded eraser to lighten them, leaving just a hint of value.

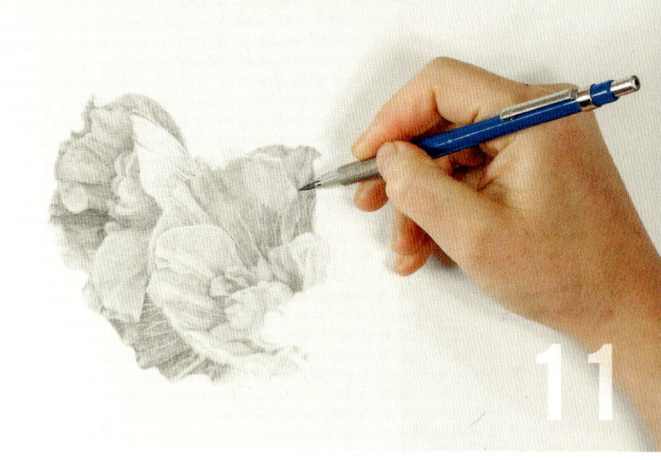

Represent rougher textures of the leaves by using slightly more pressure and layering graphite with a shaky hand—or a scribbling motion—almost like making tiny zigzag marks.

Suggest the fuzzy softness of the buds and seedpods by working with a dull, beveled side of lead rather than a sharpened point. When you are creating soft areas like this, use overlapping, minuscule oval or circular markings.

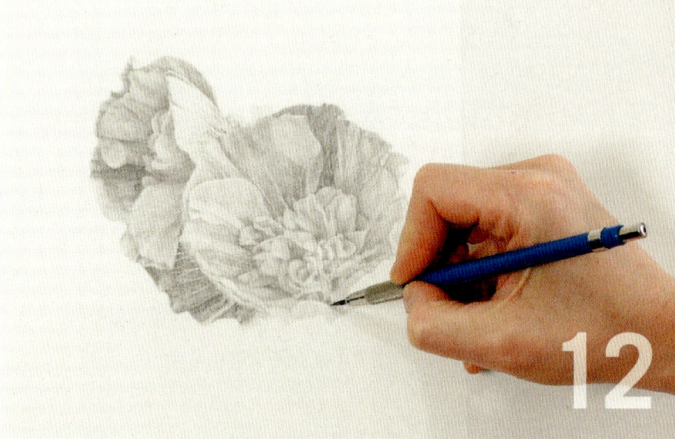

With a very sharp lead, draw dark lines for hairs at the edges of main stem and peduncles. Then, shade the surrounding areas, creating the illusion of tiny white hairs on the stem.

Working on the whole composition, add more detail and darker shadows where flowers overlap each other. Check and fine-tune the overall values with a 2B lead.

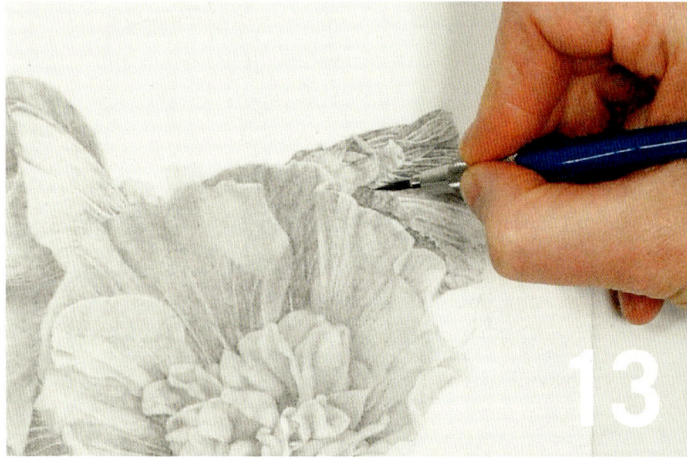

The intensity of dark shadows is increased using a 4B lead. A little more pressure can be used to achieve an intense, solid black. Increasing the range of values in this way will help convey the full dimension of the flowers' centers, developing pods, and stem, and will describe what parts are in the foreground and background.

Pull out the final highlights and clean up edges of the drawing using a kneaded eraser.

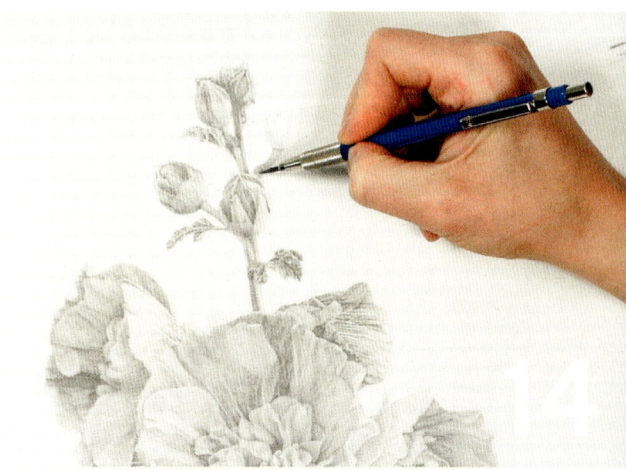

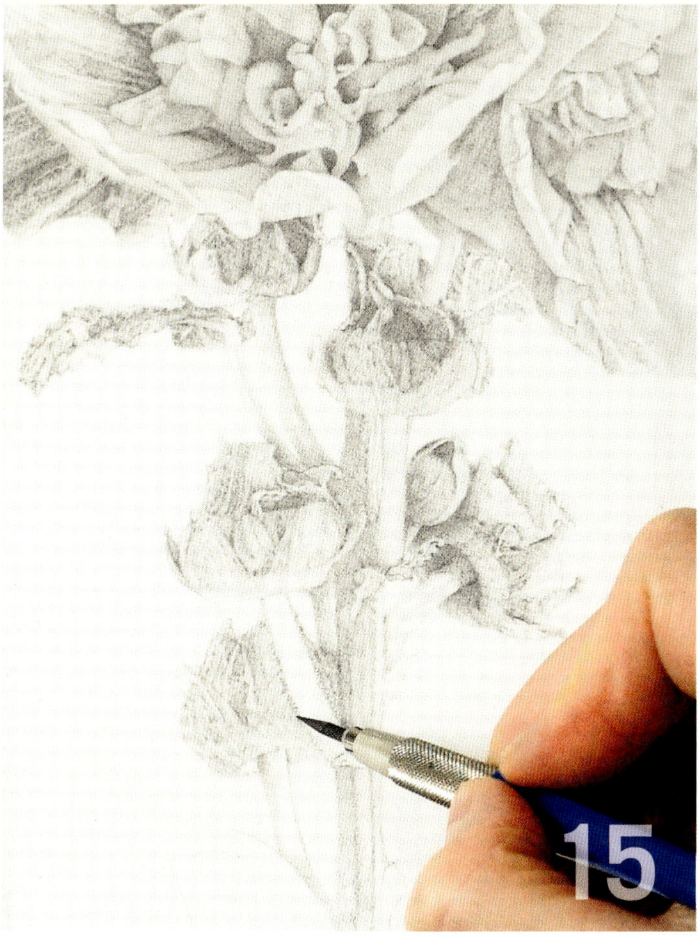

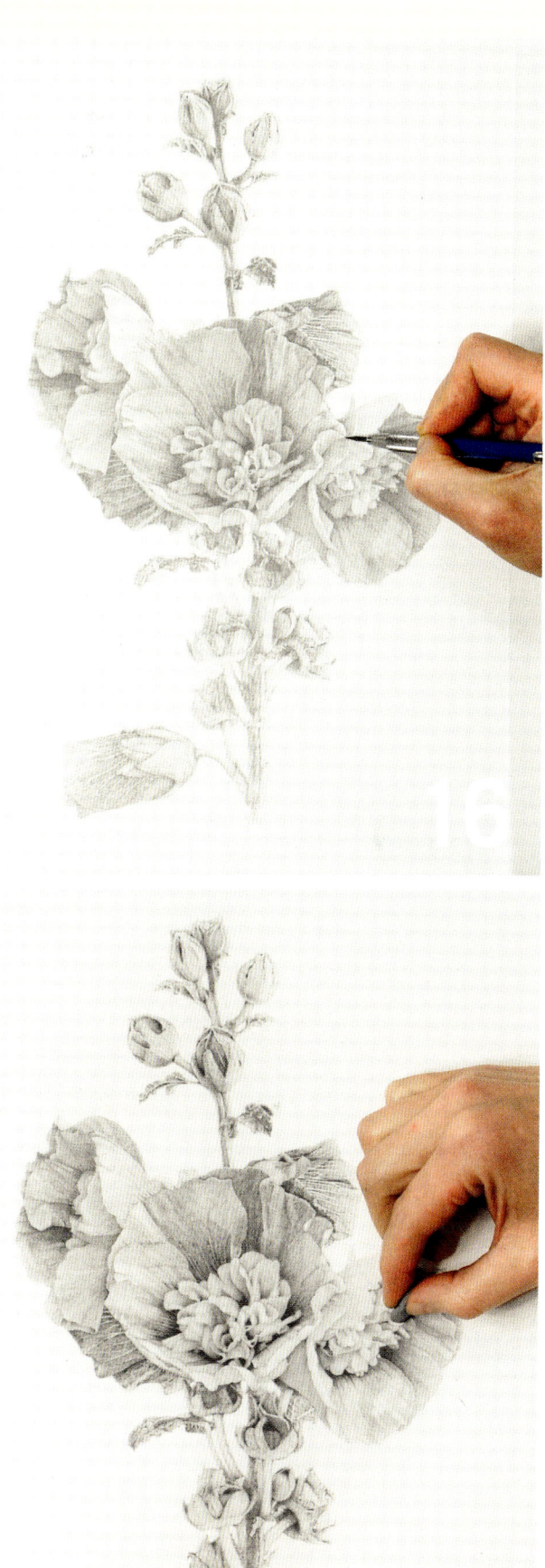

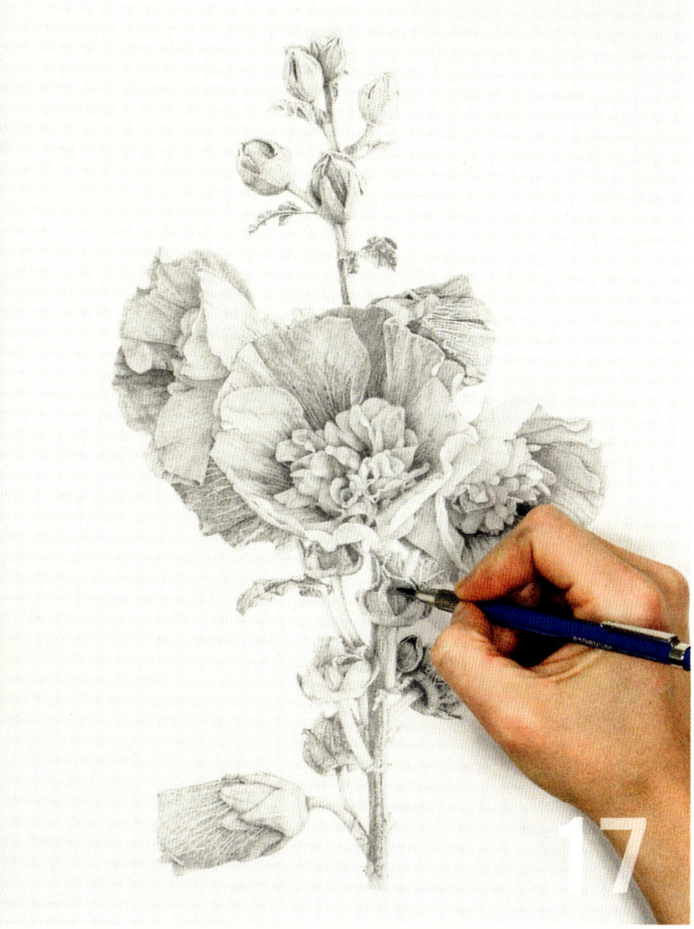

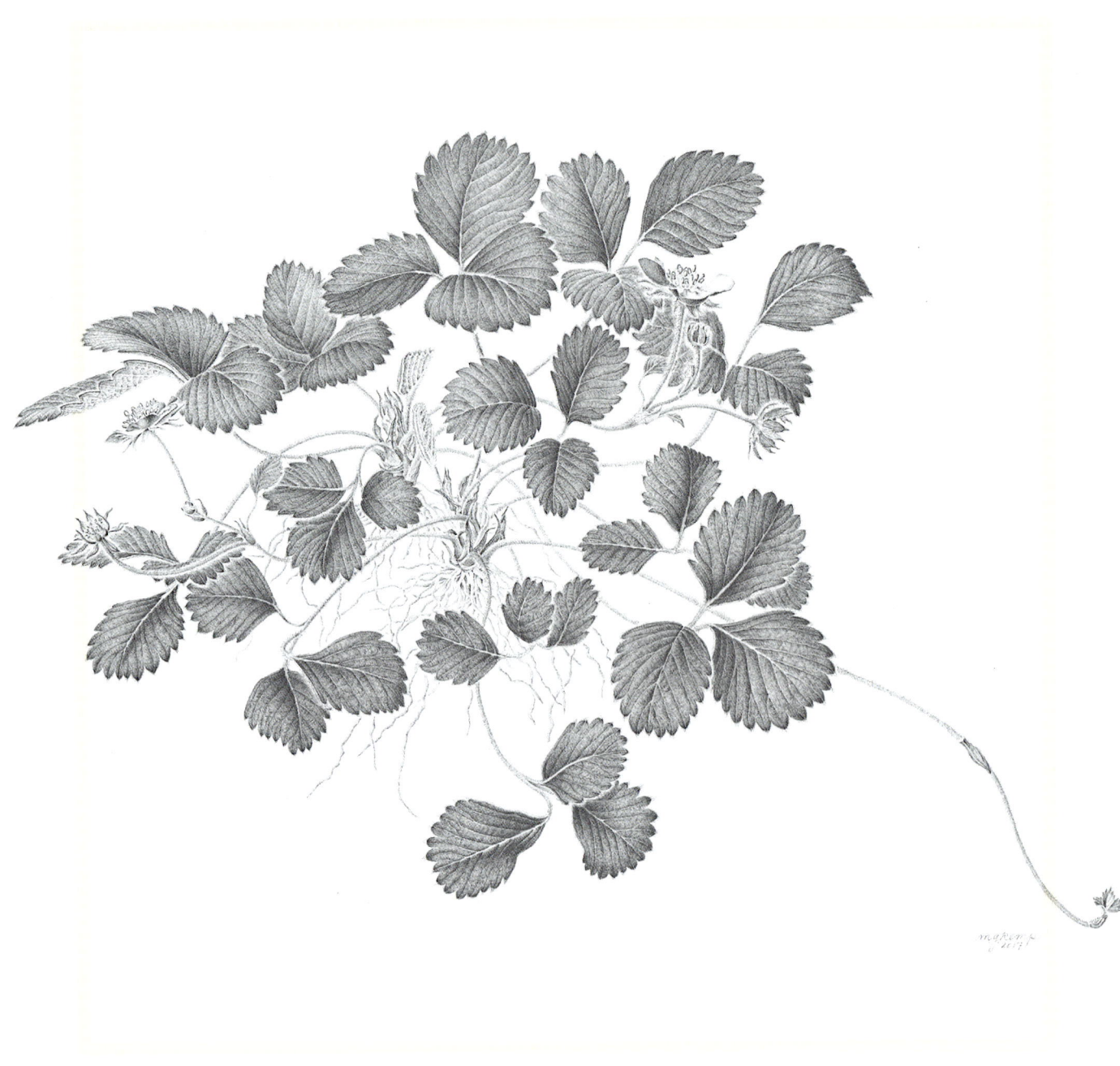

Ornamental Strawberry *Fragaria* 'Lipstick' Graphite on paper © Martha G. Kemp

<small>HOURS TO COMPLETE: 90</small>

<small>MATERIALS:</small> Clamp-on lead pointer; handheld lead pointer; white plastic eraser; low-tack frisket film; removable mounting putty; craft knife; white plastic retractable eraser; lead holders with 3B, B, 2H, H, HB, and F leads; fine-tip waterproof-ink pen; hake brush; acid-free plate-surface 2-ply Bristol paper; acid-free vellum surface 2-ply Bristol paper.

Making a graphite drawing of a complicated strawberry plant is a challenge. First, the composition is drawn out carefully, showing leaves and flowers emerging from the root mass, and specific details from leaf serrations to veining. In advancing the drawing, a number of methods of conveying characteristics in graphite are demonstrated, along with a number of methods for making corrections and removing graphite.

Illustrating a Plant Portrait from Roots to Tips

TUTOR: MARTHA KEMP

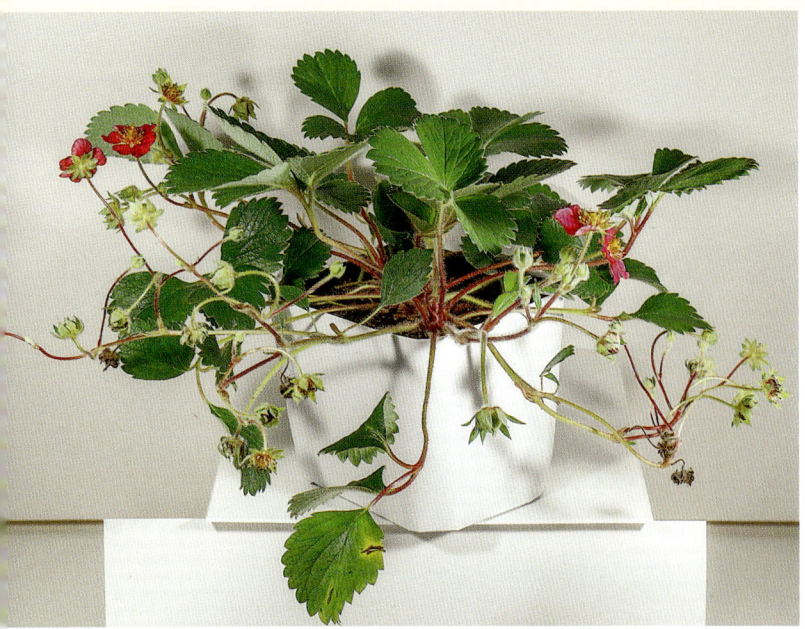

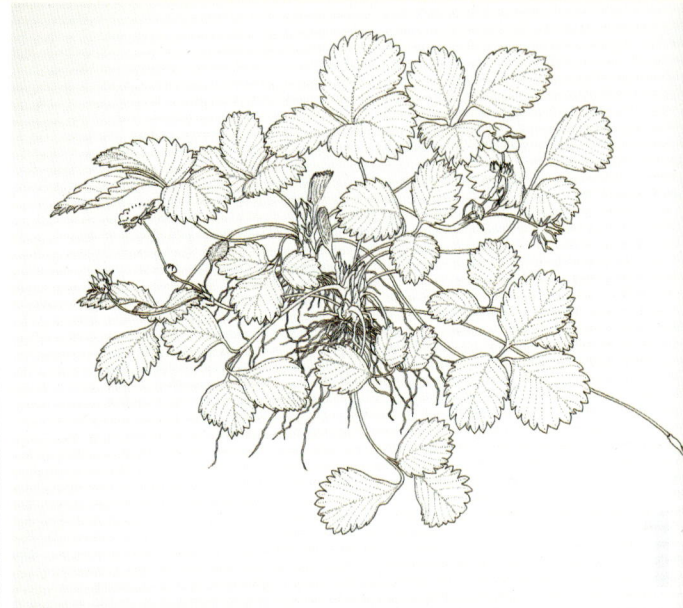

Fragaria 'Lipstick' is an ornamental strawberry. There are two *Fragaria* plants in this pot.

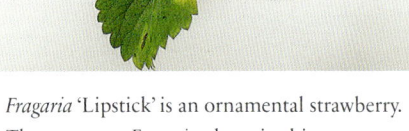

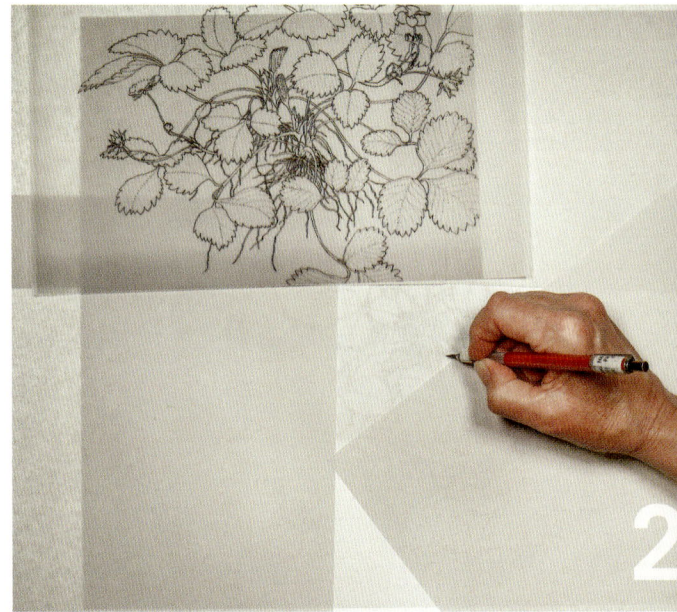

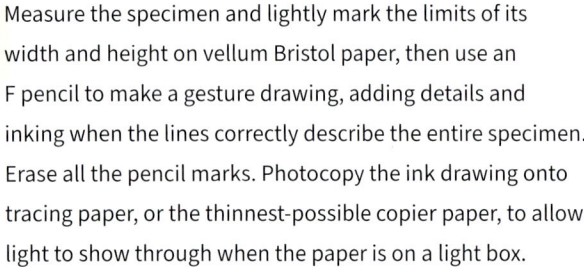

Measure the specimen and lightly mark the limits of its width and height on vellum Bristol paper, then use an F pencil to make a gesture drawing, adding details and inking when the lines correctly describe the entire specimen. Erase all the pencil marks. Photocopy the ink drawing onto tracing paper, or the thinnest-possible copier paper, to allow light to show through when the paper is on a light box.

Place the photocopy of the line drawing under a clean piece of plate-surface Bristol paper and tape it lightly to the back of the plate paper; place the taped pieces on a light box and surround the plate paper with scrap paper to protect it from your resting arm. Refer to the original line drawing, as needed, while you very lightly trace the composition onto the plate paper using an F lead.

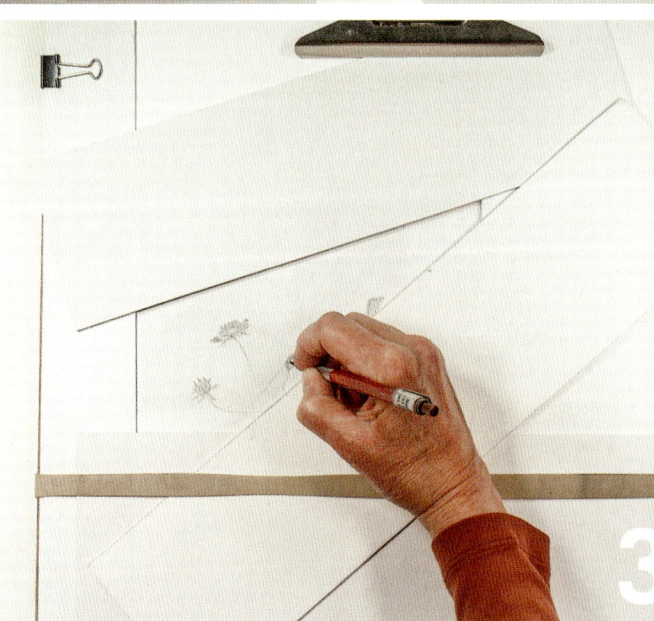

Place the traced drawing on a clipboard, and use the clip, binder clips, and large rubber bands to hold strips of matboard down over the drawing, leaving an opening only where work will be done. Place another strip of matboard under your hand and move it as needed to keep hand pressure off the Bristol paper. Reposition the strips of matboard as you work on different areas of the illustration.

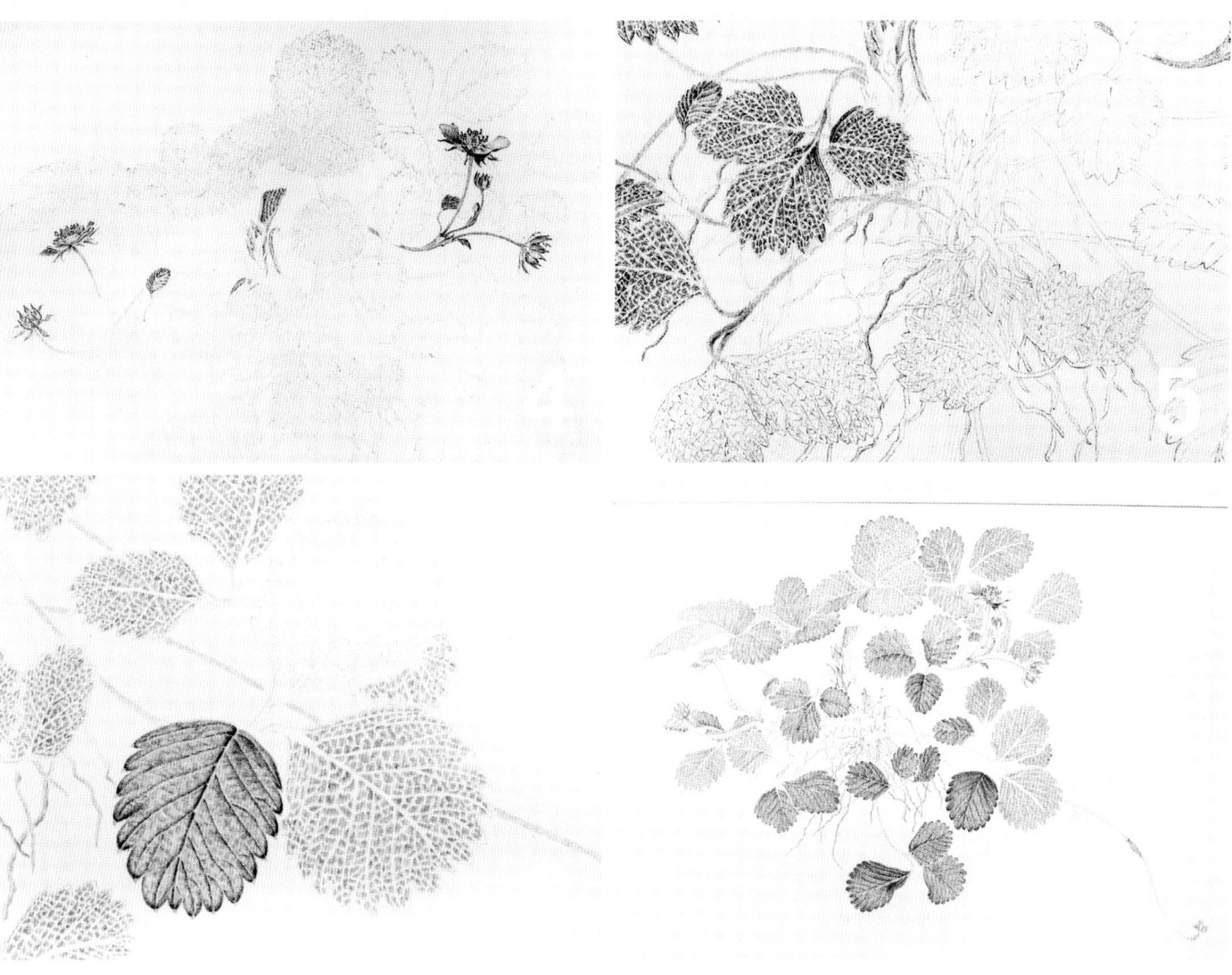

Render the flowers first, because they change most quickly. Use a sharp pencil tip to define stamens, then render sepals and petals, paying attention to keeping all the elements distinct and in sharp focus. Use a flattened pencil tip to render smooth areas of color in the petals and on the stems.

Lightly add the tiny lines that help define the veins in the leaves. These lines will be the road map for shading all the interstitial green areas among the smallest veins. Begin to shade all the tiny green areas, which will look mosaic-like, using a flat pencil tip. All the green areas should be separated by white spaces that represent minute veins.

Here are the stages in developing leaves: the tiny lines (center, barely visible), the mosaics (at left and single leaf at lower right), and a layer of graphite drawn with a flat pencil tip with long strokes parallel to the side veins to blend the little mosaics and define the shadow side of the mid- and side-veins (darkest leaf at center). Leave narrow white lines for the highlight sides of the veins. Develop all the leaves in this fashion.

This view of the drawing shows all the areas worked to varying degrees. The early lines and shading have been made very lightly and built up gradually, holding the lead holder in the writing position. Turn the clipboard as needed to suit the most comfortable direction for you to make strokes and marks.

Strokes and points will vary in a drawing. Strokes and textures created when made with an F lead are shown at top, left to right, ellipses, straight lines, and ovals. Below, the same strokes and textures are shown, made with a slightly softer HB lead. Stroke direction follows the contours of the plant part. Be constantly aware of the shape of your graphite point—sharp or flattened—rotating the lead holder to the sharper-pointed edge if needed.

Take a break from rendering leaves and begin defining the roots and bases of the leaves of both plants. The stems can be softly drawn, because they will be surrounded by tiny hairs later, but the centers of the plants need to be drawn with a sharp point so that all the parts are in focus.

Here you can see the emerging leaves in the center of each plant. Their margins—the edges of the emerging leaves—are fuzzy and indistinct, so use a flattened point to make them look soft. There are white spaces along overlapping leaf edges and overlapping stems; the entire plant is hairy, and these spaces will allow for the addition of tiny hairs later with a sharply pointed 2H lead.

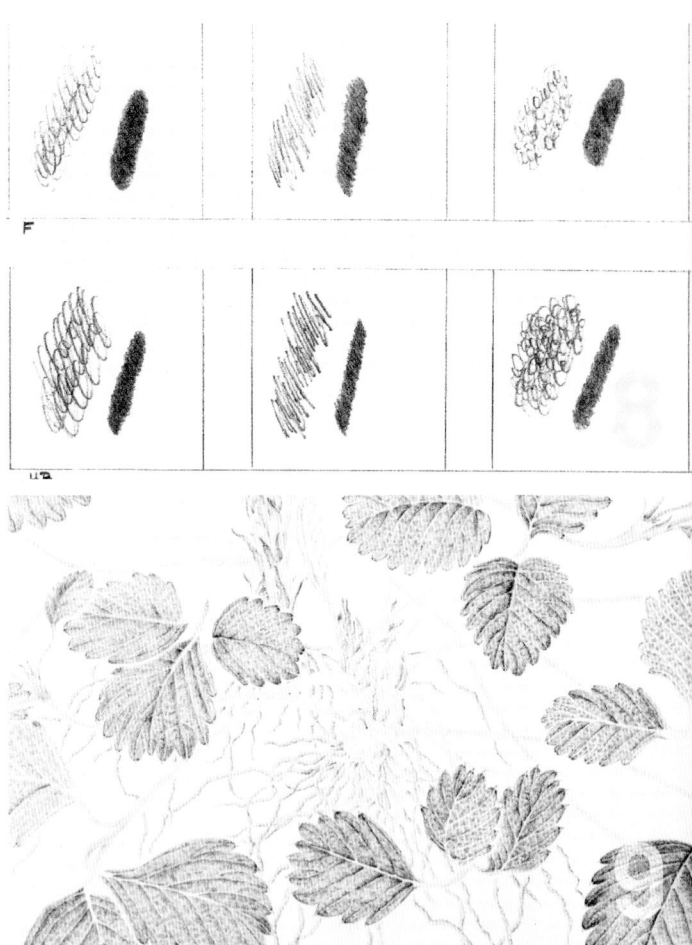

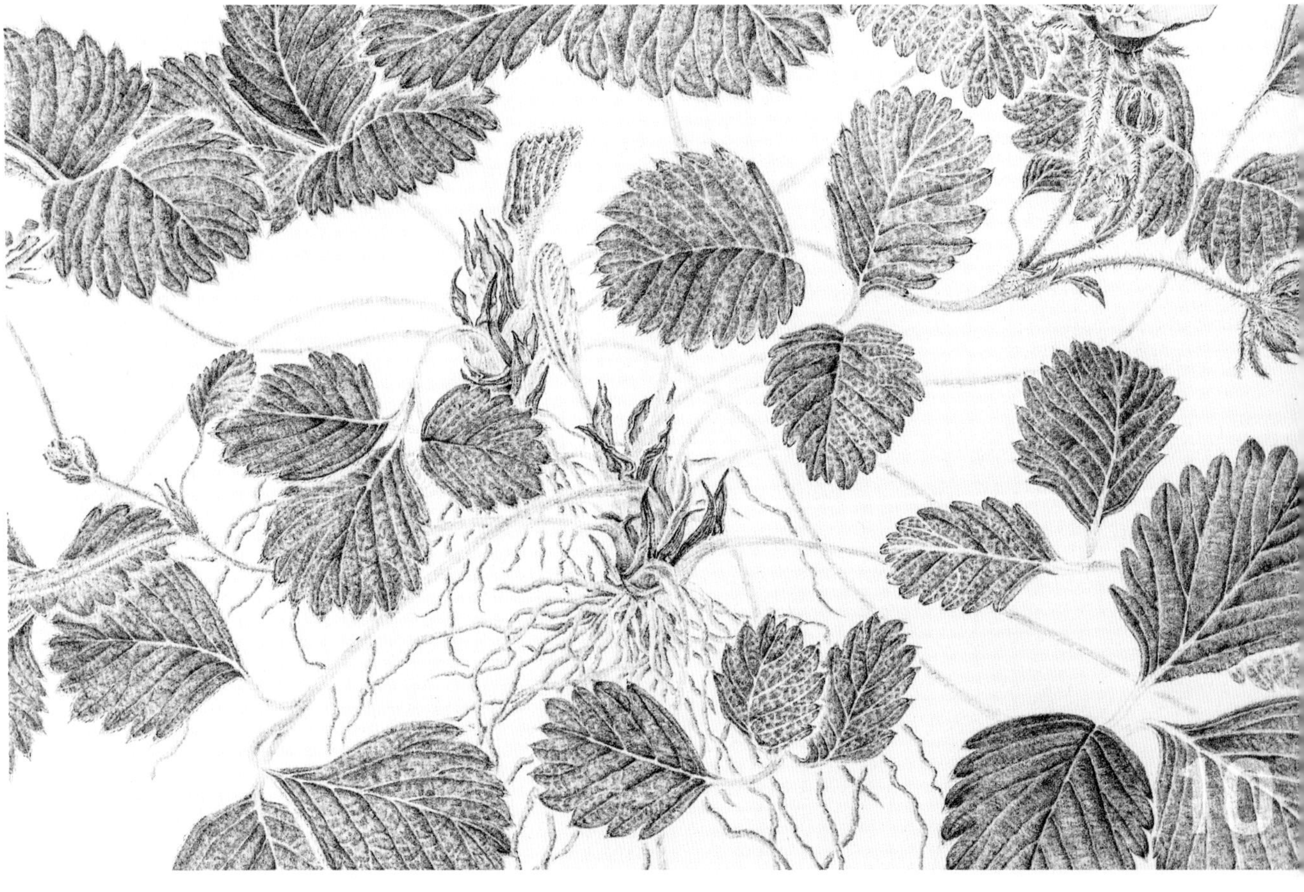

Drawing Botanical Subjects in Black and White

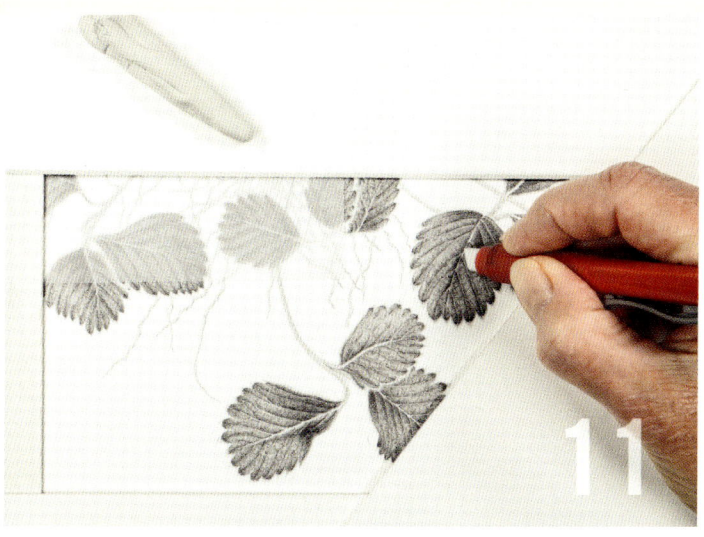

Use a craft knife to cut the end of a retractable eraser to resemble a screwdriver, making a sharp flat edge with a little tip at each end for erasing or lifting tiny areas of graphite. Clean the tip on scrap paper, so it won't redeposit graphite onto the illustration; recut the eraser as needed. You can also use a rolled piece of removable mounting putty to lift graphite by dabbing it on the selected area.

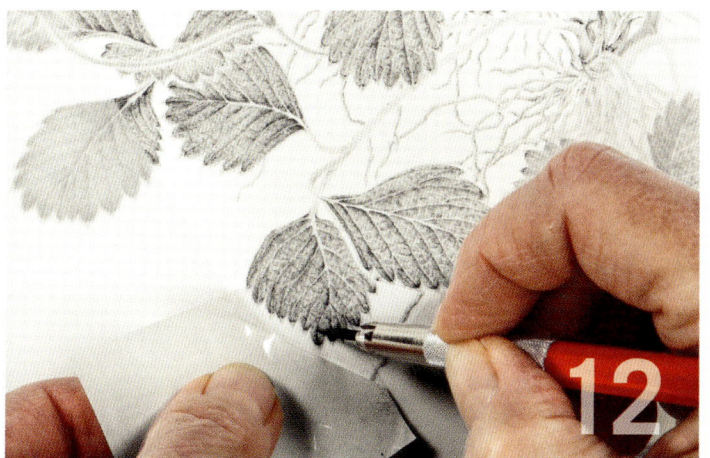

For a more surgical approach to erasing, cut a small square of frisket film and peel back a small corner of the backing paper. Place tacky side of the film lightly on the area that is to be erased and, using a dull pencil point lightly draw on the film exactly over what's to be erased, then carefully lift the film off the paper. This method should lift off the desired mark; if not, repeat the steps. Redraw any incidentally lifted graphite.

Closely inspect the drawing and add the final details with a sharp tip to make the veins crisper; clean up areas where more clarity is needed or where too much graphite was lifted.

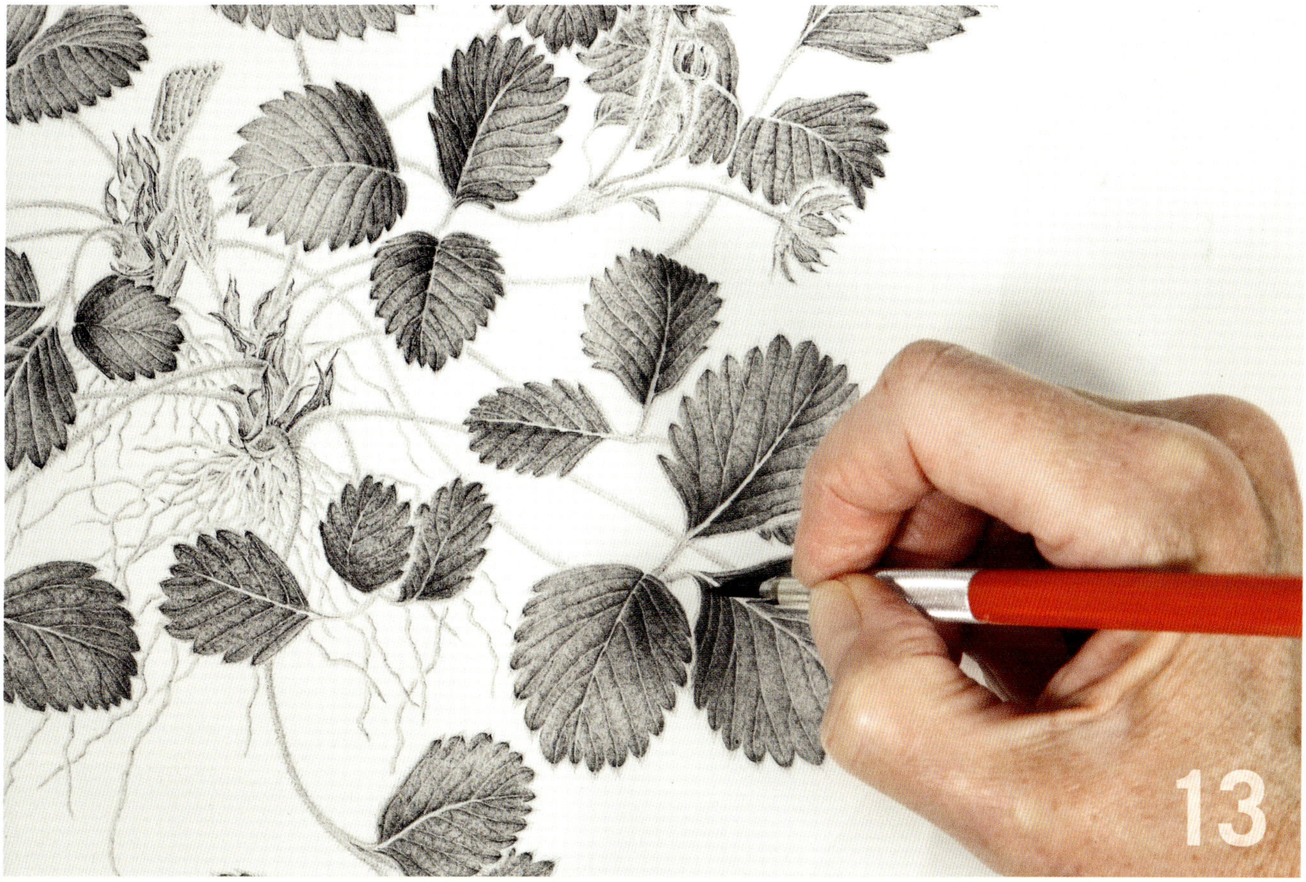

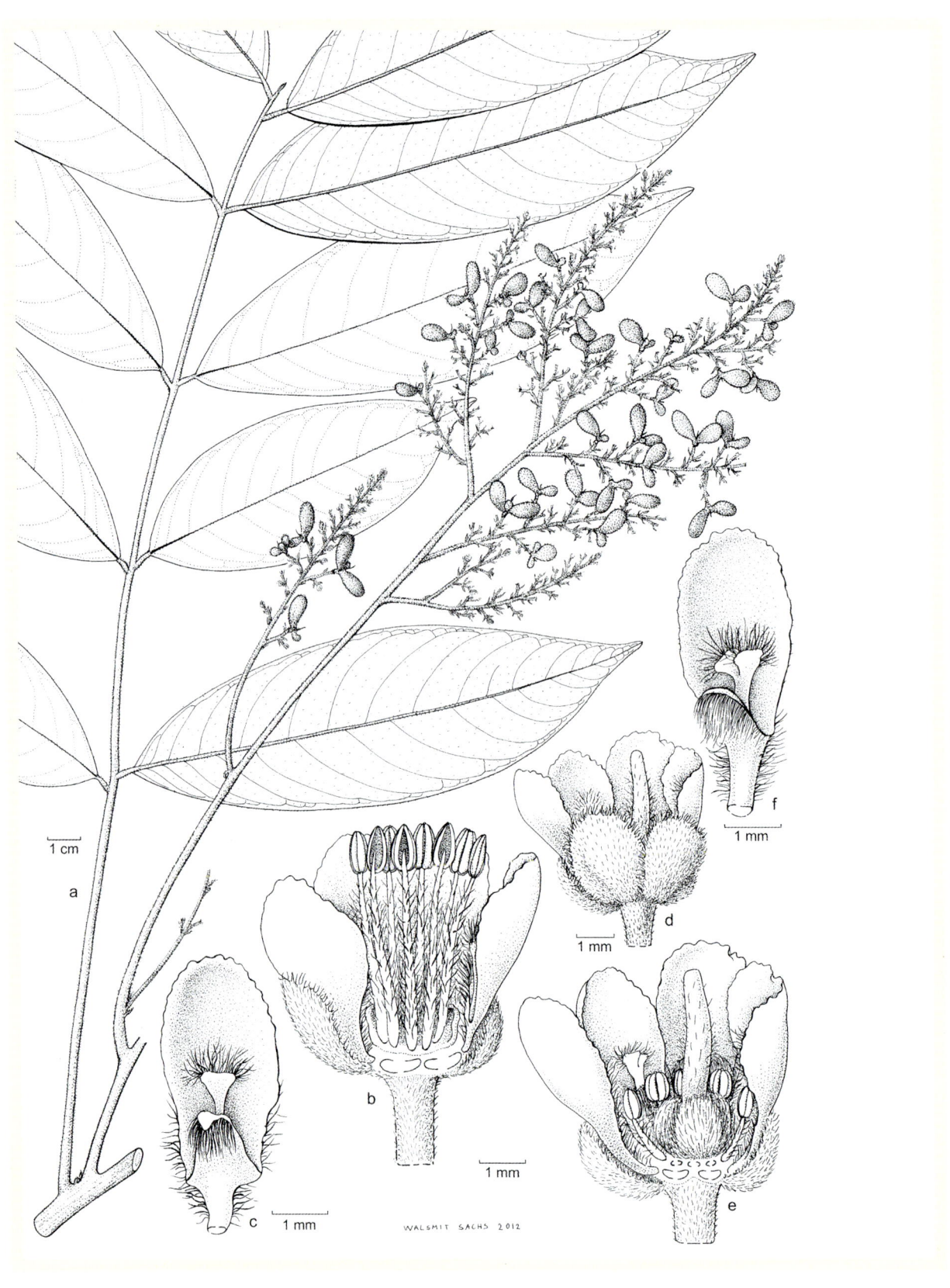

Lepisanthes rubiginosa Pen and ink on paper 14 × 9 ½ inches [35 × 23.75 cm]
© Anita Walsmit Sachs, Naturalis

Pen and ink is most often connected with scientific botanical illustration, and the best of these scientific illustrations are awe-inspiring in mastery of technique. Using a toolbox of line, stipple, and crosshatch, three dimensionality is believably conveyed. Nib pens and technical pens are supplemented by brush inking, allowing a range of characteristics in application. Botanical artists are also using pen, brush, and ink for artistic depictions of plants, expanding their utility as a medium and sometimes combining ink with other media.

PEN AND INK

Techniques and Tutorials

Pen and Ink Skills

The Basics

TUTOR: ESMÉE WINKEL

Traditional ink-filled technical pens are used by both artists and illustrators when working in pen and ink. Because of their sized nibs, they provide consistency in line thickness, and rich black ink can be used to produce a solid black line. Esmée Winkel shows basic inking techniques of line, stipple, and repairing mistakes in this tutorial.

Using and Caring for Technical Pens

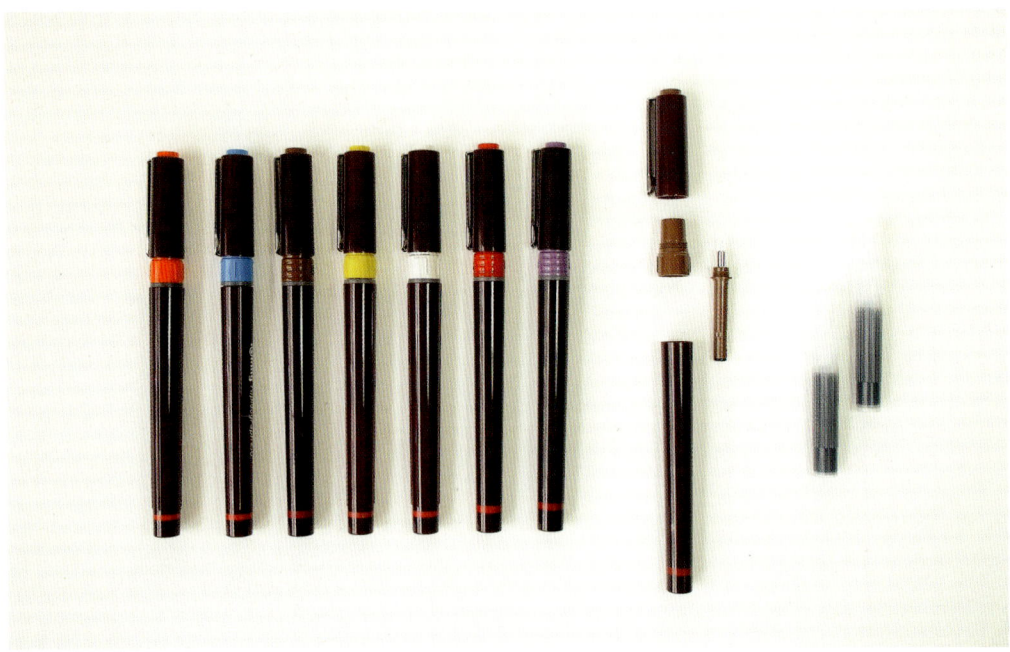

A range of technical pens are available for the botanical scientific illustrator; each brand has its own qualities. Technical pens produce detailed, elaborate botanical illustrations and require very smooth, high-quality technical inking paper, such as Bristol paper, extra-smooth-finish paper, or drafting film. Avoid using textured or loose-grained paper, the fibers can clog the pen's nib, cause lines to bleed, and make it more difficult to repair mistakes.

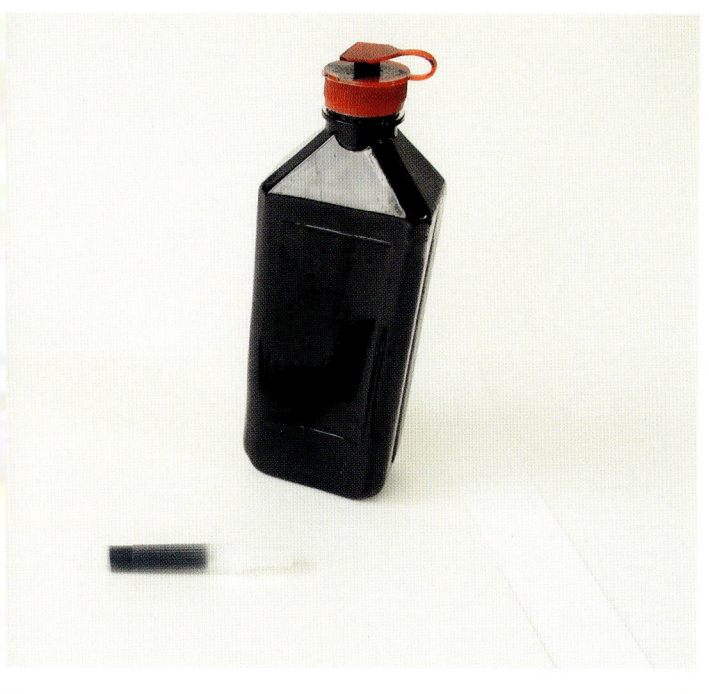

Use good-quality inks that are pigmented, lightfast, and water-resistant. They dry to a deep black color, which makes reproducing the drawings in journals and books easier. Ink in disposable cartridges can become clogged at the bottom after a period of disuse. Pens can be stored lying down, but larger pens, such as 0.5 mm and larger, may start dripping so try storing them with the nibs upright.

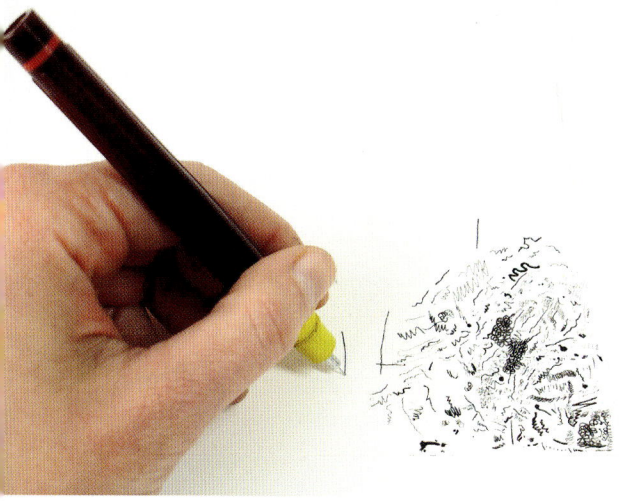

Before you begin drawing, make practice strokes on a piece of technical inking paper to ensure that the pen's ink flows readily. Don't push too hard on the paper with the pen. The ink should begin flowing from the nib easily. Always put the cap back on the pen when you finish working and clean the cap and the nib carefully from time to time with water.

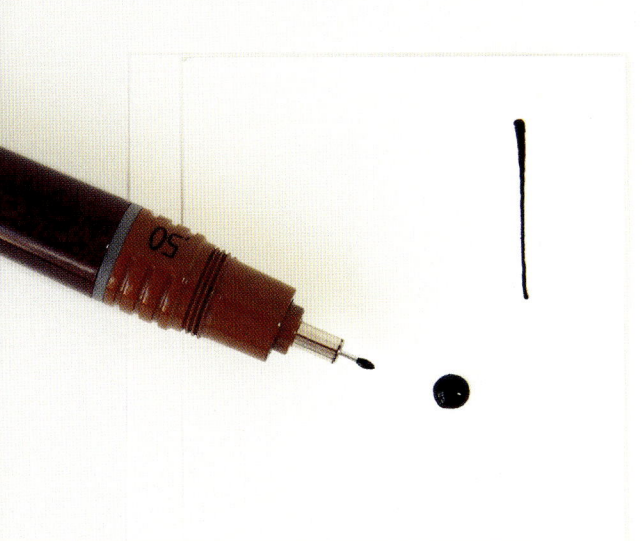

Ink starts dripping out of pens because the pressure in the disposable cartridge has changed. This often happens when the cartridge is almost empty and needs to be replaced.

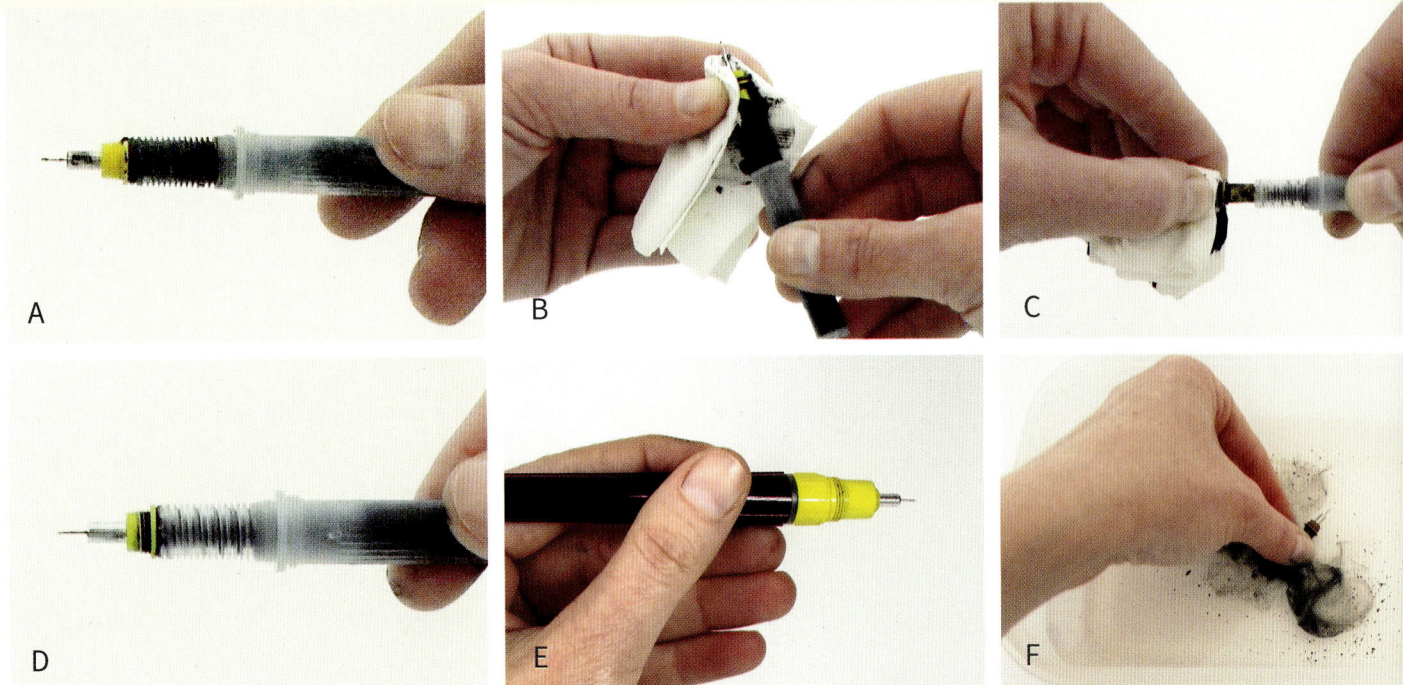

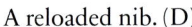

A nib with an old ink cartridge that needs to be replaced. (A)

To replace the cartridge, hold the plastic bit of the nib with a piece of cloth. Be careful not to bend the metal tip of the nib. Pull the cartridge off and throw it away (or reuse for something else). Dab the plastic base of the nib on the cloth to clean off leaking ink. (B)

Hold the plastic bit of the nib with the cloth again and push the new cartridge carefully onto it. (C)

A reloaded nib. (D)

Even if you are not working on an illustration, use the pens periodically to help prevent the ink from clogging. If a pen does not immediately work, give it a horizontal shake to get it started. (E)

If a pen seems to be clogged, try putting the nib in a bath of warm, but not hot, water and swish it carefully in the water. (If the water is too hot, the plastic will melt.) (F)

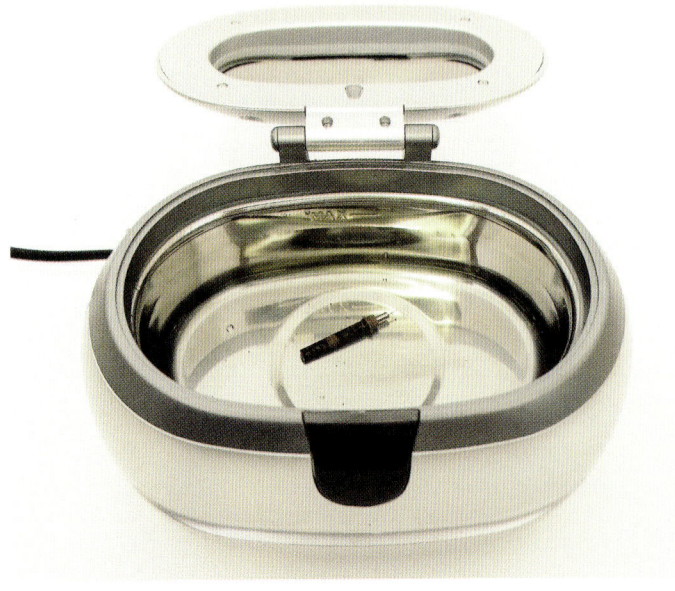

The best way to unclog pens is to put the nibs in an ultrasonic bath. High-quality baths can be expensive, but more affordable models, such as jewelry cleaners, work just as well. Drop the nib into the bath (adding a little dishwashing detergent can help) and turn it on until the nib is clean (it only takes a minute or so).

Basic Inking Techniques

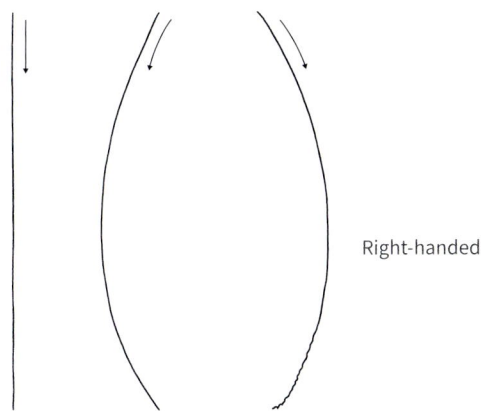

Right-handed

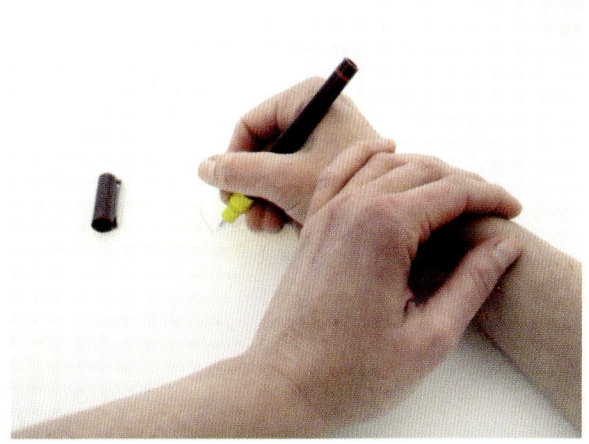

To ink a smooth, straight line, it is easier for most artists to ink lines downward instead of upward, and it is often easier to ink the line toward your body. Inking away from your hand often makes your hand tremble, creating a tremor in the line (like the tremor seen at the bottom of the line at the right). Inking toward your body means that you will have to turn the paper regularly in order to ink lines in the most controllable direction.

If your lines have a tremor in them, try supporting your inking hand with your other hand—this helps keep it stable.

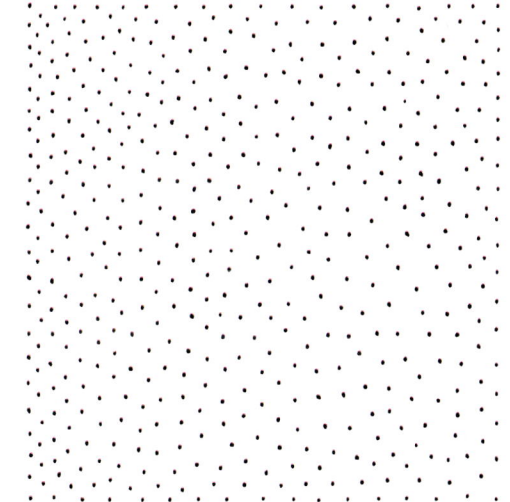

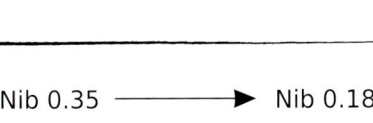

Nib 0.35 ——————▶ Nib 0.18

It is more difficult to create a line of varying widths using a technical pen rather than a flexible nib pen, such as a crow quill, or a brush. Start by inking where the line width is broadest, stop where needed, switch to a pen with a smaller line width, and continue inking the line. This line was begun with a 0.35 mm nib at the left, but a 0.18 mm nib was used near the right to make a narrower line.

The stippling technique creates volume, transparency, texture, color, pattern, or details such as leaf veins. To suggest volume, shadow and light are created by closely placing dots in shaded parts, as shown at the left in this square, and more openly in lighter parts. Place dots in a systematic and uniform way or the illustration will look chaotic and muddy; or an unwanted textural appearance may develop.

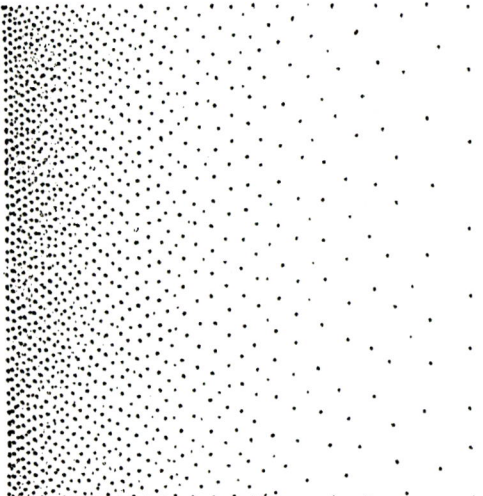

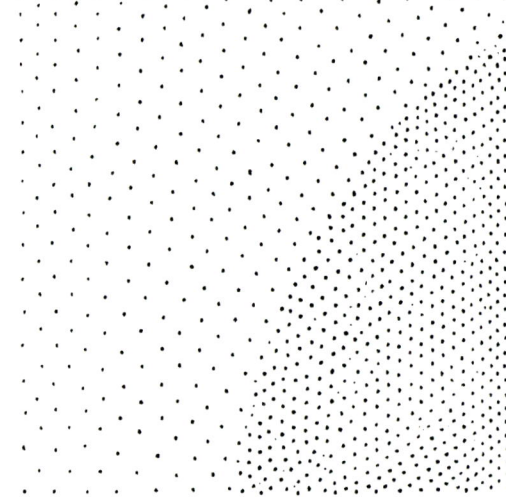

To show shadow and light, place dots in a row, add subsequent rows, creating a bit more space between the dots and gradually complete the area. The smoother the transition from dark to light the greater the three-dimensional effect. Although black-and-white illustrations reproduce very well, too many and too small dots may appear as solid black when printed.

To suggest transparency, place a layer of evenly spaced dots on top of the transparent area of the illustration. For a color pattern in a shaded area, first create the volume and then place another layer of evenly placed dots describing the color pattern.

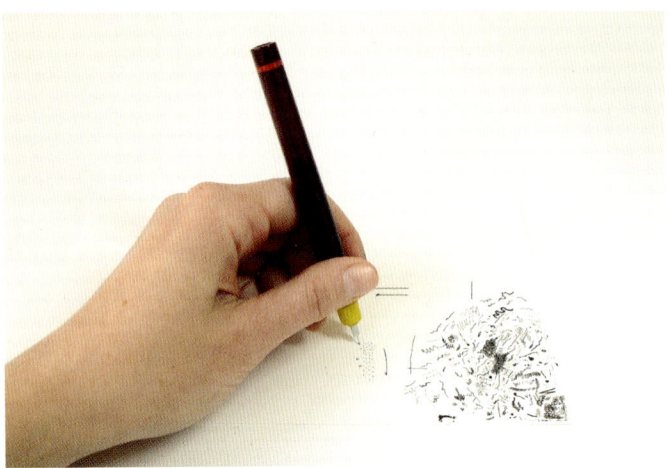

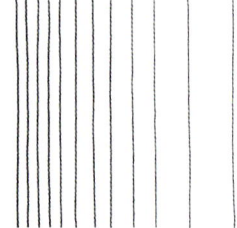

When stippling, hold the pen in a vertical position so the dot will not accidentally become a short dash. Use pens with 0.25 mm nibs and larger. Step back from your work periodically to observe if lines and dots are correctly spaced, or make a reduced black-and-white photocopy of your work. Use a 0.18 mm pen (or finer) as little as possible for lines and dots when the drawing will be reduced in size for publication. The exception is that hairs and other small details like glands are typically inked with a 0.13 mm pen.

Shading with a series of parallel lines, called hatching, instead of shading with dots, also suggests volume. The lines on the left suggest a flat tone, and the lines on the right suggest an area shading from dark to light. Hatching is faster than stippling, but it can be difficult to ink every line parallel to the previous one, and it does not make as smooth a transition from dark to light as stippling does. Hatching works well for certain leaves, but it works less well for delicate flower petals.

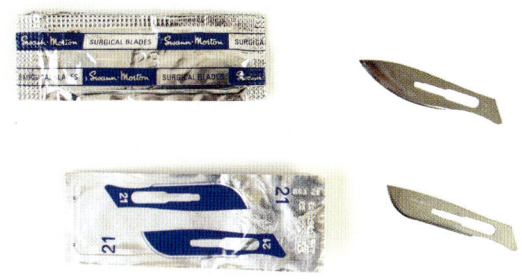

To repair mistakes, use a surgical blade, but use it with extreme caution. Surgical blades are extremely sharp—they are used by surgeons to make incisions—so be very careful when working with them. They are available in various forms and sizes. Because the blades are so sharp and slightly curved, they are helpful for removing mistakes on paper.

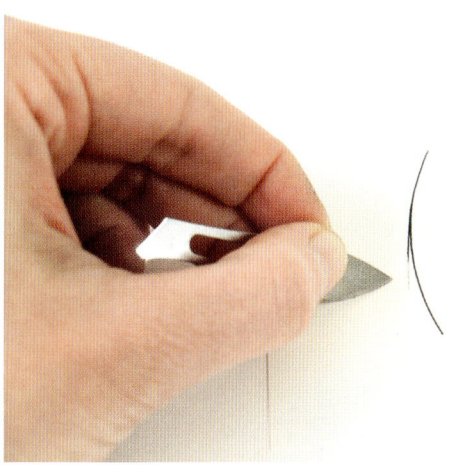

When a mistake is made, first ink the correct line and then scratch off the mistake using the surgical blade. After the error has been scratched off, the paper surface is damaged, and it becomes difficult to ink smooth lines that do not bleed into the paper.

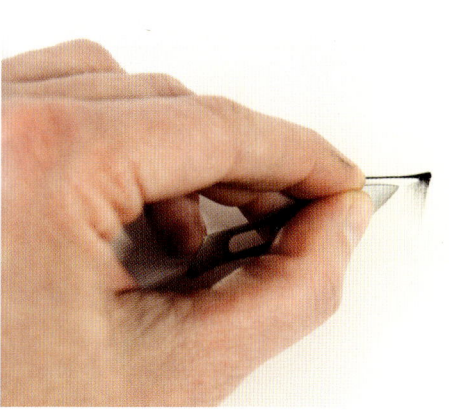

When you are repairing a mistake, use the long side of the blade—not the tip. Using the tip damages the paper even more and can easily create a large hole. Sometimes ink has not completely dried and is smudged across the surface when erasing the pencil drawing. To repair the smudge, first re-ink the line that has been smudged, let the ink dry thoroughly, then scratch off the smudge.

Pen and Ink Line Characteristics

TUTOR: DEREK NORMAN

When you are beginning a pen-and-ink drawing, first consider the characteristics of the line that will be created. A technical pen will produce a drawing with a different overall personality or look from a drawing produced by a traditional dip pen.

The major advantage of technical pens is the consistent width of the line they produce. This can be an advantage or a disadvantage, depending on what kind of drawing you wish to produce. Other distinct advantages are its ease of use (it is very convenient for a stipple technique) and its ability to execute detail—especially with the fine points, such as the 0.13 mm or the 0.18 mm).

A dip pen, by virtue of its design and flexibility, has the advantage of executing a thin or thick line within the same stroke. A swollen line is very much part of a dip pen technique that is generally considered to be more expressive.

These drawings of a spiderwort (RIGHT) and a sunflower (BELOW) show the line characteristics of a technical pen (spiderwort) and a dip pen (sunflower). Technical pens may be easier for beginners. A dip pen requires more practice and patience to master controlling its nuances and the characteristics of various pen nibs. Both pen types have their vagaries, such as making blots (dip pens) or drying out (technical pens), and all pens need to be cared for consistently.

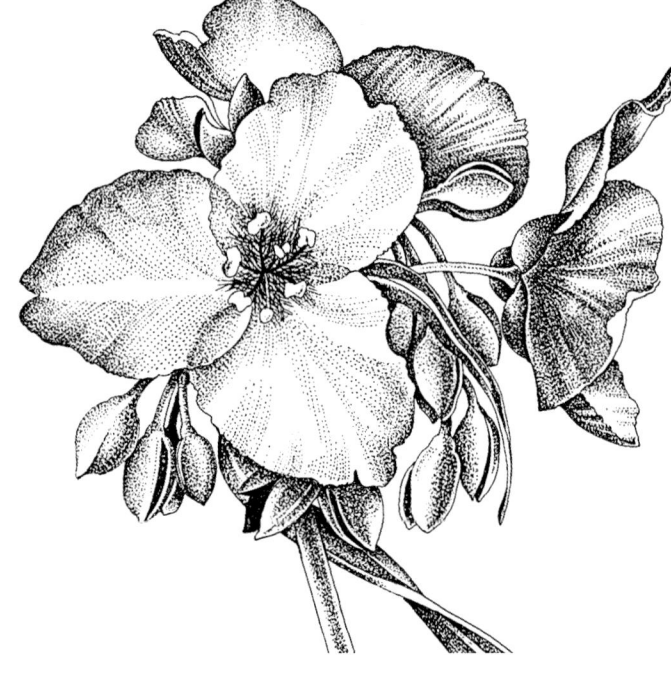

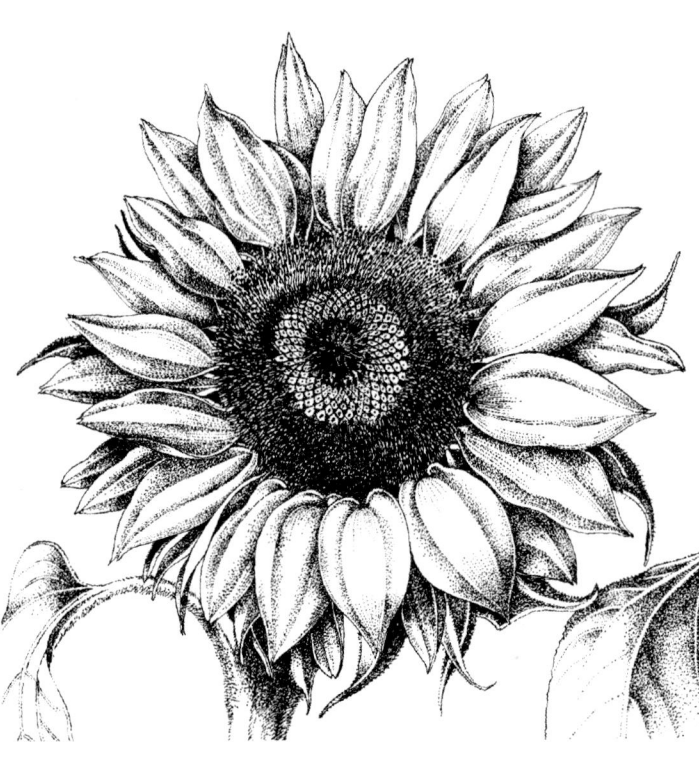

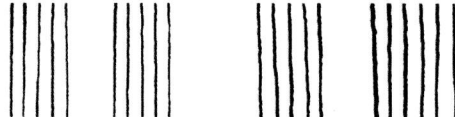

On the left, compare the straight-line characteristics of technical pens sizes 0.18 mm and a 0.25 mm to dip pen nibs no. 102 and no. 22. On the right, compare curved lines made with a 0.18 mm and a 0.25 mm technical pen and dip pen nibs no. 102 and no. 22. Once mastered, these techniques can be used separately or in combination within the same drawing.

Here are examples of thick and thin, eyelash or swollen lines using a no. 102 nib. Each type or size of dip pen nib will have a different degree of flexibility when you exert pressure on the pen, so the swollen line will vary from nib to nib.

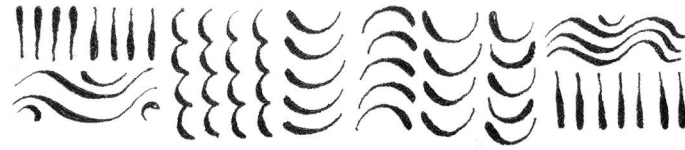

These examples of thick and thin, eyelash or swollen lines were made with a no. 22 nib pen.

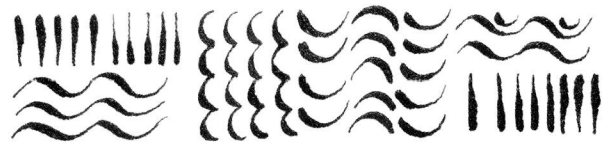

Use good-quality waterproof black India ink in a thimble-size container, properly secured so that it doesn't spill, and transfer the ink to the container using the bottle's pipette. To draw the ink into the pen nib, dip the nib of the pen to just below the open hole. While you are working, occasionally wipe any excess ink off the nib. Before storing the pen, clean the nib with a little warm water and carefully dry.

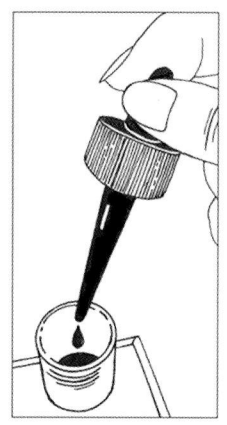
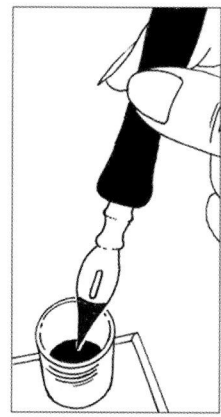

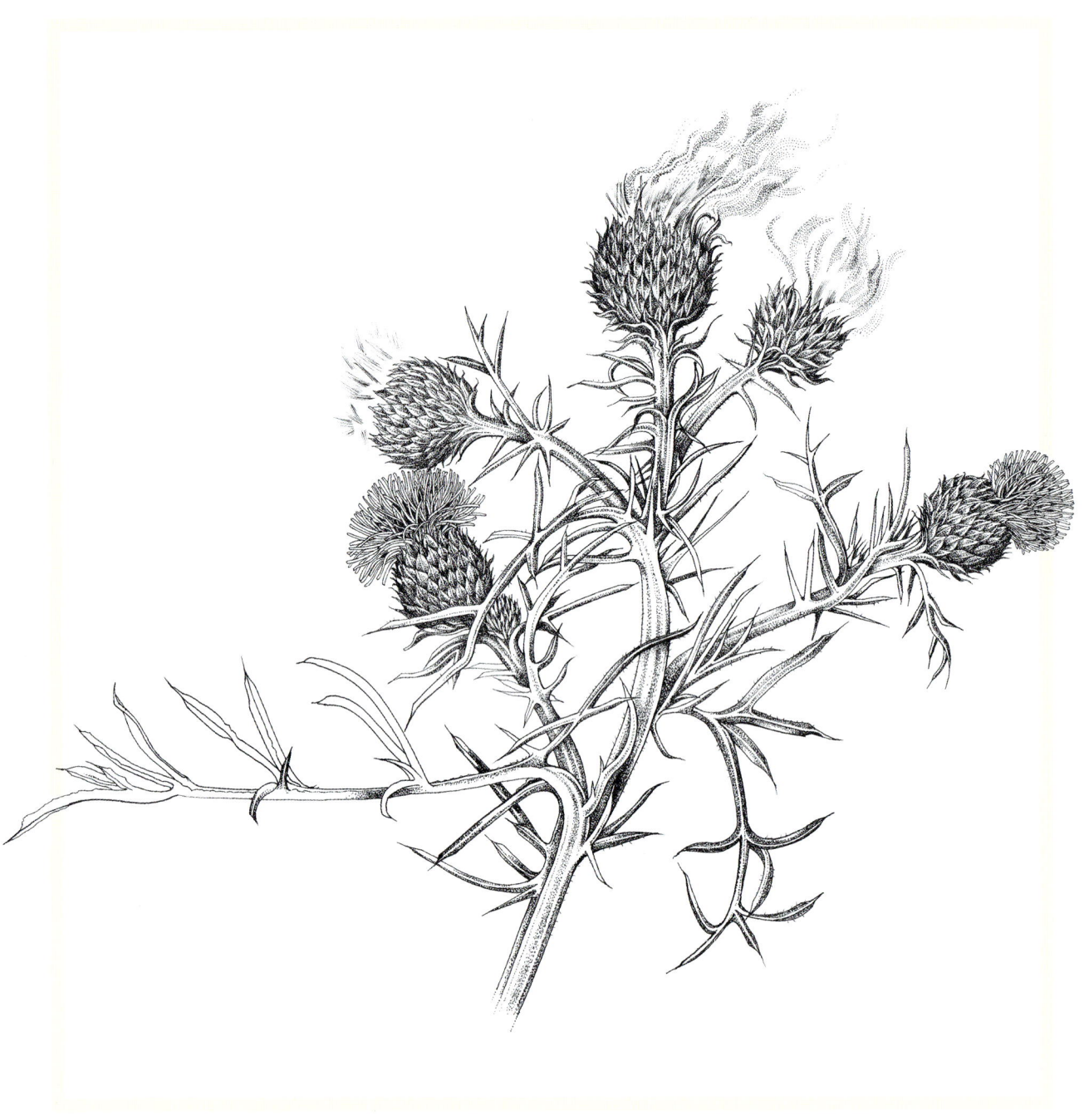

Pitcher's Thistle *Cirsium pitcheri* Pen and ink on Bristol board 9 × 11 inches [22.5 × 27.5 cm]
© Derek Norman HOURS TO COMPLETE: 75

MATERIALS: Kneaded eraser; lead holders with HB and 2H leads; dividers; pen holders and nibs (Hunt 512, 22, and 102); technical pens (0.13 mm and 0.25 mm); ruler; black waterproof India ink; India ink for technical pens; lead pointer; 16- × 21-inch [40 × 52.5 cm] drawing board; Bristol board with smooth (plate) surface (2- or 4- ply); magnifying glass; paper towel; drafting tape.

Derek Norman demonstrates drawing a thistle branch from field sketches to finished pen and ink drawing. The inking was based on a strong graphite rendering; technical pens are used where line consistency is desired, and nib pens where a variable line is preferred. The resulting drawing conveys the spikiness of the branches, the weight of the thistle seed heads, and the airiness of the thistle down.

Drawing of a Thistle Head in Seed

TUTOR: DEREK NORMAN

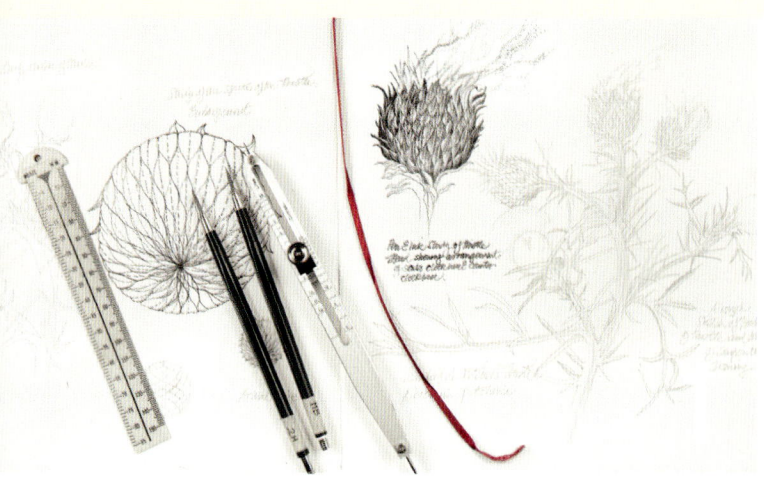

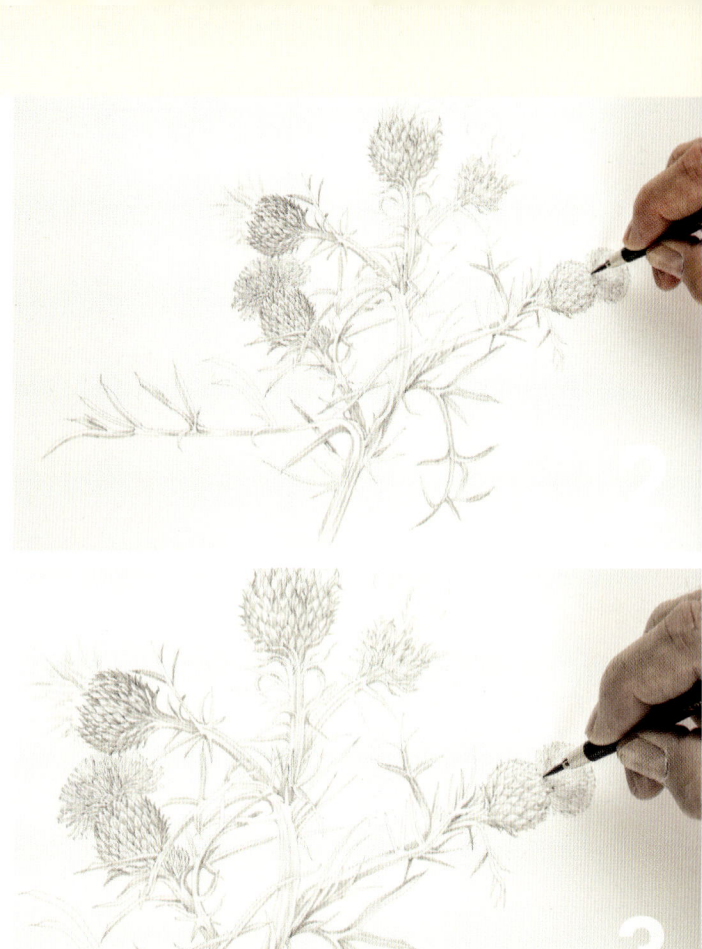

Working in the field is essential at all stages of the subject's life cycle. Make pencil drawings and studies over the course of several visits to the plant. While you are in the field, record the plant's measurements, establish accuracy, and draw intricate details. On location, sketch various arrangements and complete your preferred composition. The final drawing can be checked against the actual plant in the field, allowing you to make any necessary modifications.

Make a careful transfer of the pencil drawing to the Bristol board, using clean and precise lines to capture the detail of the plant. A careful transfer of the pencil drawing is key to a successful outcome.

Very lightly add some tonal value using an HB pencil. The shading will act as a guide during the inking process.

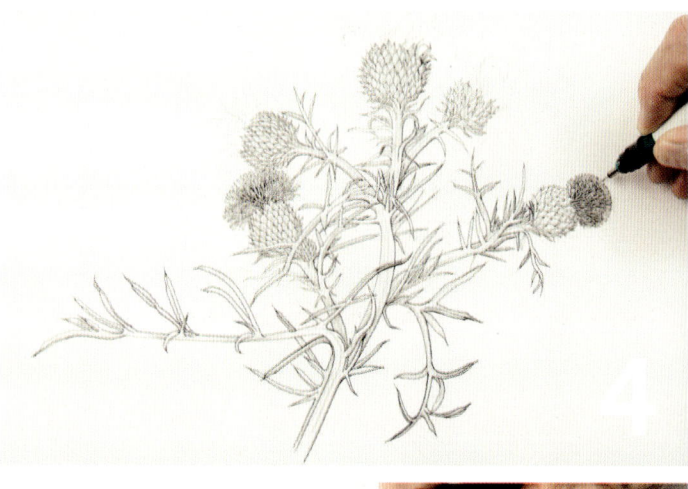

Use a no. 512 dip pen nib or a 0.25 mm technical pen to ink the outlines on the shaded sides of the stem and main branches. Ink the other outlines with a no. 2 dip pen nib or a 0.13 mm technical pen. Use the smallest tips for details (a technical pen is being used here). Practice making long lines and varying the pressure for thin-to-thick lines when using a dip pen.

Use a 0.13 mm technical pen or a no. 102 dip pen nib to make stipples—fine, regular dots—which add depth, dimension, and detail. Ensure that the ink is thoroughly dry, then remove any pencil under the ink by gently dabbing a kneaded eraser on the drawing. Don't rub the surface, because rubbing will damage both the drawing and the Bristol board.

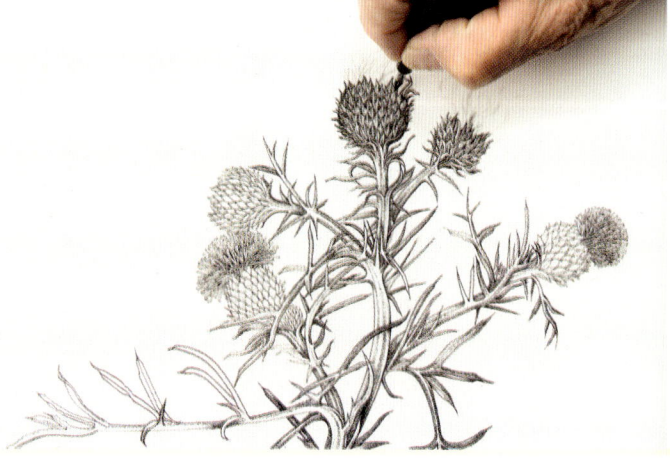

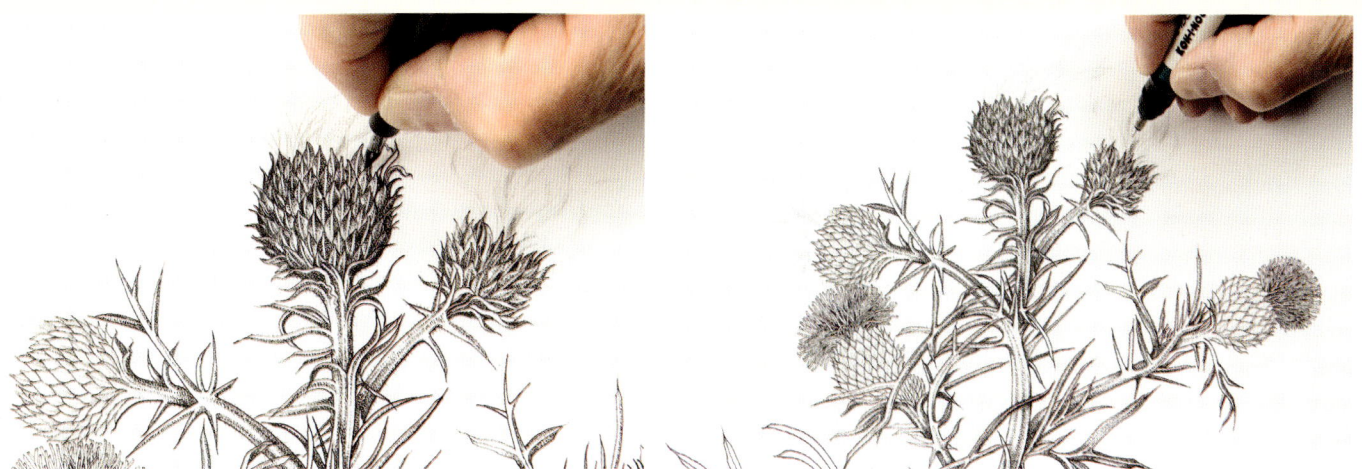

Here, a dip pen nib is used for the involucral bracts. Only the edges of the bracts are outlined, with the inner areas stippled. Keep in mind that the finer the dip pen nib or technical pen is, the finer the stipple will be. Be careful how much ink is on a dip pen nib so that it doesn't drip. To allow some parts of the leaves to look bright, they are not filled with stipples.

Use either dip pens or technical pens (used here) for stippling, depending on the detail required and your personal preference. To ensure a good, clean circular dot, hold the pen at a steep vertical angle. Note the stippling on the stems to make the dimensional ridges. Practice the technique to maintain an even look.

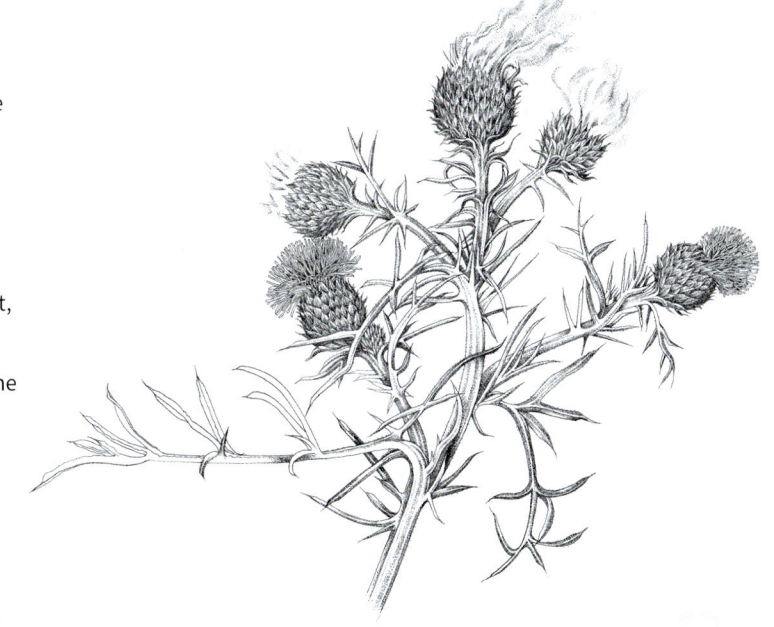

Portray the delicate thistledown (the seed's dispersal system) by using a skipping, stippling, broken-line technique. Combining broken lines with negative space results in a light, ethereal effect (see page 106). Once the ink is thoroughly dry, use the kneaded eraser to carefully remove any remaining signs of pencil. Note how the composition flows and is balanced by light airiness at the top and open areas at the bottom, with the visually heavier, darker flower heads in the center.

Note from the editors about the composition of this thistle head drawing: Derek Norman frequently leaves some areas of his drawings incomplete, as in the lower left-hand leaf of this thistle. One of his goals in doing so is to guide the eye of the viewer to that area of the drawing, usually the top, that best shows the botanical detail and enriches the visual experience. Another aim is to generate an awareness and appreciation of the varying stages that are followed in creating a detailed plant drawing. In this Cirsium drawing, his intent had been to leave the lower right leaf as incomplete but he became distracted by a phone call and then realized his mistake—too late! However, the mistake serves to demonstrate the theory; notice how it pulls the eye downward when the intention was to do everything possible to make sure the eye drifted upward.

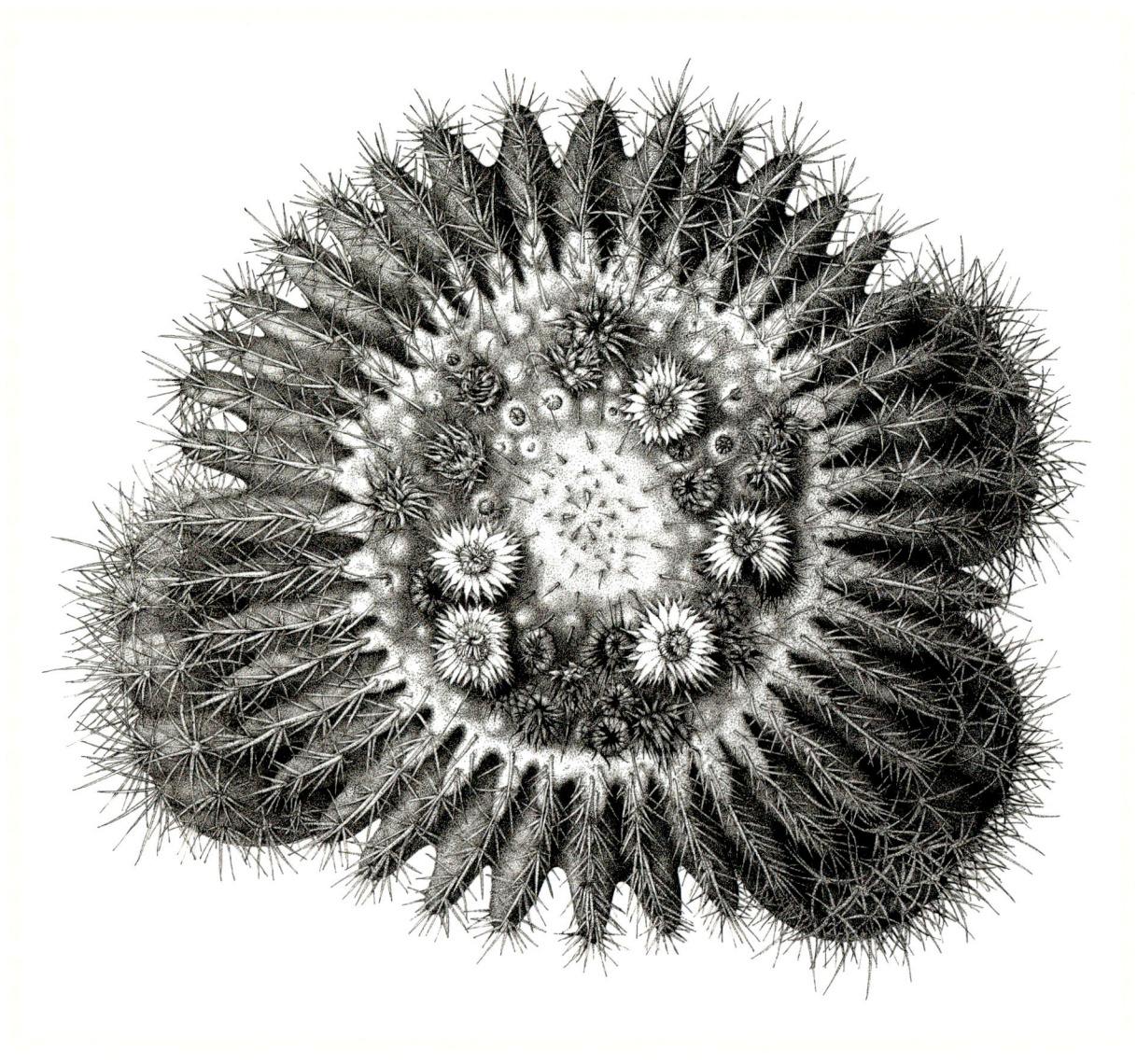

Echinocactus grusonii Pen and ink on paper 16 × 17 ½ inches [40 × 43.75 cm] © Joan McGann
HOURS TO COMPLETE: 130

MATERIALS: Blue transfer paper; hake brush; rotary lead pointer; kneaded eraser; lead holder with 4H lead; technical pens (0.25 mm, 0.3 mm, and 0.35 mm); black waterproof India ink.

Spines or thorns can be some of the most intimidating subjects to portray. In this tutorial, Joan McGann uses technical pens, first drawing outlines for the spines, flowers, and cactus lobes. Then stippling and cross-hatching are used to convey form and volume. Even the individual spines are stippled, to show their tubular shape and the different angles at which they protrude from the body of the cactus.

Depicting Cactus Spines

TUTOR: JOAN MCGANN

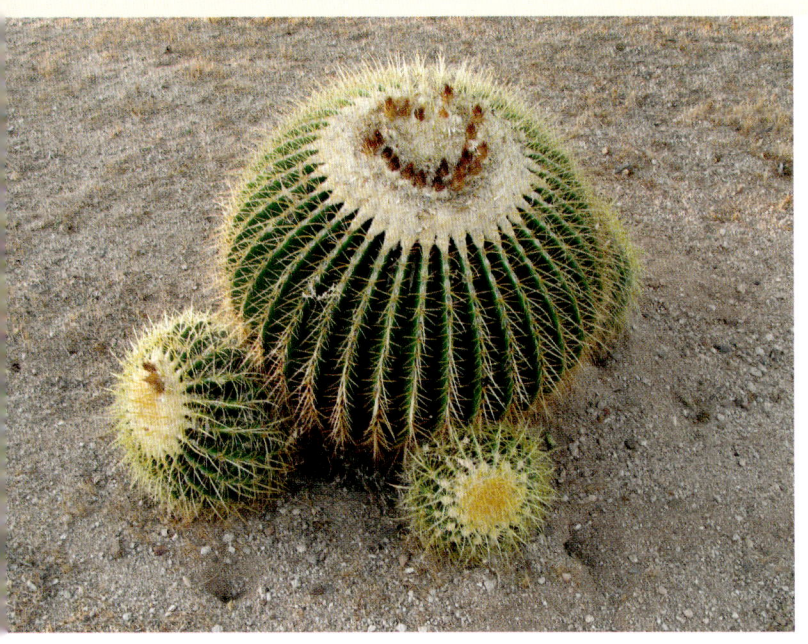

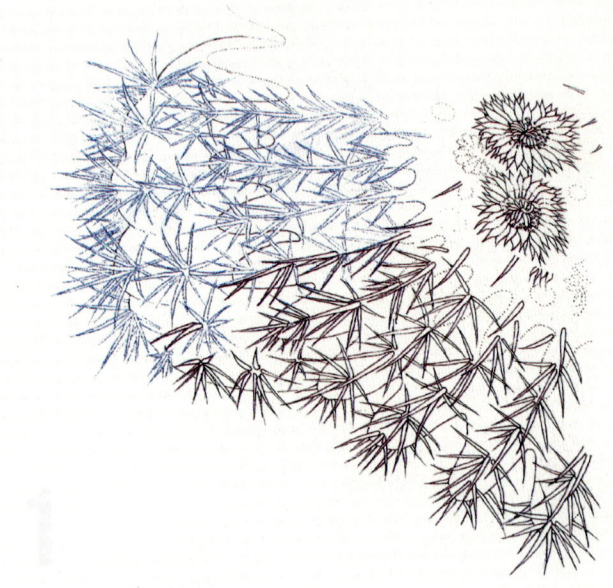

Echinocactus grusonii, golden barrel cactus, has a bright green color with light yellow spines and flowers. It is cultivated for use ornamentally throughout the southwestern United States, but it is endangered in its native habitat in the Mexican state of Hidalgo. A composite of several specimens was used to illustrate the plant from an aerial perspective.

Transfer the initial drawing to vellum-finish illustration board using blue transfer paper and 4H pencil. Using a 0.25 mm technical pen and special black India ink for technical pens, draw in the contour lines of the spines, flowers, and edges of the plant body. The lines of each spine start at its base and meet at the point.

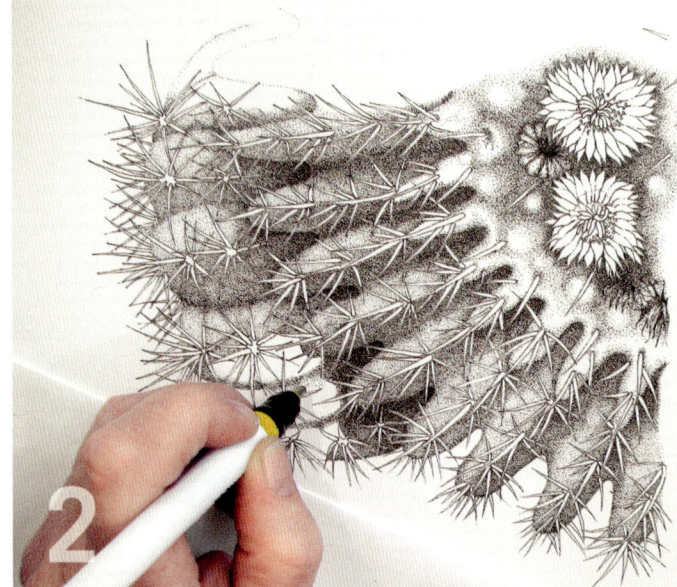

Develop the cactus by stippling a fine dot pattern that builds depth, form, and shadow. Make the dots using a 0.3 mm technical pen, held nearly perpendicular to the paper surface. To avoid a mechanical look in the dot pattern, use an overlapping circular placement of dots.

In the final stage of the drawing, delicately place stippling in the flowers and the woolly center of the plant. Use stippling within the spines to produce a rounded effect. Thicken the edges of spines in shadow and the darker side of larger spines using a 0.3 mm technical pen. Darken the form and shadow in the plant body further with 0.35 mm and 0.3 mm technical pens.

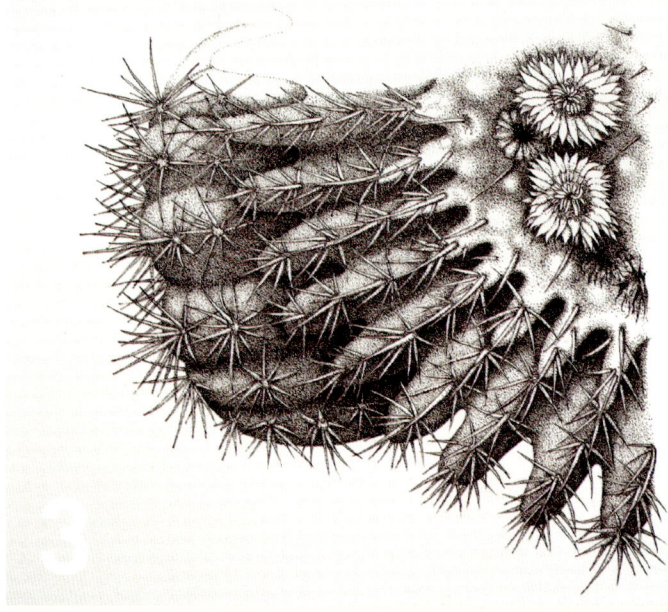

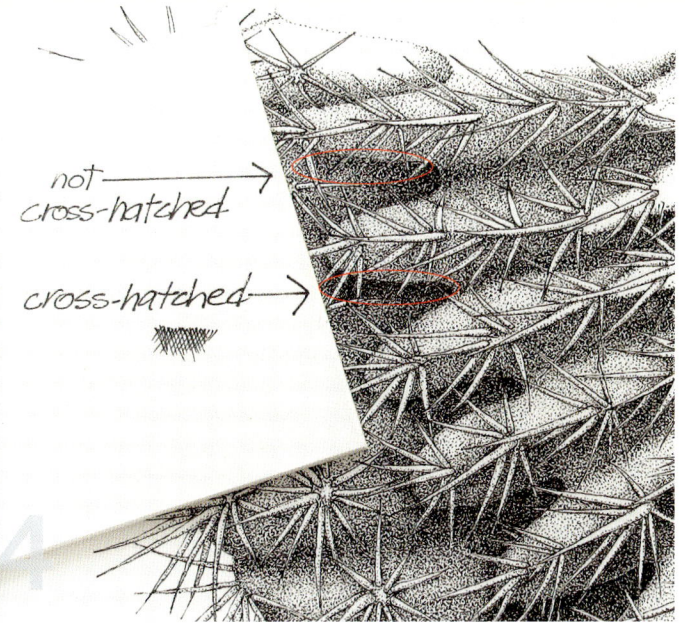

not cross-hatched →

cross-hatched →

Use crosshatching with a 0.25 mm technical pen in the darkest areas to create a textural black, rather than filling the area in solidly with ink. This is done over the stippling. The lines start at a dark edge and fade away from it. The area does not appear to be crosshatched, but using this method produces a more uniform dark area.

This is a close-up of the finished drawing, showing how less stippling makes forms stand out above the more heavily stippled areas. Show light-colored flowers with very light stippling, so they stand out, and ink the wilted flowers and buds with denser stippling as their coloration is not as bright. Remove any blue transfer lines remaining with an eraser. Their blue color makes them easy to see, so they can all be removed.

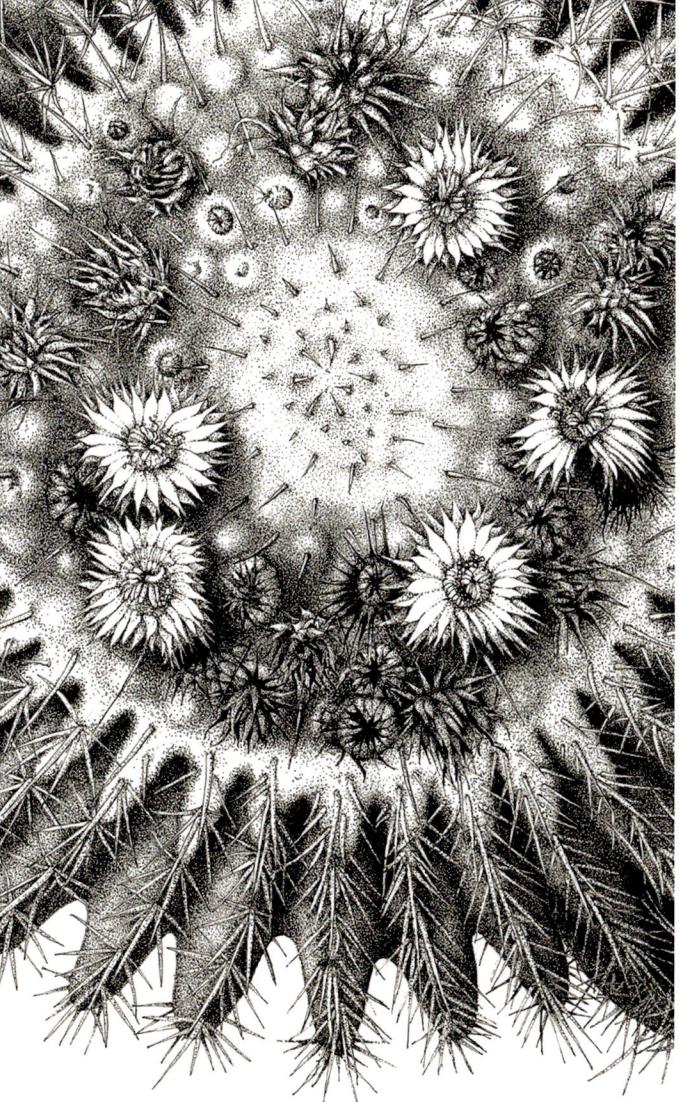

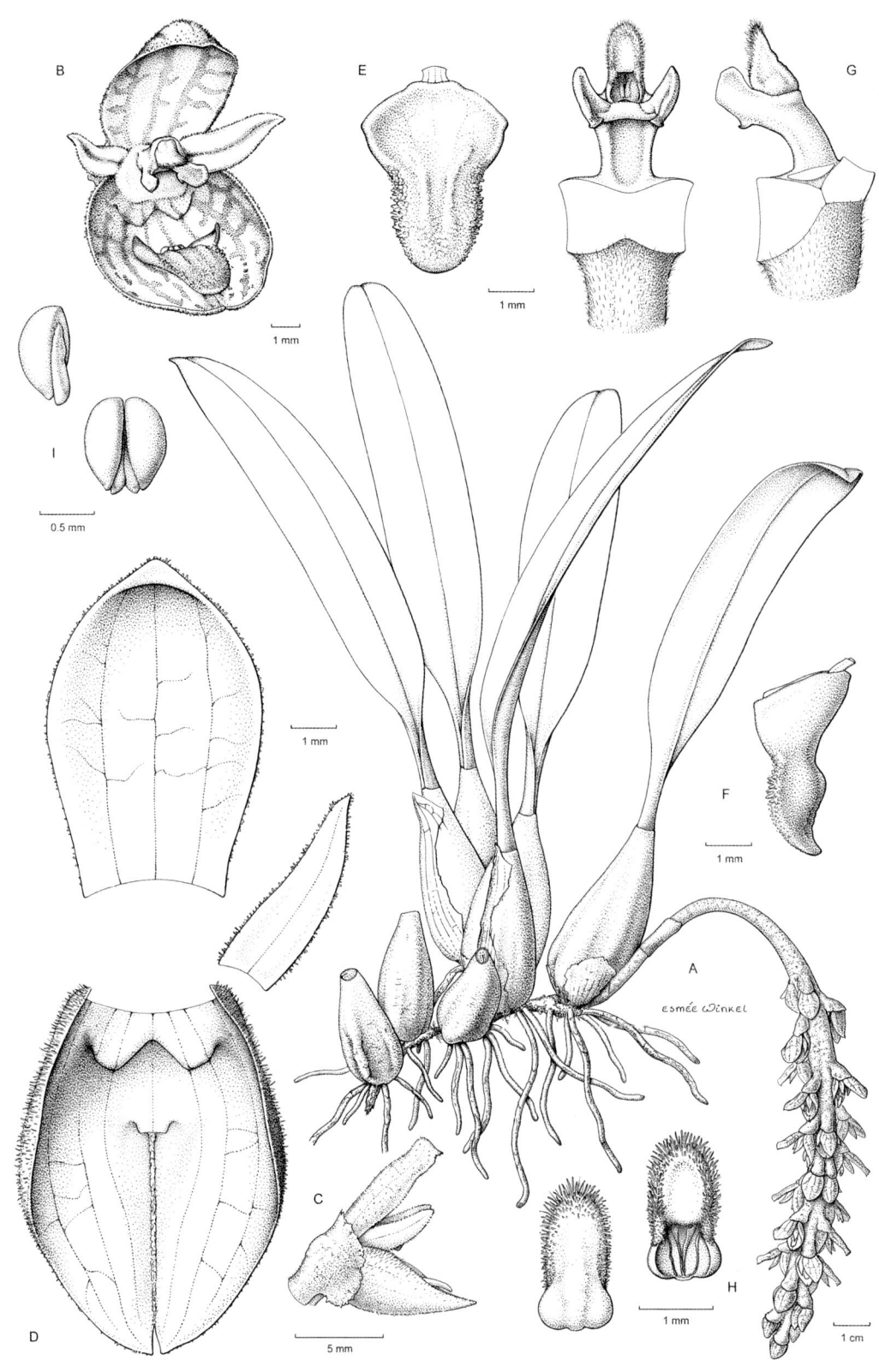

Bulbophyllum sp. aff. _ankylodon_ Orchidaceae Pen and ink on paper 14 × 9 ½ inches [35 × 23.75 cm]

© Esmée Winkel 2013/For Rogier van Vugt, Hortus botanicus Leiden

Legend: A. plant habit; B. flower; C. flower with floral bract, lateral view; D. dissected perianth; E. labellum;
F. labellum, lateral view; G. column, ventral and lateral views; H. anther cap; I. pollinia.

HOURS TO COMPLETE: 45

The goal of a scientific illustration is for the viewer to be able to understand the species. In this example, Esmée Winkel uses technical pens on smooth paper to make an illustration of a newly described orchid species. After making a series of graphite drawings of the plant's parts, scales are recorded and a composition is laid out. Line and stipple techniques are used to ink the entire drawing, then lettering and scales are inserted digitally.

Making a Scientific Ink Dissection Drawing with Technical Pens

TUTOR: ESMÉE WINKEL

MATERIALS: Ruler/square; millimeter graph paper; sheet of black paper for the petri dish; petri dish and cover; dissecting tweezers; smooth acid-free technical inking paper or board, tracing paper, sketching paper; removable tape; high-quality pigmented ink; technical pens; surgical blade; white plastic eraser; HB pencil; ethanol 70 percent; microscope with camera lucida; transparent film.

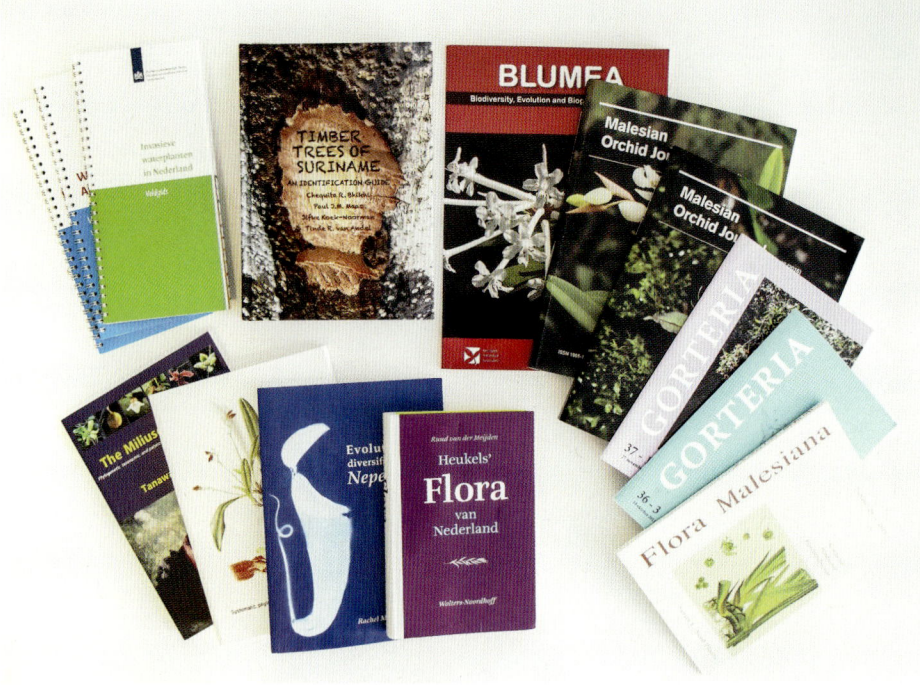

Scientific illustrations record and preserve detailed information about the subject and are published with research in scientific journals and floras. The illustrations contain critical information that supports the systematic order of species and are therefore not portraits of an individual plant but rather a representation of the characteristics of the species.

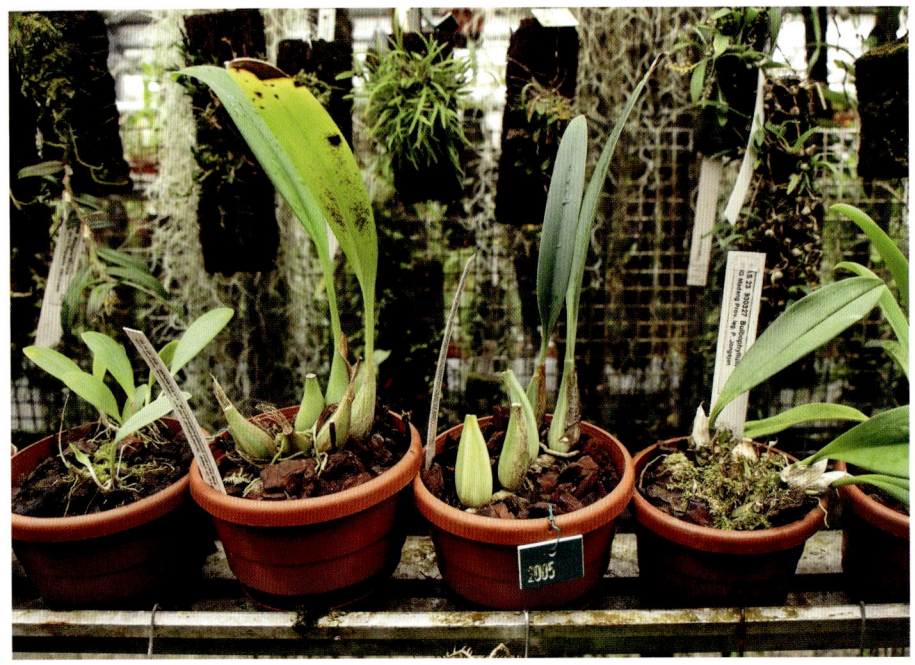

In this tutorial, *Bulbophyllum* sp. aff. *ankylodon*, an orchid species kept in the living collection at the Hortus botanicus Leiden, the oldest botanical garden in the Netherlands, is studied and illustrated. This illustration was made for Rogier van Vugt, Hortus botanicus Leiden, who is still working on this specimen.

Flower

Habit

Orchidaceae, Bulbophyllum ankylodon, Indonesia Sulawesi
Leid. Cult. 20053110, Hortus botanicus Leiden R. v. Vugt
Habit from living specimen
Dissected flower from spirit collection

Image size: 14.2 (H) x 9.5 (W) inch

The illustration should be larger than the plate reproduction size for publication, but usually no more than two times. Record the subject's scientific name, collection number, whether the subject is dried or spirit (in alcohol) material or a living specimen, and if this is a type (a specimen used for the original scientific description of a new species), a holotype (the single specimen used and designated by the scientist), or another type of specimen, such as a paratype, isotype, or syntype.

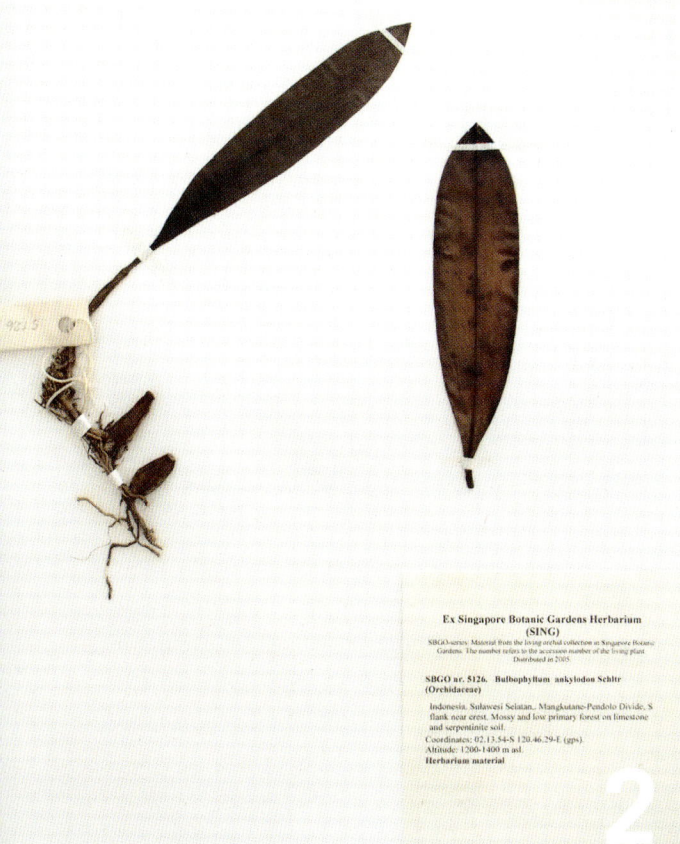

First, study as many specimens as possible. It is essential to take as much time as you need to thoroughly study the plant's form, posture, and details, and its differences from closely related species. Consult as much as possible with the scientist who requested the illustration. Take care not to damage the plant in any unnecessary way.

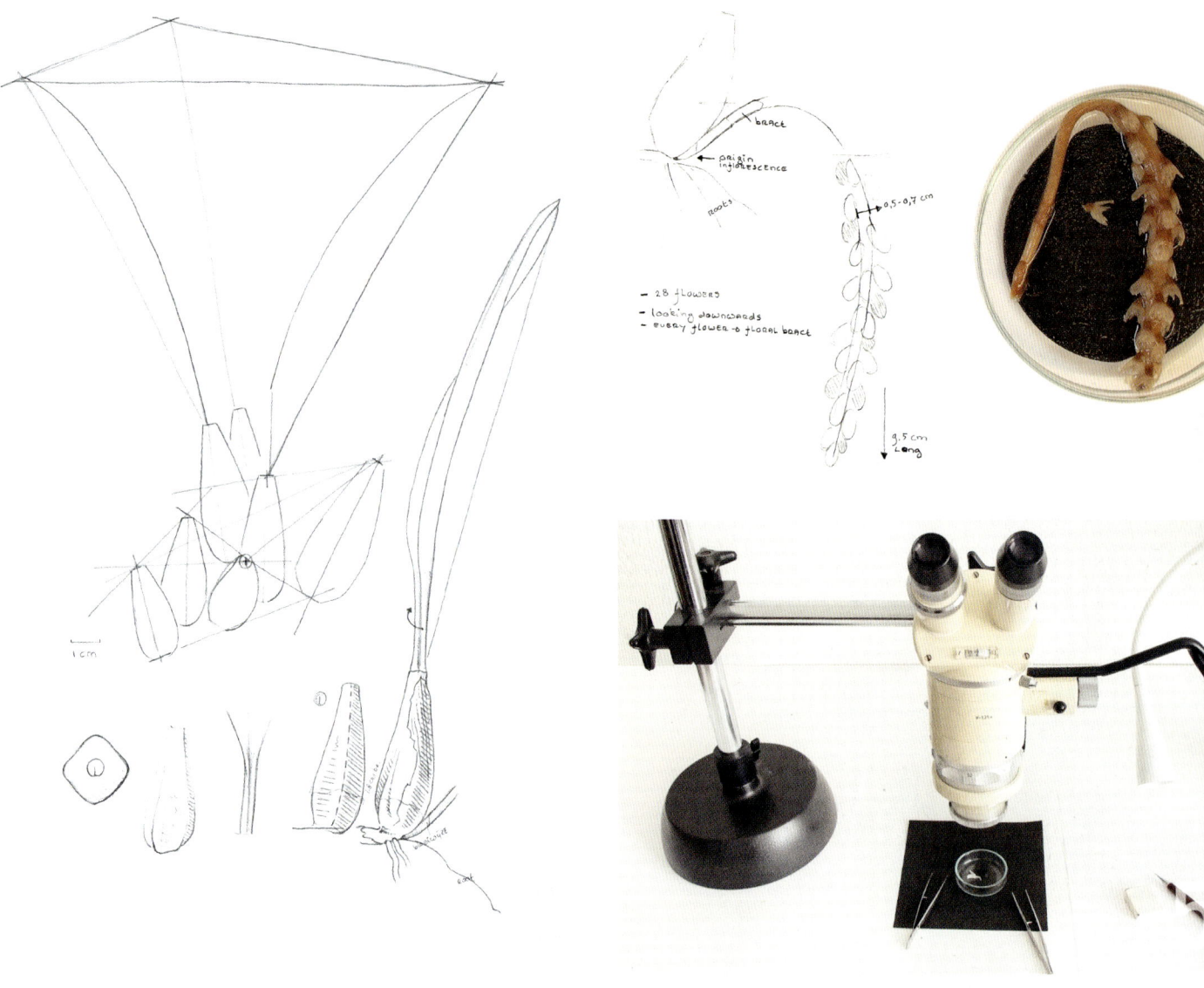

When you are sketching the subject's habit (the plant's general growth structure), first make a basic rough line drawing and decide on the direction of certain details, such as the leaves, and include the inflorescence or infructescence (or both). Measure the various parts precisely and build up the drawing from schematic to a more detailed depiction. Then start adding shadow, hairs, glands, and other important characteristics to finish the drawing. Include a scale.

Study where and how the inflorescence originates from the habit. Look for and count possible bracts, bracteoles, and flowers and measure the length and thickness of the peduncle and rachis, if applicable. In this example, the inflorescence has a very thick rachis with 28 flowers. Make notes on whether the flowers are facing upward, horizontally, or downward, and note any peculiarities.

Remove a flower and study it under a microscope; a camera lucida attachment is useful for this step. This camera lucida enables you to see both the plant material and the drawing, making it easy to precisely measure the various parts with millimeter graph paper. Make sketches of the flower from various views. Once you begin dissecting the subject there is no turning back. Include a scale.

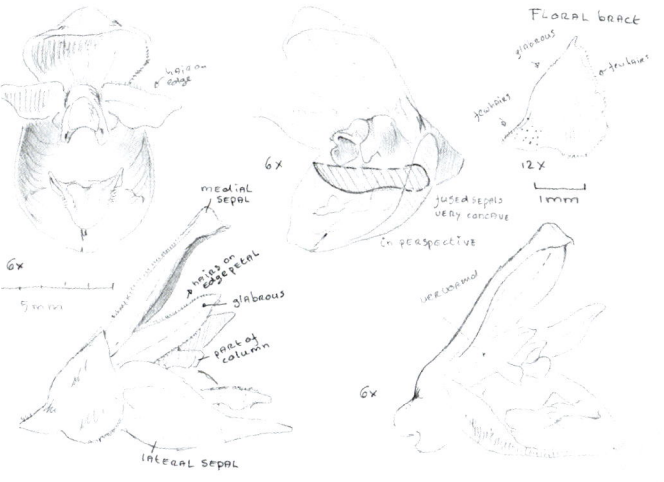

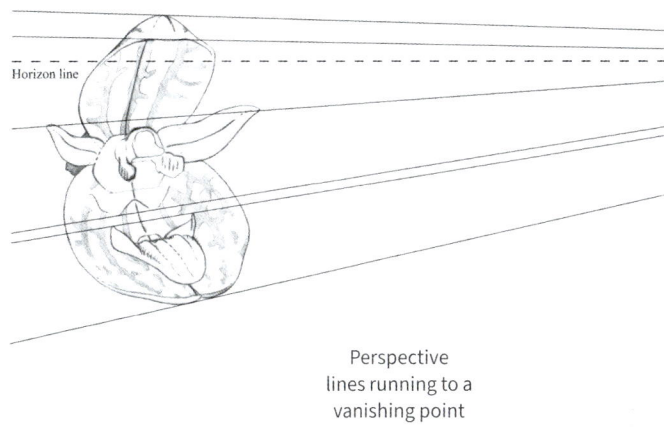

Perspective
lines running to a
vanishing point

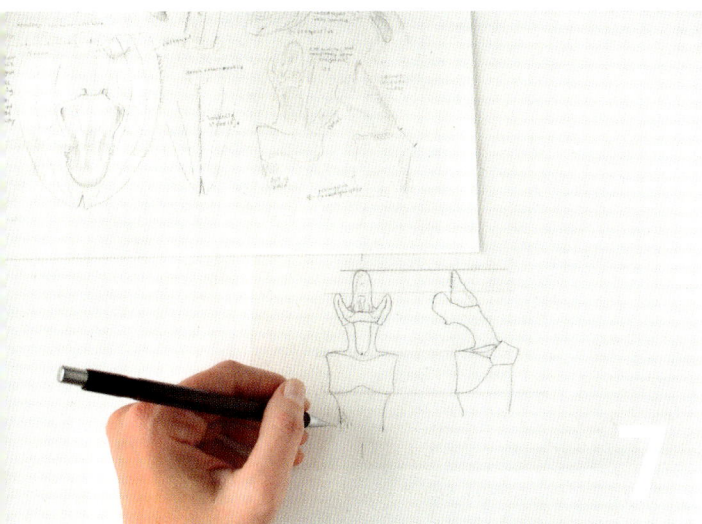

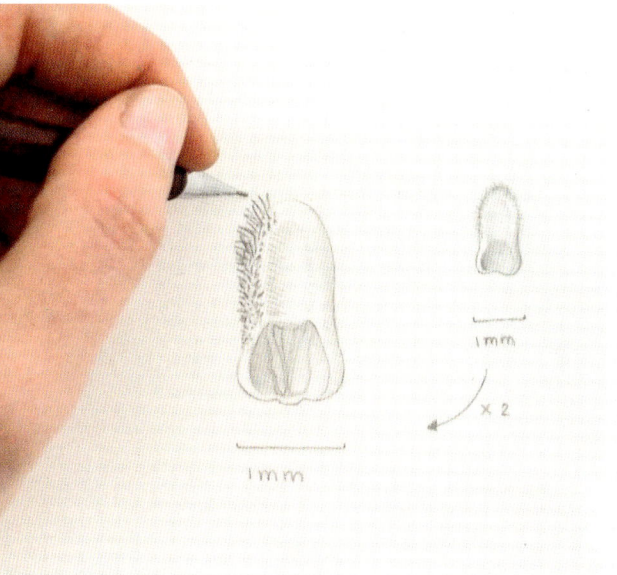

Dissect the flower and make a sketch of each flower part. To help understand the parts or how they're put together, make a sketch of the dissected flower as well after a part has been removed. Turn the parts around or move the lighting, because sometimes it is difficult to see hairs and glands. Form is important, so at the very least draw everything from a front or lateral view.

Draw the various parts in the same proportion as much as possible. When some parts are too small to clearly see the details, enlarge them and include a scale for reference. Sketching the various parts and details from different angles helps you develop a good three-dimensional understanding of the species.

After you have thoroughly studied all the parts, redraw and adjust your sketches. Work out proportions and perspective, decide what should be left out, and when necessary stipple in the color pattern. Finished drawings should be clean and clear and include all the important details. Discuss your work again with the scientist.

A basic knowledge of perspective is essential for successfully drawing convincing flowers and other plant parts from a three-quarter view (when the subject is slightly turned). To achieve perspective, lines are drawn (only if needed, and only on the sketch to aid in making the graphite drawing) converging to a vanishing point to create an illusion of depth and distance. This results in objects becoming smaller as their distance from the observer increases; to achieve this effect requires foreshortening some plant parts.

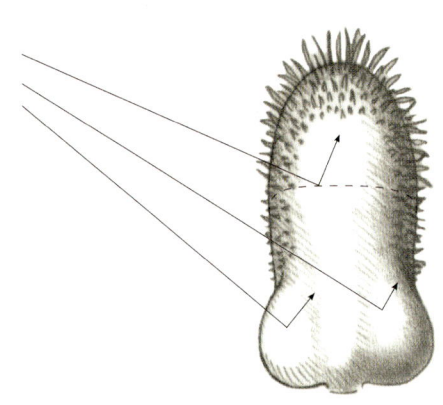

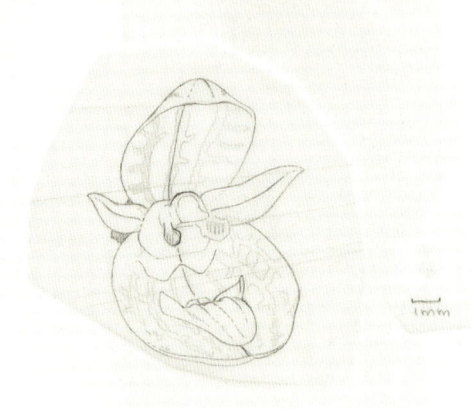

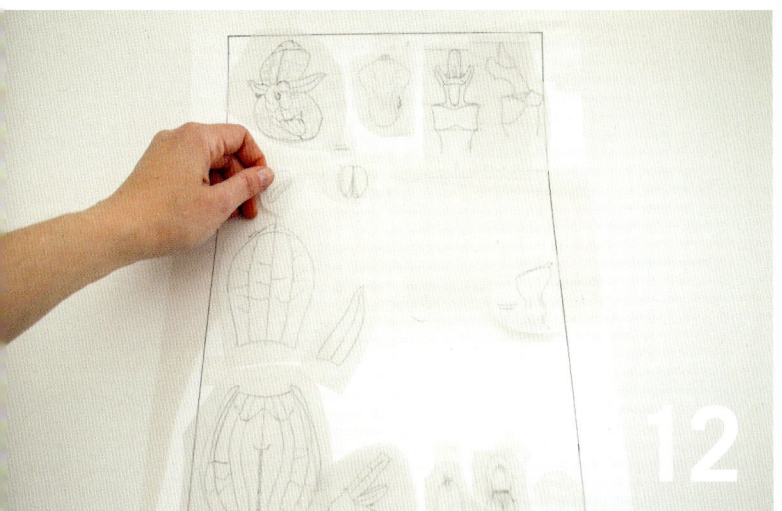

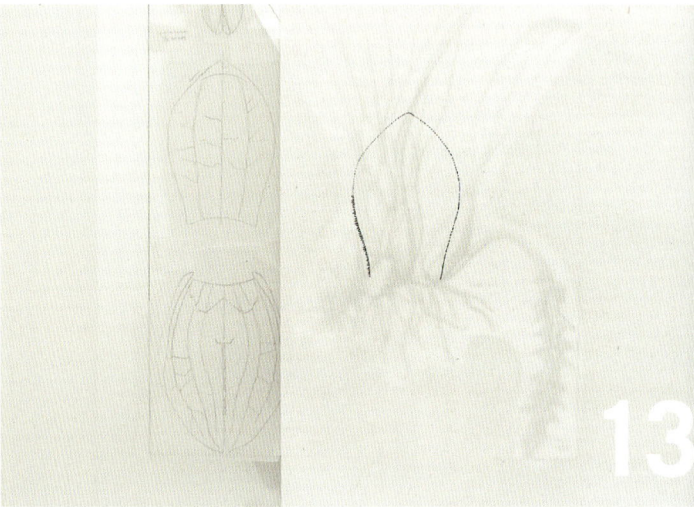

When making the sketches of floral parts, sometimes a line drawing doesn't provide enough information for later inking. Additional information on form, texture, volume, or transparency may be needed, as in the anther cap of this orchid. By creating a smooth shadow from dark to light on an object, a three-dimensional illusion is created. There are three basic surface contours to consider: flat, concave and convex.

If the scientist approves all drawings, continue with the composition within the restraints of the journal or other requirements. One method is to draw the various plant parts on pieces of tracing paper, and then tape them to transparent film. This will make it easier for light to pass through the paper and film on a light box for transfer.

Decide which element is the most important, then position all the others. Move the parts around to construct a composition that is clear, balanced, and uncluttered. If possible, keep different views of the same object next to each other and to the same scale. The goal of a scientific illustration is for the viewer to be able to understand the species. The viewer should understand the parts of the plant and how they fit together.

Once you have finalized the composition, transfer the drawings to very smooth, acid-free, technical inking paper. The drawings can be traced with tracing paper and retraced back onto technical inking paper. They can also be put on a light box with the technical inking paper on top ready for inking, and redrawn where necessary. A retraced drawing should always be checked thoroughly against the specimen and the original drawing; be sure to refer to the specimen frequently.

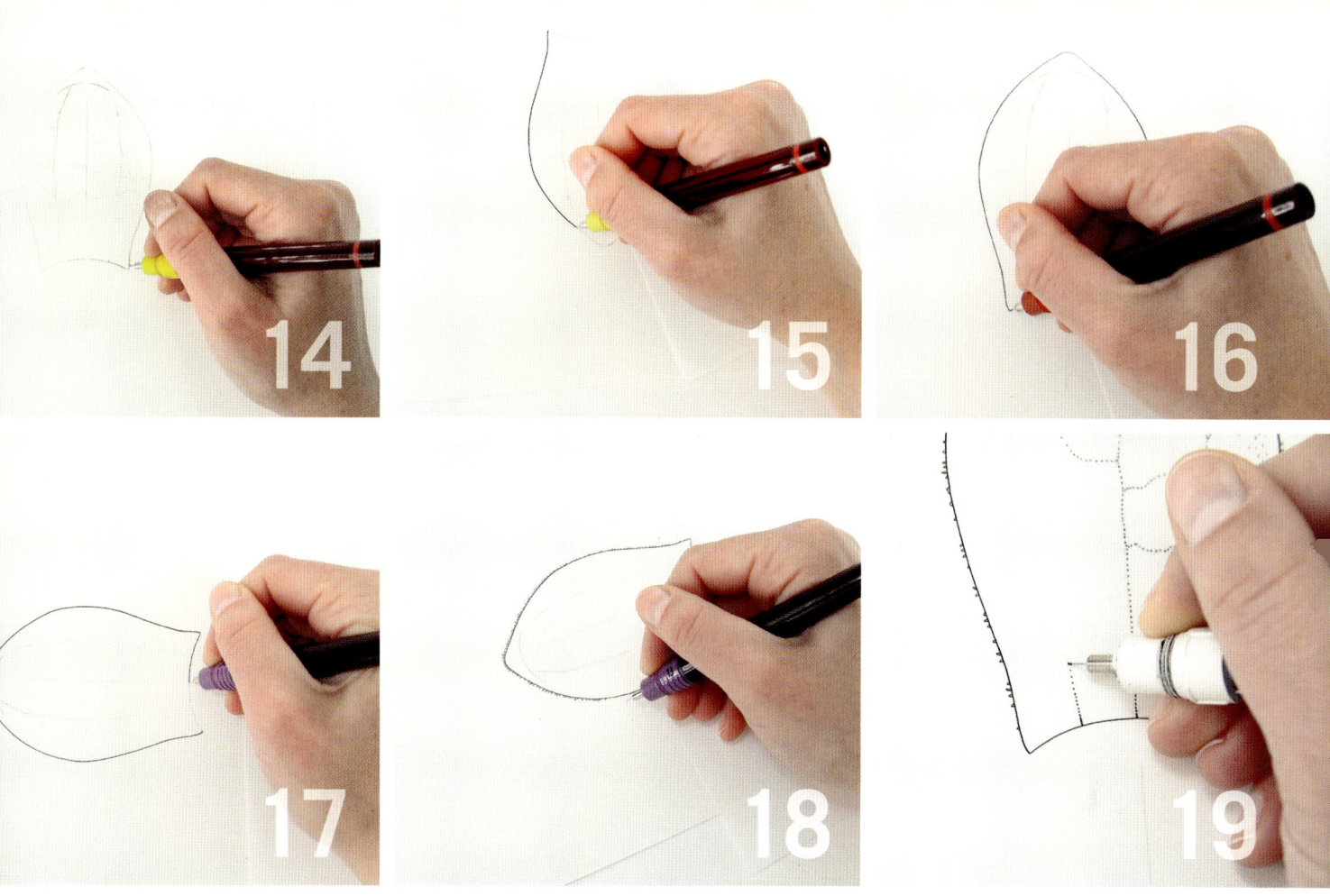

Inking is the final step in completing the illustration. By using thicker lines on the dark side and thinner lines on the light side of the object and then adding shadow, you can suggest volume. Shadow and details can be shown with stippling.

The dorsal sepal will be inked first, starting with the right side. It feels natural to draw a line in a particular direction. For example, for a right-handed artist it is easier to draw a line downward and toward the hand; to do that the paper must be turned upside down, as seen here. With a 0.35 mm pen the line on the right is inked until it turns upward.

The paper is turned right side up again. With a 0.18 mm pen the line is inked starting where the 0.35 mm line ended. Using a variation of a thicker line on the dark side and a thinner line on the light side of the sepal suggests it has some thickness.

With a 0.13 mm pen, a line is inked between the beginning and the end of the outline just inked. When a part is cut off from the whole, indicate the cut by inking a line along the cut line. This cut line is inked with a 0.13 mm pen to contrast it from the rest of the dorsal sepal outline.

Hairs from the abaxial, or outer side, of the sepal can be seen when looking straight at the adaxial, or inside, of the sepal. These tiny hairs, or details like glands, are inked with a 0.13 mm pen. This smaller point is not suitable for stippling, because using too many and too small dots fill up the shaded parts, creating solid black areas when the illustration is reduced in size and published.

Now the veins of the sepal are inked with a 0.25 mm pen. The veins are stippled (dotted) instead of drawn in a continuous line, because they are barely visible. They are not a depression in the surface of the sepal and by dotting them, they will become less prominent. Place the dots in a systematic and uniform way so the structure inked is clearly a vein.

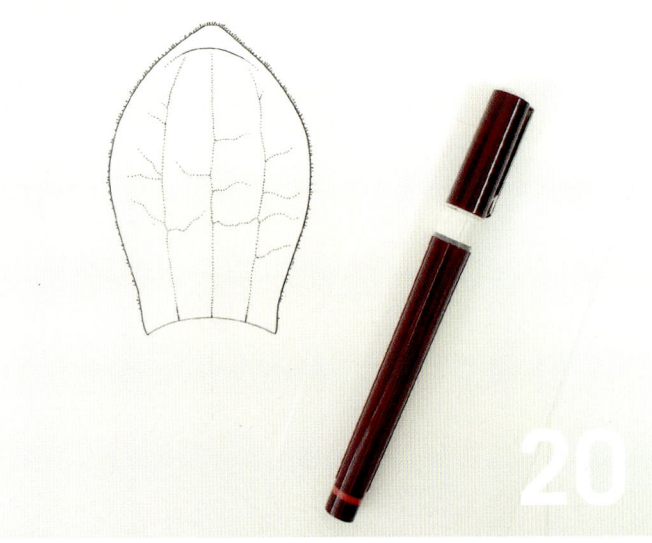

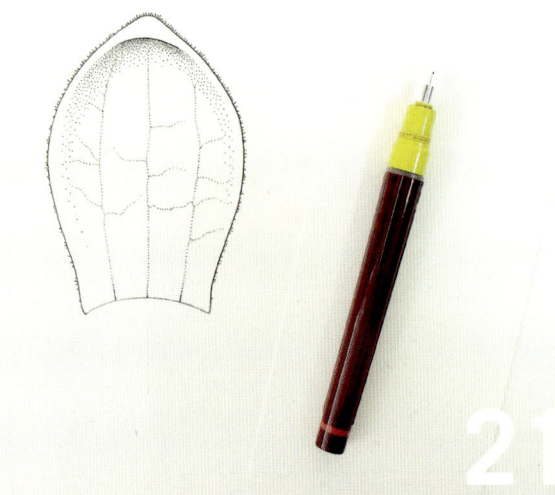

The top of the sepal is concave, creating a shadow in that area. First, the side of the concave area is inked as a solid line with a 0.25 mm pen. A solid line shows a steeper incline in the cupped shape; if the line were stippled, it would suggests a subtle incline.

Volume is suggested by putting the dots close together in the shaded part and spreading them out in the lighter part. Start by using the 0.35 mm pen for the darker part of the shadow. Beginning with a large dot saves time—large dots add value more quickly.

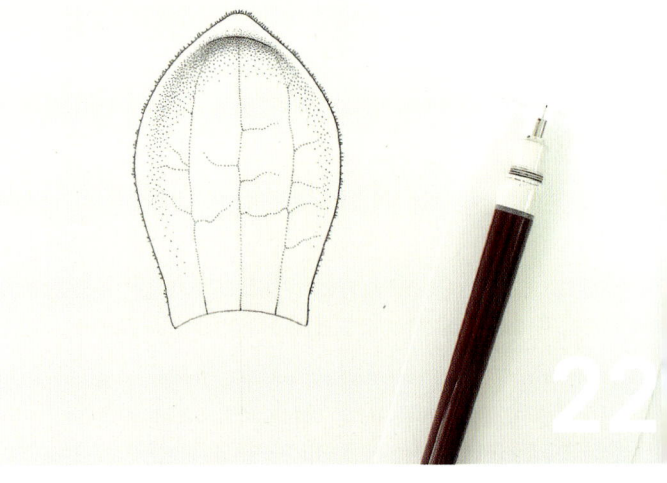

Continue shading with a 0.25 mm pen in the lighter part of the area that just has been dotted with the 0.35 mm pen. Continue stippling until the form and volume are correct and finished. The smoother the transition from dark to light, the greater the three-dimensional effect. Using two sizes of pens creates a smoother transition.

If parts of the veins have become obscured by the stippling, re-ink them. Include the scale. The sepal is now finished. Erase the pencil drawing from the inking paper. The next part of the illustration should be inked in the same way. When the illustration is finished, scan it in black and white, at 1200 DPI in a TIFF format. Edit the illustration where necessary, adjusting the scales, and add labels using a digital drawing program. The final result is then ready for publication and print.

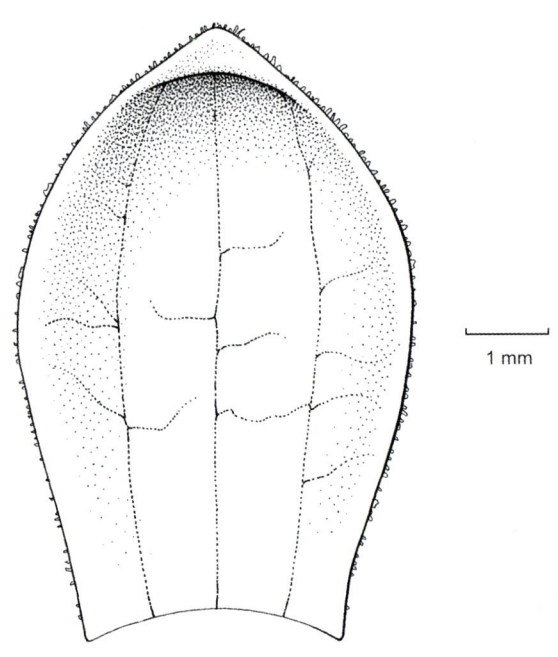

1 mm

SCALING IMAGES FOR SCIENTIFIC ILLUSTRATIONS

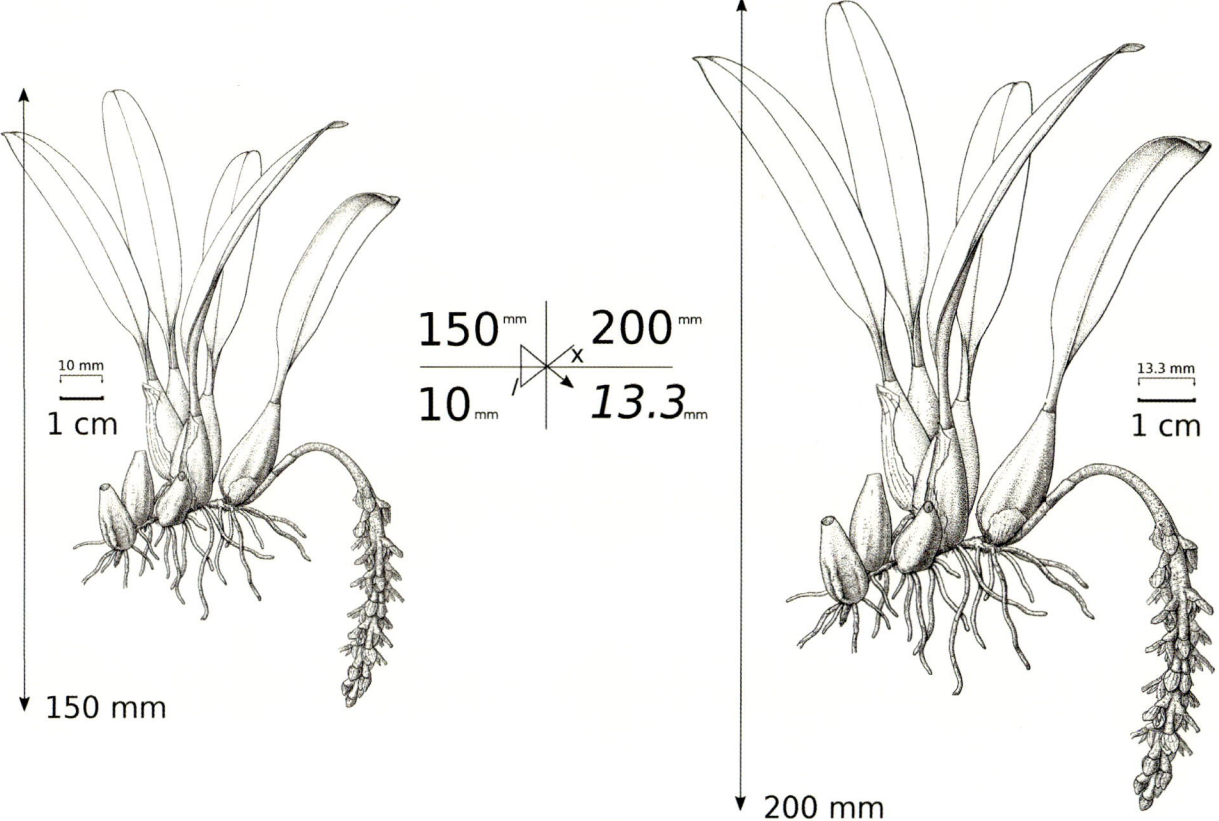

$$\frac{150^{mm}}{10_{mm}} \diagup \diagdown^{x} \frac{200^{mm}}{13.3_{mm}}$$

10 mm
1 cm

150 mm

13.3 mm
1 cm

200 mm

When you are drawing a specimen, it is easier to draw it life-size first. Working with a microscope with a camera lucida attached, an mm-grid graph paper can be placed next to the specimen, and the camera used to note the scale. To enlarge the drawing to the desired size, use a ratio calculation. An example is given in this drawing:

The actual size of the plant is 150 millimeters tall, and the accompanying 1-centimeter scale bar is 10 millimeters long. The desired size for the finished drawing is 200 millimeters tall. The formula is 10 × 200 divided by 150 = 13.3 millimeters. Therefore, if the drawing is enlarged to 200 millimeters, the accompanying 1-centimeter scale bar will actually measure 13.3 millimeters. This formula can also be applied to enlargements of individual sections at varying scales.

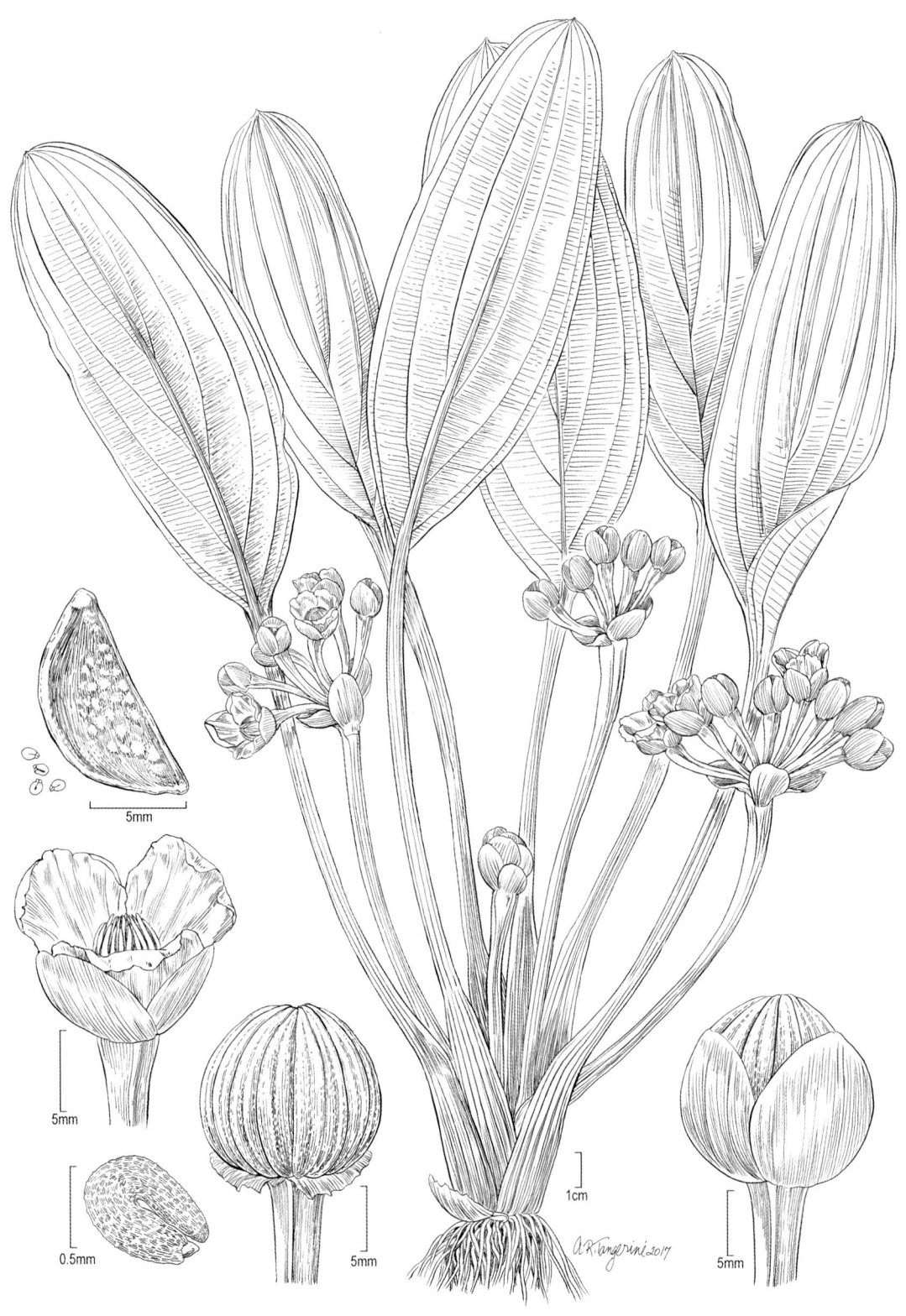

Limnocharis **sp.** Ink on matte polypropylene film 17 × 14 inches [42.5 × 35 cm] © Alice Tangerini, Smithsonian Institution, National Museum of Natural History

In a museum environment, herbarium specimens are the main source material used in botanical illustration. Herbarium specimens are dried plants that are pressed and then taped or glued to herbarium sheets made of 100 percent rag paper in a standard 11 × 17-inch [27.5 × 42.5 cm] size. A typical drawing consists of a habit (the entire plant or a partial branch—whatever is on the herbarium sheet) and dissections of floral parts enlarged from 2X to 50X. The scale of each part is shown, so the viewer can comprehend the actual size of each of the parts of the drawing.

Scientific Botanical Illustrations in Pen, Brush, and Ink

TUTOR: ALICE TANGERINI

Scientific botanical illustrations are used in descriptions of new species and in monographic or floristic treatments. A new species is one not previously known to science. A monograph is a treatment of a related group of plants, usually on a worldwide basis. A flora is a treatment of plants of a certain geographic area.

In a publication of a new species, the drawing accompanies a written description in botanical Latin and English. The artist must learn how to read the description or be in close communication with the botanist. Most illustrations for botanical journals are black and white (pen and ink), as it is the traditional medium for botanical illustrations and originally it was the least costly to reproduce. Continuous tone (using graphite or ink wash) may be used in cases where tonal quality is desired. With the advent of digital images and online journals, the use of color is increasing for a couple of reasons: There is no additional cost (as there is with printed color images), and digital color photographs taken of live plants are abundant.

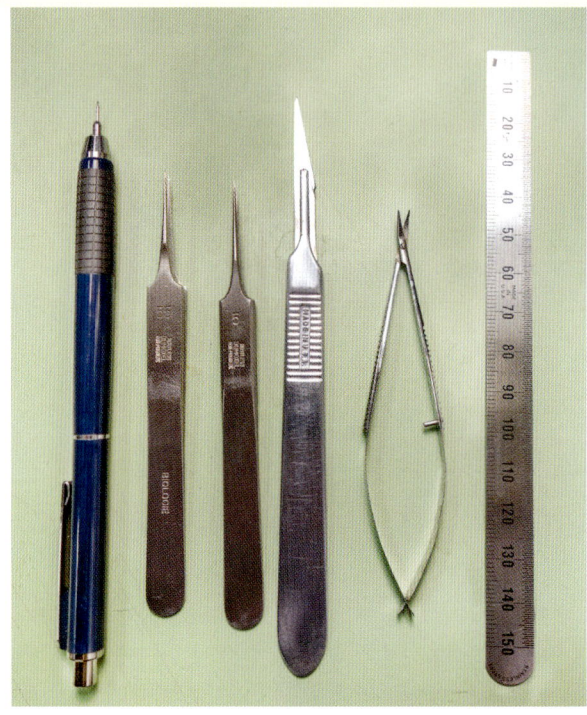

Tools: Mechanical pencil (0.5 mm or 0.3 mm with HB or H lead); two stainless steel micro dissecting tweezers with superfine points; scalpel knife handle no. 3 with no. 11 surgical blade; micro dissecting scissors (3 ½-inch [8.75 cm] curved and sharp tipped); stainless steel metric ruler.

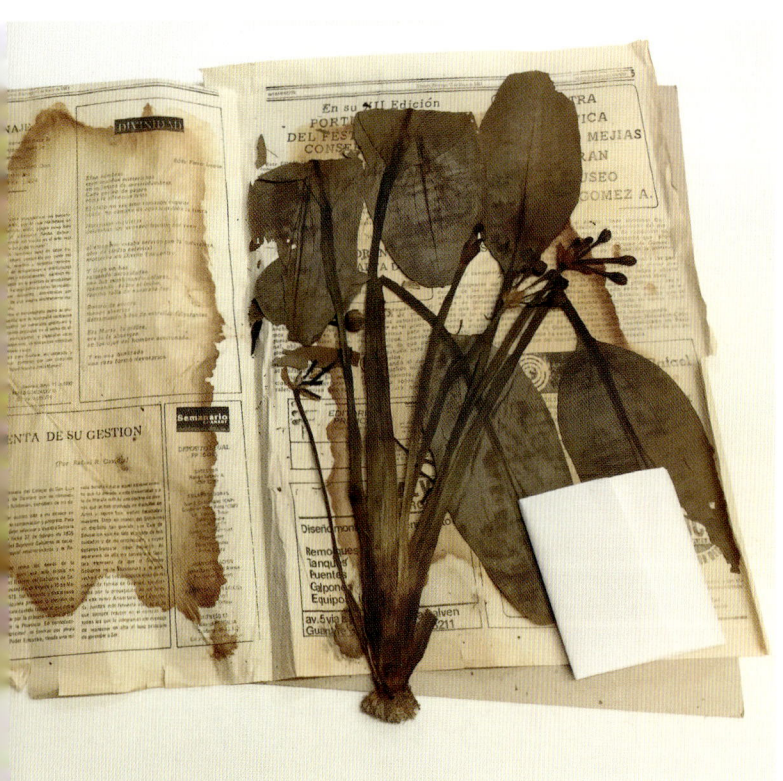

Herbarium specimen of an undetermined *Limnocharis* species (Alismataceae), pressed and dried in newspaper before mounting, with a packet of specimen fragments included.

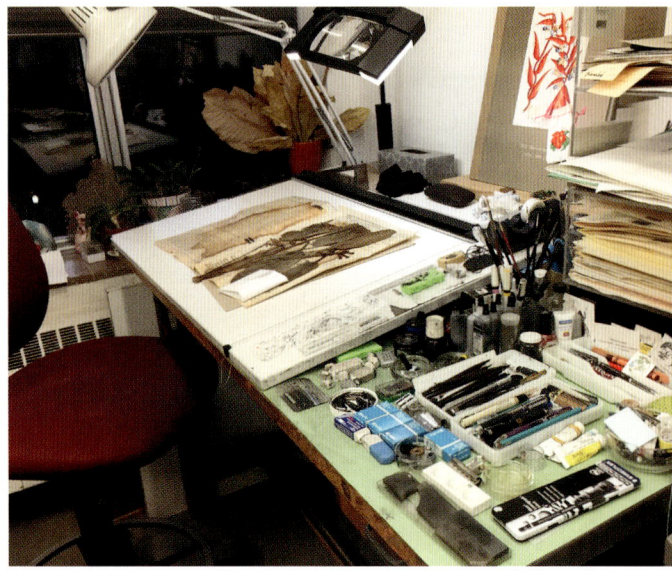

The work area displays the herbarium specimen on an elevated 32 × 41-inch [80 × 102.5 cm] drafting board. The five-foot-long [1.5 meter] drafting table generally provides enough flat area for tools and media. An adjustable swing-arm lamp equipped with fluorescent and incandescent lights provides balanced directed lighting. An additional fluorescent magnifier lamp aids in viewing specimens at 6X.

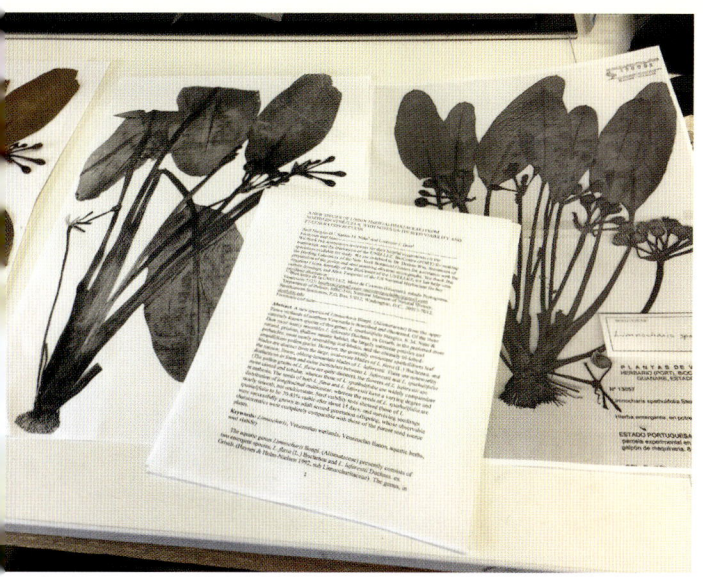

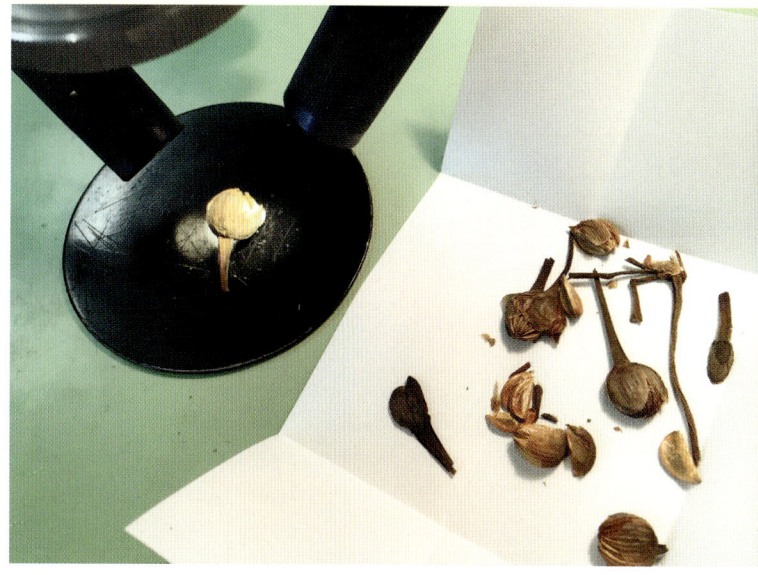

Shown here are the *Limnocharis* specimen, photocopies of the specimen, including one of an additional specimen, and a written description of the new species. An illustrator must be able to understand the botanical description of the species and also observe and highlight any differences found while illustrating. The illustrator should bring any discrepancies to the botanist's attention.

The fragment packet may include buds, flowers, fruits, or seeds, or a combination of all of these. They are best seen on the black side of a reversible metal black-and-white stage plate when viewed through the camera lucida.

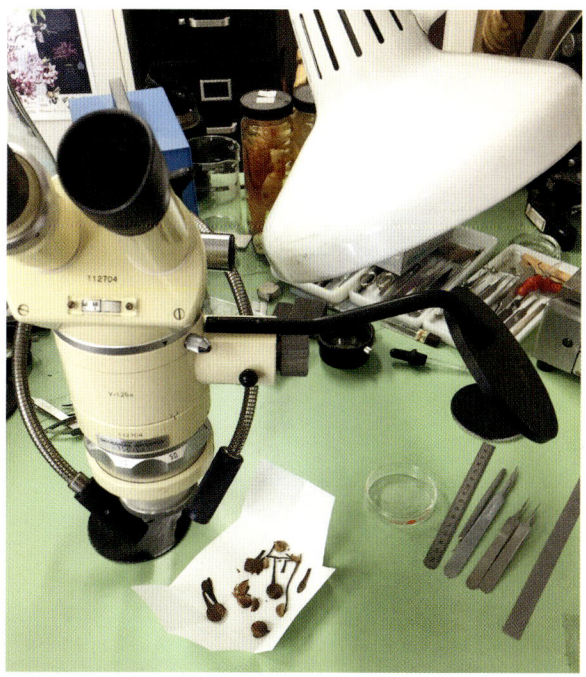

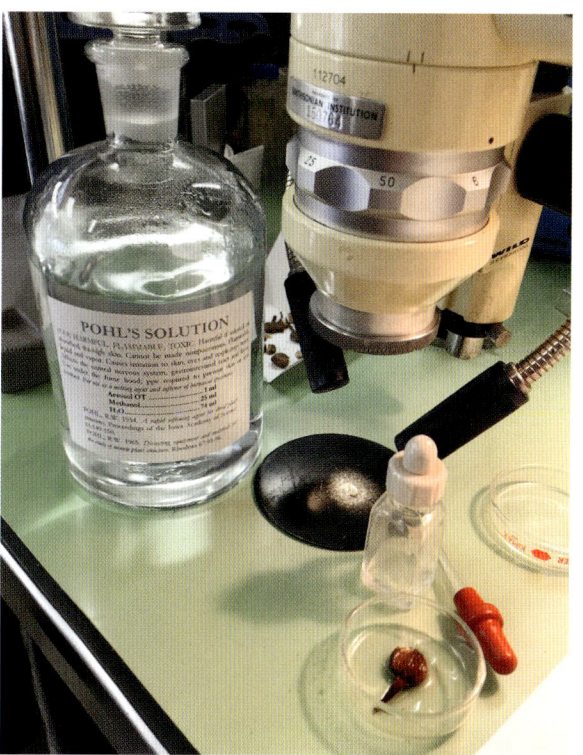

A stereomicroscope outfitted with a camera lucida (drawing tube) mounted on a swing arm stand allows enough space for viewing an entire herbarium sheet. A dual fiber-optic system (externally mounted with adjustable snake necks) provides the cool directed lighting necessary for illuminating tiny dissected plant parts.

Wetting solutions are available to soften herbarium specimens. The solutions consist of an aerosol surfactant dioctyl sodium sulfosuccinate, water, and methyl alcohol. Liquid dishwashing soap may be substituted for the aerosol. Apply a few drops of wetting solution directly on the specimen with a dropper, then float the specimen in water in a covered petri dish.

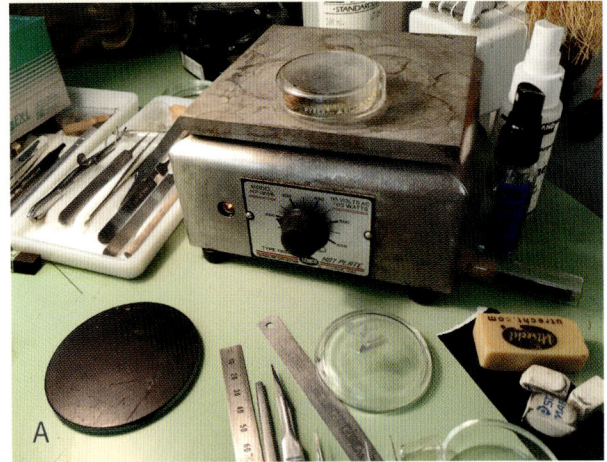

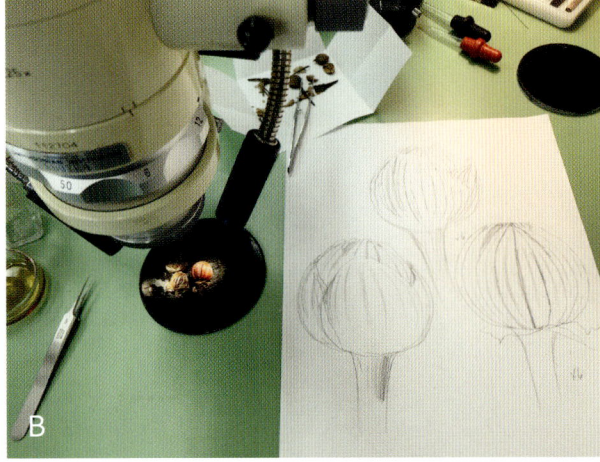

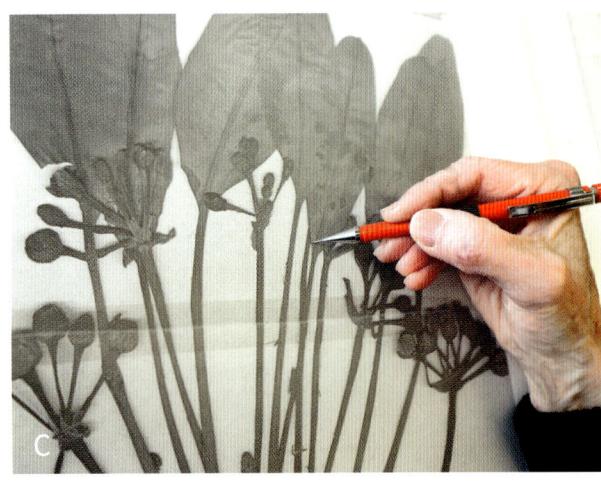

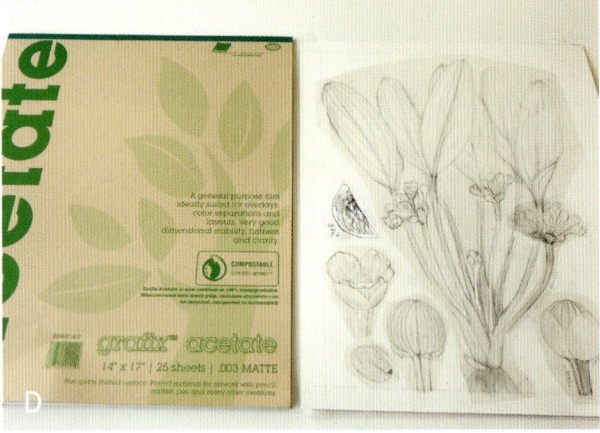

A heating device (a hot plate with temperature settings) provides the source for warming dissections in heat-resistant petri dishes. Heating the petri dish on a hot plate with temperature settings allows for warming and will soften most dehydrated dissections. (A)

The initial sketch of the compound fruit of *Limnocharis* sp. is illustrated with 12× magnification through the microscope using the camera lucida. Although drawn at 12×, the size of 6× is noted on the drawing; it will be reproduced at 50 percent, so the final scale is noted on any sketches. Views include the fruit with sepals (left), with seed poking out (middle), and without sepals (right). (B)

A photocopy of the specimen was made to serve as the model for tracing at the specimen's natural size. Outlines and other important details were traced on 0.3 mm translucent matte acetate—translucent enough to see the details of the photocopy—using a 0.5 mm mechanical pencil. (C)

A matte acetate 14 × 17-inch [35 × 42.5 cm] pad is at left, and the preliminary layout of cut-out tracings on acetate is on the right. Many journals have a page format of 5 × 8 inches [12.5 × 20 cm], so the drawing is done at 10 × 16 inches [25 × 40 cm] to allow a 50 percent reduction when printed. (D)

These are details in graphite done with the microscope. They include a fruitlet (top left), open flower, seed, and compound fruit. The cut-out figures can be attached to Bristol board with transparent tape or spray mount, but spray mounting with an adhesive allows for a very flat surface and avoids tape edges. (E)

Digital prints of living plant material provide additional information for reconstructing the pressed specimen. The completed graphite drawing is ready to be inked onto a sheet of archival polypropylene drafting film, which has a matte surface on both sides. (F)

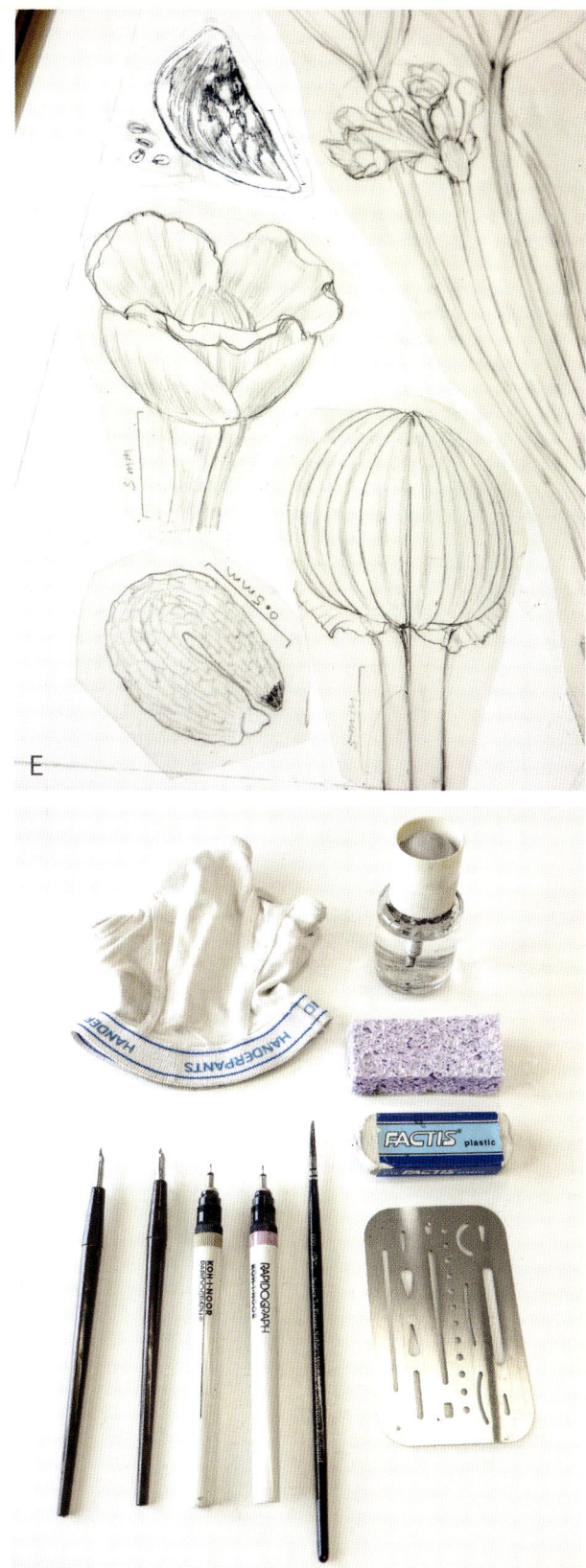

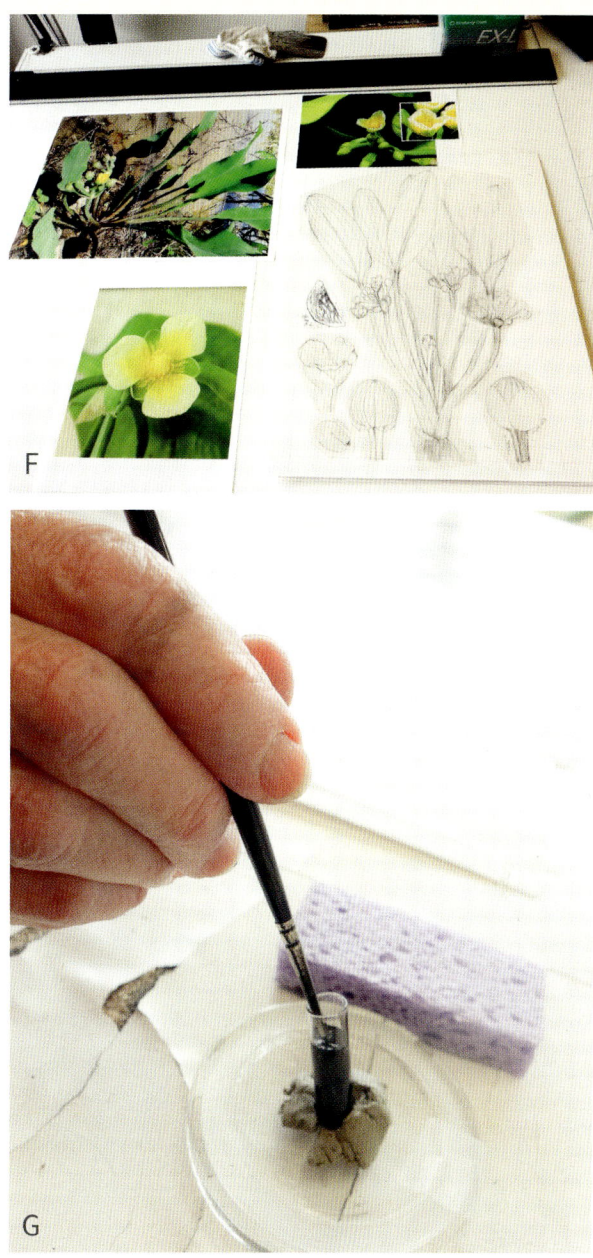

This one-quarter-dram glass vial from a lab-supply catalog is mounted in a watch glass (which is taped to the work surface so that it doesn't slide) with adhesive clay so the vial can be tipped at an angle. Any jar lid and adhesive that can hold the vial at the desired angle will also work for this purpose. Use permanent ink, suitable for drafting film and very opaque, and fill the vial to about two-thirds to three-quarters full. (G)

Tools for inking: White fingerless gloves; jar with non-sudsy ammonia; cellulose sponge; white vinyl eraser; metal eraser shield; Kolinsky brush (no. 000); technical pens (nos. 0.25 mm and 0.18 mm); pen nib (no. 104) and holder; crow quill pen nib (no. 102) and holder.

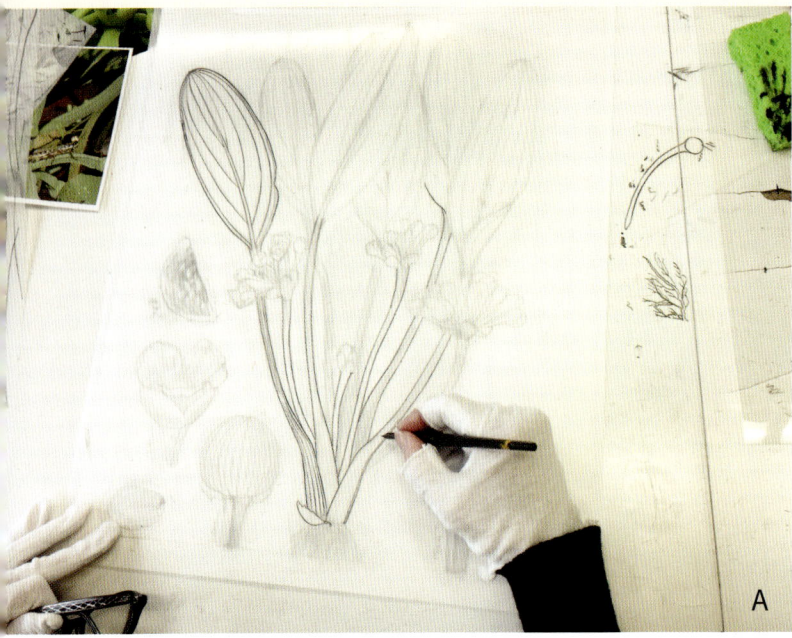

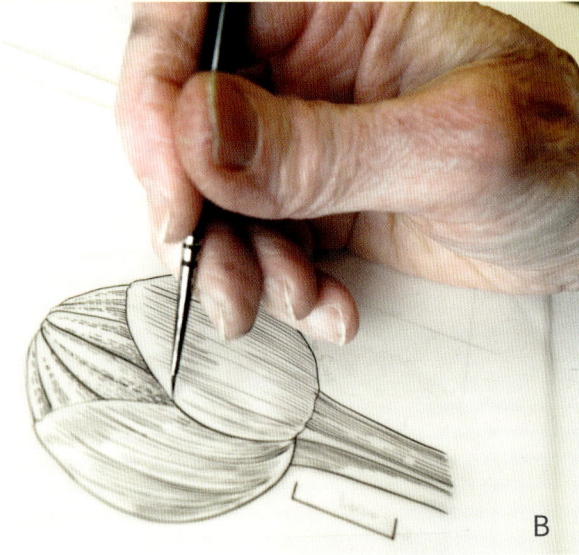

B

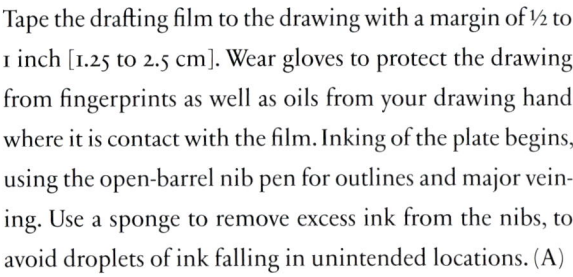

Tape the drafting film to the drawing with a margin of ½ to 1 inch [1.25 to 2.5 cm]. Wear gloves to protect the drawing from fingerprints as well as oils from your drawing hand where it is contact with the film. Inking of the plate begins, using the open-barrel nib pen for outlines and major veining. Use a sponge to remove excess ink from the nibs, to avoid droplets of ink falling in unintended locations. (A)

Some parts are inked using a no. 000 Kolinsky brush. Lines with a brush can vary substantially in width from wide to extremely fine by applying more, or less, pressure with your hand. A brush is an excellent tool for the sinewy lines in grasses or other monocots with parallel venation. (B)

A crow quill pen nib is a closed-barrel nib capable of holding more ink than an open-barrel nib. The nib is very fine but stiff and can make parallel lines of equal width. It's suitable for line-shading techniques and outlines where variation in line width must be controlled. (C)

The no. 104 open-barrel nib is an extremely fine nib capable of making the tiniest strokes in small areas. It holds less ink than the crow quill, so it is used more often for details in small areas. (D)

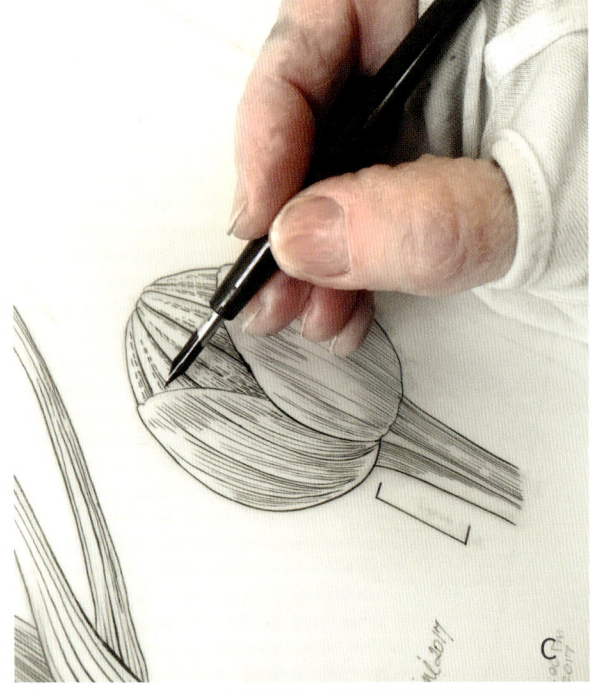

C

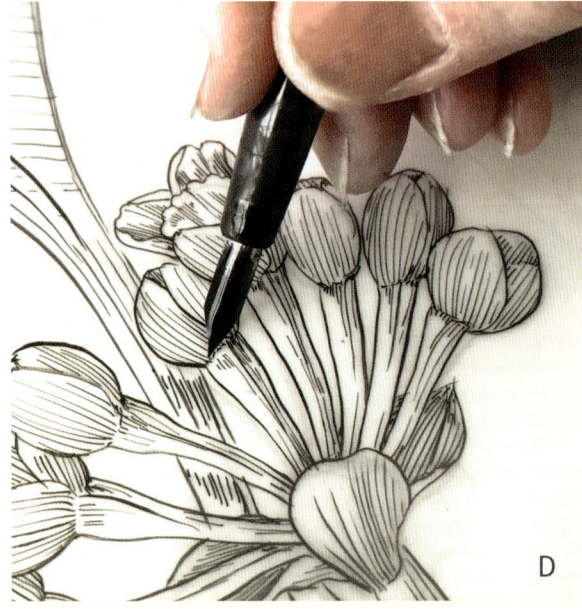

D

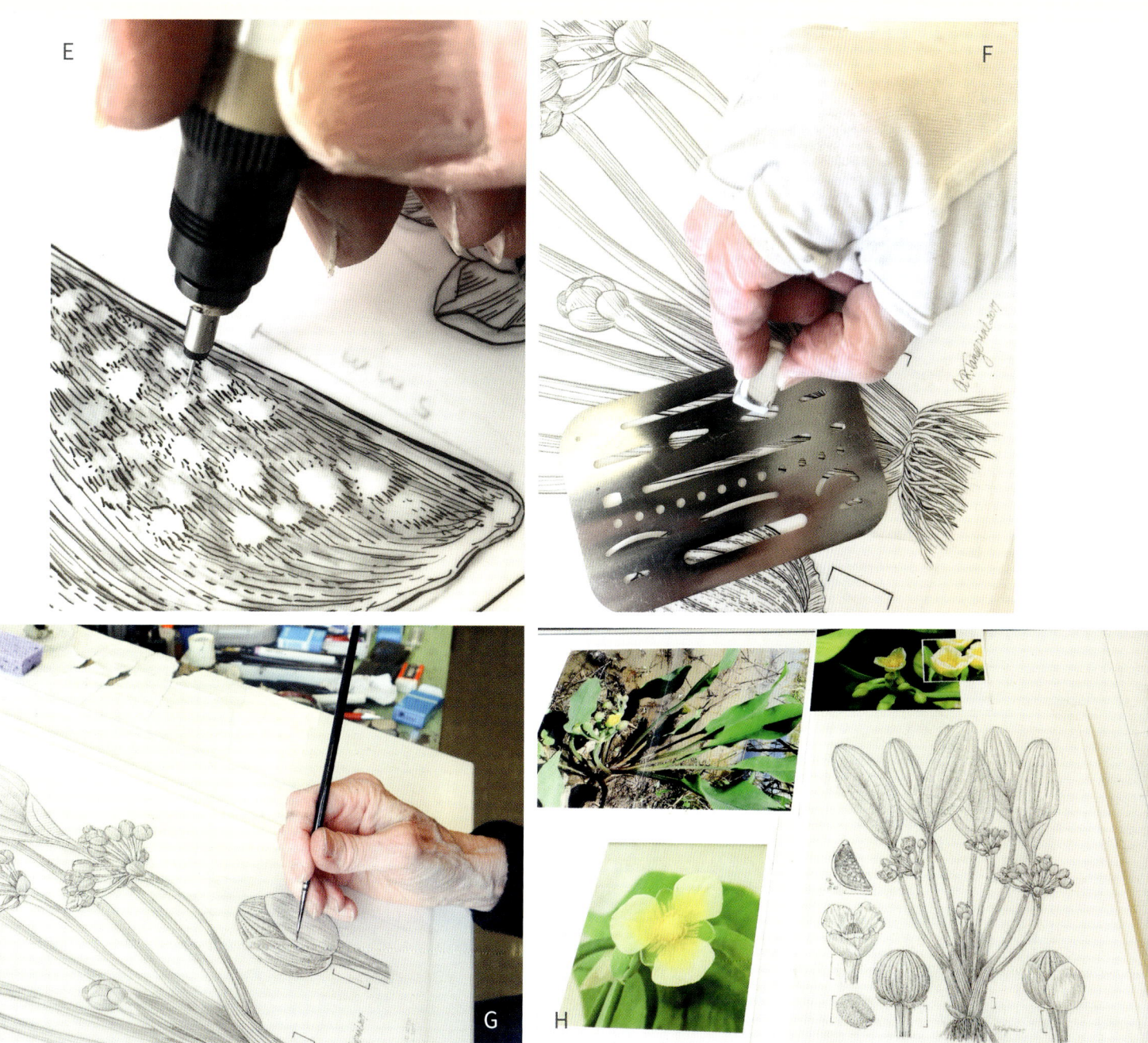

Use a fixed-width technical pen when any variation in line is undesirable—they deliver a consistent line width. It is especially useful for stippling, as the pen makes even, round dots (uneven stippling with a flexible nib can be mistaken for a surface texture rather than shading). Stipple size can easily be determined by your choice of pen size. (E)

Ink lines can easily be removed from film with a white plastic eraser and a little moisture. Just a touch of moisture is enough to remove ink from areas within the openings of an eraser shield. Discrete small areas of ink can be removed this way. Wipe the eraser before reusing it. (F)

Final touch-ups are made using the no. ooo Kolinsky brush with a light pressure for very fine lines. Scale marks have been placed to indicate magnification. (G)

The final inked drawing of the unidentified *Limnocharis* species is shown on the right on a 14 × 17-inch [35 × 42.5 cm] sheet of polypropylene matte drafting film. Detailed printed photographs used to supplement understanding of the dried specimen are shown alongside the completed plate. (H)

USING STIPPLE IN BOTANICAL ILLUSTRATION

This illustration of *Nymphaea odorata* by William S. Moye is a tour de force of pen and ink, featuring a masterful use of stipple, line, and a bit of white gouache. The piece is unusual in the botanical illustration world because it also shows the water lily's habitat.

Stippling is the process of making a continuous tone with a series or pattern of dots. Different values are achieved by the size or spacing of the dots, or a combination of the size and spacing. The dots themselves must be very round and regular, and not small lines or checks, or they will erroneously read as texture on the subject. This work was done entirely with technical pens. Technical pens are sized on a scale indicated by a number; for example 0.13 mm (very thin) to 1.2 mm (relatively thick) or a fraction of a millimeter expressed as a decimal, thus making a consistent line thickness and hence a consistent dot size.

The scale of the stipples and contour lines must be in the right proportion to each other. In general, contour lines should be heavier than internal stipples. This is clear at D. The dots are smaller, and on the larger stamen, the stipples are placed in a line to create fine form. To create a line that tapers, technical pens need to be changed mid-stream one or more times to smaller sizes. This tapering is seen in the solid contour lines defining the outer petals at B. If contours are made with stipples they can appear fuzzy. The flower in the habitat has some petal contours drawn in stipple, but in this case, it shows the very bright aspect of sunlight on the petals. There are enough petals with contour lines to create an understanding of the shape of the petals. Smaller dots are seen in the enlargement of the water lily than in the flower in the habitat; that's because the enlarged detail of the flower allows more subtle distinctions in tone.

Stippling all aspects of an illustration is not always the best solution. The grasslike leaves emerging from the water are simply drawn in different thicknesses of line using a different size technical pen for each. Very small forms are often clearer without stippling. The pedicel of the fruit at F shows a layer of parallel lines overlaid with stipple, a combination that continues up into the fruit, with the membranous covering handled only in dots. This approach separates the two textures and clarifies the form.

Care was also taken to indicate color. For instance, stippling is more closely placed and heavier in the green leaves and sepals than in the white flower. The very dark leaves underwater were made with solid black ink.

While the vast majority of this illustration is accomplished in pen and black ink, white gouache is used in selected areas to separate objects from one another or to convey some of the water's effects. To visually separate stippled areas, a line of white gouache was painted with a brush around the form; for example, white gouache is painted around detail C and around the flower petals (view B) that overlap the dark habitat area. In this same view B, overlapping petals are given a slight separation by whiting out the adjacent line of the petal underneath. White gouache is also used to indicate the water's edge and its sparkle against the large floating lily leaves.

White Fragrant Water Lily *Nymphaea odorata*
Pen and ink 14 × 9 inches [35 × 22.5 cm]
William S. Moye HOURS TO COMPLETE: 200

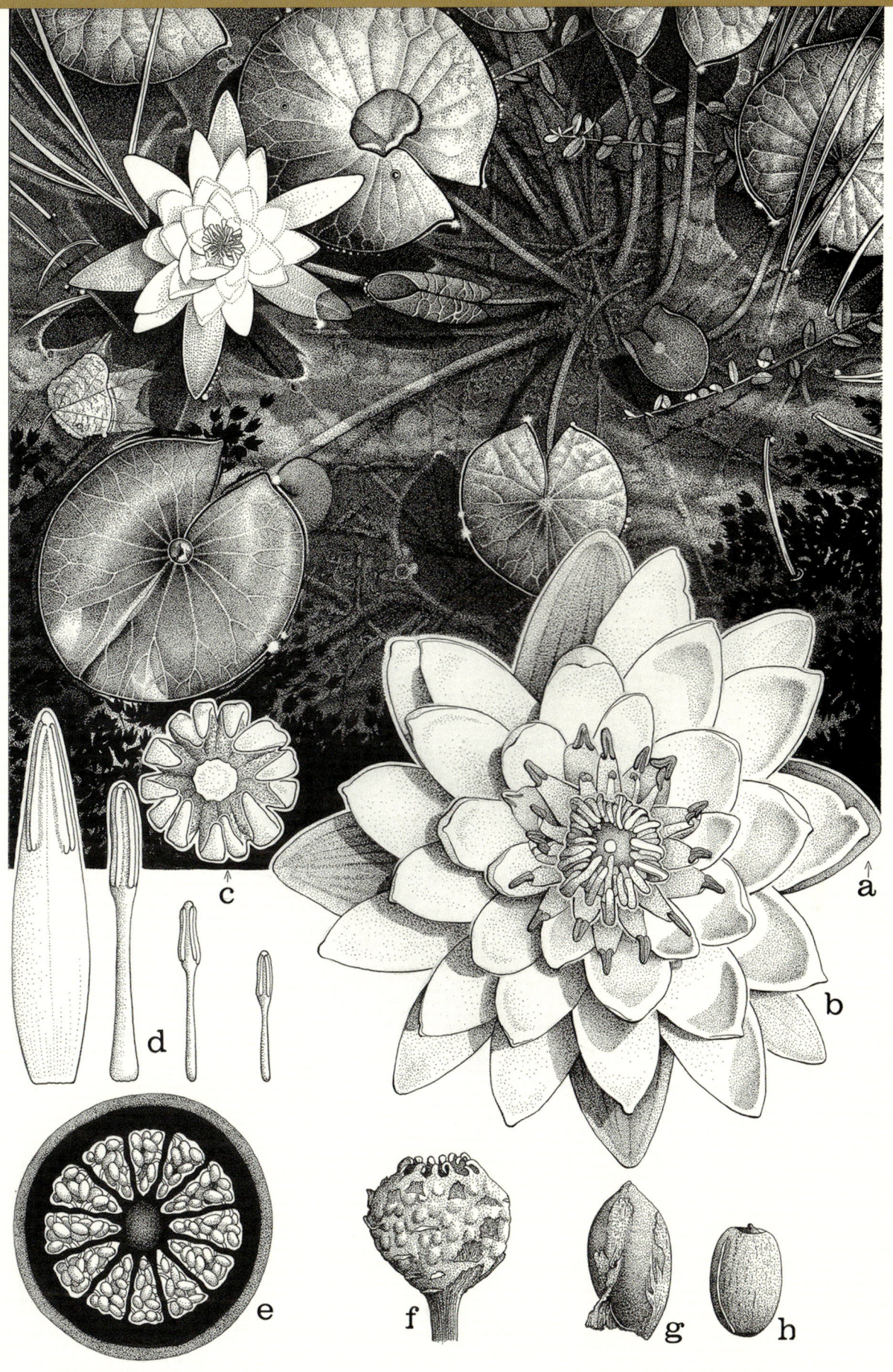

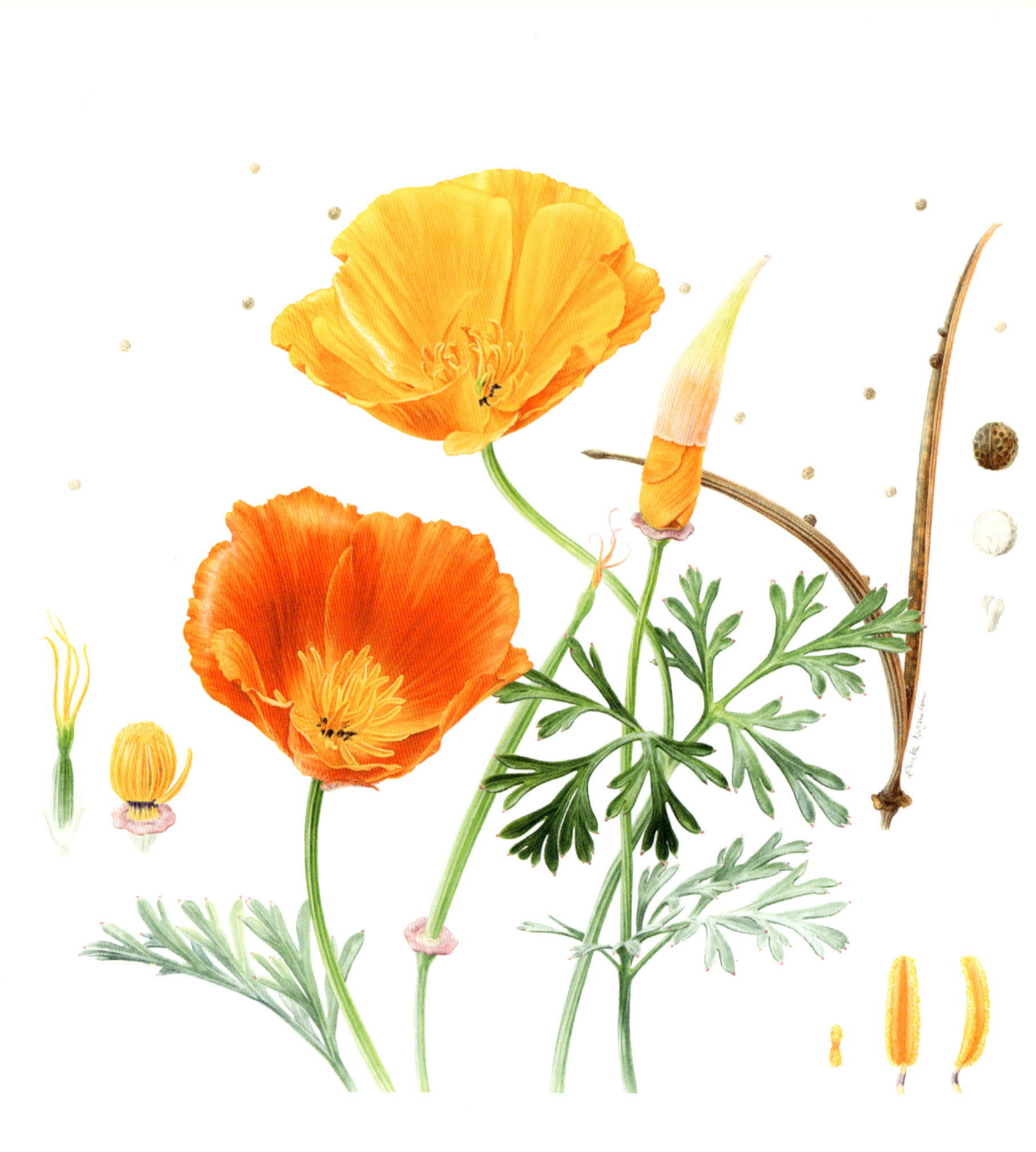

Eschscholzia californica **California poppies** Watercolor on paper 22 × 22 inches [55 × 55 cm] © Eunike Nugroho

PART 2

Botanical
Subjects in
Color

A BRIEF GRAMMAR OF COLOR

TUTOR: MARILYN GARBER

To understand color, you must be familiar with the grammar, or principles, of color. Each of the following aspects of color contributes to an artist's ability to create a three-dimensional image on a two-dimensional surface, but this basic language of color only lightly touches the surface of all that can be learned by reading about color and understanding it through experience. Time spent exploring a variety of pigments is time well spent. Understanding how the colors on your palette behave comes with practice. Once you have gained that understanding, you will find greater confidence and assurance in planning a pathway from an artwork's beginning to its completion.

Primary colors are colors that cannot be mixed from any other color. These are red, blue, and yellow.

Secondary colors are a mixture of two primary colors and include orange, green, and violet.

Tertiary colors are a mixture of primary and secondary colors, yielding red-orange, yellow-orange, yellow-green, blue-green, blue-violet, and red-violet.

Complementary colors are colors that are opposite each other on the color wheel. Complementary colors help to darken or dull a color. For example, bit of red added to green may be used in shadows of a green leaf.

Hue is a color without tint or shade and is often seen as interchangeable with the word "color." Hue does apply to primary, secondary, and tertiary colors.

Tint is a lighter version of a hue. With opaque media such as gouache, acrylic, and oils, white is added to tint a color. In watercolor, water is added, reducing the amount of pigment and allowing the substrate to be seen through the color. For example, red is a hue, pink is a tint.

Shade is a darker version of a hue. In watercolor, a complementary color or a neutral tint is added to a hue to darken it. For example, red is a hue, burgundy is a shade.

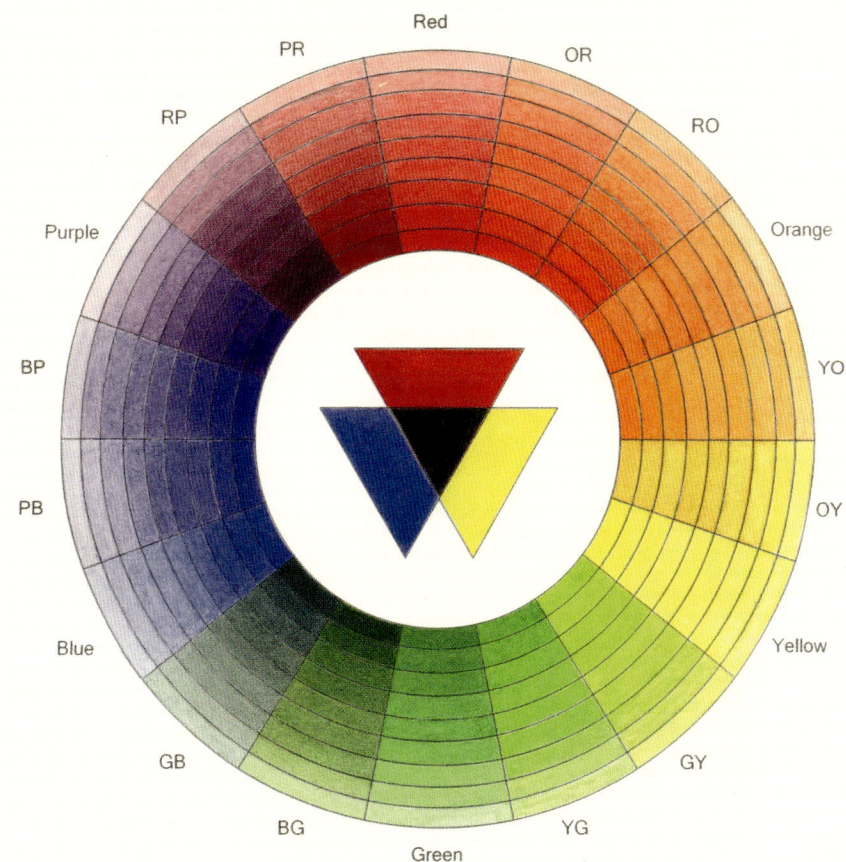

Moses Harris Color Wheel, 1766.
Reproduced by Scott Stapleton.
The prismatic color wheel begins with
the primary colors of red, yellow, and blue
in the center. As colors modulate into
their adjoining colors on the wheel, each
is also shown in a more saturated version
in the center of the wheel, then progressing outwardly to increasingly pale tints.

Tone describes the lightness or darkness of a color. It is different from shade or tint, as tone denotes dulled hues and has less color saturation or intensity. For example, both pink and red can have many variations in tone.

Saturation, intensity, and chroma all refer to the brightness of the color. A color is at its highest saturation when it exhibits hue purity, without complementary colors or white added. Intense color is high chroma, near neutral or dull color is low chroma. For example, cadmium red at full strength is high chroma. Cadmium red diluted, and subdued with the addition of green, is lower chroma.

Local color is color that is not influenced by light, high-light, tone, reflected light, shade, or surrounding colors. For example, an apple is red—red is the local color.

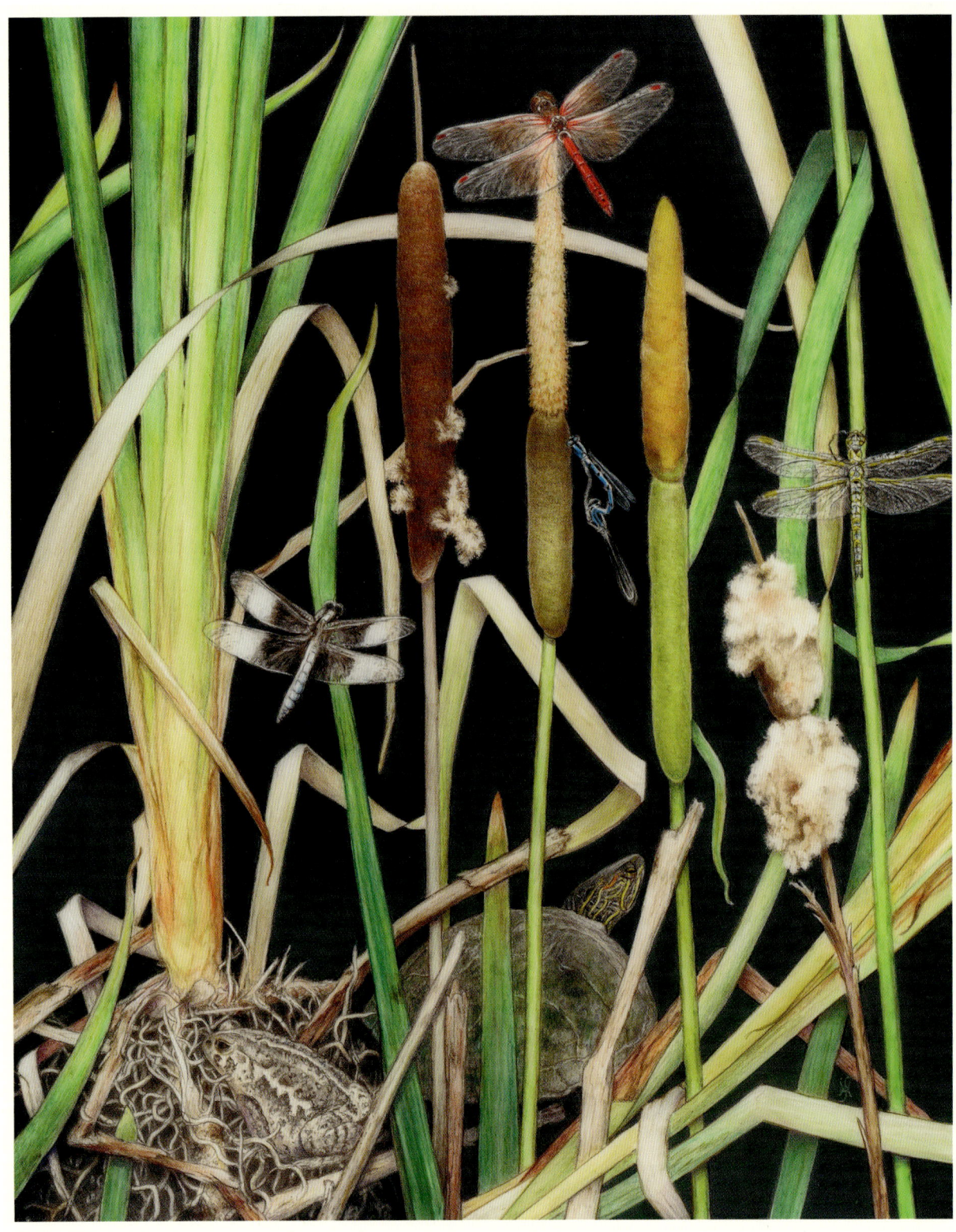

Cattails Colored pencil on film, black acrylic on reverse 20 × 16 inches [50 × 40 cm] © Heidi Snyder

Colored pencils are becoming more and more popular among botanical artists. Developed in Europe in the early twentieth century, they were originally used for commercial purposes. Over the years, their quality has greatly improved, and more long-lasting and varied pigments can be found, along with dry and wet versions. The pencils use waxes, oils, or gum arabic as vehicles for their color cores, which are carried in hardened barrels for less wasteful sharpening. Their ease of use, immediacy, portability, and control are among the aspects artists find appealing.

Techniques and Tutorials

Colored Pencil Skills

The Basics

TUTOR: LIBBY KYER

Colored pencils are wonderful pigments, mounted in a variety of mediums and wrapped in handy wooden holders. Look for pencils that feature archival-quality pigments, a large range of colors, and hardened barrels that allow you to sharpen the pencils well without using up the color core. Following are basic methods that are suitable for all colored pencils worked dry, and watercolor and wax or oil pencils worked wet.

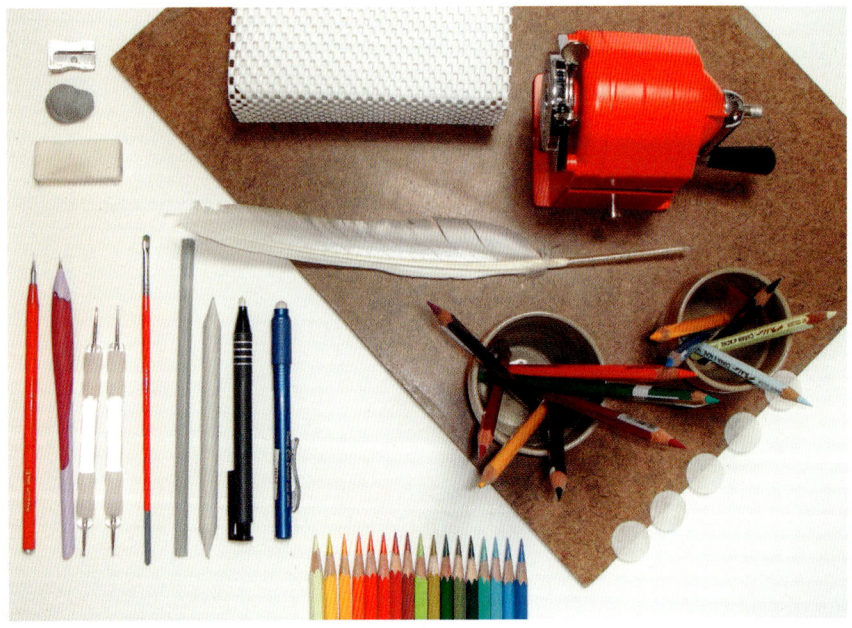

Materials: White-plastic eraser; kneaded eraser; pencil sharpener; drawing board (smooth particle-board); 2- or 4-inch [5 or 10 cm] foam block wrapped in nonslip cupboard fabric to raise drawing board; lead pointer; white feather; containers for sorting colored pencils; drafting dots; archival colored pencils; white-plastic retractable erasers; blending stump; wax blending stick; short-haired scrubber brush; four embossing styluses; plate-finish Bristol board or hot-pressed 140 lb. [300 gsm] watercolor paper; removable tape; isopropyl alcohol (ISPA) pen.

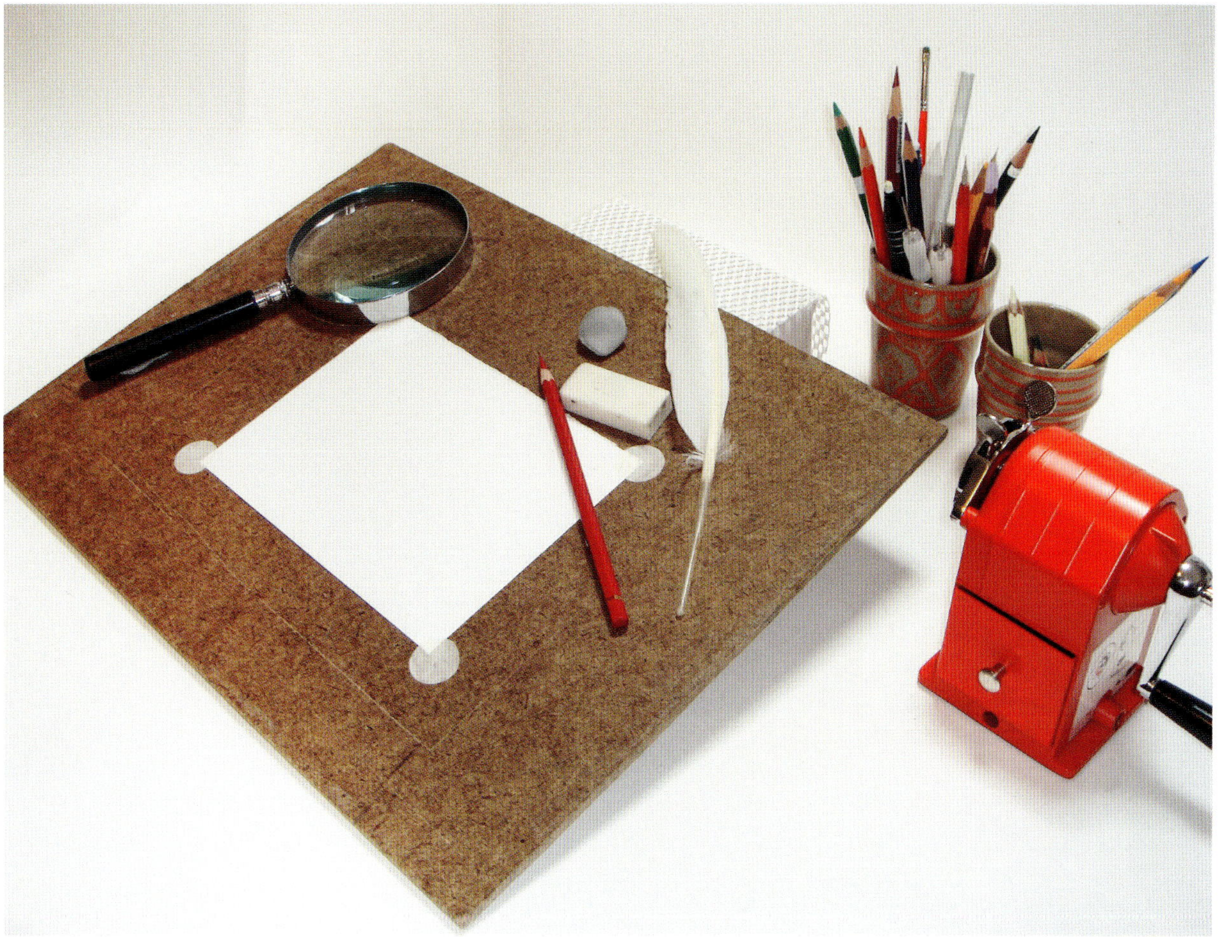

Before you begin working, raise the top edge of the mounting board on a block to ease the strain on your head, neck, elbows, and arms, and also to protect the paper from pencil points, shavings, and other debris. Tape the paper at each corner, making sure it is flat and doesn't move. Situate your colored pencils within easy reach of your drawing hand.

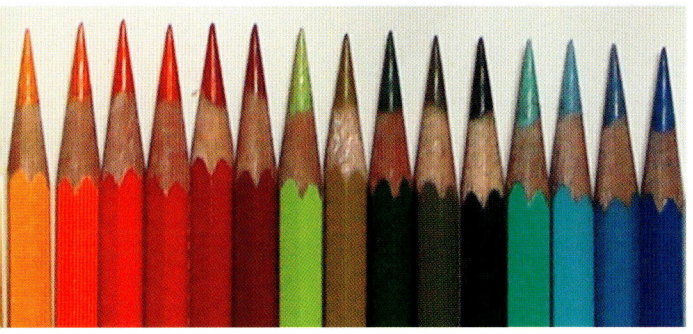

There are three "Ps" to consider with colored pencils: point, position, and pressure. The points should be kept extremely sharp. When a pencil point is sharp, a lot of pigment is exposed and the point can be configured to make various marks.

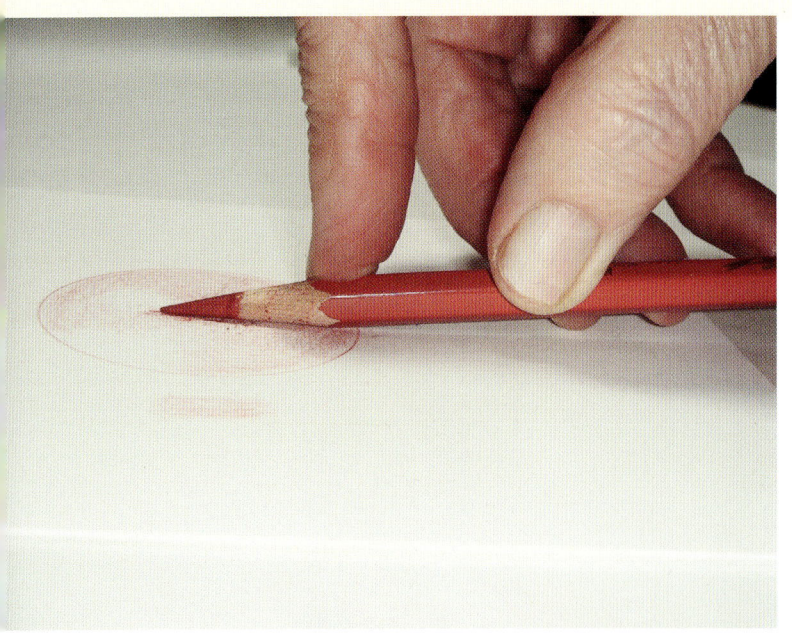

To fill in broad areas of local color, position the long side of a point flat against the paper, with the pencil tilted slightly upward so the full core is in contact with the paper. Holding the pencil near the point allows for tighter control; holding the pencil farther back allows for greater coverage. Note the rather loose open coverage (the broad soft strokes of color fill laid down when you use the side of a colored pencil).

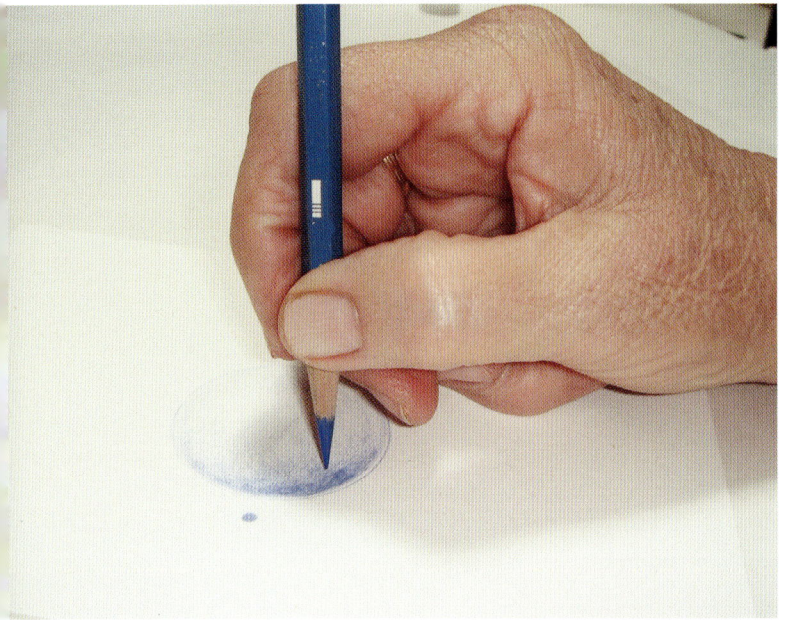

By holding the colored pencil straight up, you can deposit color deeply on the paper without applying heavy pressure. With the pencil in this position, the pigment reaches all levels of the paper's grain, unlike the side position, which skims over the grain. Maintaining a sharp point in this position is crucial to achieving an even tone.

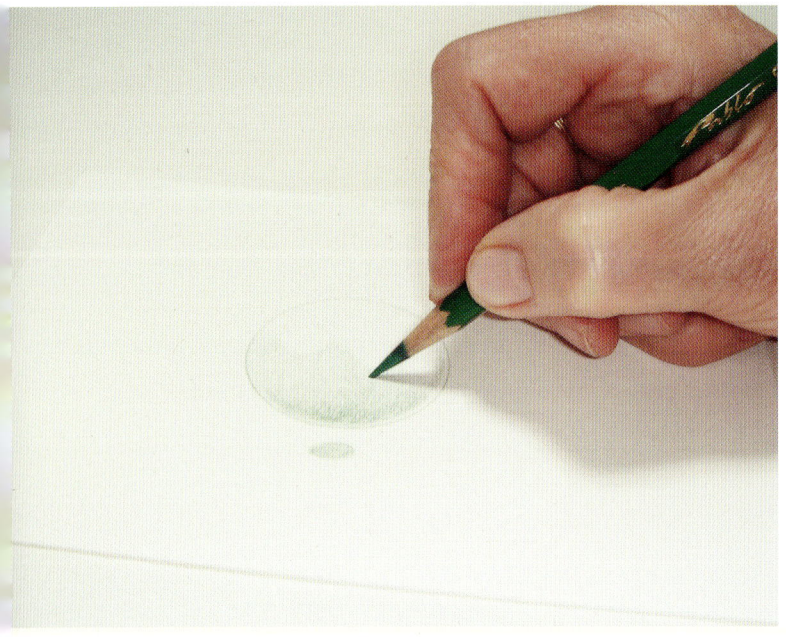

For creating line, fill, and continuous tone with a variety of strokes, hold the pencil in a comfortable writing grip. The point wears off into a flattened oval, allowing a range of pigment to be deposited. Rotating the colored pencil as you work maintains the functional oval, with a good point for color application and layering.

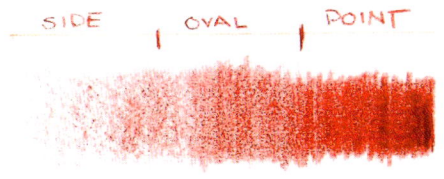

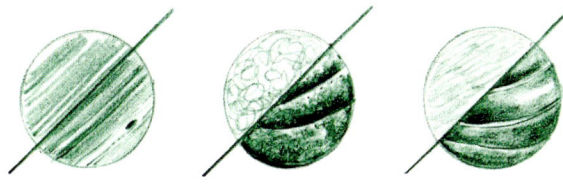

This diagram shows changes in tone you can achieve by varying the position of the pencil.

Here are three basic workhorse strokes. Using these strokes will limit voids, or areas of too-light or too-dark color. Add layers of colored pencil to develop deeper hues.

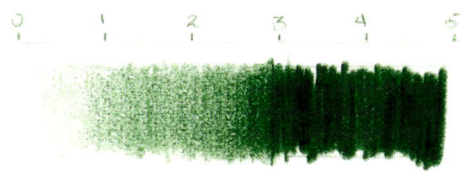

Left: Single lines create edges, veins, and texture. Draw small, linear, connected strokes to achieve a more organic appearance. Lines placed closely together create a smooth tone in small areas. The longer the line, the more difficult it is to repeat it accurately.

Pressure is a tool, but applying too much pressure hurts your hand and destroys the paper's tooth, leading to inconsistencies in further layers of color. This green bar illustrates an imaginary pressure scale from 0 (no pressure) to 5 (pressure that indents paper). Ordinary, comfortable writing falls between 1.5 and 2. Colored pencil work is from .5 to about 3, allowing hue depth in a single layer, without damaging the paper's tooth.

Middle: Scumbling, or making irregular, circular strokes, creates richly textured surfaces, with small changes in random overlapping shapes. The irregular openings between strokes allow multiple layers to sparkle through.

Right: Overlapping small flat elliptical strokes—one-quarter inch [6.4 mm] or smaller—create smooth surfaces.

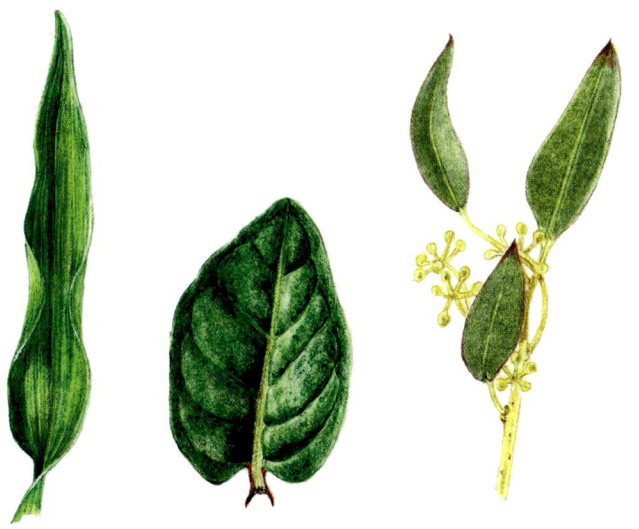

Here are three leaf studies made using the three strokes demonstrated in the previous image. From left to right: linear connected strokes, scumbling, flat elliptical strokes.

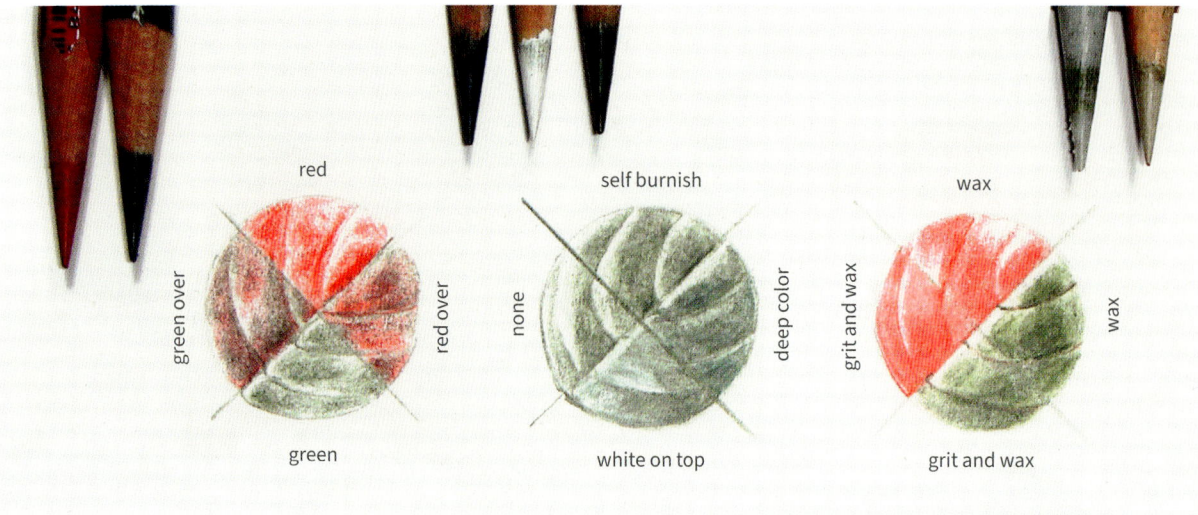

Controlling Color: Mixing, Blending, and Burnishing for Great Color

Colored pencil is semi-transparent and semi-liquid due to its wax or oil medium—that's why it can be so vibrant as well as subtle. Mix and blend color as you layer to get the best results. Try these methods for effective mixing.

Visual mixing (left): Gentle layering puts pigment grains in close or distant proximity to each other. Just like in impressionism, the eye does the actual mixing and blending.

Tips:
- The color on top has the most influence over lower color layers.
- Lighter colors on top tint or lighten the colors underneath.
- Darker colors on top tone or darken the colors underneath.
- Lay in form with darker colors, then add local colors in the upper layers so that the local colors are dominant.
- Layer gently, preserving paper tooth for further additions of color.
- Remember that point position can lay down color without a lot of pressure.

Physical mixing (center and right): Blending medium and pigment with a variety of physical manipulations results in more nuanced blends. Use the least pressure possible to get the effect you want, to keep tooth available.

Methods include:

Burnishing (center): Use the local color in the top layer, with a pressure of about 1 on point, to smooth all the colors underneath it. Use a similar stroke to the color laid down first. This unifies and shines up the surface. Clockwise from top: self-burnished (burnished with the same local color), burnished with deeper color, burnished with white on top, no burnishing.

Colorless blender burnishing (right): Use a colorless wax blender over the top of all colors, with a pressure of about 1 and using a small elliptical stroke. Pressure and the semi-liquid aspect of the medium will emulsify the lower layers just a tiny bit to bring pigments closer together. Clockwise from top: Red quarter burnished with colorless wax blender; green quarter burnished with colorless wax blender; green quarter burnished with a wax and pumice blender; red quarter burnished with a wax and pumice blender.

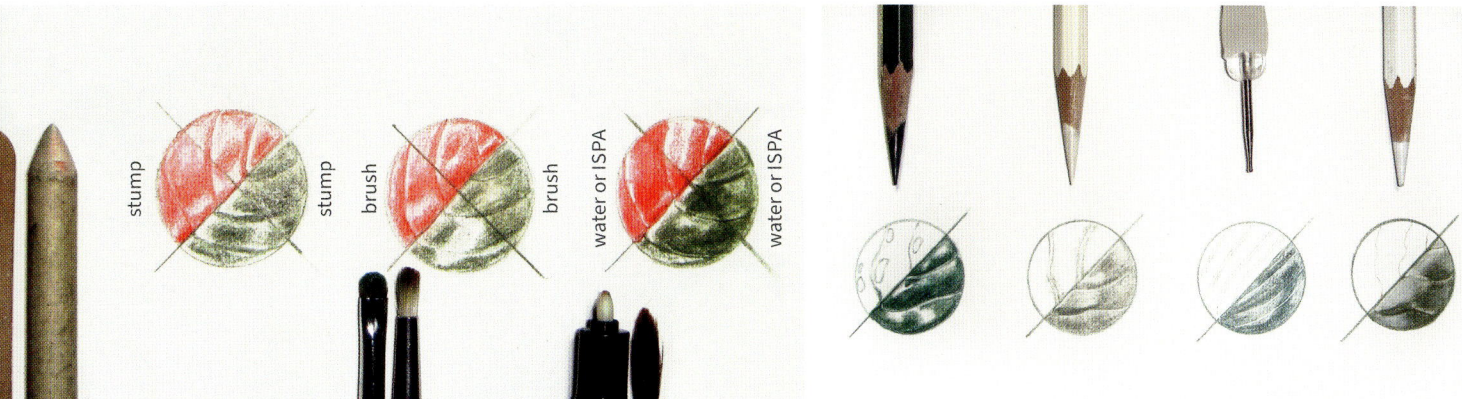

Colors blended with a blending stump (left). Using a blending stump with a pressure of 1, blend using the point or the side of the blending stump to create a soft, matte finish. Clean the blending stump on an emery board.

Colors gently blended with a scrubber brush (center). Using a small, short, stiff, filbert-shaped brush, rub the color gently in small elliptical strokes. The brush moves pigments a tiny bit and emulsifies the wax medium to smooth out the color and create a small glow from the wax that settles below the surface.

Colors blended with solvents (right): The safest solvent is water, used with watercolor pencils made with water-soluble waxes. These pencils also respond to dry-blending techniques. Colored pencils in non-water-soluble waxes can be blended using rubbing alcohol (isopropyl 80 percent). Working with color on the paper, dip a small watercolor brush in water or alcohol, or use an alcohol felt-tipped pen. Tap the brush or pen on the color to melt the wax and create a liquid blend.

Whites are critical for creating form, shape, and detail definition. Here are four ways to handle whites, from left to right:

Reserve the white: Don't put any color in the brightest highlights. Outline a highlight in local color to ensure placement of full highlights. Work color up to the edge of the white area, eliminating the outline.

Resists: For lightly tinted whites, reserve small details such as veins or tiny details by drawing them with white, cream, or colorless blenders. Colors layered over them will skip over the resist area. Use a pressure of 1 to 1.5.

Impress: For true white lines: Use an embossing ball stylus to press lines or dots into the paper's surface. The impressed lines will remain uncolored when drawn over with a colored pencil. To create tinted lines, lay the color in first, then impress the lines and work over them.

Add top layer of white: Using white on top of local color for highlights creates a lovely tint of the local color with a waxy shine. Add soft highlights using this method.

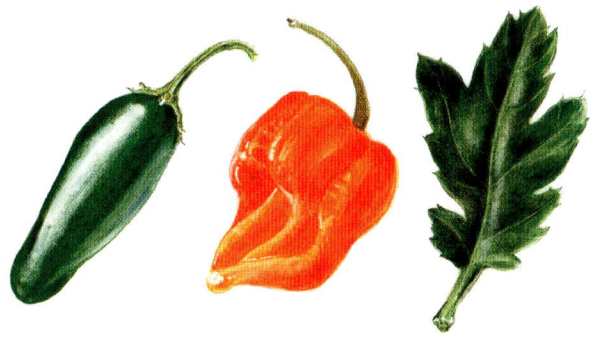

Here, these techniques of handling whites are studied and practiced on small specimens. When you are doing a more complete specimen, create the drawing on tracing paper then transfer it to the selected paper or other substrate using a 30 percent gray colored pencil over a light box.

Jeanne Reiner demonstrates drawing three types of flowers using colored pencils, with the addition of pastel dust (from pan pastels, or pastels that are packed into small containers; they can be applied using a variety of tools, including cotton swabs) in two instances. Each flower type requires its own approach. The first flower is cockscomb (*Celosia cristata*), with a dense cluster, or inflorescence, of many closely packed, tiny flowers with small colorful bracts. A petunia (*Petunia ×hybrida*), which has a velvety texture, follows. The last is a chrysanthemum; in this instance an inflorescence of disk and ray flowers.

Three Flower Types in Colored Pencil— Texture and Color

TUTOR: JEANNE REINER

Cockscomb

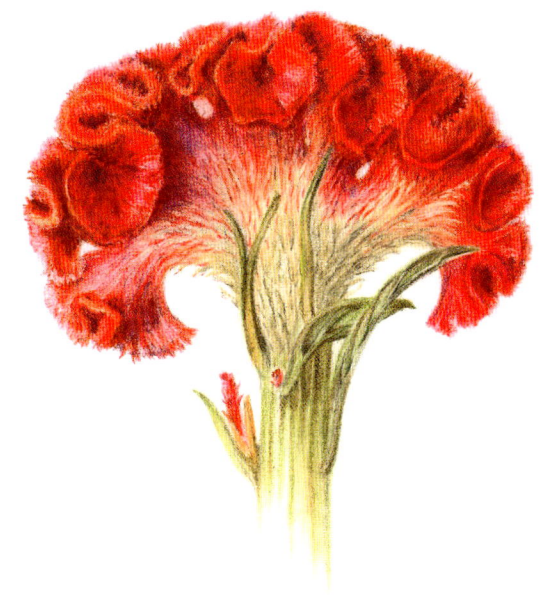

Cockscomb *Celosia cristata*
Colored pencil and pan pastel
on Bristol board
3 × 3 inches [7.5 × 7.5 cm]
© Jeanne Reiner
HOURS TO COMPLETE: 24

MATERIALS: Magnifying glass; erasing shield; feather for dusting off drawing; odorless mineral spirits; electric pencil sharpener; colorless blender pencil; thin retractable eraser; colored pencils; flat brush for applying pastels; cotton swabs; artist's tape; graphite pencil; craft knife; dividers; pan pastels.

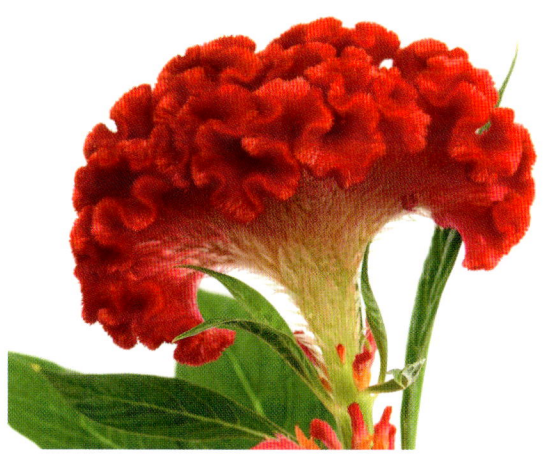

Celosias have a richly textured, undulating flower head with a furry appearance. The flowers are perched atop an expanded stem with many small bracts. The challenge is in creating the furry surface while clearly showing the undulations of the flower cluster.

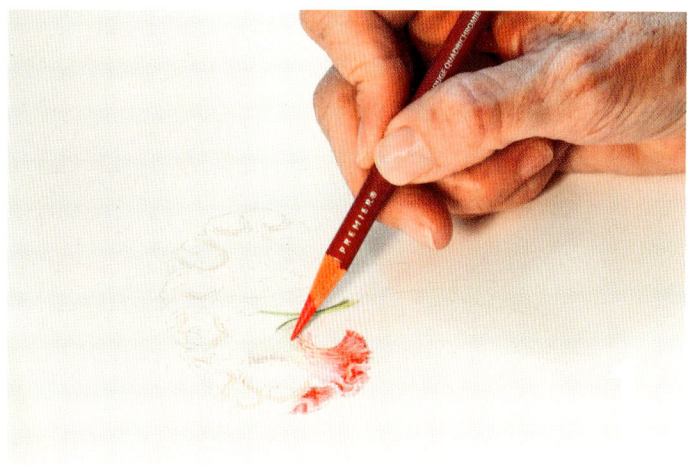

First, the rippled edge of the flower head is lightly colored. Then a slightly darker magenta is drawn around the individual flowers to delineate their shapes, as well as to suggest the shadows below the large folds of the crest.

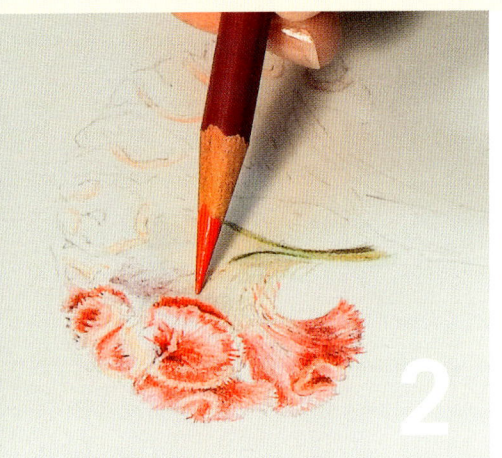

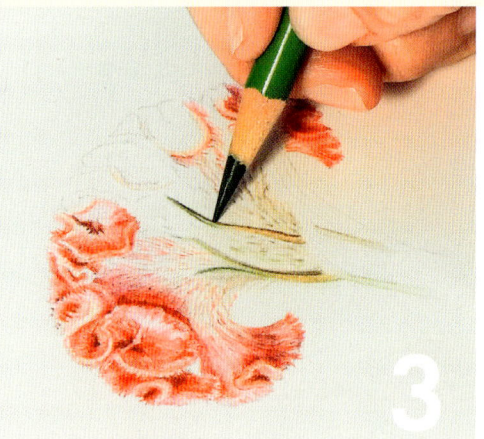

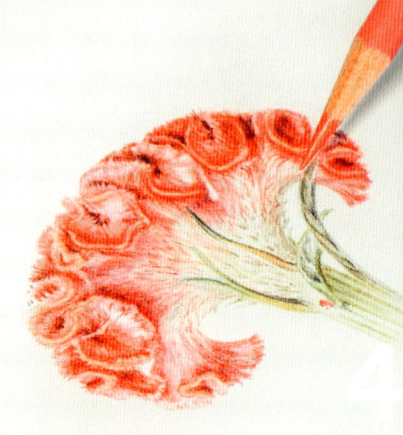

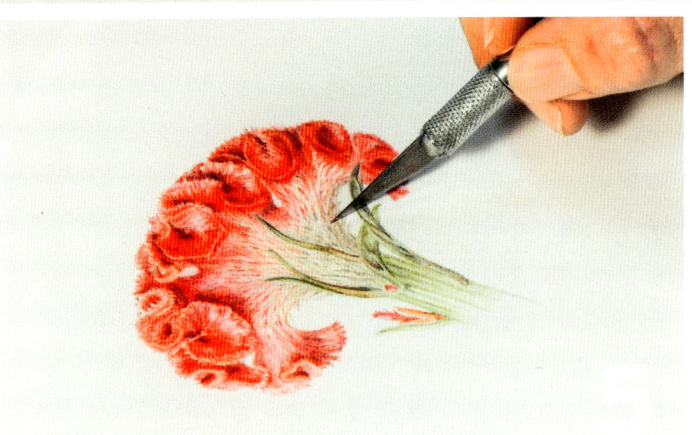

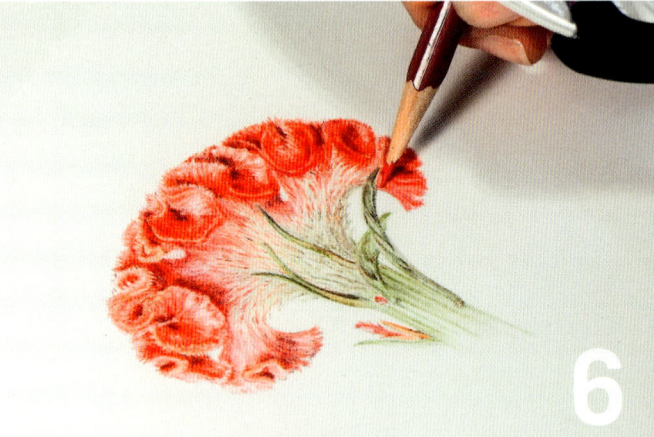

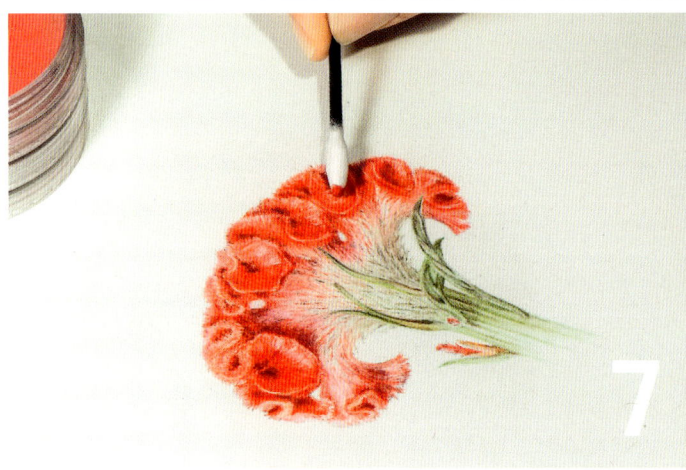

The edge of the cockscomb crest is very bright magenta. To retain the vivid hues in the shadow areas, dark purple is used as an underdrawing, or first tonal layer, rather than a typical grisaille of gray, which may contain yellow and thereby dull the color.

The receptacle that all the flowers are attached to, and the small leafy bracts, are pale sage and ivory. Draw a grisaille using French grey 50 percent, then apply several layers of sage and ivory, leaving the spikey flowers lighter. Create texture using darker colors in small strokes.

Bright pink and magenta are applied in small strokes over all the crest area including the shadow colors to unify the head of flowers. A light touch is used to keep a highlight on the edges of the undulating folds.

The tip of a craft knife is used to lightly scratch away some layers of waxy pencil, where a brighter detail is needed. Scrape very gently sideways so the paper is not damaged.

Using a magnifying glass and an extremely sharp pencil, more details and richer color are added.

Pan pastels are used sparingly at the end, applied with a cotton swab, to soften the edges of the cockscomb, enhancing its fuzzy texture

Petunia

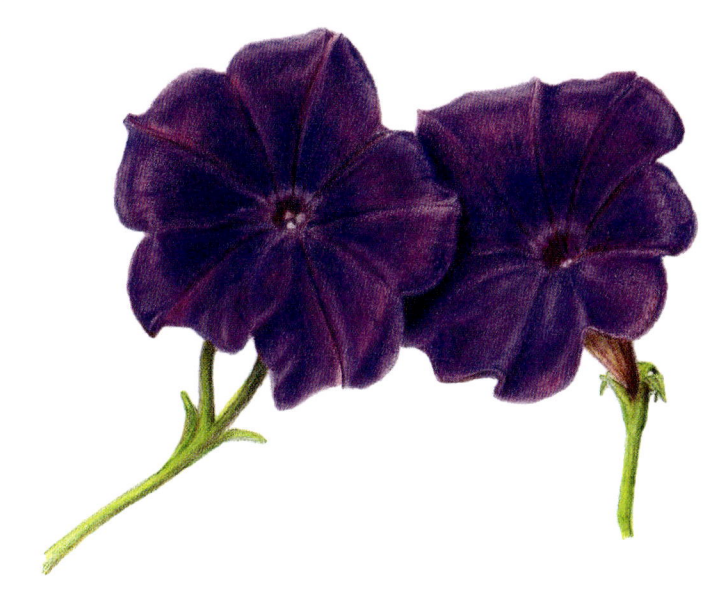

Petunias
Colored pencil and pan pastel
on Bristol board
3 ¾ × 4 ¼ inches [9.4 × 10.6 cm]
© Jeanne Reiner
HOURS TO COMPLETE: 6

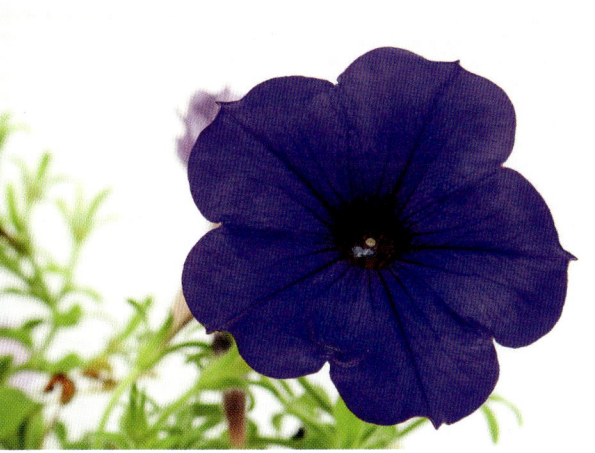

This petunia's petals are partly fused, and flowers are funnel shaped. Their surface is soft and velvety, and in this case a very dark purple. To replicate this deeply-colored velvety characteristic, a solvent is used, as well as pan pastels, to help smooth color and create depth.

To create the dark, velvety purple of the petunia, a light layer of process red is applied to the highlight and midtone areas while manganese blue is used in the shadows. Dioxide purple is then lightly layered over, everywhere but the highlights. This sequence is repeated two more times in all but the highlight areas.

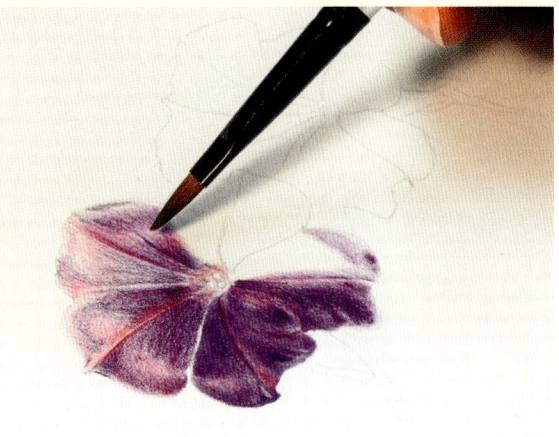

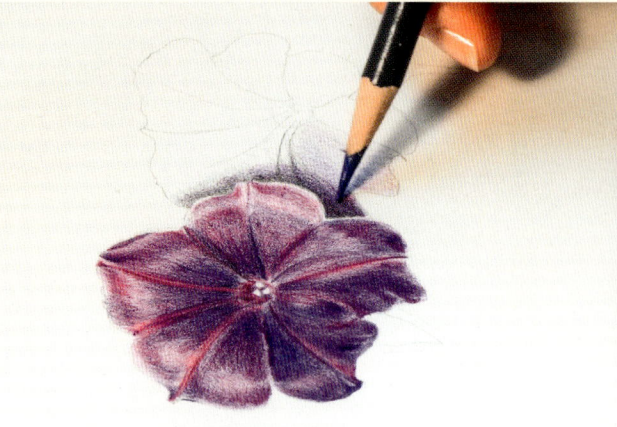

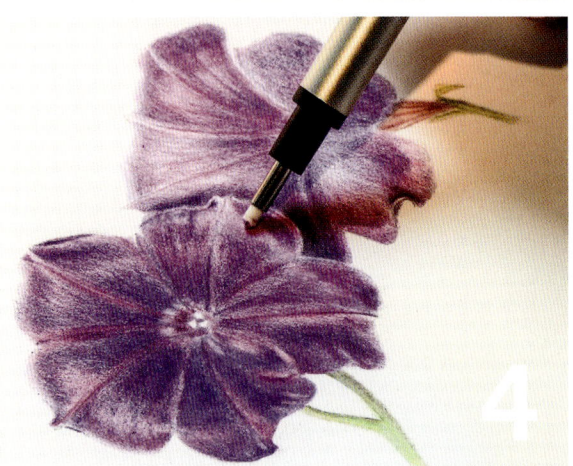

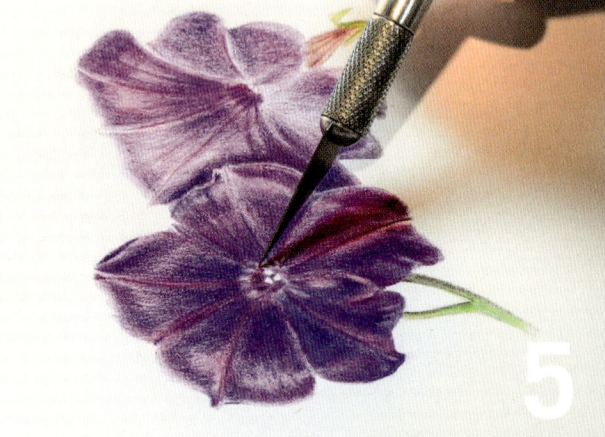

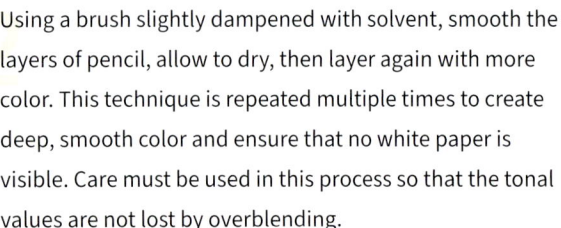

Using a brush slightly dampened with solvent, smooth the layers of pencil, allow to dry, then layer again with more color. This technique is repeated multiple times to create deep, smooth color and ensure that no white paper is visible. Care must be used in this process so that the tonal values are not lost by overblending.

Bright white highlights lend an appearance of a glossy surface. However, highlights in this case should appear as tonal variations to convey the velvety appearance of the petals. This effect is achieved by continuing to use process red in the lightest areas. Introduce the cast shadow onto the second flower using manganese blue.

Once most of the color is laid down, gently rub a small white eraser over the areas where highlights occur, creating brighter areas that are light pink (process red) but not white. Clean the eraser frequently. The rich, soft texture is maintained by the warm pink highlights.

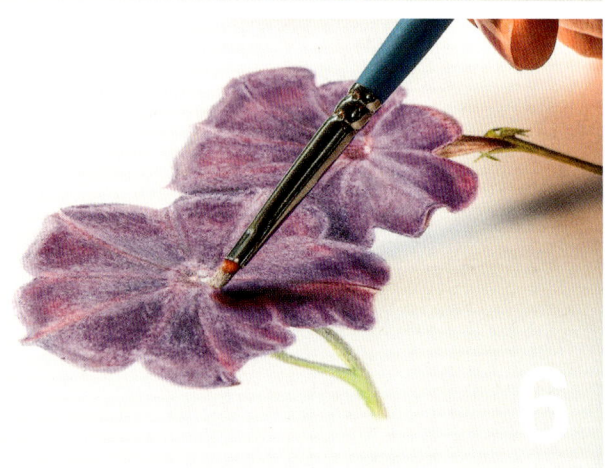

Final details of the stamens, stigma, and surrounding corolla are created by scratching color out of the brightest white areas with the tip of a craft knife.

Last, white pan pastel is applied with a brush or sponge tip applicator to enhance the soft, powdery "bloom" typical of the highlights in velvety textures.

Chrysanthemum

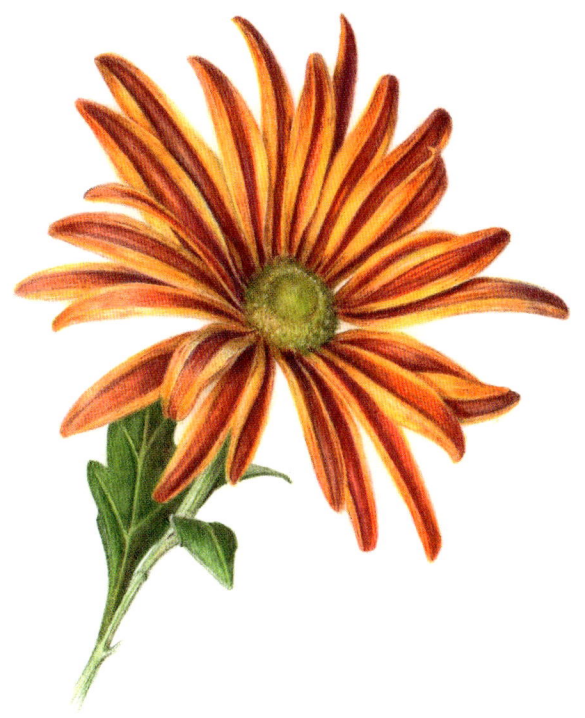

Chrysanthemum
Colored pencil on paper
4 ½ × 3 inches [11.25 × 7.5 cm]
©Jeanne Reiner
HOURS TO COMPLETE: 12

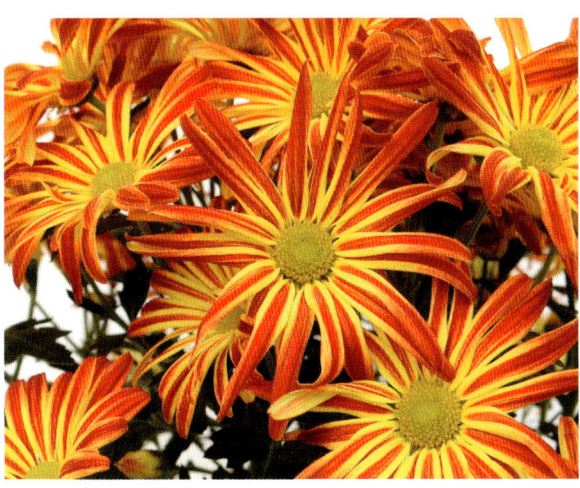

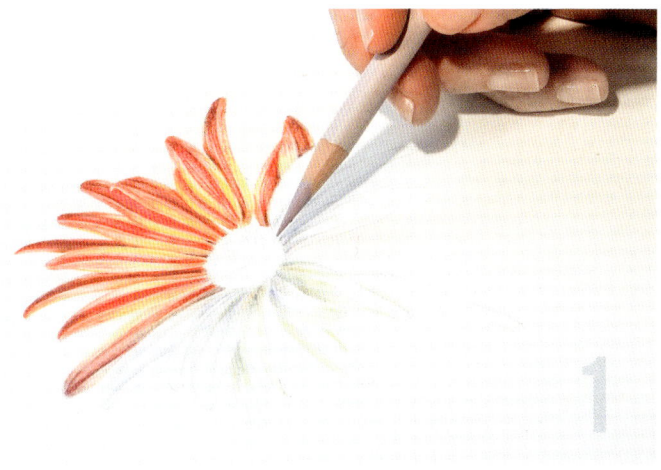

A good example of a compound flower, this chrysanthemum has both disk and ray flowers. Its basic color is yellow, with overlays of red. This flower is approached using colored pencils exclusively, to retain the areas of clear delineation between red and yellow.

The ray flowers of this chrysanthemum have cadmium yellow edges and red striations in the center. First, draw the longitudinal ridges of the ray in pale violet gradating to white.

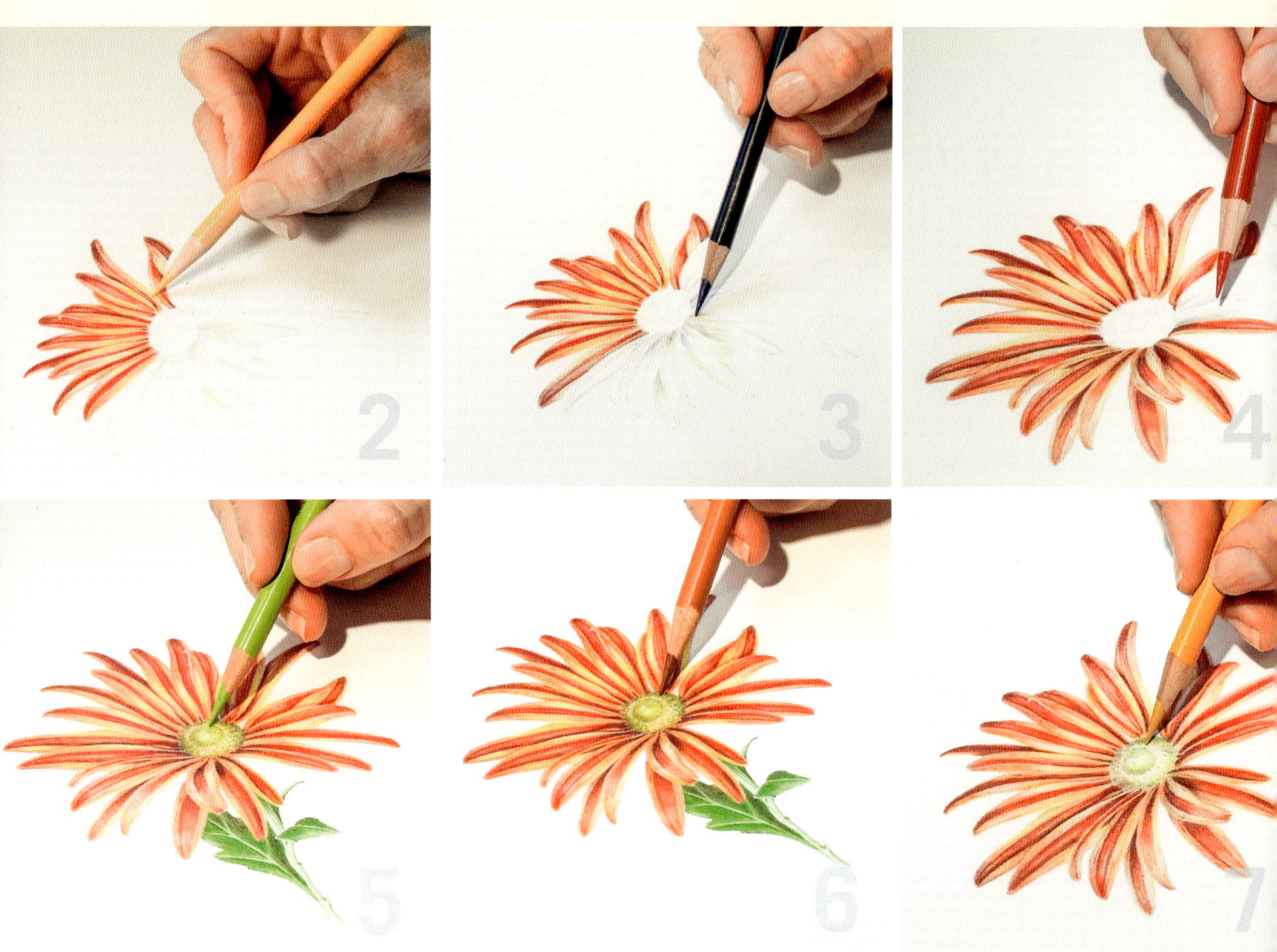

When yellow is drawn over this tone, the white will keep the yellow pure and bright in the lightest areas, and the violet will begin to add form. Before applying the red of the ray flower, apply dark red-violet, changing to yellow in the lighter areas.

The left side of the drawing is partially in shadow, making the area closest to the disk the darkest. Apply an ultramarine blue grisaille, then use red to darken it.

In order to darken the shadow side of the flower, use a French grey as a base where the flower is yellow, and darken both the red and yellow local colors.

The shape of the center disk is domed with a flat top. For the local color, choose a very clear bright yellow-green.

A light ochre (which has a reddish bias) was used in the shadow areas to darken and dull the green without causing a major color shift.

As the final step, add cadmium yellow in tiny strokes to simulate the styles of the open disk flowers.

Karen Coleman demonstrates the use of colored pencil on three leaf types: one with a fuzzy texture, one with fall color, and one that is shiny with bright white highlights. In these three tutorials, several techniques are shown including embossing, the addition of watercolor pencil, and the use of colored pencils on film and paper.

Depicting Leaf Texture with Colored Pencil

TUTOR: KAREN COLEMAN

Lamb's Ear

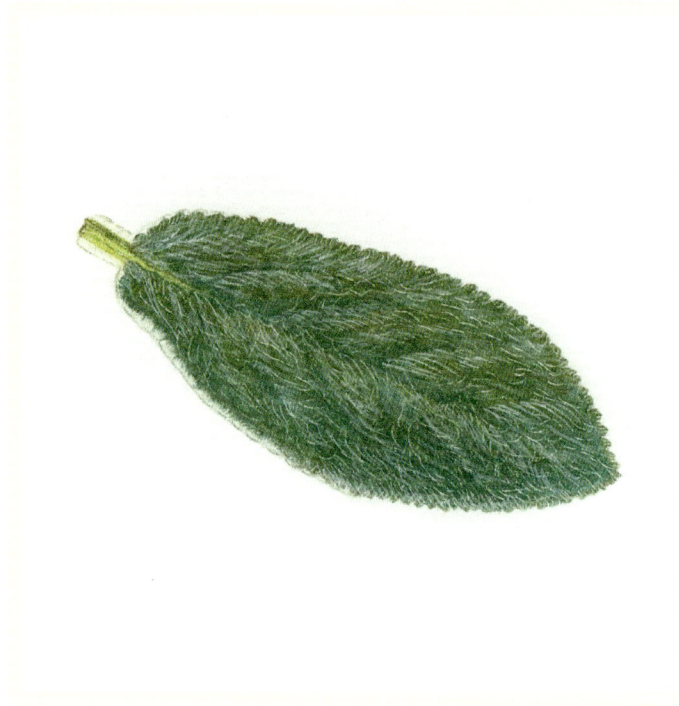

Lamb's Ear *Stachys byzantina*
Colored pencil on paper
5 ½ × 7 ½ inches [13.75 × 18.75 cm]
© Karen Coleman
HOURS TO COMPLETE: 3

MATERIALS: Magnifying glass; colored pencils; electric pencil sharpener; duster brush; kneaded eraser; white-plastic retractable erasers (medium and fine); emery board; fine-tipped embossing tool; watercolor brush (no. 00); white watercolor pencil; hake brush.

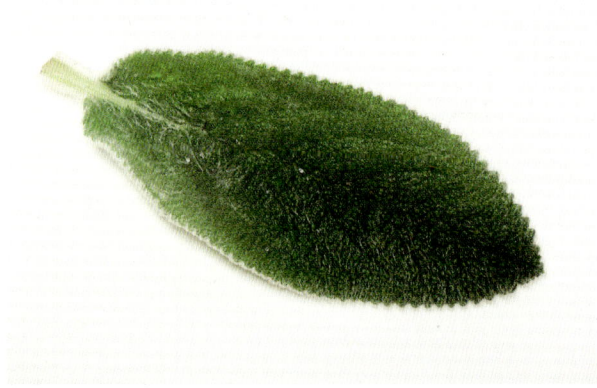

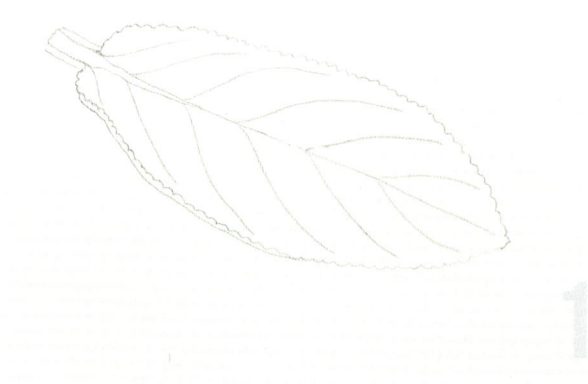

This lamb's ear leaf is mossy green and covered with fine white hairs that give it a silver-gray cast. Ideally named, it is thick, soft, and velvety and feels just like a wooly lamb's ear. The leaf is oblong-elliptic with serrated margins. The underside is pale and visible when the leaf edges turn up.

Make a sketch of the leaf and transfer it to watercolor paper. Use a kneaded eraser to lift graphite from the line drawing, leaving only a pale outline of the leaf.

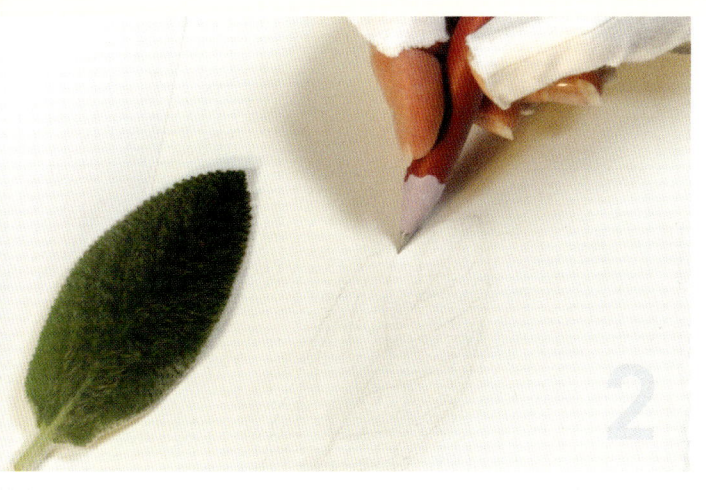

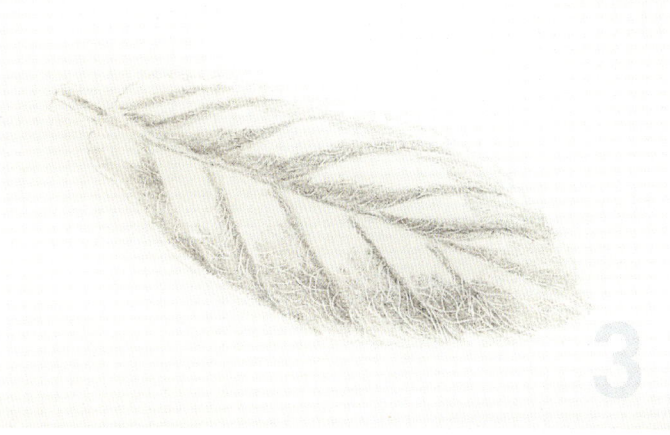

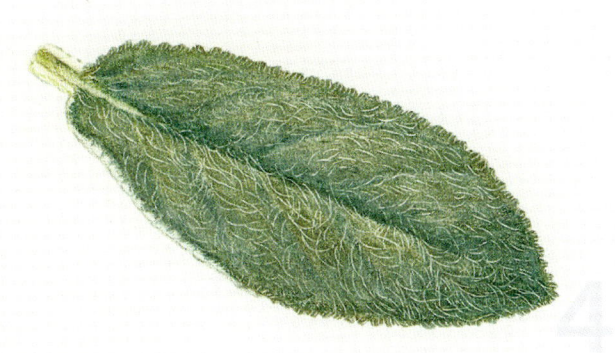

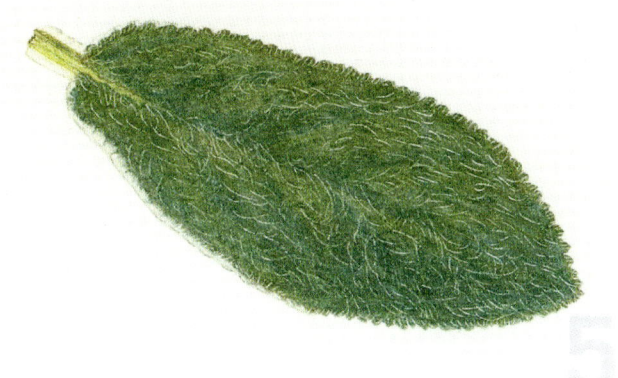

Use an embossing tool with a fine tip to make line impressions in the paper to show hairs on the leaf. To find the right pressure, test the embosser first on a scrap piece of watercolor paper. Then, observing the directions of the hairs, impress them on both the body and margins of the leaf.

Shade the shadow areas with a medium-warm gray pencil. Pay particular attention to the midrib and the main veins, because they almost disappear into the thick, fuzzy lamina. With this first layer of color, the impressed hairs are showing clearly.

Color in the short stem, midrib, and main veins with a pale yellow-green. Using different degrees of pressure, layer the colors over the entire leaf: layer peacock green lightly over the gray shadow areas; then moss green, using firmer pressure; and finally jade green, using stronger pressure.

Use olive green and Kelly green to warm up the leaf, and use celadon green to blend and burnish. Detail the stem and further define the leaf margins. Use peacock green to give some of the hairs subtle shadows. Draw in hairs with white watercolor pencil and then smooth them using a no. 00 Kolinsky brush dipped in water.

Black Gum Leaf

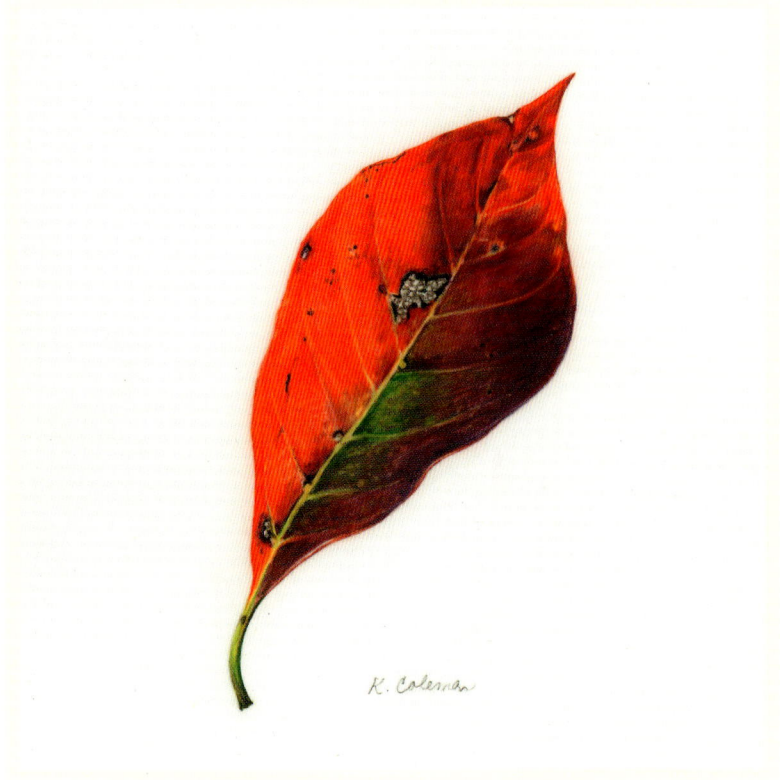

K. Coleman

Black Gum *Nyssa sylvatica*
Colored pencil on drafting film
8 × 7 inches [20 × 17.5 cm]
© Karen Coleman
HOURS TO COMPLETE: 5

MATERIALS: Magnifying glass; harder and softer core colored pencils; electric pencil sharpener; duster brush; hake brush; eraser shield; kneaded eraser; white-plastic retractable erasers (medium and fine); emery board; colorless blender pencil; small cotton cloth.

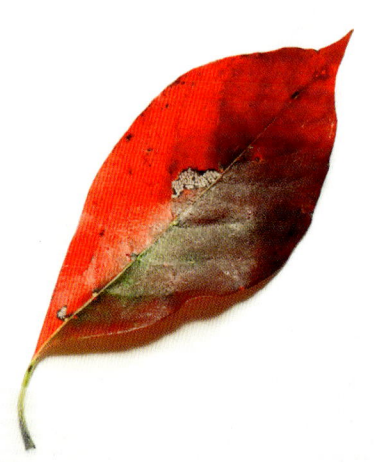
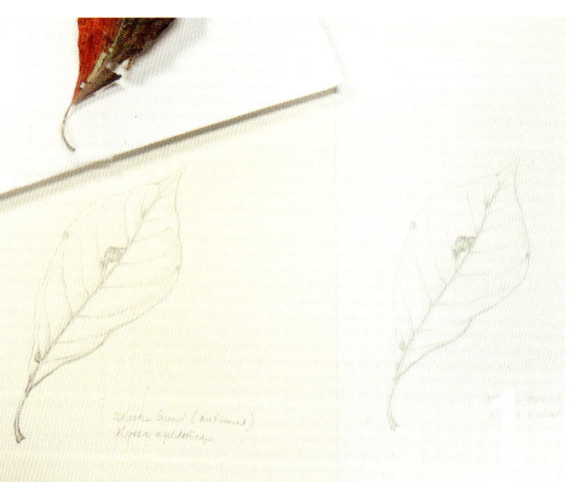
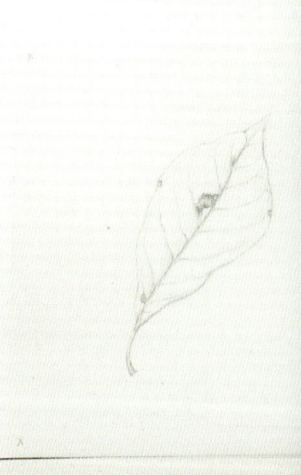

A harbinger of autumn, the black gum is one of the first trees to begin changing color. Its leaves are broad with a simple elliptic shape and smooth margins. This specimen retains some of its dark green color, but it has mostly changed to scarlet and burgundy. Skeletonized veins, caused by insect damage and resembling transparent netting on the lamina, are characteristic of the black gum.

Draw the leaf. This leaf is drawn showing outline, midrib, main veins, and insect damage (left of the main vein). The drafting film (on the right) has a matte finish on both sides and is translucent. Make a photocopy of the original drawing and place the film on top of it to avoid getting graphite on the film. Set aside the original drawing for future reference.

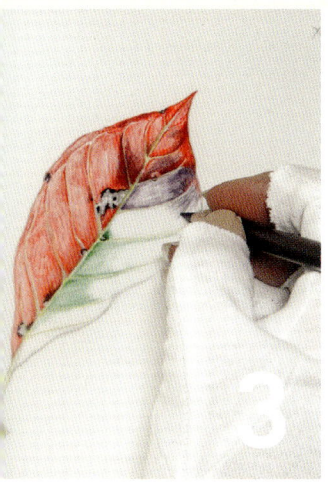
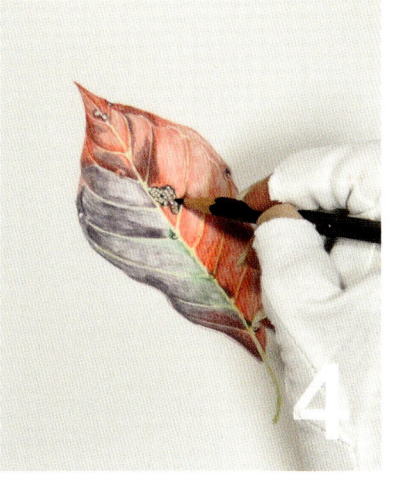
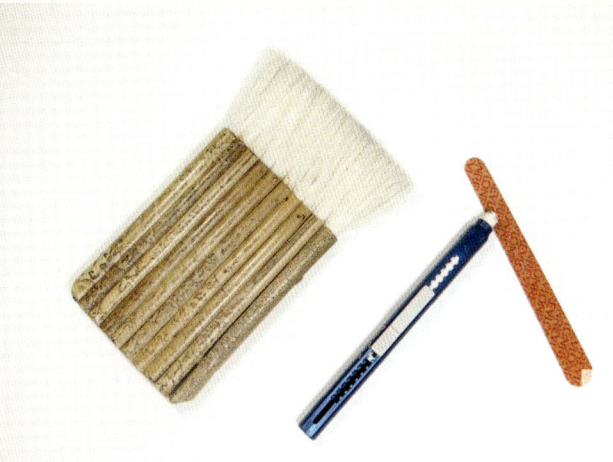

Color will be applied to both sides of the film, so it will need to be perfectly aligned with the photocopied drawing. To achieve this, mark an X in each corner of the photocopied drawing and then lightly trace them onto the film. The X's will help realign the film when it is turned over from front to back. There is no need to transfer as the drawing can easily be traced through the film.

Using fingerless cotton gloves will keep the film clean. Draw the stem, midrib, and veins with lime green. Lightly apply dark green, crimson, black cherry, and black grape to delineate color transitions. Use an oval pencil point, following the contours. Preserve the insect-damaged areas by applying color around them. To keep a record of the colors you are using, list them on a spare piece of film.

The film is turned to the reverse and a sheet of white paper inserted underneath. Insect-damage netting is outlined with a hard, dark umber, and light edges on the right side of the leaf are further defined. Throughout the process, periodically insert a clean sheet of paper under the work to check for any corrections that need to be made on the front and the back of the film—the paper can highlight gaps in the drawing.

Before using an eraser, clean it with an emery board or sandpaper to ensure any color remaining on the eraser is removed. Clean up any pigment crumbs or dust appearing on the film immediately. To prevent smearing, use only a duster brush or a similar tool to sweep away crumbs— never use your hands.

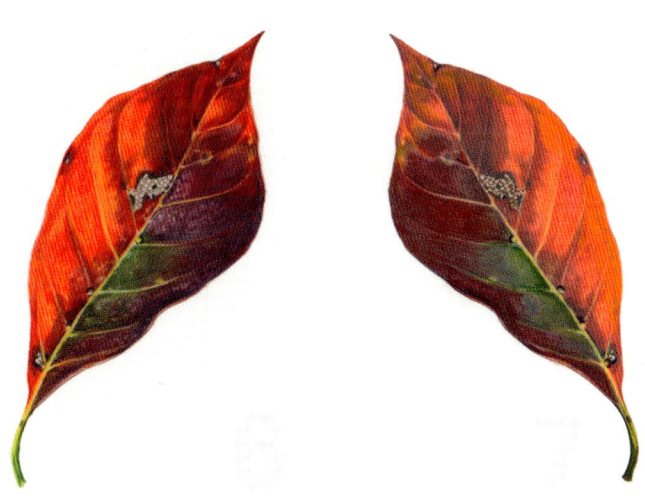

Film is not porous, like paper, so it accepts fewer layers of color than paper. With film, color glides on more smoothly, so apply colors using a lighter touch than you would use with paper. With a sharpened pencil point and soft circular strokes, add warmer hues to begin layering and blending the colors together to make the leaf glow—lime green, olive green, crimson lake, scarlet lake, carmine red, hot pink, pale vermillion, yellowish orange, and sunburst yellow.

Add some warm colors to the back of the film. Use the colorless blender pencil very carefully (to avoid scratching the film) to blend and clean up edges. To finish, intensify the hues on both sides. Refine the details and use hard pencils to define edges. Erase smudges and gently buff any visible strokes with a cotton cloth.

Magnolia Leaf

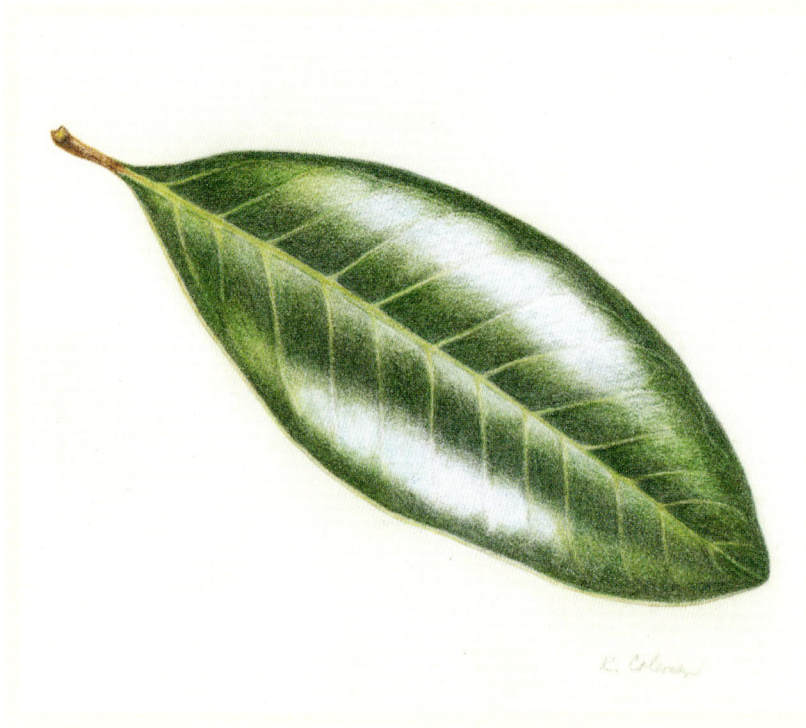

Southern Magnolia
Magnolia grandiflora
Colored pencil on paper
7 × 9 inches [17.5 × 22.5 cm
© Karen Coleman
HOURS TO COMPLETE: 4

MATERIALS: Magnifying glass;
harder- and softer-core colored pencils;
electric pencil sharpener; duster brush;
small cotton cloth; HB pencil; colorless
blender pencil; white-plastic retractable
erasers (medium and fine); emery board;
kneaded eraser; blending stump;
hake brush.

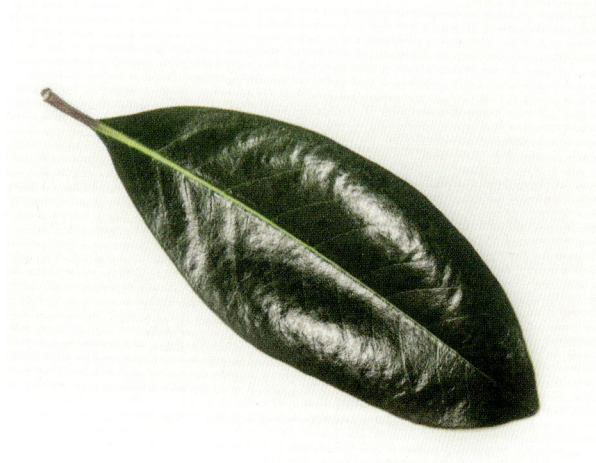

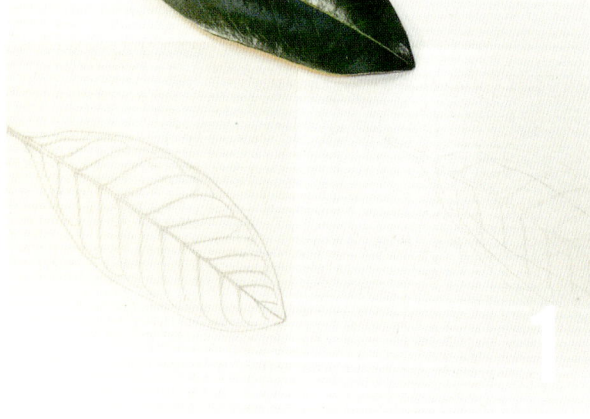

The southern magnolia is an evergreen tree whose leaf is simple and broadly ovate with smooth margins. The midrib is thick and extends to the tip of the leaf. Light reflects strongly off this dark green, leathery leaf, which results in bright highlights.

Make a sketch of the leaf and transfer it to the art paper. Softly outline the strong highlights on the leaf with an HB pencil as a reminder to save the white of the paper there. Then use a kneaded eraser to lift graphite from the line drawing, leaving only a pale outline.

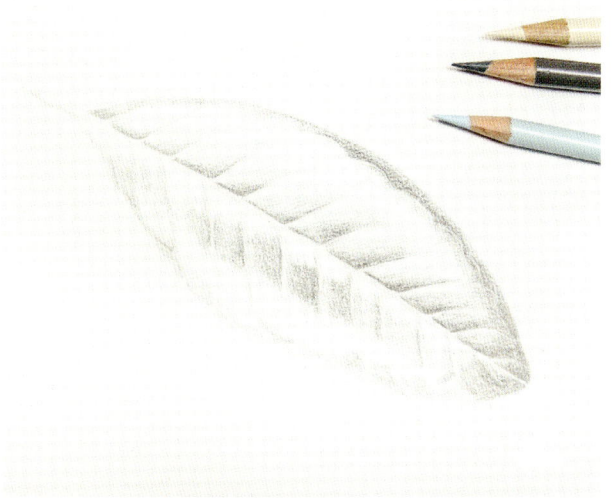

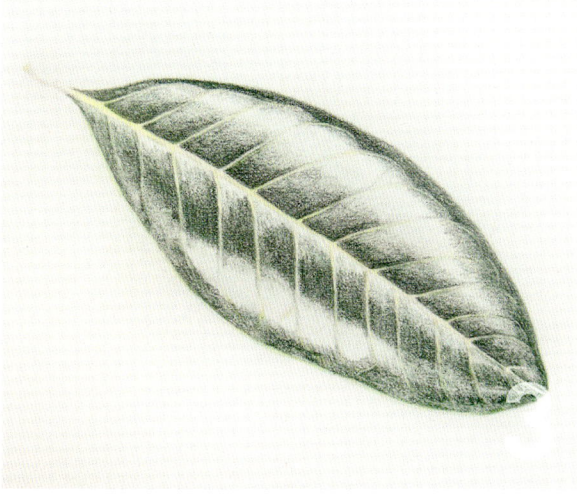

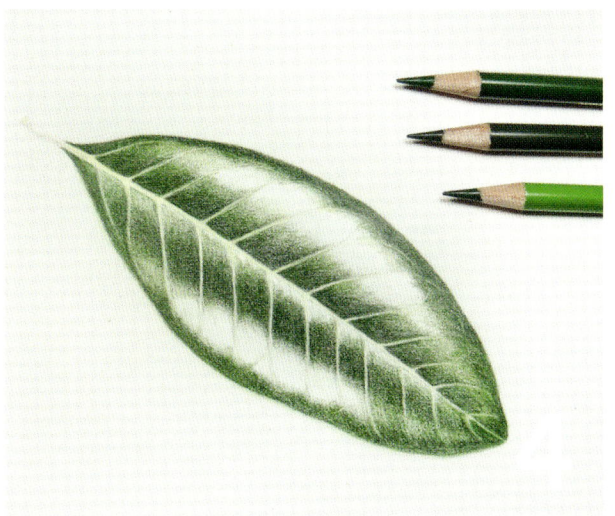

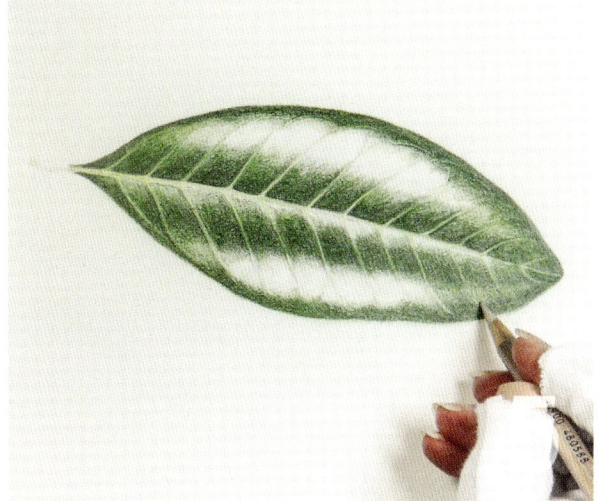

With firm pressure, use an ivory-colored pencil on the midrib and veins to save these areas. Soften the edges of bright highlights with a light sky blue. Shade in shadow areas with a medium-warm gray with varying pressure, using it heaviest in the darker shadows. Lay down color very smoothly, using soft strokes.

Add lemon yellow to the midrib and veins and to the lower edge of the leaf. Using a sharpened point and a smooth circular stroke, layer juniper green over the whole leaf blade except in the highlights. Cover the gray shadow areas using medium pressure and the lighter areas using less pressure.

With varying pressure, add olive green all over except in the bright highlights. If too much color goes into the lighter areas, lift it out with a kneaded eraser. Then add chrome green over the darker areas and yellow green over the lighter areas, blending lightly into the edges of highlights.

Olive green is added to the veins darken them slightly. Use a colorless blender pencil to burnish over the greens and blend some of the color into the highlights. Burnishing presses the pigment into the tooth of the paper, which helps give the leaf a smooth, shiny appearance. Strengthen the darks and lights with additional layers.

Complete the stem by layering it with brown ochre, burnt sienna, and burnt umber. Add brown ochre to the lower edge of the leaf. Clean up all the edges with hard pencils. Use a blending stump to add touches of light turquoise to the highlights in the leaf blade, reflecting the sky. Buff any apparent pencil strokes with a cotton cloth.

Tammy McEntee demonstrates the use of oil-based colored pencils in three examples of fruits and vegetables.
A bumpy gourd, smooth eggplant, and papery shallot
offer a variety of textures to challenge an artist. Colored
pencils consist of a binder (either wax or oil) and pigment. Whatever binder you prefer, the most important
consideration is a high-quality pencil.

Fruits and Vegetables
in Colored Pencil

TUTOR: TAMMY MCENTEE

Gourd

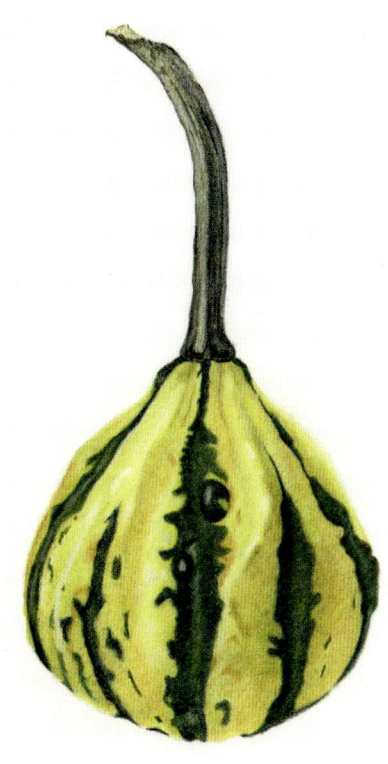

Gourd *Cucurbita pepo*
Colored pencil on paper
7 × 4 inches [17.5 × 10 cm]
© Tammy McEntee
HOURS TO COMPLETE: 20

MATERIALS: Round synthetic brush (no. 3); sandpaper block; oil-based colored pencils; blending stump; lead holder with HB lead; burnisher; retractable erasers; kneaded eraser; odorless mineral spirits.

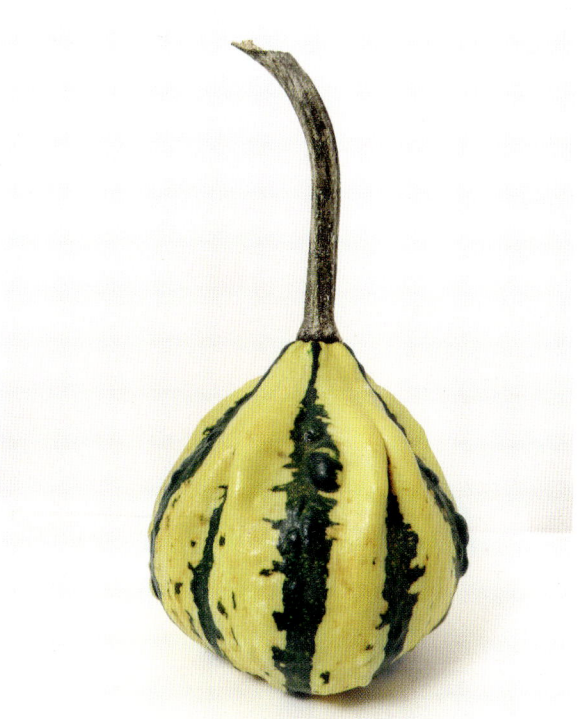

This ornamental gourd is the fruit of *Cucurbita pepo*, a genus whose variants include pumpkins, zucchini, and winter squash. Gourds are inedible, but they are popular for decoration due to their colorful and often warty rinds.

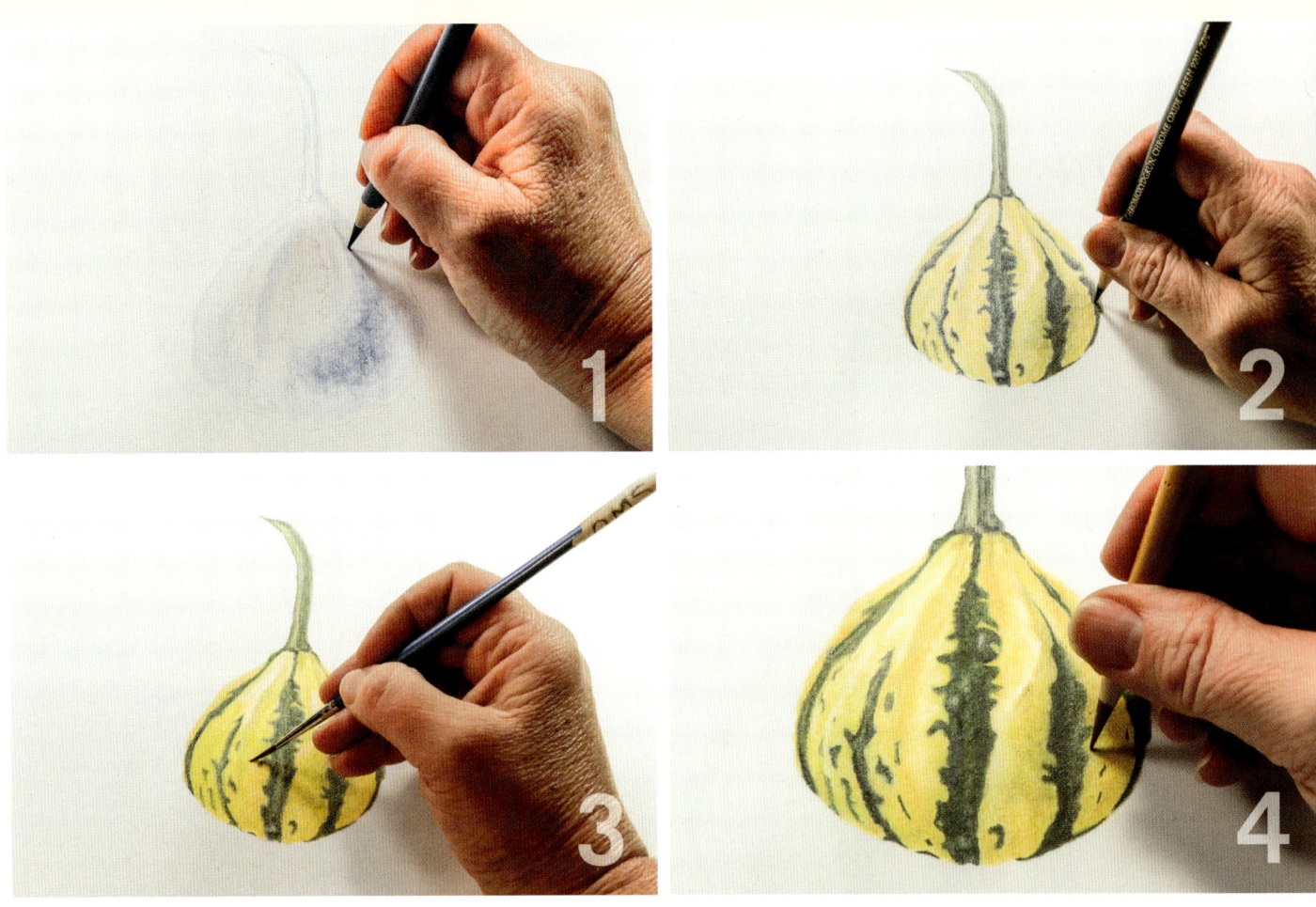

First, draw a grisaille (an image drawn entirely in shades of one color, usually gray) with indanthrene blue to establish shadow and form. Layer cadmium yellow over the indanthrene, creating a soft green-gray—the desired color of the shadow for this subject.

Cover the body of the gourd with one layer of cadmium yellow, except for the highlights. Use chrome oxide green in the stripes, which will be layered alternately with dark indigo to darken the shadows in the stripes. Continue to layer in the body of the gourd with the yellows, then layer the stripes.

Dip a brush in odorless mineral spirits and use it to blend the layers of colored pencil. Clean the brush after blending the green areas, to prevent the green from staining the yellow and to maintain a clear delineation between the colors. Allow the odorless mineral spirits to dry before layering more colors, then blend again with odorless mineral spirits.

Once the main areas of the gourd are complete, refine the details by adding light yellow ochre for some of the blemishes and white gradating into ivory for the highlights. To deepen the shadows of the warts, use dark indigo.

Eggplant

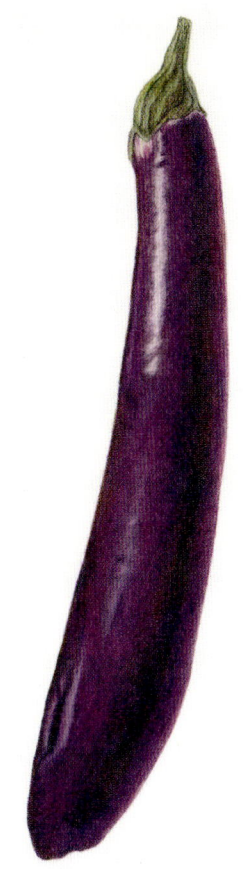

Japanese Eggplant
Solanum melongena var. *esculentum* 'Ichiban'
Colored pencil on paper
10 × 3 inches [25 × 7.5 cm]
© Tammy McEntee
HOURS TO COMPLETE: 20

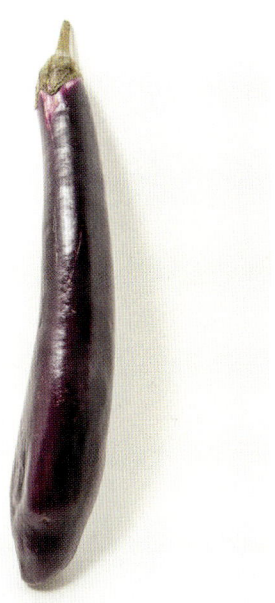

The Japanese eggplant, *Solanum melongena* var. *esculentum* 'Ichiban', is a member of the nightshade family, which includes tomatoes and potatoes. Its rich purple skin is glossy, presenting a challenge for the artist in creating contrast.

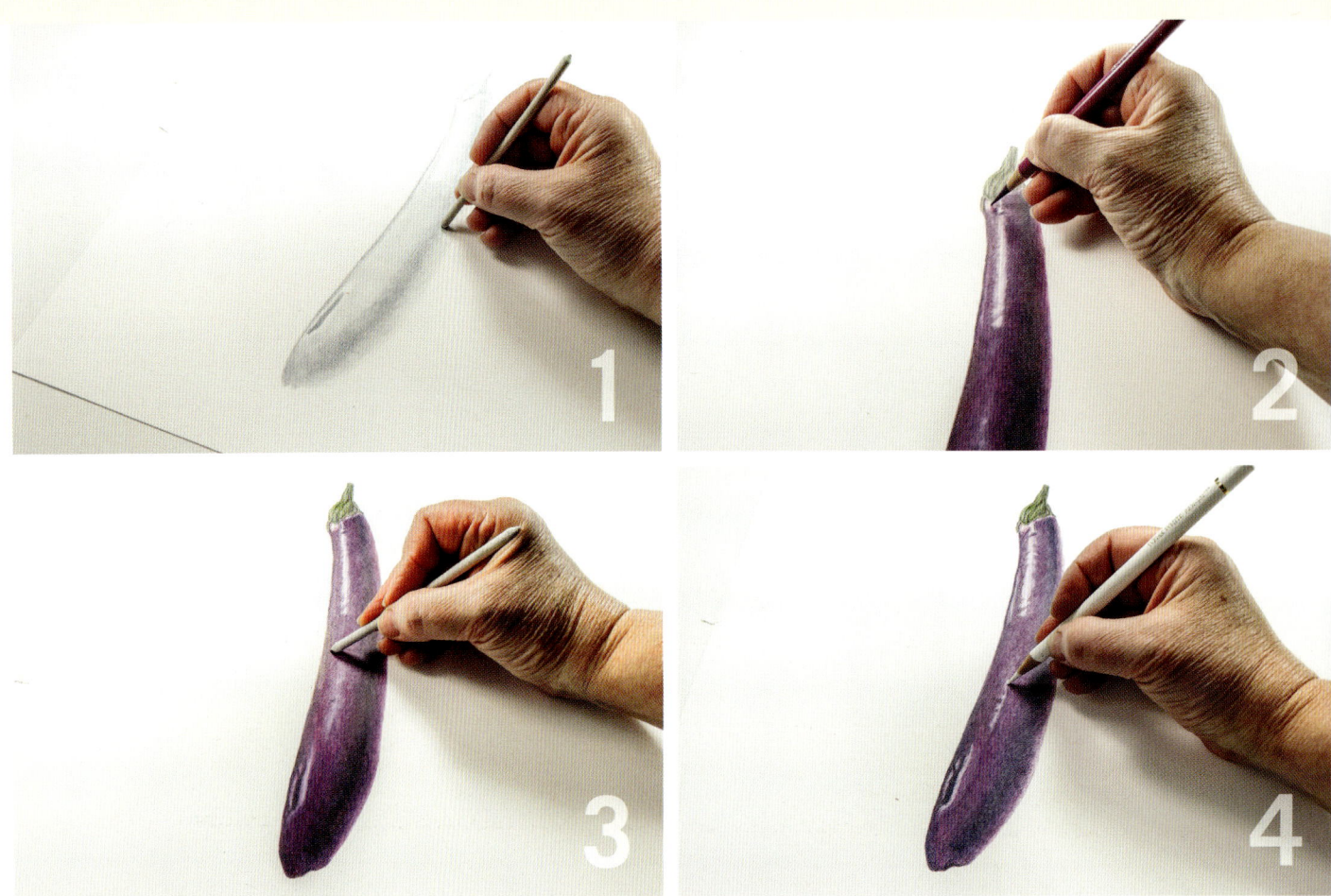

Draw in the outline, then begin to shape and shade the form using a dark indigo pencil. Use a blending stump to gently smooth and contour the shading of the eggplant.

Alternate layers of black grape, manganese violet, and fuchsia, keeping the right edge of the eggplant a lighter value. Concentrate the black grape in the shadows, and layer cadmium yellow over the darkest value to achieve a rich deep shadow. Add light red violet and crimson striations to the top of the eggplant just below the sepals and stem.

Layer the body of the eggplant, always avoiding the highlights, with fuchsia pencil and blend with a clean blending stump (rub the blending stump on a sandpaper block to clean it). Use chrome green opaque, chrome oxide green, and raw umber to color the sepal and stem.

Apply white pencil to create long linear highlights, softening their edges with warm gray. This portrays the waxy, shiny, almost rubbery quality of the skin. The right side of the eggplant still has a lighter tone of reflected light, suggesting the cylindrical nature of the fruit, and avoiding a flat, cutout look.

Shallot

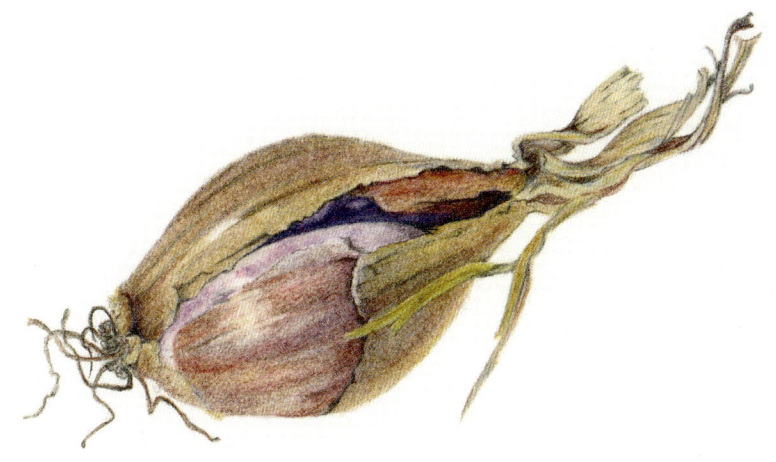

Shallot
Allium cepa var. *aggregatum*
Colored pencil on paper
3 ½ × 5 inches [8.75 × 12.5 cm]
© Tammy McEntee
HOURS TO COMPLETE: 12

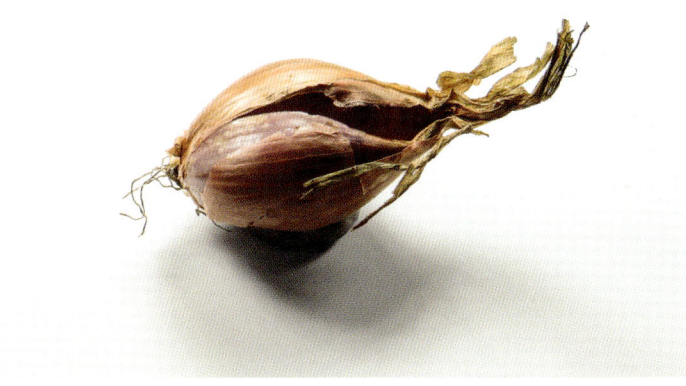

Allium cepa var. *aggregatum*, the scientific name for shallot—is a cluster of bulbs. Onions are a perennial favorite of botanical artists, partly because their papery covering (called a tunic) provides an interesting textural component. The shallot is held in position by placing it on a kneaded eraser.

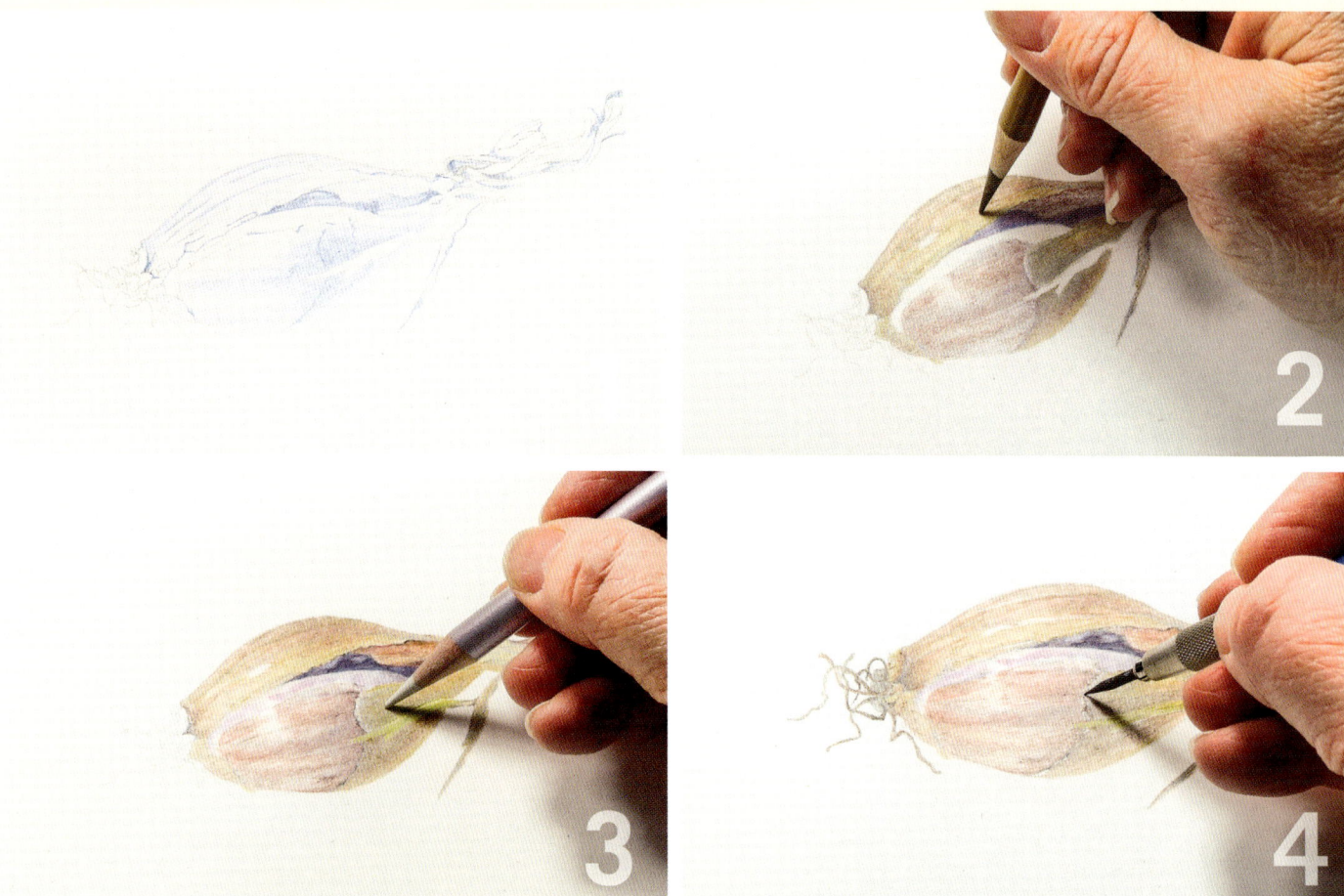

Begin this drawing with a grisaille in ultramarine blue, being sure to darken the space between the two bulbs. This monochromatic underdrawing provides structure for the rest of the drawing, with the darker shadows cast by the lighting on the lower right side of the lower bulb.

Layer caput mortuum, caput mortuum violet, burnt sienna, fuchsia, and brown ochre in the papery skin, lightly and loosely rather than trying to achieve one color. Follow the natural lines of the skin from the root end to the top, emphasizing the growth pattern. Use violet, purple violet, fuchsia, and indanthrene blue on the exposed section of the bulb.

Gently burnish the skin colors to just slightly blend them again in the direction of the growth; the beauty of the skin is lost if it is too heavily burnished. Add highlights with a very sharp ivory pencil. Continue to deepen each of the colors throughout, while maintaining the almost stripy quality of the coloration.

Draw the roots using burnt umber, burnt sienna, and brown ochre, then dab them with a kneaded eraser to soften the color. Use a lead holder with HB graphite to strengthen the thin shadows of the skin's layers and folds. Draw root bases with warm gray pencils and add detail with sharp graphite.

Grisaille technique has been used for hundreds of years in botanical illustration, especially in printmaking to achieve a grey-scale, which was often later hand-colored. In this tutorial, light and shadow are first drawn in with a dark sepia pencil. Color is then applied in layers on top of the grisaille, using both watercolor pencil and colored pencil.

Grisaille Techniques on Rose Hips with Colored Pencil and Watercolor Pencils

TUTOR: WENDY HOLLENDER

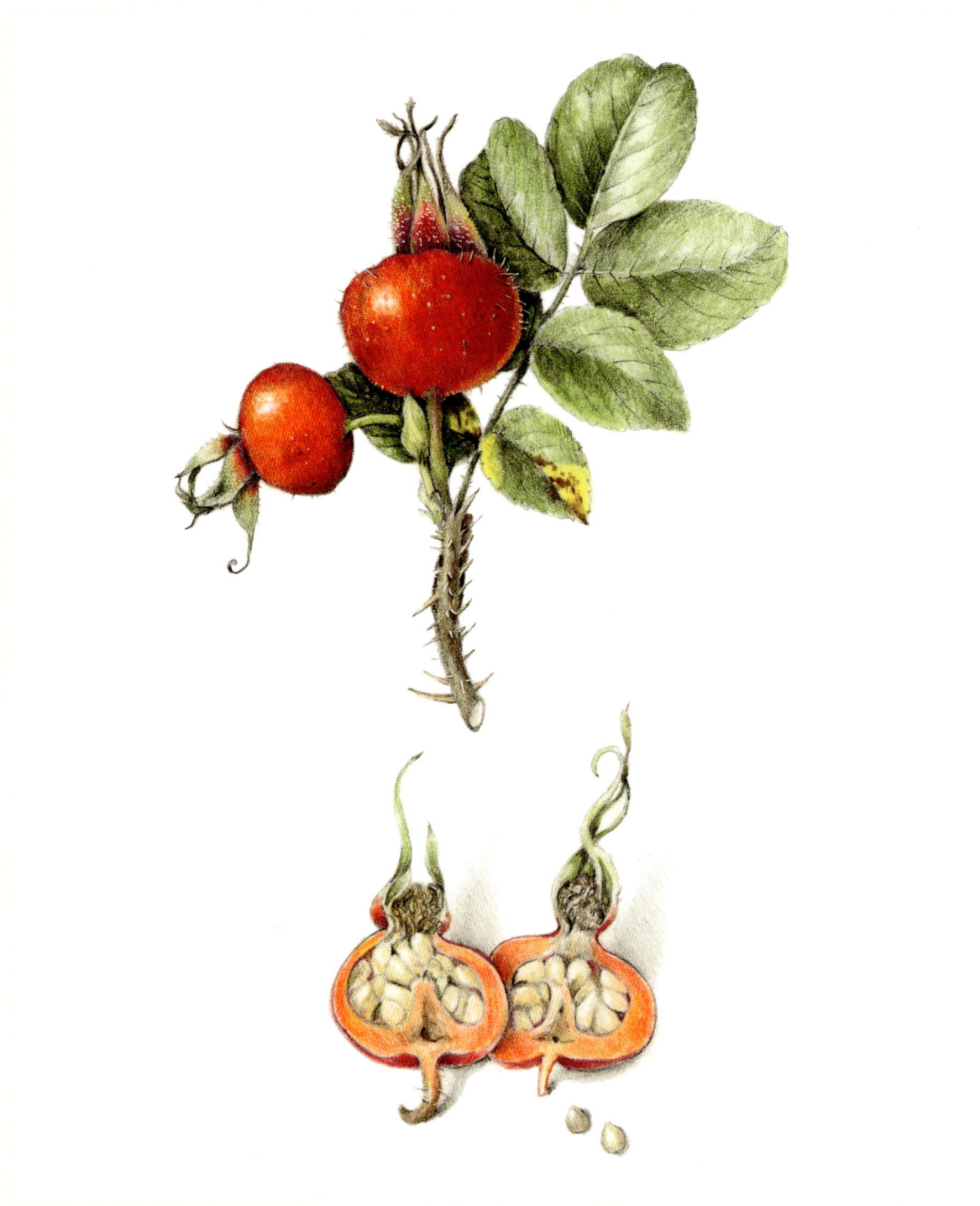

Rose Hips Colored pencil on paper 7 × 7 inches [17.5 × 17.5 cm] © Wendy Hollender

HOURS TO COMPLETE: 10

MATERIALS: Pencil sharpener; drafting brush; clipping shears; container for water; magnifying glass; paper towels; watercolor pencils; watercolor brushes (nos. 000, 3, 6); 140 lb. [300 gsm] hot-pressed watercolor paper; sand eraser; kneaded and white-plastic erasers; transparent ruler; high-quality colored pencils; graphite pencil H; embossing tools.

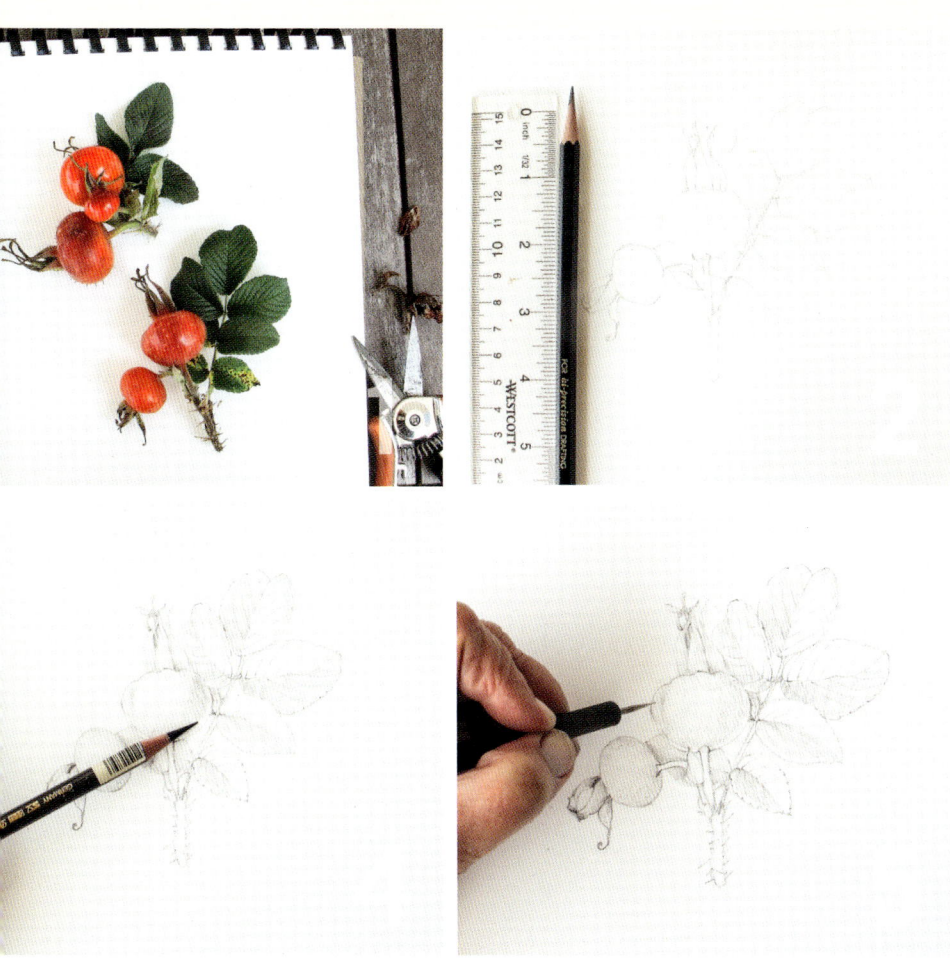

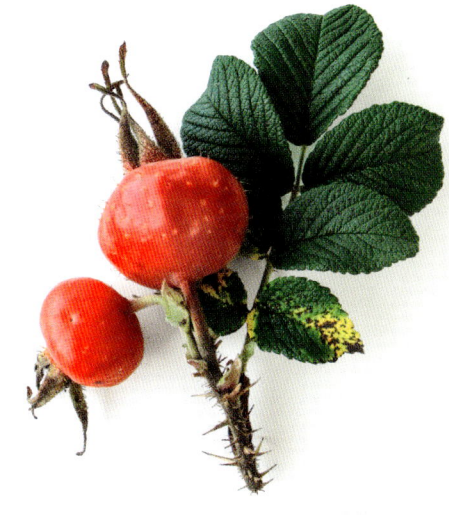

Collect cuttings of rose hips with some leaves and stem attached. Watch out for the sharp prickles! Cut more than one specimen so you can plan a pleasing composition on the page and choose the best specimen. Cut a long branch, then at your drawing table cut up samples to compare and measure for your composition.

Measure your subject and draw it life size on a sheet of paper with a graphite pencil. Use light pressure while making this drawing. Erase as needed and remeasure for a precise drawing. Be sure to have some overlapping areas of fruit, leaves, and stem for good contrast and depth. Plan a focal point for your drawing.

Illuminate your subject with a light source from the front and upper left. This creates a clear shadow side with a good highlight on the upper-left quadrant of the rose hip.

Grisaille drawing uses a single neutral color to develop form before adding color. Begin the grisaille drawing with a dark sepia-colored pencil. Always work with very sharp pencils and sharpen them often. Map out the tones from light to dark. Indicate highlights, shadows, overlaps, and reflected highlights. Add tone to the form with a clear shadow side and leave highlights of empty paper.

Using a fine embossing tool, press into the paper to create fine light hairs on the rose hips. Add tone over these embossed areas using the side of a colored pencil. The finely embossed hairs will resist the pencil and begin to show up. Avoid using color over areas that should appear white. Darken the objects behind overlapping areas to create clear spatial distinctions between objects.

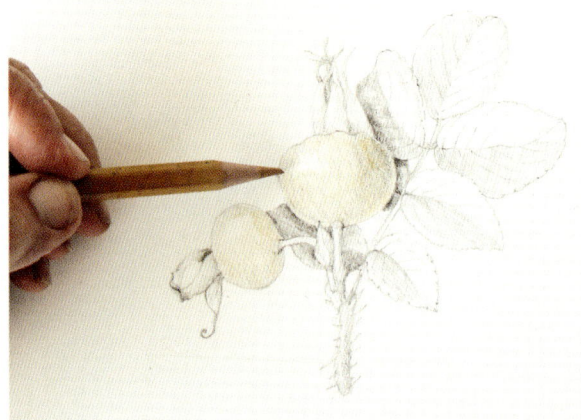

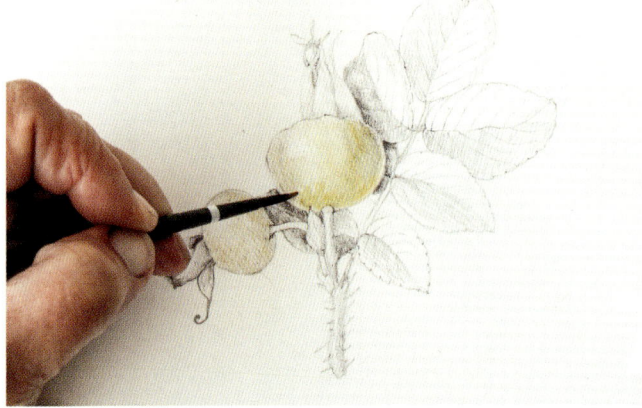

Introduce color over the grisaille drawing. Apply a yellow ochre watercolor pencil in a dry technique, as if it is a regular colored pencil. Graduate the values from light to dark and leave the highlight areas empty. Apply the color directly over the dark sepia-colored pencil. The grisaille will continue to define the form as color is layered.

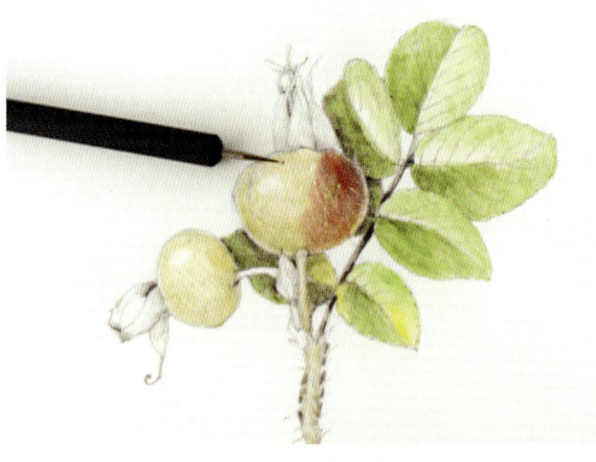

Wet a watercolor brush and use the wet brush to carefully spread the pigment of the watercolor pencil. Work from the highlights out so the highlights remain empty paper. Gradually transition the pigment from light to dark in the shadow areas. Be careful not to obliterate the finely embossed hairs with color.

Using an embossing tool, add more hairs and spots on the rose hip. By pressing into the drawing in an irregular way, create the fine hairs and spots that look natural. Do not use wet watercolor pencil over the embossed areas, as the color will penetrate those areas. To keep those areas light enough to show, use dry pencils over these areas.

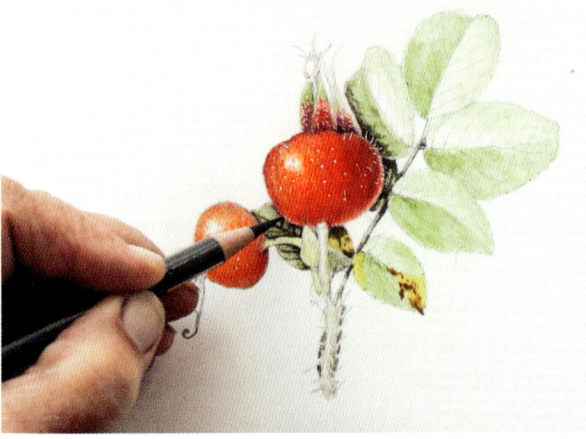

With a variety of colored pencils, add color to the fruit, sepals, leaves, and stem. The embossed areas will begin to appear, because the pressed-in areas resist the pencil. Continue to develop overlaps with darker pencils, and saturate color—remembering to keep the form looking three-dimensional.

Next, apply a yellow watercolor pencil in a dry technique on areas of the leaves that are yellowed. Then add green watercolor pencil on the leaves, carefully creating a darker and lighter side of the leaves. The dark sepia grisaille from step 4 is still visible and sets up the different lighting on the two sides of the leaf.

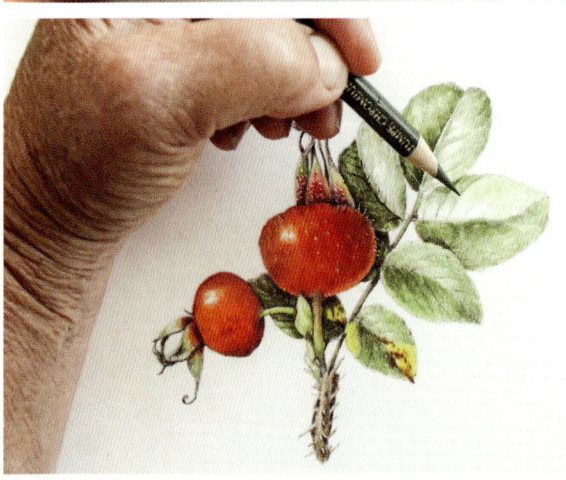

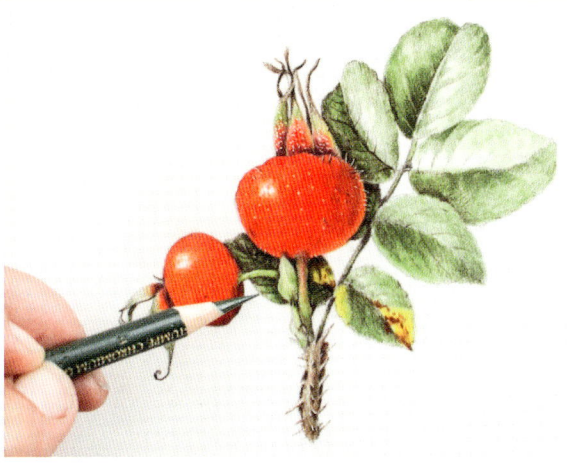

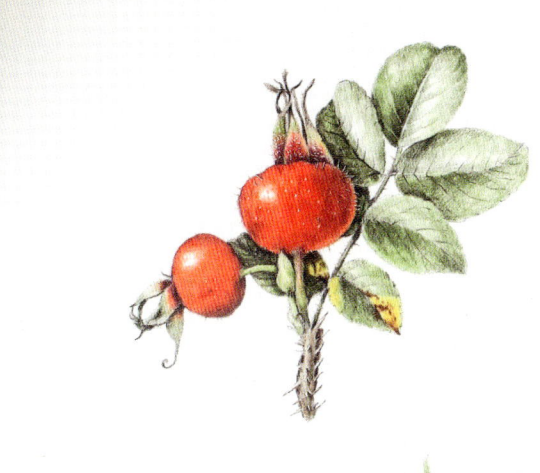

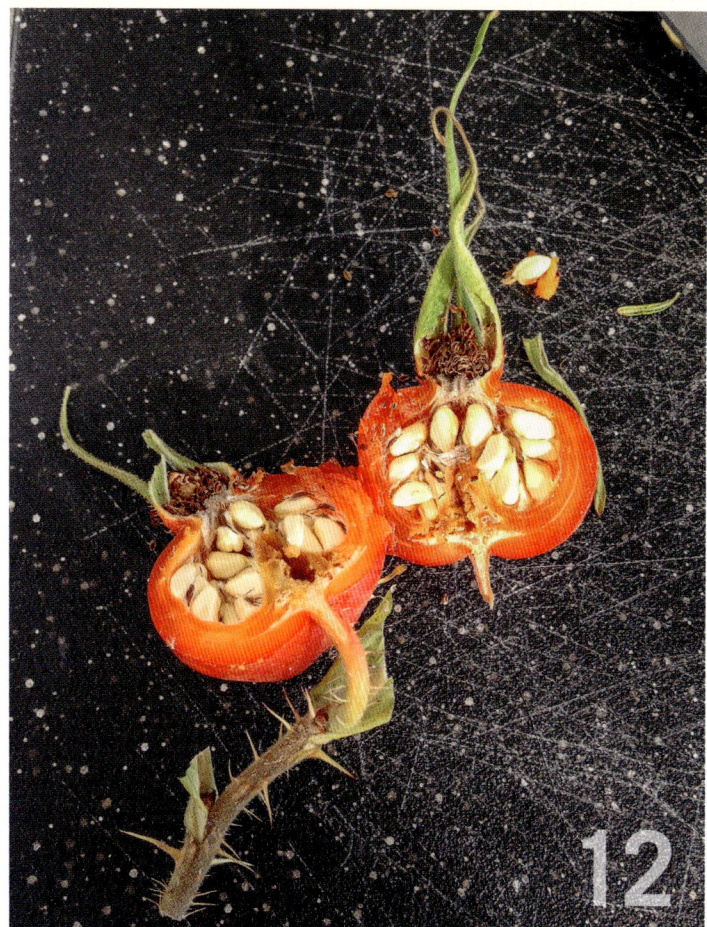

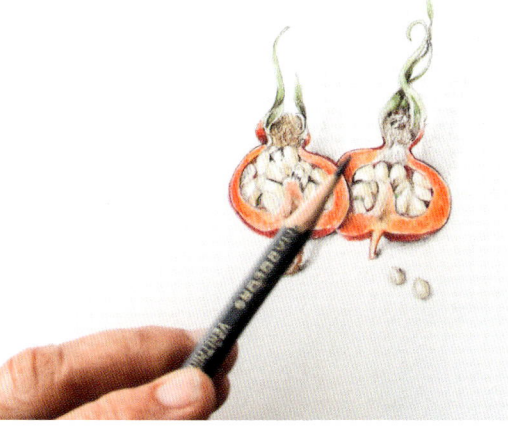

Add the veining and browning details to the leaves. Layer color with various dry colored pencils, saturating the color and using sufficient pressure. Keep a range of tones from light to dark. Darken behind the fruits, so that the rose hips seem to sit on top of the leaves. Maintain the reflected light on the dark edge of the rose hip.

Cut open a rose hip to add a longitudinal section of the fruit. This adds interest to the composition as well as information about the fruit. Approach this illustration in the same way as the original drawing: First draw the subject with graphite pencil, then complete the dark sepia grisaille, and finally add the details and many layers of colors.

Add cast shadows from the dissected fruit, suggesting that the halves are sitting on a surface. Using a hard-lead gray colored pencil creates a fine, subtle texture. When you are creating a cast shadow, place the darkest tone next to the fruit, then gradually lighten the value until the shadow fades into the paper, without a strong outline. Toward the end, burnish over the fruit and near the highlight with a cream pencil to make the colors blend together. To do this, press hard with the pencil and make the highlight smaller so that it does not look like an empty space.

ONE SUBJECT, TWO MEDIA: PEN AND INK AND COLORED PENCIL

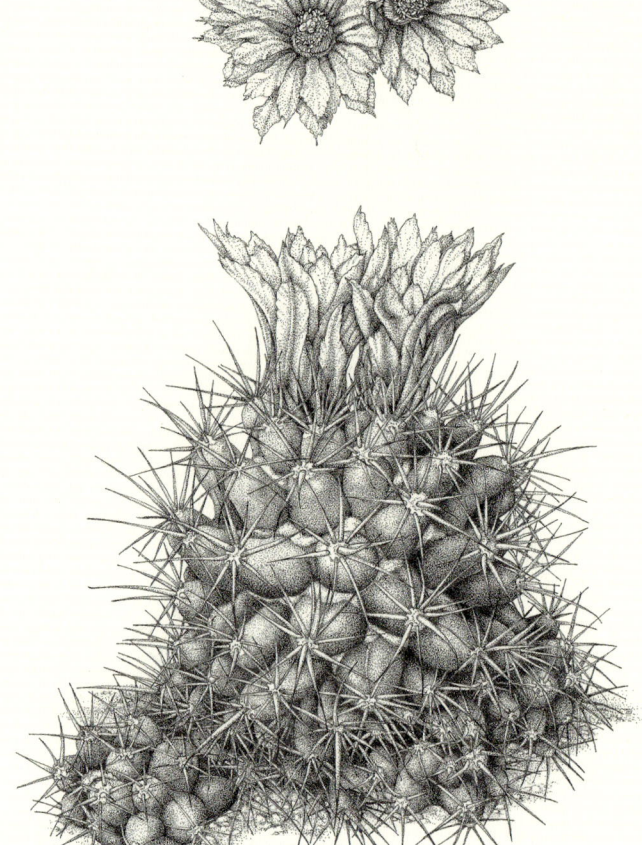

Artist Joan McGann specializes in illustrating cacti and desert plants. The first time she was able to draw a Pima pineapple cactus, she chose to render it in pen and ink. The unusual depth and volume of the tubercles and the thickness of the spines were of interest, and with pen and ink, the contrast created can be dramatic. A more delicate hand was needed for the flowers, and that delicacy is conveyed through a stippling technique.

Technical pens in sizes 0.3 mm and 0.25 mm were used in the drawing. The line work around the spines was inked first, using a slightly heavier line on the shaded side. The 0.25 mm pen was used to outline all the forms in the body and flower of the cactus. The remaining parts of the drawing are stippled from dark values to light, creating depth and form. Some stippling was added in the spines to create volume there as well.

Pima Pineapple Cactus
Coryphantha robustispina
Pen and ink on illustration board
16 ½ × 12 inches [41.25 × 30 cm]
© Joan McGann
HOURS TO COMPLETE: 100

While inking the drawing, McGann became enamored with the delicate pale yellow petals of the flowers and the creamy greens and blue-greens of the cactus body. The original drawing was transferred to illustration board using wax-free blue transfer paper. Using colored pencils, the spine outlines were drawn in with shades of violet, brown, and neutrals to define their edges in front of the tubercles. Then the outlines of everything else were drawn in the appropriate colors.

Color was built up in layers, avoiding the spines until all the volume had been created. Once the remainder was nearing completion, the spines were drawn in. Then, using a light cream pencil in light areas and darker colors for darker areas, pressure was applied to burnish the surface of the cactus body to create a smooth finish. The white of the wool between the tubercles was strengthened, along with the highlights on the spines. A little bit of surrounding ground was added at the bottom to soften the image into the page.

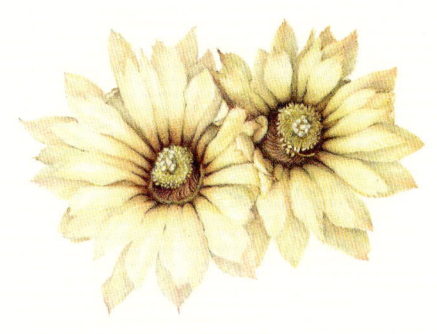

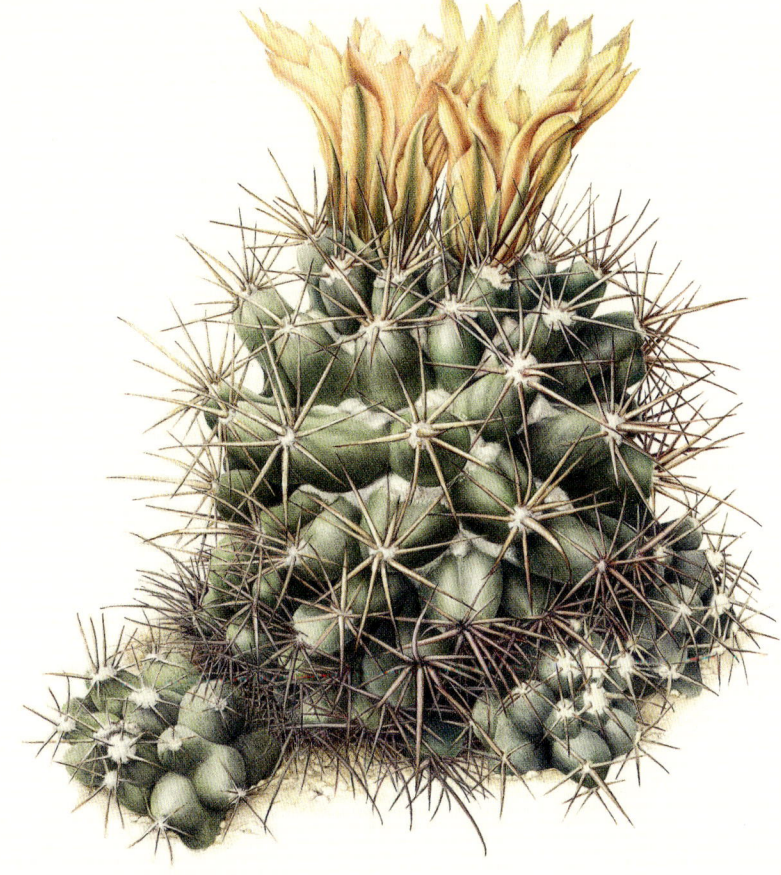

Pima pineapple cactus
Coryphantha robustispina
Colored pencil on illustration board
28 × 19 inches [70 × 47.5 cm]
© Joan McGann
HOURS TO COMPLETE: 100

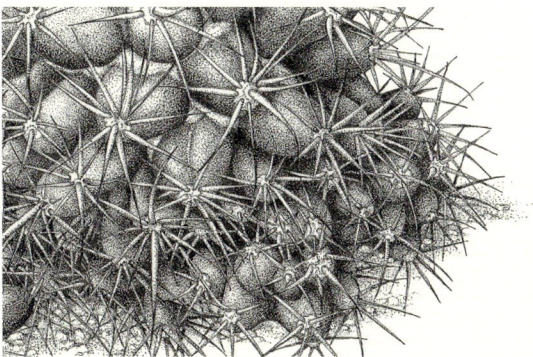

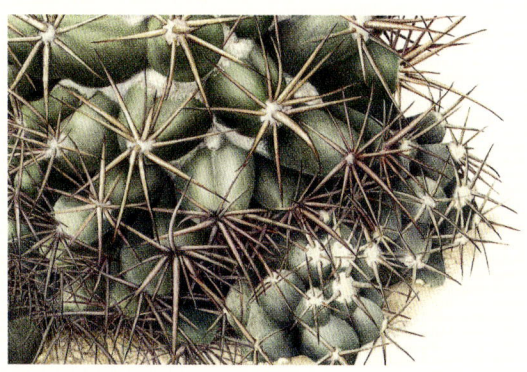

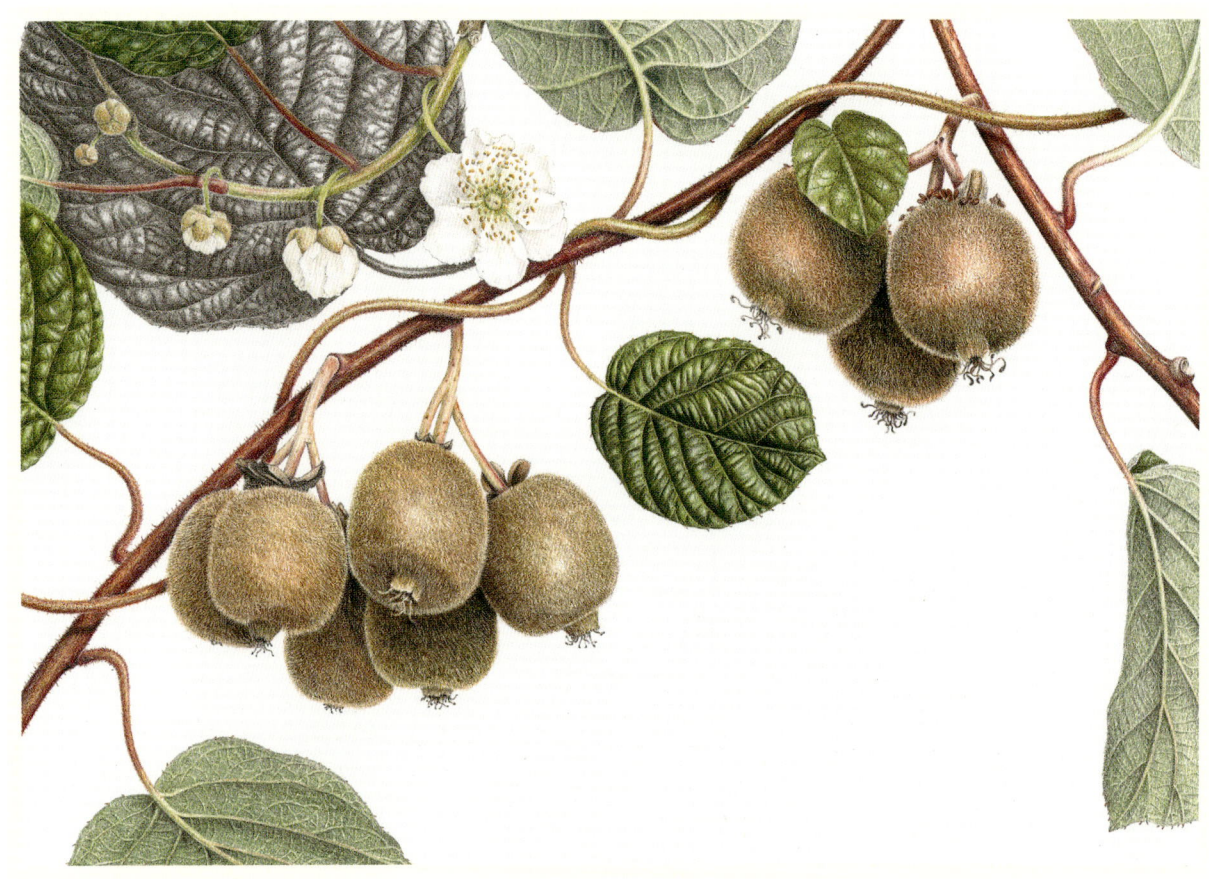

Kiwi Life Cycle Colored pencil and graphite on paper 10 ½ × 15 ½ inches [26.25 × 38.75 cm] © Ann Swan

HOURS TO COMPLETE: 36

MATERIALS: Colorless blender pencil; a selection of green, ochre, brown, and dark red colored pencils; alcohol-based solvent pen; 0.5 mm embossing tool; larger embossing tool; synthetic filbert brush; lead holders with HB and 2B leads; 2H 0.3 mm retractable pencil; a selection of graphite finely hand sharpened pencils 9H, 3H, H, F, HB, 3B, and 9B; craft knife.

A combination of colored pencil and graphite is used to depict this complicated kiwi vine in its flowering and fruiting stages. A variety of techniques, including embossing, burnishing, resist, and color and graphite layering, are used. The graphite leaf serves as a backdrop and adds interest and dimension. The entwined, curving stems lead the eye through the picture and create interesting negative spaces.

Kiwi Vine in Colored Pencil and Graphite

TUTOR: ANN SWAN

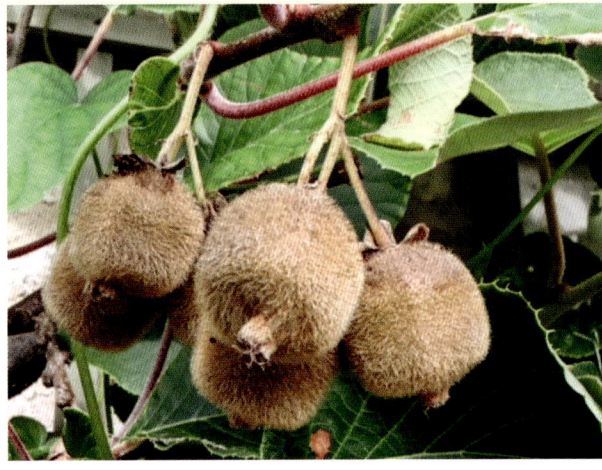

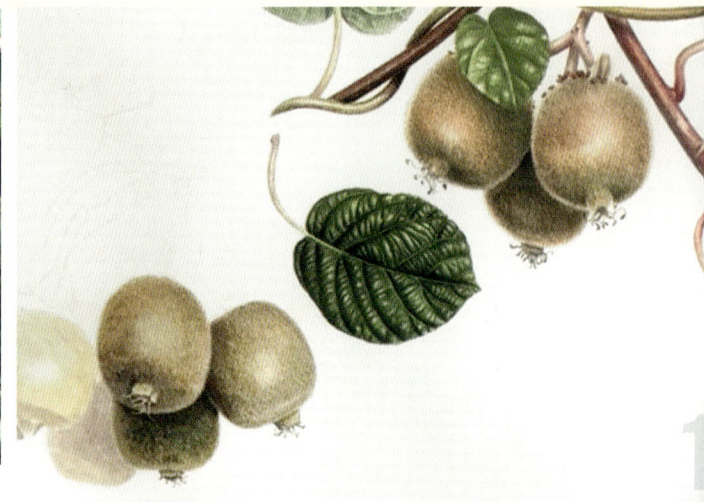

The artist has a kiwi vine growing in her own garden, but she hadn't seen it fruiting until traveling to the Loire Valley in France, where she was inspired by its profusion of fruit. The plant is nearly completely covered in hairs, with shiny leaf tops and velvety backs.

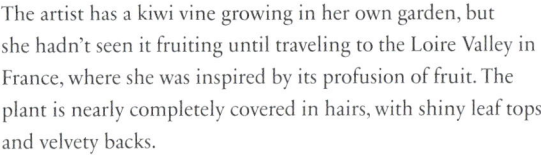

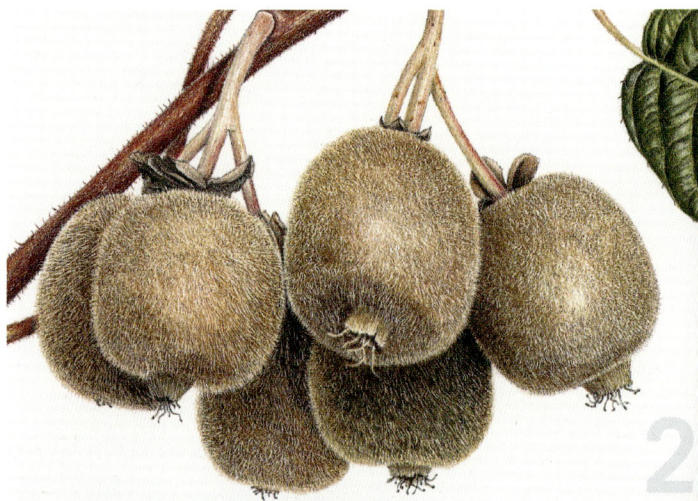

Shade the fruits first using a mix of dark sepia and various grays, as seen at the far left, with white paper saved for highlights. Then blend these pale undertones using an alcohol-based solvent pen.

Create the hairs on the surface of the fruits with a fine 0.5 mm embossing tool. The embossing should be done all at once, to avoid leaving bald patches, using firm multidirectional strokes over the entire surface of each fruit. The body colors of the fruits—olive green yellowish, bistre, nougat, brown ochre, and ginger root—are then layered over the fruits, making the hairs pop out.

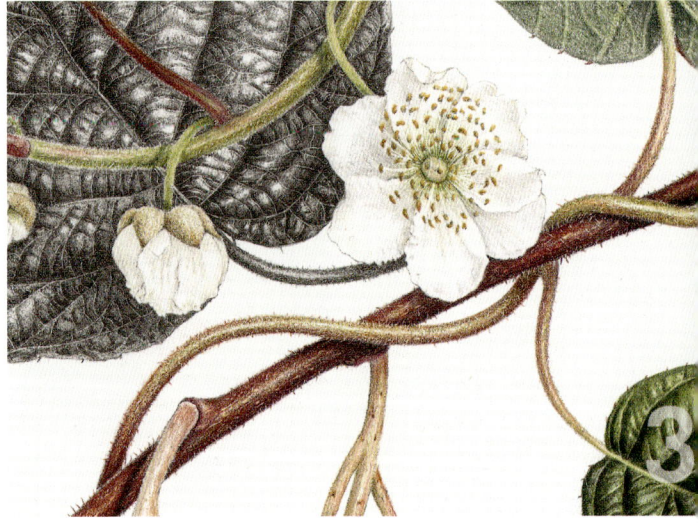

After drawing a very faint outline around the flower, incise the filaments with a 0.5 mm embossing tool, then draw in the anthers with light yellow ochre and shade them with the 0.3 mm retractable graphite pencil. Shade the petals across the embossed lines using a combination of May green in the center and light violet so the filaments are revealed. The edges of the petals are slightly emphasized with these soft shade colors, so the flower is more visible on the white paper. The graphite leaf acts as background for some of the petals.

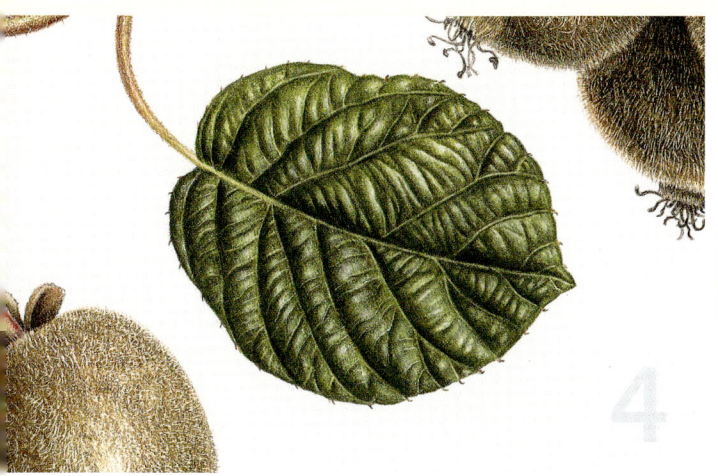

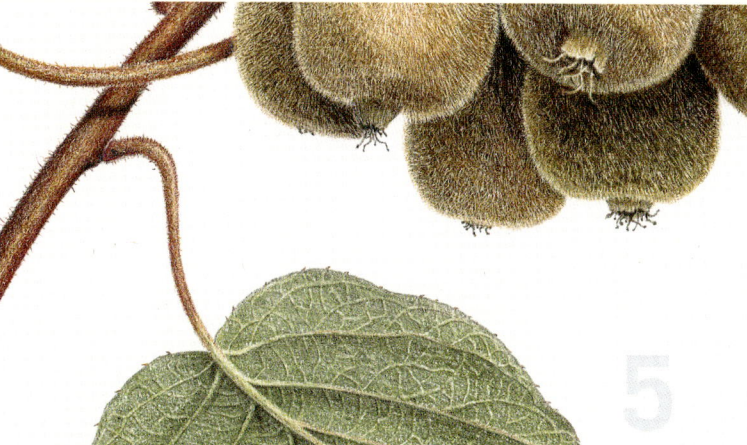

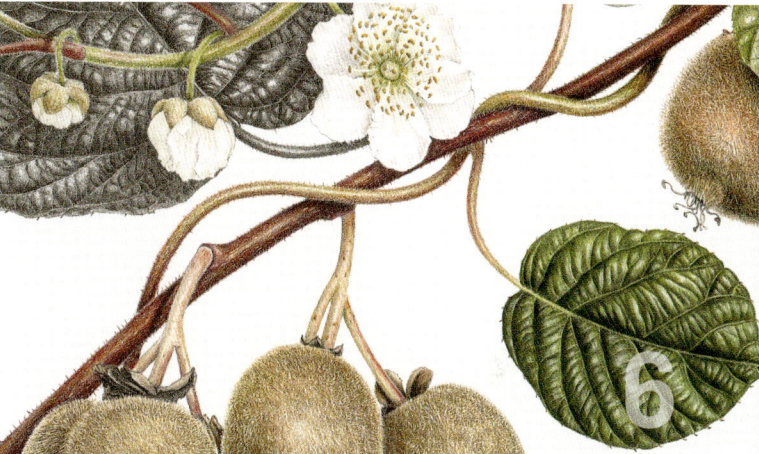

On this glossy leaf top, first incise the veins using a sharp ivory pencil applied fairly heavily to create a resist effect. The colors for the leaf are a combination of chromium green opaque, earth green yellowish, and May green. Layer these up from dark to light using a darkish grey for any shadows. Leave the white of the paper for any highlights, and soften those highlights using a colorless blender pencil applied with pressure to smooth the colors together. Each vein causes an undulation in the leaf, and values are varied to show these undulations.

For the backs of the leaves, strongly emphasize the veins with ivory, drawn with pressure. Emboss the hairs along the veins and randomly over the leaf surface. To create a wider, softer point, colored pencils in earth green, chromium green opaque, and May green were deliberately blunted on one side using fine silicone paper and then applied evenly across the surface to pick up the grain of the paper and create the soft, velvety leaf texture. Finally, after burnishing with pale sage to soften the color, draw the cast shadows under the veins using a sharply pointed earth green.

To create the soft creamy glow of the stems, first apply a cream blender pen, leaving highlights as white paper. Next, emboss the stem hairs and create the larger light highlights with ivory resist. Apply dark indigo and Payne's gray for the stem shadows, and use red-violet, burnt carmine, Venetian red, earth green and May green in various combinations to build up the color. Burnish the paler stems using ivory to soften them. Finally, use extremely sharp burnt carmine and red-violet pencils to flick out the colored hairs from the stem edges.

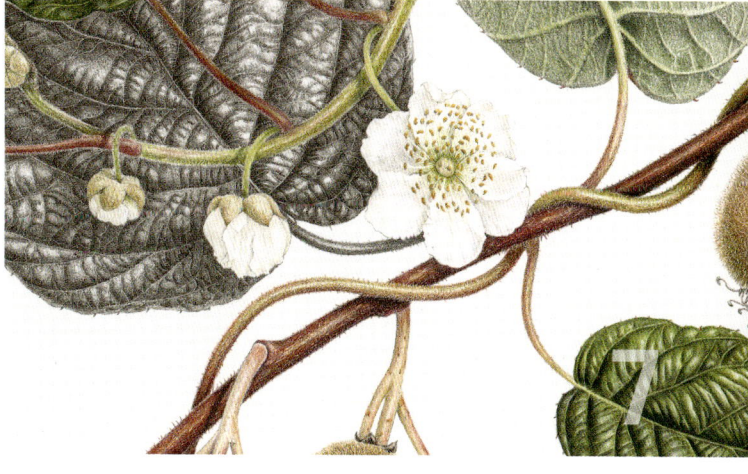

Draw the graphite leaf last so that the embossed hairs along the edges of the stems and leaves pop out as white paper and to avoid smudging. Incise the veins using 1.0 mm and 0.5 mm embossing tools, and use a 9H pencil in the shaded areas. Then apply the leaf shading, using a range of pencils from 3B to 3H and using a shallow elliptical stroke to produce an even coverage and smooth tonal gradations. Leave the highlights as white paper and then soften them by gently brushing the graphite across them with a small filbert brush.

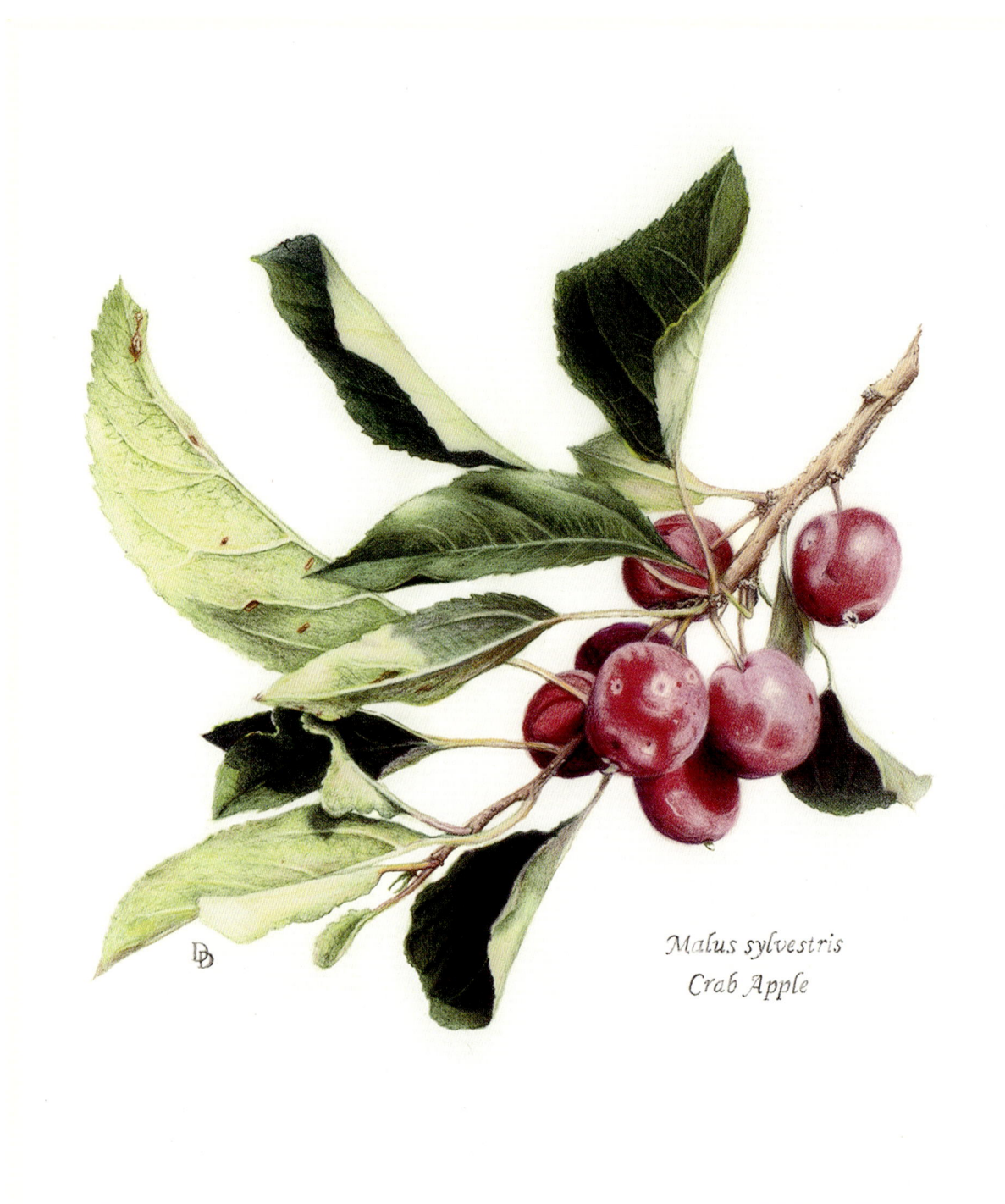

Malus sylvestris
Crab Apple

Common crabapple *Malus sylvestris* Colored pencil on drafting film 8 × 8 inches [20 × 20 cm]
© Dorothy DePaulo HOURS TO COMPLETE: 9

MATERIALS Pencil sharpener; double-sided (frosted on both sides) drafting film; household cleaner; old paintbrush; abrasive sponge; cotton swabs; retractable eraser; five brands of wax-based colored pencils with varying degrees of hardness, waxiness, or pigment; standard waxed paper.

A Crabapple Branch in Colored Pencil on Film

TUTOR: DOROTHY DEPAULO

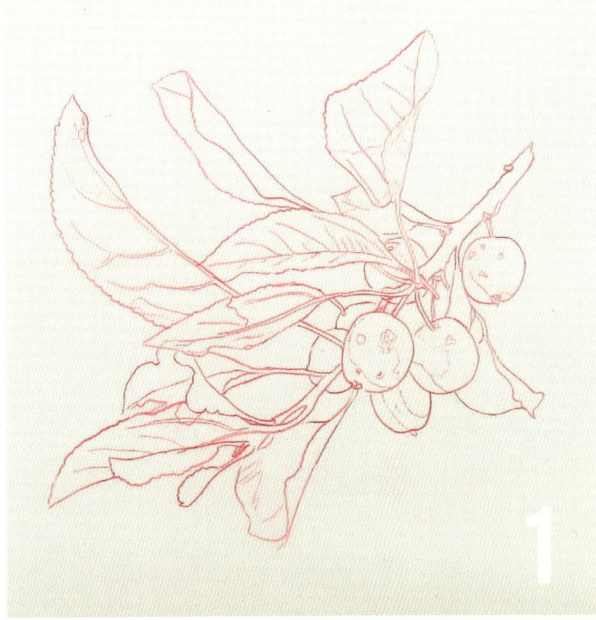

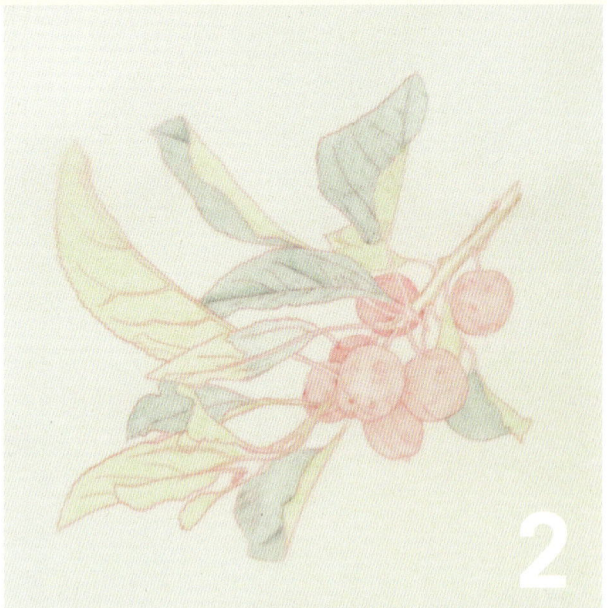

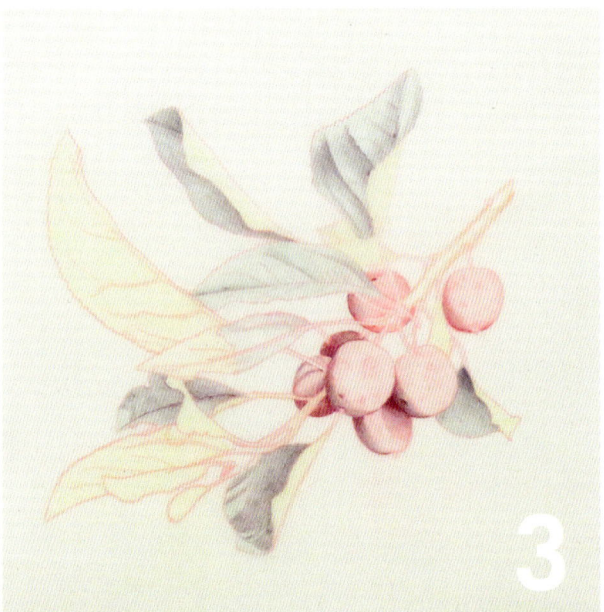

To begin, make a detailed line drawing in a bright color using a hard colored pencil on paper. A sheet of drafting film will be placed over the line drawing, so it is important that the lines be bright enough to show through the translucent film.

Lightly tape the line drawing to the drawing board, then tape the drafting film over it. Using extremely light pencil pressure, make very small overlapping circles to apply the first layer of color, making it as even as possible. There is no need to go over the outlines—they just serve as a guideline for where to place the color.

Next, apply a layer of a very dark hue of purple where the shadows are the darkest. It is difficult to get an even dark layer over an area that already has several colors on drafting film, so place the darkest tones first.

Match the colors to the plant specimen as closely as possible. Using as many different colors as necessary, create the rich color of the fruit by building up layer upon layer. A mix of different brands of colored pencil may be used—choose the pencils by color rather than brand.

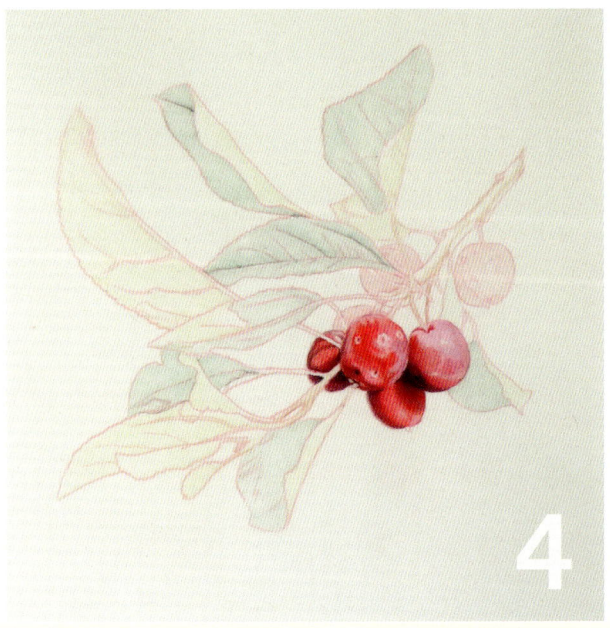

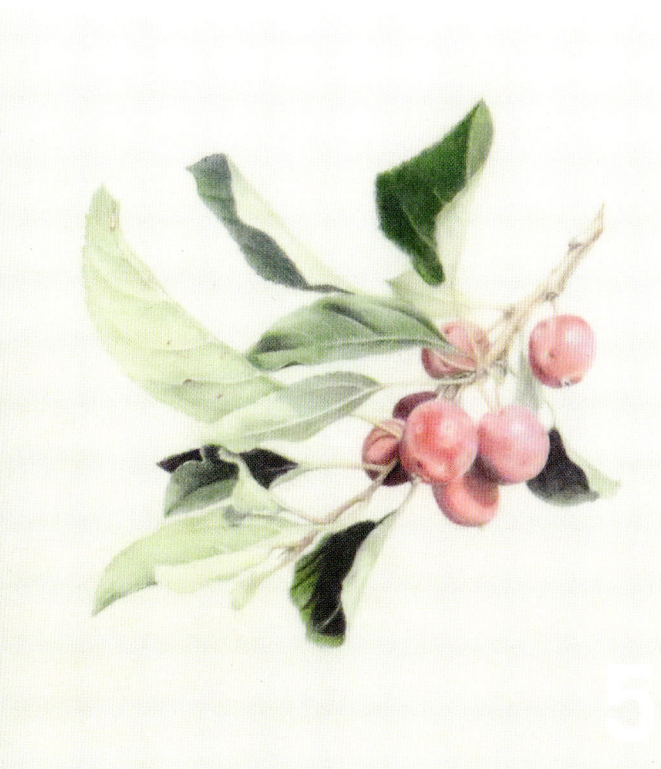

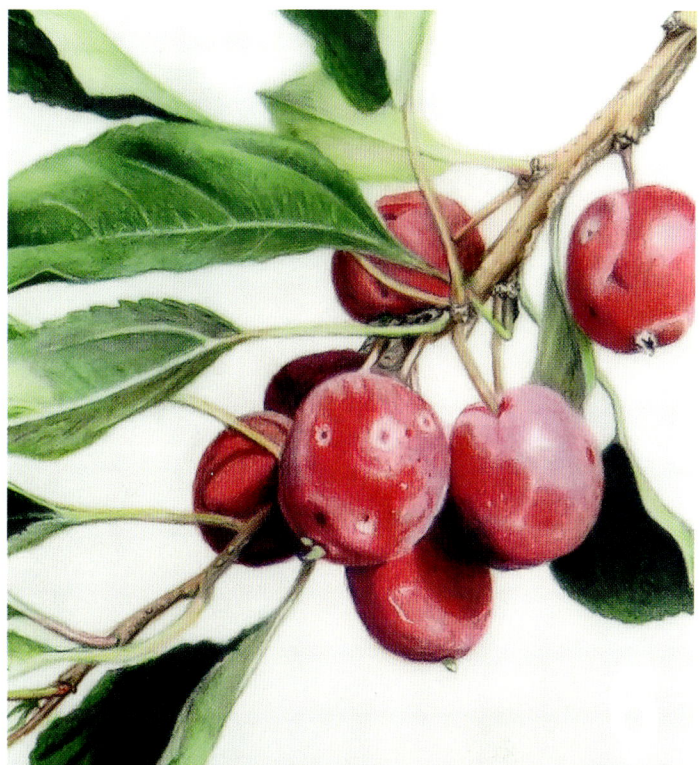

To achieve very dark or intense colors, turn the drafting film over and add dark purple to the reverse side of the drafting film in the very darkest areas. Shy away from using blacks or grays as they tend to deaden the colors.

Begin in the center of the drawing and work outward. Always consider each part of the drawing in relationship to the whole image. For instance, a green leaf near a red crabapple will reflect red more than a leaf that is farther away. Once the entire painting is defined, remove the line drawing from underneath.

To make the small veins, place a piece of waxed paper over the leaf and draw firmly with a hard, colored pencil, lifting the color from the film underneath. Make improvements, such as erasing to lighten color, adding deeper tones, and sharpening edges as needed. Finally, using household cleaner on a cotton swab, remove any smudges or minute flakes of colored pencil pigment.

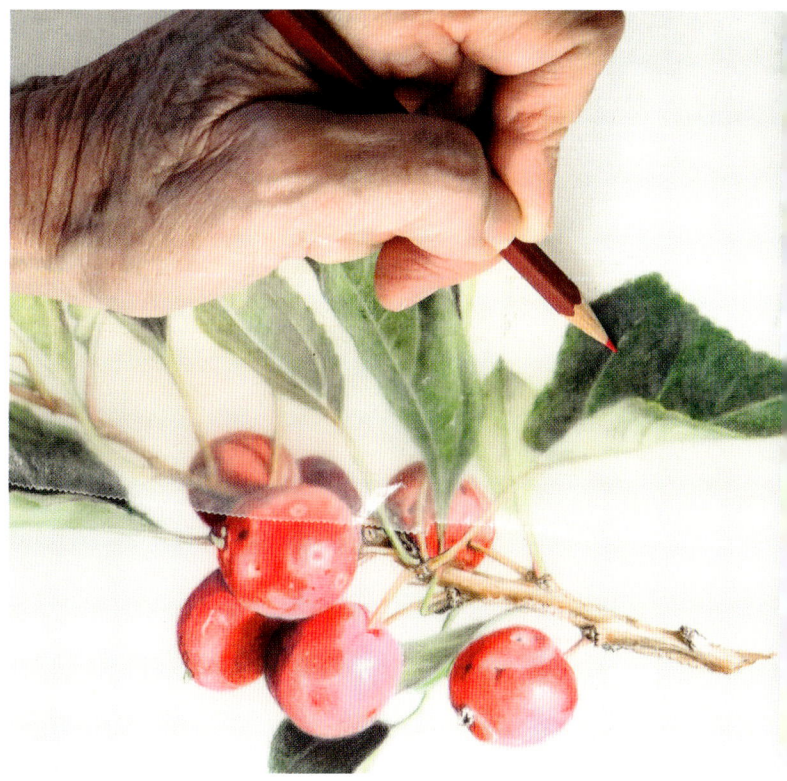

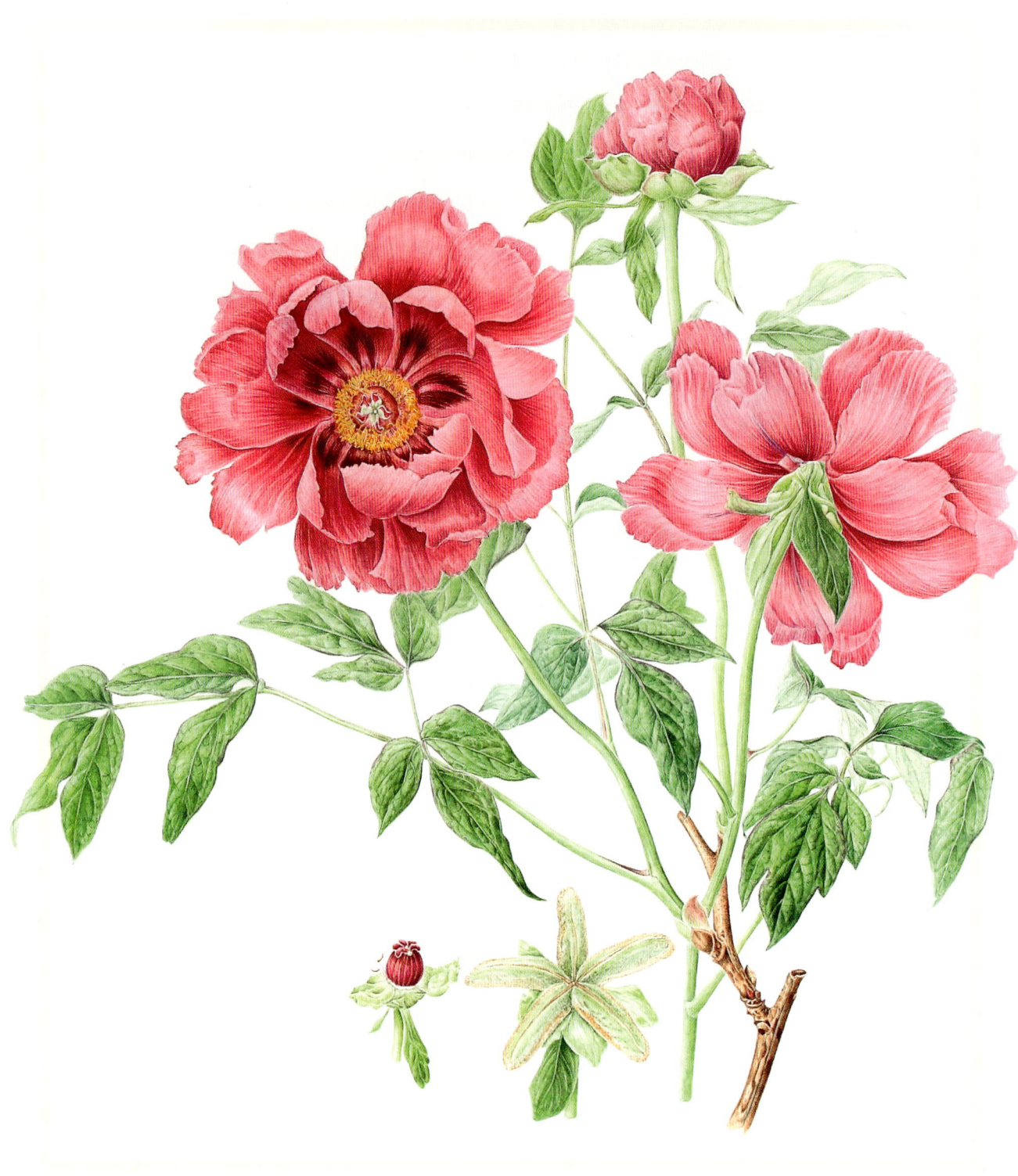

Paeonia suffruticosa Watercolor on paper 21 × 19 inches [52.5 × 47.5 cm] © Jee-Yeon Koo

WATERCOLOR ON PAPER

Watercolor has historically been the most used medium for creating botanical artworks, and it continues to be so today. Watercolor's broad range of techniques for application, expansive range of pigments, transparency, and ability to portray fine details are some of the reasons it dominates the field. Manufacturers are continually innovating and introducing new pigments and binders, and focusing more on pigment permanence. Their liquid nature provides for some wet techniques not available in most other media, and these can be used alongside drier techniques.

WATERCOLOR ON PAPER

Techniques and Tutorials

Watercolor on Paper

Properties of Watercolor Paints

TUTOR: SUSAN T. FISHER

For artists, there are many good reasons to become familiar with the properties of watercolor paints, among them are mastery of the medium and conservation of the resulting artwork. Artists need to know their materials and predict how the materials will perform during the working process. Following is a guide to help artists understand the properties of watercolor paint, and additional information can be acquired from watercolor manufacturers and on the internet.

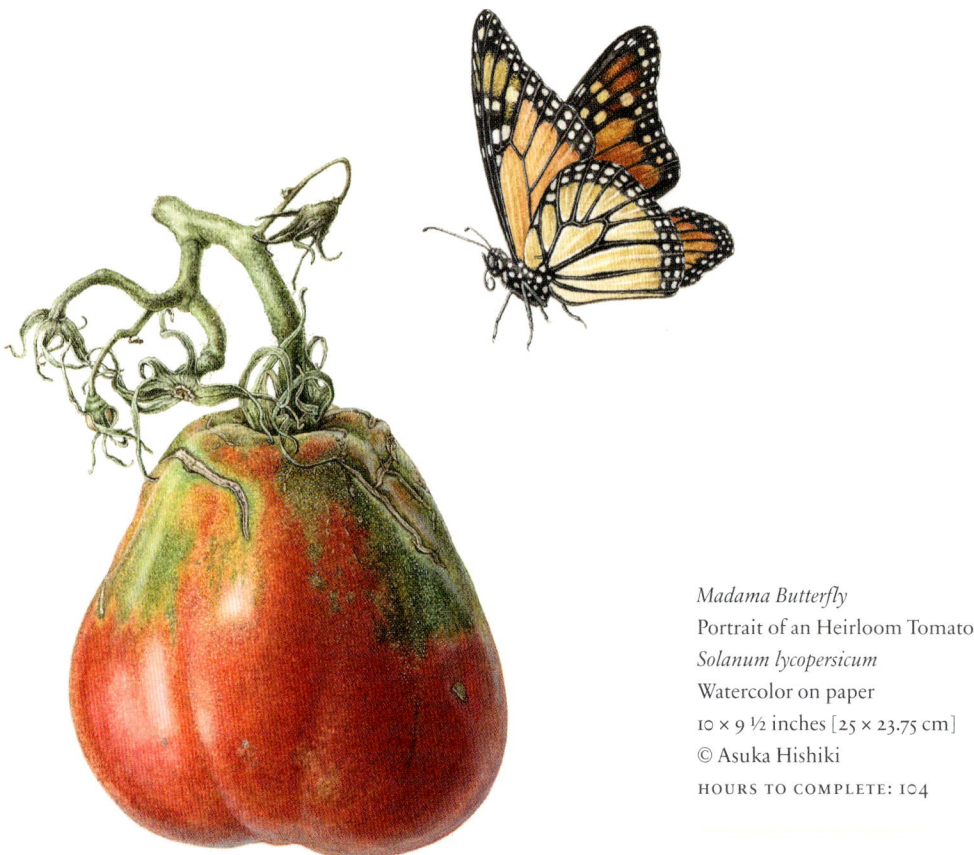

Madama Butterfly
Portrait of an Heirloom Tomato
Solanum lycopersicum
Watercolor on paper
10 × 9 ½ inches [25 × 23.75 cm]
© Asuka Hishiki
HOURS TO COMPLETE: 104

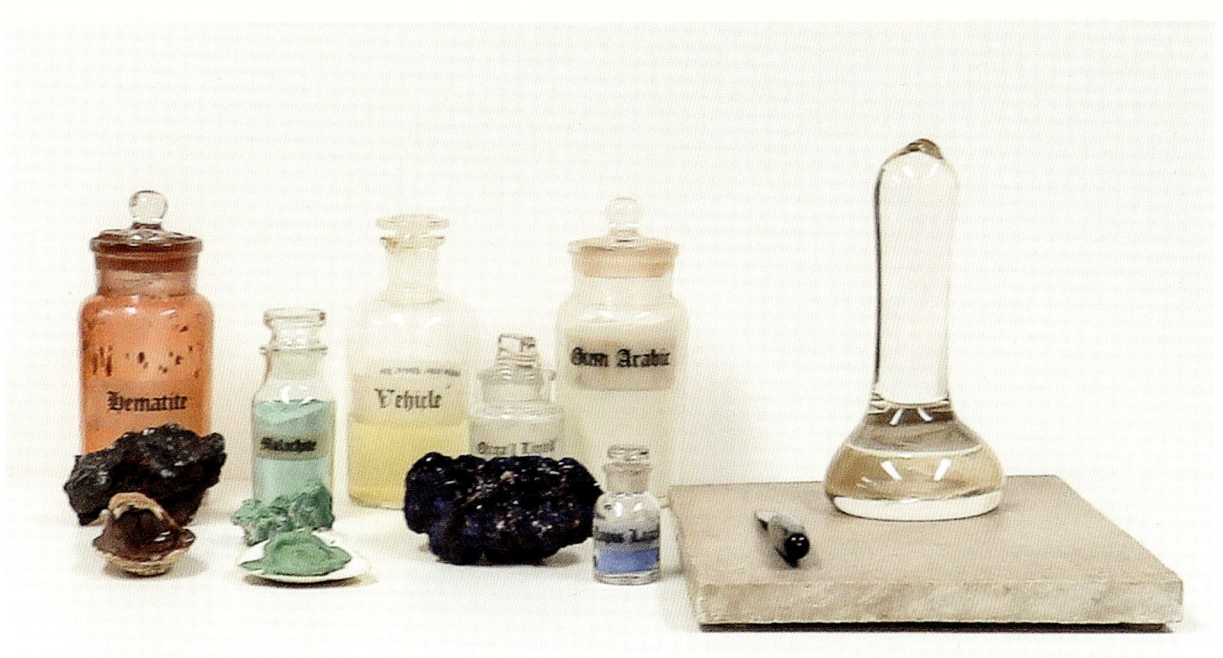

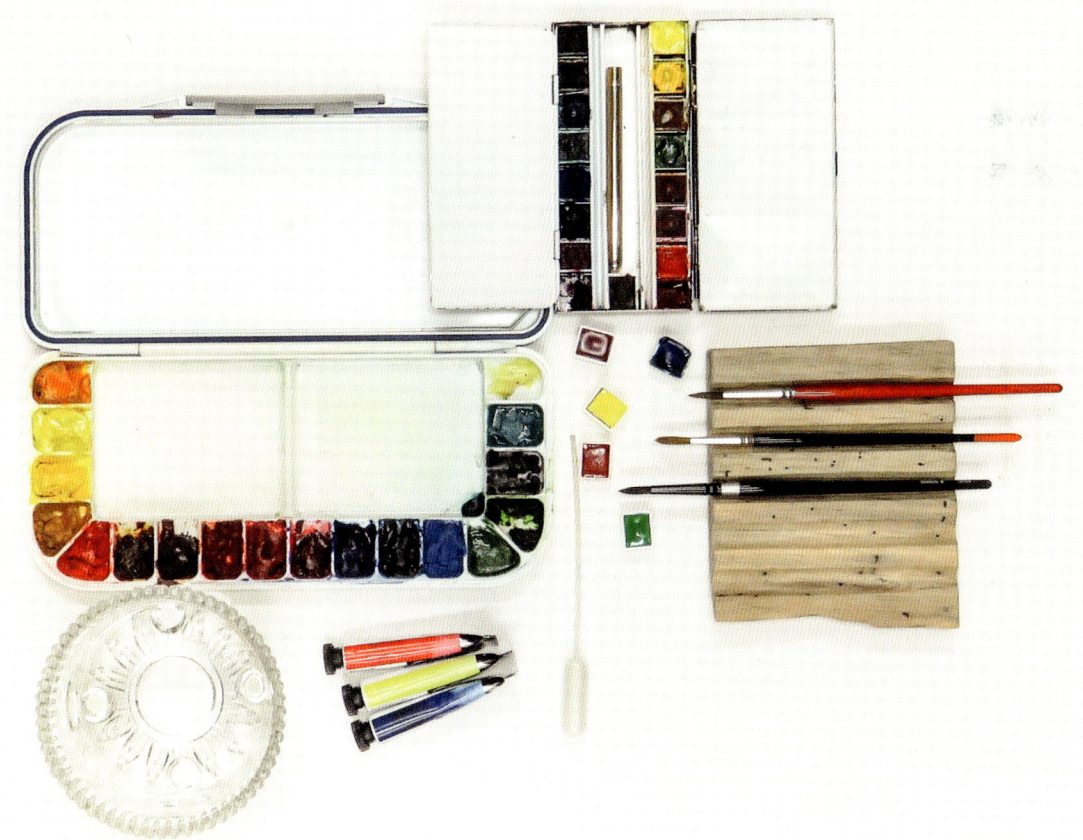

TOP Some of the components of watercolor paints, including minerals, ground pigments, and gum arabic. Also shown is a glass muller sitting on a grinding stone (it is still possible to make paints using a muller, pigments, and other ingredients).

ABOVE Watercolors are available in tubes or pans. Also shown are palettes, a glass of water, a pipette for delivering a measured amount of water to the paints, a retractable travel brush in a field palette, and brushes on a brush tray.

There is more than meets the eye when it comes to ingredients in watercolor tubes or pans. Every watercolor brand includes and excludes a variety of ingredients to suit their own specific needs. Typical ingredients in watercolors include a binder along with humectants to keep the paint moist, and deodorizers to keep the paint smelling as pleasant as possible. Extenders are often used to improve the paint's handling qualities, and brighteners are used to enhance the color. Dextrin or glycerin can maintain moisture content or smooth out the mixing ability of the paint and fungicides keep the paint from molding. Tube paints provide a moist ready-to-go color and pan paints are convenient for travel. Many artists have a preference, because they appreciate the handling characteristics of one type over the other. More commonly, artists keep both options available. Watercolor pencils used both wet and dry share similar properties with tubes and pans, although in a pencil form.

Binders

There are a variety of binders for artists' paints, including linseed oil in oil paint, milk proteins in casein paint, egg in egg tempera, and acrylic polymer binders in acrylic paints. Gum arabic is often the binder in watercolors, and like the others, it holds the pigment to the paper. However, unlike some binders, gum arabic does not prevent the final artwork from fading or turning dark. It never becomes impermeable, so it is always re-wettable, requiring the protection of glazing for completed artworks. It should be mentioned that colored pencils have oil or wax binders (in addition to a dry combination of pigments) and are therefore different from watercolors.

Pigment

Watercolor paint manufacturers buy their colors from a variety of distributors. These color distributors also sell colorants beyond the scope of art supplies. There may be twenty distributers selling a specific color to manufacturers or there may be only one. This is important because it helps the artist understand there can be a difference in color substance and appearance from one distributor (or brand) to the next. Each watercolor brand adds their own preferred ingredients to the colors to produce a line of products for the competitive art-supply market. They may also make a student grade of watercolors that is not addressed here.

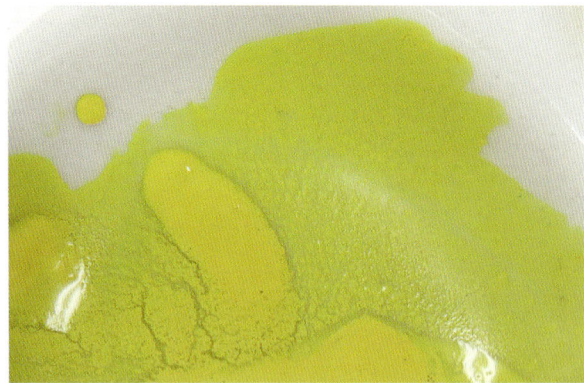

An example of flocculating paint, where the particles clump together like small clumps of clouds.

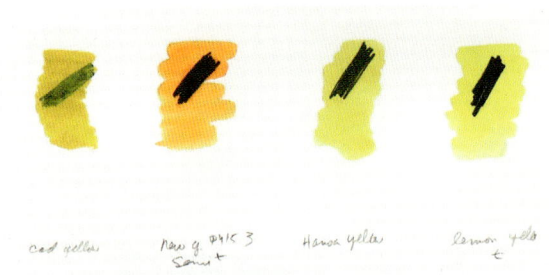

A variety of yellow pigments painted over black marker demonstrate the degree of opaqueness or transparency the different types provide. From left: opaque, semi-transparent, semi-opaque, and transparent watercolors. The degree of opaqueness or transparency also depends on how heavily or lightly the paint is applied.

Pigments are particles, and even though they can be minute they do not completely dissolve in water. Some particles can separate and settle into the tooth of the paper to give the paint a granulating or sedimentary appearance. Flocculating color refers to pigments that tend to draw together in clumps to create an uneven appearance. Transparent colors tend to permanently stain, and they can be difficult to remove without damaging the paper.

Opacity and Transparency

Opaque paint can also be considered semi-opaque, and either way the category is obvious: It presumably has a greater ability to cover what is beneath it, unlike transparent paint. However, it does not stain the paper to the same degree as some transparent colors. Like all colors, a lot depends on how the paint is managed by the artist. Opaque colors can be applied so that they appear transparent, and in certain applications, transparent colors can cover quite well. Color choices as well as opacity or transparency are preferences of individual artists—one is not inherently better than the other.

Changes in Paint Ingredients

Change happens in a lively market, and artists should be aware of the changes paint manufacturers sometimes make to their products, often with positive results. Manufacturers work hard to find solutions to toxicity concerns or scarcity issues, and therefore paint ingredients are altered or switched out for a variety of reasons. The color new gamboge, which used the pigment PY153, is a recent example of change. The pigment PY153 has become scarce and therefore different pigments are being sought to replace this orange-yellow colorant. Note that although the pigments used to create a paint may have changed, the name on the tube may remain the same. Hence a tube of new gamboge purchased two years ago may not contain the same color ingredients as one purchased this week. This is a critical bit of knowledge to have at hand, because the revised combination of ingredients may affect the paint's characteristics, such as transparency and permanence. Read the contents on the paint label. Look for the pigment designation numbers and the lightfast category. Be aware of a different and perhaps confusing situation where the paint labels have the same name and even the same pigment designation numbers across brands but the colorants might be slightly different in both appearance and handling characteristics. Again, this is the result of ingredient preferences by the producer of the paint.

Pigment Identification System

Pigment designation numbers identify the colors yellow, red, blue, green, orange, white, black, brown, and violet. They are denoted (same order) this way: PY, PR, PB, PG, PO, PW, PBk, PBr, PV and are followed by a number. Pigments are catalogued into large Colour Index volumes, now found online. These volumes are a reference database jointly maintained by the Society of Dyers and Colourists and The American Association of Textile Chemists and Colorists. In addition to the pigment designation number there is a more specific five-digit Colour Index number. This five-digit number refers to an exact pigment and is accompanied by a description of the characteristics of the pigment. These numbers are applied to all colors manufactured; for example, the art market, the home-improvement market, and the industrial-colorant market. The Colour Index number is often noted as "CIN" or "CI#." It may not always be on the tube or pan, but the pigment designation number should be. Remember that the name of the color on the label, such as "sap green" or "alizarin crimson," is not a useful way to choose or describe a color, because manufacturers can change their pigments and dyes to reflect a variety of changing needs or expectations. For example, a color called "Burnt Sienna" may be a PBr7, or it may be PR101. These are different pigment designation numbers, but the name of the color on the label remains the same. However, the appearance of the paint and its working properties may be different. Be aware that many PBr7 pigments can vary across brands. The name on the label does not indicate this variation nor the change that has been made to the ingredients. Again, it is important to look for the pigment designation numbers on the label.

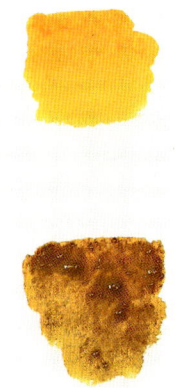

Two versions of new gamboge from the same brand: Above is a former new gamboge color and below is the current new gamboge. They have different pigments, but the same label.

These are four different brands of ultramarine blue, PB29. The samples have visible differences in sedimentation, granulation, and flocculation.

Labeling

Obviously, the label on a tube of paint is not a property of watercolor paint. However, it is critical to understand what is written on it to avoid frustration when the color doesn't perform as anticipated. Here are some things to either look for or note when they are absent. The lightfastness rating is very useful when it is present and perhaps revealing when a manufacturer does not include it. Although there may be other factors, lightfast designations are often avoided for two main reasons: One is that the pigment inside is known to fade or turn dark, such as genuine rose madder, alizarin crimson, or genuine indigo; and the other is that the manufacturer chooses not to disclose this information for proprietary reasons. When you are working in watercolor, it is important to choose pigments that do not fade. Fugitive colors, which fade or shift in color rapidly, can mean unpleasant and unwanted shifts in color over short periods of time.

The American Society For Testing and Materials (known as ASTM International) is an independent testing body that tests colors submitted to them. Not all manufacturers choose to submit their colors; some have their own tests and their own ratings. The ASTM lightfast rating is ASTM I, ASTM II, ASTM III, ASTM IV. The ASTM has official wording that describes lightfast ratings, not included here, but to give a sense of the ratings the Roman numeral "I" in this system is the best. It means that the color may not begin to show signs of degradation for one hundred years. ASTM II means that a color can begin to alter near the hundred-year mark. ASTM III indicates a color that could endure for twenty to a hundred years before showing signs of fading or turning dark. The ASTM IV rating means the paint will most likely degrade in twenty years or less. Different watercolor paint companies may use the ASTM rating, or they may have their own lightfast rating system. Bear this in mind as you choose your paints. It's possible to request the information about lightfastness from the paint manufacturer, but many artists simply avoid paints that do not come with disclosures about their lightfastness.

The toxicity of paint is an ongoing concern for artists. A toxicity description for watercolor paints is available at art-supply stores, from the manufacturer (on their website, for example), or from other online sources. A Safety Data Sheet documents the potential hazards (or not) of

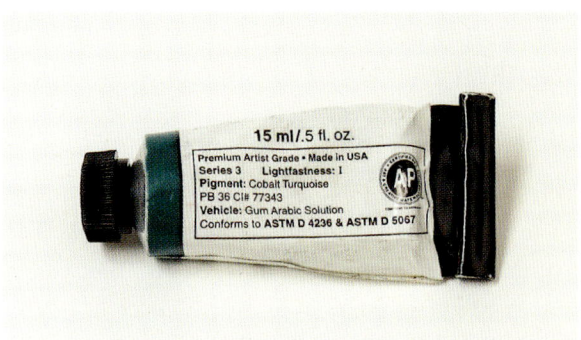

An example of excellent labeling on a tube of watercolor paint. Notice all the information provided: pigment designation number, CI#, lightfastness rating, and other ASTM ratings.

watercolor paints. The American Society For Testing and Materials notes the information this way, "Conforms to ASTM 4236," confirming that the paint is properly labeled for chronic health hazards. This means the information is available to consumers if they wish to seek it out.

Water

One way to think about watercolors is to think of the pigments and dyes as substances and not colors. With this mind-set an artist is more apt to look for the handling characteristics that will guide their mixing possibilities. Water, no matter how much or how little, becomes a property of watercolor once it is added into the mix. You must be alert to how much water is being added to the paint or how much water is evaporating out of the mix. Consider the amount of water in the paintbrush. Water on the paintbrush, and water mixed into the paint on the palette, both affect how the watercolor behaves when placed on paper.

Light

Light is an important aspect of both watercolor painting and watercolor viewing. Light affects the appearance of watercolors in a dramatic way. The light under which the subject is painted and the light in which the final work is viewed can be different and most definitely affect the appearance of a work.

Get to Know Your Paints

Last, but not least: It is the responsibility of the artist to understand the qualities of the watercolor paints being used and to keep up with changes in the industry. It is also important to consistently practice with the

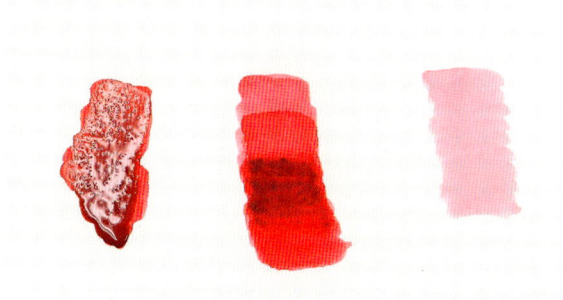

Light's effect on paint, from left to right: Reflected light, absorbed light, and scattered light. It is a good idea to let watercolor paint dry before judging its color and values.

Sir Isaac Newton's Color Wheel, 1704. Reproduced by Scott Stapleton.

materials—there is no substitute for hands-on experience. Only you can decide which brand, which colors, and which materials work best for your work—making these determinations is a unique voyage for every brave artist.

Palette Philosophies

TUTOR: MARILYN GARBER

Botanical artists who work in watercolor use a wide variety of colors on their palettes. Some use every color available. Others stick to a limited palette of six colors all their lives. Many experienced artists choose 12 to 15 colors that become their standards. Some botanical art certificate programs recommend limiting your palette to 12 to 15 colors; these colors may vary from program to program.

When a beginner is learning about color, it is often helpful to work with a limited number of colors in order to understand the extent of the color variations they can achieve. A select palette of six colors, featuring warm colors and cool colors, can create an infinite number of colors when they are mixed in various pigment combinations and tints. An artist's palette will continue to evolve with experience, since getting that just-right shade of lavender may not always be possible with a limited palette.

"Everything that you can see in the world around you presents itself to your eyes only as an arrangement of patches of different colors variously shaded."

—

—John Ruskin (1819–1900), Slade Professor of Art, Oxford University, 1869–1878

Color palettes will vary in different parts of the country and world. The colors used in the tropics versus those used in the desert or those used to depict plants in the midwestern United States will differ from one another. The character and quantity of light varies around the country and the world, as do the plant species and the pigments they produce. Still, there are aspects of color that they all have in common. What follows is an exploration of the different approaches to color palettes and the color terminology affecting these choices.

What is color?

In 1666, Sir Isaac Newton, the English physicist and mathematician, discovered that color was in light and that when all the colors of the spectrum are combined, they create white light. There are many colors in the visible light spectrum, made up of different wavelengths of light. Color is light separated into its varying wavelengths. When light strikes an object, its wavelengths are either absorbed, transmitted, or reflected. The color we see is the light reflected back to our eyes.

Trying to categorize color, Newton began to experiment, and his first paper featuring his color system was published in 1671–72. The system was included in *Opticks*, in 1704, his treatise on his study of light, and consisted of yellow, green, blue, indigo, violet, red, and orange. He included seven colors to match the seven tones of the Dorian musical scale (F, G, A, B, C, D, and E). As we understand it today, color is an impression of the relationship between light and the light-reflecting surfaces with which it interacts.

The Six-Color Limited Palette

The primary colors—red, yellow, and blue—are the basis of the six-color palette. Although paint manufacturers have attempted to develop pure reds, yellows, and blues, all colors have biases toward a second primary color.

The colors in the six-color palette have the following biases:

Cool colors: lemon yellow (blue bias), permanent alizarin crimson (blue bias), ultramarine blue (red bias)

Warm colors: Hansa yellow deep (red bias), cadmium red (yellow bias), cerulean blue (yellow bias)

Knowing a color's bias can help you mix either clear colors or dulled colors. Mix a cool color with a cool color, and you will get a clear color. Mix a warm color with a warm color and you will get a clear color. Cross the palette by mixing a warm color with a cool color and you will get a more neutral color. Many colors in nature are dulled or contain an element of neutrality. An infinite number of colors can be mixed from this six-color palette. It is helpful to learn how they perform when mixed with each other in varying amounts, and how they are affected by different ratios of pigment and water. In addition, understanding their transparency, opaqueness, and other characteristics will help you sort out the complicated subject of color.

An Unlimited Color Palette

Nature presents us with an unlimited range of color, and while much can be accomplished with a limited palette, many artists use an expanded palette to capture the colors they see in nature as accurately as possible. Paint manufacturers have developed many choices for artists, and some are convenience colors. In many cases, these colors can be mixed using colors already on your palette. Always consult the pigment numbers on paint containers, because they provide information about the contents that is not evident in the color name.

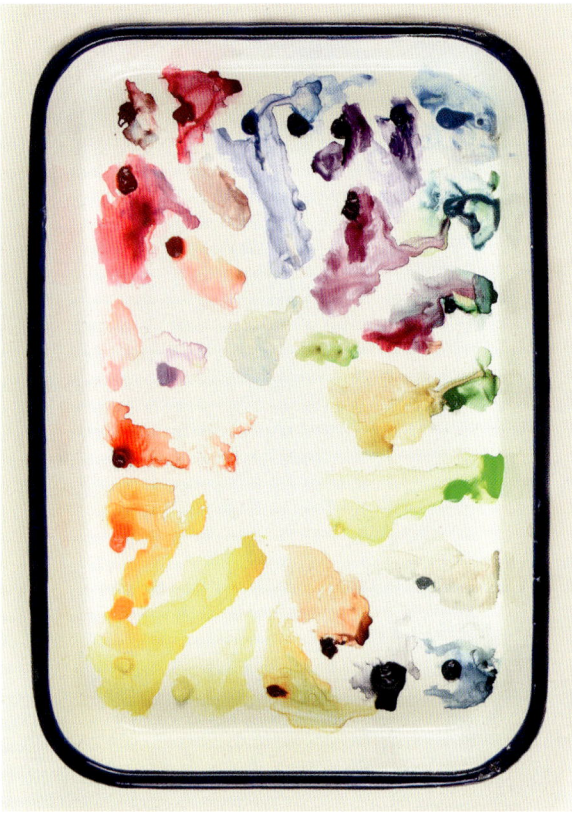

Jean Emmons's Watercolor Palette

When Jean Emmons, known for her beautiful, complex color, first learned botanical painting, her teacher used a limited palette of eight colors and mixed everything, trying to match the local color of the plant. Emmons believes this was a good way to learn, as it was helpful to approach the subject within a structure. Over the years, her palette and approach changed. She said, "Color is mysterious to human beings, as we don't see it very well. However, we see in black and white extremely well. When I reach for a color, I am thinking about its black and white value, not its hue. The irony is, if I can visualize my subject in black and white, it will look dimensional, no matter what colors I use." Emmons currently has many colors on her palette. She prefers layering colors to mixing colors and particularly appreciates transparent colors, such as the quinacridones. Her paintings progress through underpainting with unusual colors, followed by more logical and local colors of the subject painted over the top in drybrush.

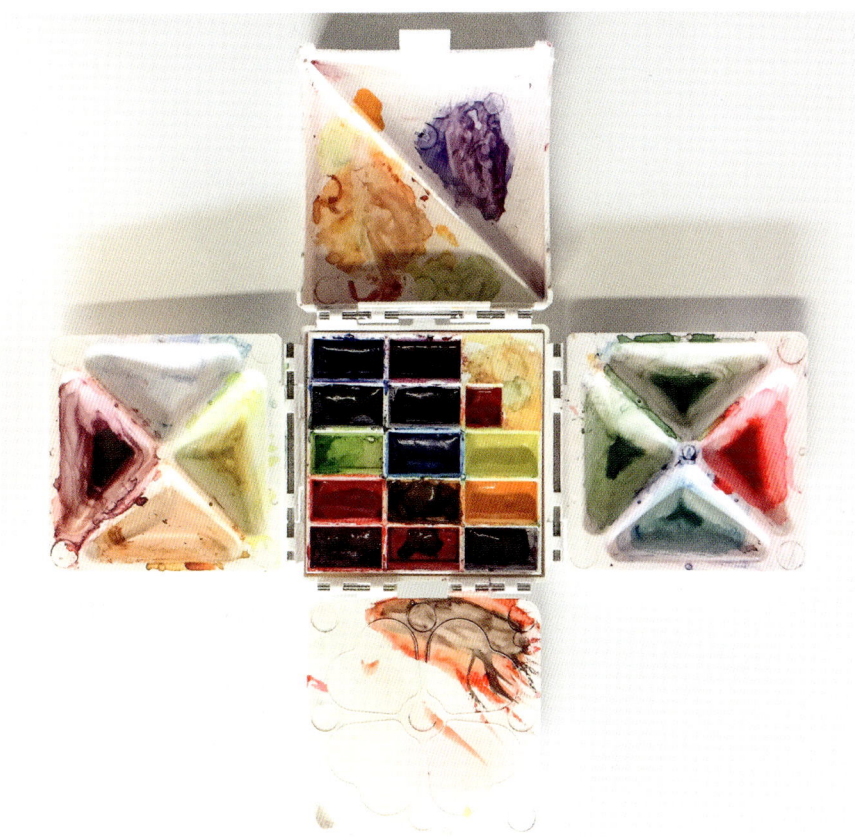

John Pastoriza-Piñol's Watercolor Palette

John Pastoriza-Piñol works with transparent and more modern synthetic paints, mixing the color on the paper in layers, rather than mixing them on a palette. His limited selection is based on the Wilcox Split Primary Palette. He extends his palette to enhance his available color range of pigments. John's limited palette includes the following pigments: vanadium yellow, quinacridone gold, quinacridone red, perylene maroon, cerulean blue hue, and ultramarine blue (green shade). His extended palette includes: May green, brilliant blue violet, brilliant red violet, Indian yellow, deep red, perylene violet, perylene green, and madder lake deep.

Looking back to historical botanical artists, Dr. Richard Mulholland, an art historian and research fellow at the Bodleian Libraries, University of Oxford, England, has researched the pigments used by Austrian botanical illustrator Ferdinand Bauer (1760–1826) for the ten-volume *Flora Graeca*. Oxford University holds all of Bauer's extant annotated field sketches and watercolors for this classic work. Bauer developed a unique system of making drawings from life and annotating them with numbers. His chart included numerical codes for up to 140 different red, yellow, blue, and green color tones. The codes allowed Bauer to accurately record detailed color information for each of the study drawings he made on expeditions, so they could be finalized later as paintings, sometimes years after completing the drawings. By identifying and analyzing the pigments from the original *Flora Graeca* watercolors and numbered sketches, a team at Oxford created a historical reconstruction of what a missing color chart based on this coding system might have looked like.

The approach to color is and always has been unique to each individual artist. While some take a very technical approach and develop annotated color swatches to record aspects of a subject's color, others work through it as they progress through a painting, adjusting color by improvising. No matter what approach an artist uses, a familiarity with color is an indispensable tool in creating botanical art and makes it possible to achieve the nuances of color present in the plant world.

There are several ways to transfer a compositional layout drawing onto paper or vellum. The two methods discussed here are the most frequently used. Carbon transfer paper or homemade graphite paper is not recommended for transferring drawings onto vellum, as they can drop graphite in places where it is not wanted. Be sure to leave enough open paper or vellum around the drawing so that there is at least additional half inch [1.25 cm] on all sides to go under a mat for framing.

Transferring a Drawing onto Paper or Vellum before Painting Begins

TUTOR: CAROL WOODIN

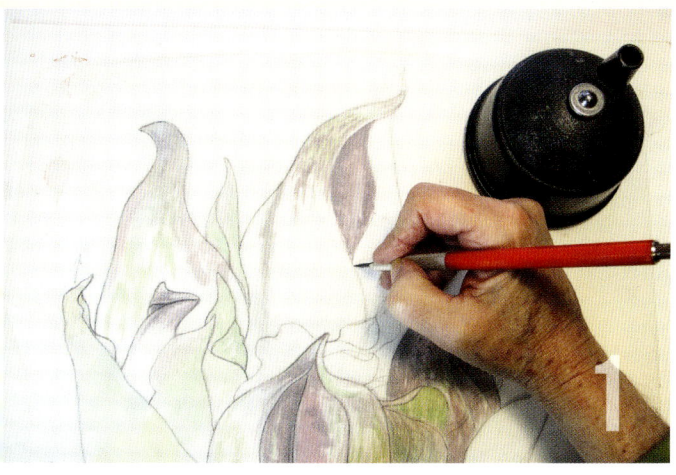

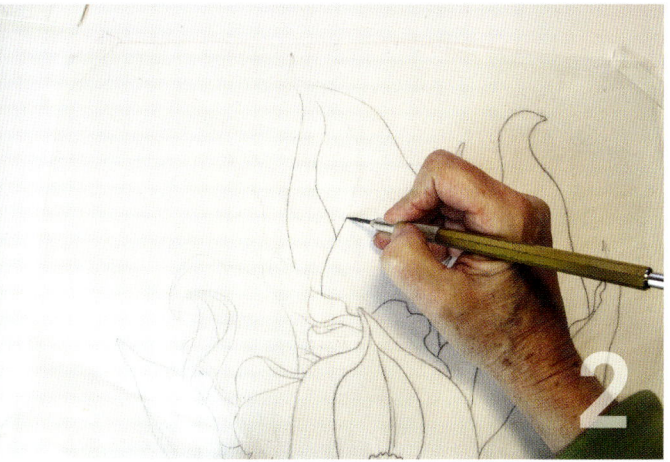

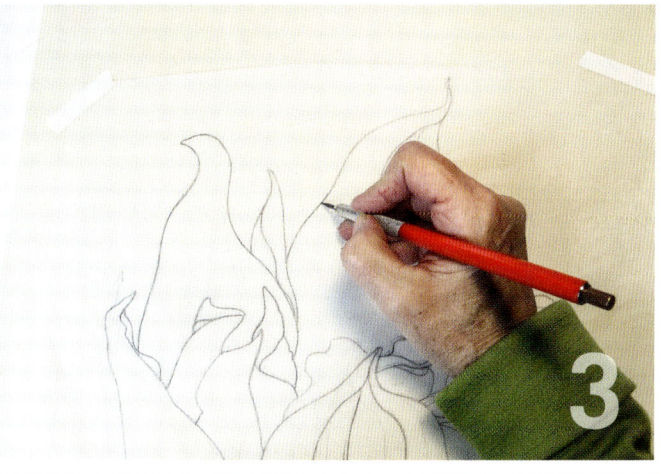

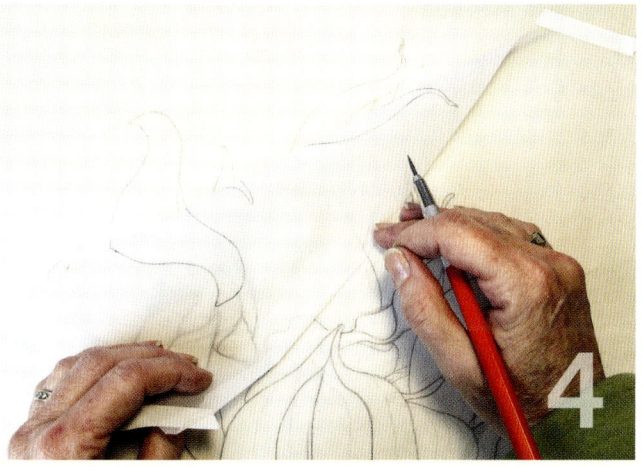

To transfer a drawing using tracing paper, lay a sheet of tracing paper over the final composition drawing and tape it down lightly with acid-free artist's tape. Using a sharply pointed hard lead (2H to 4H), make a precise tracing of the outline and any other important lines you need to follow during your painting process.

Turn over the tracing paper and, using a sharply pointed softer lead (HB to 3B), trace over the lines on the back of the tracing paper. If you are transferring the drawing onto paper, then HB or B leads are good choices. Each piece of vellum responds differently to graphite, so if you are transferring to vellum you may need to use an HB, 2B, or 3B lead.

Turn the tracing paper over again so the drawing is facing up, and tape it lightly to the paper or vellum. Trace over the lines with slight pressure using a 2H to 4H sharply pointed lead. As you trace over the lines, the drawing on the other side of the tracing paper will be transferred onto the paper. At this stage, elements may be adjusted by repositioning the tracing paper, as can be seen through the tracing paper at the bottom of this drawing.

While you are working on the tracing, peek under the tracing paper occasionally to ensure that the transferred drawing isn't either too light to see, or too heavy, leaving too much graphite on the paper or vellum. If the transferred drawing is too light, apply more pressure, sharpen your 2H or 4H pencil, or increase the lead on the back. When working on paper, take care that increased pressure with a very sharp lead doesn't incise the watercolor paper. If the transfer is too dark, lighten the pressure you are using to transfer the drawing. On a complex tracing, it may be useful to put a checkmark or an X next to the components as they are transferred, so that you do not miss anything.

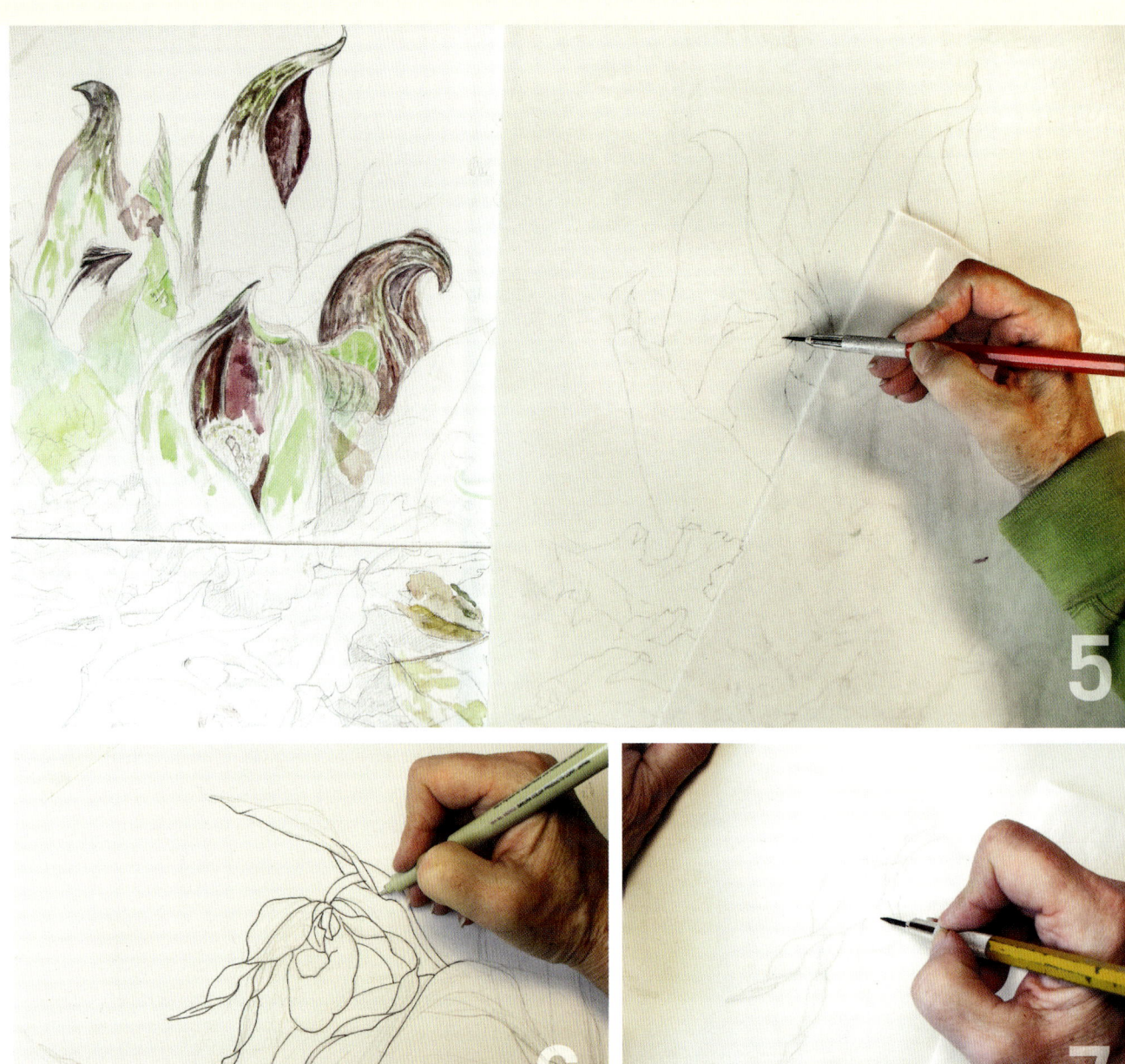

Once the tracing is transferred, sharpen up the drawing, referring to the original composition and the subject plant, if available. Gaps in the transferred drawing can be filled in, and excess graphite lifted using a white-plastic retractable eraser.

Instead of using a tracing paper transfer, some artists use an extra-fine marker pen or technical pen to draw over the initial graphite layout drawing. Ink over the parts of the drawing you want to transfer, let them dry, then place the paper or vellum over the inked layout and trace the drawing using a graphite pencil.

The thickness of the paper or vellum determines how easily the underlying drawing can be seen. If the drawing is difficult to see clearly, place the drawing and paper or vellum on a light box to increase the light through both layers. Sometimes this will work even if the drawing has not been inked and is still in graphite.

Rose Marie James demonstrates the basic techniques of working with watercolor washes. She shows us a flat wash (the application of an even layer of color to fill a shape), a graded wash, and the technique of charging. A graded wash creates a gradual transition from a more to less saturated color. Charging involves mixing two colors onto slightly wet paper. The word charging refers to the way wet paint reacts when the two colors come together. All these applications work best when the watercolor paper is positioned at a slight angle on a board so that gravity can help the wet pigment flow.

Watercolor Wash and Wet Techniques

TUTOR: ROSE MARIE JAMES

Flat Wash

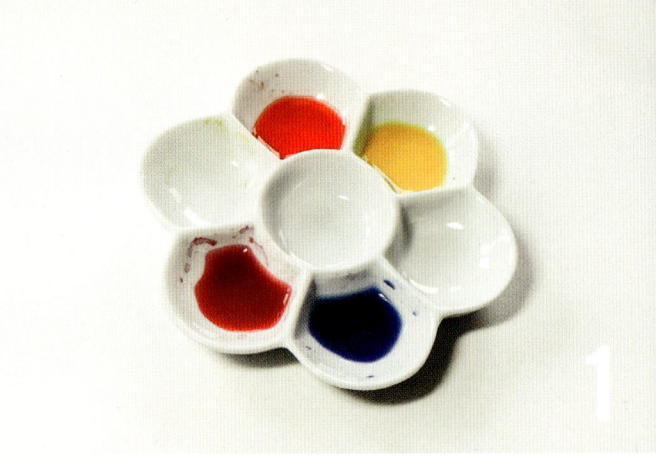

MATERIALS: Clipboard with watercolor paper; round watercolor brushes; tube watercolors; paper towels; palette with wells; containers for water; water dropper; cotton glove.

A flat wash can be applied to a dry or damp paper surface depending on the size of coverage needed. Small areas—less than a 1-inch [2.5 cm] square—can often be done on dry paper. First, mix up a well of color—pigment plus water—to the strength of saturation desired for the wash. Generally, this is a dilute concentration. Transfer the drawing very lightly with graphite to good-quality watercolor paper.

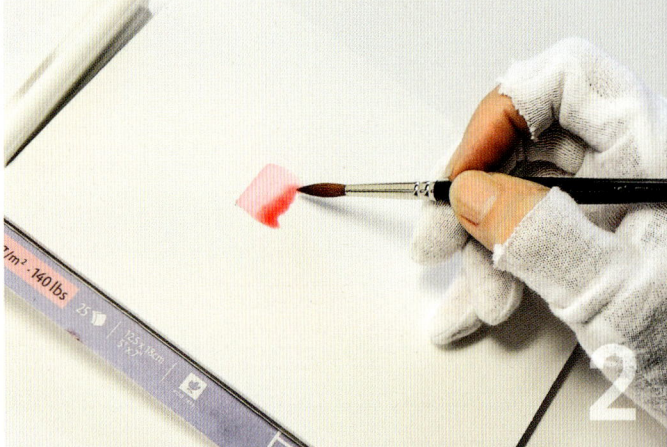

Using a clean brush and clean water, slightly dampen the area to be painted—damp paper prevents the pigment from drying before the entire area is covered. The area should feel slightly damp with a matte—not shiny—appearance. Load the brush with pigment, and wipe the excess off onto the well. Starting at the top of the shape, apply pigment across, allowing some of the paint to puddle at the leading edge of where the paint is flowing.

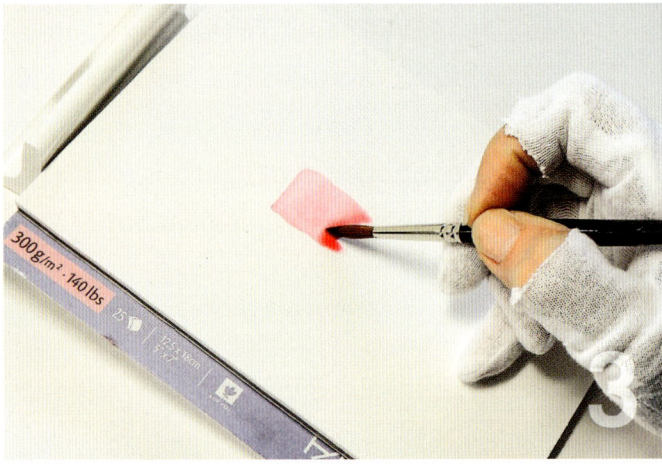

Always maintain the puddle as the pigment is moved along into a new area. This will prevent an unwanted edge when the paint dries. Reload the puddle with pigment by dropping in more of the mixed pigment. Don't allow the puddle to dissipate before the shape is completed.

If a bit of pooling is left at the bottom of the area, it must be removed. Without cleaning the brush, dab it on a paper towel. Barely touch the puddle's edge with the brush tip. Capillary action will draw extra paint into the brush. Avoid reworking any area of the flat wash until it is totally dry.

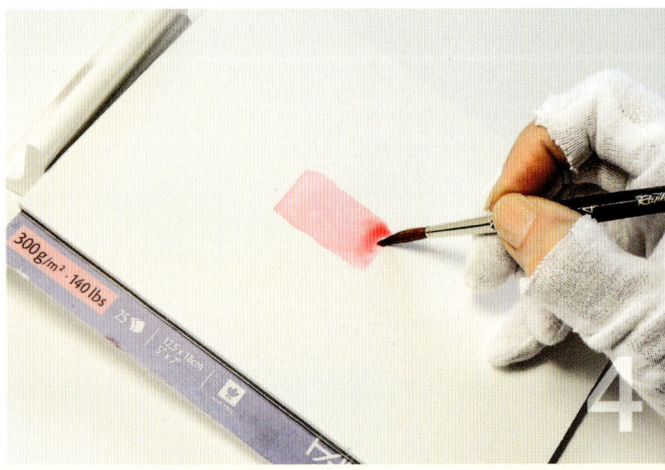

Graded Wash

For a graded wash to be successful, the area being painted should be only slightly damp. The area shown in this image is too wet, which will cause the applied paint to migrate and leave a dark outline. Use two brushes—one for water, the other for pigment. To wet the paper, dip a brush into water and wipe it on the edge of the container to remove the excess water. Gently cover the area with water, then wait until the surface becomes matte.

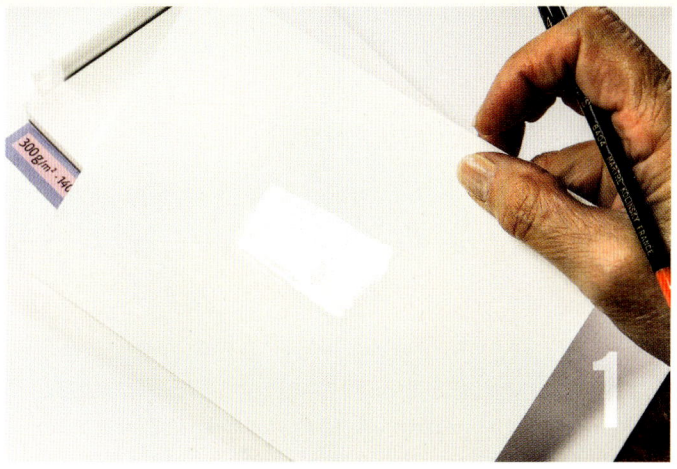

Position the paper at a slight slant, with the area to be painted dampened. Dip the painting brush into the darkest value desired. Gently wipe the brush on the paint well to avoid overloading the brush with paint. Starting at the top, paint the area by sweeping from side to side to about a third of the way down.

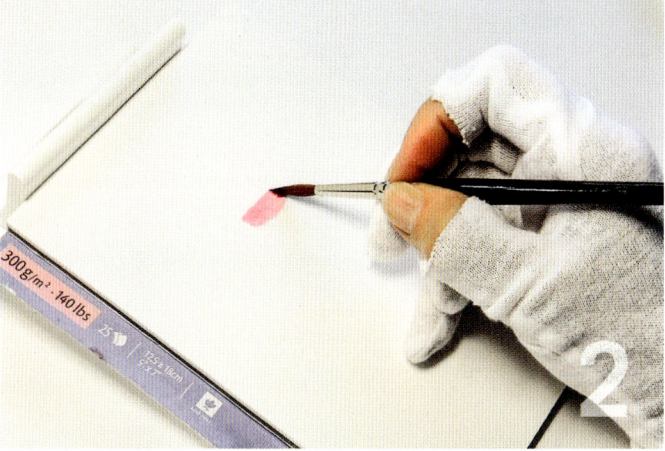

Immediately rinse your paintbrush in water, then blot it to release *some* of the water. Quickly go into the painted area, about a third of the way above the leading edge (where the first application stopped), and pull the pigment down by moving the brush from side to side across the area. Because the brush does not contain any pigment, it will now dilute the existing color, creating a transition from dark to light.

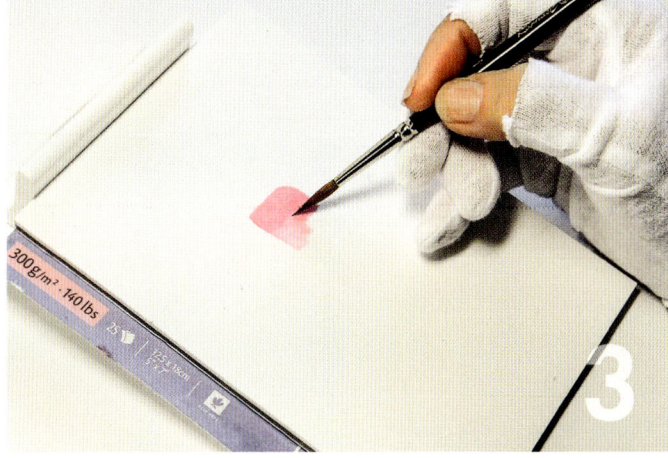

When the color stops moving, rinse the brush again and continue the process above the leading edge, being sure not to go back into the original wash (it will create unwanted dilution). An imperfect transition can be somewhat corrected later using the drybrush technique, but avoid going back into a wet area to try to fix it. This process can be repeated as needed. It can be done all at once or in a series, allowing each finished transition to dry before the next layer of transition. This is one of the most difficult watercolor techniques to master, and it requires much practice, not only to become adept with the technique, but also to familiarize yourself with how pigments behave with this technique.

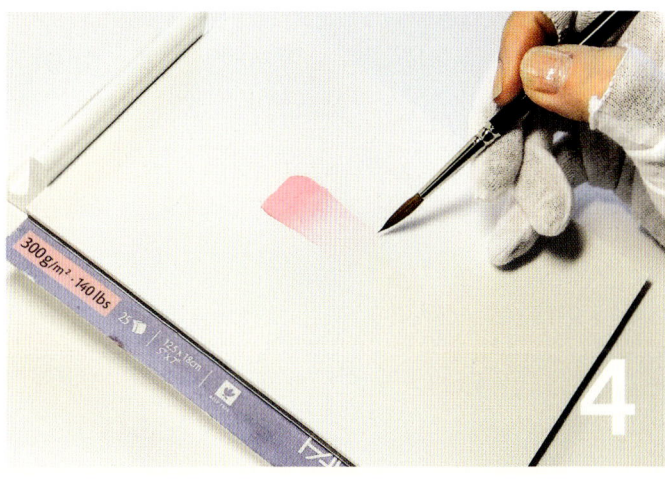

Charging
Watercolor Washes

Charging is a technique that blends two colors seamlessly in an area, and is usually done on dry paper. Begin by loading a brush with the first color and paint the desired area on dry paper, keeping a puddle of paint along the leading edge.

Rinse the brush in water, blot it to remove excess water, and load it with the second color. Using the tip of the brush, drop this color into the puddle on the paper. The colors will "charge," or mix in the pool.

Pull the mixed color down a bit by moving the brush from side to side across the area, maintaining the puddle on the leading edge.

Again, rinse the brush, blot out the water, and reload the brush with the second color. Dip the new color into the puddle at the edge of the previous color.

Pull down the second color to its finish point. As in the other washes, if a puddle remains, wipe the brush and touch the tip to the edge of the pooled remainder to wick up the excess.

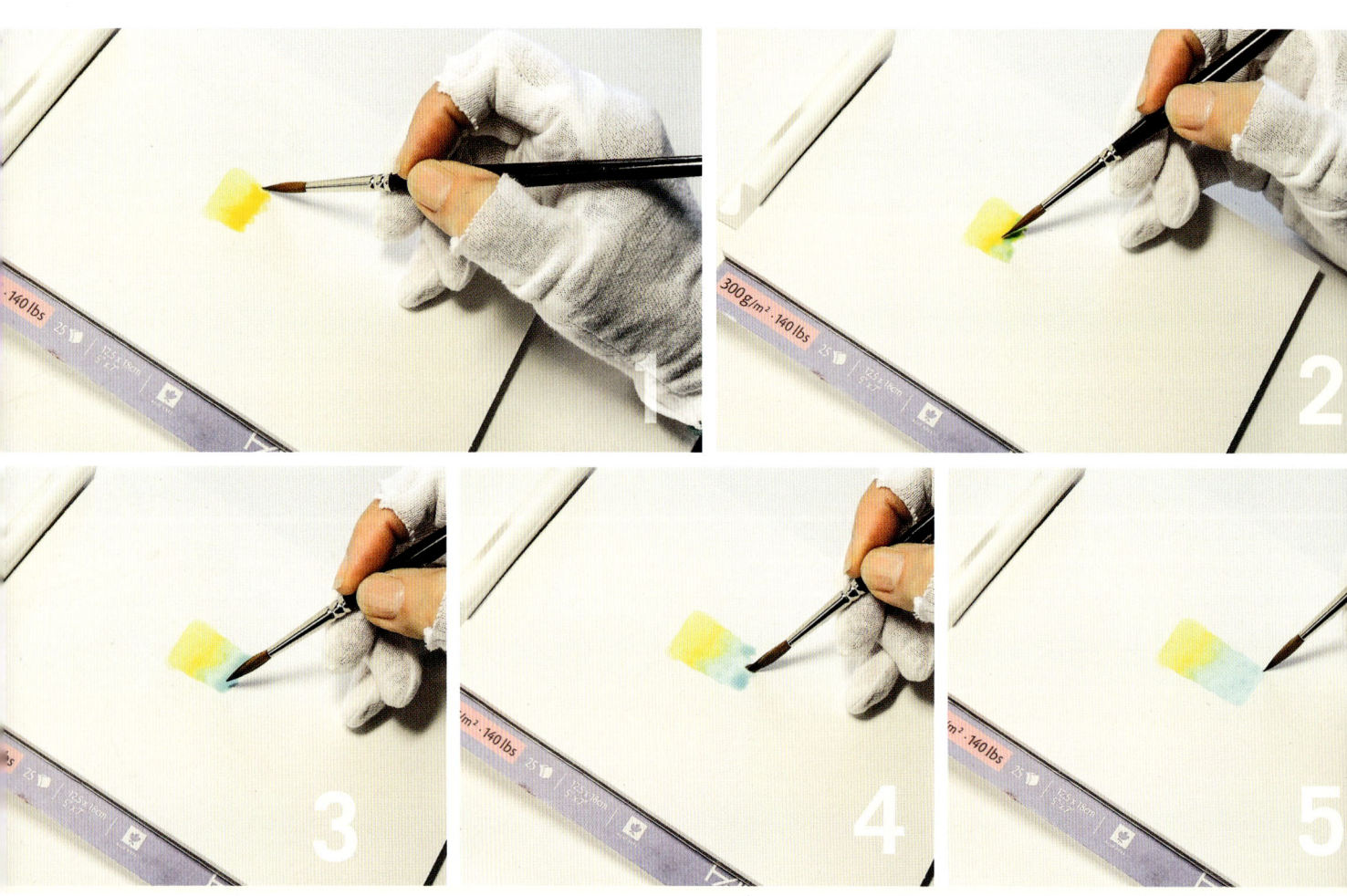

Once you have chosen the perfect apple to paint, observe it closely. Look at it from all sides and feel it to understand its density and texture. The more familiar you are with your subject, the more lifelike your painting will be. After a basic wash, use a combination of drybrush layering, glazing, and drybrush detailing to create surface textures, color and form.

Drybrush Layering, Glazing, and Detailing

TUTOR: CATHERINE WATTERS

Drybrush Layering

MATERIALS: Magnifying glass; extra-fine retractable eraser; 2H and 4H graphite pencils; kneaded eraser; dividers; retractable brush with lid; ceramic palette; paper towel; Kolinsky brushes (nos. 1 and 3); shader brush (bright; no. 4); scrap piece of watercolor paper. Watercolors: Alizarin crimson; sap green; new gamboge; burnt umber; magenta; ultramarine violet; ultramarine blue.

Drybrush layering is a controlled way to map out the stri-ations and local color on an apple. Although a wash can be controlled for areas of light and dark, drybrush layering allows for more specific depiction of surface patterns and texture. You will see the form develop after the first few coats of paint.

On a pale yellow wash, lightly paint the red striations. Dip the brush halfway into a small amount of diluted paint, twirl it at the edge of the well to remove excess paint, then lightly swipe the brush on a paper towel or cotton cloth. Barely touching the surface of the paper with the side of the brush, allow the yellow wash to show through.

Continue applying the striations all over the apple, avoiding the highlight and reflected light. Carefully observing the direction of the striations, start at the top of the apple and work down. When you are close to the bottom edge, turn the paper around to make sure the strokes stay within the edges.

With a barely damp brush and using dilute ultramarine violet, apply a transparent shadow, leaving reflected light unpainted. Brush in the shadow in the same direction as the striations. The shadow should be clean and very pale, allowing the local color to show through.

Apply another coat of shadow to deepen the color, and let it dry. Then, deepen the striations with another drybrush coat of red. Use a light, sketching motion of the brush, in combination with the paper's texture, to enhance the speckled appearance of the apple's surface.

Apply a brighter and more saturated coat of red to emphasize the darker striations and the shadow. Do this using the same drybrush method. The apple's form will develop with the contrast of highlight, shadow, and reflected light.

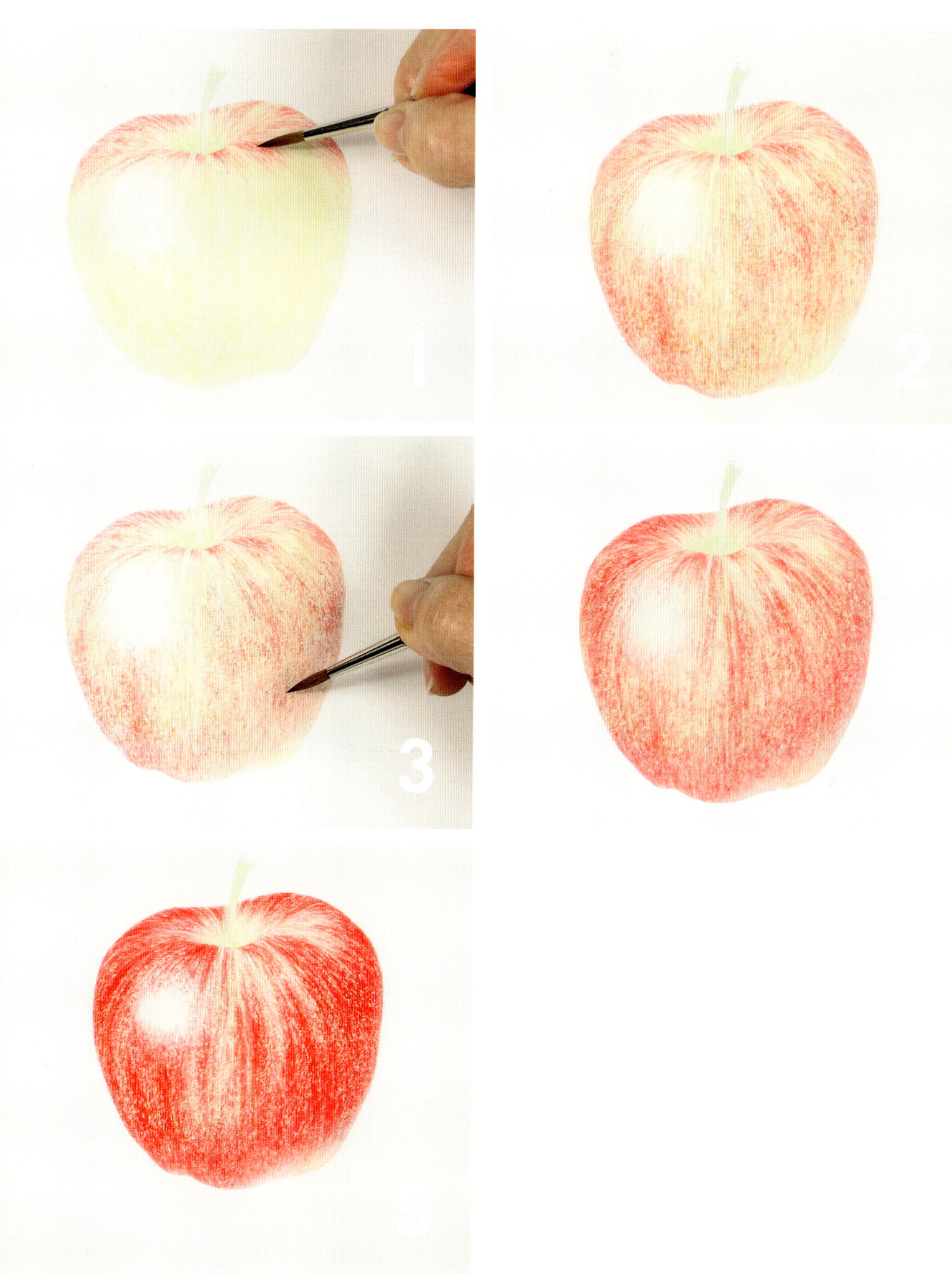

Glazing

A glaze is a thin and transparent layer of paint applied over an existing painted area to either alter or deepen the color. Glazing can also soften and assimilate the colors beneath and make them glow. Although a glaze is similar to a wash, do not wet your paper first. Before applying a second glaze, the paper must be completely dry.

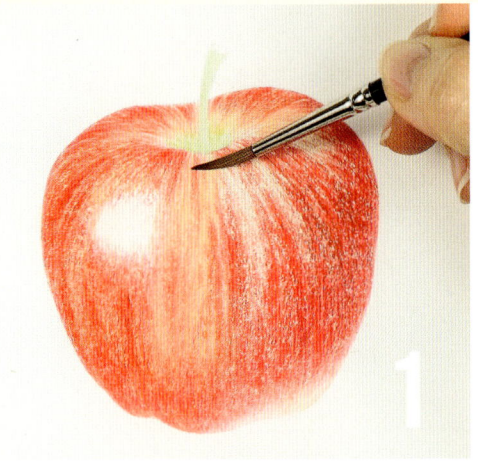

Apply a yellow glaze using the side of the brush for maximum coverage. This should be done quickly, because hovering in one spot may lift the previous coat. The brush should be damp, but not dripping wet. Dip the brush into the well, and twirl it at the edge of the well to remove excess water. Notice the effect of the glaze on the shoulders and left side of apple.

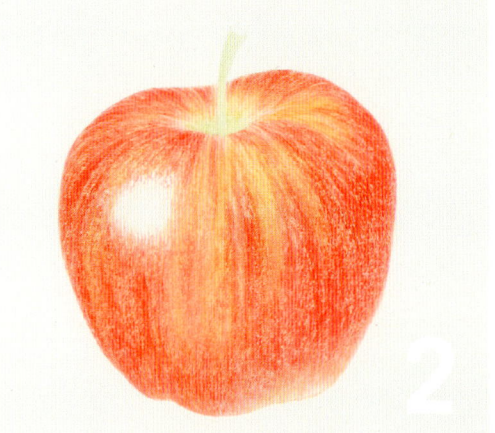

Finish glazing yellow all over the apple, avoiding the highlight and reflected light. Remember to turn the paper upside down to keep the bottom edges of the apple clean and crisp.

Apply a red glaze here and there to further saturate areas of darker patterning and areas in shadow. To deepen the color of the well (the indentation around the stem), apply a glaze of one or two light coats of pale green with a touch of brown. Although a fairly large no. 3 Kolinsky is being used, its fine point allows for close control.

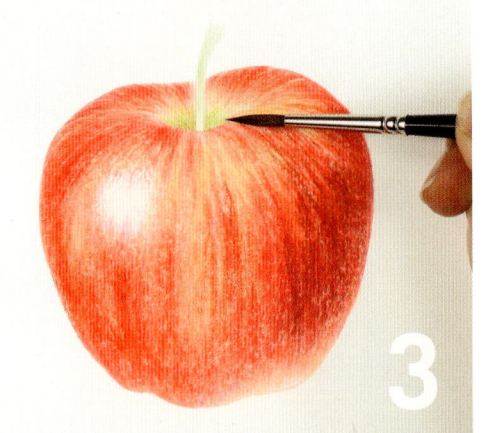

Apply a green glaze over the stem. Apply a thin water glaze over the entire apple to soften the striations. The brush should be just damp, with no color, and applied in the direction of the striations. Keep moving, using a light touch so that previous layers are not pulled up.

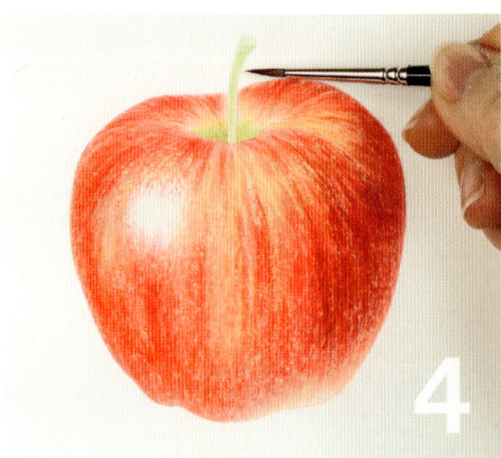

Drybrush Detailing

This is the stage when the subject leaps off the paper. The finishing drybrush details are very important, so take the time to do them well. Think of this stage as creating the illusion of a three-dimensional object on a two-dimensional surface.

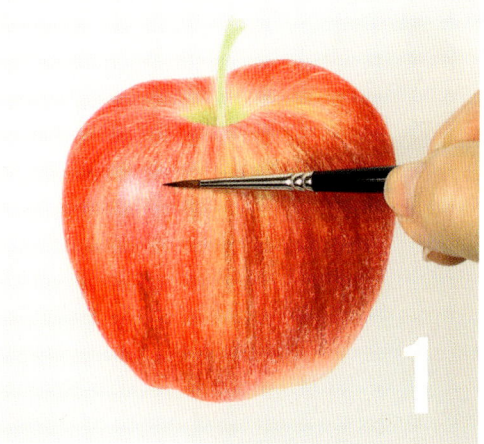

The apple's highlight should look like a sparkle of light, not a hole. With a small detail brush and very little paint, carefully weave yellow and red into the highlight to make it smaller. The edges must be soft so that the highlight gently transitions into the local color. Use a rimless magnifying glass while you paint to see every detail.

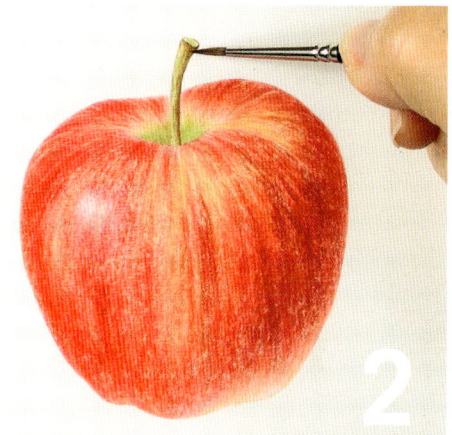

The stem needs to look strong and firmly placed in the indentation. Using very little paint, drybrush medium brown here and there, letting some green show through. To appear three-dimensional, the stem needs to have a highlight on one side (on the left side of this stem) and a shadow (on the right). Apply shadow with a deeper brown.

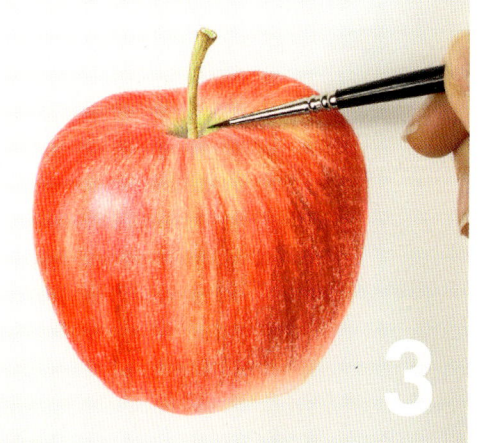

To anchor the stem in the indentation and create depth, paint a light transparent shadow to the left of the stem and gradually darken it. The left edge of the stem and the edge of the well must be very crisp. To create the shadow cast by the stem onto the right shoulder, paint a curved shadow that gently fades into the shoulder.

To lift little spots on the apple, use the corner of a small, barely damp shader brush. Then define the edges of the spots with a little bit of red.

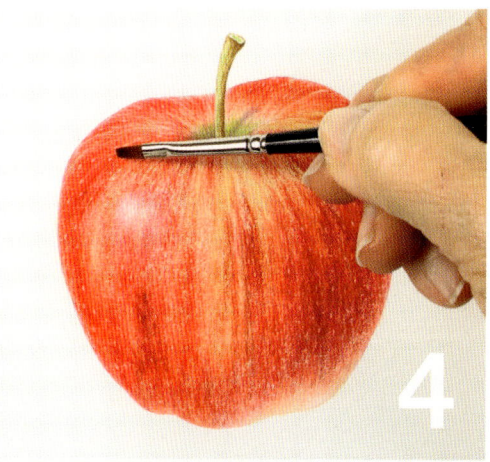

When you are applying the final details, the apple's shape can be slightly altered if you feel it's not quite right. In this painting, the left shoulder of the apple was gently raised by lightly outlining the new shape with a 4H pencil. With a damp brush, the old edge was softened and pushed into the new one. A little red paint was carefully applied to fill in the space.

For the final review, place the painting on an easel and step back to view it. Just a few more details are needed here. Add a little red in the dark striations and the shadow area. Tone down the reflected light by carefully weaving in a little diluted red. Make the edges of the apple crisp; they should be defined but not outlined.

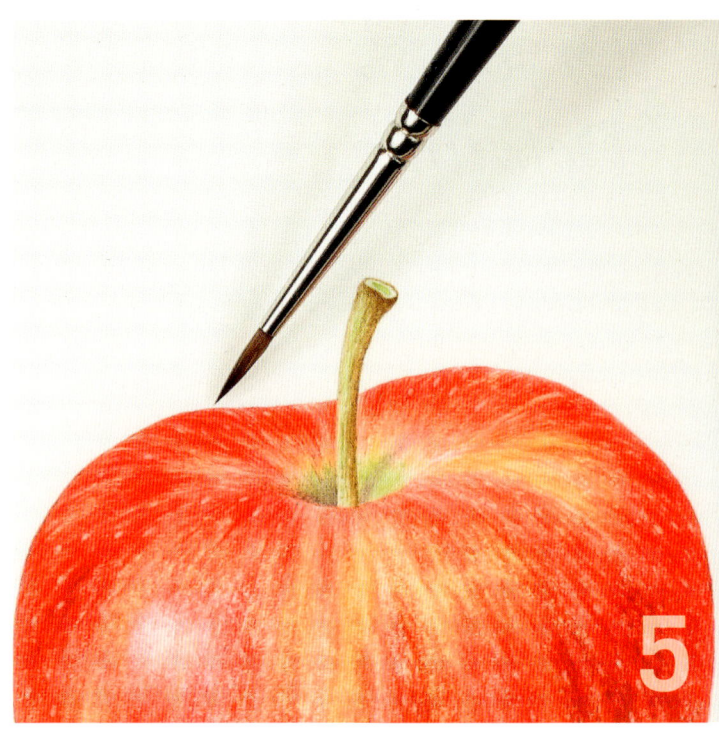

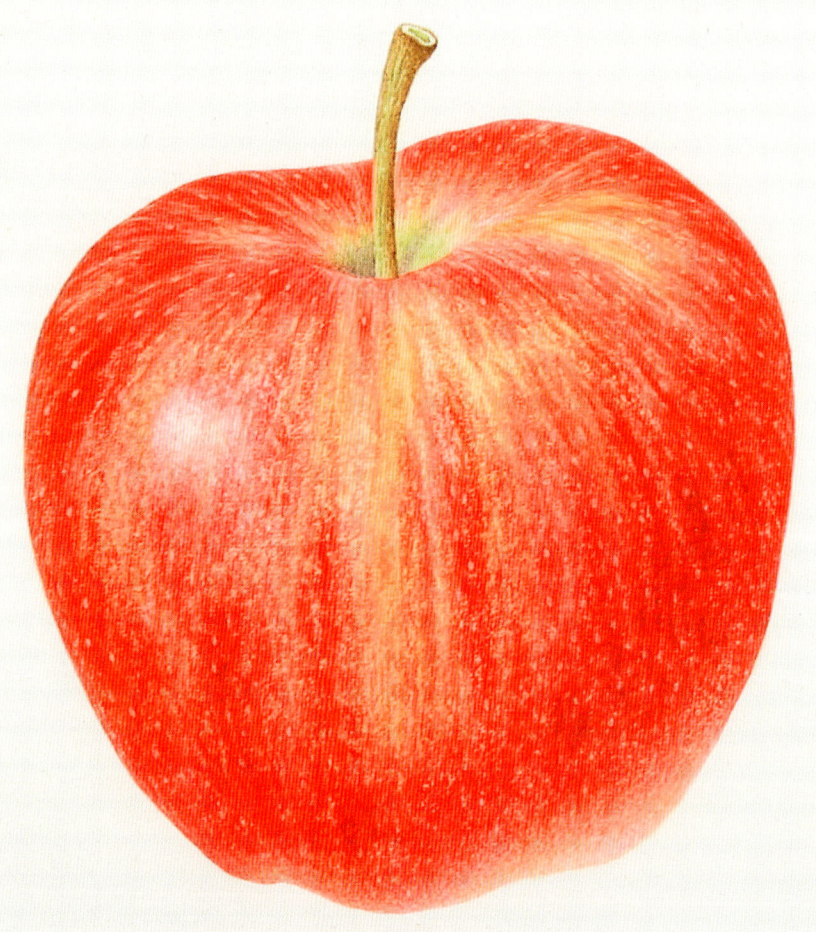

Gala apple
Malus domestica 'Gala'
Watercolor on paper
7 ½ × 7 inches [18.75 × 17.5 cm]
© Catherine Watters

Constance Sayas demonstrates painting three types of flowers using watercolor on 300 lb. [640 gsm] hot-pressed paper combining wet-on-wet and drybrush techniques. The simple tulip is a good first step with its satiny petals. The textures of the iris's velvety falls and delicate standards each require a different approach. Finally, with its many petals, a floribunda rose is a challenge. The illustrations took between 50 and 70 hours to complete, but most of those hours represent research, drawing, and observation—creating the actual paintings took about a quarter of the time shown.

Flowers

TUTOR: CONSTANCE SAYAS

Tulip

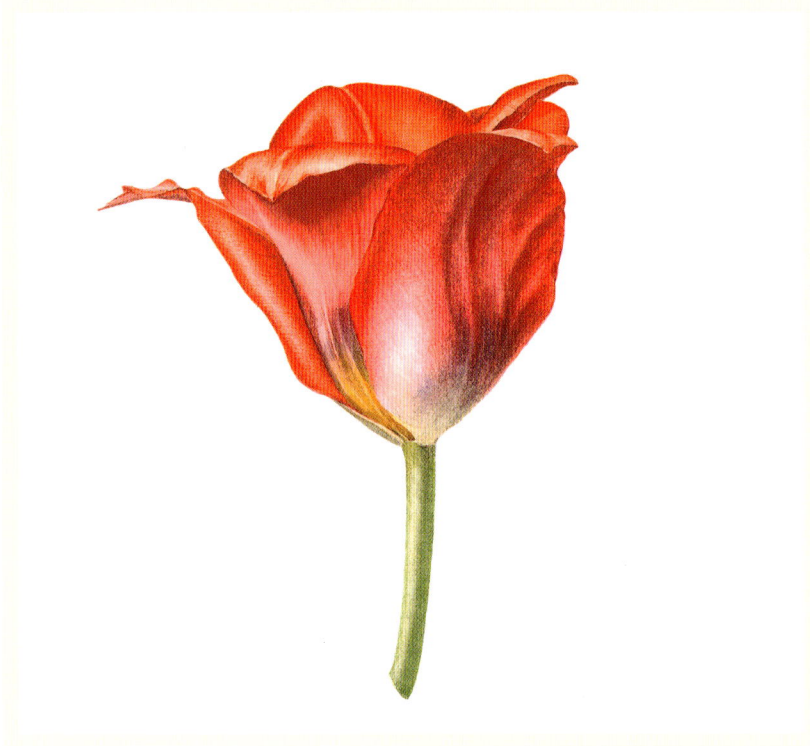

Greigii Tulip
Watercolor on paper
7 × 8 inches [17.5 × 20 cm]
© Constance Sayas
HOURS TO COMPLETE: 60

MATERIALS: Kneaded eraser; lead holder with HB lead; paper towels; Kolinsky watercolor round brushes (nos. 4 and 2); scrap piece of watercolor paper; container for water; ceramic palette. Colors (tube watercolors): Hansa yellow; pyrrol scarlet; quinacridone red; ultramarine blue; cerulean blue; phthalo green.

After some study, this species, *Tulipa greigii*, quickly revealed a strategy for painting. The variety of reds seen on the outsides of the petals, in transition from orange-red to violet-red and dark violet, are scenarios for wet-on-wet color blending and some drybrush color blending techniques.

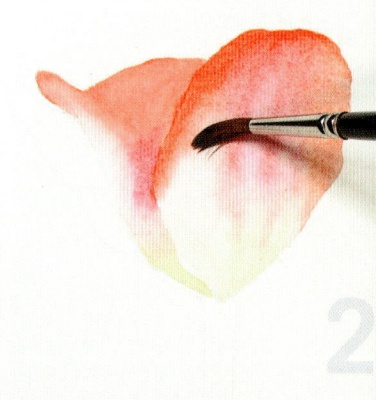

Begin with wet-on-wet color blending. Wet the paper, apply a yellow wash to the base of the petal, let dry, then rewet the paper. Starting at the top of the petal, apply strong orange-red and brush it down the petal. Drop some quinacridone red into the wet paint. Colors will merge naturally, but they can also be blended with a brush. Refrain from extraneous brushwork once the paint begins to absorb into the paper.

Use the same wet-on-wet color blending technique on the adjacent petal. Then, while the paint is still wet, lift color with a clean, damp (not wet) brush. Press down on the brush in a sweeping motion to mop up wet paint. The wet paint will flow back into the lifted area a bit, retaining the desired soft edges. This will start to map out areas of lighter and deeper values.

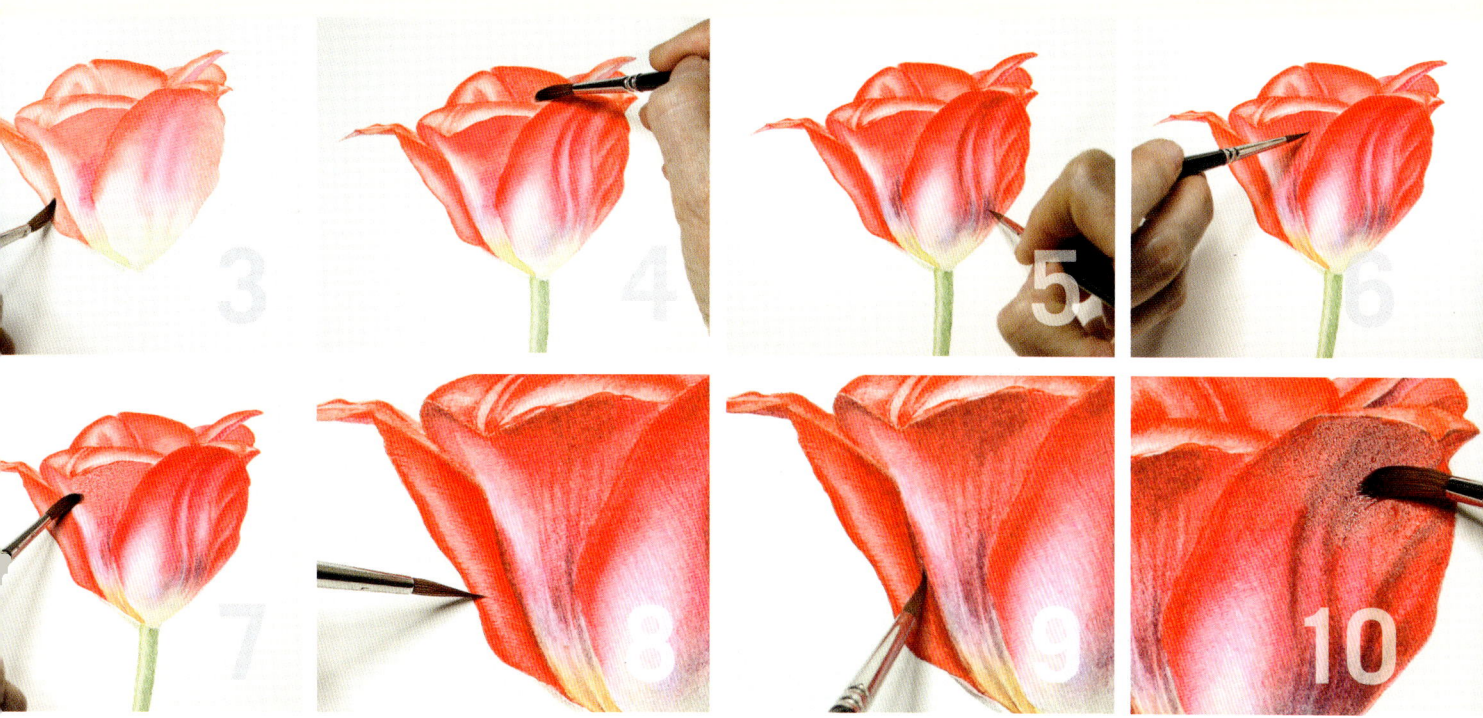

Paint washes on the insides of petals, reserving white highlights as needed to depict shine. Then, sweep a single wide stroke of orange-red along the dark side of the curled petal. Follow this with a clean, damp brush, swiping the edge of the paint to soften and control the spread of paint as needed.

When the paint is completely dry, rewet the paper and apply a second layer of local color washes to the damp paper. Add washes throughout the flower to build depth of color, value, and form. Few strokes are needed on wet paper, because the paint is easily guided into position before being absorbed into the paper. Using a few intentional strokes will keep the paint layer intact.

A violet-gray mixture of complements quinacridone red and phthalo green will serve two purposes. First, it is drybrushed onto the petal, marking a dark violet color shift in the tulip. Later, a much more dilute form of the same violet-gray mixture will be used as a glaze for shadows, even over the pale-yellow color at the base of the flower.

Add texture lines to the backs of the petals. When brush-strokes are applied to damp paper, a subtle softness in edges results. This conveys the veins' texture. Using the tip of a no. 2 brush, and using the same shadow mixture as above, stroke faint shadow lines onto the barely damp paper.

Thus far, local color has been maximized in creating values to describe the tulip's overall form. Shadow colors are now needed in the areas of core darks and cast shadows. Rewet the paper, then brush a dilute violet-grey mixture onto the outside of the petal, taking care that the edges of the shadow remain soft. The shadow color will darken the red.

Some textures and edges require crisp lines. Here, the tip of the no. 2 brush draws vein lines on dry paper. Note that the veins follow the shape of the petals. The veins appear most in the mid-tones, while fading in the highlights and hiding in the shadows.

It is time for final details. Add more texture such as striations on the backs of the petals using drybrush, and, in some instances, soften them with a clear water glaze. Here, a line of the violet-grey mixture was drawn onto dry paper to show a cast shadow. Add other edges and lines as needed for definition.

Make any final adjustments. Step back to evaluate the values relative to the entire flower. Do highlights need to be toned down, or do shadows need to be darkened? After reviewing the tulip, use a glaze of local color to soften a paper-white highlight. Here a local-color glaze of dilute red unifies a shadow area.

Bearded Iris

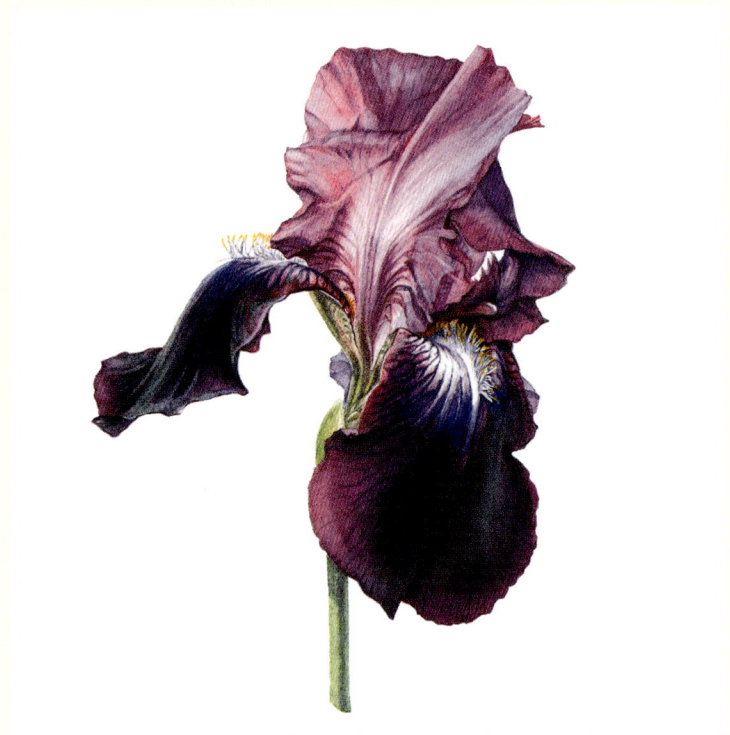

Bearded Iris
Watercolor on paper
9 × 8 inches [20 × 22.5 cm]
© Constance Sayas
HOURS TO COMPLETE: 70

MATERIALS: Lead holder with
HB lead; kneaded eraser; Kolinsky
watercolor round brushes (nos. 2
and 4); water container; paper towels;
scrap piece of watercolor paper for
testing color and brush load; ceramic
palette.Colors (tube watercolors):
cadmium yellow; burnt sienna;
quinacridone red; ultramarine blue;
phthalo green.

This bearded iris features visual contrast
in its petals, color, value, opacity, and
texture. Depicting its iridescent, delicate,
crepelike upper petals (standards) in
comparison to its dark, opaque, velvety
lower petals (falls) requires different
painting strategies; both layered color
blending and wet-on-wet color-blending
techniques can be used here.

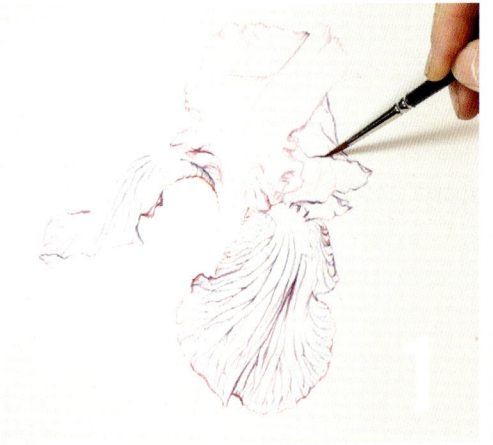
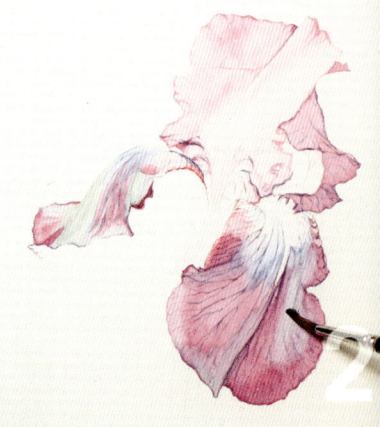

Paint watercolor lines on top of the pencil line drawing,
tailoring the line weight, color, and value to the iris subject.
The falls are opaque, so dark lines here will aid painting,
acting as a template seen through the dark layers of paint
that will follow. To trace the lighter standards, paint these
lines in a lighter color and weight.

Map the initial color areas onto the falls. Working wet-
on-wet, drop in ultramarine blue and quinacridone red
and guide them to blend. Use a different color-blending
method to convey the pale luminosity in the standards:
paint different colors as glazes in separate layers, letting
each layer dry between applications. A first glaze of dilute
quinacridone red is the layer shown here.

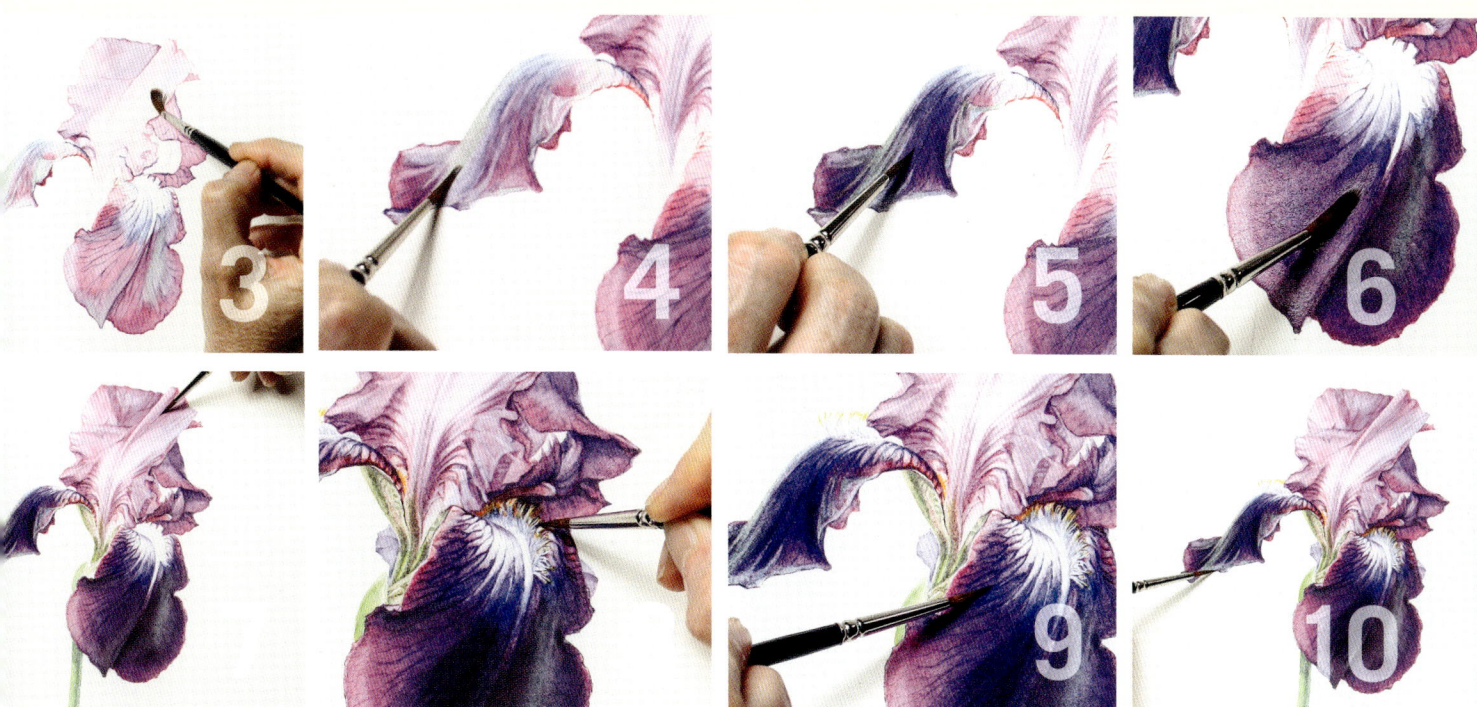

When the quinacridone red glaze on the standards is completely dry, rewet the paper and wash a layer of dilute ultramarine blue over the quinacridone red. The separate alternating layers of transparent quinacridone red and ultramarine blue will mix optically to create varied violets with iridescent hints of red and blue showing through. Let the paint dry thoroughly.

Once they are dry, the falls are ready for another layer of color. A green-grey mixture of quinacridone red and phthalo green is used here to represent the sheen of the diffused highlights that appear on velvety petal textures. This lighter sheen of color needs to be applied first before the final dark color is laid on top.

A layer of concentrated paint is needed to achieve the deep color seen in the lower petals. A less dilute mix of quinacridone red and phthalo green is used to make a rich violet black. With a few intentional strokes, carefully brush this color onto the falls, avoiding the lighter green-grey sheen areas. Follow this step with a clean, damp no. 4 brush, using it to soften and blend as needed.

Glaze the larger petal with water first to ensure the pigment stays on the surface long enough to be guided into position, then drop the same violet-black mix as on the adjacent petal. Retain select areas of undercolor, conforming to the falls' shape. Working wet-on-wet also ensures blurred edges

of the dark paint, essential to conveying the soft, velvety petal texture.

The shadow creases in the standards are strengthened with strokes of local color. When painted on barely damp paper, the shadow lines will blur slightly while maintaining the definition needed to simulate the crepe-like texture of the petals.

A section of white paper was reserved to render the beard in drybrush. Some of the beard detail is simply drawn in as color lines and shadows against white. Other beard detail is defined by painting into the white area, painting the surrounding dark color into the hairs of the beard.

Dark lines of striped pattern are stroked over the dark template lines that were applied early on. The thick paint lines drawn onto damp paper will bleed slightly. Then, as the paper progresses from damp to dry, redraw paint along the centers of the lines to reinforce the pattern markings. Pattern often includes combinations of both soft and hard edges.

Add hard-edged details late in the painting when they do not run the risk of being disturbed by further washes. Fine lines, shadow edges, and other definition should be painted on dry paper. Here, a shadow line is drawn along the edge of the petal using the tip of a no. 2 brush on dry paper.

Floribunda Rose

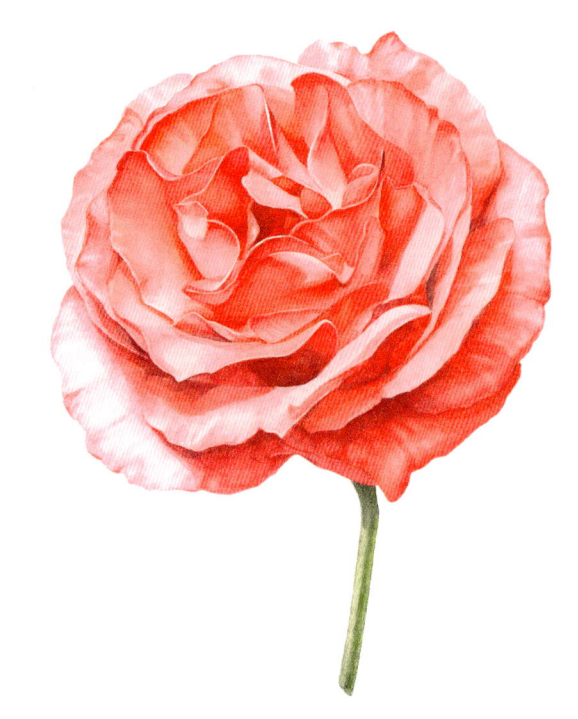

Floribunda Rose
Watercolor on paper
7 × 8 inches [17.5 × 20 cm]
© Constance Sayas
HOURS TO COMPLETE: 50

MATERIALS: Lead holder with
HB lead; kneaded eraser; Kolinsky
watercolor round brushes (no. 2 and
4); small, synthetic angle shader
brush; water container; paper towels;
scrap piece of watercolor paper for
testing color and brush load; ceramic
palette. Colors (tube watercolors):
cadmium yellow; pyrrol scarlet;
quinacridone red; phthalo blue.

This rose can be rendered using
primarily wet on-wet painting
techniques to blend color and build
form. Painting on wet paper requires
minimal brushwork. Flowing paint stays
on the surface of the paper long enough
to be easily guided into place. Only two
layers of paint, with refinement, are
needed to keep the appearance of the
painting as fresh as the flower.

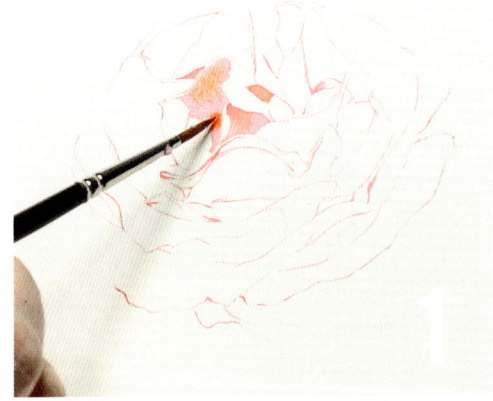

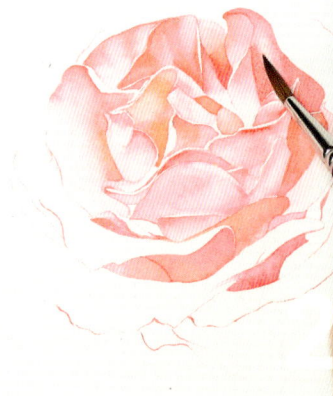

Replace the pencil drawing of the rose center with watercolor lines. Varied in weight and value, the colored lines act as a map to help you navigate the inner maze of abstract petal shapes. Then, apply washes of violet-red color to the petal sections with the no. 2 brush. Coral mixtures are then charged (dropped) into the wet paint. With minimal brushwork, guide colors to blend.

Moving outward to the petal sections bordered by dry paper, continue the same wet-on-wet color blending. Pay careful attention to retaining light areas according to form, sometimes reserving lights with graded washes, other times lifting color. Here, wet paint is lifted, mopped up with a clean, damp (not wet) brush. Lifting wet paint ensures soft edges around the lifted area.

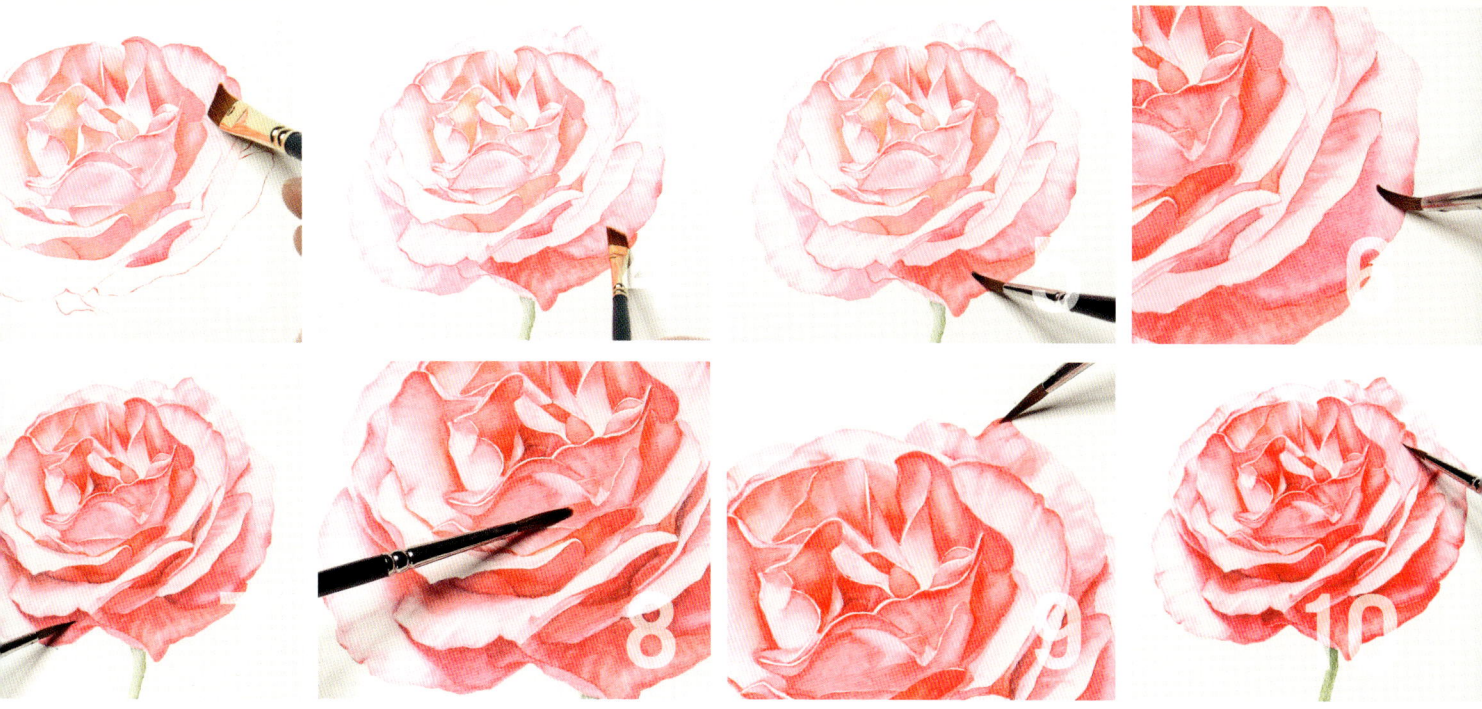

Apply graded washes to individual petals. Once the paint begins to absorb into the paper, further brushwork will disturb the paint layer. Disrupting the settling paint intentionally, however, can create desired textural effects. In this painting, a damp angle shader brush held upright and stroked down the established wash lifts out lines of light to depict the petal's subtle ridges.

You can create different petal textures by maneuvering an angle shader brush over a settled wash. Held upright, the angled brush lifts out linear highlights. Held on its side, as seen here, the brush lifts out spots of color to mimic a mottled petal texture.

In addition to creating texture by lifting paint, you can enhance texture by adding color, applying wide strokes of violet-red on damp paper to blur the strokes. To match the subtle undulations seen in the rose's petals, texture marks made with those wide strokes should be close in value to the color underneath. If necessary, texture marks can always be subdued with a glaze.

Apply a second layer of washes throughout the flower to build color, value, and form. Add cast shadows in local color help to separate and define petals. Here a wash was applied to form a cast shadow, and one edge was swept with a clean, damp brush to soften. The diffused shadow edge suggests distance between petals. The crisp edge defines the petal above.

More local color red and orange values have been intensified to build form. After evaluating values relative to the overall rose, some darker areas were added to give depth to the flower. A dilute neutral mixture of phthalo blue, pyrrol scarlet and a touch of cadmium yellow is used for select shadows in the darkest recesses.

Always look for opportunities to boost color and contrast. With that goal in mind, a color accent was added here by dragging a dab of bright coral paint across the petal. The deep color reinforces the petal's structure. Other colors were added to capture the vibrancy seen in some recessed areas of the rose.

It is time to refine edges. Painted lines that define edges should show form in thickness and value and should read as shadows rather than outlines. This petal tip is reinforced with a line of red paint, which is then blended into the petal. In other places, tone down the white lines of the petal edges with single strokes of dilute color.

Review the rose for final enhancements. Additional glazes act to unify areas and subdue some texture marks. Here a generic shadow shape was reconfigured to better fit the petal's specific form. Attention paid to nuance in shapes and details will produce a more natural-looking painting.

Many artists use a combination of wetter and drier watercolor techniques to achieve color and form. In this tutorial, colors are mixed in mixing-tray wells, creating a supply of consistent color to draw from over the course of an entire painting. Some of this color is applied to reusable, plastic-based paper and allowed to dry into skins for use in drybrush areas. Here, a silver maple leaf and a bur oak leaf are painted with blended first washes, followed by additional layered colors, then drybrush work for details.

Leaves

TUTOR: MARGARET BEST

Silver Maple Leaf

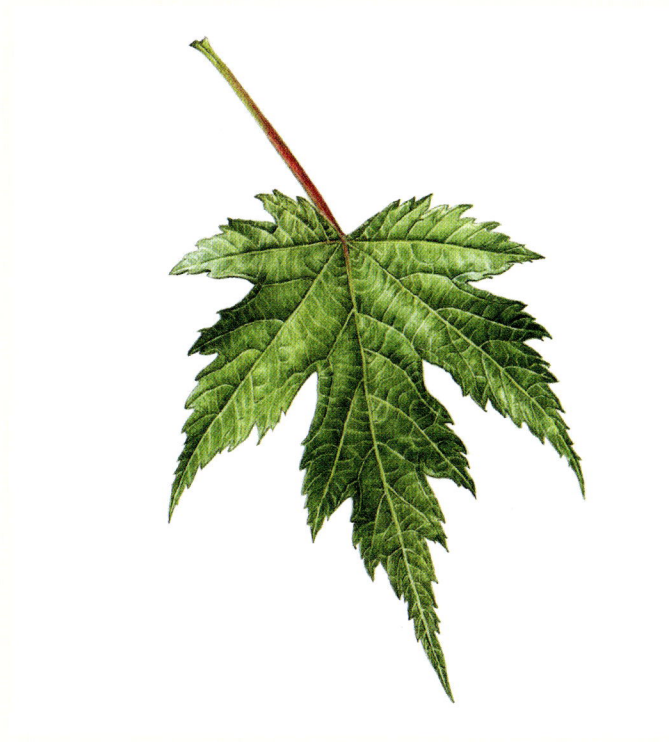

Acer saccharinum
Watercolor on paper
6 ½ × 4 ½ inches [16.25 × 11.25 cm]
© Margaret Best
HOURS TO COMPLETE: 22 HOURS

MATERIALS For drawing: Light box; tracing
paper; tape; 2.3 mm retractable eraser;
mechanical pencil (0.3 mm with
H or HB lead). For painting: Container for
water; brushes: synthetic mixing brush (no.
4); synthetic brush (no. 000); flat lifting brush;
Kolinsky rounds (nos. 4 and 1); pipette; mixing
tray; paper towel; reusable polypropylene
synthetic paper; hot-pressed watercolor paper.
Paint colors: quinacridone gold, leaf green,
phthalo blue, quinacridone red, transparent
red oxide.

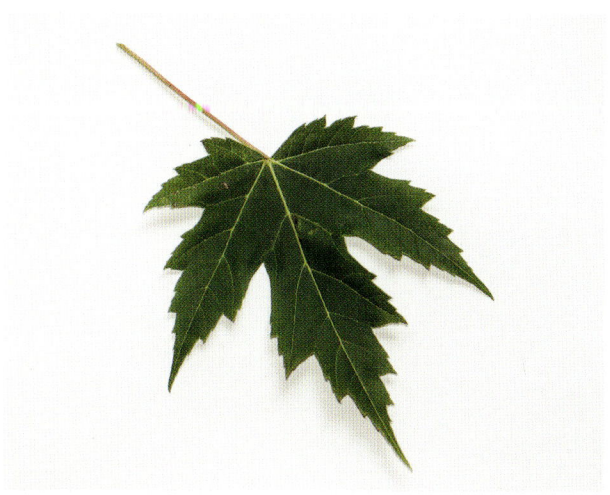

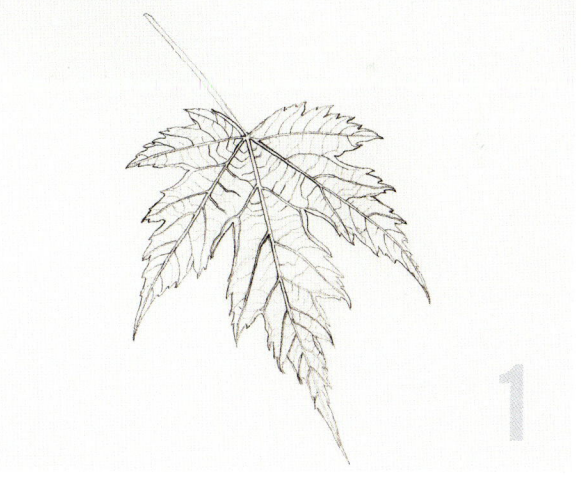

A silver maple leaf (*Acer saccharinum*) is lobed with a serrated margin and many fine veins. It is fine in texture, and light passes easily through it, leading to its bright yellow-green color. For the artist, the challenges of illustrating this leaf include capturing the numerous visible small veins and holding the sharply defined edges on a complex leaf structure.

Complete an accurate line drawing of the specimen directly onto tracing paper. Using a 0.3mm mechanical pencil with H or HB lead, draw the main veins, showing their very fine dimension (not a single line). Include all the visible vein lines on the tracing paper. The lines must be dark enough to show through paper on a light box.

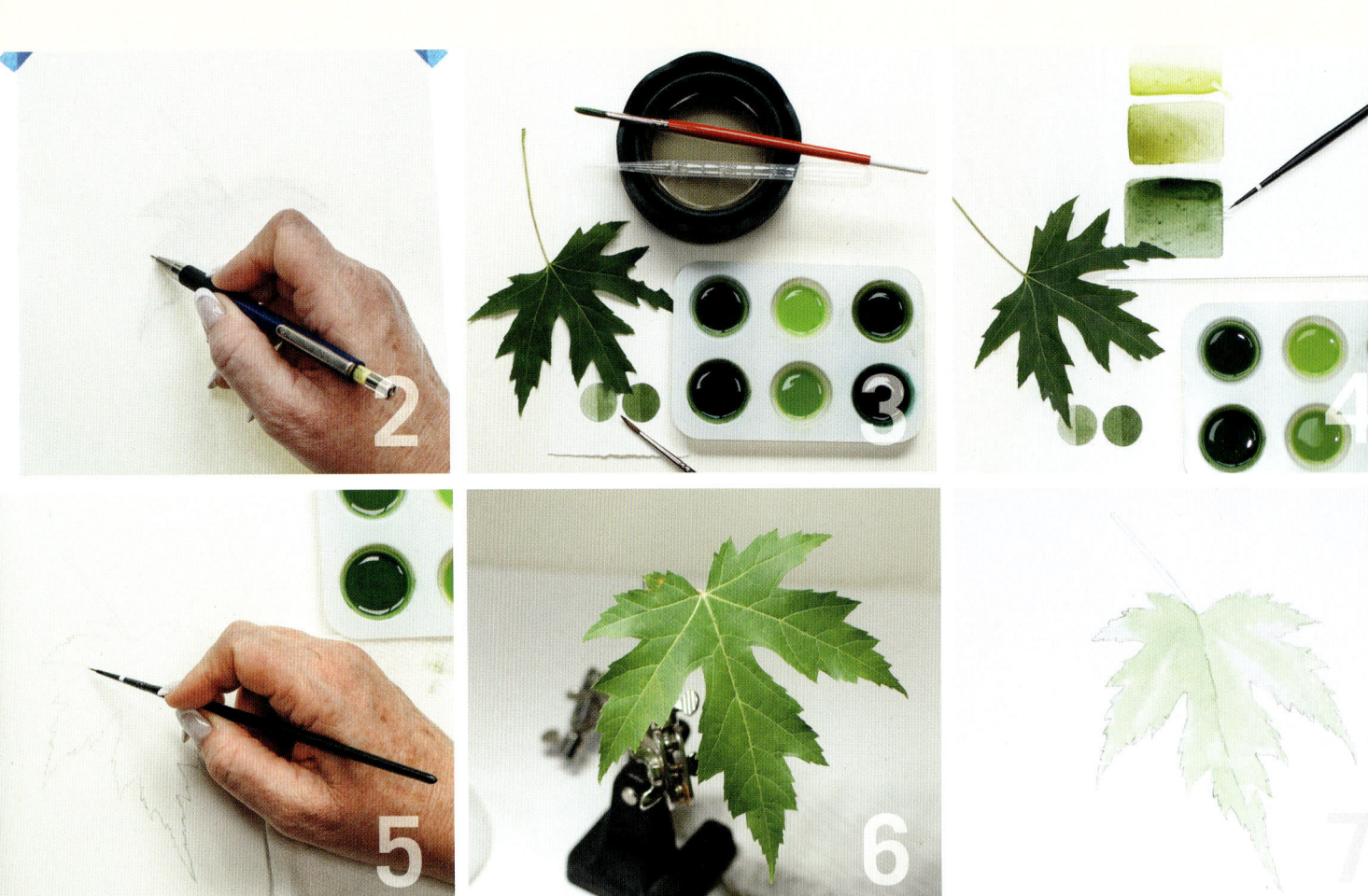

Attach the tracing paper to the light box with hot-pressed paper taped in position over it. Using a mechanical pencil, transfer the outer-edge outline drawing only, and apply very little pressure so that it is barely visible. Avoid erasing any part of the drawing to prevent damage to the surface of the paper.

Mix colors to match the specimen. Using a clean pipette, measure 2 ml of water into each well of the mixing tray. Blend colors with a dedicated mixing brush, then test each color for accuracy on a scrap piece of watercolor paper. Create pigment skins of matched colors on the polypropylene paper. When the skins are dry, pigment can be lifted for fine details.

The leaf is a mix of Prussian blue and Indian yellow. Use leaf green with a touch of matched leaf color for the exposed veins and the first wash. Use a weak phthalo blue mix for highlight areas, and, for the leaf stem, use leaf green, quinacridone red, and transparent red oxide. Note how color can be lifted from the skin using a fine detail brush.

With a weak blend of the leaf's matched green color and using a no. 000 brush, carefully paint a fine line over the pale graphite outline of the leaf. Once the paint is completely dry, lift any evidence of remaining graphite very gently with a retractable eraser so as not to damage the surface of the paper. Paint a single line to indicate one edge of the midrib.

Illuminate the leaf with a small lamp at a 45-degree angle from the upper left or right side. Lighting the leaf at this raking angle will illuminate the its dimension, surface texture, and value range.

Using a no. 4 Kolinsky brush, dampen the paper evenly over the left half of the leaf to the midrib edge, allowing water to seep into the paper slightly. With the tip of the brush, add weak phthalo blue to the damp surface in areas where highlights are observed on the specimen. Rinse the paintbrush with water and load it with the vein color. Apply the vein color to the remaining areas of the leaf, and blend while the paper is still damp. Repeat on the other half of the leaf.

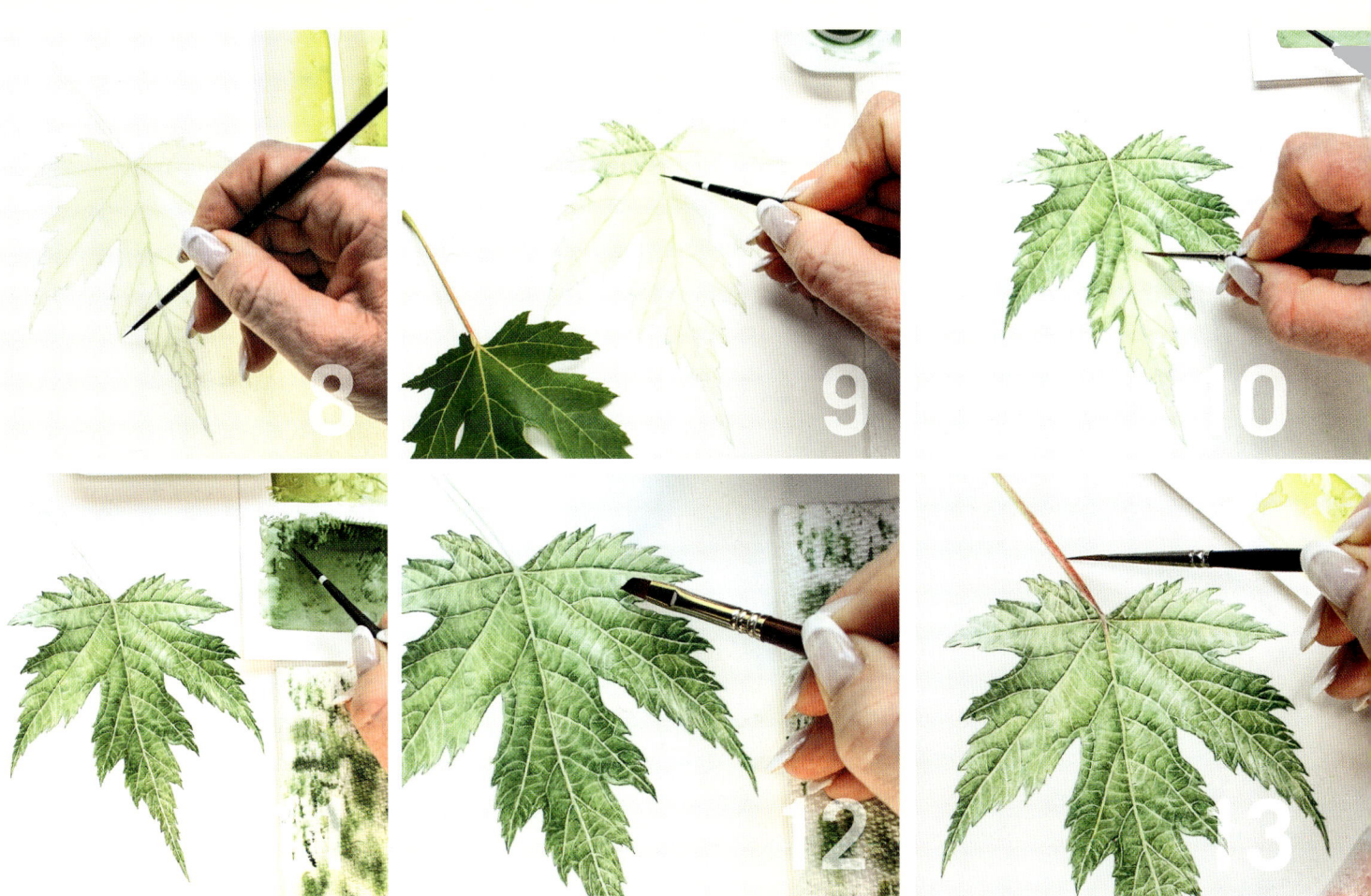

When first washes are completely dry, return the painting to the light box, align it with the original tracing, and secure it with tape. With a damp no. 000 brush, lift some of the vein color from the pigment skin and carefully trace only the larger, more defined veins connecting at the leaf base and midrib.

Refer to the leaf specimen and detailed drawing to check for accuracy. Add small, pale washes with matched leaf color using the tip of a no. 1 or no. 000 brush to define the spaces created by the veins. Layer each section between the main veins and margins, leaving visible vein lines open to expose the first wash of vein color.

Allow each layer of wash to dry fully before adding the next. Work from the top of the leaf downward on both sides of leaf. In addition to the blue highlight areas, show bright green areas on the left side of the leaf using vein color mixed with leaf color. Build value ranges with layering and leave the darkest fine lines for the detail stage.

Review the shadow areas of the leaf and stem for the strength of color and depth of value. Use drybrush work to add the finest dark-value details where noted, lifting pigment from blended colors or dried paint skins with a damp no. 000 brush. Clarify the serrations along the leaf edge.

Step back from the painting and consider the highlight areas. If lighter-value areas are needed for contrast, use a damp lifting brush to carefully lift paint layers. To avoid damaging the surface of the paper, allow it to dry completely after each attempt. Lifting is a legitimate technique—not only a remedial correction method.

Using the tip of a no. 1 brush, paint leaf-green wash on the stem. Allow the wash to dry. Apply the red color match in the relevant areas of the stem, leaving some of the leaf green exposed. Picking up color from the pigment skin with a no. 000 brush, carefully add some leaf green to make the exposed veins more vibrant. Review the whole leaf carefully for any stray graphite that needs to be erased, and any less-than-sharp edges that need to be touched up. Know when to stop rather than overwork the paper.

Bur Oak Leaf

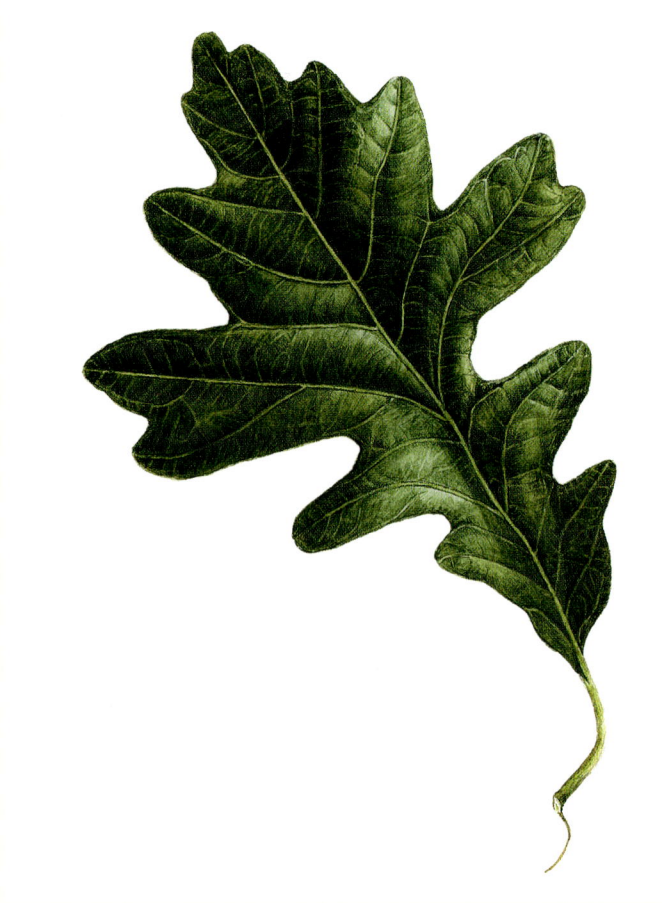

Quercus macrocarpa
Watercolor on paper
6 ½ × 4 ½ inches [16.25 × 11.25 cm]
© Margaret Best
HOURS TO COMPLETE: 25

This bur oak leaf is a dark green, and its thicker texture allows less light to pass through the leaf. A palette of Prussian blue, leaf green, phthalo blue, quinacridone gold, and transparent red oxide is used to convey these characteristics, along with its deeply lobed margins that curl toward the underside of the leaf.

Complete an accurate line drawing of the specimen on tracing paper, using a 0.3mm mechanical pencil with an H or HB lead. Be sure to draw both sides of the main veins to show their thickness. Include all the visible vein lines on the tracing paper—the lines must be dark enough to show through 140 lb. [300 gsm] hot-pressed paper on a light box.

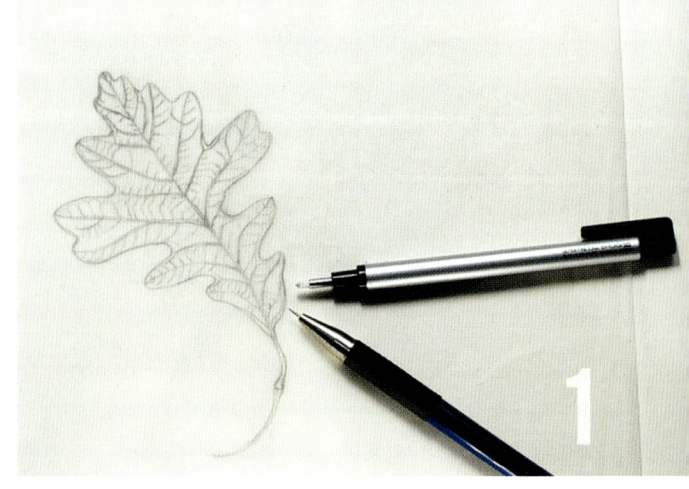

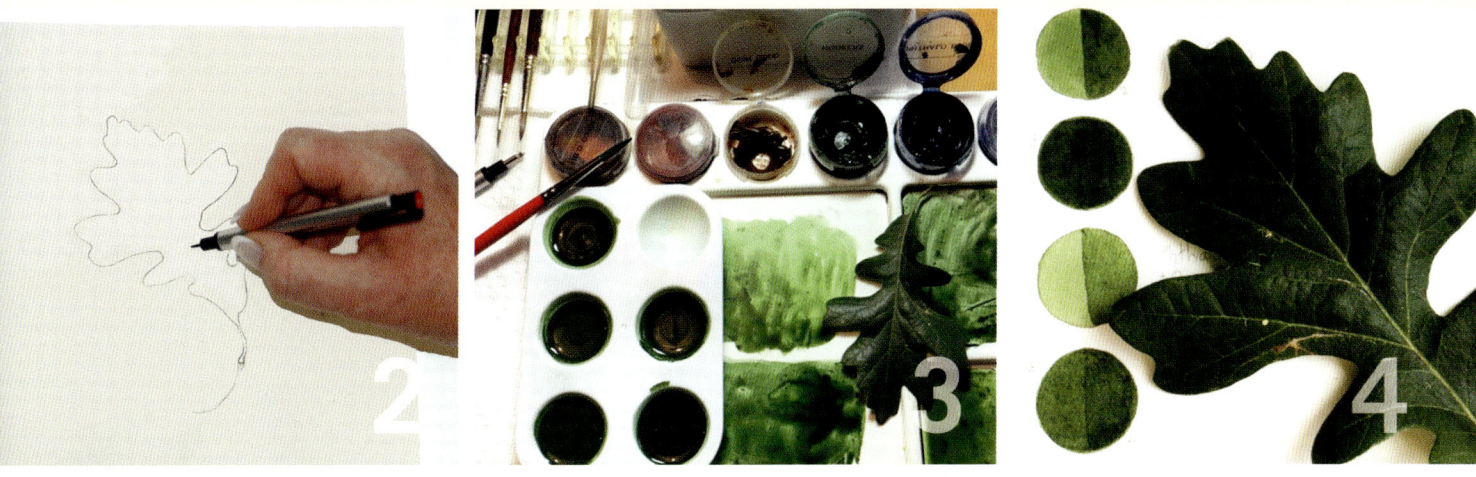

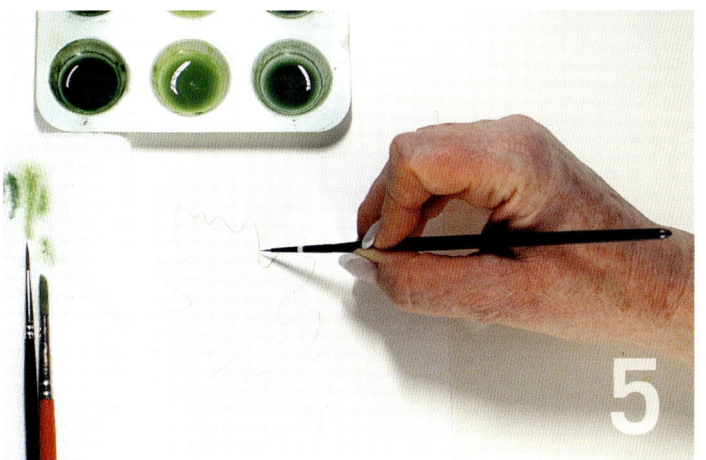

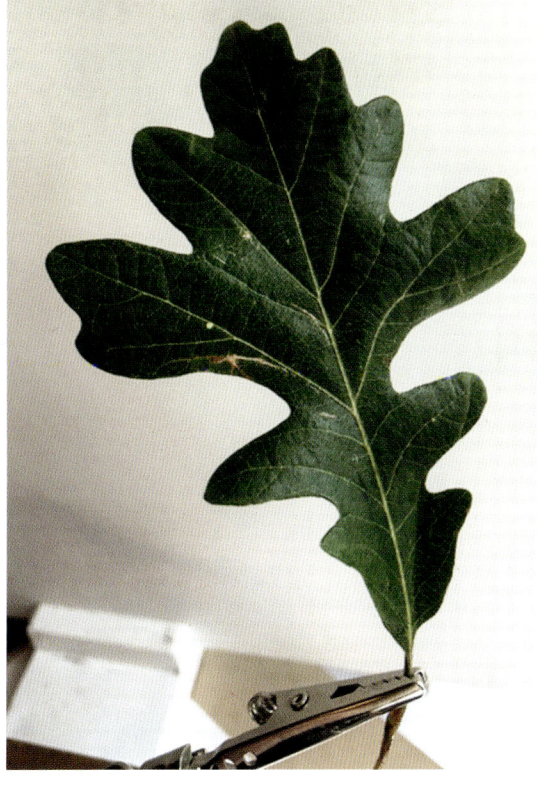

Attach the drawing to the light box with hot-pressed paper taped in position over it. Using a mechanical pencil, transfer the outline of the drawing only. Trace lightly, with as little graphite as possible, so the drawing is just visible. If needed, gently erase any excess graphite with a fine retractable white-plastic eraser.

Mix colors to match the specimen. Using a clean pipette, mix 2 ml of color to match each of the different leaf areas in the wells of a mixing tray. Blend colors with a dedicated mixing brush, then test each color for accuracy on a scrap piece of watercolor paper. Create pigment skins of the matched colors on a palette or polypropylene paper. When the skins are dry, lift the pigment with the pointed tip of a damp brush for fine details.

The leaf color is a mix of Prussian blue and quinacridone gold. The exposed veins and the first wash of leaf uses leaf green with touch of the leaf's matched green color. Highlight areas are a dilute phthalo blue. The petiole (leaf stem) is a mix of leaf green and transparent red oxide.

With a diluted blend of the leaf's green color and using a no. 000 brush, carefully paint a fine line over the pale graphite outline of the leaf. Once the paint is completely dry, lift any remaining graphite gently so as not to damage the surface of the paper. Paint a single line to indicate one edge of the midrib.

Using an alligator clip to hold the leaf, illuminate it with a small lamp at a 45-degree angle from the upper left or right side. Lighting at this raking angle will increase contrast between light and shadow, revealing highlights and surface texture.

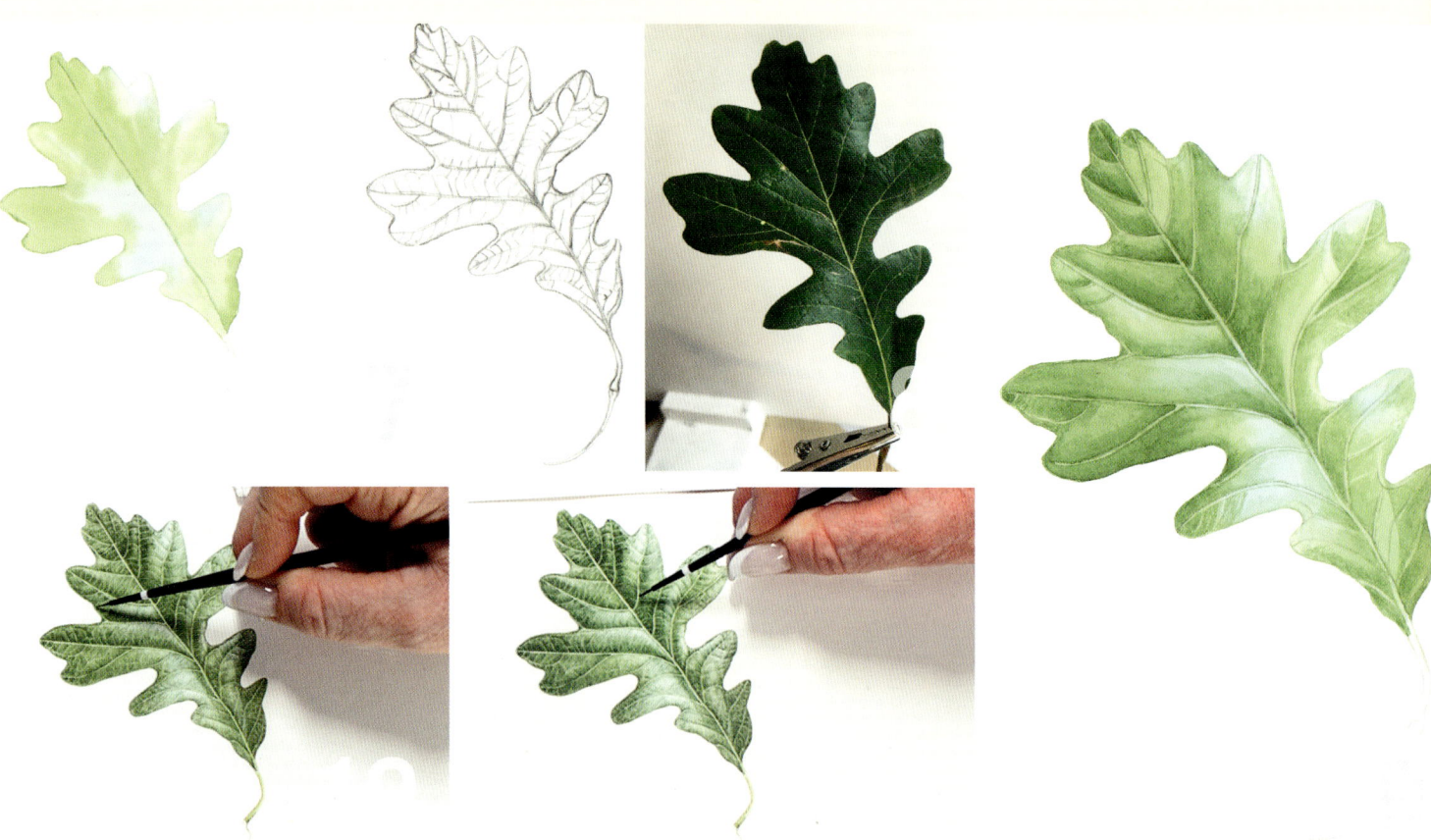

Using no. 4 Kolinsky brush, dampen the paper evenly over the left half of the leaf to the midrib edge, allowing the water to seep into the paper slightly. With the tip of a no. 4 brush, apply diluted phthalo blue in the highlight areas. Blend to soften the edges while the paper is still damp. Rinse the paintbrush with water and load it with the vein color. Apply the vein color to the remaining areas of the leaf, and blend while the paper is still damp. Paint the other half of the leaf in the same way.

Return the painting to the light box, align it with the original tracing, and secure it with tape. With damp no. 000 brush, lift some of the pigment skin from the polypropylene paper and carefully trace only the main veins connecting at the midrib. Refer to leaf specimen and detailed drawing for guidance. Veins are more than lines in a leaf; they often cause undulations in the leaf, leading to areas of tonal variation.

Layer each section between the main veins and margins with leaf color, going around the visible veins to expose the first wash of vein color. Avoid painting the blue highlight areas. After the second layer has been applied, use a less diluted blend for successive layers. Observing the center and secondary veins, lay in the light and shadow they create.

Build value ranges with layering, and leave the darkest fine lines for the detail stage. Allow each layer of wash to dry fully before adding the next.

It is important to avoid building layers with weak color blends when you are painting leaves of dark value in watercolor, because too many layers of paint will cause the paper to become overworked. Try to achieve the darkest values with no more than four to five layers to avoid overworking the paper.

Using a damp no. 000 brush, pick up pigment from the dried paint skins to sharpen the vein edges where needed. Using the same technique, sharpen and darken the leaf margins to show how they curl downward. This fine-detail drybrush work is very important and should be completed after all the washes have been laid in place and have completely dried.

With the tip of a no. 1 brush, paint a leaf green wash on the stem. Allow the paint to dry. Then apply a blend of leaf green and transparent red oxide in the relevant areas of the stem, leaving some leaf green exposed. Review the leaf for any needed repairs or stray graphite that needs to be erased.

The cylindrical form is found throughout nature, especially in stems and roots. Stems and roots are the unsung heroes of any botanical painting, and they are central to its composition. They convey information about the light source, as well as the structure and habit of a plant.

Stems, Twigs, and Roots

TUTOR: SARAH ROCHE

Cylinder

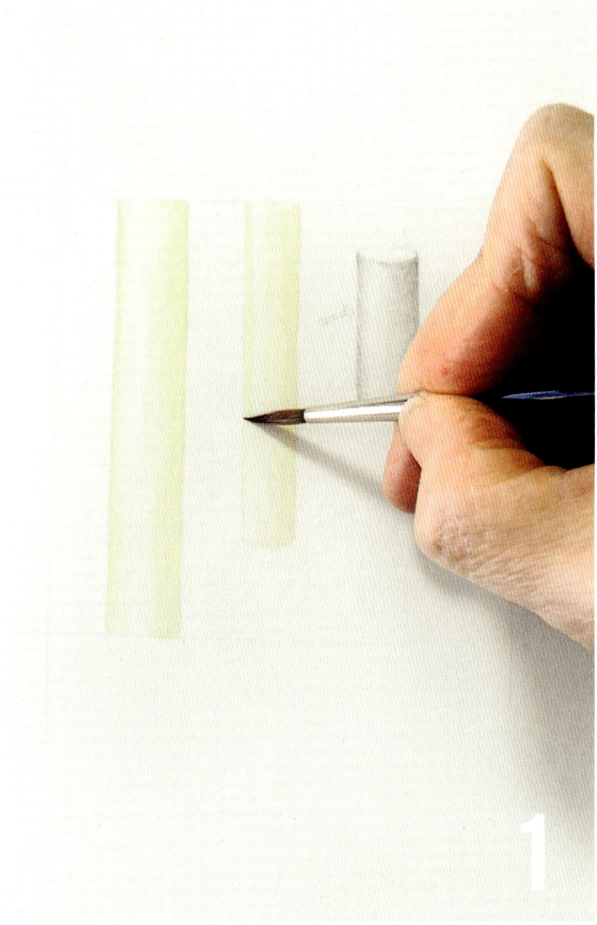

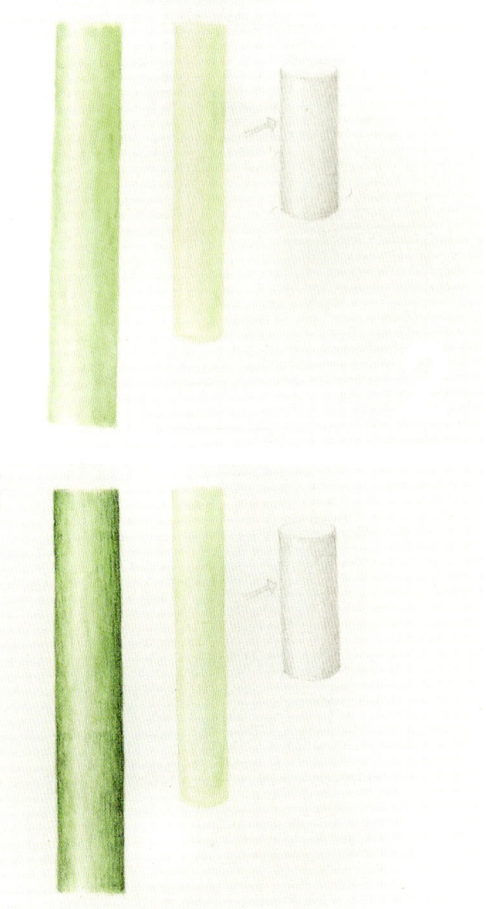

A simple stem or root is essentially the same shape as a cylinder or tube. Here, two cylinders are lightly laid out in watercolor, alongside a graphite study of a cylinder, showing the cylinder's circular form and stronger value away from the light source. Using a dilute wash of lemon yellow, lay in the areas of color along the left edge and right side, leaving an area of white paper for the highlight. Soften the edge of the wash with a clean damp brush. Let it dry.

Mix lemon yellow and ultramarine blue to make a yellow-green wash. Intensify the value in the darker area, blending the tonal edge toward the highlight. Establish the left edge of the cylinder with a very fine brushstroke.

Add more ultramarine blue to the mix to deepen the value and reinforce the sense of form. Use a damp, clean brush to smooth any obvious brushstrokes.

MATERIALS: Container for water; two ceramic palettes; Kolinsky round brushes (two no. 4's and one no. 2); shader brush (bright; no. 2); cotton cloth; dividers; HB, 2H, and F pencils; emery board; extra-fine retractable eraser; craft knife; ruler. Colors (watercolor pigments): lemon yellow; nickel titanate; new gamboge; raw sienna; burnt sienna; permanent rose; scarlet lake; pthalocyanine green; ultramarine blue.

Tulip Stems

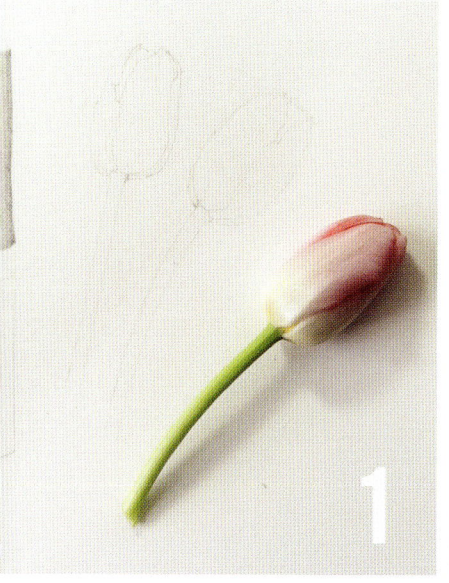

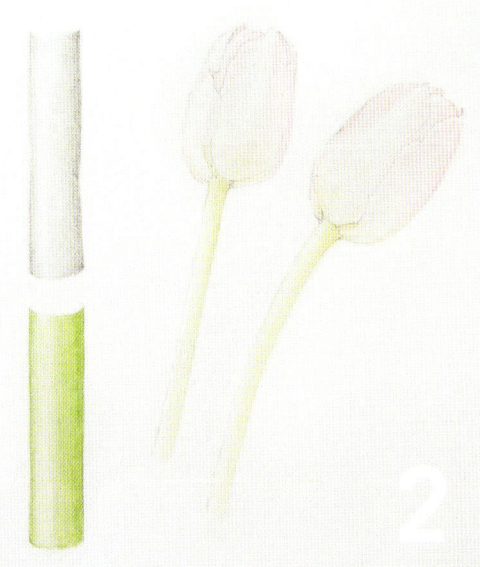

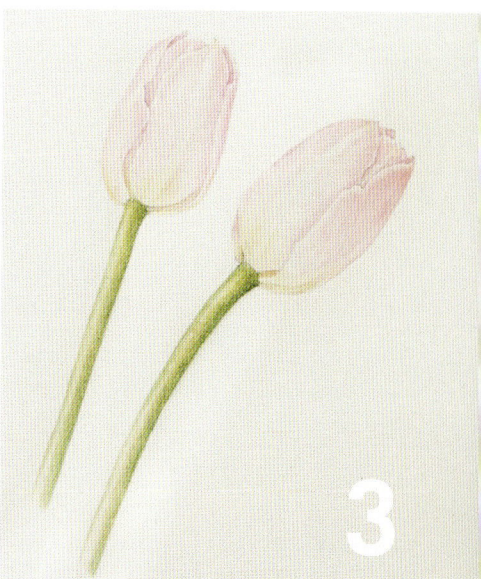

A graphite sketch of two tulips is made, alongside a stem drawing showing tonal sections.

Using the yellow observed in the base of the tulip petals, lay down an initial wash to establish the form. Since the stem is smooth, run the paint stroke down the right side of the stem and blend the edge into the highlight area with a damp brush.

Intensify the green, adding ultramarine blue to the yellow used in the first wash. Soften the green into the highlight area with a clean damp brush.

Continue to add layers of paint to the darker areas to emphasize the stem's roundness, allowing the previous layer of paint to dry before adding another.

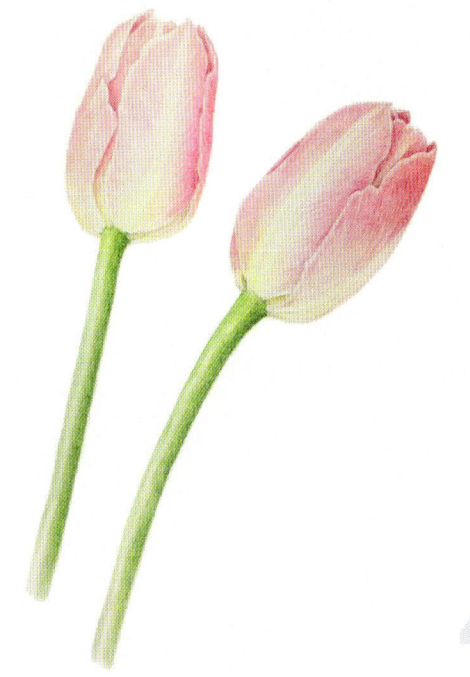

Thorny Stems

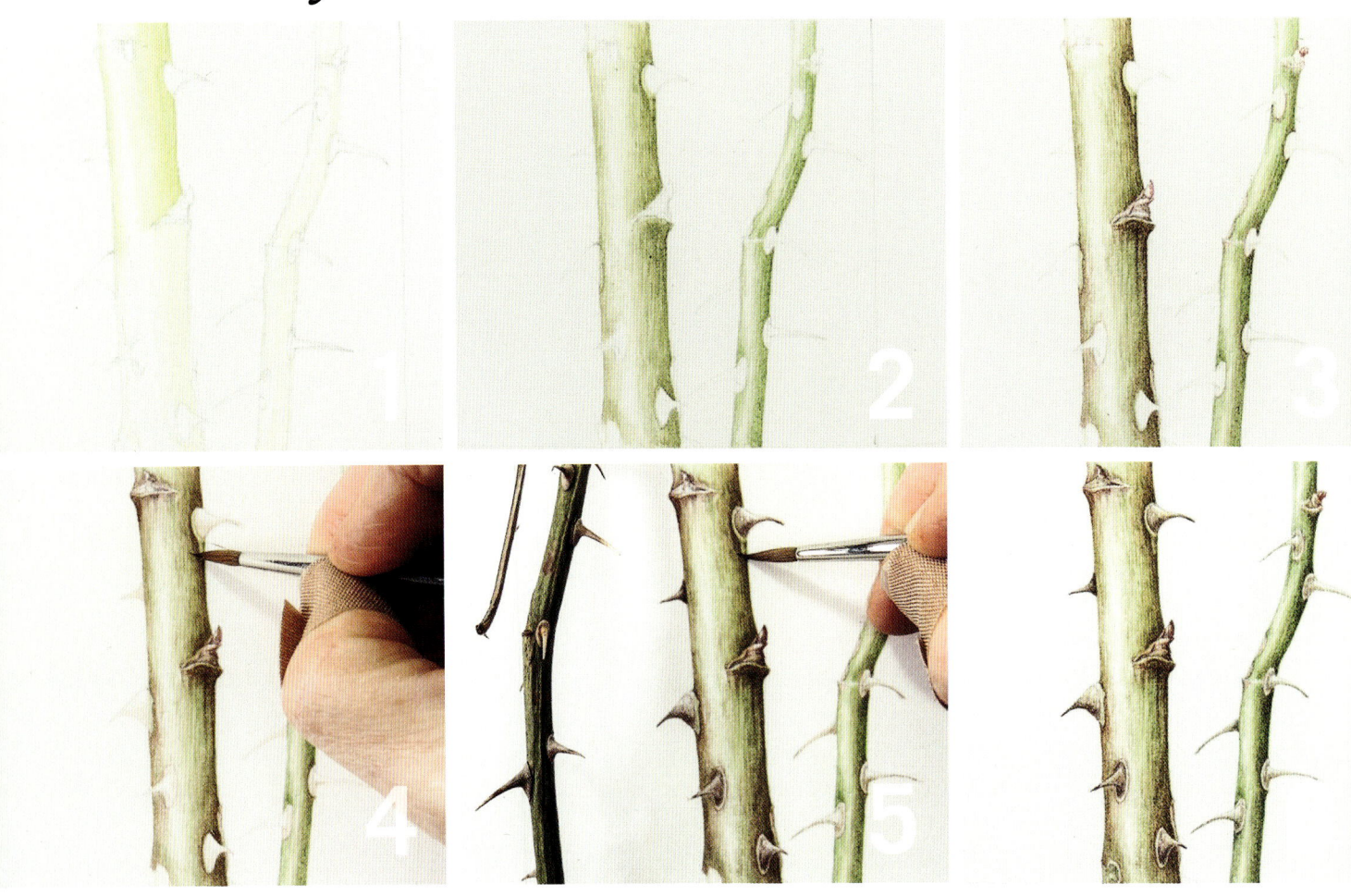

Stems are generally thicker toward the base of the plant, and they become progressively thinner as they become longer. Stems with thorns are basically a cylinder with external attachments. Draw the stems carefully, observing the placement, form, and attachments of the thorns.

Work out the color mixes for each stem and then, leaving the thorns unpainted, paint the stems, establishing their round, smooth form. Note the small rises in the stems where they intersect with the thorns.

As the form is established, add some of the flower color to deepen the values. Both of these specimens have pink flowers; the one on the left is a dark pink, and the one on the right is a lighter pink. Use a smaller brush to add detail, working with small drybrush strokes. Once the stems are painted, begin the thorns.

Each thorn is also a tapered cylinder, so observe where the light hits each thorn and build up the color. Use some of the flower color to help describe the thorns' shape, leaving a lighter area where they are attached to the stem. Keep your brushstrokes small and accurate, using a fine, fairly dry brush.

Add layers of pink and green to the stems, and clarify the intersections of stem and thorn by darkening the areas around the thorns with a drybrush. Add shading to the lower sides of thorns to convey their three-dimensionality.

Be sure to retain the highlight in the stem as you add the final details, intensifying color by using the tip of the brush.

Rose Stems (Early Spring)

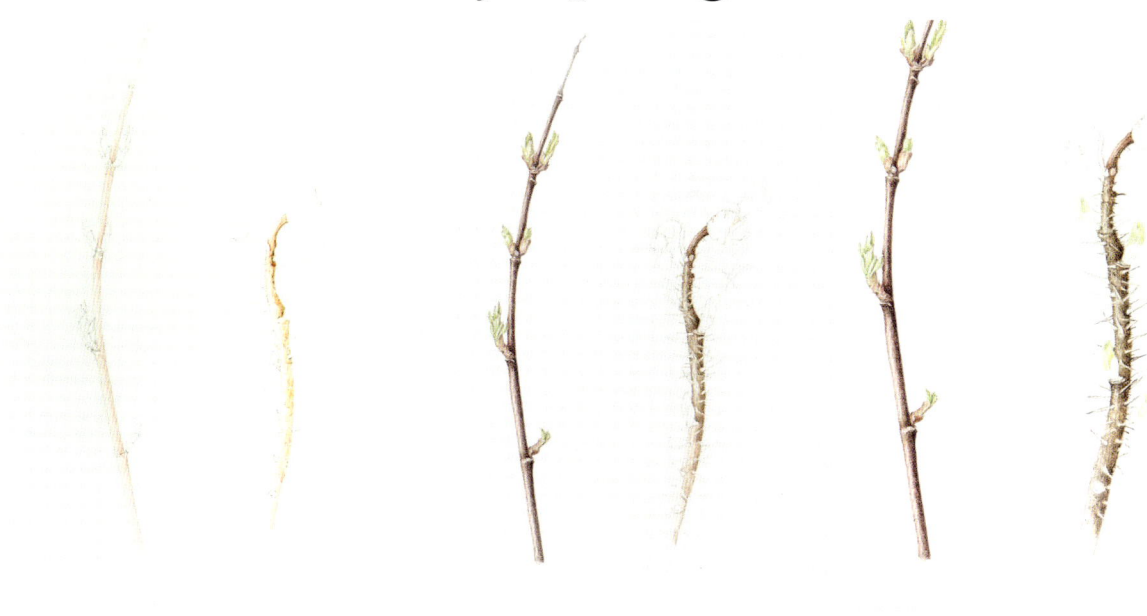

For the smooth knockout rose stem on the left, establish the form using a very light tea wash, and when it is dry reinforce the form. The colors found in the stem of a plant will often echo those of its flower; in this case it is a pink rose.

This prickly *Rugosa* (at right) was carefully drawn, with special attention paid to the direction and distribution of the prickles. Beginning with a lemon yellow wash, and then introducing the bud color (lemon yellow and pthalocyanine green), begin to build up the cylindrical form of the stem. Add the leaf buds in a light value to the rose stem on the left.

A mix of permanent rose and burnt sienna will introduce the colors in the rosehip to the stem on the right and help deepen the values. Using a damp pointed brush, carefully work between the prickles, leaving them—and the area they emerge from on the stem—unpainted. Pale green is added to the tips of the leaf buds on the stem on the right.

Build up the layers of paint with a fairly dry brush, smoothing out any unwanted hard edges with a damp clean brush. Each prickle is a tiny cylinder, so carefully darken one side more than the other to explain its shape. Paint the tiny prickles, which emerge between the larger ones, in a darker mixture, which gives them emphasis along the margins of the stem.

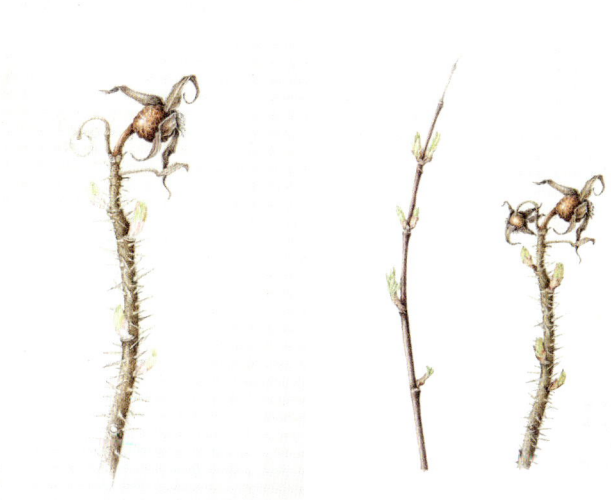

Paint the rose hips, along with the dried sepals, and lay shading between the sepals and hips. Paint the details in the emerging leaf buds using the pinks and reds in the bracts, and greens and pinks in the emerging leaves. Deepen the shadows around the leaf buds, and, where needed, in the hips. Balance the color and value between the two stems.

Hairy Stems

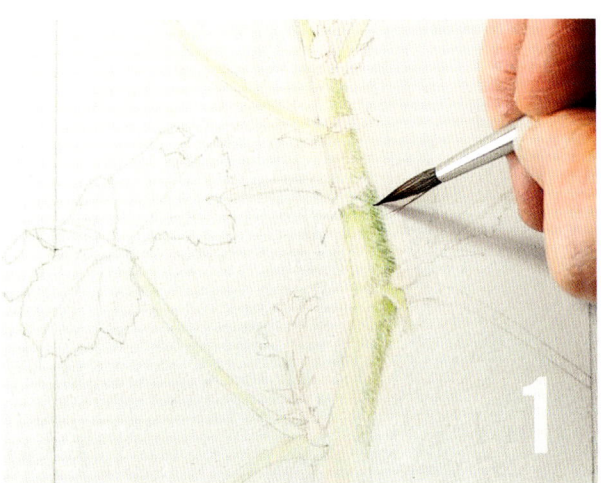

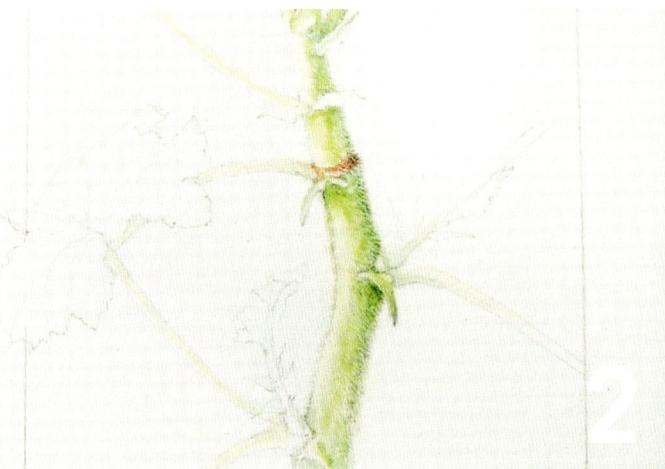

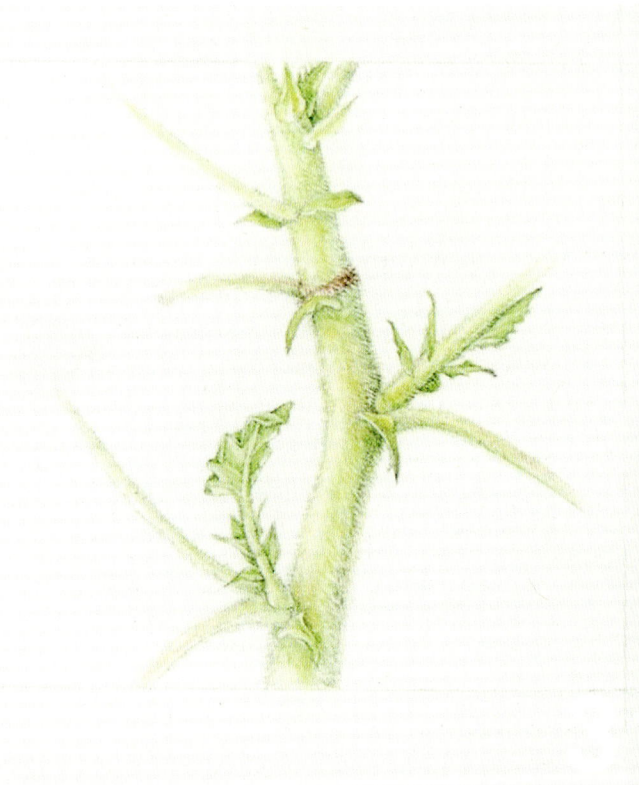

First, draw the stem carefully with a very fine light pencil line. In this specimen, the hairs were white, so the form was established in very light values. With a no. 2 brush and a mid-green color, use small brushstrokes to establish the direction of the hairs, painting the dark areas between them to suggest their texture. Aim to give the impression of them, rather than to paint every one.

Use pthalocyanine green, lemon yellow, ultramarine blue, and burnt sienna to suggest the hairs in the body of the stem. Next, darken the lower side of each hair with a very dilute mix, and then increase the value of both edges of the stem.

On the light side the hairs will show as a dark value, and on the dark side they will appear lighter. Make sure that the edges of the actual stem are obvious. Use a stipple line to suggest them, inside the margin of the hairs that you have established.

Twig (A Woody Stem)
Viburnum carlesii

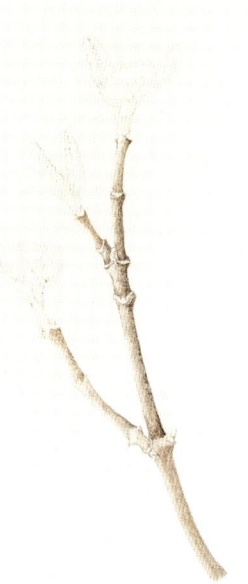

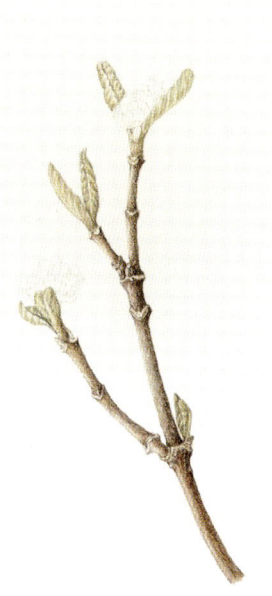

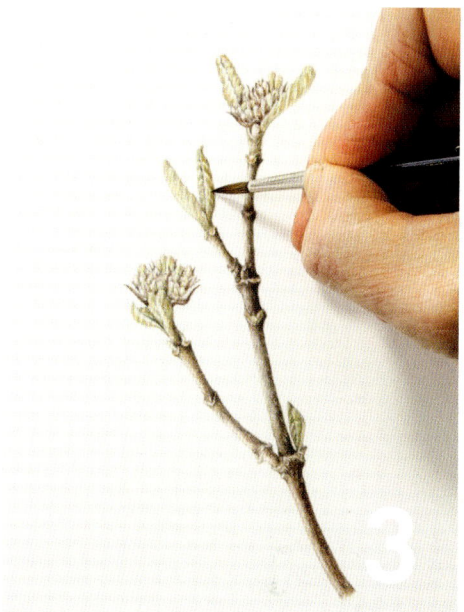

With a 4H pencil, carefully draw the specimen onto hot-pressed paper, making sure to accurately render the intervals of growth, the buds, and the leaf scars at each junction. Add a light wash of raw sienna and ultramarine blue to establish the roundness of the stem structure.

Begin to intensify the color in the stem through additional layers of color, mostly built up on the shadow side of the stem. With a light wash of yellow green, lay in the leaves that are just beginning to unfurl. Add a little of the leaf color into the main stem to unify the composition.

As the leaves take form, use the stem mix of raw sienna and ultramarine blue to show their ridged texture. Reinforce the stem margins with drybrush. Use permanent rose to add definition to the stipules between the buds and the deep values at each growth point on the stems.

The pink and creamy white buds were achieved with the yellow of the leaf color, and their form was established with a light pink-grey line. The floral sepals are painted with a permanent rose mixed with green. All the edges and transitions are further clarified in drybrush.

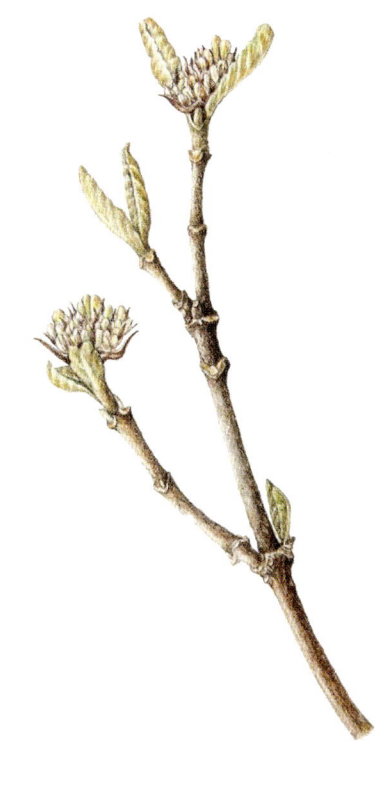

Roots

Roots are usually painted in the later stages of a composition, with the color mixes that have already been used. Study the roots carefully to determine what type of roots they are; for example, hairy, smooth, branching, or not branching. Observe the roots' habit, then draw them carefully with a 4H pencil and a very light line. Begin with very dilute washes.

Start with the most dominant roots, the ones at the front of the clump, then add the ones that emerge behind them, drawing from the front, then painting from the back. Lift any dark graphite with a retractable eraser, then, starting from the roots at the back of the drawing and using a fine paintbrush, begin defining the cylindrical form and subtle value changes.

Each root will be slightly different. Add more blue-violet tones to the back roots, and more sienna and warm beige tones to the roots that are more dominant. Reinforce their form, even in the extremely light values. Finally, erase any pencil lines with a retractable eraser and replace them with painted lines in the same value. Define the tips, which are often green, and emphasize contrast in the darkest areas.

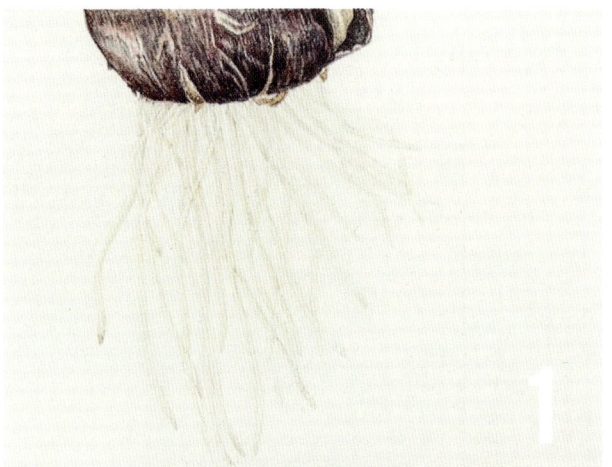

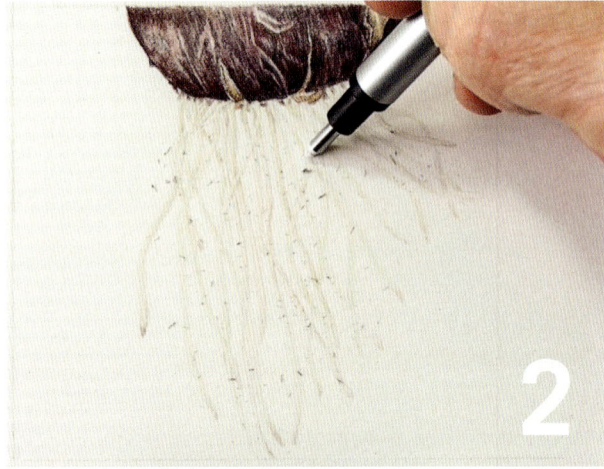

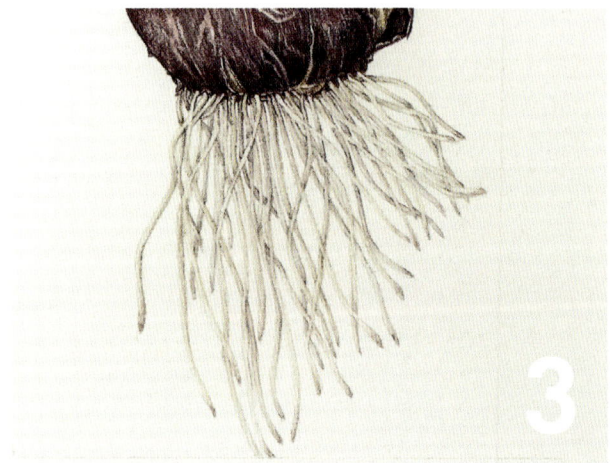

Sepiatone is ideal for emphasizing the architecture of a plant specimen. With its reddish-brown hue, it adds warmth to what would be a grey-scale painting. As a tonal rendering, local color is eliminated and form and detail become the focus of the resulting painting. When used in a drybrush technique with controlled brush-work, it can create fine texture and detail.

Painting a Leaf in Sepiatone

TUTOR: LARA CALL GASTINGER

Elm Leaf

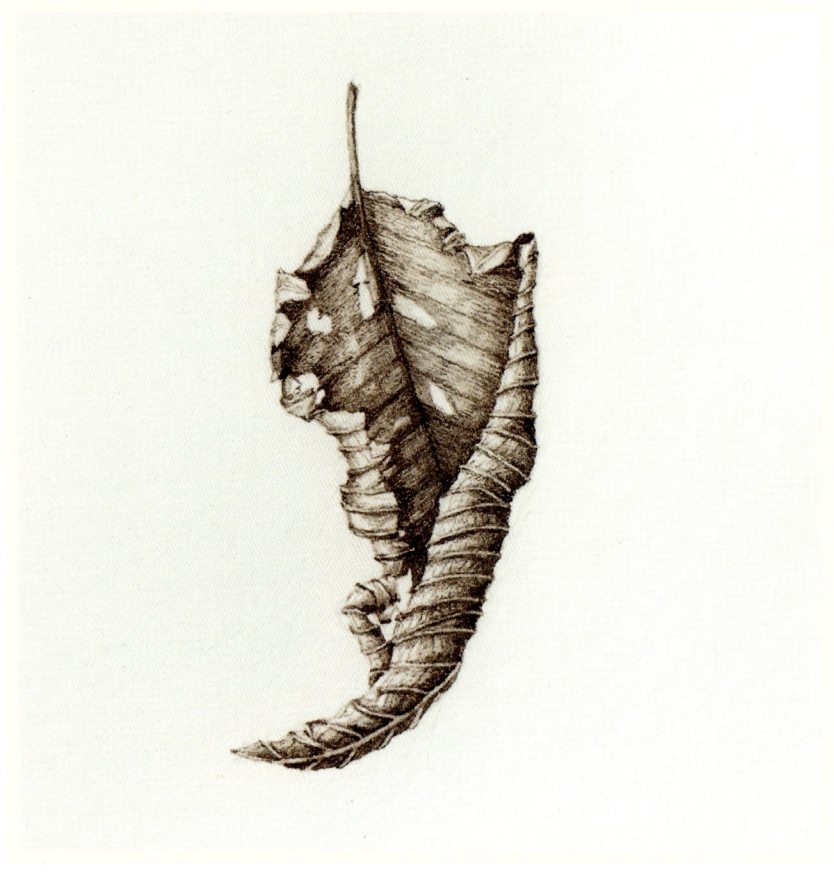

Elm Leaf *Ulmus* sp.
Sepiatone watercolor
on paper
4 × 2 inches [10 × 5 cm]
© Lara Gastinger

HOURS TO COMPLETE: 3

MATERIALS: Container for water; a
plate to use as a palette; sepia paint;
drafting brush; kneaded eraser;
Kolinsky brushes (nos. 0 and 2); HB
pencil, paper towel; pencil sharpener.

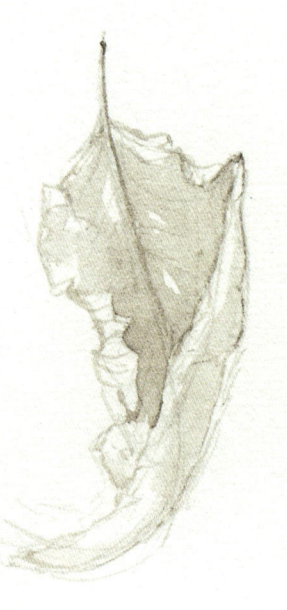

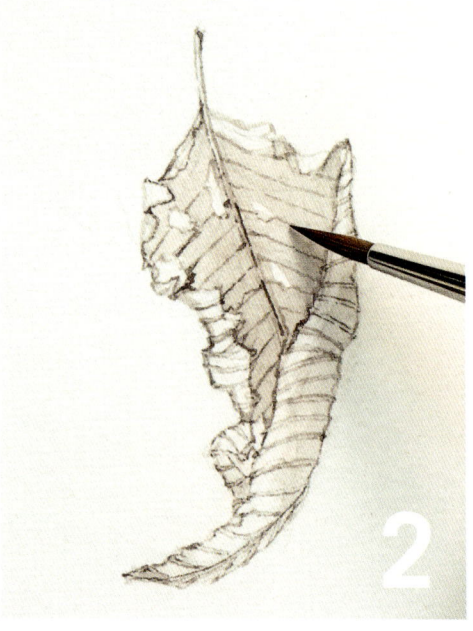

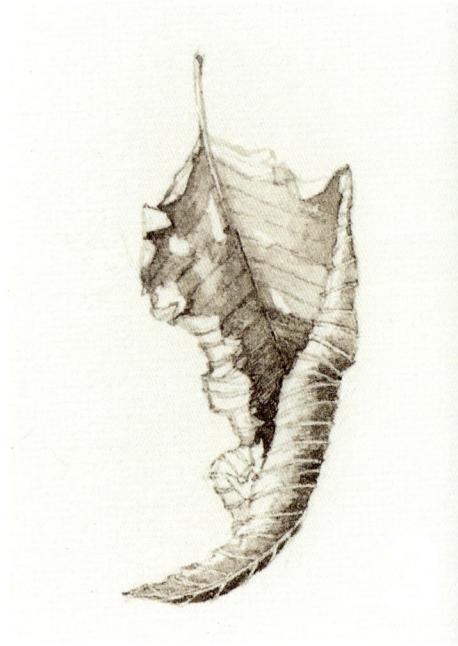

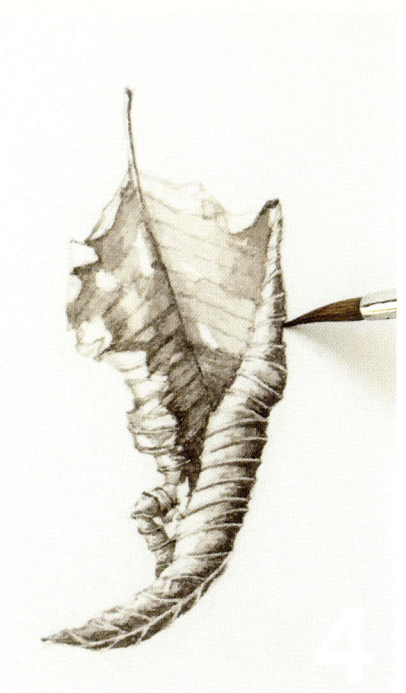
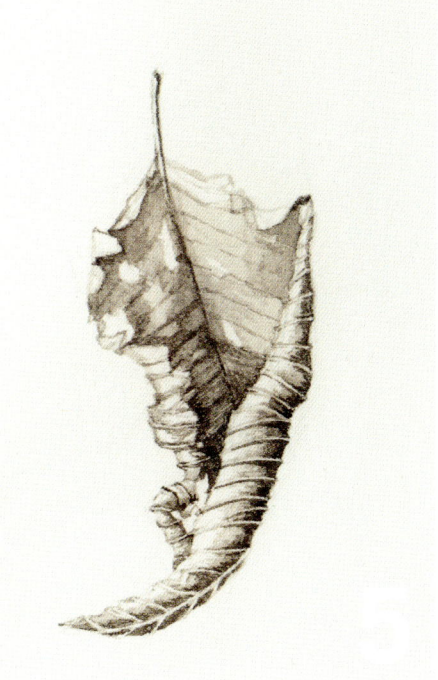
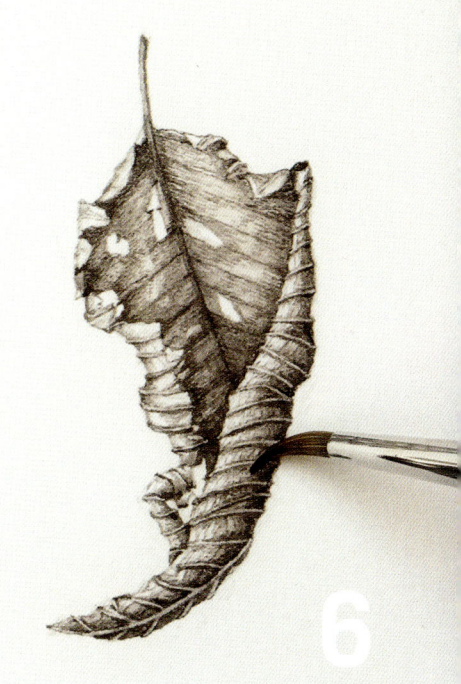

Sketch the leaf, making sure the center line continues from the top of the leaf through the curled-over underside. Lay down a dilute wash of sepia paint, focusing first on the darker areas of the leaf. This helps to lay out the general shape and values of the specimen on the paper.

Dab up any excess graphite with a kneaded eraser. Using a relatively dry, well-pointed brush (with not too much water, just pigment), draw the details of the leaf with paint. In this example, leaf venation is being painted. Jumping into this level of detail right away provides controlled and focused painting.

With the leaf venation established, add more paint with the no. 2 brush, starting with the darkest areas. Darken the top of the leaf where the edges curl forward. On the underside of the leaf, paint around the completed venation lines in such a way that these veins appear raised and lighter.

Depicting the curled area on the back of the leaf requires retaining the highlight area while darkening the shadows. Use the tip of a no. 2 brush to darken the edge of the leaf's back while keeping the veins lighter.

Continue to darken the shaded areas to add contrast, but keep the lightest areas of the leaf untouched. Intensify the contrast where the back of the leaf curls around the front of the leaf, and along the center vein so the three-dimensionality of the leaf is conveyed.

Last, put in the smaller leaf veins and clarify and smooth the background tones with small lines, crosshatching, and dots with a no. 0 brush. If the painting seems to have too many lines and textures, use the larger brush, dampened, to blend in and soften some of those textures. The completed leaf shows crisp shadows set against the highlights of the curling leaf.

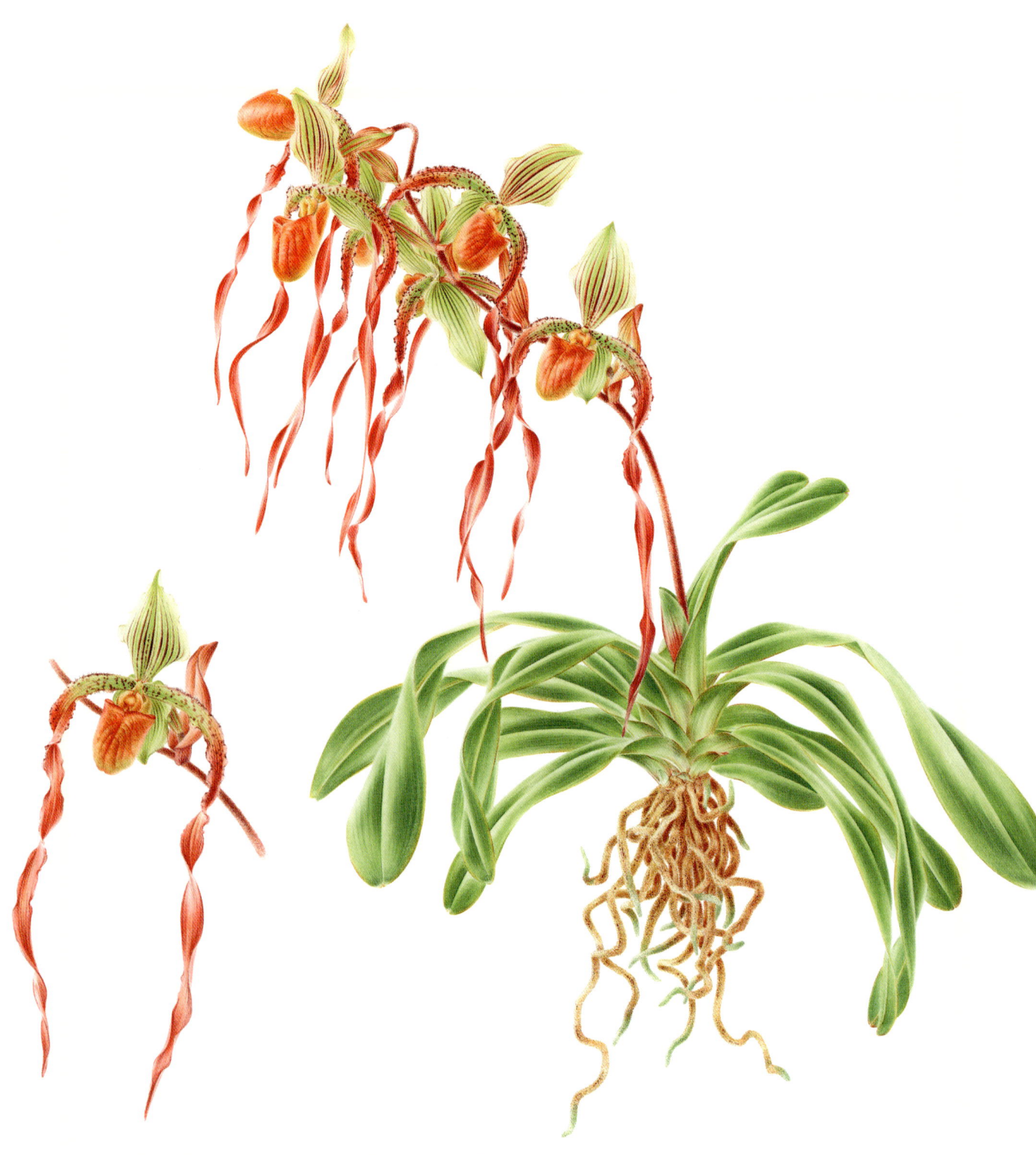

Paphiopedilum ×sanderianum 'Screaming Eagles' Watercolor on paper © John Pastoriza-Piñol
16 ½ × 12 inches [41.25 × 30 cm] and 30 × 22 inches [76.2 × 55.9 cm]
TIME TO COMPLETE THE FULL PAINTING: ONE MONTH   SMALLER PAINTING: 20 HOURS

MATERIALS: 4H pencil; retractable eraser; mechanical pencil; sable brush (no. 8); ¼-inch Taklon comb brush; blending brush
(no. 6); adders tongue brush (no. 2); spotters (nos. 4 and 3); fine spotter (no. 0); nib pen; white plastic eraser; drafting film; watercolor
paper 140 lb. [300 gsm] smooth; masking fluid; palette. Colors: perylene green, vanadium yellow, quinacridone gold, quinacridone red,
cerulean blue, perylene maroon, May green, perylene violet, brilliant blue violet, ultramarine blue (green shade), indathrene blue.

Masking fluid is used to isolate key details and floral parts in this painting of a slipper orchid. Then water-color washes are applied to build color quickly, allowing each layer to dry completely. When the masking fluid is removed, these veins, hairs and edges can be either lightly glazed in highlight areas, or darkened where they appear as red stripes.

Painting a Slipper Orchid Using Wet Techniques and Masking Fluid

TUTOR: JOHN PASTORIZA-PIÑOL

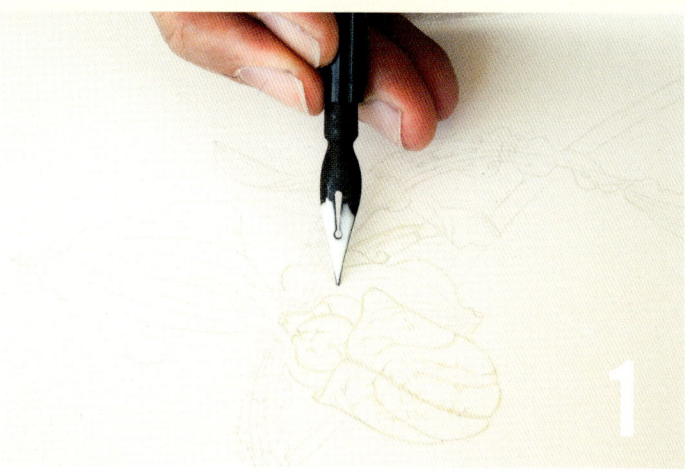

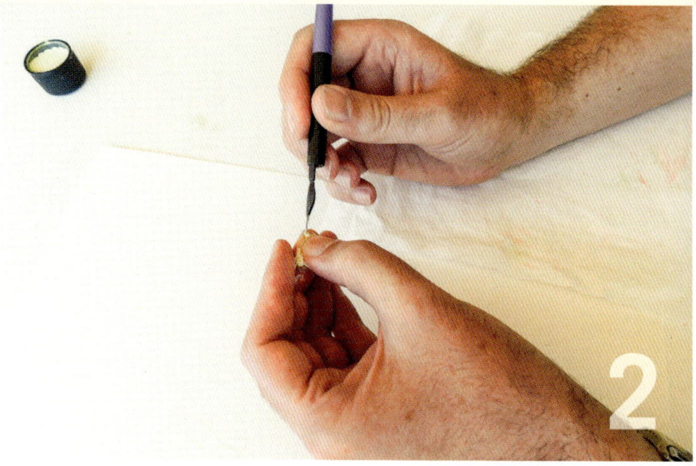

Prepare a basic sketch capturing the important morphological parts of the subject: dorsal sepal, synsepals, petals, labellum, and column. Transfer the sketch onto smooth watercolor paper using a 4H pencil via a light box or window. Apply masking fluid with a pen nib directly on the pencil lines. This helps delineate the floral parts. Apply fine masking fluid lines on the stem to create hairs.

Masking fluid dries quickly, so it is necessary to continually pull off dried masking fluid from the pen nib with your fingers or a paper towel before re-dipping. This ensures clean, smooth lines. The area of the painting you are working on should not be reworked until the previous layer of masking fluid and washes are completely dry.

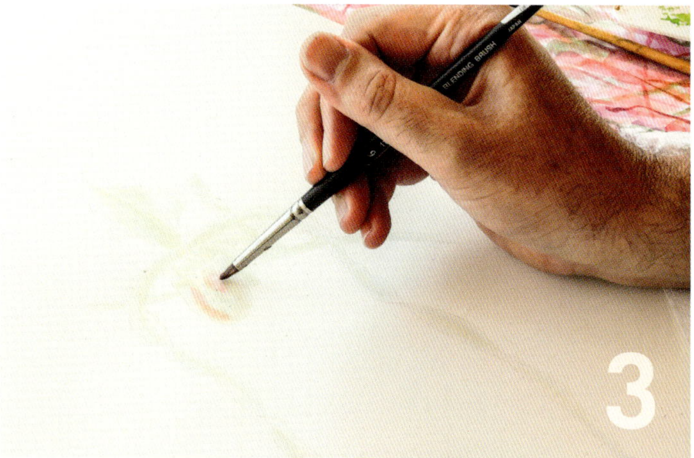

Once the masking fluid has dried, after about five minutes, evenly wet the watercolor paper in the subject area and apply a light wash of cerulean blue to indicate the cooler hues of the specimen. Keep the lightest areas free of any pigment. When the area is dry, follow with a light wash of quinacridone red to the labellum.

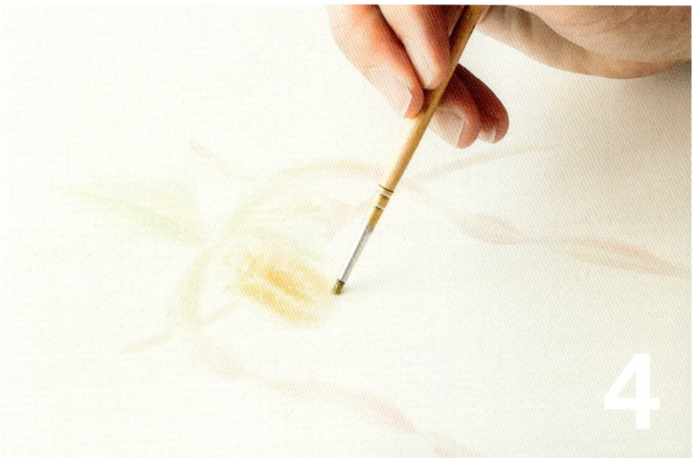

Begin the many layers of wet washes that will build rich and luminous tones by laying down a pale wash of the local color throughout the flower. Once the wash has dried, rewet areas of the flower with a warm yellowish hue and apply a weak wash of vanadium yellow. These washes will yield variations of hue in the local color.

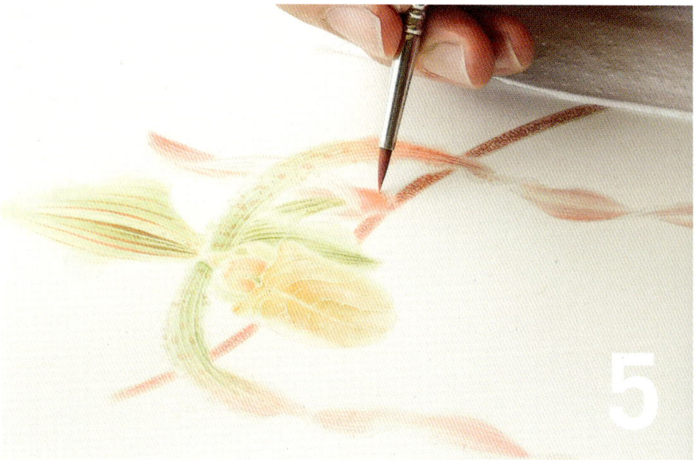

Wet the petals and the labellum and enrich the color with another light wash of quinacridone red. Next, apply a light wash of green (cerulean blue and vanadium yellow) for the dorsal and synsepals and allow them to completely dry. Keep the original sketch nearby for guidance. Rest your arm on a paper towel as you work to keep the paper clean.

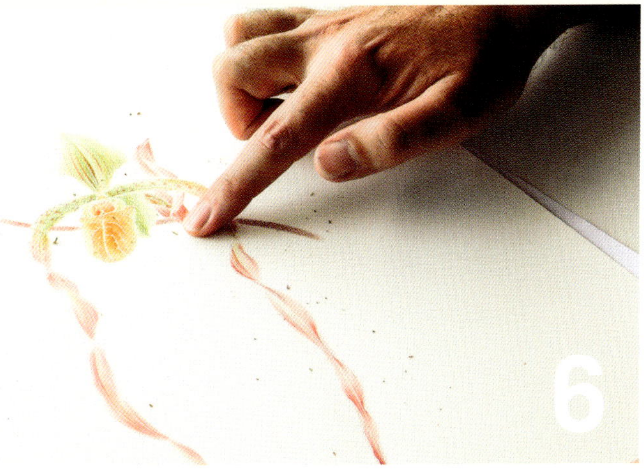

Remove the dry masking fluid by gently rubbing it with your finger (be sure that your hands are clean and the paper is dry). If there are any stubborn masking-fluid areas, reapply masking fluid directly to them, allow to dry, and remove.

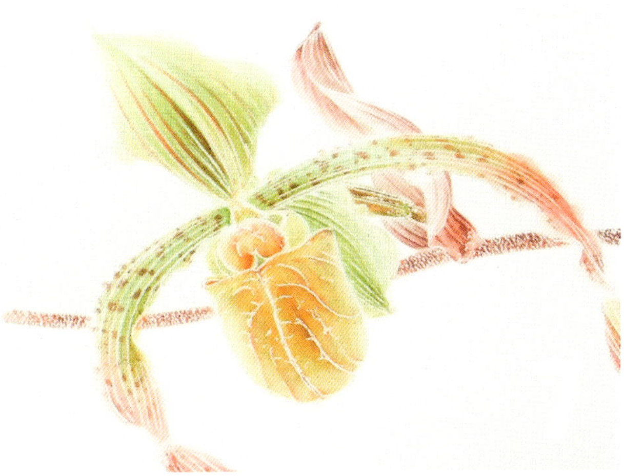

Observe the white lines left behind from the masking fluid. When transparent layers are built up over the lines, the lines will continue to glow through. While the lines appear sharp-edged at first, careful treatment will maintain their light quality while also integrating them into the tones and form of the orchid.

It is often necessary to turn the paper to apply strokes in the optimum direction. Soften the revealed white lines using clean water and a soft brush. Gently brush the pigment, moving it from the painted areas into the spaces left by the masking fluid rather than the other direction, to avoid unwanted blooms or splotches of color. A small, flat synthetic brush holds a lot of water and is excellent for this purpose.

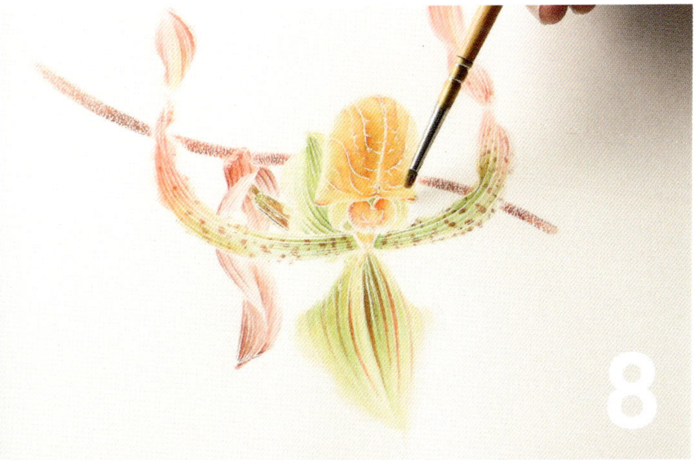

Using drybrush, apply a layer of quinacridone red to the sepals and labellum and continue to conserve the reflected-light areas. Continue to build and apply paint to all the flower parts, using fine brushwork and the flat, feathered tip of the comb brush.

When finished with the masking fluid, apply cling film or laboratory film to the lid to stop any leaks during transport and keep it from drying out.

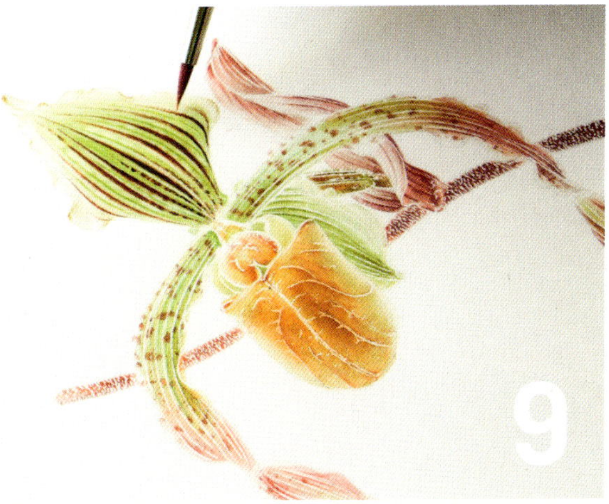

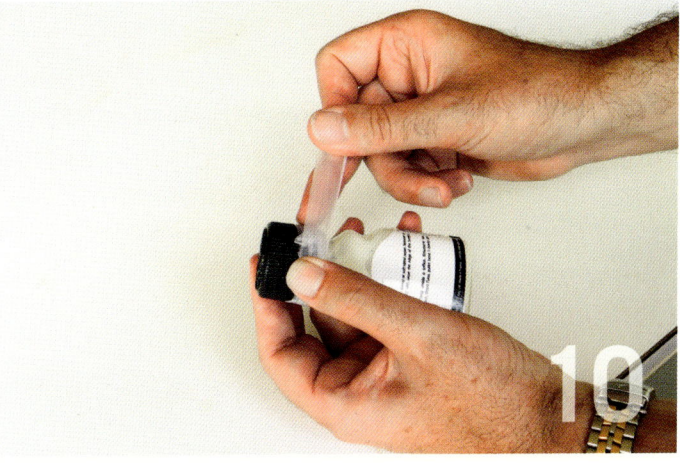

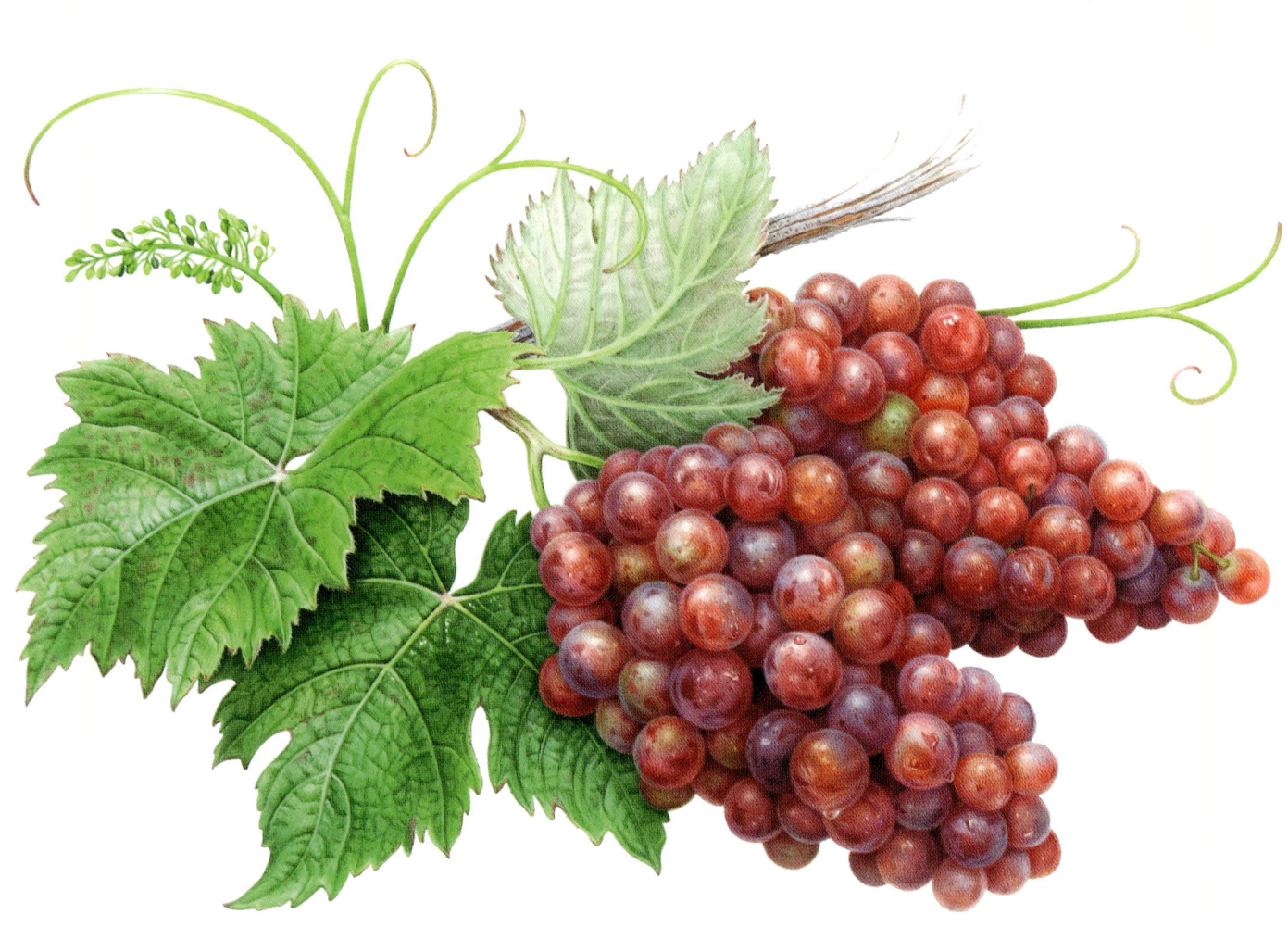

Joie de Vivre Watercolor on 500-pound Bristol plate paper 8 ½ × 11 ½ inches [21.25 × 28.27 cm] © Karen Kluglein

HOURS TO COMPLETE: 90

MATERIALS: Kneaded eraser; white plastic power eraser; dividers; HB, 2H, 6H pencils; palette; Kolinsky brushes (nos. 000 and 1); scrap paper; a container for water; paper towels; hake brush; tracing paper; transfer paper; artist's tape. Colors: perylene maroon; cadmium yellow; cobalt blue; manganese blue hue; permanent sap green; green gold; dioxazine violet; cobalt violet; permanent alizarin crimson; cadmium orange; olive green; Naples yellow; terre verte; perylene green; Hansa yellow.

Depicting fruit with a bloom is a complex interplay between the color of a shiny fruit and the waxy coating (bloom) with a blue cast. One of the keys is to map out the bloom areas and take care not to paint into them with the warmer fruit colors. In a cluster of fruits such as these grapes, reflected light on each grape should be shown, as well as shading between grapes to create depth in the cluster. Leaves in this composition show a broad range of values, from light blue highlights to very dark cast shadow on the lower leaf. The painting is accomplished by using two fairly small brushes and mainly drybrush technique.

Painting Gloss, Bloom, and Reflected Light in Grapes

TUTOR: KAREN KLUGLEIN

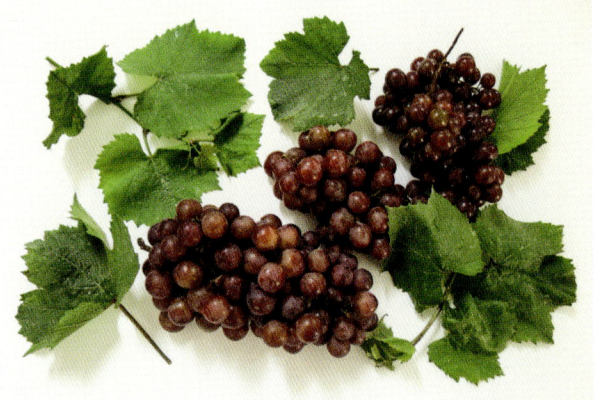

These grocery-store grapes had ample bloom on them, showing a nice contrast between the dark and light areas on the fruit. The leaves were collected at a local vineyard. When you are working with leaves, take many photographs of them for reference purposes later, because leaves can wilt quickly.

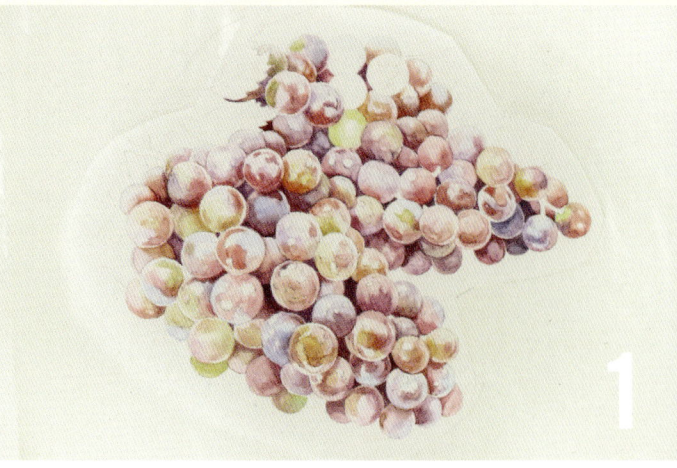

Once you complete your drawing, cut some tracing paper to expose only the area of 500 lb. plate-finish Bristol paper being painted. Put down washes of color in small sections of each grape to map out color, including for the bloom (the powdery blue that can be brushed off), and keep track of your progress. As you add more layers, these colors will overlap, deepen, and blend together.

Add a second layer of color. Work each grape (mostly) with the tip of a no. 1 brush. After the brush is loaded with paint, blot it on a paper towel to remove any excess paint before applying it to the paper.

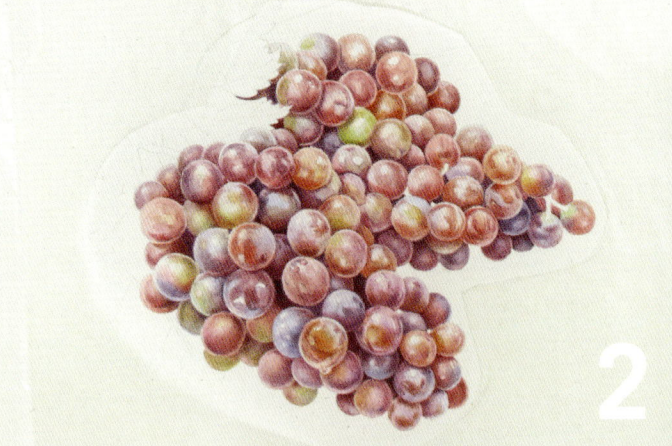

The cluster in the back has been further advanced in this image. Indigo blue was added to perylene maroon for the deepest shadows. Delineate dark and light areas from the beginning and begin to darken shadows. Convey dimension using shadows from one grape to another and within each grape. At the same time, avoid overdarkening light areas, keeping in mind it is always easier to add paint than to take it away.

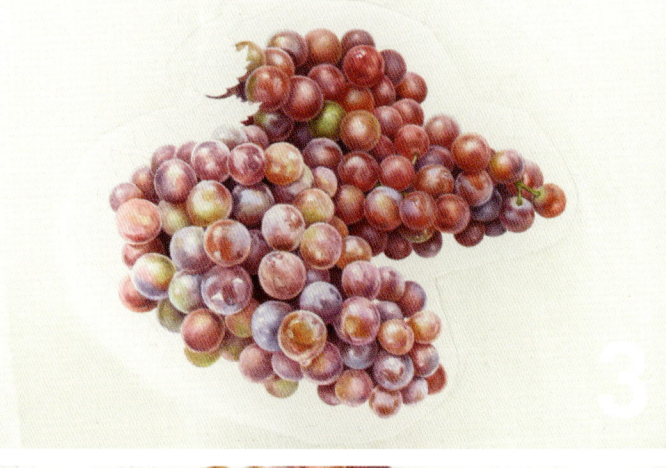

Pencil lines that are showing through the watercolor can be removed with a battery-powered eraser or kneaded eraser. To avoid tearing or otherwise damaging the paper, be sure the paint is completely dry before you begin erasing. If you remove any paint, carefully replace it using the tip of a brush.

Areas of blue and light purple indicate bloom (the powdery blue that can be brushed off). These blue areas were indicated from the beginning mapping stage so that the color is clean. Although they are paler in value than the shinier parts of the fruits, they still require shading in complementary colors to add dimension. Add shadows and imperfections to the bloom areas with slow, precise, and careful painting.

Color and shadow are reflected from one grape to the surface of another. With the tip of the brush, strengthen shadows on the undersides of each grape. Grapes have a lot going on in a small space: you can observe many different areas of color when you look closely at them. Try to retain this color variety in the grapes, to avoid a formulaic look to the cluster once completed.

Adjust the light and dark areas within each grape. When you want to lighten an area, you can pick up color by brushing the area with a damp brush, then blotting the area with a paper towel. Do this carefully, with very little water in the brush to maintain control over the gradation.

Even though the main subject may not be finished, it can be helpful to work on a different section of the painting to ensure that everything flows together. Here, paint colors have been determined for both the top and underside of the leaves. The first washes of color have been applied, and the surface of each leaf has been broken down into highlights, shadows, and mid-tones.

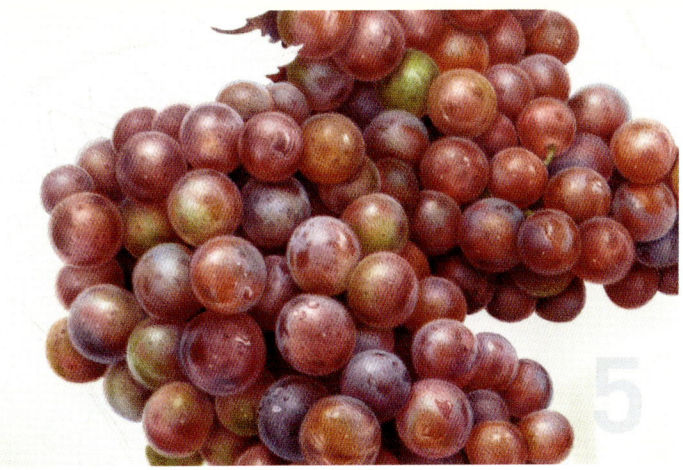

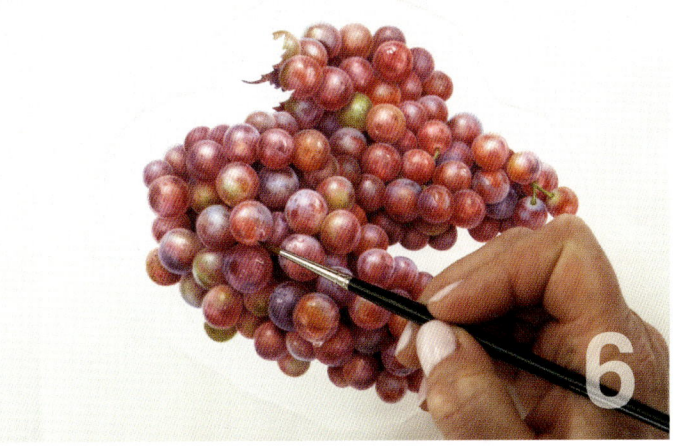

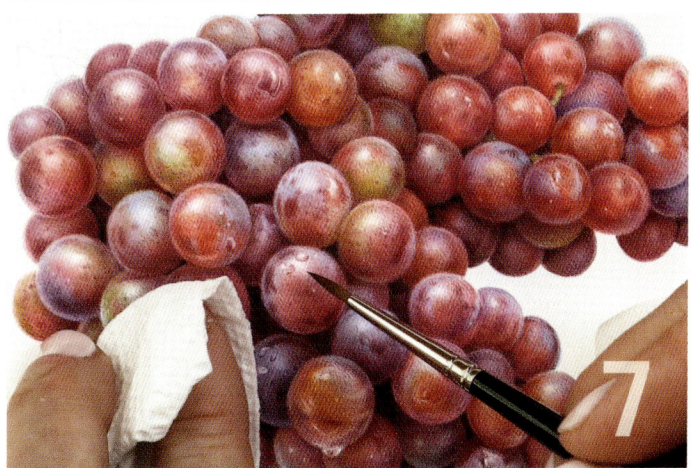

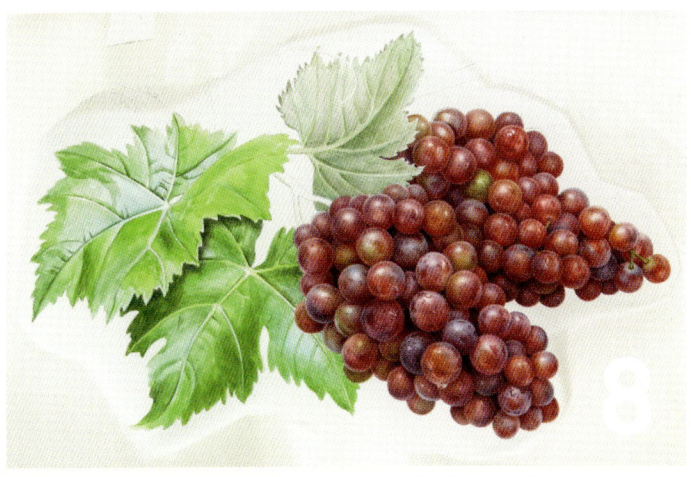

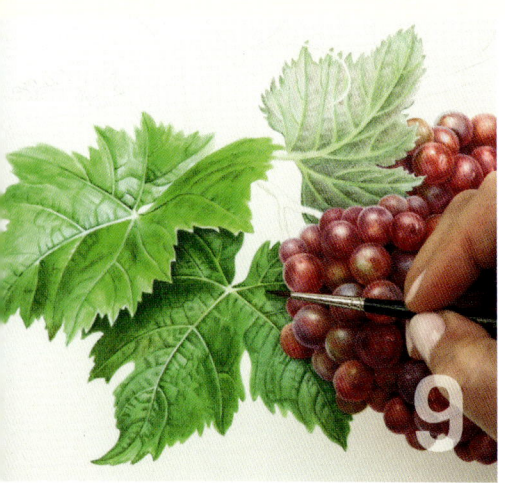
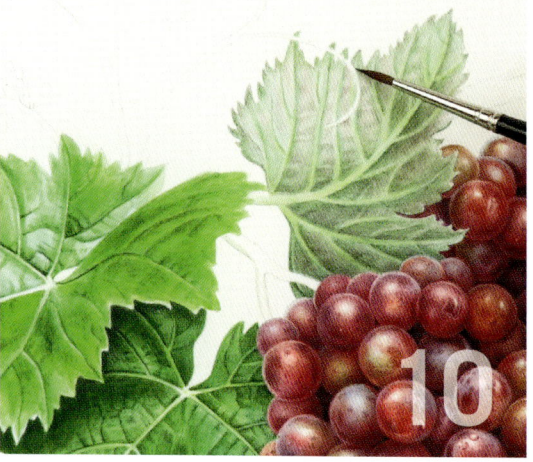
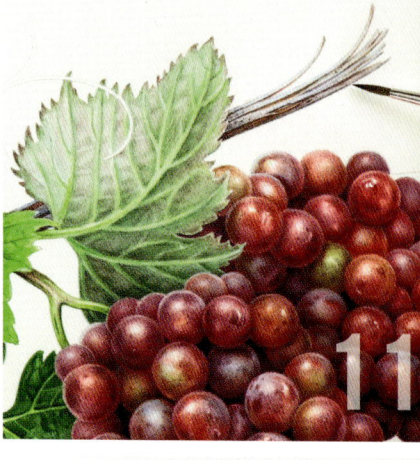

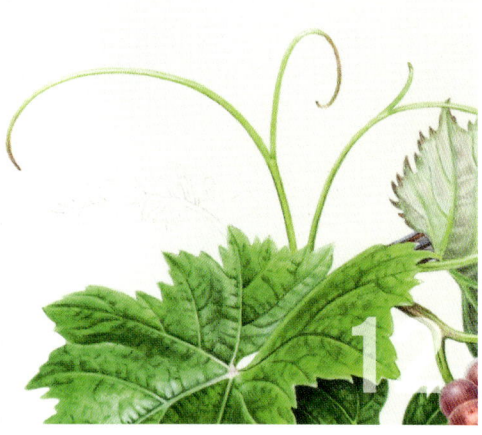
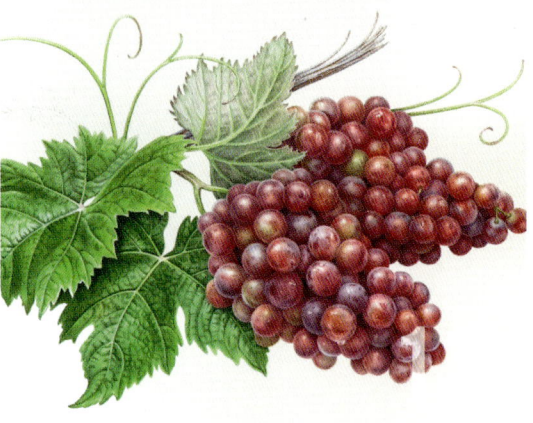
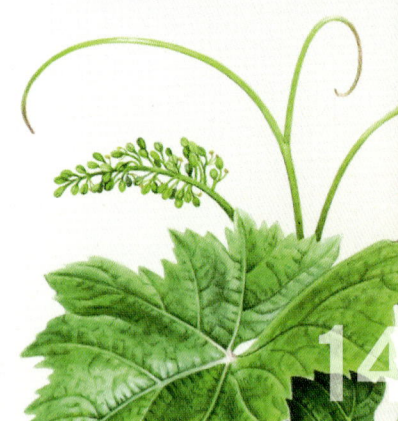

Continue mapping the color of the leaves with consecutive washes. Add line and some shadow to the small veins so that texture begins to show. Use a hint of red and purple on the underside of the leaf on the right. Add texture to the leaves by paying close attention to the light direction and adding shadow to each little bump. This also serves to increase the overall value of each leaf.

Leave this overlapping tendril without paint while you put washes on the leaf around it. On the back of the leaf, overall color is paler, and the veins are similar to a narrow tube laying on the top of the leaf. Each of these veins casts a shadow, which is painted in violets and blues on top of the pale green.

For the branch, use the same colors that were used in the grapes, along with sepia and yellow ochre.

Add the curling tendrils and stem. The color of the curling tendrils changes gradually from green to yellow or red; they are decorative and add to the overall design.

Take a moment to assess the entire painting. At this point, it still needs more contrast and detail, clearly noticeable when you compare this image to that of the final painting.

Adding a growth of small buds contributes new texture and a different scale to the painting. All the leaves, tendrils, and buds have been removed from grapes available at supermarkets, but if you can source plant material from a nearby garden or farm, you can use them as subjects for adding special details such as stems, buds, or tendrils.

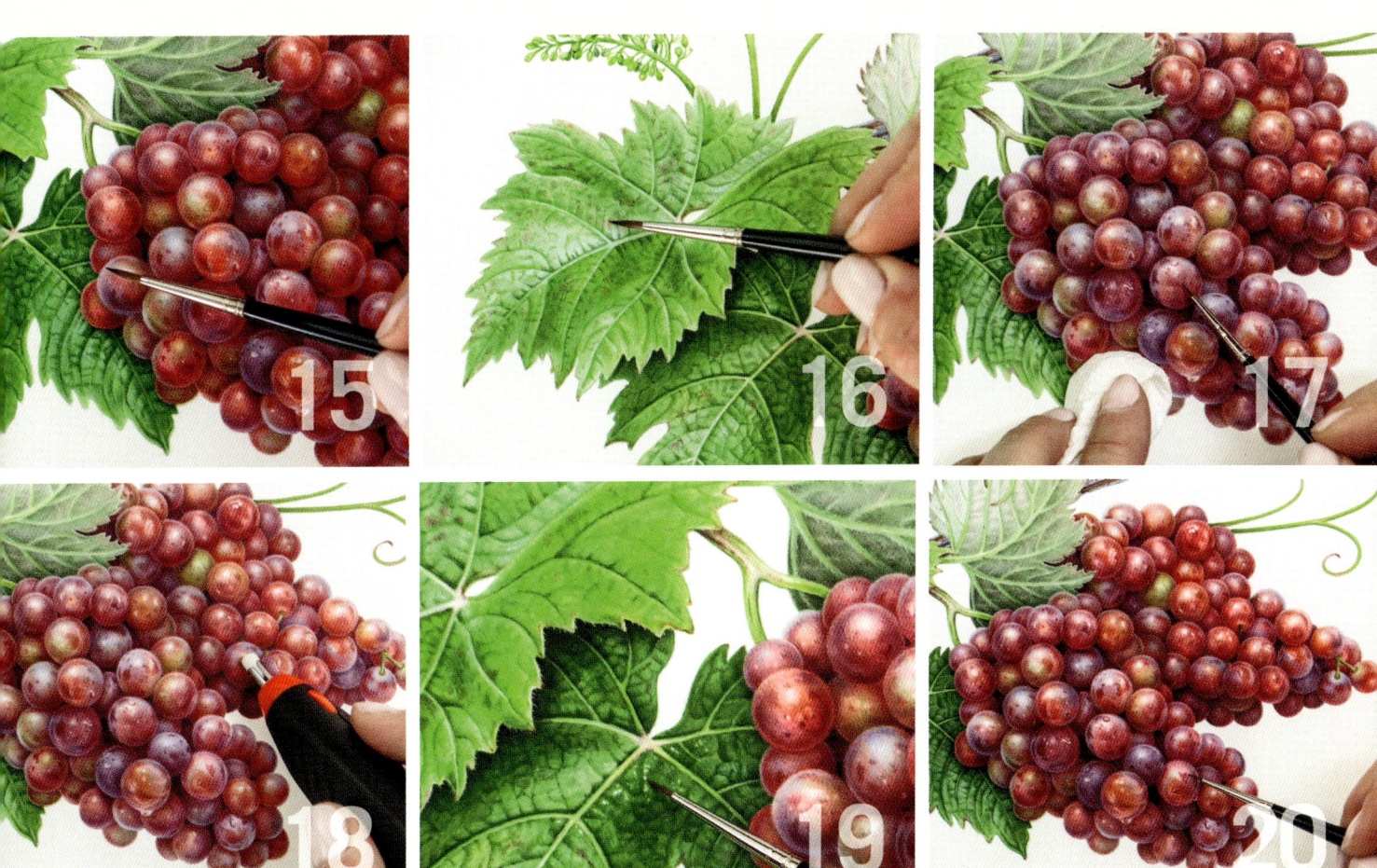

Areas where the grapes meet the leaves may need to be adjusted so that they work together. For example, the green of a leaf reflected on the surface of a grape may need to be added, or the shadow on a leaf may need to be darkened where grapes lie over it.

Paint mottled red or purple lightly into areas of the leaves to make them more realistic and more imperfect. If this red were added into darker green areas it would appear brown, but when it is applied in light areas it will look redder.

Using the no. 000 brush, both add and lift specks on the grapes. These specks are most obvious in dark areas, but lifting can be repeated in the light areas until the specks become apparent. Dabbing with a clean paper towel while the spot is damp can help to lift color.

Observe the actual grapes and notice the lightest highlight areas. A battery-powered eraser can be used to pick out the highlights on some of the grapes. Make sure the surface is completely dry when you do this; otherwise the paper will tear. Use light pressure so only color is gently lifted.

Lift small, irregular spots to represent moisture on the lower leaf. On the upper leaf, add tiny hairs to some of the leaf edges with Naples yellow paint, especially where the leaf overlaps dark shadow. The shapes of the serrated edges of the leaves should not be perfect. Touches of red, brown, and ochre are found along them.

Sharpen the detail in the water drops last—each drop has at least one highlight and a cast shadow. Use a final touch up with the no. 000 brush to smooth and deepen the color in the painting. Throughout this process, paint has been added and very rarely is it taken away. The painting is finished when you feel you cannot go any further with smoothing gradations; the dark, medium, and light values are correct and work well together; and there is ample detail.

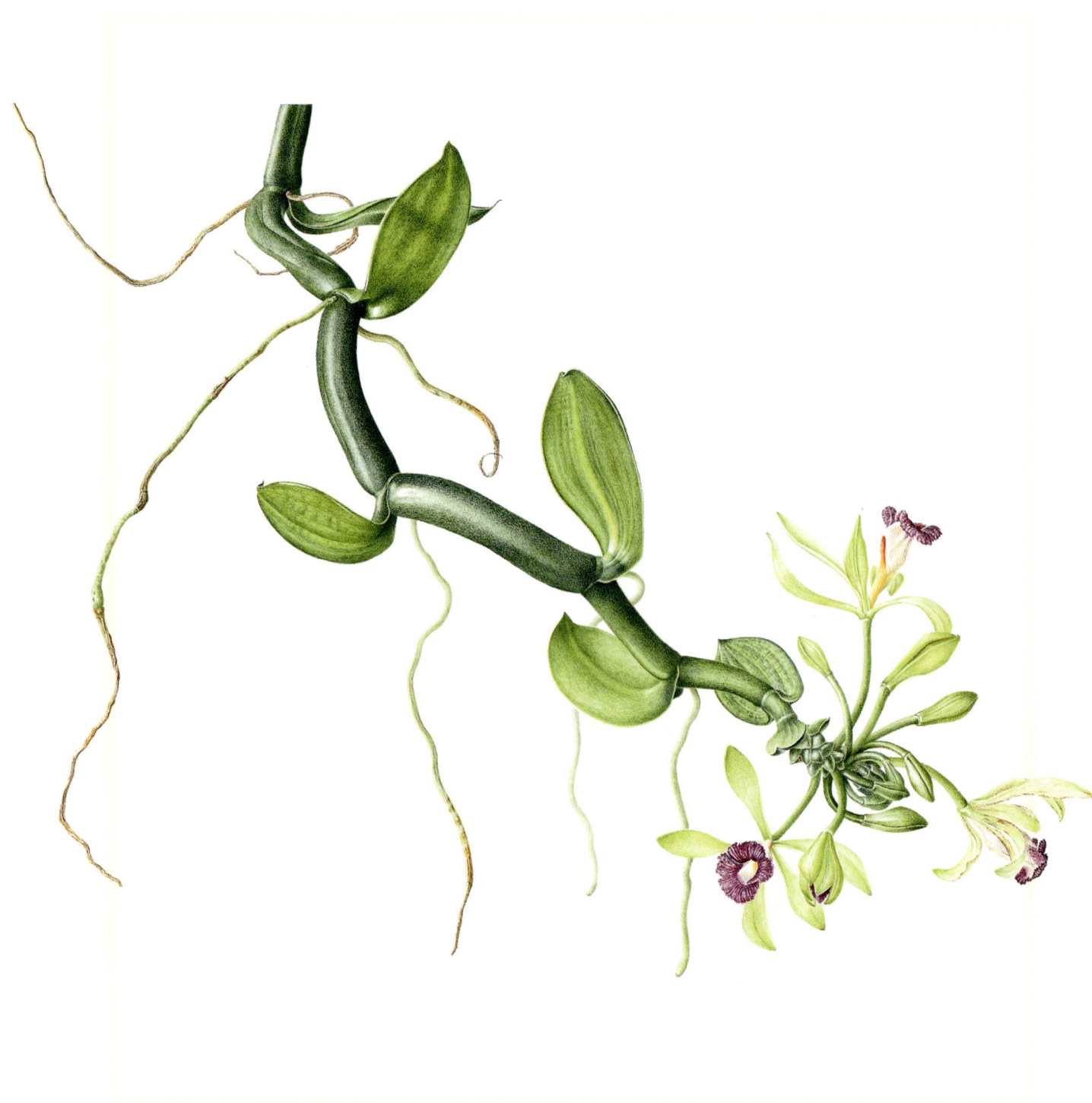

Vanilla orchid *Vanilla imperialis* Watercolor on paper 18 × 24 inches [45 × 60 cm] © Lizzie Sanders

HOURS TO COMPLETE: 86

MATERIALS: Ruler; magnifying glass; paper towels; container for water; pencil sharpener; scalpel; synthetic flat brush for lifting; Kolinsky miniature brushes (nos. 3, 2, and 1); lead holder with HB or F lead; white-plastic eraser (cut into pieces); ceramic plate. Colors: gold ochre; burnt sienna; yellow ochre; Payne's gray; new gamboge, quinacridone magenta, indanthrene blue.

Using a limited palette and drybrush technique, Lizzie Sanders completes a complex composition in two stages—first painting the leaves and stem, then adding flowers from another specimen later on. By laying down brushstrokes with little liquid, control is exerted over light, shadow, and color. Greens vary from cool blue-greens to warm yellow-greens using Payne's gray and yellows, with the occasional use of burnt umber for warmth. Magenta is added to the palette for the flower labellum, providing a splash of color.

Drybrush Watercolor and Color Mixing

TUTOR: LIZZIE SANDERS

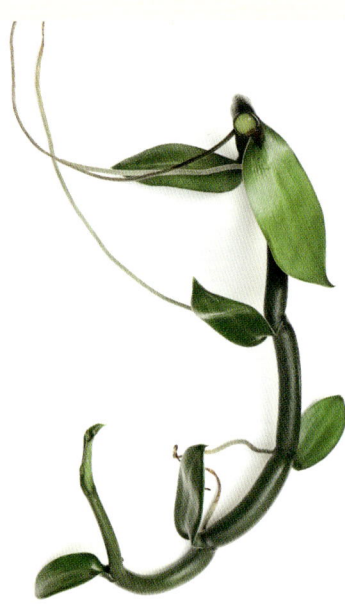

Vanilla imperialis (Vanilla orchid) is a robust plant with thick fleshy leaves, fat shiny stems, and delicate flowers. Apart from the flowers, the vine changes little once cut. This specimen was photographed in many positions to plan the composition, without flowers, which will be added later. If you are adding elements at a later stage, be sure they are attached correctly and are botanically accurate.

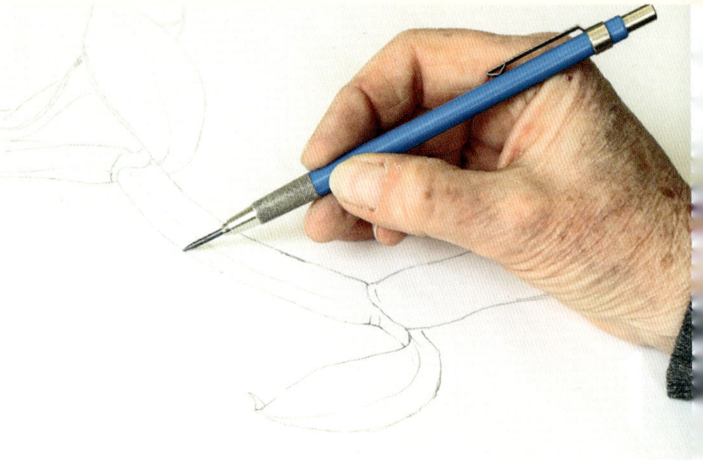

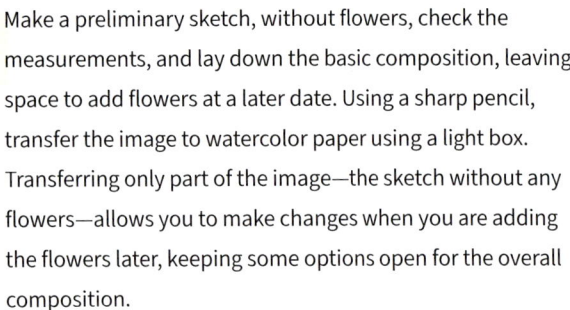

Make a preliminary sketch, without flowers, check the measurements, and lay down the basic composition, leaving space to add flowers at a later date. Using a sharp pencil, transfer the image to watercolor paper using a light box. Transferring only part of the image—the sketch without any flowers—allows you to make changes when you are adding the flowers later, keeping some options open for the overall composition.

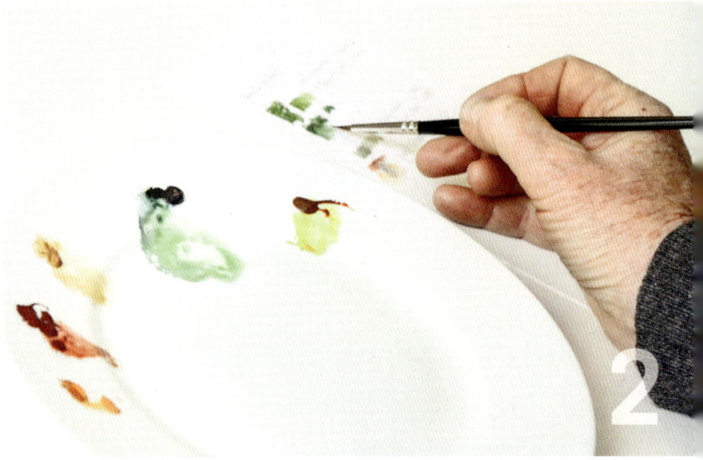

Mix and test colors along the way, rather than working with a premixed pool of color. Dilute the colors (here Payne's gray and new gamboge) with a wet brush and test them on a scrap piece of watercolor paper. Record the percentage of the mix. For pale colors, dilute to the required tone and allow the paint to dry before picking up with a dry brush.

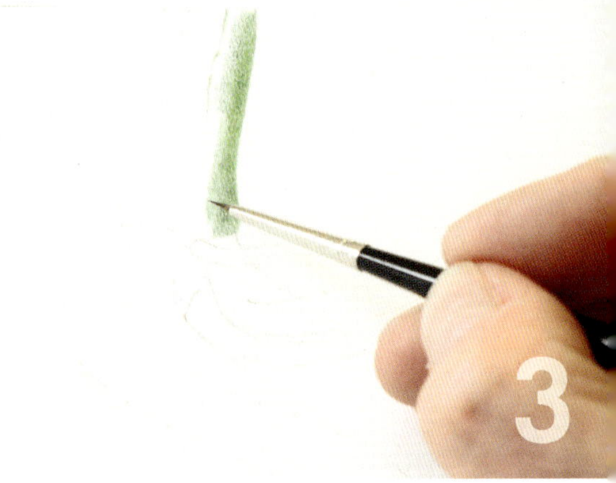

Before you begin painting, lift out the graphite with an eraser. Wet the tip of a damp brush, pick up paint, wipe the brush on a tissue and start to lay down tiny strokes, all in the same direction. Build up layers as you move across the area. The strokes must be very smooth and even—avoid creating unintentional patterns.

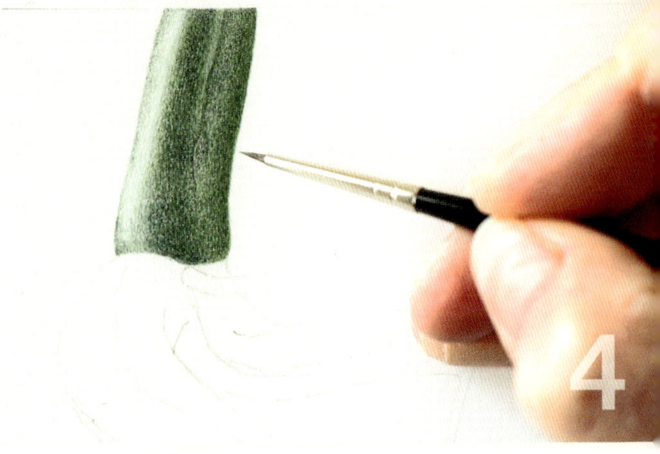

Finish each area as you go, building up enough dry pigment with the brush until the tonal values match the specimen. Follow the growth pattern of the plant. The paper surface helps create the texture. As the pigment is stroked on, tiny white spaces are left—this is the paper showing through, which adds sparkle to the painted area.

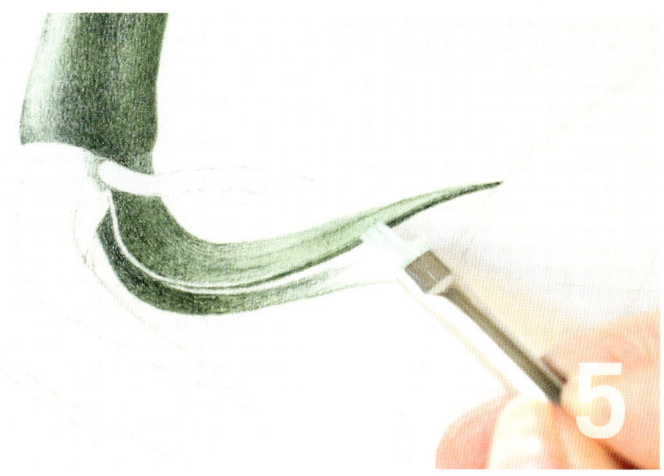

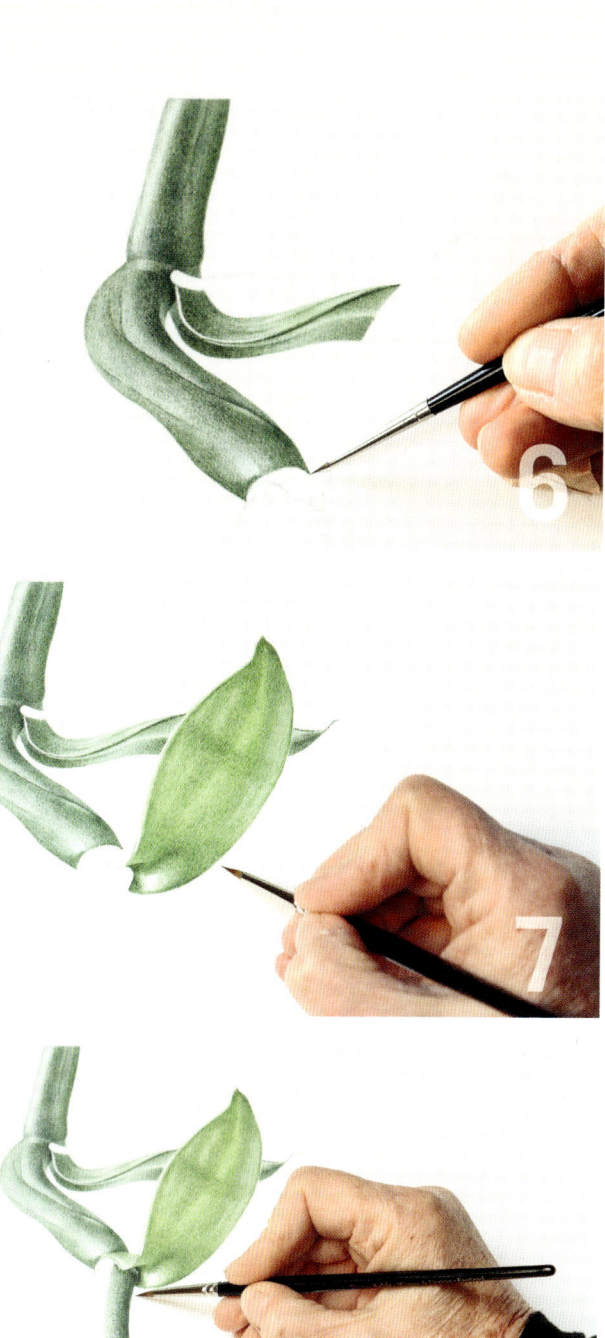

Moving to the next area, continue to work with tiny strokes. Use the flat brush to lift a soft highlight. Dampen the brush and dry it on a tissue, then sweep the brush across the mid-tones and blot immediately. Repeat for a lighter highlight. Keep in mind that dampening and lifting too often will damage the paper. For a sharp white highlight, leave the paper unpainted until later.

As each distinct area is completed, move on using the same tiny strokes, working across the next section. The strokes can vary in size—from stipple to tiny lines—according to the surface texture to be rendered. They can also vary in direction, following the growth pattern. Notice that some highlights are almost blue.

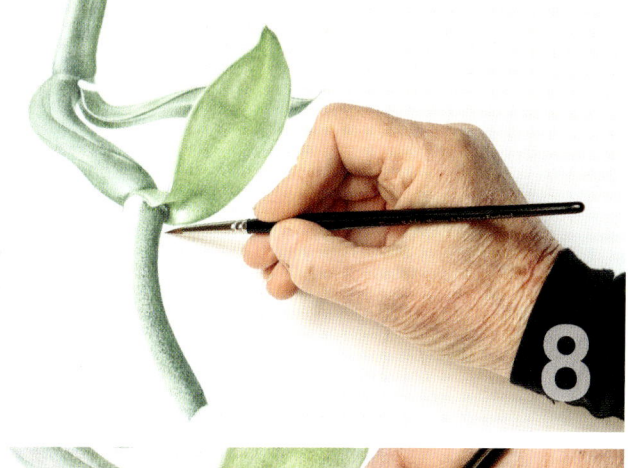

For smoother surfaces, use a no. 3 brush and a little more water—still quite dry but with enough water to almost blend the strokes. Keep going back and filling in any white gaps between the strokes until the leaf surface is almost smooth. Leave bright highlights white and build layers of strokes to render the correct tonal values.

Using a stipple technique, create a dark texture in the shadow areas by building layer upon layer with a dry brush—stroking and stippling almost-dry pigment onto the paper. Only two colors are being used—Payne's gray and new gamboge. Keep the edges sharp.

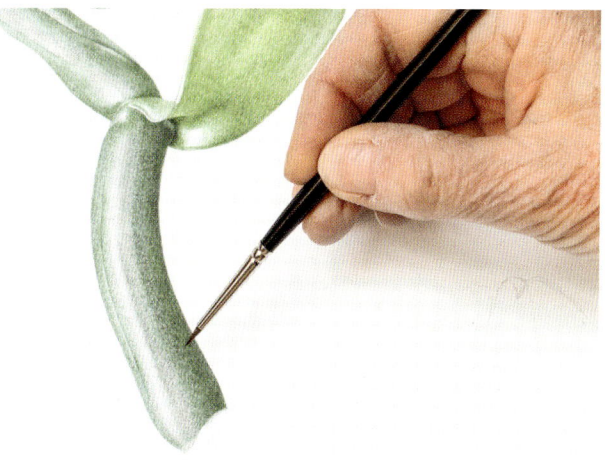

Using a damp brush, sweep down the darkest shadow area of the stem to blur the texture where it is barely visible. Too much water will destroy the texture completely. Varying the color mix from light to dark, paint over the speckled texture until real three-dimensional weight is achieved.

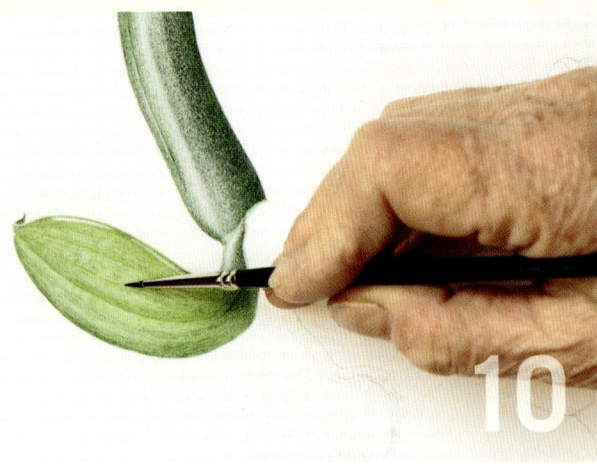

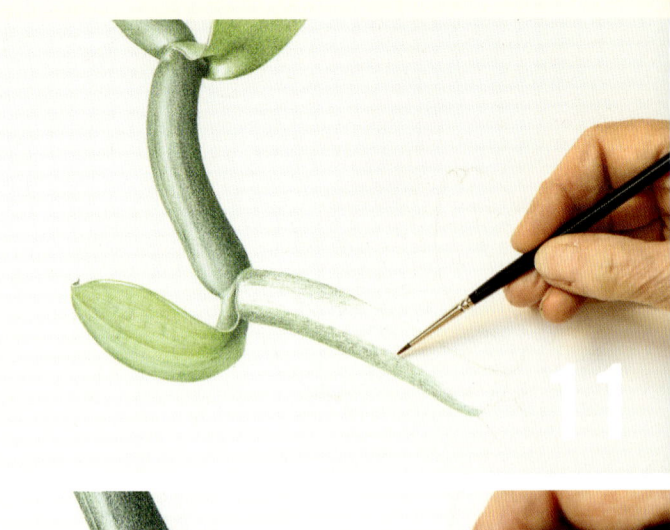

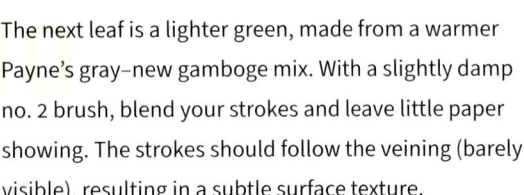

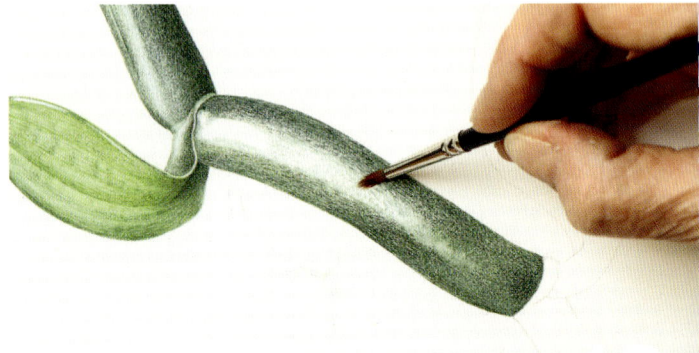

The next leaf is a lighter green, made from a warmer Payne's gray–new gamboge mix. With a slightly damp no. 2 brush, blend your strokes and leave little paper showing. The strokes should follow the veining (barely visible), resulting in a subtle surface texture.

Leave the highlights white on this section of the stem. Work forward and back, edging toward the highlight and building up the depth of color with the same tiny strokes. If a heavy stroke or blob appears, wet it with a tiny brush and blot immediately. Allow the area to dry before painting over it.

Start to fill in the highlights using a pale blue-green. Squint at the color to make sure it's even, and use the stipple technique to fill in the holes so the color is very smooth. Blur the edges of the highlight with a damp brush dragged across the paper.

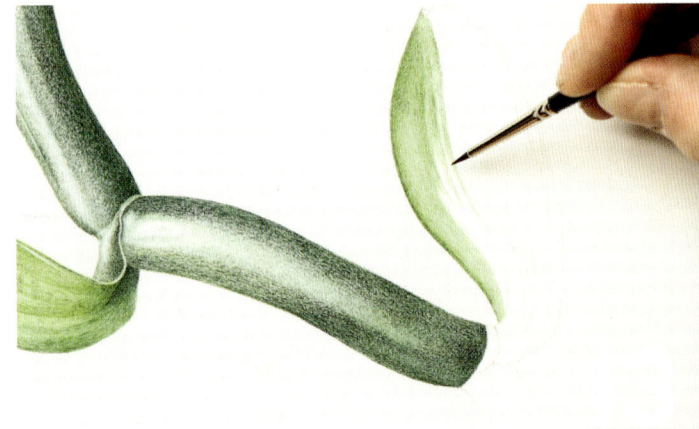

The veins on the underside of this leaf are much more distinct than in other leaves. Paint a fine line very close to the graphite vein line and then lift off the graphite using an eraser. Using a slightly damp no. 2 brush, lay down long strokes in the direction of the veining. Build the color with longer strokes, but use a brush that's just as dry as the one you were using to make tiny strokes.

Build up each section of the leaf until the depth of color and tonal values match the specimen. Using no. 1 brush, draw in the darkest veins in smooth curves. Finish the fleshy edge of the leaf by showing a tiny, dark sliver of the front of the leaf.

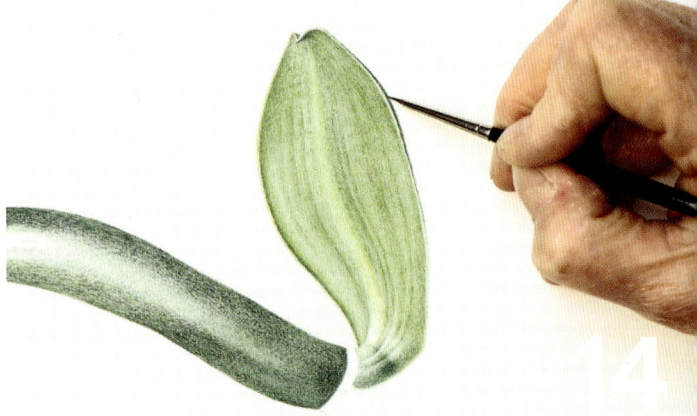

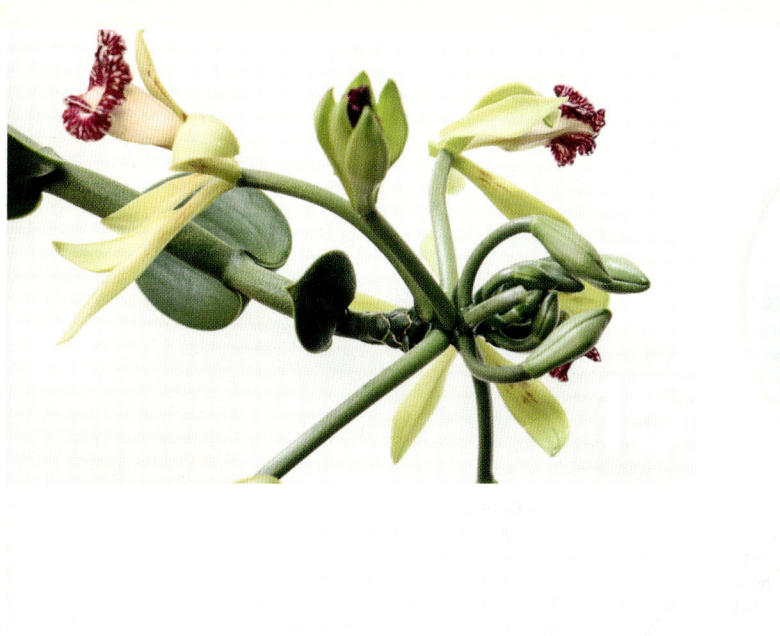

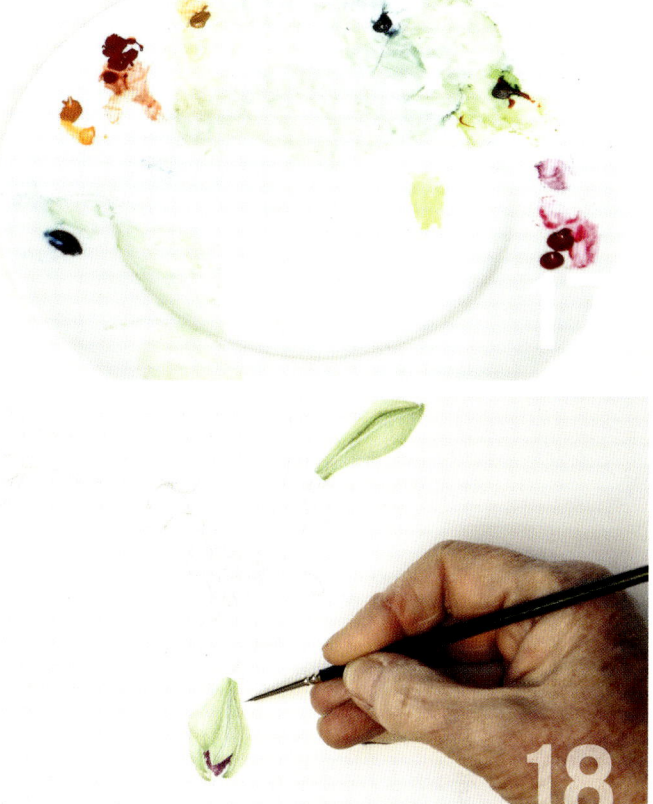

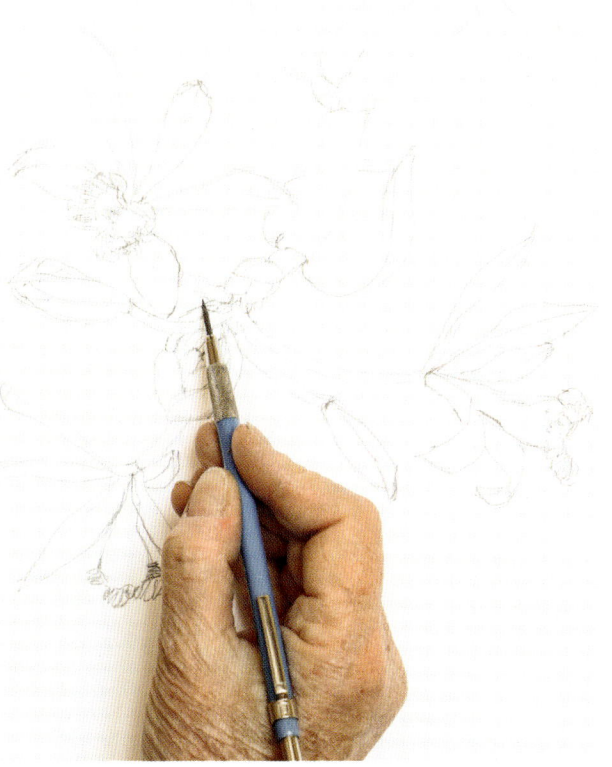

After making several sketches, fitting the new buds and flowers to the half-finished painting of the stems and leaves, the first part of the final drawing was transferred to watercolor paper using the light box. Because flowers change and fade quickly, it is important not to have to erase and redraw them, so add one or two buds or flowers at a time.

Additional colors were added to the plate to be used for the buds and flowers. On the left is indanthrene blue, and on the right is quinacridone magenta. This additional blue, combined with new gamboge, will provide the sharp, pale green of the sepals and petals. The magenta is an almost perfect match for the labellum edges.

Work on the buds first. Dilute the mixed pale green, then allow it to dry on the palette completely. Using a damp brush, pick up the paint on the tip of the brush and apply it in tiny strokes. Stipple the tightly pleated labellum edges in magenta. Here an old, worn no. 1 brush is used to draw in veins.

A fresh specimen of flowers was obtained to finish the painting. Flowers do not last long, so document them quickly, taking compositional photographs as well as close-ups of their details. The flowers' three sepals and two lateral petals are pale green and almost transparent. The labellum seems solid and waxy, cream colored with a strong, magenta, frilly edge.

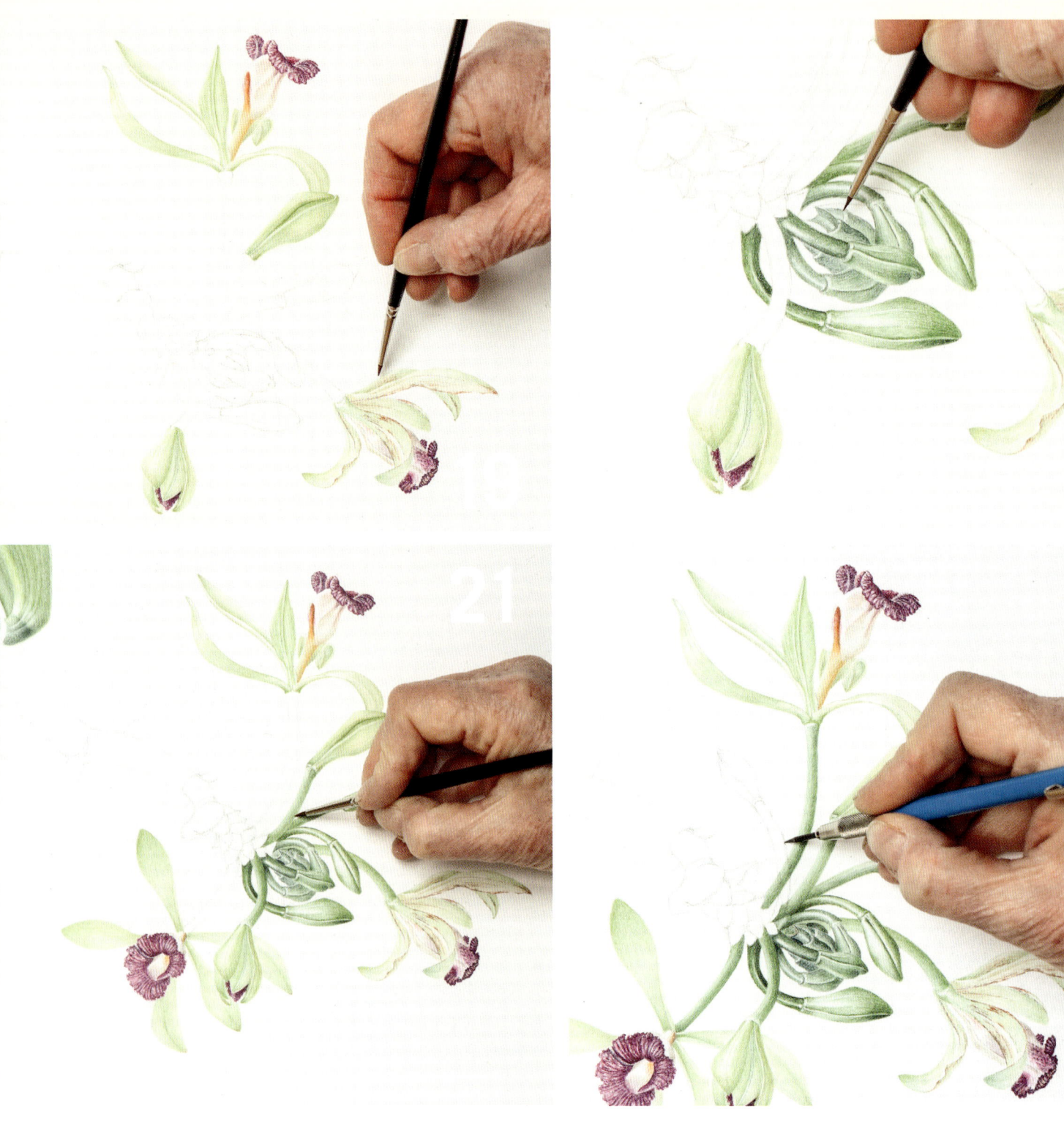

Moving to the flowers, use a range of pale green mixes for the sepals and lateral petals. Paint the labellum in tones of cream, ochre, and magenta. On the oldest flower, which is past peak, touches of burnt sienna were added to the edges and some very dry color dragged across the back of the sepals.

Lay down the complex central area of unopened buds in a variety of greens to ensure separation between each. These greens are all made from Payne's gray and new gamboge. With a no. 1 brush, use stippling and tiny strokes to produce the required surface texture.

A third flower was added and the drawing adjusted to ensure the two sections join accurately. Build up the shadow on the pedicel in tiny strokes using the same green mixed from Payne's gray and new gamboge. Notice that the shadow areas are built up by adding more and more layers, not by using an additional color.

Once the pedicels were completed, the composition seemed to be too regular and symmetrical, and another bud was added to cross an existing one. This change involved lifting the paint on the under pedicel, and, when thoroughly dry, painting in the new pedicel, taking great care, as the paper surface had now been disturbed.

Complete the bracts using a combination of small strokes and stippling. Pick out the edges in burnt sienna. Small imperfections help to make the image believable.

Add the last two leaves, one with strongly textured veins, the other extremely smooth. Achieve these textures by precisely controlling the brushstrokes, by varying the sizes and direction of the strokes, and by leaving white spaces or blending gently.

The roots are a combination of dried roots and newer roots. The positioning of the roots in this illustration is botanically accurate but chosen to balance the composition. The older roots are painted using ochre and burnt sienna with a no. 1 brush. Blemishes and split areas were drawn in, using the brush as if it were a pencil.

The newer roots were added using different tonal values to create an illusion of space and depth, the palest being farthest away. The newest roots are smooth with pale ochre tips. Once you have finished a whole painting, check it and make finishing touches, such as sharpening edges or adjusting the tone of the highlights.

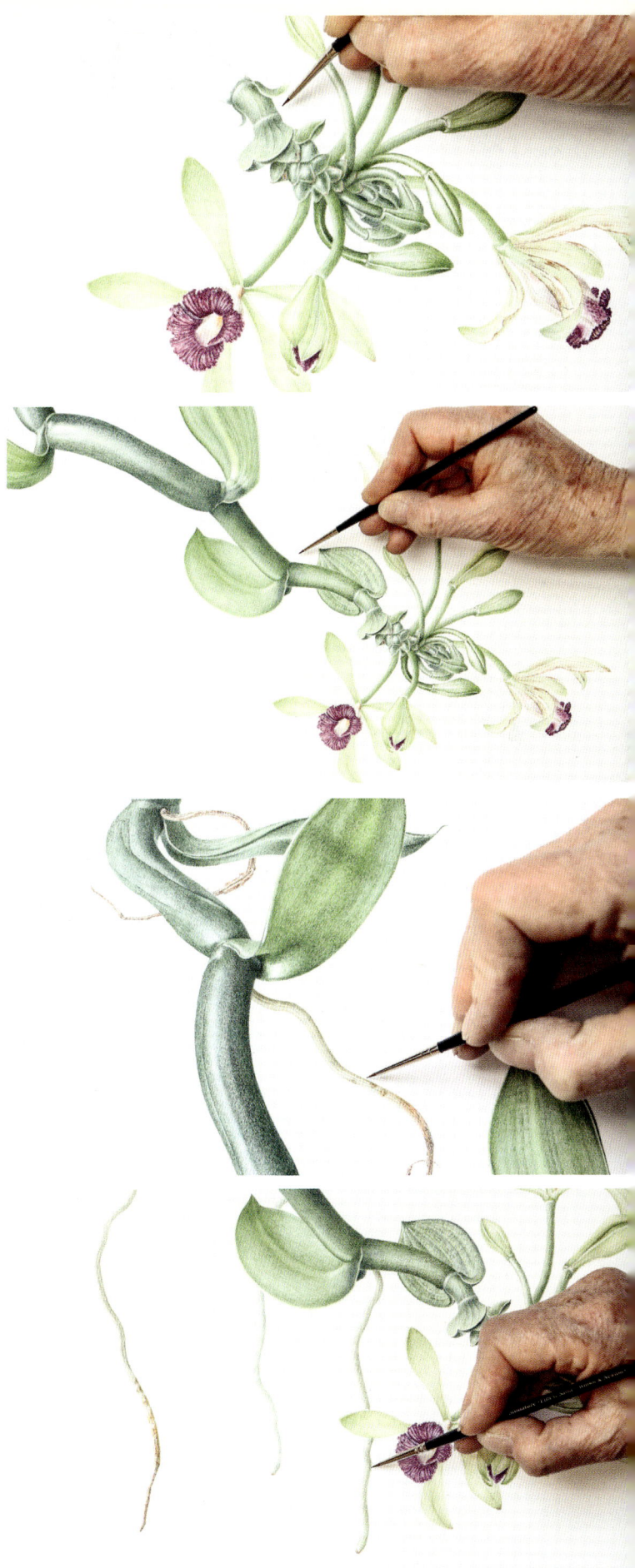

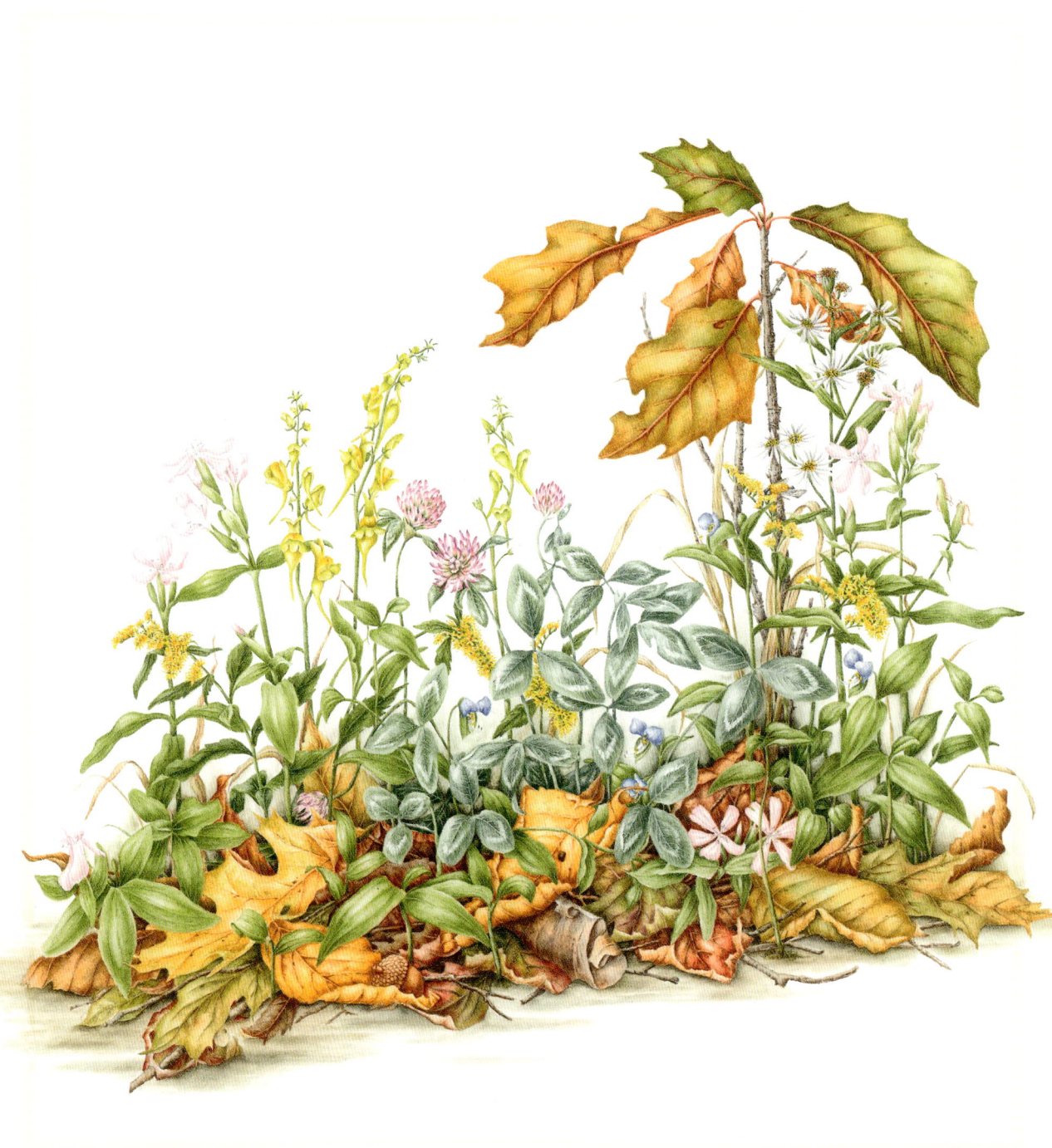

Roadside Wildflowers Watercolor on paper 16 × 19 inches [40 × 47.5 cm] © Betsy Rogers-Knox

HOURS TO COMPLETE: 70

MATERIALS Helping hands specimen holder; metal dividers; artist's tape; glass jar for water; paper towel; porcelain palette; mixing brush (no. 4); blending brush (no. 4); Kolinsky watercolor brushes (nos. 2, 0, and 1); soft brush (no. 10); lead holders with HB and 2H leads; medium white-plastic retractable eraser; ultrafine white plastic retractable eraser; kneaded eraser; rotary lead pointer.

Ground litter is often overlooked when we seek the beautiful wildflowers blooming above, but the ground offers important information about the plants that thrive in it, and it is full of rich color and form. Creating a painting that includes the complexity of in-situ elements can be a challenge. By breaking down the painting into a step-by step process, working from the darkest background for the ground litter, forward to the mid-ground, and ending with the foreground, you can establish the depth necessary to successfully create a small habitat.

Creating an In-Situ Painting

TUTOR: BETSY ROGERS-KNOX

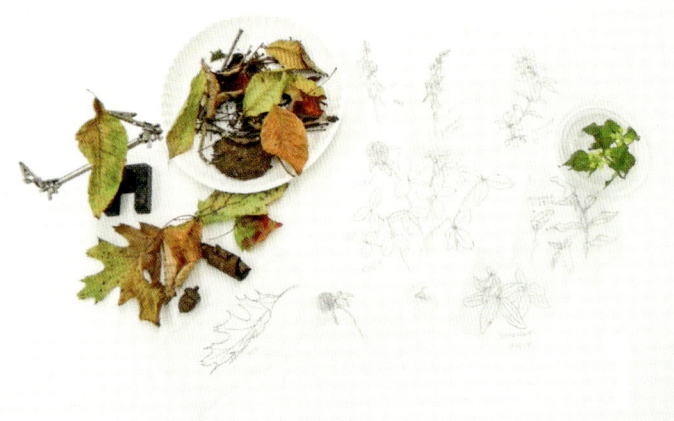

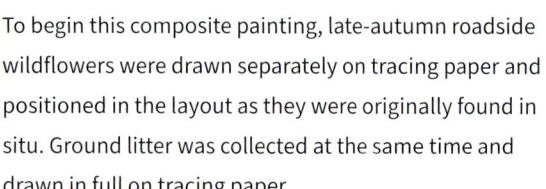

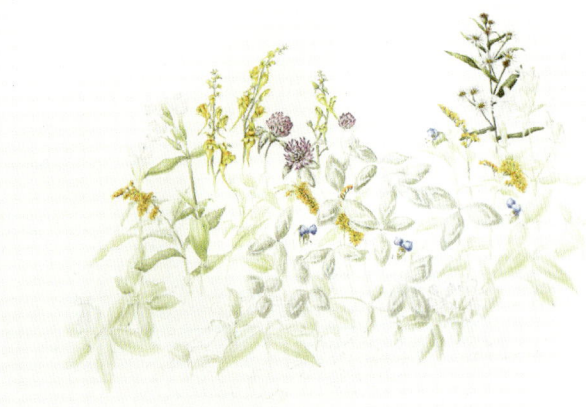

To begin this composite painting, late-autumn roadside wildflowers were drawn separately on tracing paper and positioned in the layout as they were originally found in situ. Ground litter was collected at the same time and drawn in full on tracing paper.

The tracings were transferred to 140 lb. [300 gsm] hot-pressed paper, and a light initial wash was applied to all the foreground flowers and leaves. Flowers that would be gone soon, with a frost pending, were painted first to ensure the accuracy of their shape and color.

To create a mid-ground, several layers of wash were added to the leaves, bark, and ground litter (just behind the wildflowers). The mid-ground foliage was painted using a slightly darker wash. The final details and drybrush of foliage were done last.

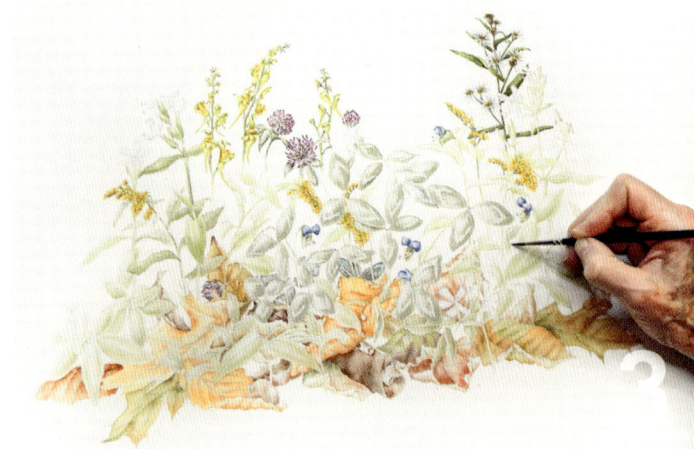

The leaf litter was painted to full strength to create a sense of depth and to highlight the wildflowers and foliage in front. Developing the background completely at this stage sets the dark tones and avoids possible overpainting of the mid and foregrounds.

To give the sense of leaf litter being underneath and below the other elements in the composition, darker shadows were used where these elements intersect with others; for example, where dried leaves lay atop one another and where foreground elements appear. Foliage color and detail were built up in drybrush. To create a vertical element, an oak sapling was added, and a light wash at the bottom softens the edge of the composition.

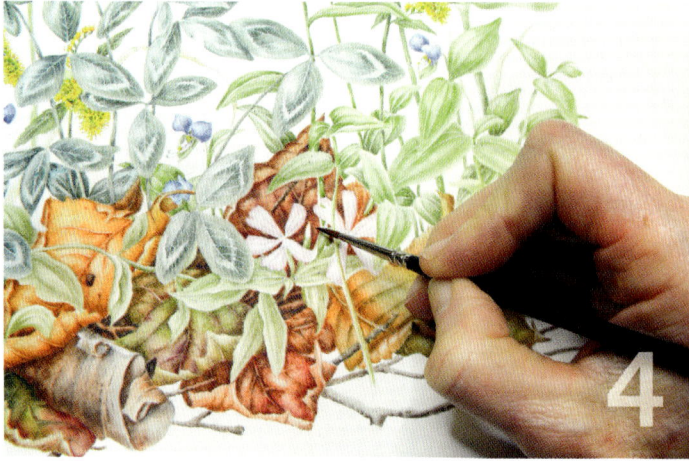

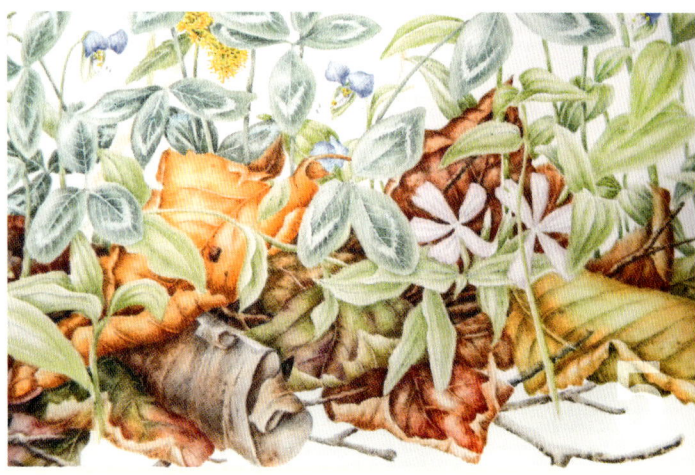

A variety of wash and wet techniques helps to advance this painting of a magnolia quickly through color building. Flower tones are richer at petal bases, and fade out toward the tips. Violets and yellow are used to shade white parts of the petals. The bumpy bark of the branch provides textural contrasts, along with the fuzzy green leaf buds, each requiring different handling with dry-brush detailing.

Painting a Magnolia with Watercolor Washes

TUTOR: BEVERLY ALLEN

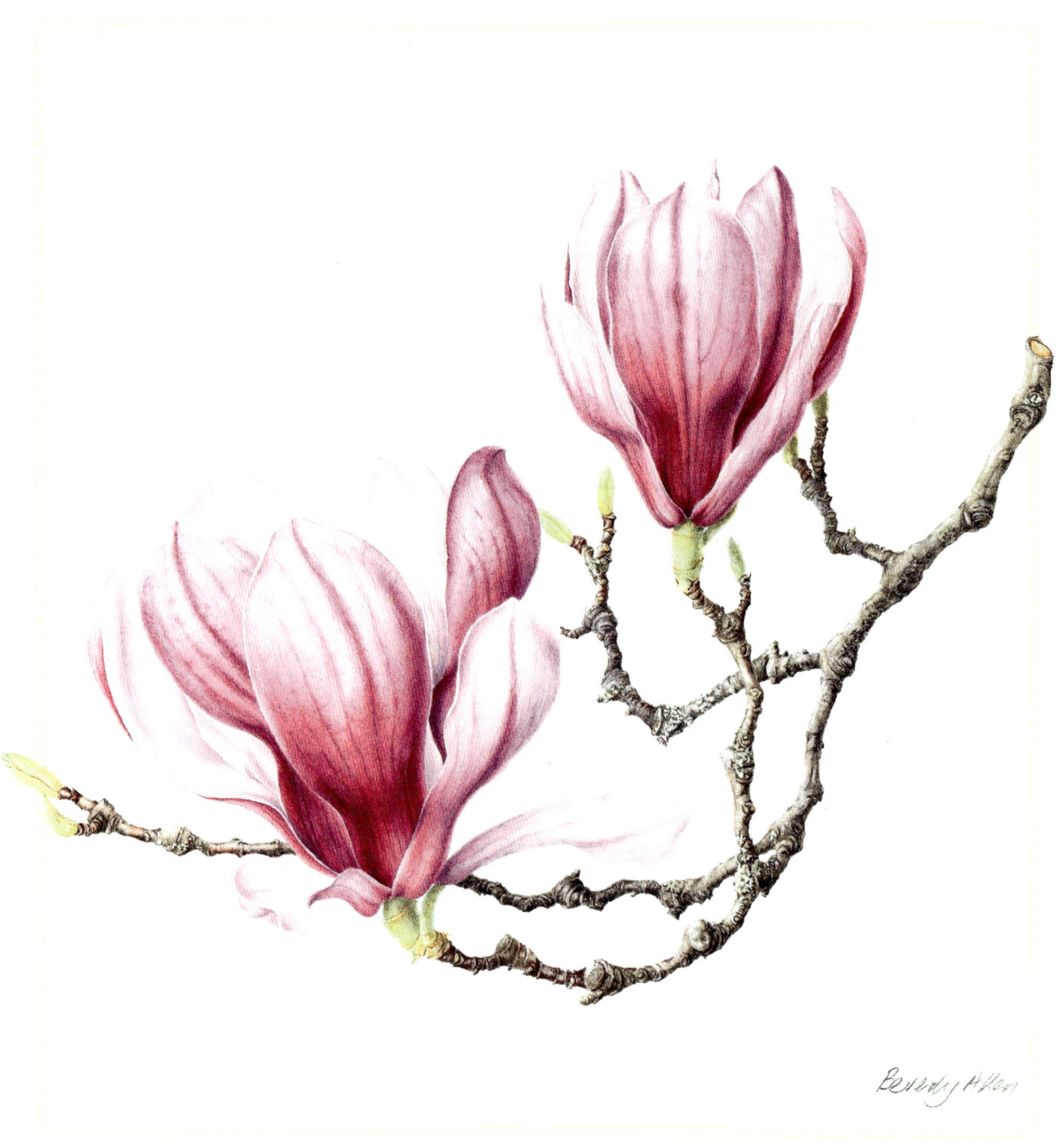

Magnolia ×soulangeana Watercolor on paper 10 × 10 inches [25 × 25 cm] © Beverly Allen
HOURS TO COMPLETE 35

MATERIALS: Scrap paper; jars for water; 2H and HB pencils; mechanical pencils (0.35 mm with 2H and HB leads); dividers; retractable eraser; kneaded eraser; white-plastic erasers; dip pen, masking fluid; cloth; flat bright brush (no. 4); spotter (no. 1); Kolinsky brushes (nos. 1, 2, 3, and 4); synthetic mixing brush; soft cotton brush; palette with basic and extra colors for this work.

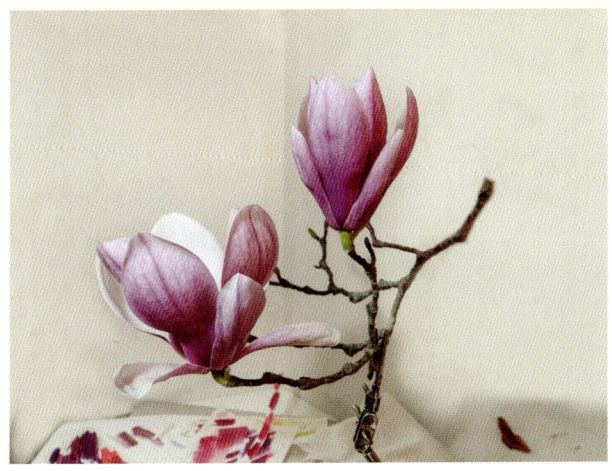

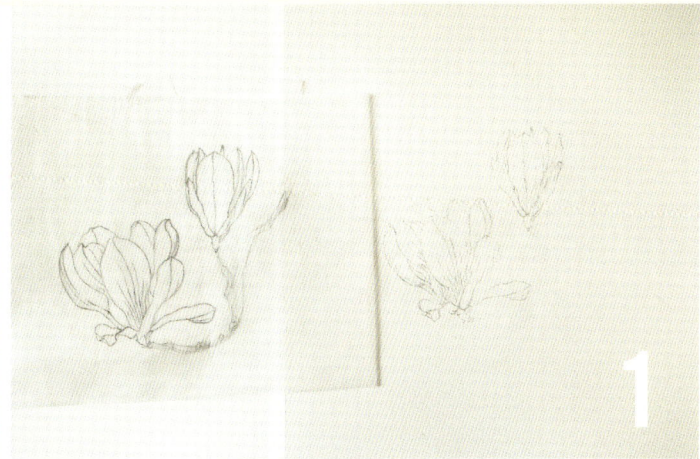

The classic shapes, color, and soft texture of the petals of this *Magnolia ×soulangeana* contrast well with the intricacy and rougher character of the branch. Its graceful curve, ending with the upright posture of the flowers, and the touch of fresh green buds serving as a counterpoint to the pink flowers, makes it an appealing subject.

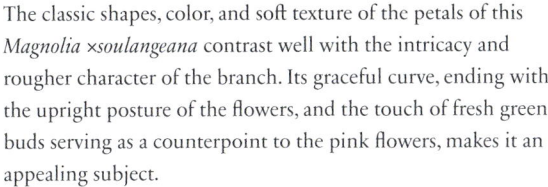

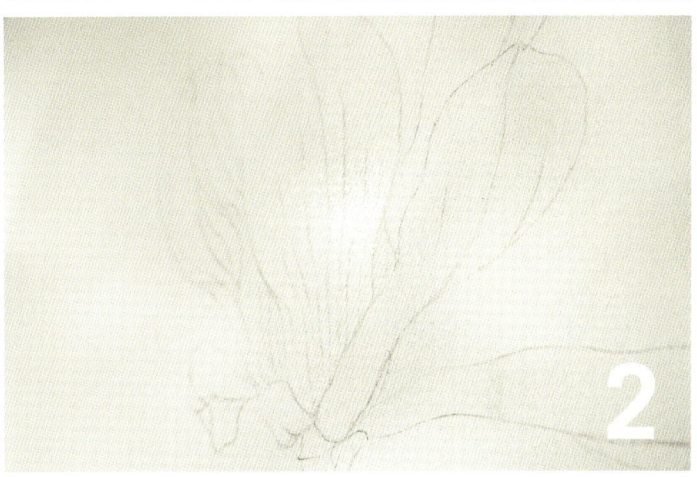

Draw the flowers in detail on tracing paper before they fade. This drawing was transferred to 140 lb. [300 gsm] hot-pressed painting paper using a 2H pencil. Apply masking fluid to the edges of the petals using a simple pen nib only where retaining the white is essential.

The petal is well primed with clean water, which is left briefly to partially dry to a velvety sheen in preparation for the next step.

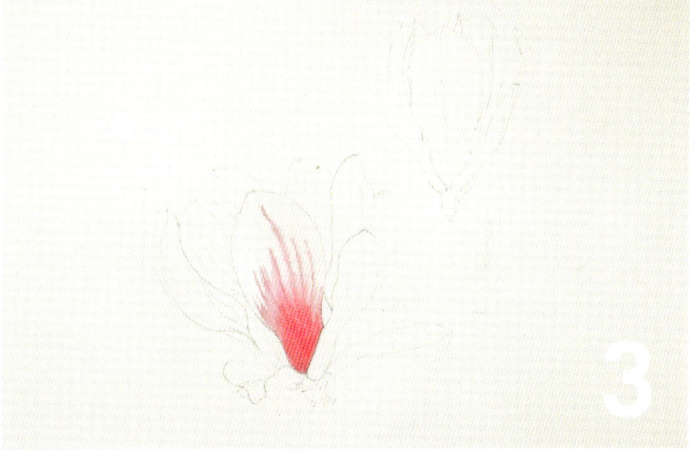

Wet a no. 4 brush and wipe off the excess water with a cloth, then dip the tip into a creamy mix of permanent rose. Control the amount of paint on the brush by wiping the brush on a cloth as needed. Lay down the permanent rose onto the damp paper where the deepest color is desired and gently draw it out into the paler area.

The rose color is more evident in the brighter foreground areas and will glow through the later layers of the main flower color mix (see next step). Apply an underwash of rose to all the areas where it is visible. Allow it to dry before the next wash is applied.

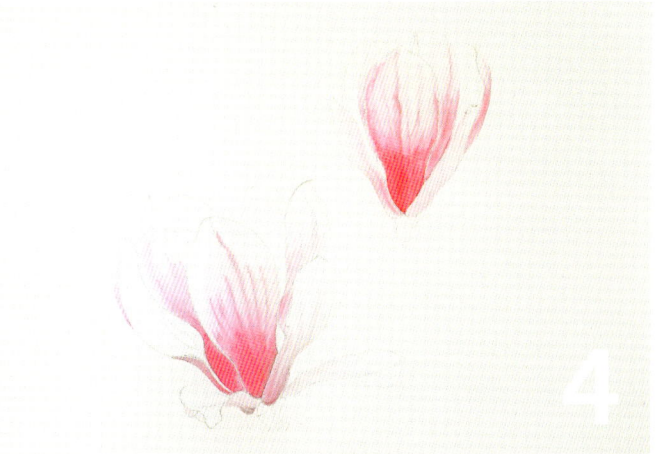

Dampen the white inside of the petals, then apply soft washes of pale rose or a shadowy color mix of rose and ultramarine blue. For soft color edges, dampen beyond the area needed, and wash in from a darker edge. To dull the shadow mix, add lemon yellow. Use fine shadows and crinkles to delineate the petals from the paper without outlining them.

Prime each dried petal with water, then apply the main flower color, a mix of rose and ultramarine violet, with a no. 3 brush. Draw out from the strongest color into the pale areas, feathering pigment while the paper is still damp to create veins and texture and picking up additional skinned color (dried washes on palette) onto the brush tip as necessary.

Move alternately around the petals, adjusting the mix as appropriate, making them pinker where they are brighter in the foreground and in areas of stronger clear light; or making them bluer, also adding ultramarine violet, in shadow areas. When the color washes in the larger areas are strong enough and totally dry, rub off the masking fluid using a light brisk movement with a clean, dry finger.

Soften the hard edges left by the masking fluid with a damp flat bright brush. Place the tip of the brush into the white area, hold it for a second to soften the edge, then pull it gently back with a lifting movement. Turn the paper so the brushstrokes are always pulling away from the white area. Wash the pigment off the brush after each stroke.

With a barely damp brush, pick up either skinned pigment or slightly creamy paint to strengthen color areas and build the form, including the duller shadowy areas. The painting should be dry at this stage, and no additional dampening is needed. Gently lift pigment from any overpainted highlights with the flat bright brush, washing pigment off between each stroke.

Look for the venations that show the form and ensure they are as strong as they are on the flowers. Pay close attention to how and where they fade out, their direction, and the varying degrees of fineness, particularly in the highlights. Vary their color as observed.

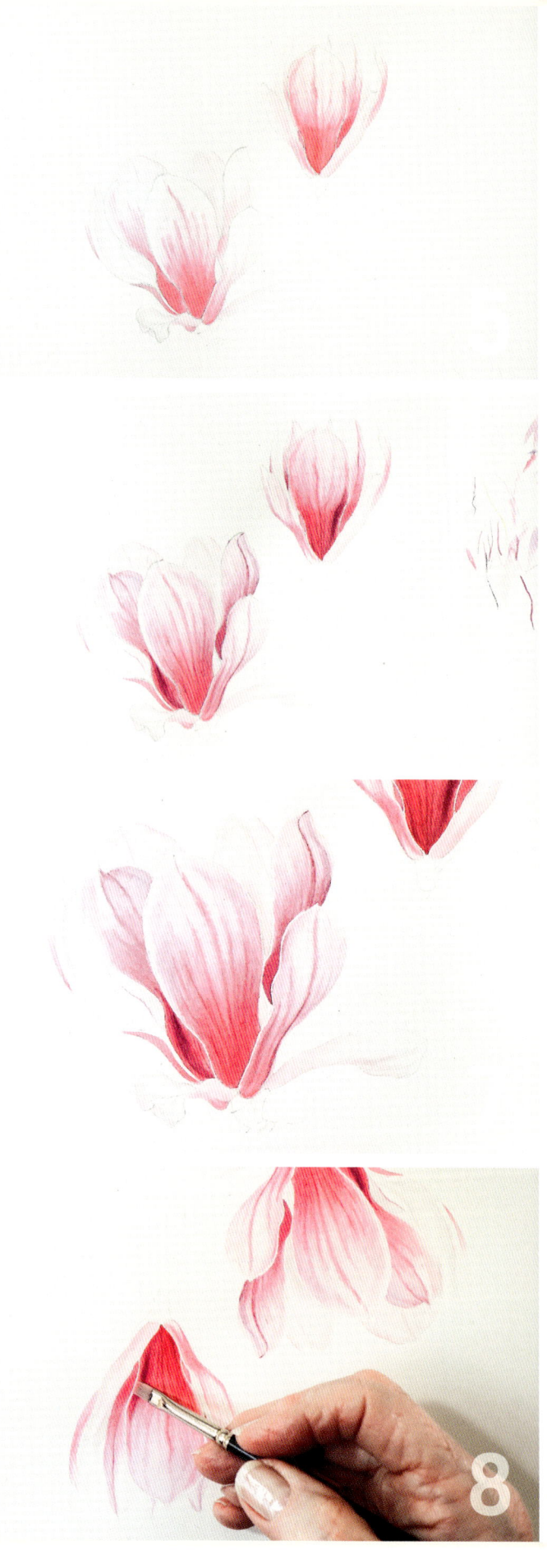

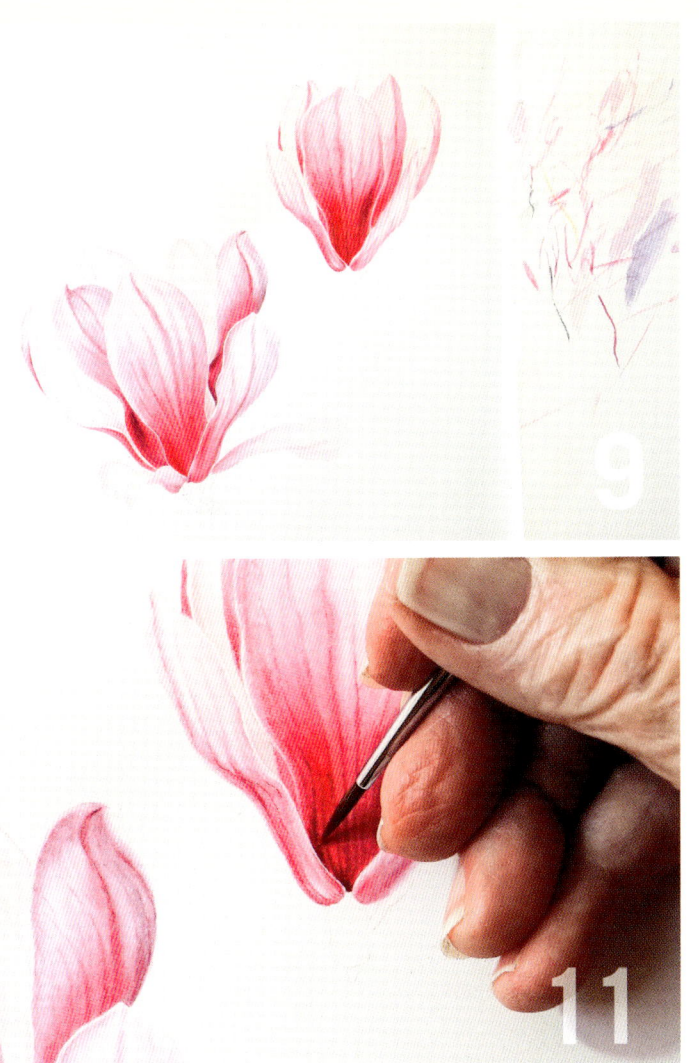

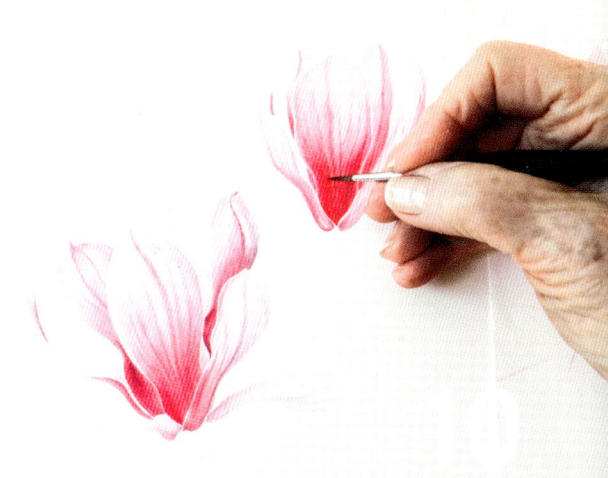

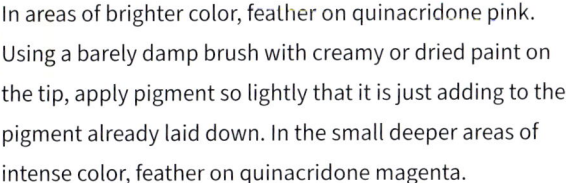

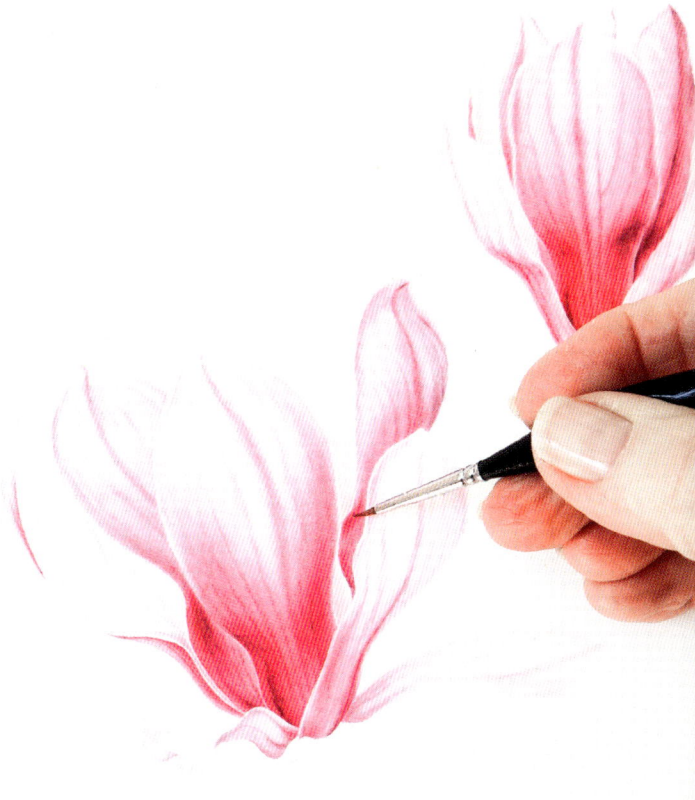

In areas of brighter color, feather on quinacridone pink. Using a barely damp brush with creamy or dried paint on the tip, apply pigment so lightly that it is just adding to the pigment already laid down. In the small deeper areas of intense color, feather on quinacridone magenta.

Dull and deepen small shadows by adding lemon and ultramarine violet to the main color mix. Make the very tiny darks as deep and fine as possible; even a little shadow area makes a difference in conveying form. Be sure that the cast shadows are painted on the surfaces they fall on; do not create a line between those two surfaces that doesn't belong to either of them

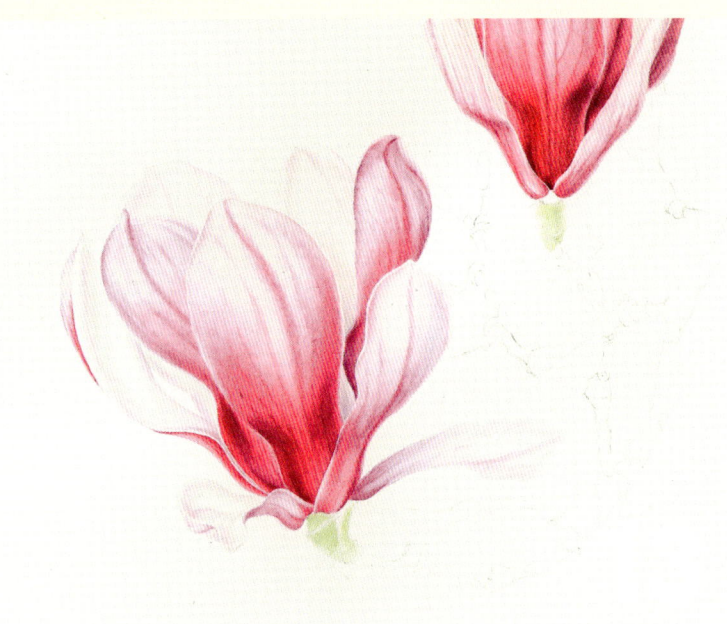

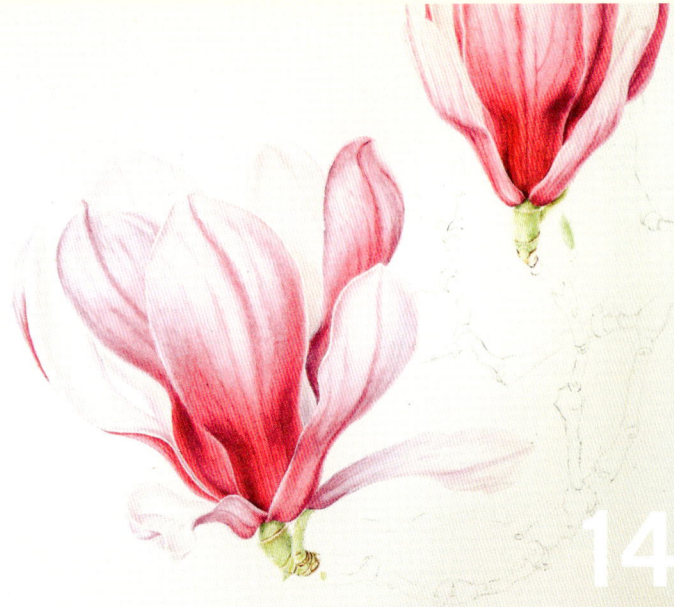

For the fuzzy green flower stalks and leaf buds, use a small amount of masking fluid for the highlighted hairs. Then dampen the paper beyond the area to be painted and apply paint well inside it for a very soft furry edge. Use mix of lemon and ultramarine violet first, and, while the paper is still damp, wash in a slight touch of cerulean to shade the green.

When the paint is dry, gently rub off the masking fluid using a light brisk movement with a clean, dry finger and add fine strokes for hairs and soft edges using no. 1 spotter. Paint in lemon and ultramarine violet mix for the deeper shadows under the flower itself. Use raw umber for the fine rings with Van Dyke brown in the darker parts.

For the branches, only minimal pencil guides are necessary, sketched in with geometrics and perspective in mind. Paint washes in, only lightly wetting the paper where soft highlights are needed, and add the details once the washes have dried. The colors used here are an ultramarine blue and burnt sienna mix for grays, a perylene violet and burnt sienna mix for purplish areas, and raw umber as needed.

Paint the lichens on the branches in lemon and ultramarine blue. Wash the shadowed areas over lightly with an ultramarine violet and lemon mix in some areas and an ultramarine blue and burnt sienna mix in others, without losing the form and texture.

Complete the branches, with the detail in the foreground stalks in higher contrast and the detail in the shadows and the rear areas with less contrast. Add the remainder of the pale green leaf buds in the same way the flower stalks were created.

The dark shadows on the branch make it necessary to adjust the flower's color, its shadows, and the outer lower petals to equalize their strength. Finally, using a magnifying glass, examine the whole painting, sharpening edges where necessary and smoothing out any brush marks, dotting in paint or moving the pigment on the paper with a fine brush tip.

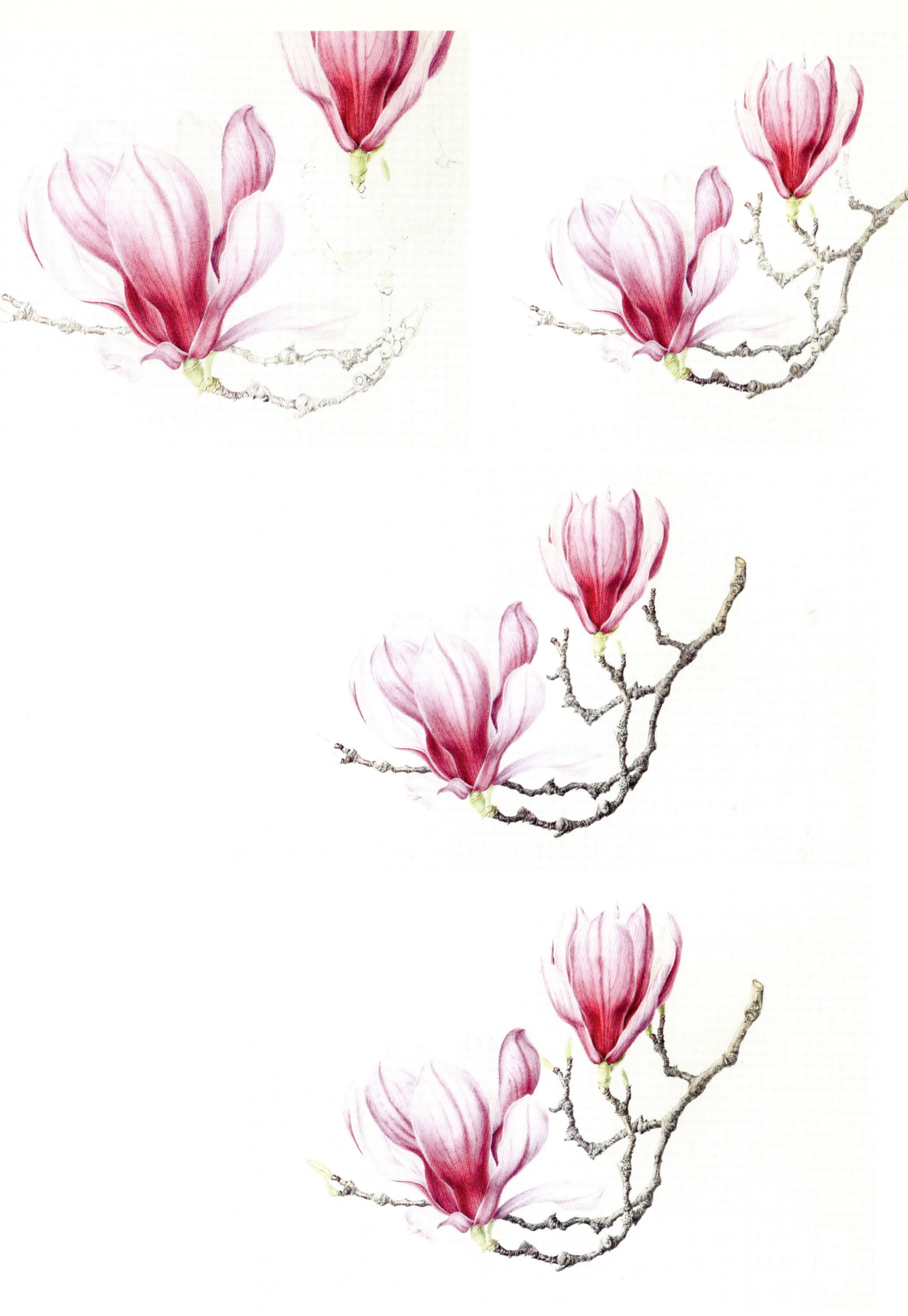

ATMOSPHERIC PERSPECTIVE: HOW TO CREATE AN ILLUSION OF DEPTH

When designing a painting with layered components, some artists choose to use atmospheric perspective, wherein objects in the background are paler and have lower contrast and lower chroma than those in the foreground. This focuses attention on the objects up front, which are painted with greater brilliance and contrast. Elaine Searle color-codes her layout drawing to clarify which parts of the painting belong in which layer.

Searle color coded the initial drawing of this *Helleborus* 'Penny's Pink' for teaching purposes to clearly show the five layers in the composition from foreground to background. Each layer is discussed below. One of the large foreground leaves sits across two layers. Searle likes to compose in three dimensions, as nature does, rather than arranging elements within a flat plane.

- Layer one (orange) contains the "hero" of the composition. It is painted to full strength with true colors, maximum contrast, and detail. This where the viewer is meant to focus their attention.

- Layers two (blue) and three (green) contain secondary focal points and convey key plant characteristics. Color, contrast, and detail are progressively muted with each layer, from front to back. These changes are subtle.

- Layers four (purple) and five (gray) are most affected by atmospheric perspective. Colors are muted, and scale, contrast, and detail are further reduced, allowing these elements to recede in space and form a backdrop to the main players on layers one, two, and three.

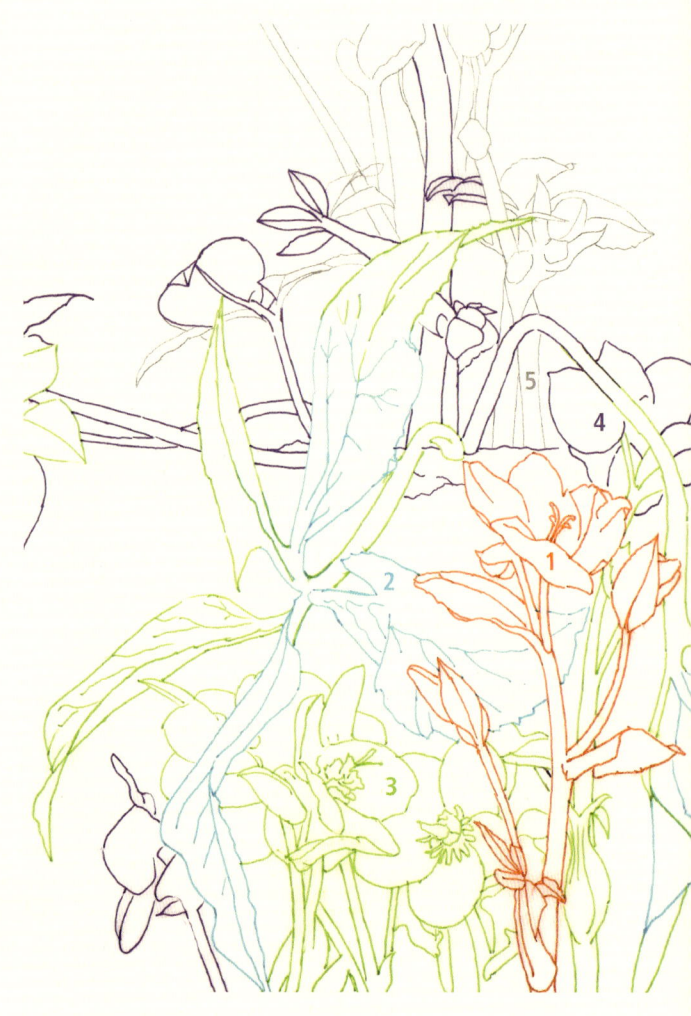

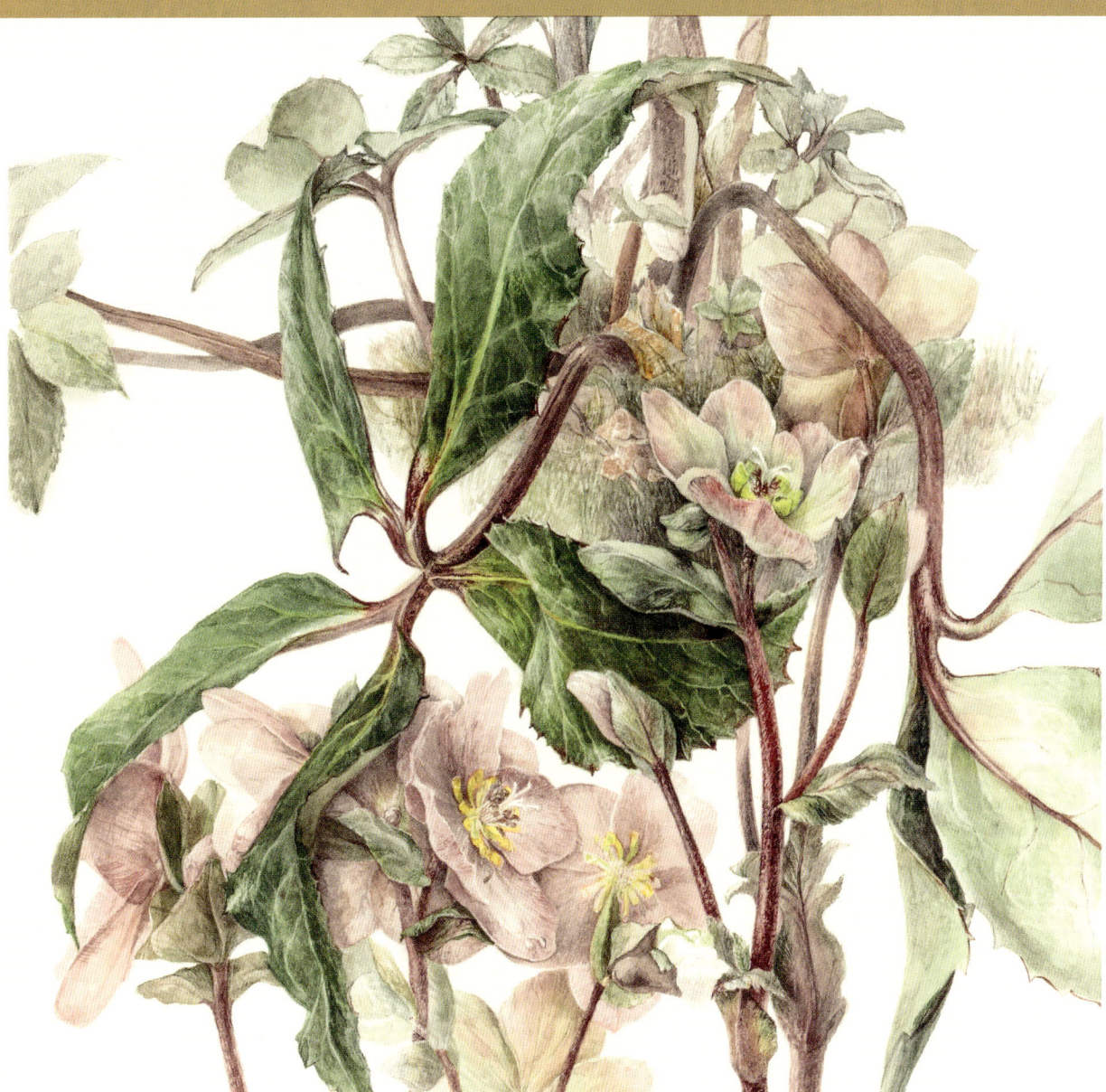

Helleborus 'Penny's Pink' Watercolor on paper 10 × 10 inches [25 × 25 cm] © Elaine Searle
HOURS TO COMPLETE: 70

Searle worked on several areas of the painting at the same time, and chose the areas to begin painting strategically:

A. The focal point, or focal points, of the painting (typically on layer one), while also addressing parts of the areas adjoining them on the mid and background layers. With this approach, Searle can evaluate their impact and show local color and full detail.

B. An area in the painting receiving maximum light (typically down the left side nearest to the single light source).

C. An area of deep shadow (typically bottom right), where little or no light is reaching the subject.

In the beginning stages, Searle would not finish any area up to full strength. Moving around all areas, the painting grows in color, contrast, and detail. She often takes photographs of the stages to help evaluate her progress. All the finishing touches, using drybrush, are done together in the final stage.

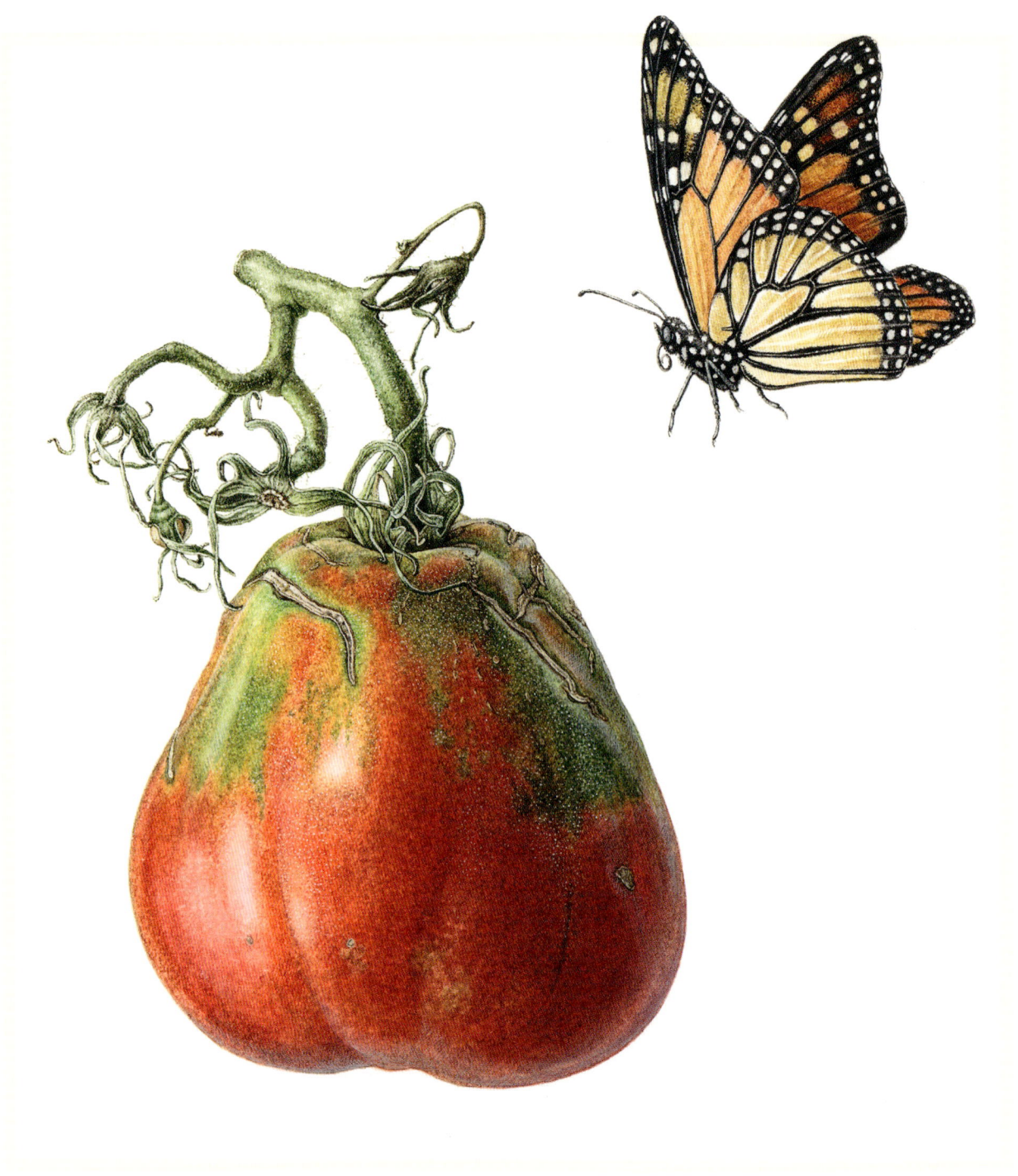

Madama Butterfly: Portrait of an Heirloom Tomato *Solanum lycopersicum* Watercolor on paper
10 × 9 ½ inches [25 × 23.75 cm] © Asuka Hishiki HOURS TO COMPLETE: 104

MATERIALS: Porcelain palette; handmade transfer paper; water bottle; scrap piece of watercolor paper for testing color; small dish for masking fluid; masking-fluid remover; masking fluid; glass for water; paints dried in pans; tracing paper and tissue paper; nib pen; synthetic watercolor round (nos. 3X0 and 6X0); flat brush (no. 2); Kolinsky round (no. 4); old brush; graphite pencil 2H; tissue; kneaded eraser; white-plastic eraser; drafting brush; tape.

An heirloom tomato is painted in watercolor without using broad washes. Colors are gradually built up with a series of dilute, but dry, layers of color. Highlights, small dots, and sepal edges are first painted with Chinese white, then protected with masking fluid. In this way, white areas are retained and textures enhanced while color is being strengthened throughout. The resulting tomato is glossy with a variety of surface textures and precisely depicted sepals and stem.

Drybrush Tomato with Masking Fluid

TUTOR: ASUKA HISHIKI

First, complete the drawing on tracing paper. Transfer the drawing to the final paper using transfer paper; this will keep the watercolor paper from being damaged by an eraser. If necessary, touch up the drawing lightly to fix any distortion that may have occurred during the transfer. Redraw the graphite lines with thin watercolor lines and gently erase all the graphite.

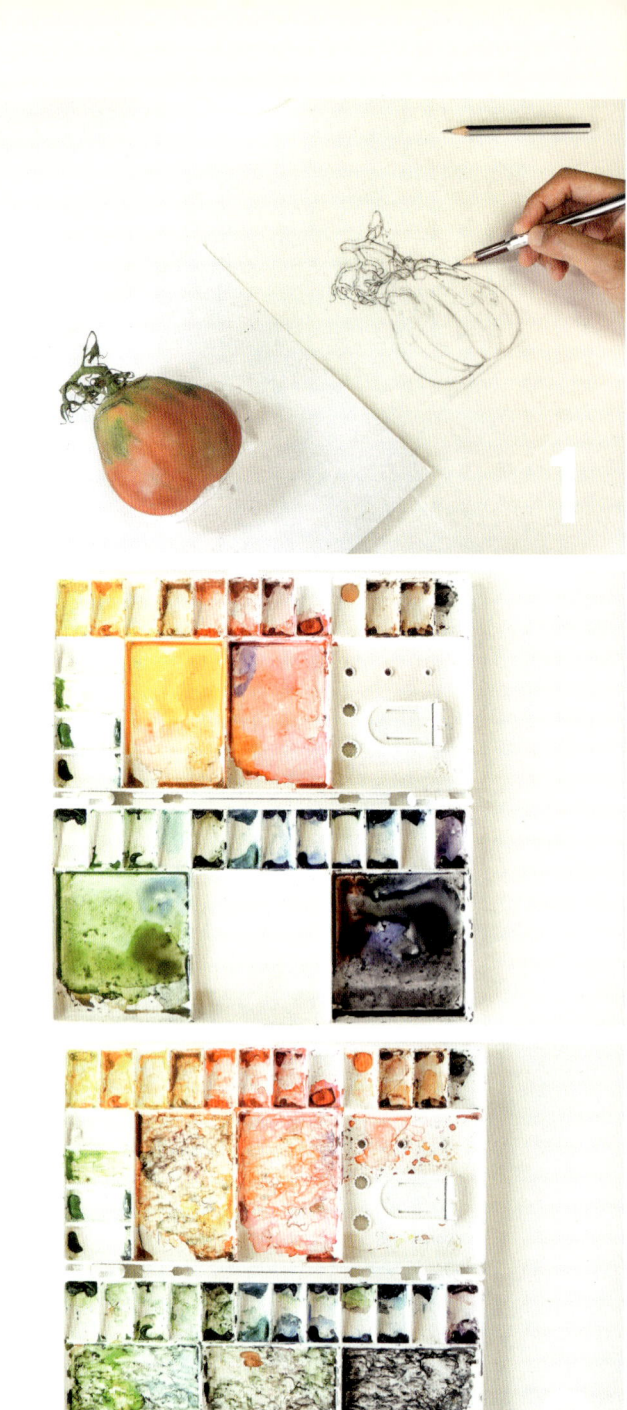

Two views of the palette at the beginning of work and as work progresses: Begin with mixes of yellow and red for the tomato, leaf greens, and blue and burnt sienna for the shadows on a palette. The colors in the tomato vary; some areas contain purple and others contain orange, so create a rainbow of colors to start. With the tip of your brush, lift a selected color from the rainbow. Over time, by mixing more specific colors for different areas, a more complex rainbow of color develops.

Use masking fluid to protect the highlight, small brown scars, and the thin sepals overlapping the tomato. Before applying the masking fluid, first paint a thin wash of diluted Chinese white on the areas where the masking fluid will be used. This protects the paper and will help to blend the masked border later if necessary. To cover a bigger area, use an old brush.

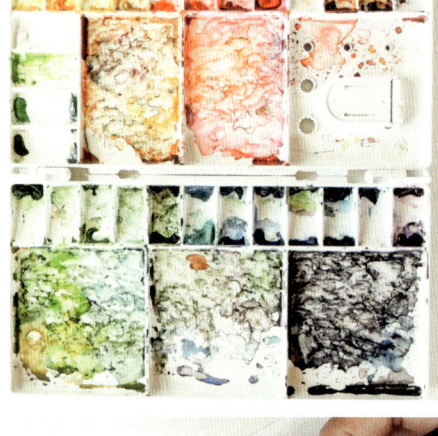

Always make sure the paper has completely dried before adding another layer. Build up small hatching lines following the contours of the subject to create the tomato's curved surface. The washes and hatching lines should be extremely diluted compared to the color of the finished painting. Frequently check the color and wetness of the brush (3X0) on the testing paper. More water makes softer lines; less water makes sharper lines.

There are many tiny white specks within the translucent tomato skin. To re-create that quality, use a nib pen to apply tiny dots of masking fluid all over the surface. Make sure the dots are evenly placed—they may look like scars rather than texture if they are placed unevenly. Add color throughout the whole area with thin washes and hatching lines. Areas that are masked will not accept color.

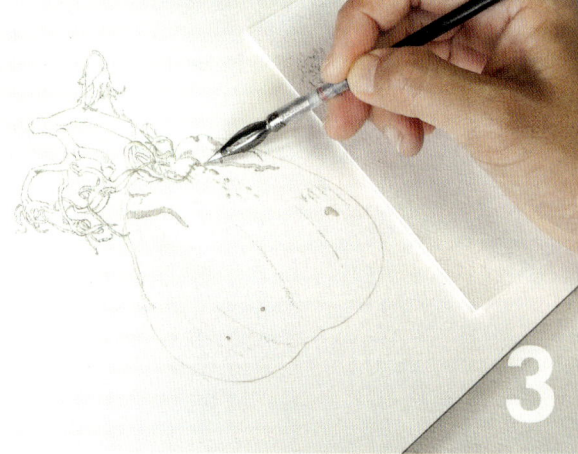

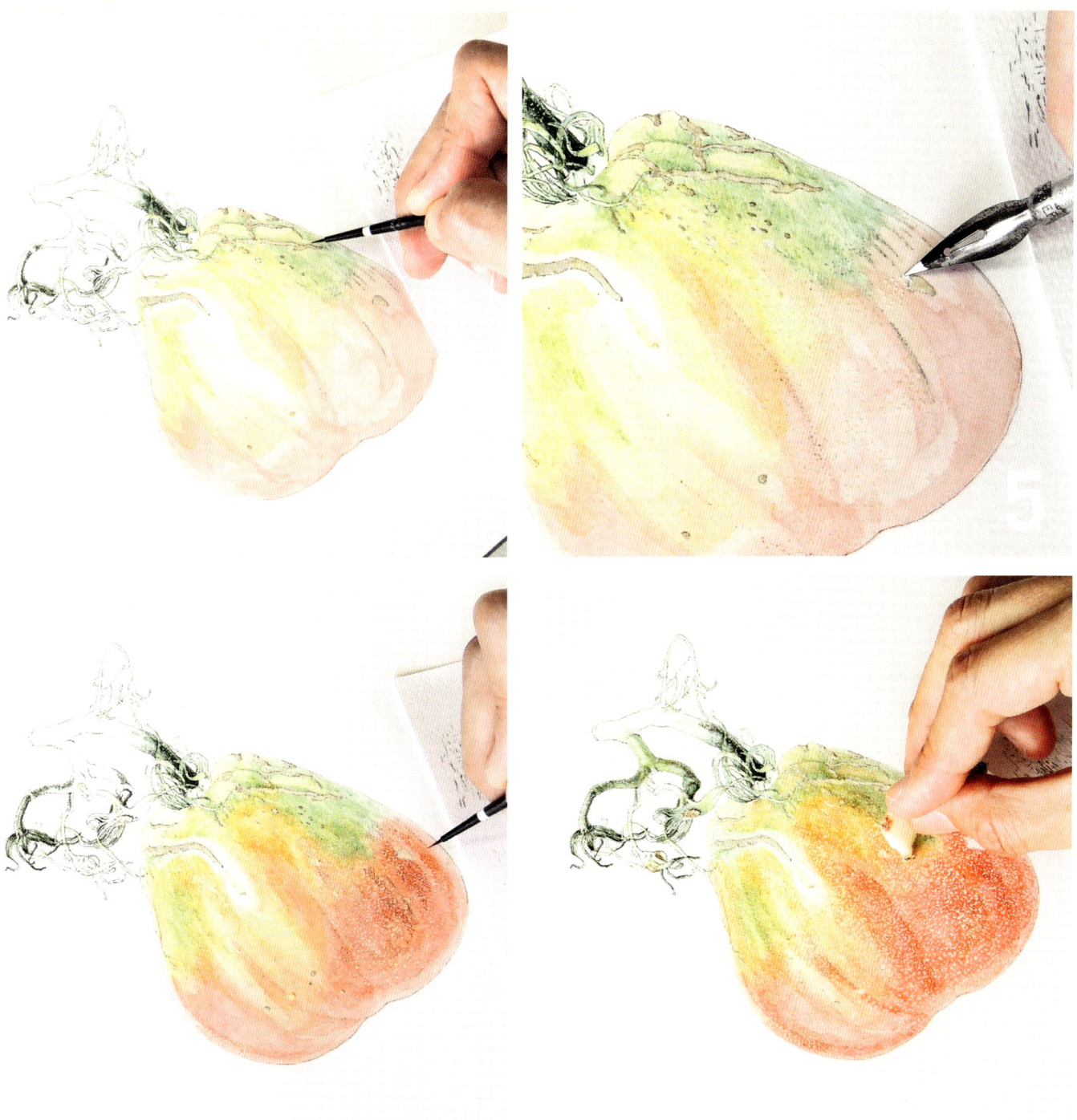

Continue adding layers of hatching and wash, to build overall color. Using masking-fluid remover, gently rub off masking-fluid dots and add new ones in different locations several times. Think of masking fluid like white paint. This process gives the dots in the tomato skin different tints of red, making them appear to be at different depths in the skin.

After applying several layers, remove the masked dots with masking-fluid remover. Hold the sheet of paper up and look for small bumps or shiny spots from the side of the painting to make sure all the masking fluid has been removed. Add more layers of paint until the desired color and texture are achieved.

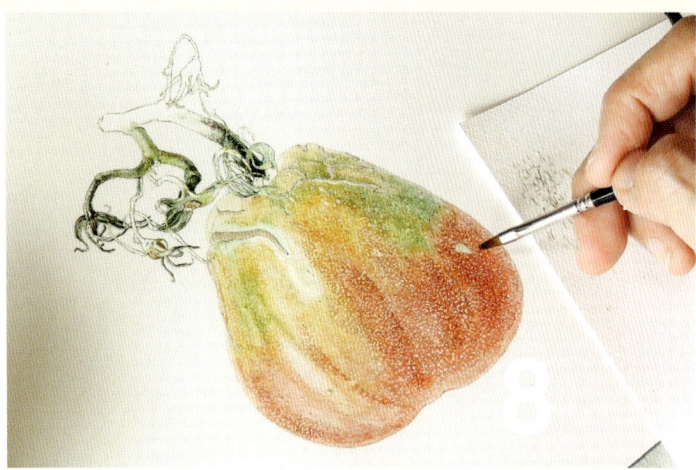

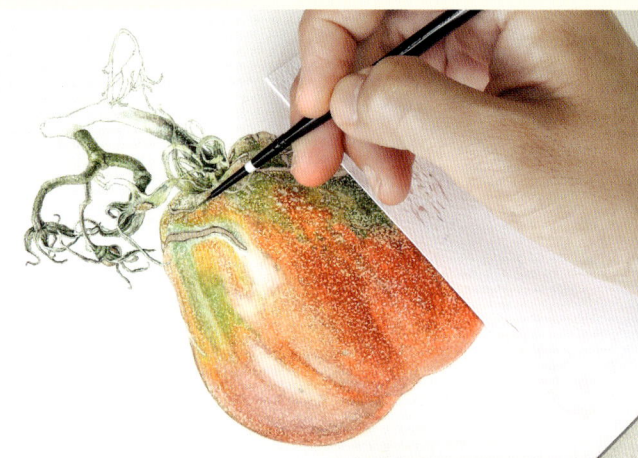

If the hatching lines are too strong and prominent, smooth them with a brush that is barely dampened with clean water. One or two strokes will soften the lines. The amount of the water should be just right—touch the back of your hand with the brush; if it's wet but no liquid is left, that's the right amount.

Often when one layer of masking fluid is removed, it must be reapplied, especially in a highlight area. Before reapplying masking fluid to the same place, add another layer of Chinese white to protect the paper; it's hard to work with the paper once it has been damaged. Fill and smooth the sharp edges left behind from removing the masking fluid.

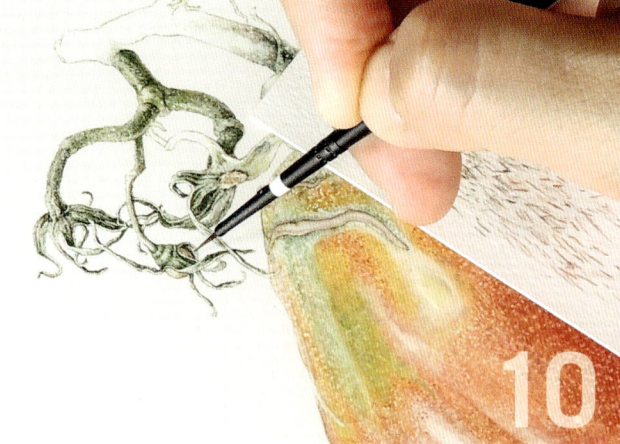

To keep the half-dried sepals sharp, leave the paper white between the painted edges. Let it dry completely, ideally waiting one or two hours before beginning the next step. Then add light tone into the white area. If the painted edges are completely dry and stable, they will stay solid even when a light wash or hatching lines are added.

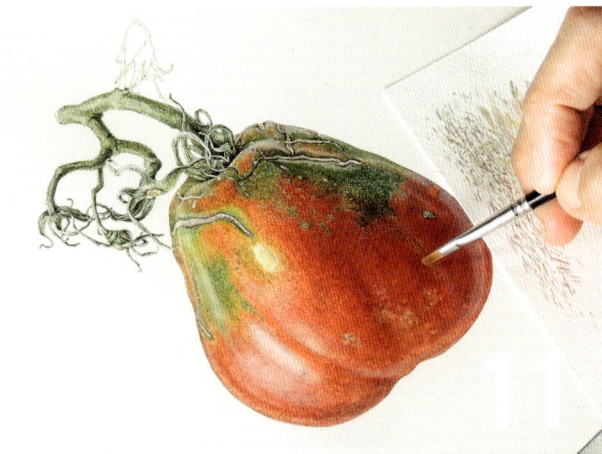

As the work progresses, it is important to step back and take in the entire picture. Because of the tendency to compare colors only in the small area being developed, the balance of the whole subject may shift out of tone. Add shadowy blue to the dark side of the tomato and airy pink to the light side, using a flat brush.

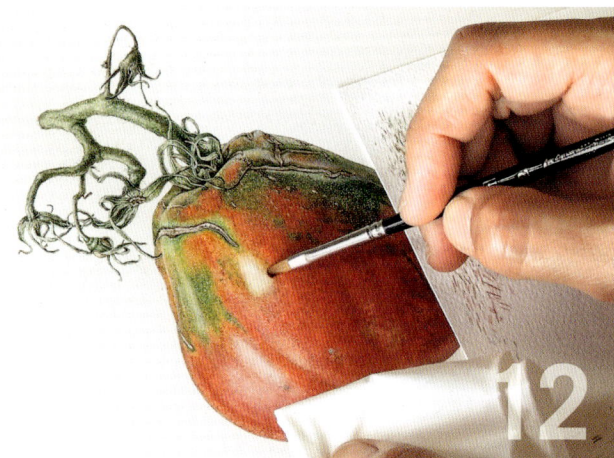

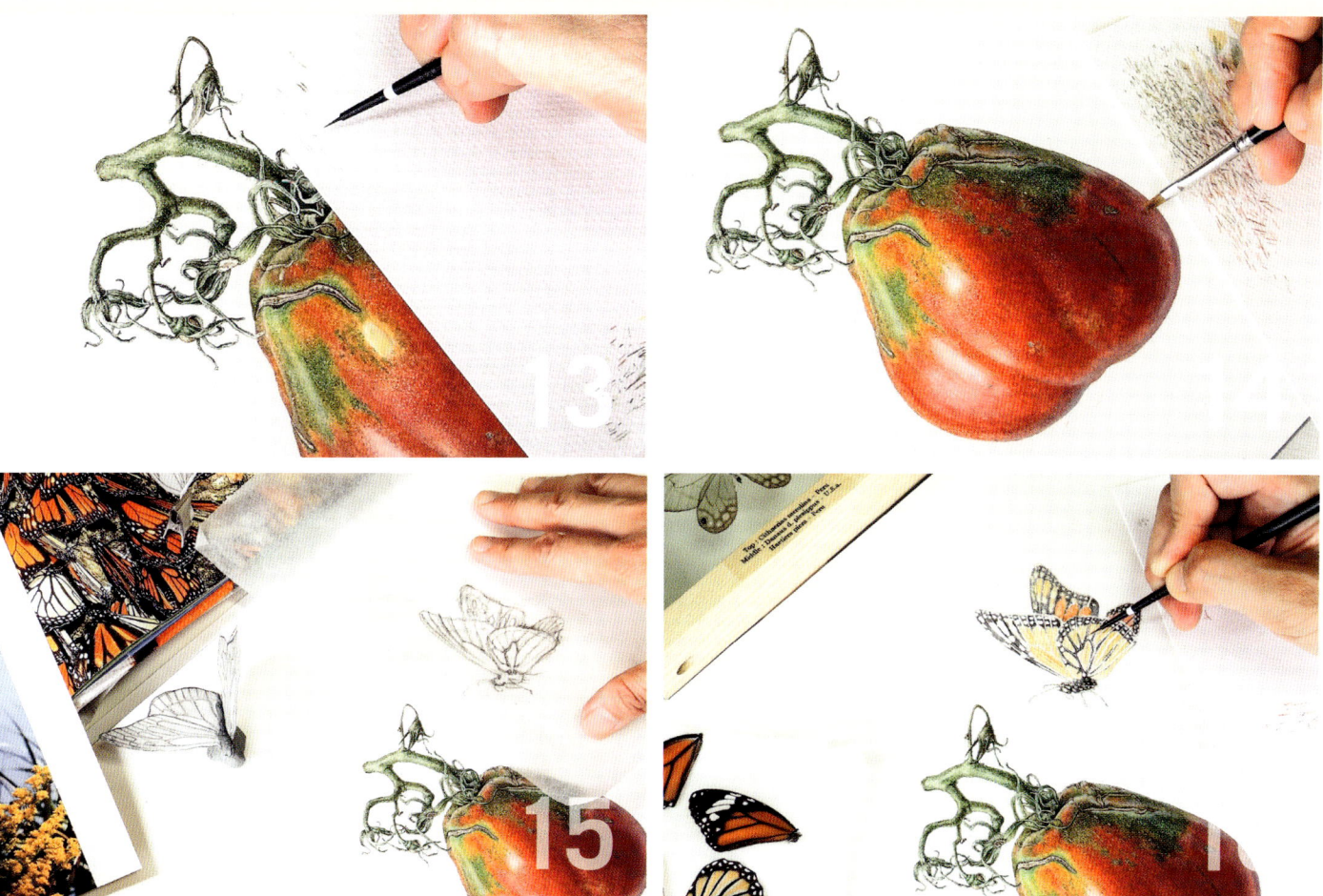

After removing the masking fluid from the glossy highlight, smooth the edge of the area with a slightly wet brush. Use only clean water and rub gently. The Chinese white underneath helps blend the paints used on top. If necessary, lightly blot with soft tissue to absorb any excess water and paint. Do not overwork the area, and let it dry untouched for a long while.

Tomato hairs are very fragile. To draw the delicate lines, use a nearly dry no. 6X0 brush. Pick up a small amount of paint from the palette skins, and roll the brush on test paper several times to dry the brush. This helps point the brush as well. To draw the tomato hairs, the tip of the brush should barely touch the surface of the paper.

True white is paper white, and white paint never reproduces that whiteness. However, white paint works well to add reflected light. A soft brownish-blue white is introduced to the reflected-light area (note that the color turns much bluer when it dries). Do not blot the area with a tissue or rub it with a watery brush when applying; blotting normally lifts more than desired.

The benefit of using tracing paper for composing and underdrawing is that elements can be moved to create the final composition. Draw the butterfly on tracing paper, then try out different positions to determine its final placement.

Butterfly veins are very delicate. Make the masking-fluid lines wider than needed. Paint in the wing colors and dark markings, then remove the masking fluid from the veins. Narrow the vein lines by painting into the edges of the white lines from both sides. Here, use stronger lines with less water and more paint. A watery, soft brush will weaken the edge and lose the papery crisp texture of the wing.

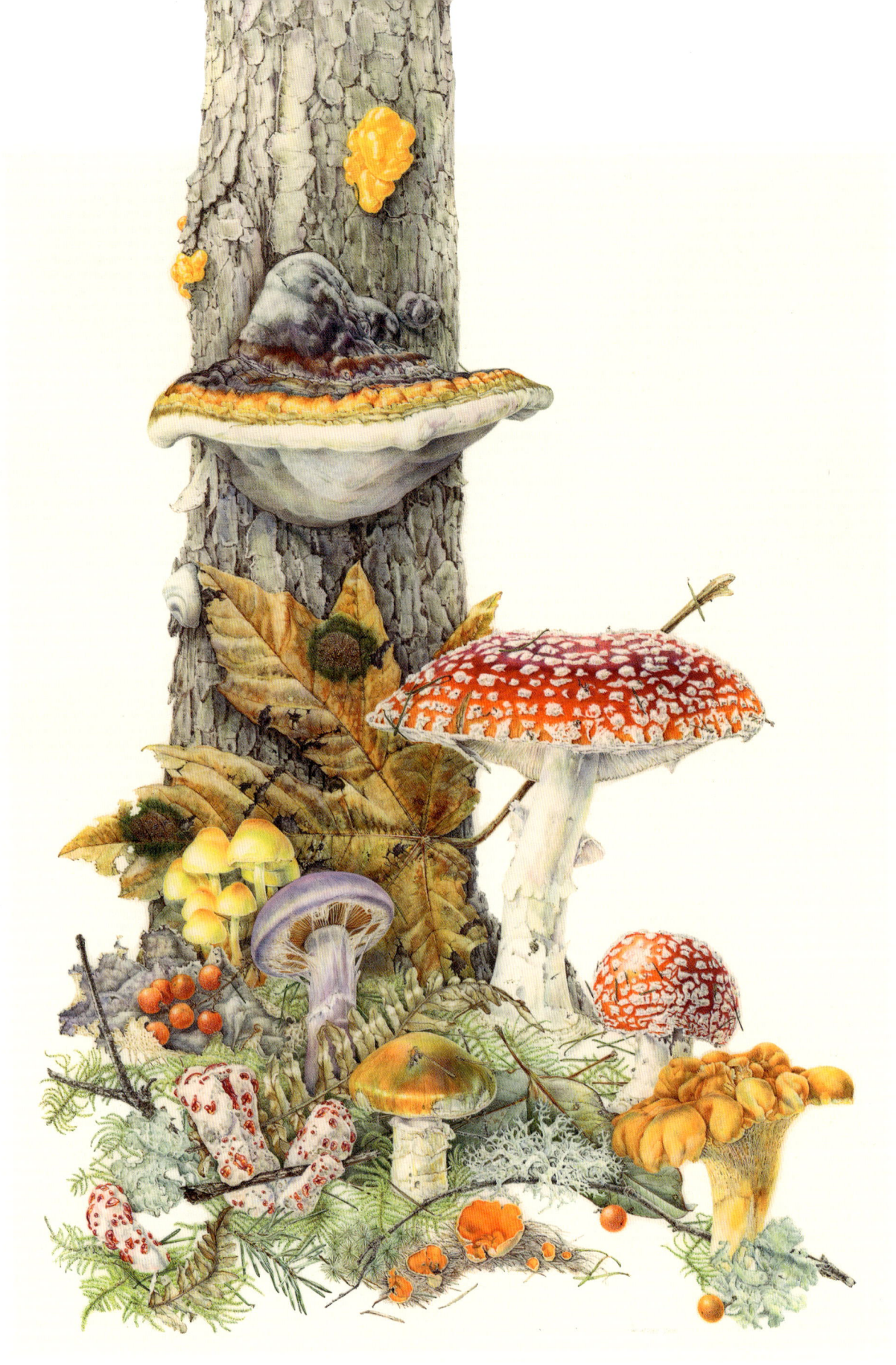

Pacific Northwest Mushrooms Watercolor on vellum over board 18 × 12 inches [45 × 30 cm] © Jean Emmons

WATERCOLOR ON VELLUM

Vellum is another material that is growing in popularity among botanical artists. When its natural translucency is combined with watercolor, the resulting works can be luminous. Its range and modulation of tone provide an organic background for plant paintings, and its smooth surface allows for close detail. When non-fading pigments are used, the resulting paintings can last centuries.

Techniques and Tutorials

Watercolor on Vellum

A Brief Overview of Vellum

TUTOR: CAROL WOODIN

Vellum is a type of untanned leather that has been prepared so that it accepts paint, graphite, ink, adhesives, and other materials used in artistic endeavors. When vellum is stored properly and kept free from insects and other damaging conditions, it can last indefinitely. Vellum's desirable properties include its extremely smooth surface, its warmth and modulation of color, its ability to accept corrections, and the uniqueness of each piece, which allows for matching vellum's surface coloration with subject matter. Vellum has a natural alkalinity that makes it a conservation-friendly surface. It also has some properties that make its use daunting to artists, such as its sensitivity to moisture, its distortion through cockling (puckering) over time, and the uniqueness of each piece, which means it can be inconsistent in handling.

These samples show a range of vellum's colors and surfaces. Most vellum used by artists is derived from calves; however, goat, deer, and sheep vellum is also used. Vellum varies a great deal in thickness. Artists prefer vellum that has some thickness to it, so that moisture from water-based media remains on the surface and doesn't soak all the way through (very thin vellum cockles easily from the moisture in watercolor). Kelmscott vellum is hand-coated with a specialized, gypsum-based material on both sides, which creates a more uniform color and also makes it thick and stiff, preventing much of the typical response to liquid.

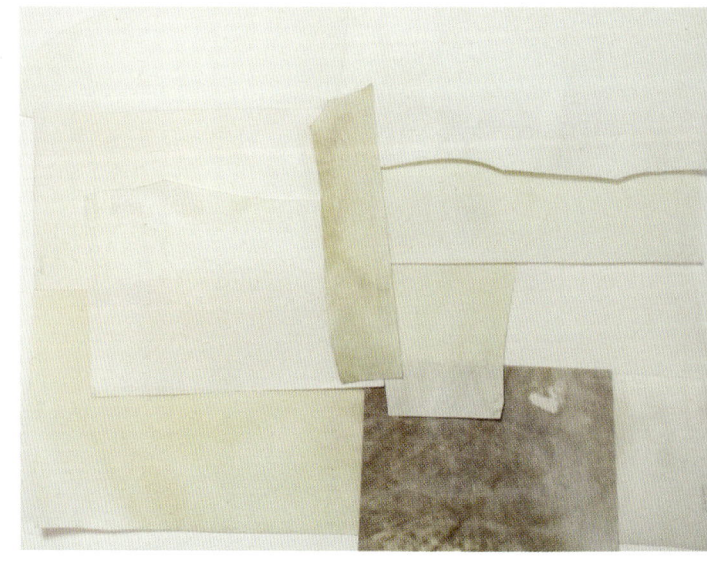

Following is the range of calf vellum most commonly used by botanical artists, placed atop a sheet of hot-pressed watercolor paper.

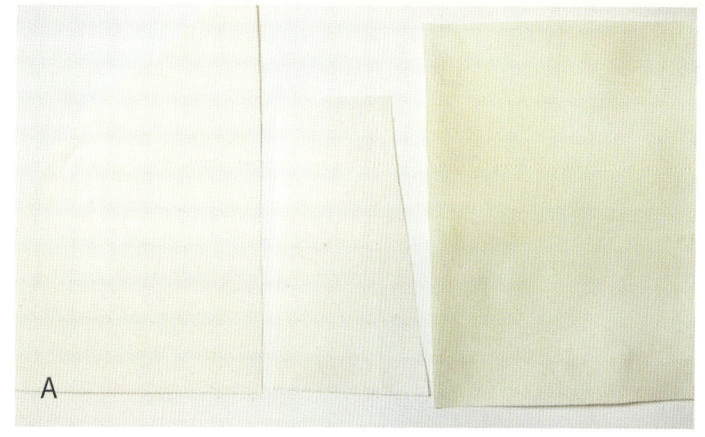

LEFT TO RIGHT: Kelmscott vellum has a specialized polished and sanded coating; it has an even, smooth, and whitish surface. It is thick and cardlike and coated on both sides.

Manuscript (white) vellum is whitest in color and is finished on both sides. The other vellum examples in these photographs are finished on only one side.

Classic (cream) vellum is slightly more golden in color, but it is fairly uniform with no heavy markings. (A)

Honey (natural) vellum is golden in color with some streaks, mottling, and veining. The darker vellum underneath is showing through this piece of honey vellum—nearly all vellum is translucent, except for Kelmscott.

Veiny vellum is dark, heavily veined, and sometimes marked with strong patterning. (B)

With the exception of vellum that is prepared for manuscripts, only one side of vellum is prepared to accept paint, graphite, and ink. The prepared side is smoother and more polished, and, for most vellum, is a darker tone. The other side—which is not suitable for accepting paint, graphite, and ink—can sometimes have an almost suede-like surface. The piece of vellum on the left shows the prepared side up; the vellum on the right shows the back side up (its front side is similar in color to the vellum at left). (C)

Techniques of Watercolor on Vellum: The Basics

TUTOR: CAROL WOODIN

By making a few simple preparations and mastering a few specific techniques, anyone who is accustomed to working in drybrush can adapt its methods to vellum. With practice, these techniques can help you avoid the most common issues artists have with vellum. Most difficulties that arise are related to the way watercolor adheres to and lifts from the vellum. Each of these techniques is further elaborated upon in subsequent tutorials.

MATERIALS (clockwise from left): Drafting brush; white plastic eraser; lead pointer; porcelain palette with flat mixing surfaces; container for water; leather paper weight; gum arabic; paper towel; dry cleaning pad; Kolinsky brushes (nos. 0, 1, and 3); lead holders with HB and 4H leads; retractable blade; retractable erasers.

Cleaning Vellum

The first step before putting pencil or paint to vellum is to remove any oils from its surface. Using a dry cleaning pad in a circular motion, clean the surface of the vellum, especially where the work will take place. Clean the area thoroughly, but don't scrub vigorously enough to abrade the surface of the vellum. (A)

These six pale color blocks were laid down as a first coat of color would be. The row at bottom, where color beading has occurred, was laid down without cleaning the vellum with a dry cleaning pad prior to painting. The row at top, where the color adheres smoothly, was applied after cleaning the vellum. If any areas of color beading are discovered after transferring a drawing and beginning painting, the vellum can be further cleaned with a white plastic eraser. (B)

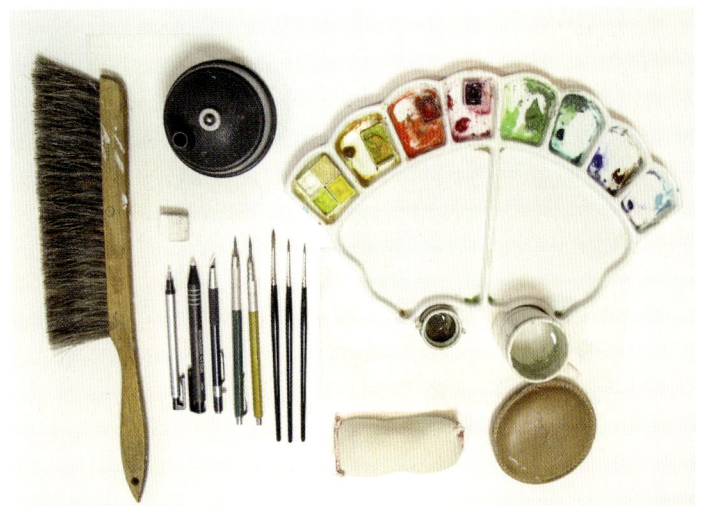

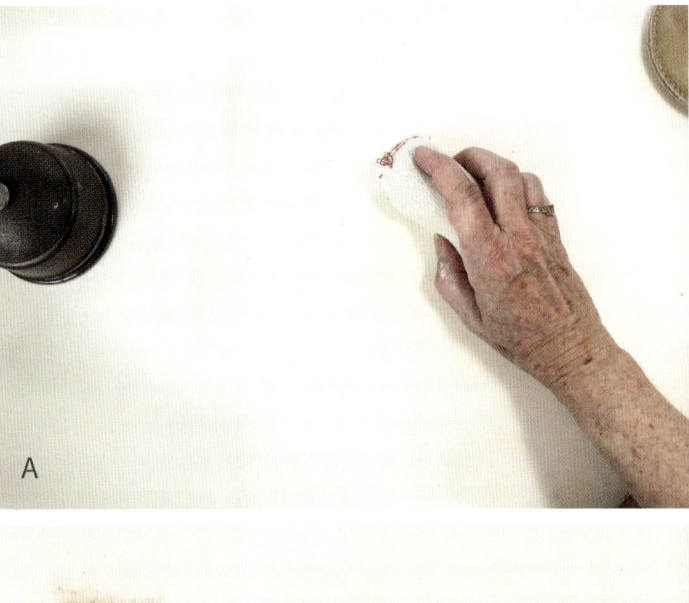

A

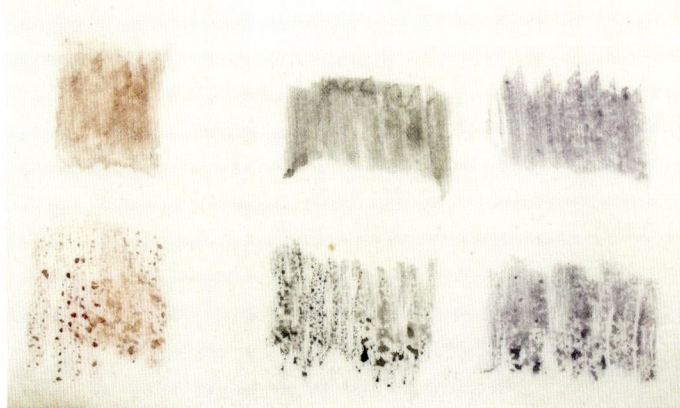

B

Brushstrokes

Success on vellum requires having as little liquid in one's brush as possible. The brushstrokes on the left have made a small puddle of color at the end because the brush has too much liquid, and a flat brushstroke has been made. On the right, the brush has less liquid, and a feathering stroke has been used to taper the beginning and end of each stroke. (C)

Finely detailed work can be achieved by using the same feathering stroke but by using the tip of the brush instead of the side. The stroke begins with a light touch, full contact through the desired stroke length, then gradually lifted at the end, making the individual marks taper at each end. (D)

BRUSH ANGLE

These broader strokes are made using the side of the brush, holding the brush farther away from the ferrule. The angle of the brush is more oblique, leading to a broader stroke. Multiple layers of paint can be added in this way without pulling up color as long as there is not a lot of liquid in the brush. (E)

Pick up a small amount of color from your palette with the brush, dab your brush on the towel while rolling the brush to point the tip, then proceed to the vellum with a light touch on the tip. The brush's angle is more acute, and it is held closer to the tip. (F)

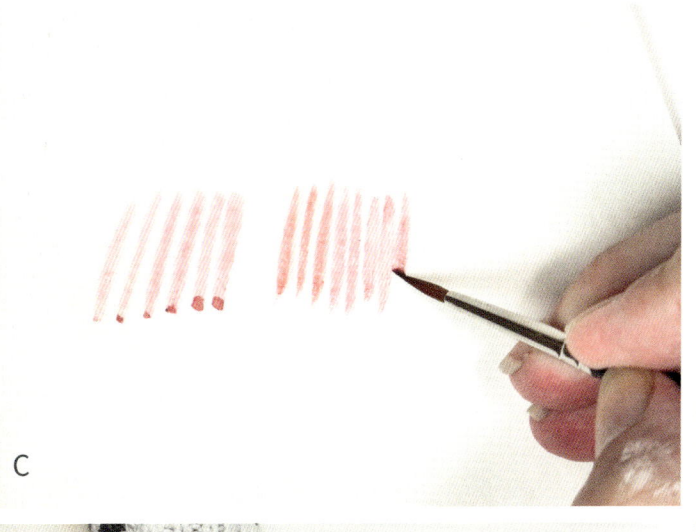

C

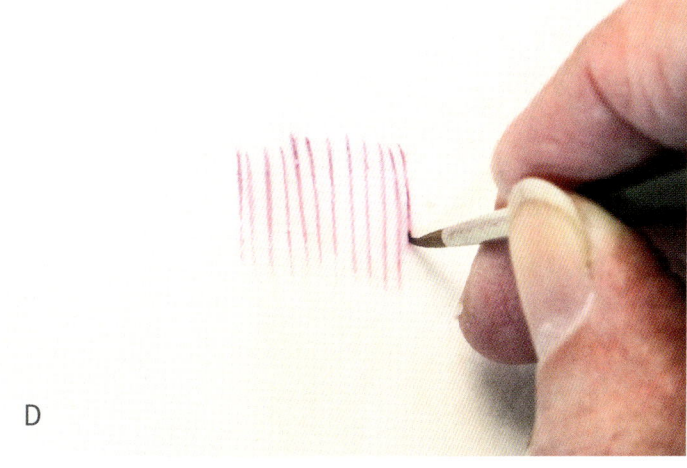

D

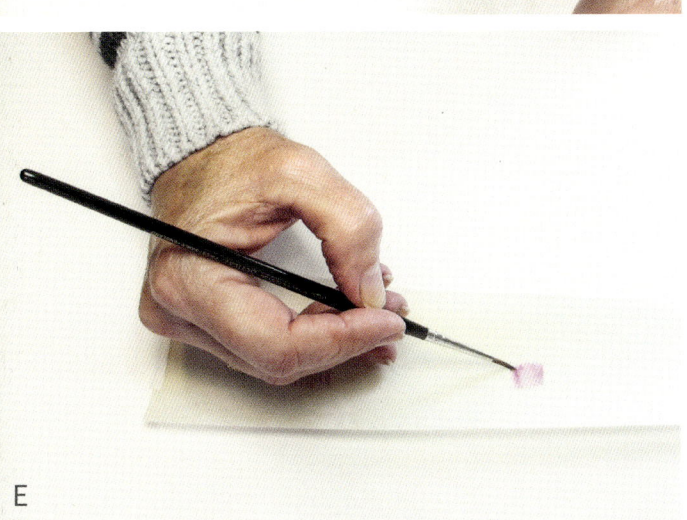

E

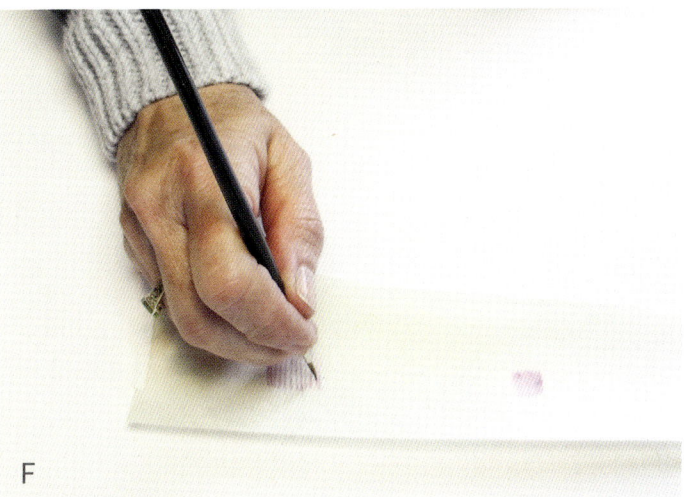

F

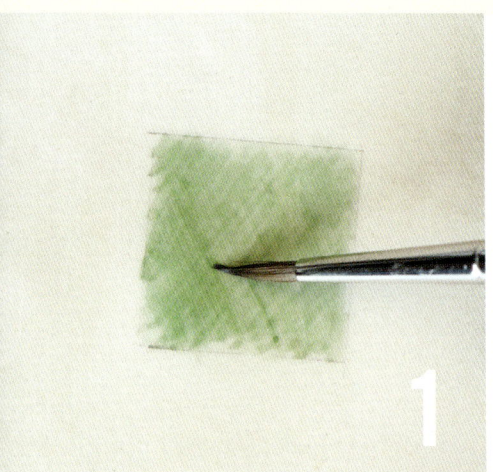
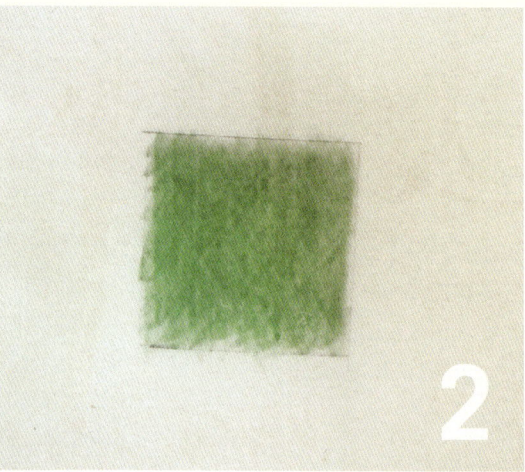
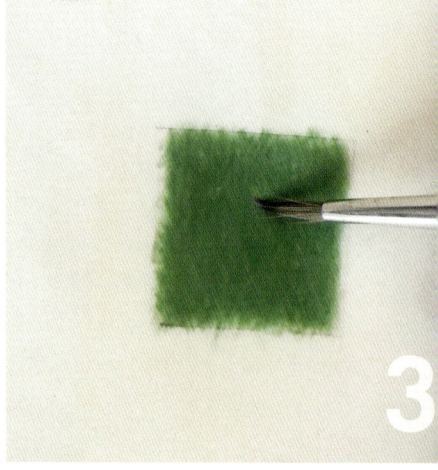
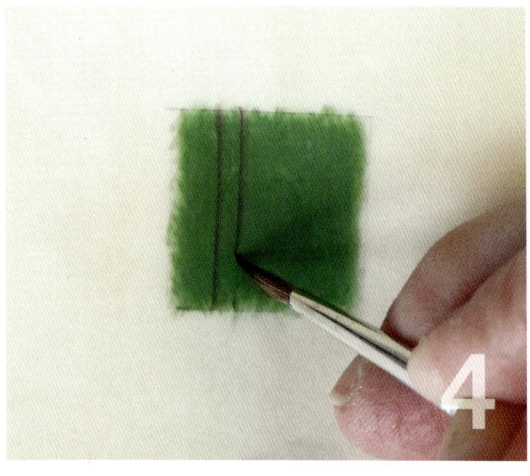
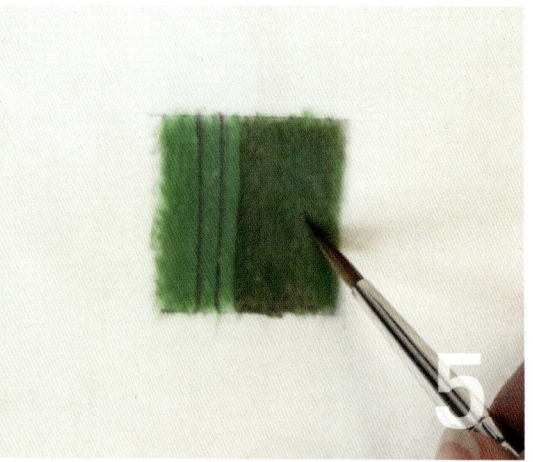

Drybrush Layering

1. Using a no. 1 brush in this dry technique, paint multiple layers of a single color, varying the direction of the strokes used in each layer. Keep moving along across the area to be painted so that the pigment laid down has a chance to dry before another layer is added on top of it. If the technique is dry enough, the strokes will dry almost immediately.

2. Gradually add more layers of color, ensuring your brush is dry but the color is fairly dilute. If the vellum under the square of color begins to bow upward, allow the square to dry. Then begin again, taking care that no puddling is occurring at the end of the strokes.

3. Continue to build up 10 layers of a single color, yielding dense but smooth color. Use a light touch and fill in small gaps with the tip of the brush. The color does not have to be perfectly smooth for this exercise, but it should be relatively uniform.

4. It can be a challenge to lay detailed lines over many layers of drybrush. Using the complementary color and the tip of the brush, paint two strongly pigmented, narrow lines without pulling up the layers underneath or leaving a pool of paint at the end of the stroke.

5. Now using a more dilute complementary color on the palette, dip the brush hairs only halfway into the color. Dry the brush and roll the tip to a point on a paper towel. Lightly paint a layer over the top, keeping the paint as smooth as possible, without pulling up the previous layers of the original color. Try to lay in softer strokes as in the previous layers.

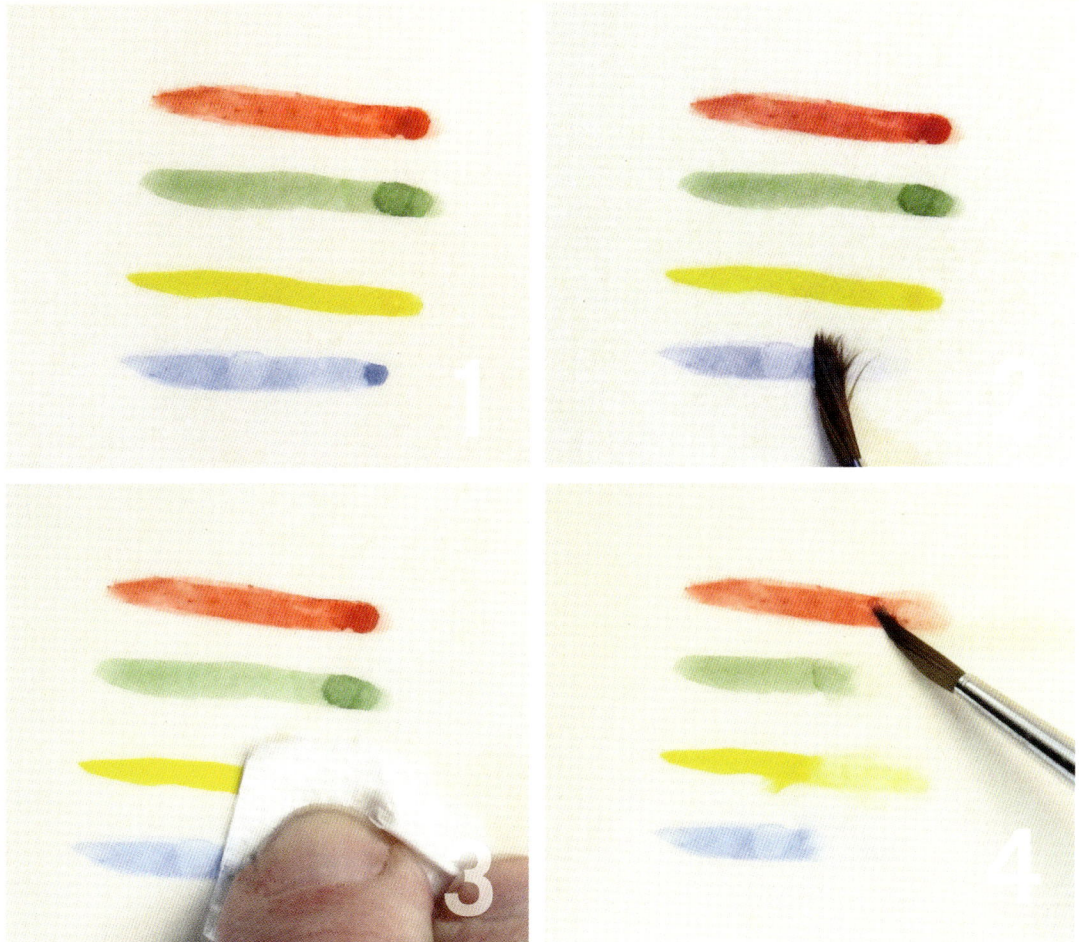

Lifting Color

1. Color on vellum can be removed or moved to varying degrees, depending on the staining qualities of the pigments being used and the surface quality of the vellum itself. Here, four different colors have been painted on the vellum in a single stroke.

2. Clean a no. 1 brush thoroughly in water, and dab some of the excess water out of the brush on a paper towel. Then, using the brush at a raking angle, push the color while spinning the brush, and the color will be picked up by the brush. This can be repeated to pick up more color.

3. To remove more color from the same area, dampen the area and dab it with a paper towel or cotton swab. Take care not to rub the surface of the vellum—this can roughen the surface. Press and dab until you have removed as much pigment as possible.

4. Repeat with each color, first moistening and lifting color by spinning the brush over the area. Then try to remove more color by rewetting the surface and dabbing with a paper towel.

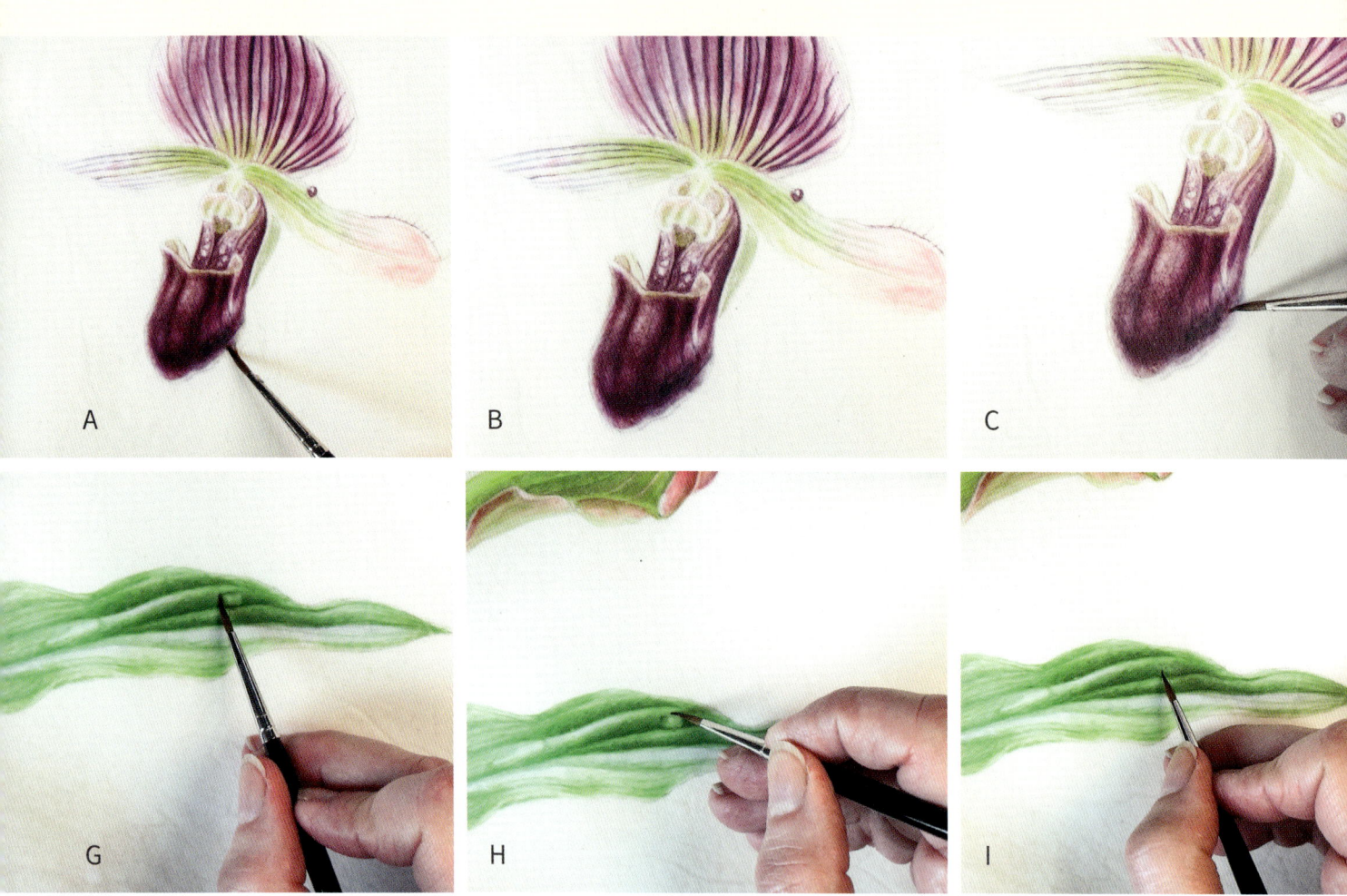

A

B

C

G

H

I

Apply these lifting techniques to a work in progress. With clean water and a no. 1 brush, moisten the area you'd like to remove, and remove the color by spinning the brush and lifting it. (A)

Here you can see the darker line of pigment created at the edge of the wetted area. This line should be removed before repainting the area. (B)

Using a damp, well-pointed brush, gently pull up the darker line using the same spinning and lifting technique. (C)

Dab the area with a paper towel or cotton swab to remove the remainder of the color in the affected area. The edge will become soft, so repairs can be painted in with smooth transitions. Wait for the area to completely dry before reworking it. It may need to dry for an hour if it is saturated. (D)

In this in-progress leaf, an errant brushstroke was placed outside of the desired area and will need to be removed. When you are removing color with water, sometimes a small amount of paint remains, which is easier to see when it is outside of the painting area. (E)

To remove this pale color, scrape off the mistaken brushstroke with a sharp blade. Try to use the side of the blade as much as possible to prevent incising the vellum itself. Scrape gently, removing only the color and not the surface of the vellum. If the vellum needs to be smoothed out, extra-fine sandpaper or micro-abrasive film can be used. (F)

One of the challenges artists have when working on vellum is preventing color from lifting up when painting over previously applied color. Using a brush with too much water in it, or using a brush that is too stiff, results in the lifting of color. When color is lifted, it is often also pushed to the edge of the area accidentally lifted, leaving a dark line around the lifted area. (G)

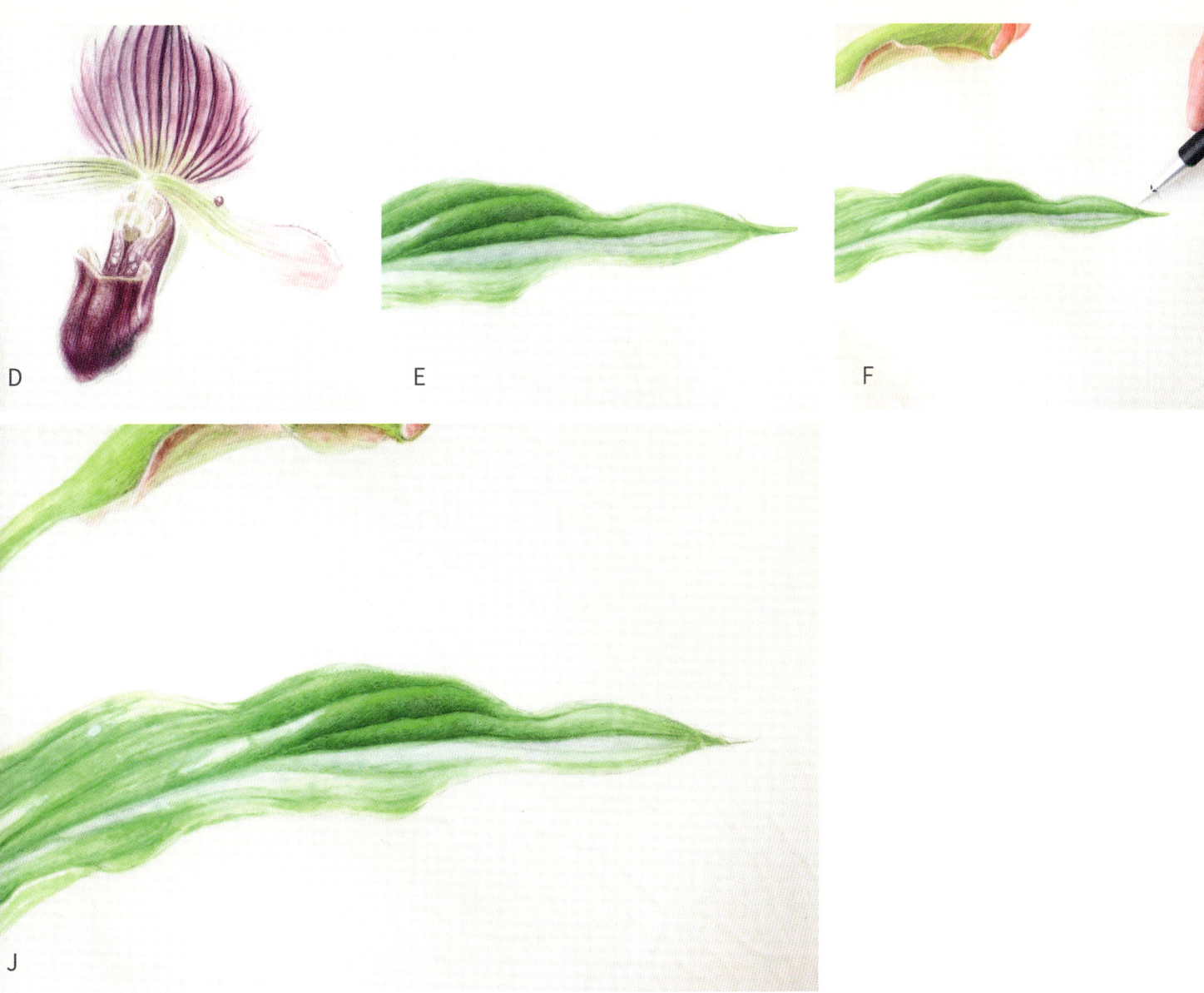

D

E

F

J

To repair the accidentally lifted area, first remove the dark lines around the edges. Clean the brush, then soak up most of the water from the brush on a paper towel, then roll and point the brush. Lightly brush over the dark line, lift and clean the brush again. Repeat in other darkened areas where pigment has pooled. (H)

When the hard edges have been removed and the area has completely dried, replace the drybrushed layers gradually with small feathering strokes. (I)

Once the color in this area has been equalized with the color surrounding it, then the leaf can be advanced altogether again with further layering. (J)

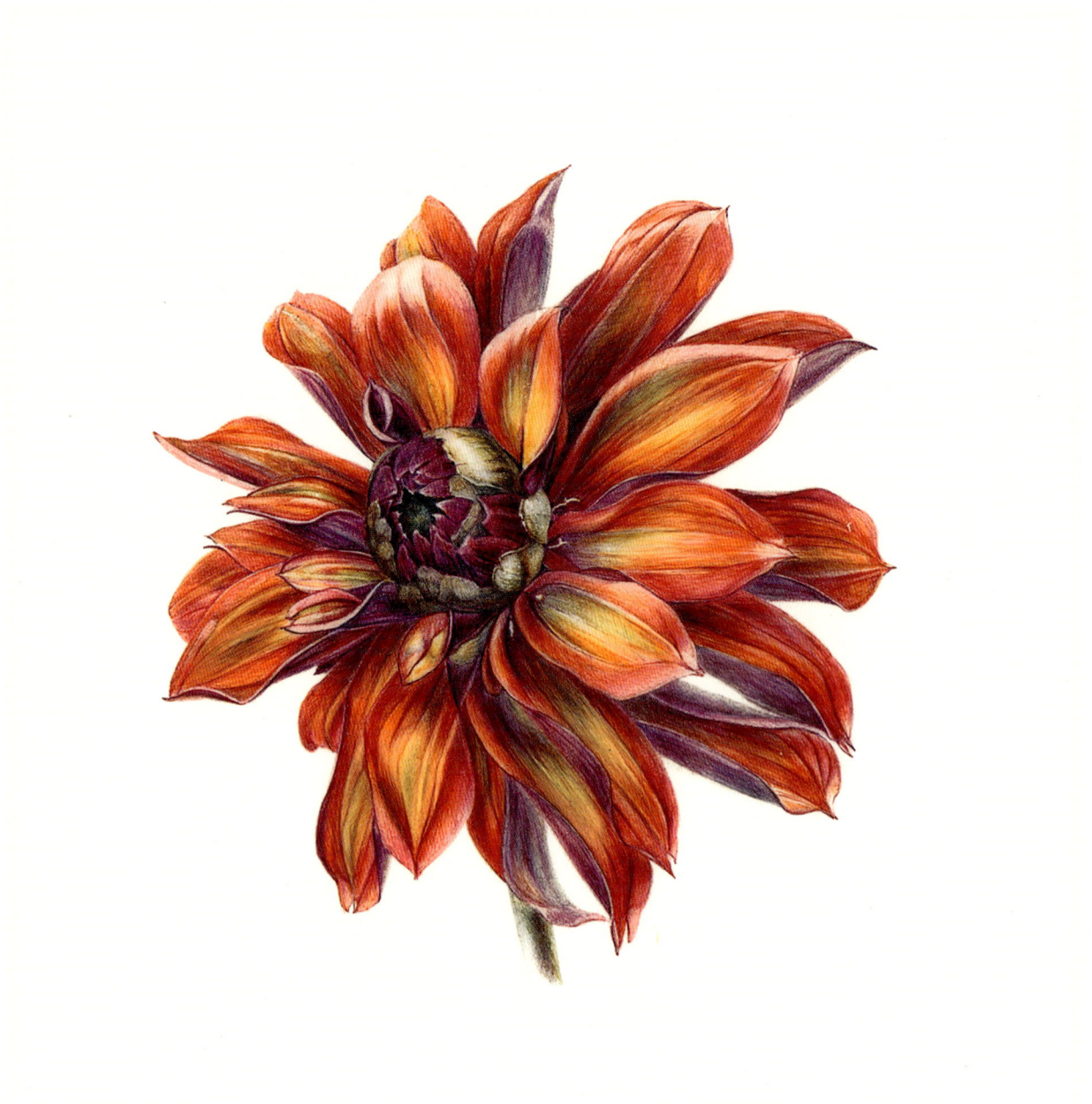

Dahlia *Dahlia* 'Groovy' Watercolor on Kelmscott vellum 4 × 4 inches [10 × 10 cm] © Jean Emmons
HOURS TO COMPLETE: 30

MATERIALS: Butcher tray palette; lint-free cotton towel; artist's tape; kneaded eraser; ultrafine sanding film; scrap piece of paper for testing paint; eraser shield; round bristle brush (no. 1); Kolinsky round brush (no. 4); mechanical pencil (0.3 mm with a 2H lead; tiny retractable knife; electric eraser; container for water. Colors: Hansa yellow light; Hansa yellow deep; permanent orange; pyrrol orange; shell pink; lilac; rose dore; quinacridone coral; Indian red; quinacridone red; ultramarine blue; phthalo blue; quinacridone purple; quinacridone violet; cobalt blue violet; cerulean blue; cobalt turquoise; phthalo green; oxide of chromium; May green; Davy's grey; indigo; neutral tint; transparent brown oxide; quinacridone gold; nickel titanate.

Jean Emmons uses a number of drybrush techniques to create works of extraordinary depth and luminosity. She maps out a broad range of colors with dilute strokes of color, and adds many layers of color, retaining brilliance and hue by laying strokes next to one another. Lower petals are set below upper petals with the use of violet shadows, conveying the depth and roundness of the flower while retaining its local coloration. Three color removal techniques are also demonstrated.

Drybrush Lines, Washes, and Crosshatching on Kelmscott Vellum

TUTOR: JEAN EMMONS

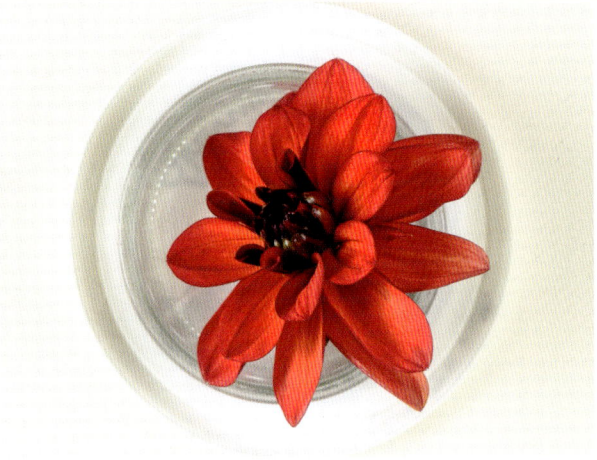

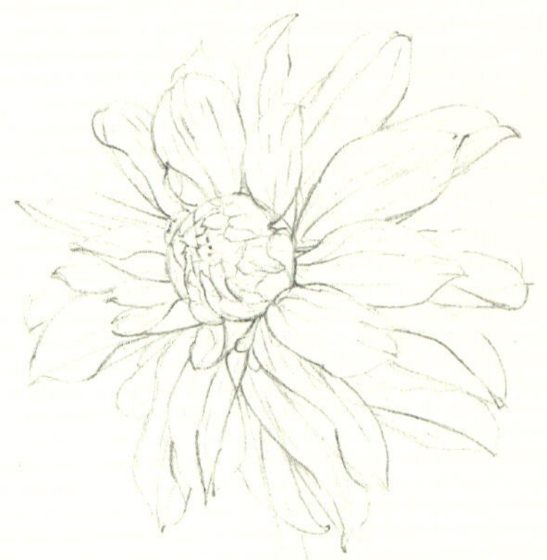

Dahlia 'Groovy' has rusty red petals with undertones of salmon and peach. The petals reverse to a deep purple, creating a striking combination. The flowers change color depending on their age, the time of day, and the weather. Dahlias are constantly opening, making them a challenging subject, but they can be slowed down if they are refrigerated between painting sessions.

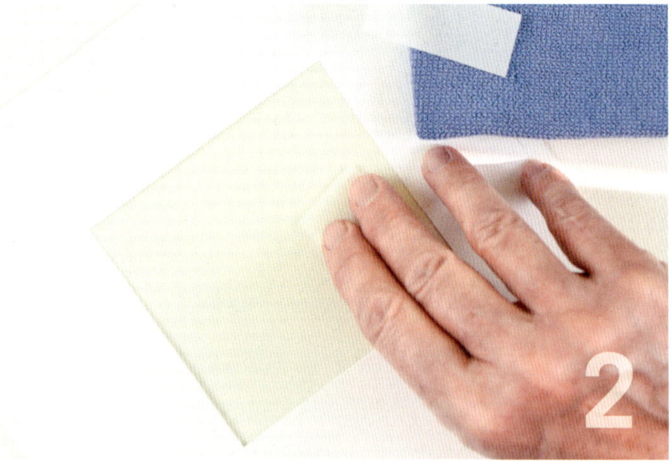

As excess graphite can cause smears on Kelmscott vellum, create the drawing on paper. Place the vellum on a light box and use a mechanical pencil with a 2H lead to transfer the basic lines of the drawing to the vellum. To avoid creasing the vellum, tape it to a piece of white mat board after you transfer the drawing onto it.

Prepare the Kelmscott by sanding it with small pieces of ultrafine sanding film. Use a gentle circular motion. Wipe off the sanding dust with a microfiber cloth. Cover the vellum with a paper mask to protect it from skin oils and water drops—random drops of water or paint that sit on the vellum for too long can permanently disfigure it.

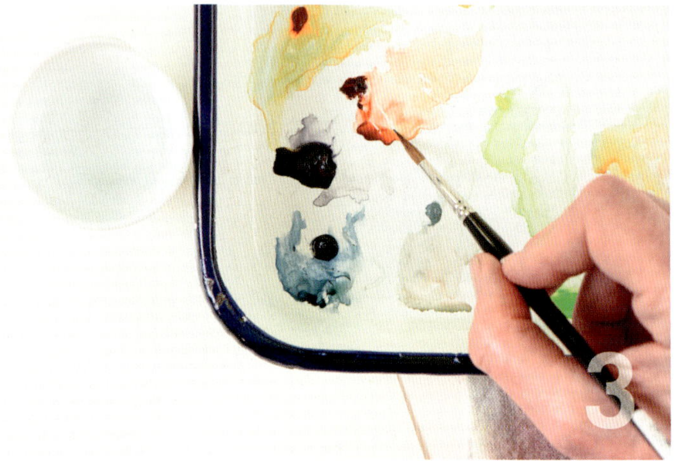

Begin with drybrush lines. Lay out skins of color on the palette and let them dry. With a damp no. 4 Kolinsky brush, dip the brush tip in water, barely disturbing the water. Remove any excess on a lintless cotton towel while rolling the brush to repoint it. Pick up a tiny bit of pigment from a color skin, roll it on the towel, and repoint.

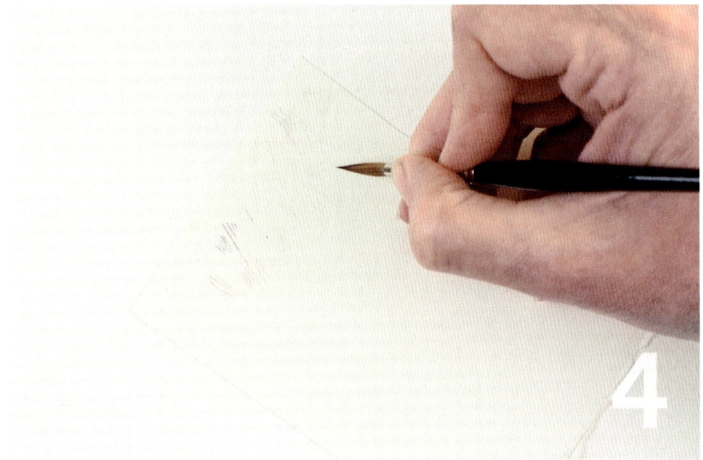

Use any dilute color, but test it first on a piece of scrap paper for the right amount of water. Puddles at the beginning or end of a line mean there is too much water on the brush, while dry rough lines indicate there's not enough water on the brush.

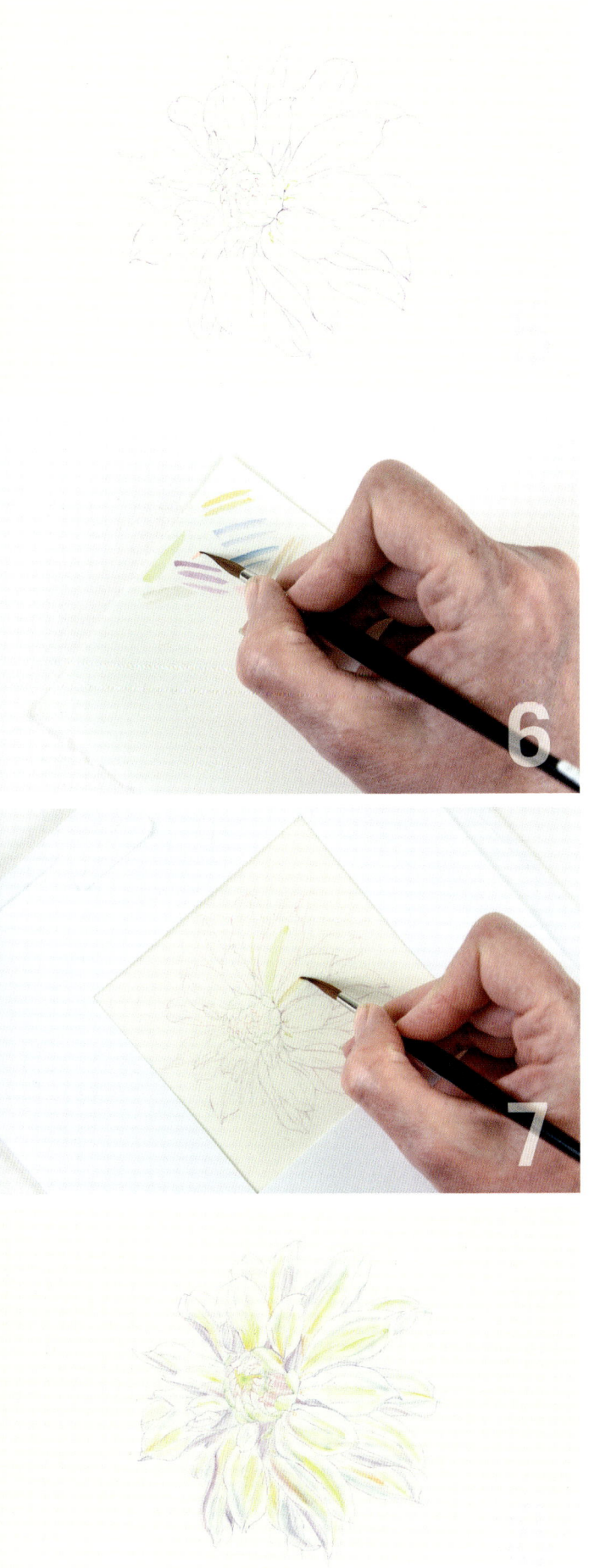

Using drybrush, redraw the pencil lines. Use a delicate touch and stay on the tip of the brush. Once the paint is dry, excess graphite can be gently lifted by dabbing it with a little artist's tape. The rest can be erased with a clean kneaded eraser. If necessary, graphite lines can be "slimmed" with a little ultrafine sanding film.

Begin the washes. Because vellum is nonabsorbent, washes must be much drier than they are on watercolor paper. Dip the brush ½ inch [1.25 cm] into the water, then pick up a little color from a skin on the palette. Test for the right amount of water and paint on a piece of scrap paper. Using the side of the brush, lay down a small wash in one direction without backing up, or moving your brush into the color that has just been laid down.

Begin the underpainting. Most problems with washes are caused by having too much water on the brush. If the color is applied too wet, quickly blot the area with a tissue and wait until it is dry. Never fix a mistake while the paint or vellum is wet. Lay a wash over another wash only after the previous wash has dried. Always use a light touch with washes.

First, lay in any clear yellows and oranges that must remain clean—unsullied by other colors. It is difficult to lay these in later without picking up other colors. After the yellows and oranges dry, start laying in small areas of other dilute colors. Begin to think about the value range of your subject, without trying to match individual colors.

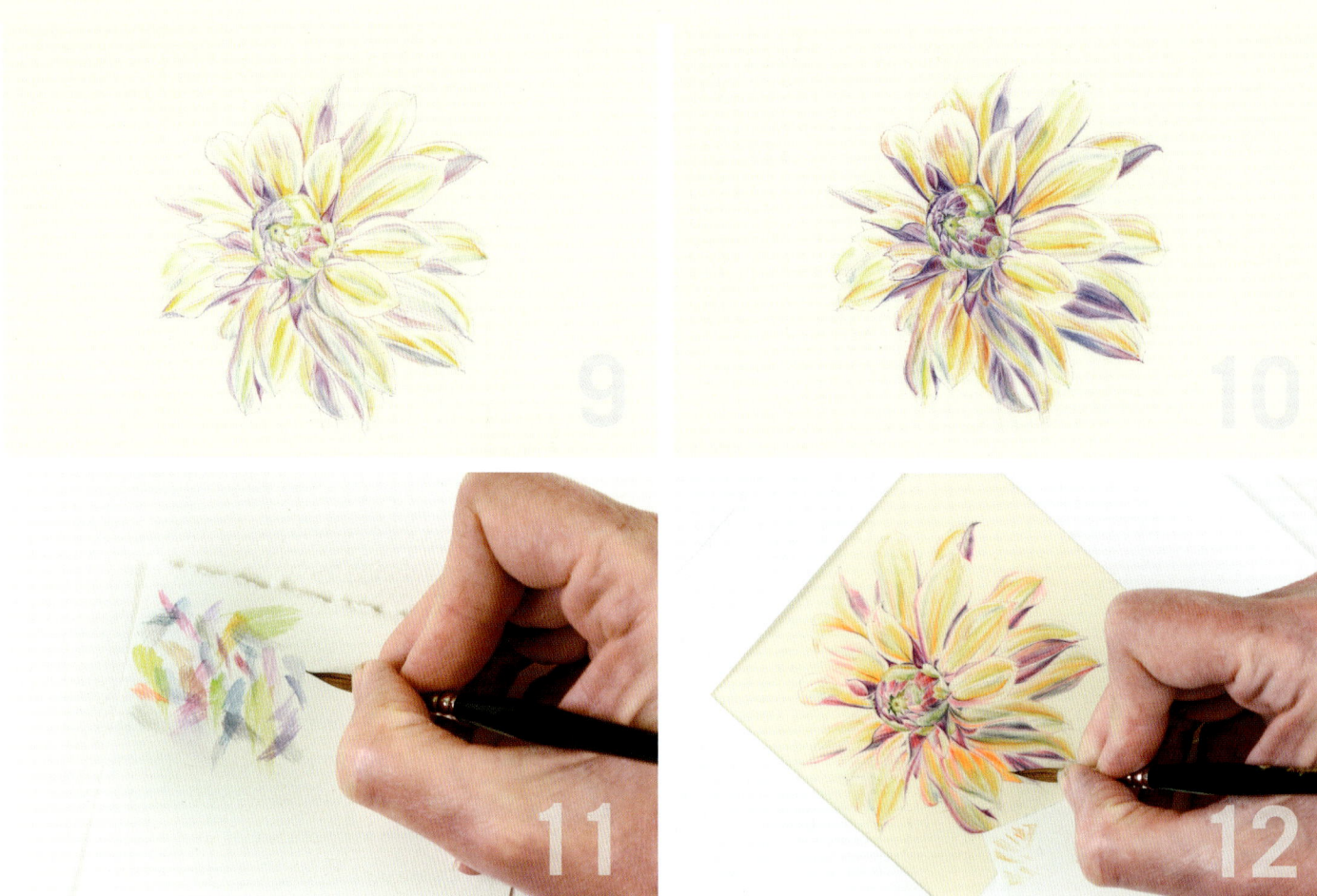

Continue building in the midrange and dark values, and stay out of the highlights and any reflected light areas. Rather than mixing on the palette, try layering transparent colors on top of each other. Try some unusual colors, while keeping the value range of your subject in mind. Make the layers drier and drier, eventually working toward drybrush.

Often, the underpainting has very little of the local color. At this stage, it can look patchy, but if the values are correct all will be well. Subsequent drybrush layers will cover up the choppiness. In the dahlia's center, start moving to drybrush detail quickly as there is not much room for washes. Continue building washes with broader strokes in the outer petals.

Begin the drybrush hatching. Load the brush for drybrush and hold it like a pencil. Grip the ferrule close to the brush hairs. Anchor the edge of your hand on the painting (be sure to protect the painting with a mask). Keeping the tip of the brush pointed, feather delicate parallel strokes. The strokes should barely touch with no space between. Go in one direction, never back up into just-painted (still wet) areas.

Using the plant's local color, move to drybrush hatching exclusively. Once an area is dry, overlay it with more drybrush. Try some warm and cool variations of the local color. Search for a comfortable hand rhythm. To work from different angles, turn the painting rather than your wrist. Keep building with drybrush.

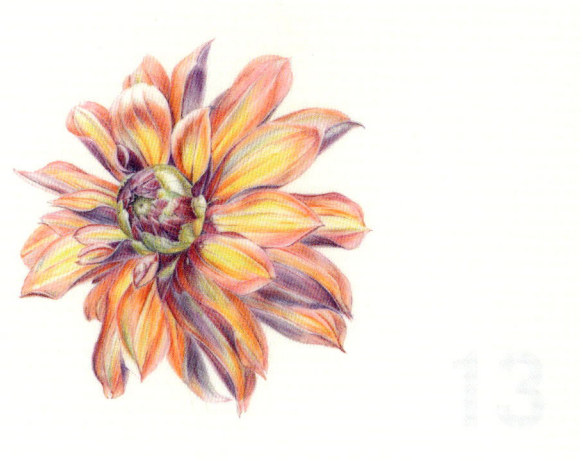

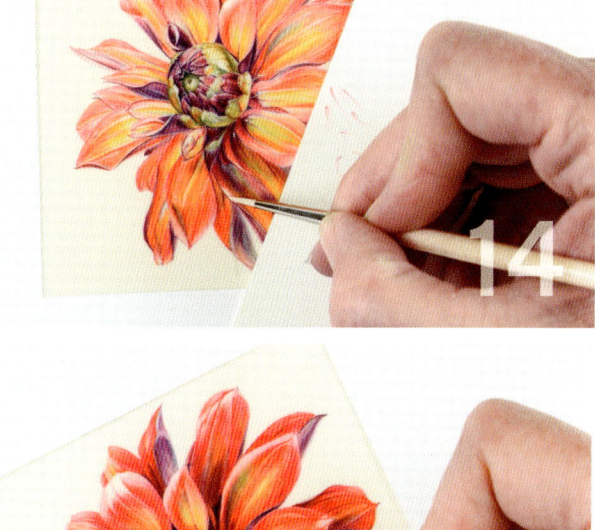

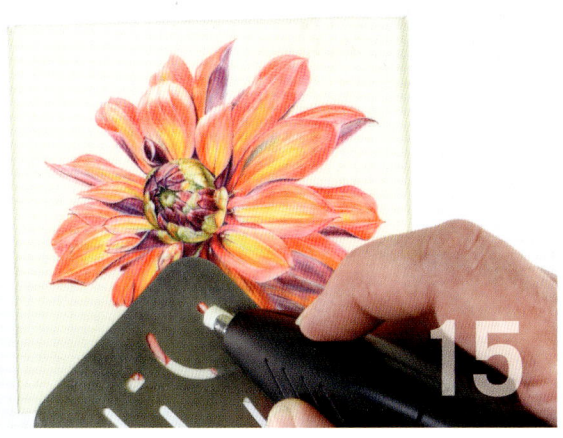

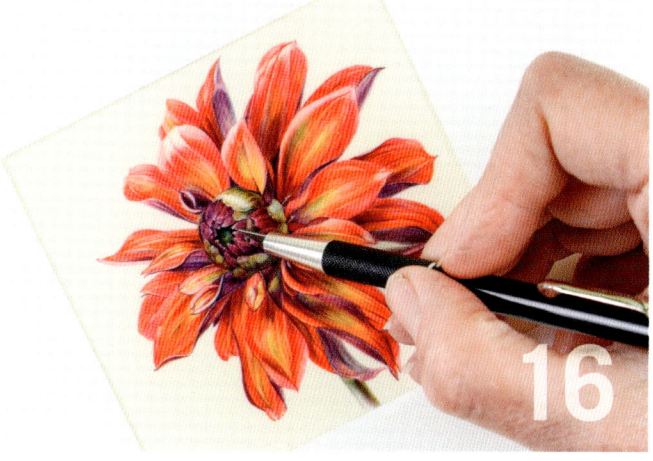

The local color will start to cover up the patchiness of the underpainting and help bring the disparate groups of color back into a logical form. Knit the color together with drybrush to create smooth transitions and to balance values. Feather local color carefully into the highlights and reflected light areas to integrate them. Refine any thick edges by cutting into them with tiny drybrush lines.

To lighten an area or move a line, wet a stiff-bristled brush with a tiny amount of water. Use the brush to gently loosen and lift a little paint from the area, then wipe the lifted paint onto a piece of scrap paper. Repeat, lifting only a small amount at one time, until the entire area is lightened.

When you have finished lifting, let the area dry totally. Some little ridges may have been created by paint being pushed around. In order to smooth the ridges out, sand them with a tiny piece of sanding film, or use an electric eraser and an eraser shield. Repaint the area with drybrush or even little dots.

Tiny details like hairs or petal tips can be scratched out with a small mat knife or scalpel. They may need to be repainted with a few transparent dots to tone them down. Try painting some large areas of thin transparent drybrush veils, or glazes, across multiple petals. Any details obscured by painting the drybrush glazes can be sharpened later. Laying down layers of color this way creates a rich surface. Forty layers of paint is not unusual. Think of the plant as being held in fine spider webs of color. Squint. When the values look correct it's done.

Akiko Enokido demonstrates how to paint three different types of leaves on classic vellum. A thick, waxy camellia leaf with glossy highlights is painted, then an ivy leaf with heavy, three-dimensional veining, and finally an autumnally hued hydrangea leaf with lobed and serrated margins. Each demonstration successfully captures its varied characteristics, using drybrush hues and values to convey not only the lifelike details of the leaf but its surface texture and three-dimensionality.

Painting Leaves on Vellum

TUTOR: AKIKO ENOKIDO

Camellia Leaf

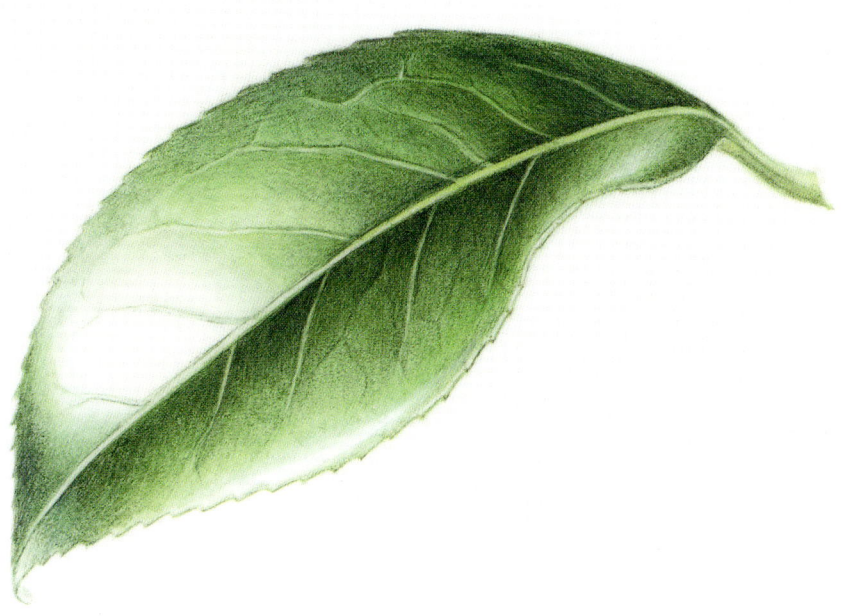

Camellia cv. Watercolor on vellum 2 ¼ × 3 ⅛ inches [5.6 × 8 cm] © Akiko Enokido

HOURS TO COMPLETE: 4

MATERIALS: Watercolors and metal paint box; 2B pencil; mechanical pencil (0.3 mm); tracing paper; dividers with lead in both tips; Japanese fine brush; spotter (no. 2); round Kolinsky brush (no. 2); flat synthetic brush; ceramic palette; container for water. Colors: cerulean blue, indanthrene blue, transparent yellow, Payne's gray, Hansa yellow, phthalo green yellow shade, perylene maroon, Van Dyke brown, burnt umber, perylene green.

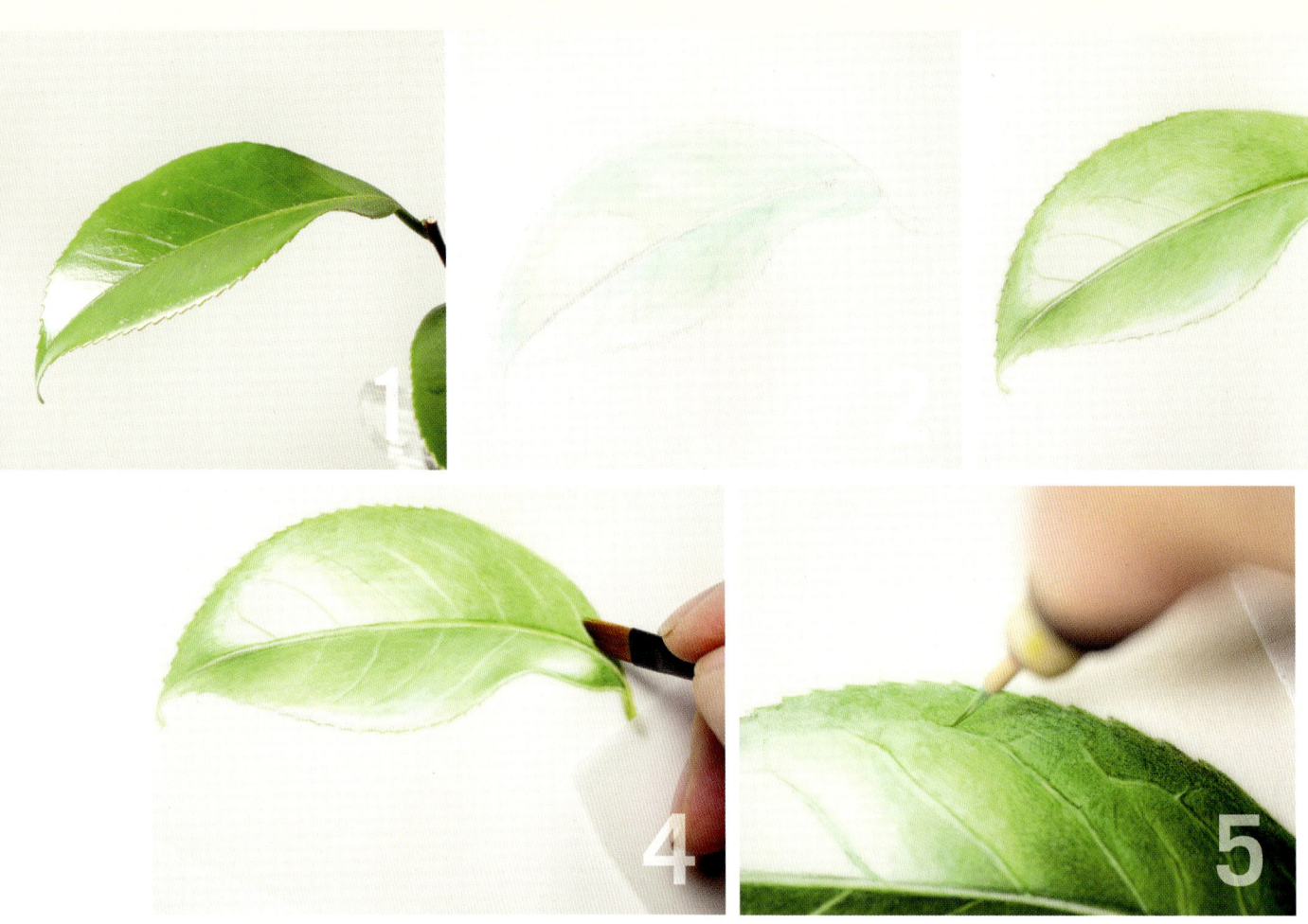

Camellia leaves have a shiny, waxy surface and a thick texture. Confirm the direction of the light source and observe the highlight and shadow areas carefully. Make a sketch of the leaf on a piece of paper, then transfer it to vellum.

Block out the highlight areas on the edge of the leaf and at the tip of the leaf with a thin layer of Chinese white. Using a no. 2 round brush, begin painting from the shadow toward the highlight area with diluted cerulean blue. Do not wet the brush too much. It is fine if brush marks are visible at this stage. Let it dry completely.

Mix a mid-tone color using indanthrene blue and transparent yellow. Paint the leaf using drybrush technique with the no. 2 spotter brush. Brush lines next to each other without overlapping. Imagine trying to create a flat surface covering the entire leaf. Dark shadow areas need more layers with the same color.

Lift color for the primary veins. Wet a flat brush and pinch out the excess water with two fingers. Place the brush tip on a vein, and do not move the brush until the paint moves to the tip of the brush. Then move the edge of the brush along the vein to lift color. For the secondary veins, use a fine brush tip in same way. Pigment lifts easily from the vellum surface.

Mix a darker green using Payne's gray and Hansa yellow. Using drybrush technique, work on details and build progressively deeper color tones with multiple layers. Narrow down the vein lines and add shadows. This leaf surface is flat, so be careful not to make bumps between secondary veins. Clean up the leaf edge, and paint the thickness of the leaf with a light yellow green color. Use additional layers to darken the most shaded areas of the leaf. Take care to save the glossy highlight areas. Use a magnifying glass to check your work and make sure all the hatching is nearly invisible and smooth.

Ivy Leaf

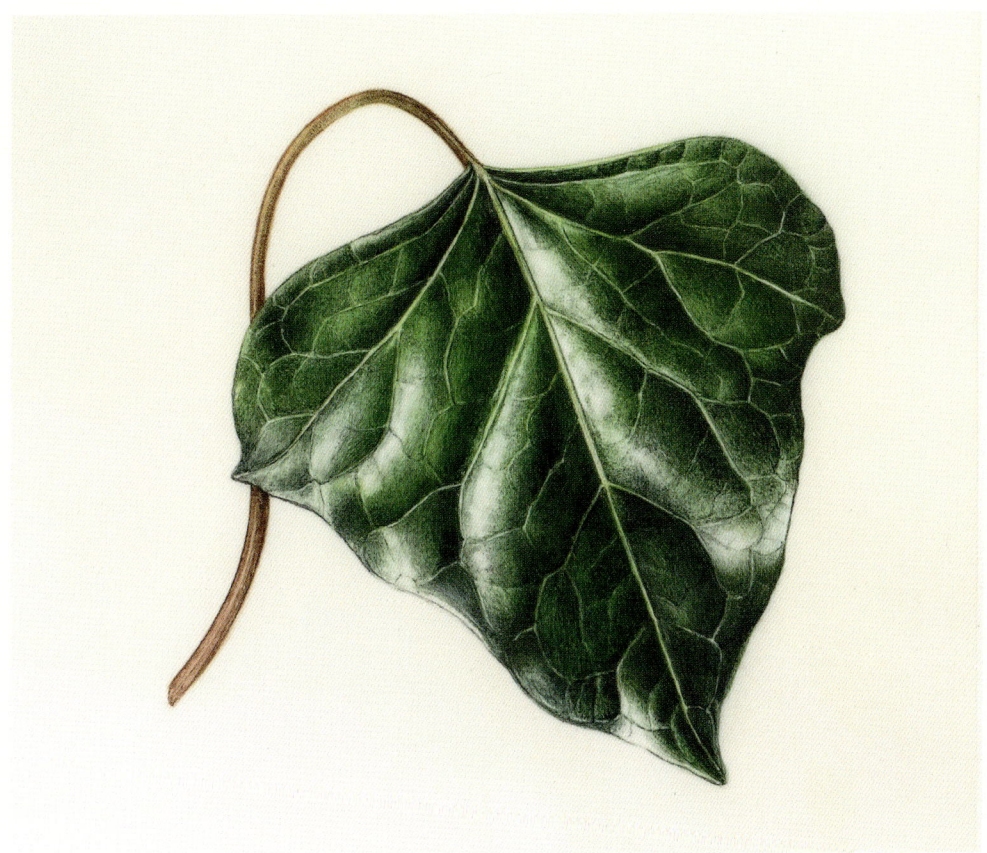

Algerian Ivy *Hedera canariensis* Watercolor on vellum 5 ½ × 6 inches [13.75 × 15 cm]
© Akiko Enokido
HOURS TO COMPLETE: 16

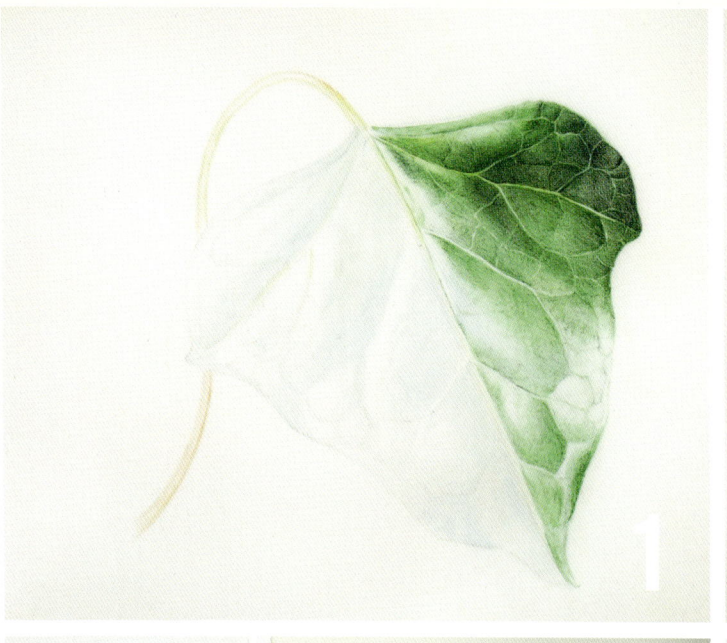

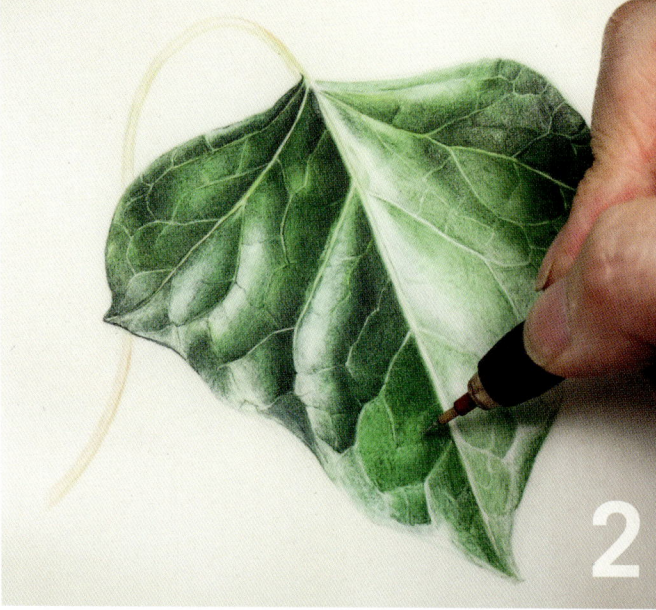

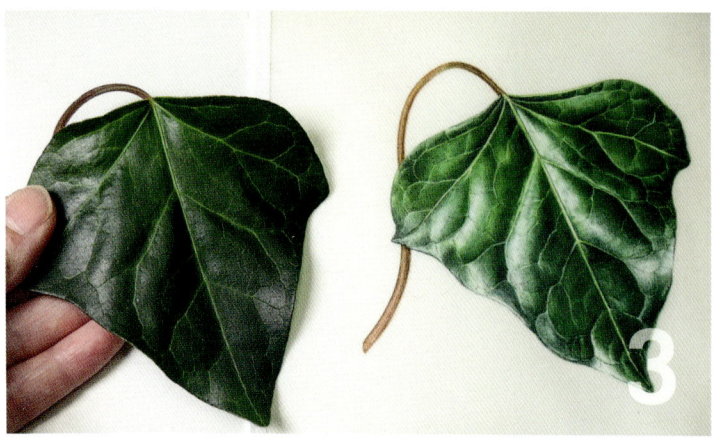

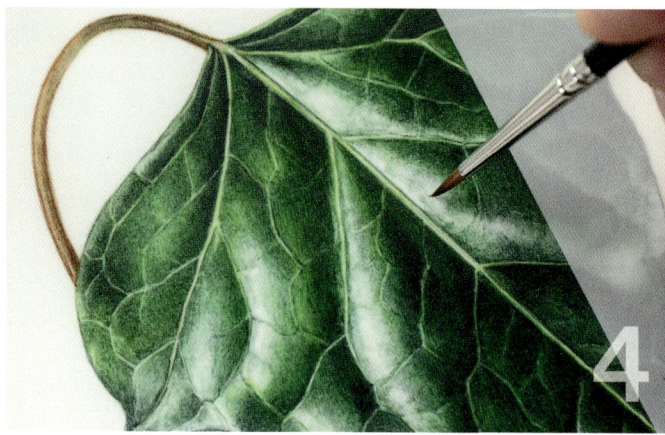

This ivy leaf has silvery highlights. After transferring the drawing to the vellum, paint the leaf form with a grayish blue color for the first layer. Do not paint the highlight area. In this photograph, the right side of the leaf is already painted with a second layer in a mixture of phthalo green yellow shade and burnt umber.

Be careful when adding a third layer; the brush tip can lift off previous color layers. To prevent this, do not put too much water on the brush. Try to fill in color where you did not paint the second layer, and let the painting dry well between each layer. Keep the main veins white, then show the thinner veins by painting the shadows around them.

Match the color saturation and brightness with the actual leaf. Apply a dark green color made with perylene green, burnt umber, and indanthrene blue. It takes five or more layers to make dark green areas. Add red to the green mix to create the darkest greens for shadow areas. Paint veins with a dilute mix of yellow and green, except in the light parts. Very gently paint yellow as a thin layer of drybrush over the leaf to warm up green areas that appear too blue.

Blend the highlight areas into the blue gray and surrounding colors with a small dry brush, softening the border by making tiny dots. Using fine drybrush, intensify the deepest shadows. Enrich the warmer areas by adding warm yellow-green, and paint the darker areas with the shadow mixture noted previously. Sharpen the edges and shadows around the veining. Paint the stem with a mixture of raw umber, perylene maroon, and Van Dyke brown, and darken in the shadow where it emerges below the leaf.

Hydrangea Leaf

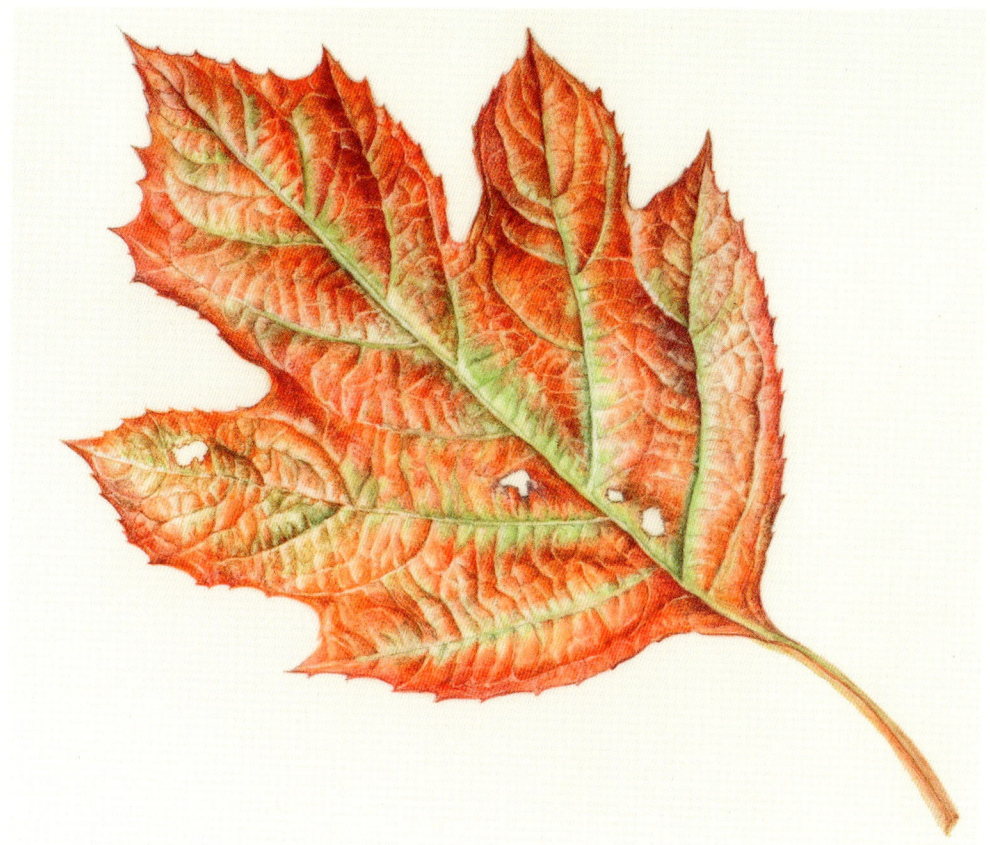

Oakleaf Hydrangea *Hydrangea quercifolia* Watercolor on vellum

5 ½ × 6 ⅝ inches [13.75 × 16.8 cm] © Akiko Enokido

HOURS TO COMPLETE: 20

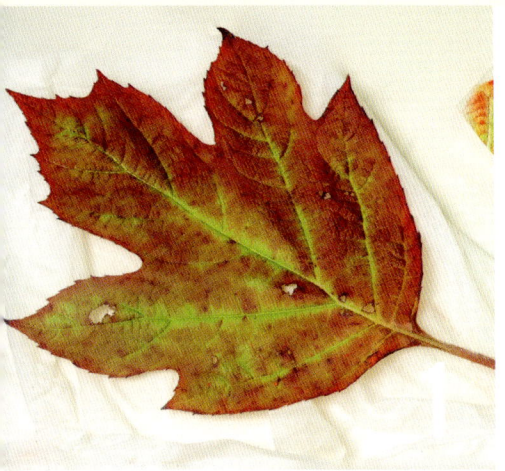
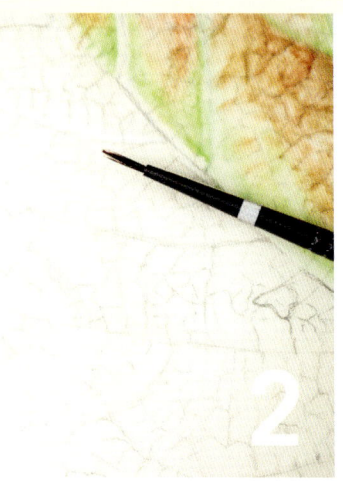
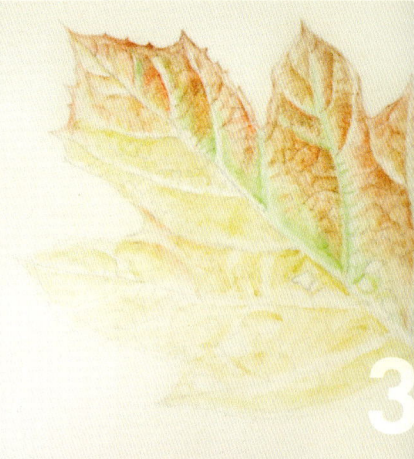

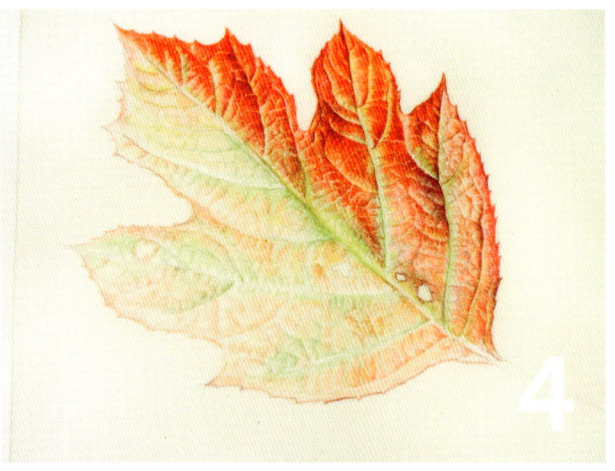
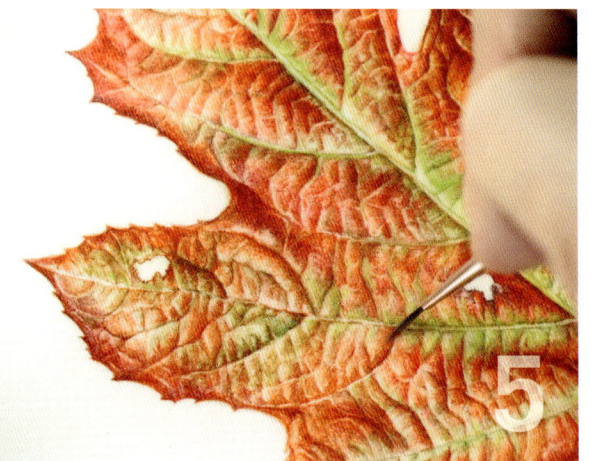

Place the *Hydrangea quercifolia* leaf on a wet paper towel and keep the paper towel moist while you are working to prevent the leaf from drying out. Test colors on a scrap piece of vellum before starting to paint.

Transfer the drawing with all detail lines to the vellum. Start the first layer with yellow and orange red. Green should be applied last, as color can turn muddy when mixing red and green. Sketch in the fine veins in color and paint around the major veins with a fine brush.

Try using one brush for yellow-orange-red and another for green—that makes it easier to paint multiple color layers. After laying in the base yellow color, refer back to the leaf for the deeper red areas. Start to lay in the green areas around the main veins.

Carefully add more layers of color. Take notice of the leaf's richness of color, and the shadows cast around the veining. Some veins are shown here by painting the brighter red shadows adjacent to them; other veins are shown by leaving them light and painting around them. Observing the leaf carefully, pay attention to the three-dimensional feeling of the whole leaf. In the light area, apply fewer details and color, working the darker areas with more layers.

Draw the details of each vein. Hydrangea leaves are bumpy, so not only the major veins are highlighted, but also the tiny secondary and tertiary veins are important to convey. Brighten the green areas, and deepen the shadows along the left side of the central vein. Clarify and refine the leaf edge and teeth. A variety of deep shadow tones, mid-tones and highlights are conveyed throughout the leaf, and holes in the leaf are outlined in brown.

The different varieties of vellum are worth exploring for their wide range of color, tones, and patterns. Vellum with brownish streaks and colorations complements dried specimens, such as this leaf, especially well and becomes part of the artwork's overall composition.

Painting a Dried Leaf on Vellum

TUTOR: DEBORAH B. SHAW

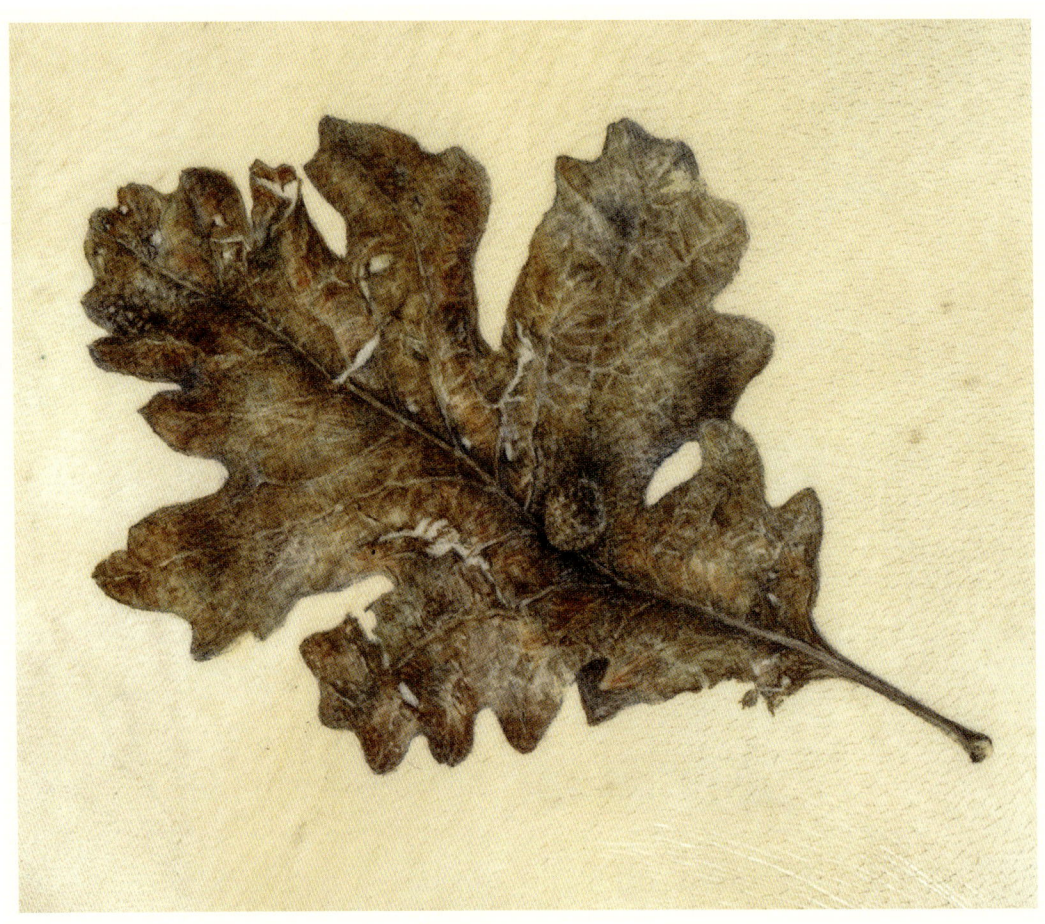

Valley Oak with Oak Gall   *Quercus lobata, Besbicus conspicuus*   Watercolor on vellum
4 ¾ × 5 ½ inches [11.9 × 13.75 cm]   © Deborah B. Shaw   HOURS TO COMPLETE: 24

MATERIALS: Synthetic brush (no. 00); Kolinsky brushes (nos. 00 and 2); Kolinsky detail brush (no. 2); squirrel brush (no. 6); kneaded eraser; dry cleaning pad; white extra-fine sandpaper (P400 or finer); retractable eraser; mechanical pencil (0.2 mm); dividers; cotton gloves; porcelain plate. Colors: yellow oxide; quinacridone burnt orange; red iron oxide; quinacridone gold; raw sienna; ultramarine blue; olive green; dioxazine purple.

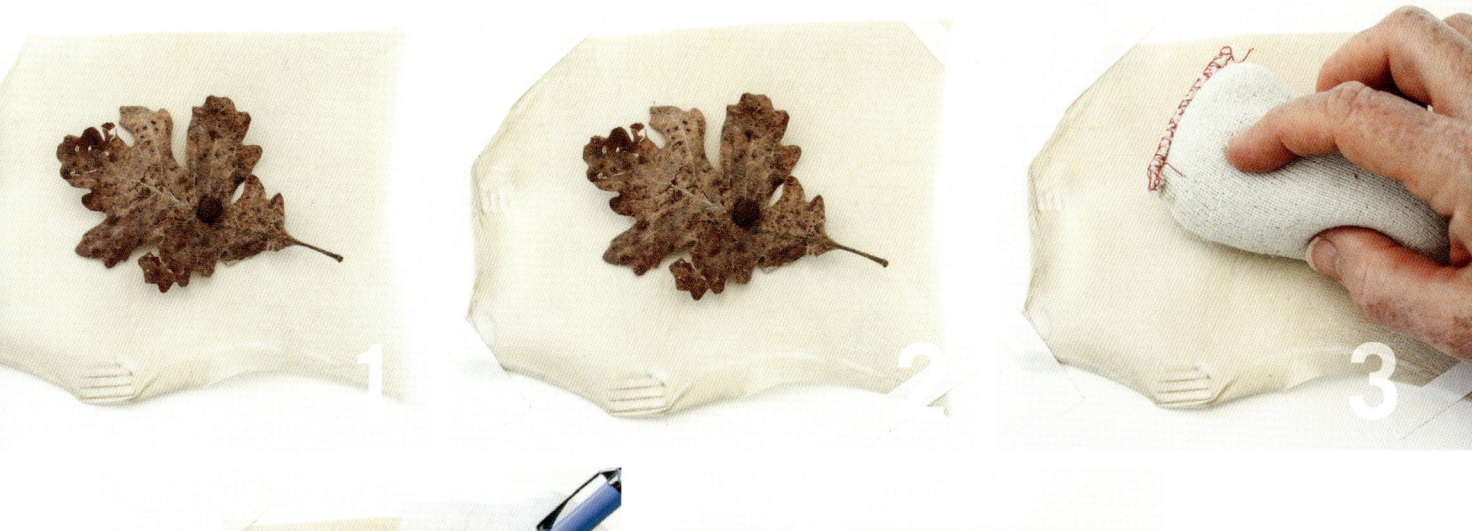

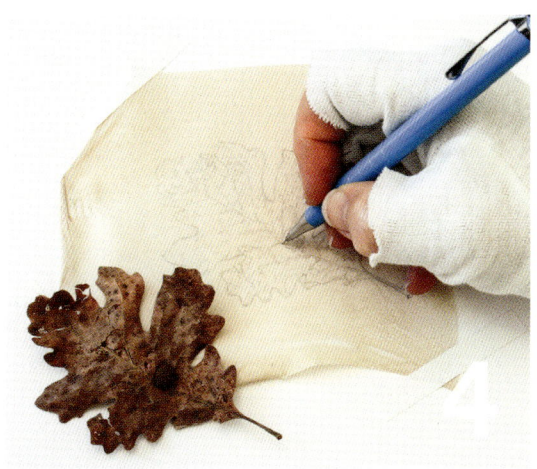

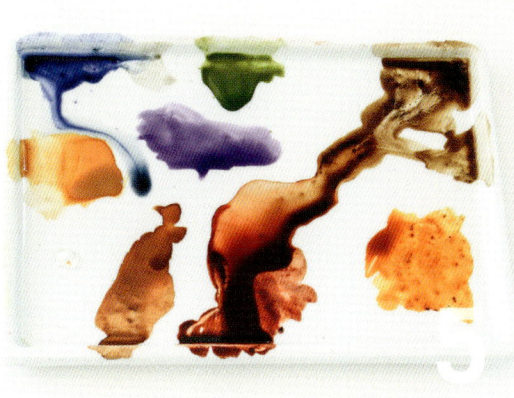

Each piece of vellum is unique and should be considered a part of the overall composition of your painting. Lay your specimens or drawings on the vellum to see where the vellum's natural markings and grain interact with the subject. Scrap pieces of vellum are fun (and less expensive) to use for small paintings or studies for perfecting techniques.

Vellum responds to atmospheric conditions and will cockle and warp with changes in humidity and temperature. Artists use different methods to allow for this while working, including stretching the vellum over board, securely taping all sides to a board or other surface, or lightly taping the vellum in place as seen here.

Before drawing on the vellum, scrub it with a dry cleaning pad to remove any oils. Do not use the cleaning pad after you have drawn on the vellum—you will erase the drawing! Irregular surfaces on the vellum can be sanded smooth with white extra-fine sandpaper (use P400 or finer). Keep

skin oils off vellum, or the paint will bead up. Wear cotton gloves, or place a piece of tracing paper under your hand to protect the surface.

Transfer your drawing to vellum using a graphite transfer technique, or draw your composition directly on the vellum with any graphite pencil. Keep in mind that graphite pencils harder than 2H may be more difficult to remove or may indent the surface if too much pressure is used. Softer lead can smear, so it should be lifted with an eraser as much as possible.

Using too much water in a painting can distort vellum's surface texture; avoid this by painting with drybrush techniques. When you are dipping your brush into watercolor on your palette, dip just the tip so that you are not picking up a great deal of liquid. Mix colors on the palette with a larger brush, and put that brush aside when painting.

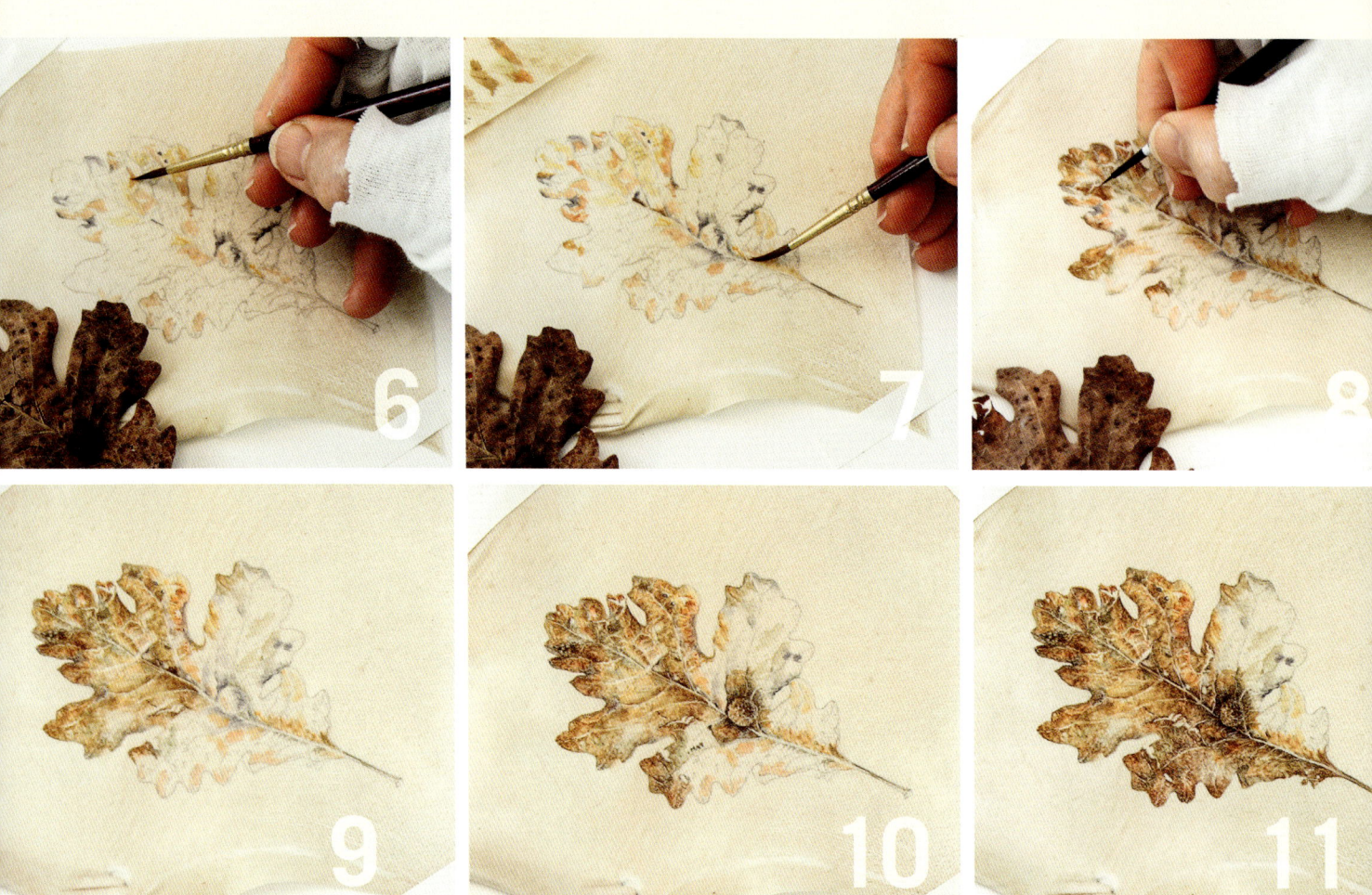

Use drybrush techniques to add undercolors of the dried leaf's hues in patches. Patches in shadow areas begin to describe form. Having a scrap of the same or similar vellum on hand is useful for testing color.

Continue adding patches of color. The painting will look spotchy at this stage. In brown subjects, an orange or pink undercolor in the mid-tone areas can help warm up the color while increasing its value. Mix a variety of neutrals using complementary or almost-complementary colors within your selected color palette.

Begin adding layers of color. As the layers build, paint underneath can be picked up unintentionally when too much liquid is in the brush. Use a bottle cap, or a similar small container, with little water in it to dip only the brush tip. Twirl and wipe the brush on a paper towel or cotton cloth to remove excess water. Detail brushes with shorter hair length can be easier to control when you are working on vellum.

Continue adding areas of undercolor where appropriate, then begin adding local color over these areas. Work all over the painting, moving through different areas. This allows each area to dry thoroughly and helps to keep the colors balanced across the painting.

Adding highlights or special details can be helpful—they act as reference points for laying out other details. Placing a few key dark areas early in the painting provides visual cues about where to add stronger, darker colors. The gall and surrounding shadow were painted to a more advanced state than the rest of the leaf to help clarify the range of tones needed.

Weave colors by using different colors in between strokes of local color. Work up the next section of the leaf, retaining a variety of discrete neutrals to prevent the leaf from becoming monochromatic.

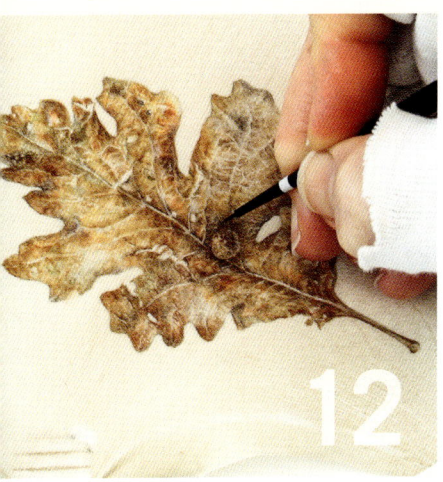
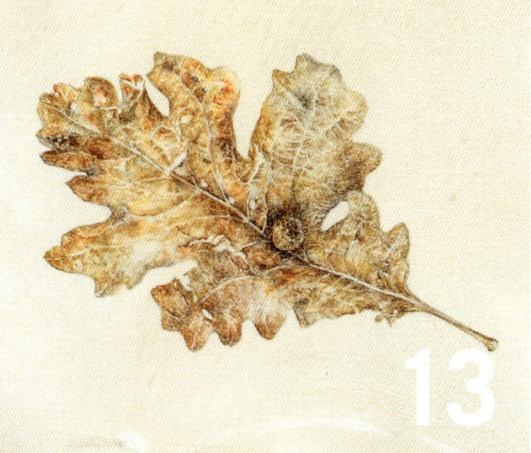
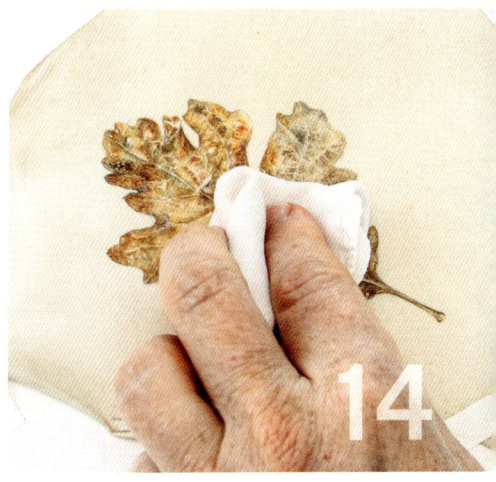

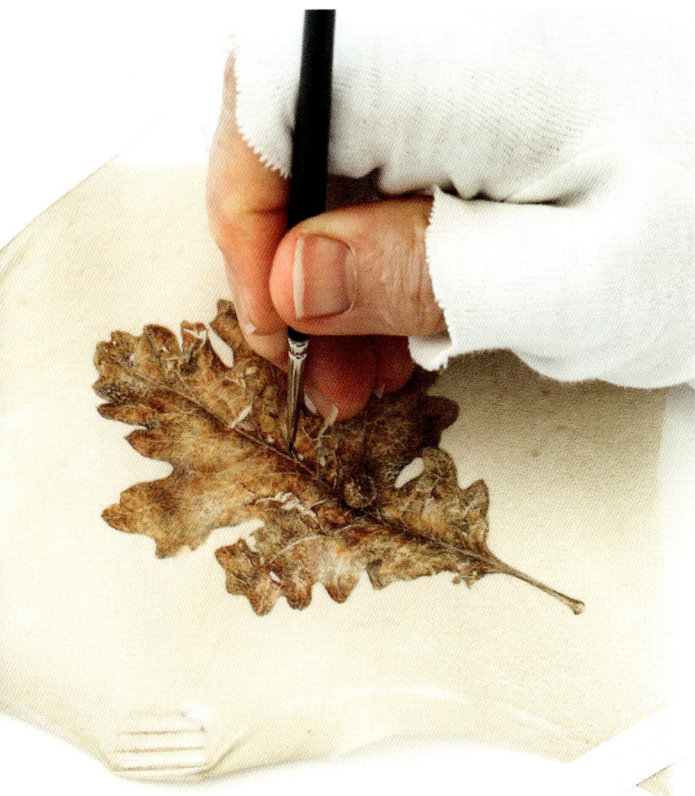

Begin adding details using a brush with a very fine point. Use a light touch, so the paint lays on top. A tiny brush is not necessarily a better brush; most important is an impeccable point with very little moisture in the brush. A magnifying glass may help you see tiny details such as the veins in a dried leaf.

Continue to add layers to define form and shadows. Use a clean, damp brush to soften edges and move paint as needed. A damp brush also can also be used to lift any remaining graphite that may be showing from the initial drawing. Stipple colors into areas where the paint is lifting too readily, or where tiny details are required.

To remove or correct larger areas of color, moisten the area with a damp brush until the paint comes loose. Then use a clean, white cotton cloth to blot the area. Repeat, using a clean, dry part of the cloth, until the paint is removed. Let the area dry thoroughly before repainting. Gently scraping with a knife is also effective, but be careful to only scrape the paint—not the vellum itself.

Color can also be lifted to add detail (for example, veins in leaves) or to make small corrections. Use a clean, damp brush to just moisten the paint you want to lift. Lift, rinse the brush, wipe it on a paper towel, and repeat as needed after each stroke. Work throughout the leaf to make final adjustments, smoothing transitions and clarifying details.

A shiny persimmon with areas of waxy bloom is navigated using layers of drybrush. After transferring the layout drawing to vellum, a first pale layer of color is used to plan areas of color. Through a series of drybrush layers that become increasingly detailed, strong value contrasts are achieved as well as a clear delineation between the orange fruit and its bloom.

Painting
Bloom on Fruit

TUTOR: DENISE WALSER-KOLAR

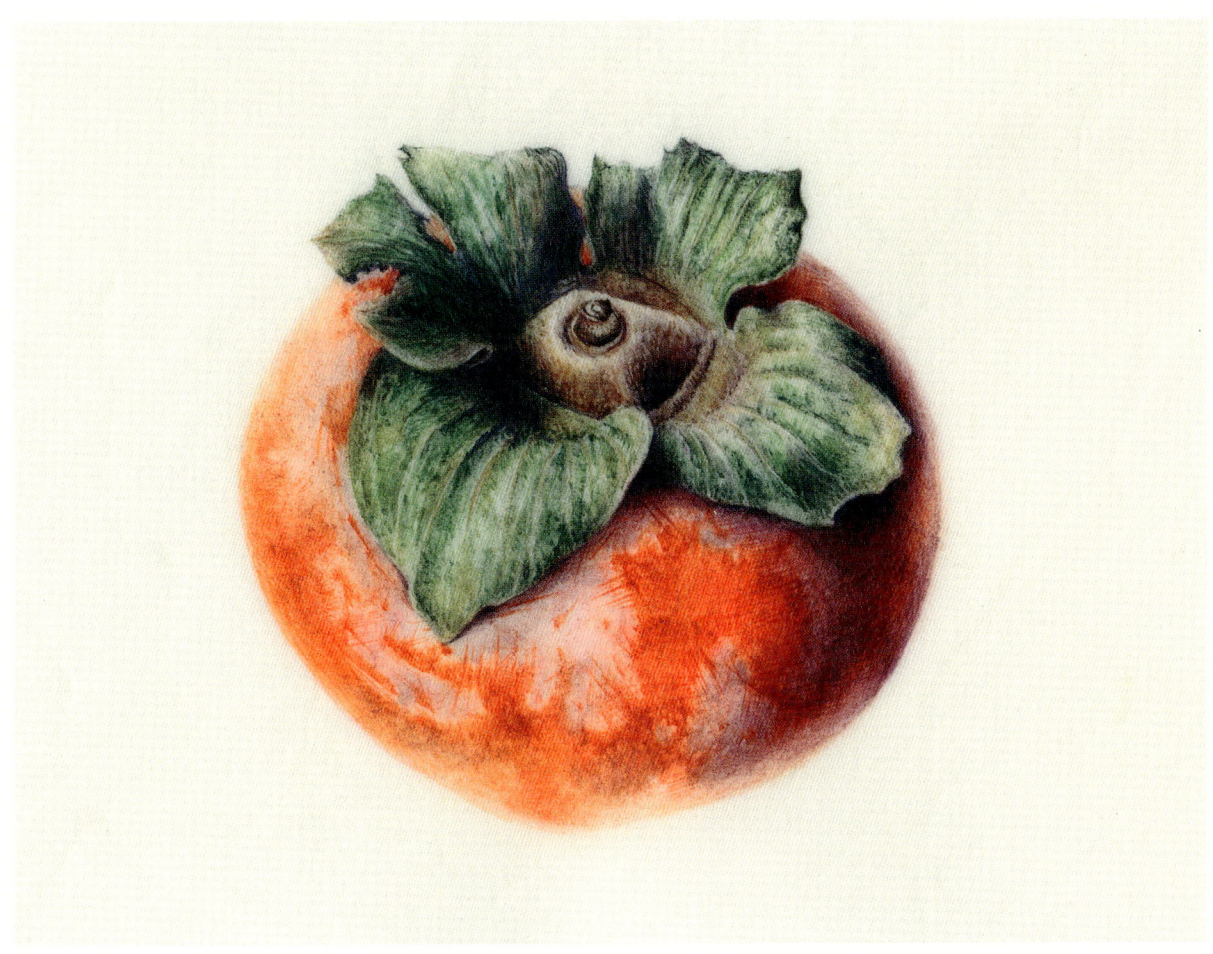

Persimmon Watercolor on Vellum 5 × 5 ½ inches [12.5 × 13.75 cm] © Denise Walser-Kolar

HOURS TO COMPLETE: 30

MATERIALS: Porcelain plate; covered palette; fingerless cotton glove; magnifying glass; tube watercolors; cotton swabs; pointed round Kolinsky brushes (no. 4), 3H pencil; kneaded eraser; drafting tape; container for water; additional container for water; cloth; acid-free foam board. Colors: quinacridone gold, quinacridone pink, quinacridone coral, manganese blue hue, green gold, rose of ultramarine, ultramarine blue, permanent alizarin crimson, transparent brown oxide, sap green, and Payne's gray bluish.

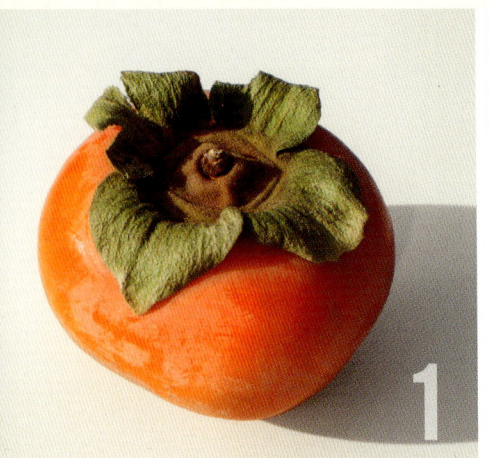

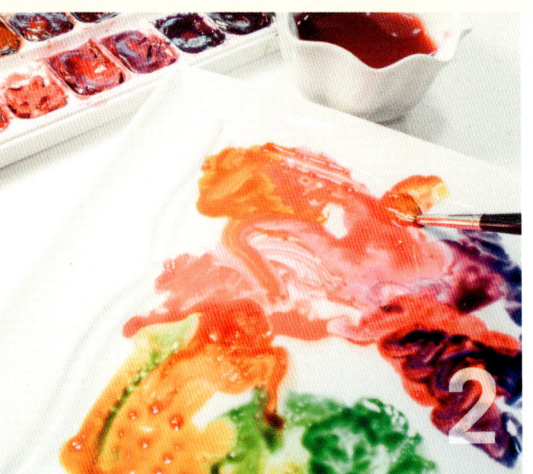

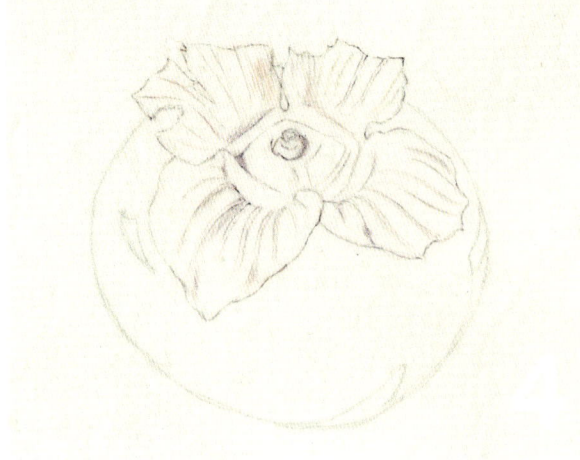

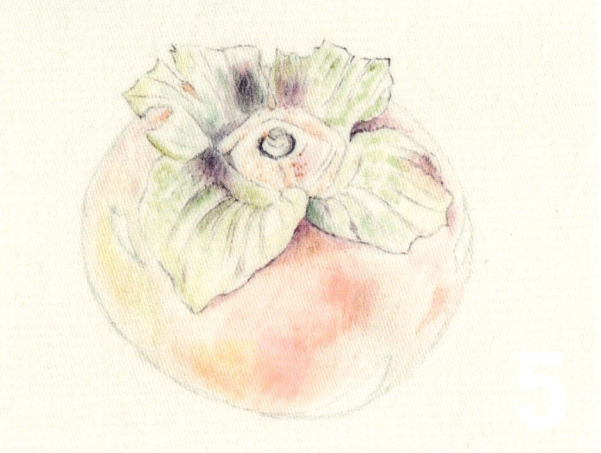

Observe the subject in bright sunshine. Note color, details, and the whitish powdery coating known as bloom. A finished painting is only as strong as the drawing, so make a very detailed drawing on tracing paper.

Squeeze the tube watercolors into a covered palette and let them dry. Using an old sable brush, take color from the palette and place it on a white porcelain plate, making sure to have a wide variety of concentrated colors to choose from once the painting is started. The colors selected are lightfast and transparent.

Tape the vellum onto white acid-free foam board. Transfer the drawing to the vellum, then refine it with a 3H pencil. On very detailed areas, make additional refinements using drybrush watercolor. The tip of the brush can be much finer than the point of a pencil, so it can be used to draw fine details.

After drawing the details in watercolor, and once the paint is completely dry, gently erase the pencil lines by lifting them with a new kneaded eraser. The edge of the persimmon is not drawn with paint, as further refinement was not needed. Take care to draw all highlights and reflected light so that they are not painted over accidentally. When drawing veins, draw a line for each side of the vein.

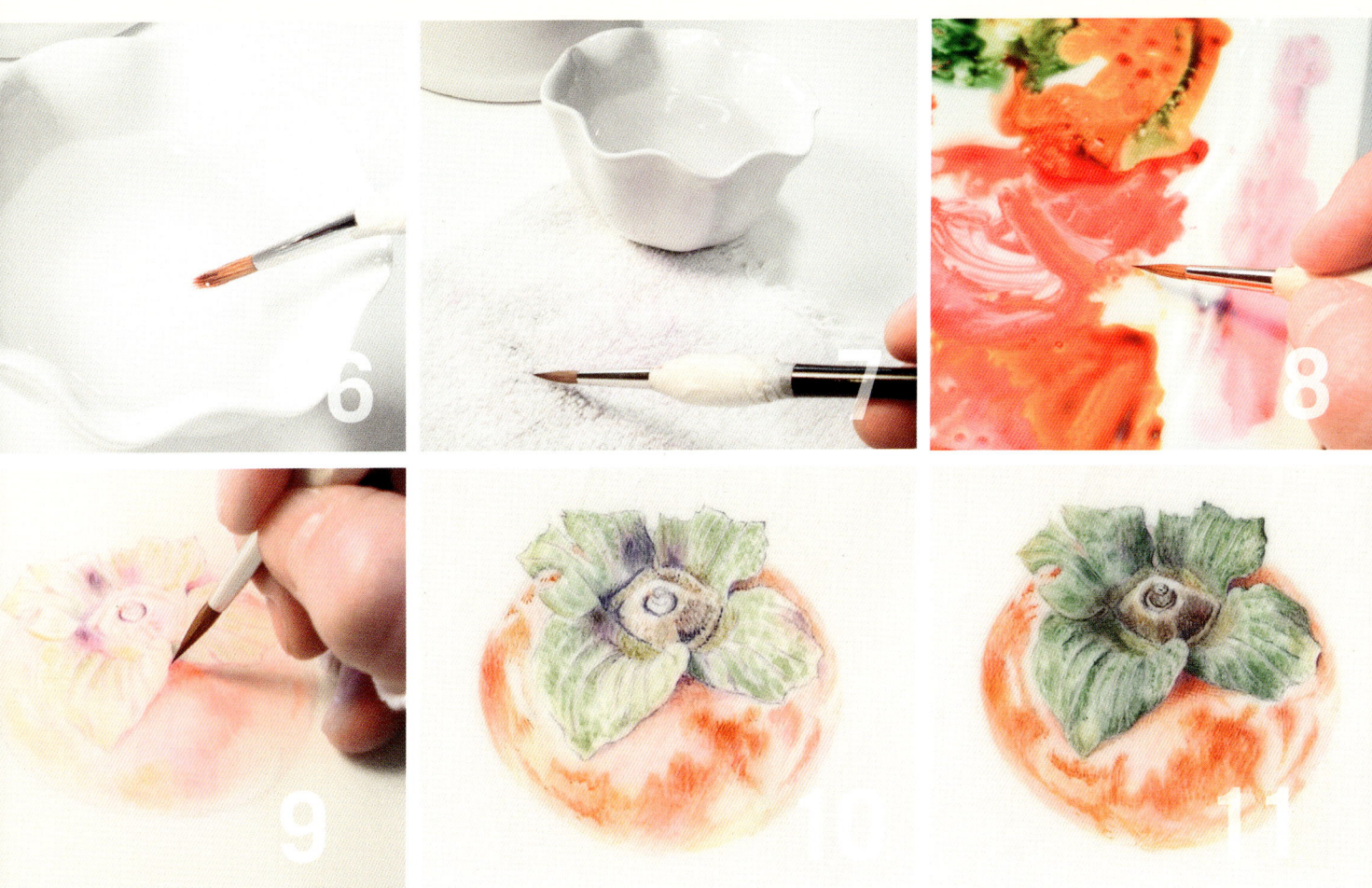

Keeping in mind the colors you observed in the persimmon in bright sunshine, begin painting with very small areas of washes to plan out the desired colors, always avoiding any highlights. Note that there is usually bloom on recessed or protected areas. Use small washes of purple in the shadow areas, with rose of ultramarine as a first layer where the shadows are deep.

The rest of the painting will be done in drybrush. Drybrush takes a bit of practice, but the more you practice, the more comfortable it will become. Begin by dipping the brush into water. Keep water away from the ferrule of the brush—only dip it about halfway up the hairs.

Roll your brush on a towel to remove excess water and bring it to a very fine point. Old cloth towels are gentler on fine brush hairs than paper towels. Don't use new towels; they have too much lint, and it will get into your paint.

Hold the brush at a sideways angle and roll it across the dry paint. This loads the paint into the brush and maintains a sharp point. Test your color and paint consistency on a piece of paper before you begin painting.

Start in a dark area and work out to the lighter areas. Make small strokes, similar to hatching with a pencil. Keep the brush as vertical as possible to get the smallest brushstrokes. Dip the brush in a slightly different color each time you go back to the palette.

Work from dark to light, taking care to avoid painting in the highlight, reflected light, and bloom areas. Save all the light areas for painting at the end.

Continue to layer color. Start creating texture in the calyx lobes. Leave the parts that catch the light unpainted for now. It is easier to make something darker than to get light back once it is lost. For the velvety fuzz on the calyx disk, use stippling rather than strokes.

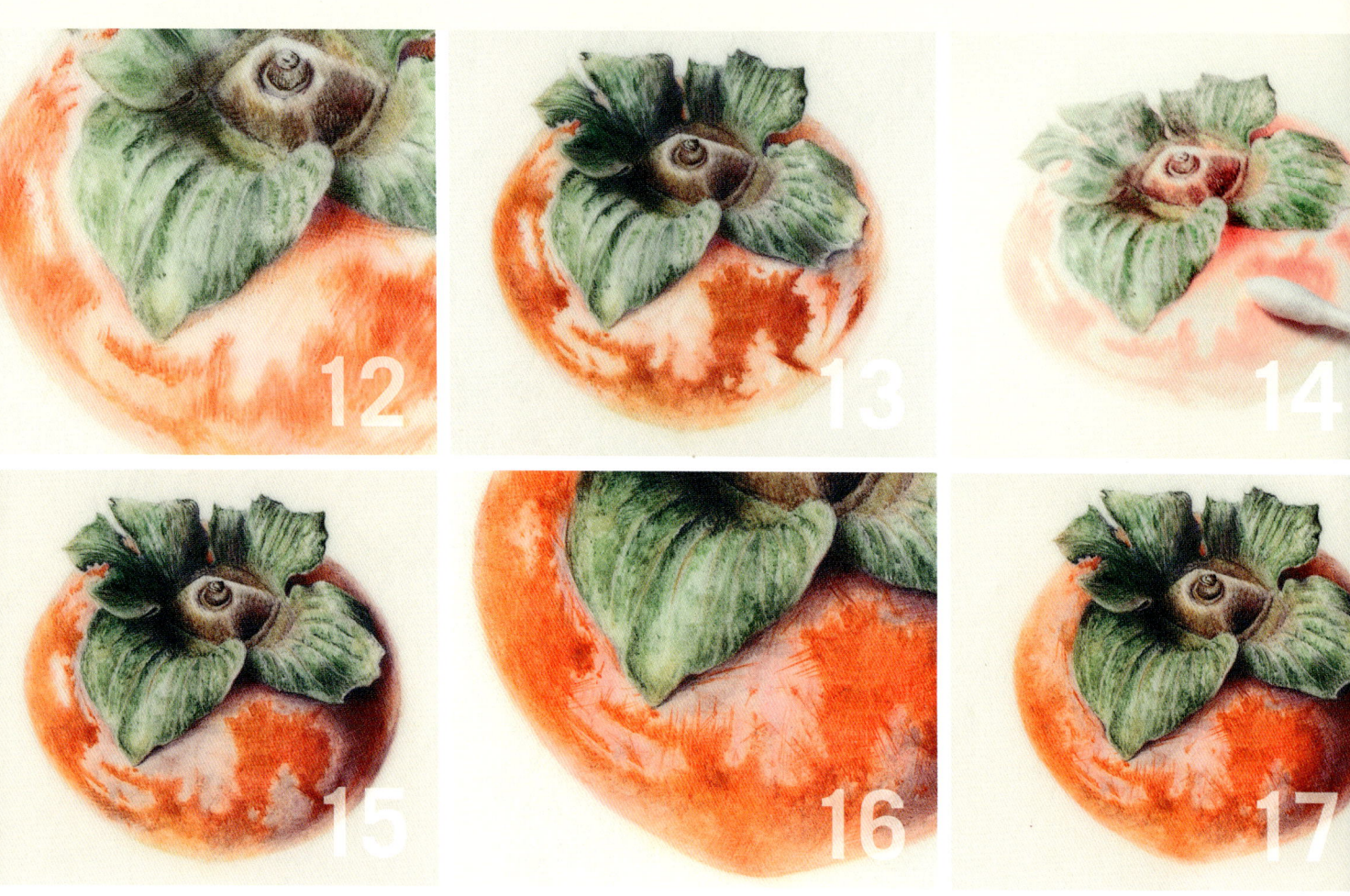

At this stage, the brushstrokes look very rough. The more layers that you add, the smoother the painting becomes. If the painting looks choppy, add more layers of drybrush.

Continue drybrushing. Avoid the temptation to blend the edge of the bloom into the skin color. The bloom should have very distinct edges. Build up color in the cap, working from dark into light. Add enough layers to make the persimmon skin look very smooth.

Vellum is very forgiving. A damp brush can remove paint layers all the way back to the vellum. To remove only the top layer, use a cotton swab. Dip it into clean water, roll any extra water off on a towel, then use the damp swab to roll off a layer of paint.

Shade the bloom area with pale purple and pink. Deepen the shadows and adjust the color where needed. To get very dark shadows on green, use a purple mix of permanent alizarin crimson and ultramarine blue. For dark shadows on the orange areas, use rose of ultramarine and the purple mix.

The last step is to paint the natural scratches in the bloom. Observe the bloom on the fruit very carefully, and try to capture its unique patterning. Draw the scratches with orange mixes, using multiple layers if needed to match surrounding areas of skin.

In order to add a little more bloom on the left side, some orange was lifted with a cotton swab and that area was repainted as bloom.

Kelmscott vellum has a very smooth surface, which can lead to color easily lifting off unintentionally. However, with the right combination of drybrush techniques, color can be stacked layer after layer, yielding very dark colors alongside bright highlights. Roots are included in the composition, providing an underground perspective and information about how root crops come to be.

Achieving Deep, Rich Color in Watercolor on Kelmscott Vellum

TUTOR: CAROL WOODIN

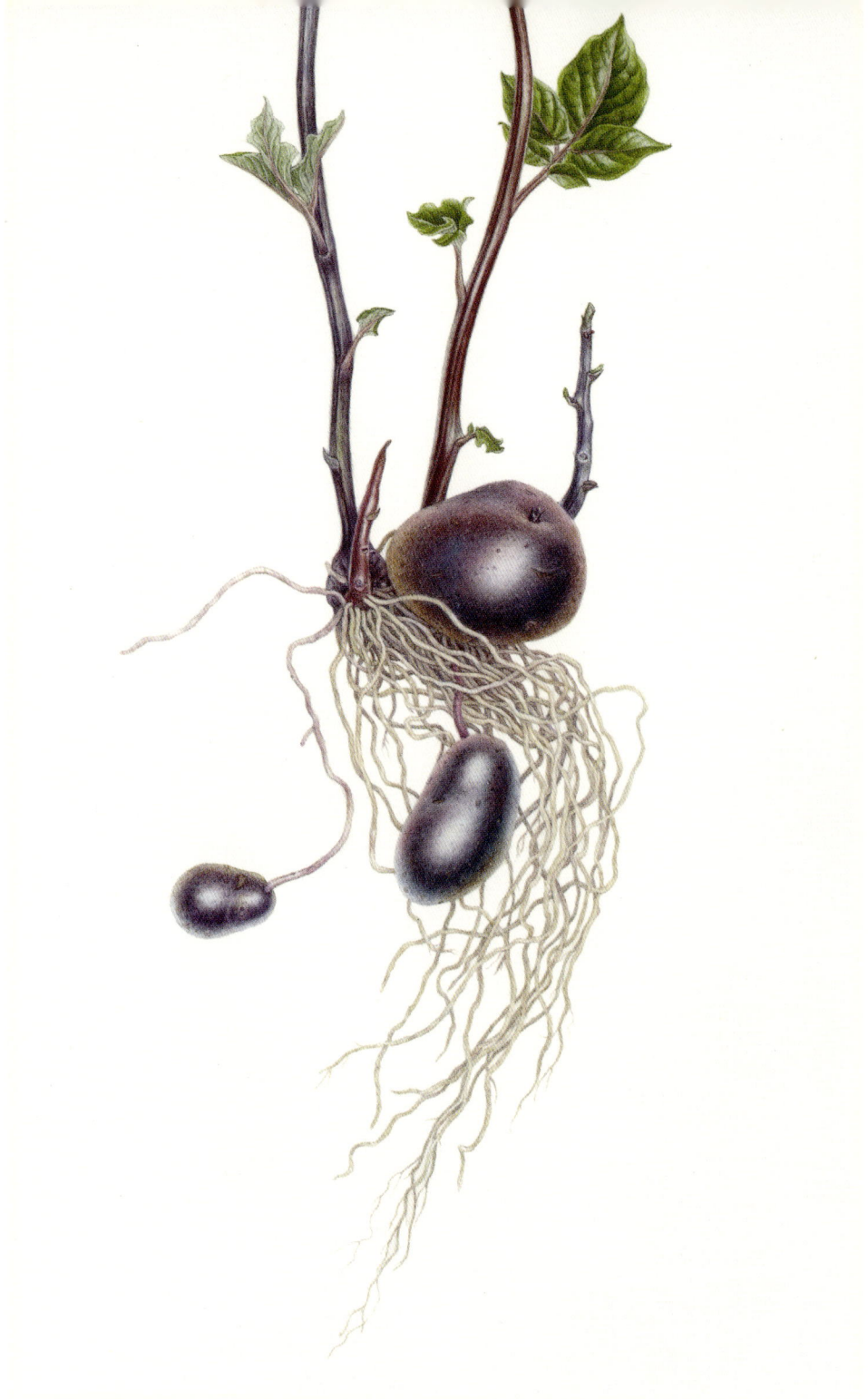

Purple Potato *Solanum tuberosum* Watercolor on Kelmscott Vellum

17 ½ × 13 inches [43.75 × 32.5 cm] © Carol Woodin HOURS TO COMPLETE: 80

MATERIALS: Drafting brush; abrasive film; white-plastic eraser; lead pointer, porcelain fan palette; container for water; gum arabic; drafting weight bag; paper towel; dry cleaning pad; Kolinsky brushes (nos. 0, 1, and 3); lead holders with 4H and H leads; fine craft blade; white-plastic retractable erasers. Colors: Chinese white; cadmium lemon; cadmium yellow; quinacridone gold; cadmium orange light; cadmium red light; cadmium red deep; quinacridone rose; quinacridone magenta; cadmium green pale; chromium oxide green; phthalo green; cobalt blue; burnt sienna; ultramarine violet; cerulean blue.

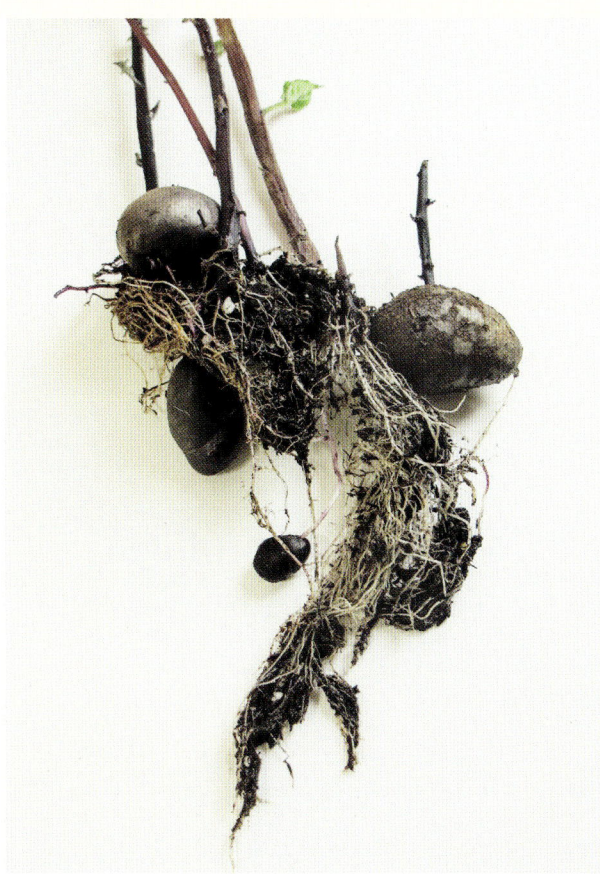

These purple potatoes were grown in pots over the winter, then unearthed for the painting. Plants were studied carefully from various directions to settle on a composition that included some elements, and edited others out.

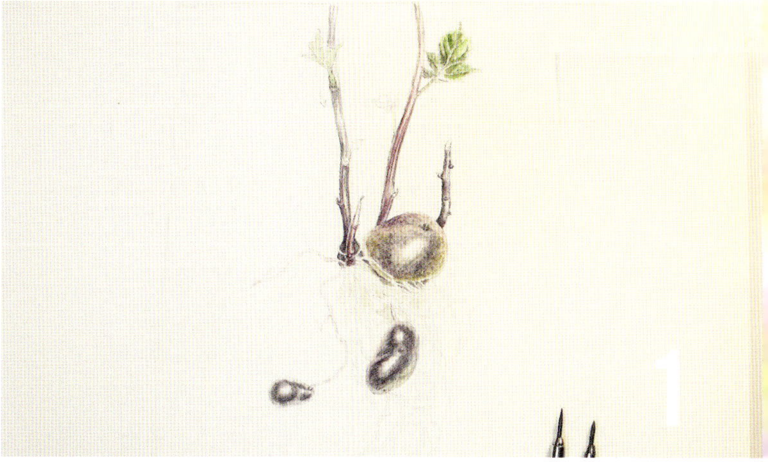

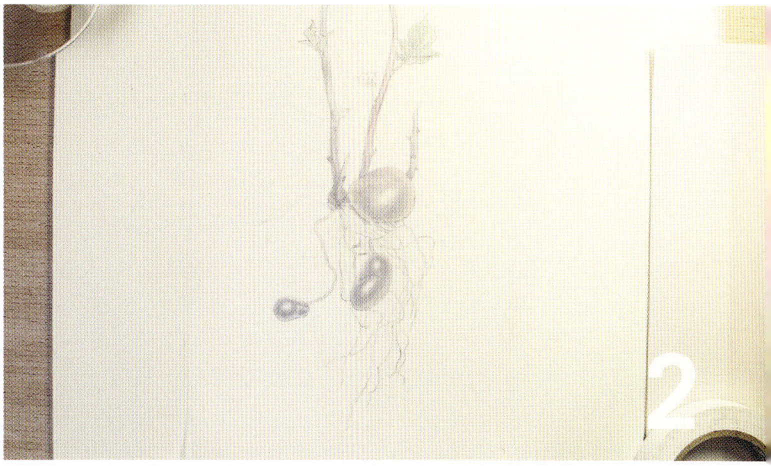

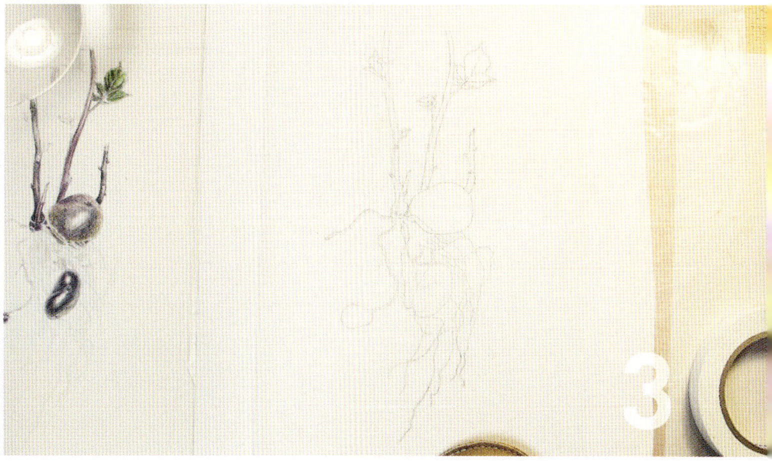

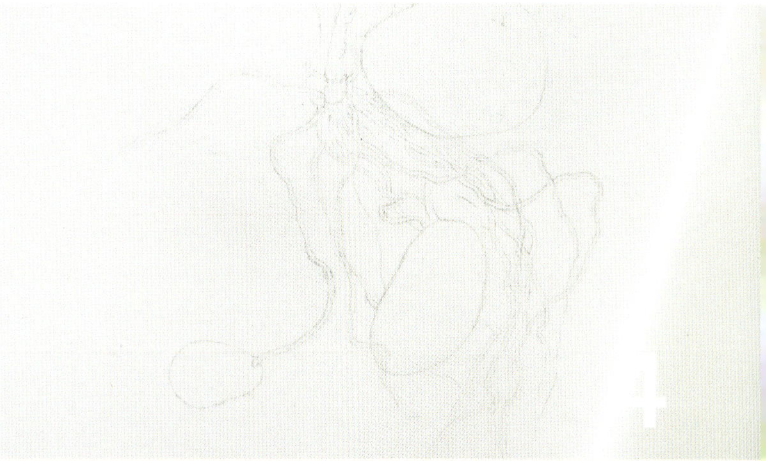

Draw the composition, focusing on what is occurring underground. For this composition, drawn on a piece of scrap matboard, the long stems with leaves were cropped out, and three potatoes and their roots became the focus. Make basic color studies of the major components.

Lay tracing paper over the compositional drawing, and trace the major components with a sharply pointed 4H lead.

Turn the tracing paper over and redraw the tracing with an H lead. Tape the tracing paper to the vellum right side up and transfer the drawing to the vellum using a 4H lead.

Once it has been transferred, tune up the drawing using the original drawing and the plant subject for reference.

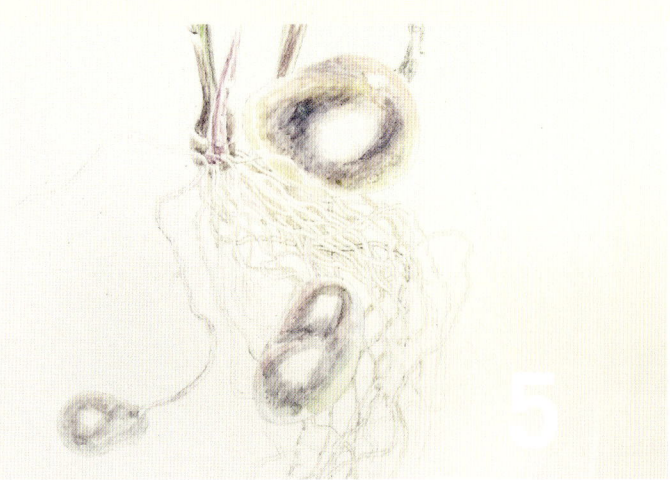

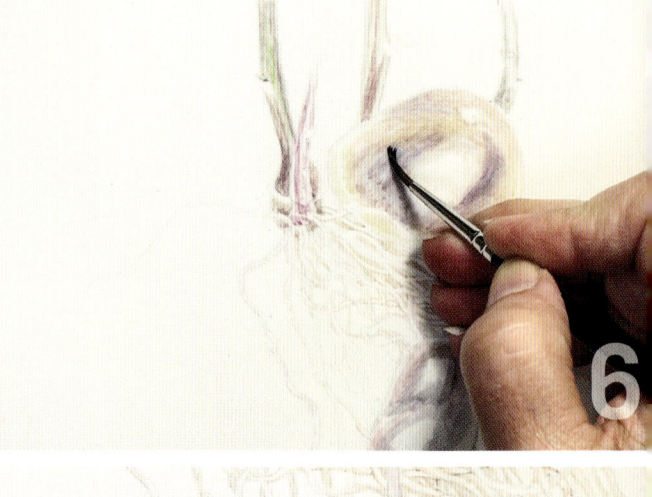

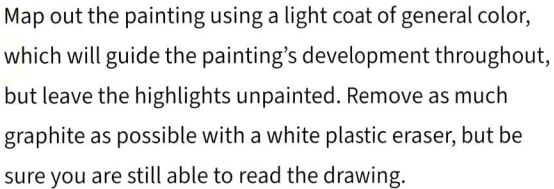

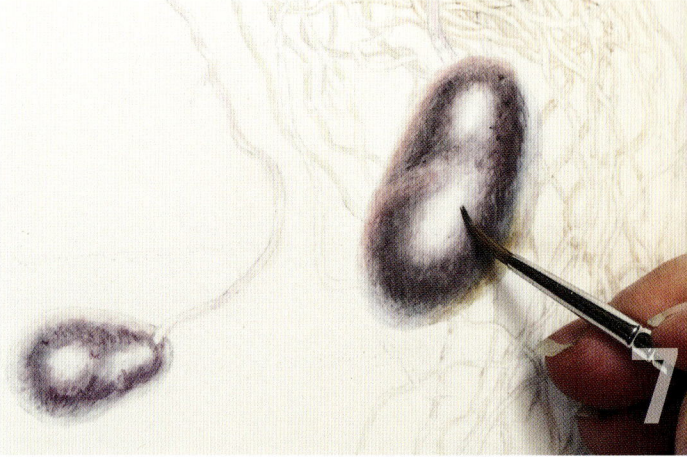

Map out the painting using a light coat of general color, which will guide the painting's development throughout, but leave the highlights unpainted. Remove as much graphite as possible with a white plastic eraser, but be sure you are still able to read the drawing.

Following the color map and using the side of a no. 3 brush, lay in a second coat of color, working the whole painting up to the same stage. Keep moving throughout the painting to avoid painting over areas that are still wet.

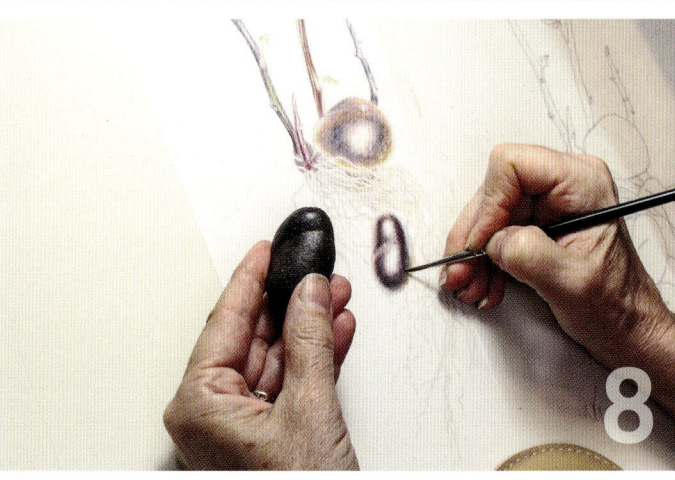

Using the side of the brush, brush dilute color into some of the highlight area to soften the edges. Work darker color into the shadow areas using quinacridone rose and magenta, ultramarine blue, quinacridone gold, and phthalo green. Don't worry about the choppiness of the brushstrokes at this stage.

Referring to the subject, continue to build the density of the color, progressing to less diluted pigment and using the tip of the brush. By building layer upon layer, color intensifies. Continually use your original reference material, including the color study, graphite drawing, and the plant material itself, if it is available. The eye is a more sensitive instrument than a camera.

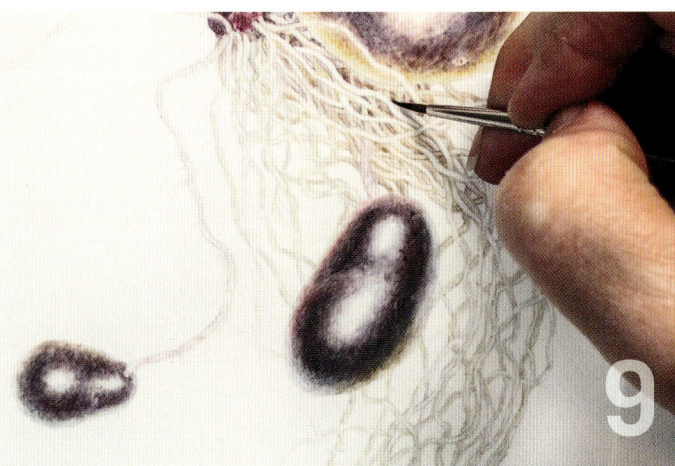

As color is built up and clarified on the potatoes, also bring up the roots and stems to a similar level. Lay in the shadows using ultramarine violet and burnt sienna to push the roots in the background into the shadow while the roots in the foreground are left brighter.

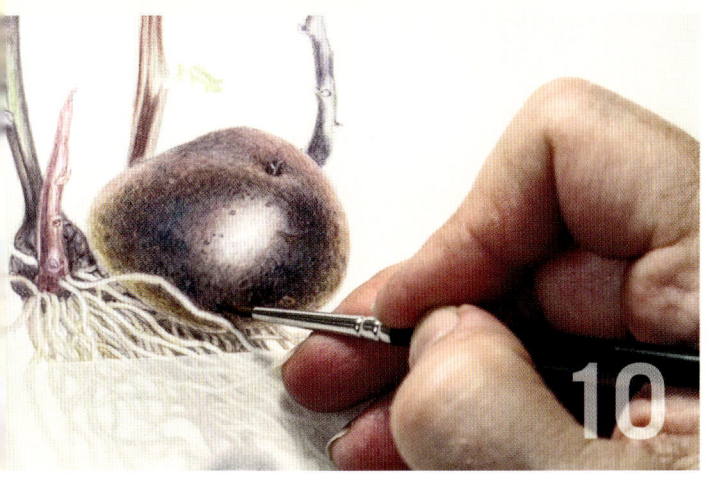

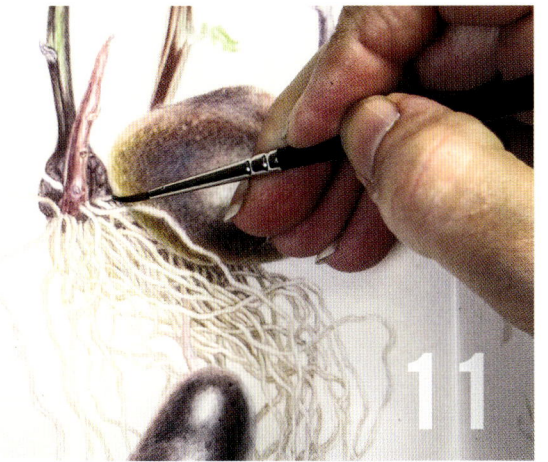

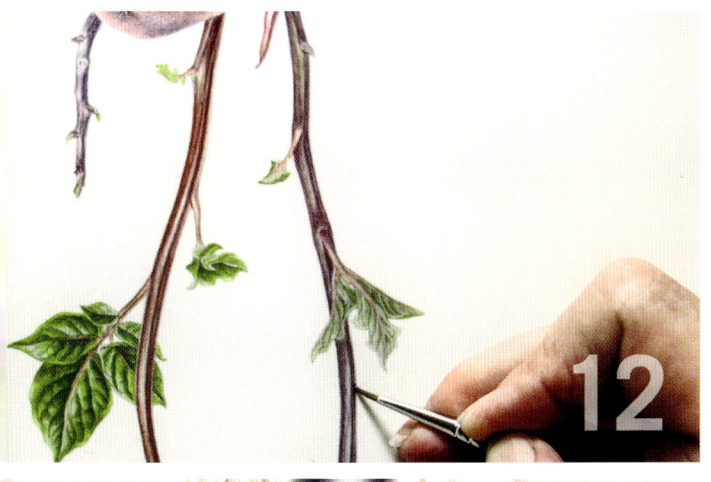

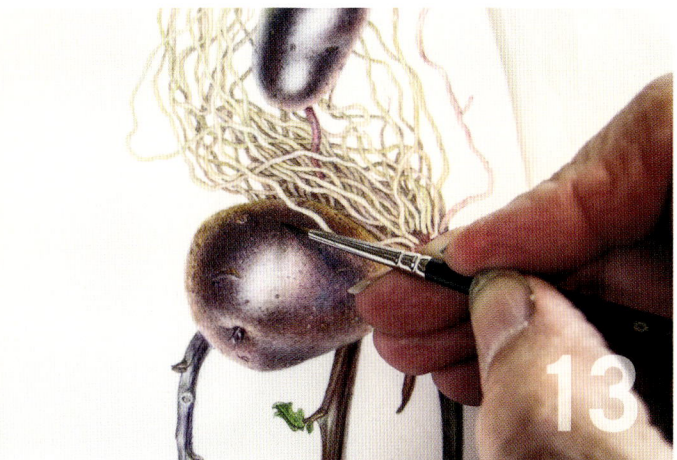

With a no. 1 brush, darken and refine the color with a mixture of phthalo green and magenta. In the brownish areas, add quinacridone gold, and in the pinker areas, add quinacridone rose. Add and detail the imperfections in the potato. Include soft shading and highlights around the just-emerging eye.

Darken the shading below the larger potato using phthalo green and quinacridone magenta, along with quinacridone gold and ultramarine blue. Add another layer to the middle potato, smoothing and darkening the mid and shadow tones. Add diluted color with a no. 1 brush to convey the undulations of the roots and where they pass behind other roots.

Invert the painting to develop the stems and leaves. The stem on the right uses a mix of phthalo green, cadmium green, and quinacridone magenta, and the reddish-brown one on the left contains more cadmium red and chromium oxide. The leaves are nearly completed, with the upper sides a warmer color with more contrast, and the undersides (right) a grayer green mixed with chromium oxide and cobalt blue.

Feather additional drybrush layers of color into the darker areas of the potatoes. Soften the transitions using a very light touch. Each potato color is slightly different, with subtly nuanced color—retain these color variations throughout. The roots leading to the potatoes are pink rather than whitish; mix the color with quinacridone rose and a smidgen of cadmium green pale to dull it slightly.

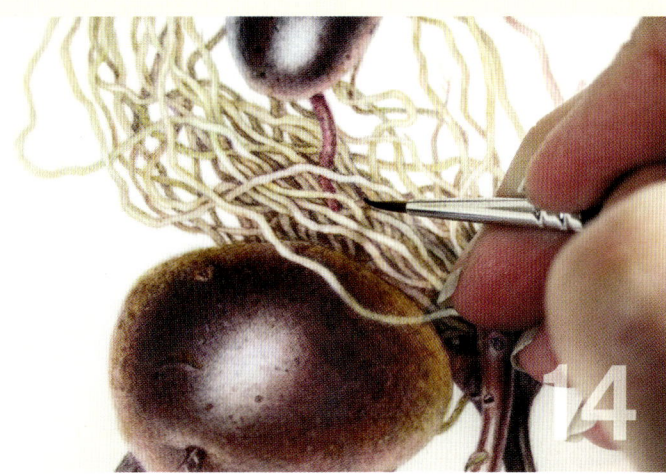

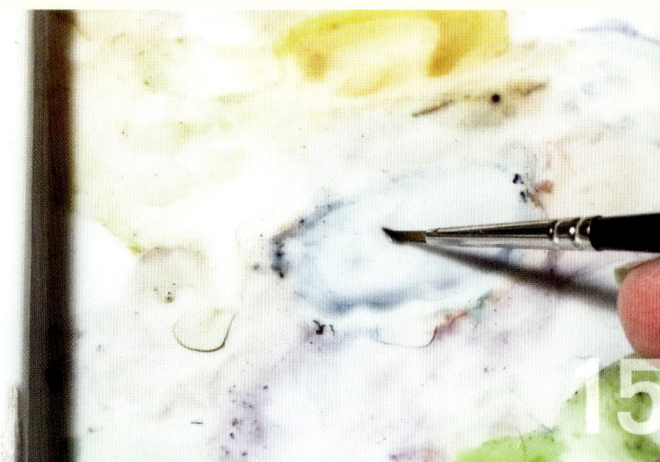

Give some attention to the roots where gradations of color are used to differentiate the many layers. Paint the roots that are the farthest back with thin layers of phthalo green and magenta, and paint the roots in the middle range of the painting with burnt sienna and blue. Add some very dilute quinacridone gold and permanent rose to the roots in the front, and shade them with mineral violet.

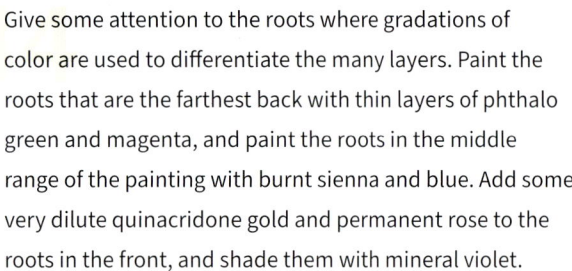

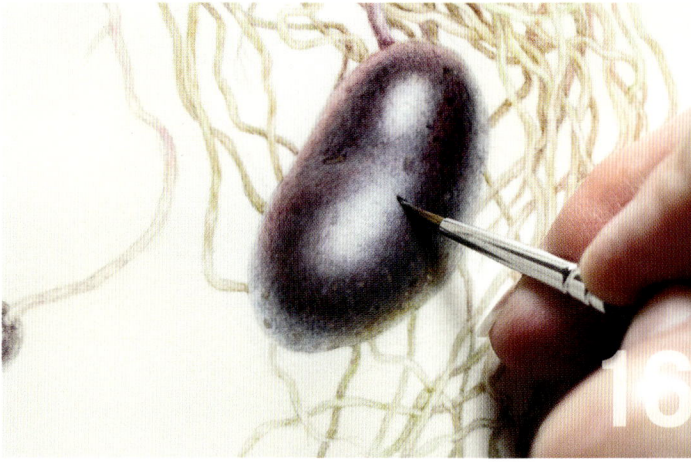

Mix some very light, thin blue violet for toning the highlight areas. Dip a no. 0 brush into the color, then dry it off on a paper towel. While you are drying the brush, roll it so that the tip becomes pointed and the brush quite dry, but still containing pale dilute color.

Lightly sketch the dry but dilute color into the highlight area to soften the transition between the highlight and mid-tones.

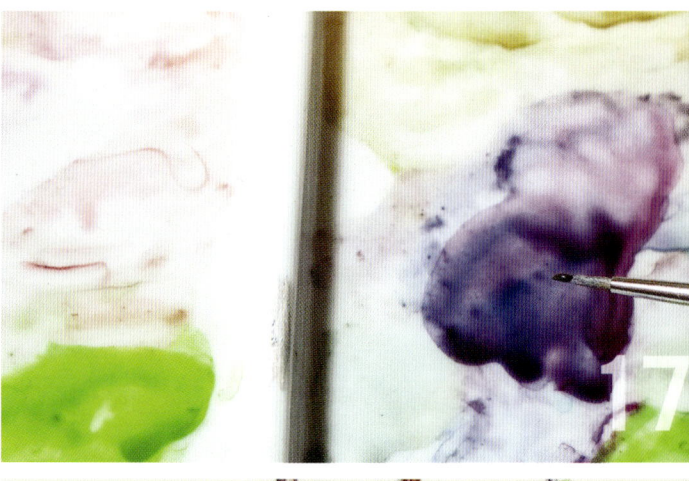

In order to continue adding dry layers of color on top of the many layers already present, make a rich mixture of phthalo green and quinacridone magenta. Then dip the tip of the brush into gum arabic, and mix this small amount of gum arabic into the pigment on the palette.

Increased color density and intense darks are achievable on vellum. Vellum is so smooth that it's easy to pick up color if the brush is too stiff or too moist. By making the paint a little stickier with a tiny amount of gum arabic, color can be added even if it's diluted, without picking up previous layers. Use a size 0 brush to fine-tune and adjust the entire painting, amplifying darks and sharpening details.

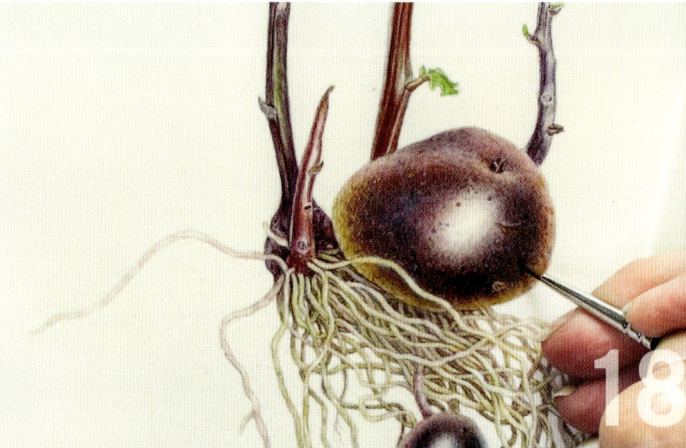

The goal of this painting was to establish depth by uniting fore, mid, and background elements. Although there is a lot going on in the composition, the Indian pipes take center stage because opaque white paint has showcased their translucent and waxy beauty against a dramatic dark ground.

Using Opaque Watercolors on Dark Vellum

TUTOR: ESTHER KLAHNE

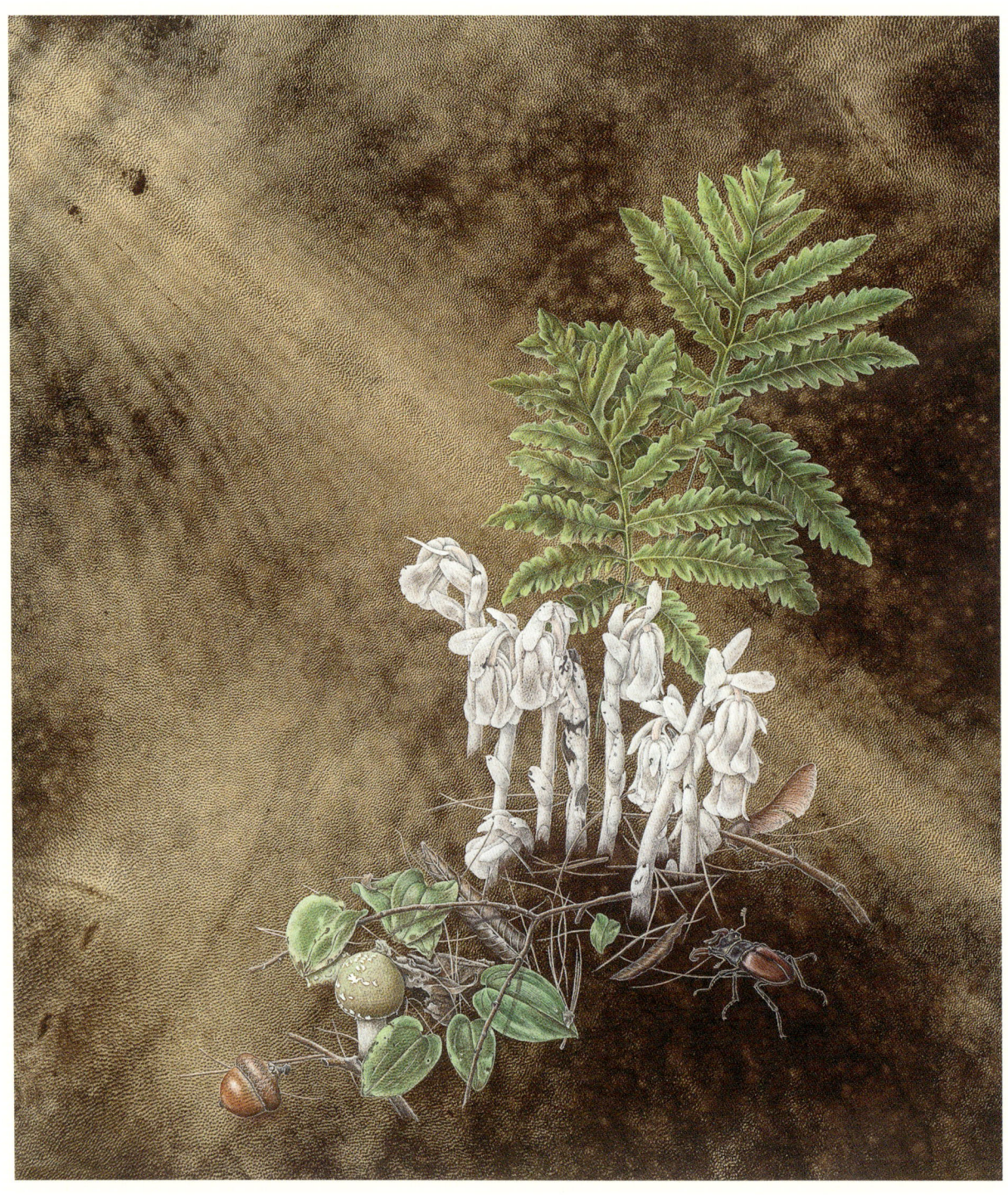

Indian Pipes *Monotropa uniflora* Watercolor on vellum 16 ½ × 11 ½ inches [41.25 × 28.75 cm] © Esther Klahne

HOURS TO COMPLETE: 125

MATERIALS: Drafting brush; dry cleaning pad; white transfer paper; ceramic palette; containers for water; tracing paper; synthetic round brushes (nos. 3 and 4); mechanical pencil with a 2H lead; kneaded eraser; white plastic eraser; magnifying glass; low-adhesion tape. Colors: titanium white; Hansa yellow light; Hansa yellow deep; scarlet lake; quinacridone violet; ultramarine blue; burnt sienna; raw sienna.

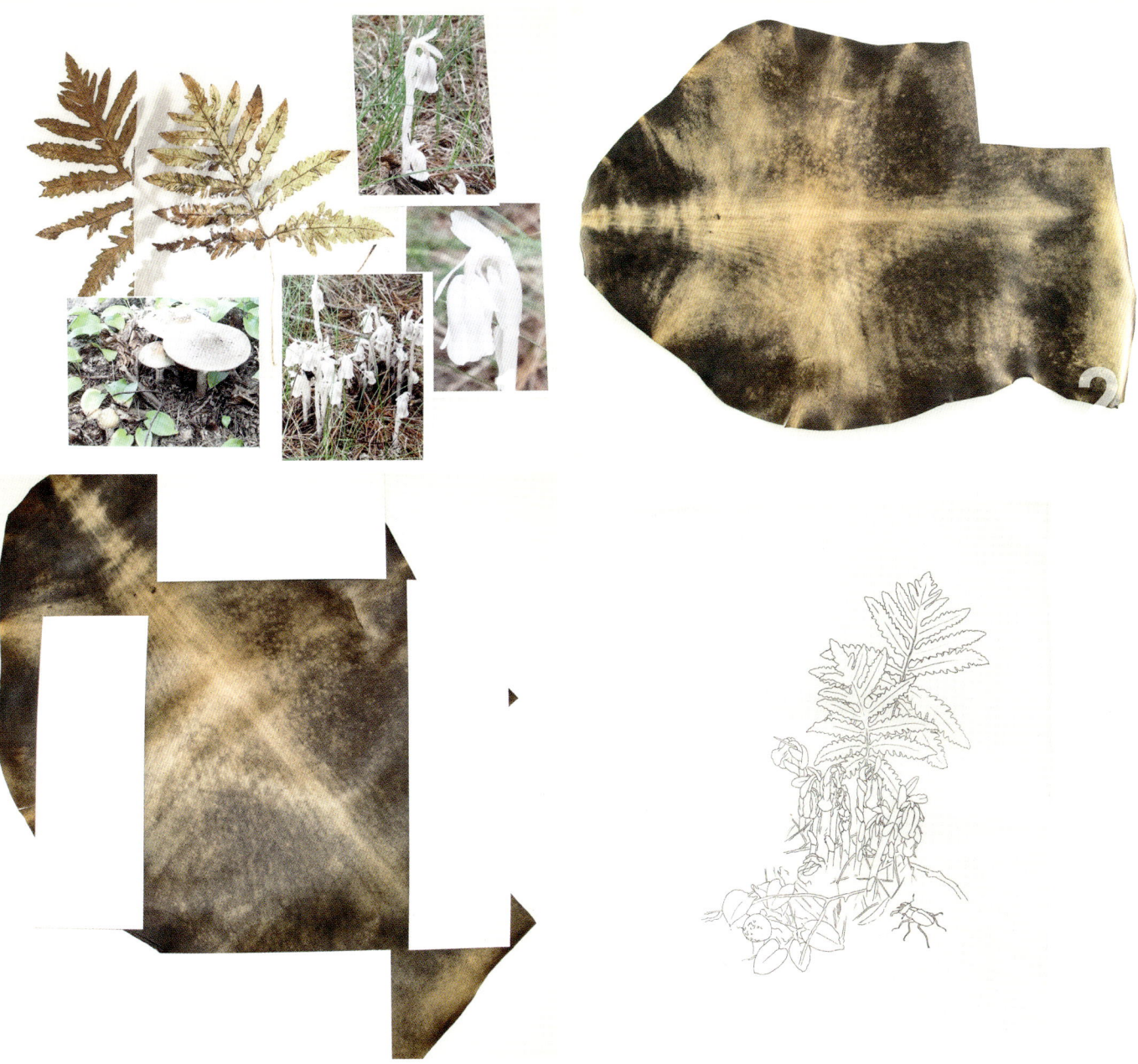

When you are working on a botanical painting of a subject that is not in season, refer to previously completed studies, good-quality photographs, dried specimens, and various reference materials to help you understand the subject's structure and growth habits, and to work out the design of your composition.

Vellum often has distinctive colors and markings that provide special opportunities. The goat vellum used here has a pronounced lighter central band that radiates outward, creating the effect of light shining through trees in a forest.

The vellum was shifted so that the band of light is angled, further enhancing the effect of sunbeams and dappled light. The composition was designed around this apparent light source.

Indian pipes (*Monotropa uniflora*) are the central focus of the composition, ferns form the backdrop, and pine needles, a mushroom, a Stag beetle, and bits of leaves form the foreground. Over the course of this tutorial, the composition evolved slightly from the original drawing.

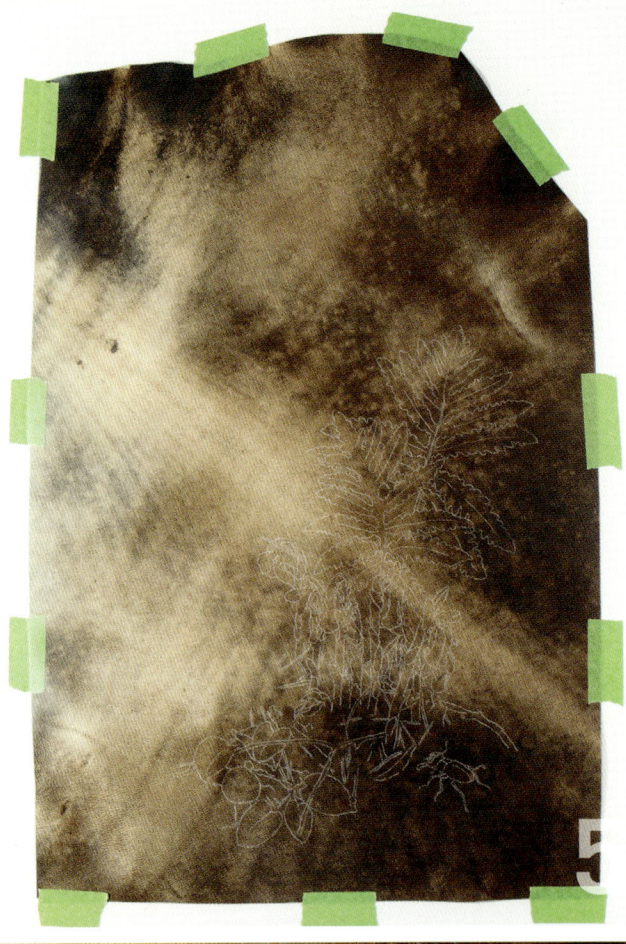

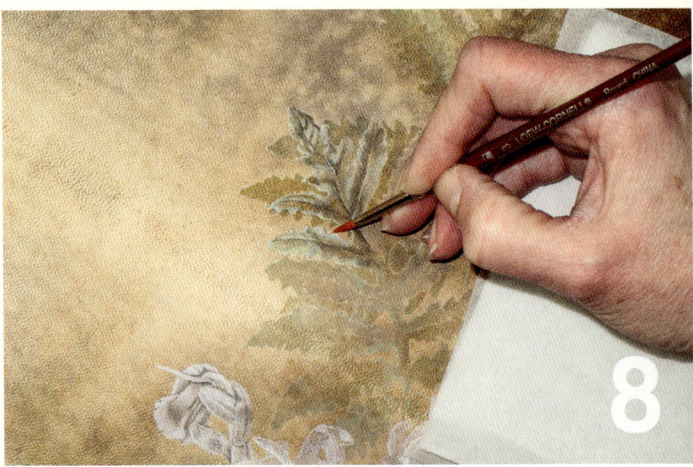

Transfer the design onto the vellum using a light box, with the vellum laid down first, then the white transfer paper, and then the tracing paper with the sketch placed on top. The drawing on tracing paper was inked to make the drawing's details more visible. A light box can help you position a composition in the best location as it relates to vellum's markings—in this case, the sunbeams.

Lay down the first layer of paint. This is often the most challenging step because the vellum's surface is not always completely receptive. The paint may bead slightly, but with persistent strokes, this layer will smooth out and become an even paint application. Use a thin layer of titanium white to define the Indian pipes.

For the ferns, use a mix of Hansa yellow light with ultramarine blue and a small amount of titanium white. In order to build up color on darker vellums, white paint is often added to colors to make them slightly opaque and stand out against the dark ground. When watercolor has white added to it, and the paint becomes opaque, it is sometimes referred to as "bodycolor."

Once the first layer of paint has dried, add a second layer to define the highlights and shadows on the fern.

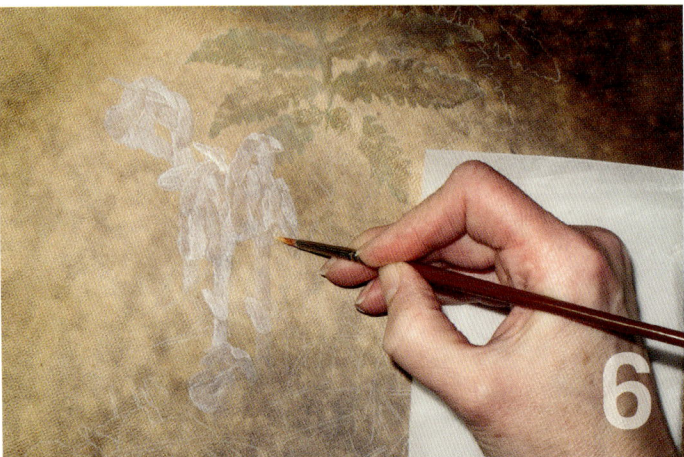

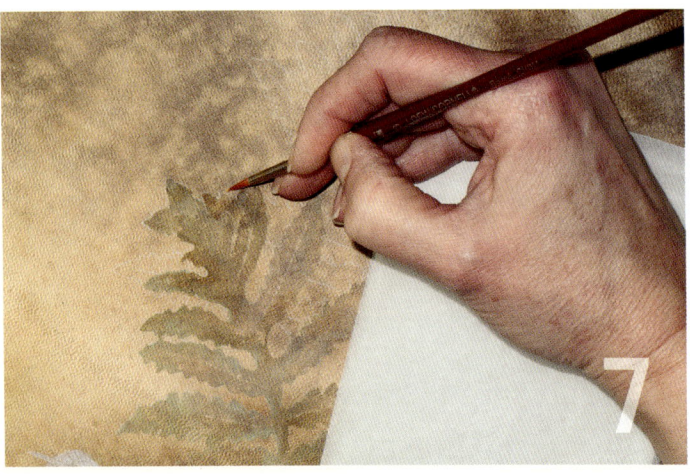

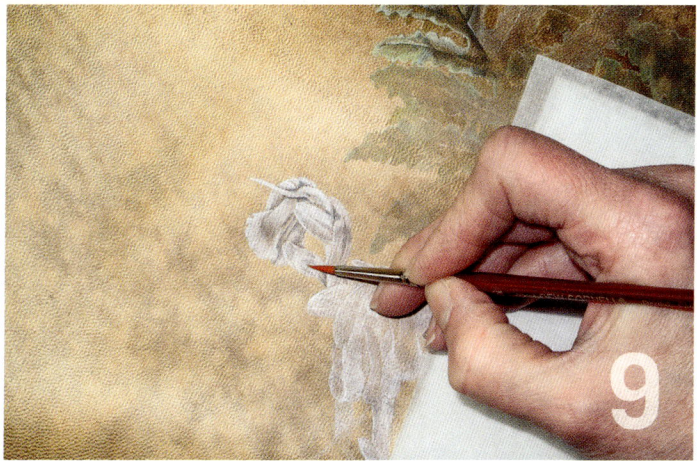

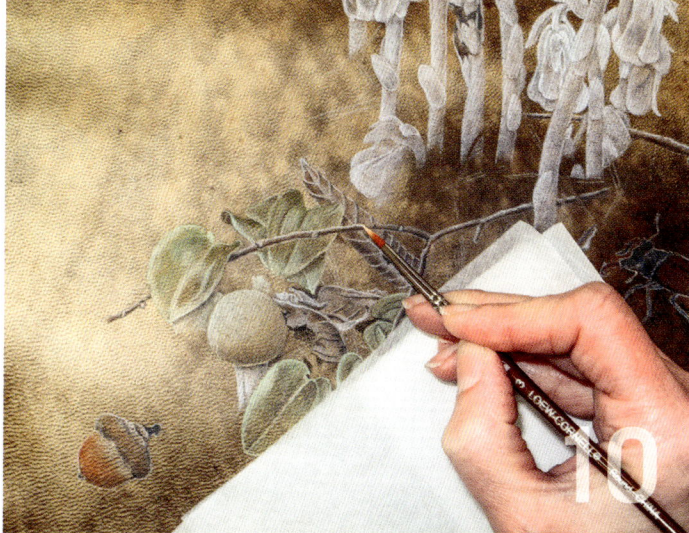

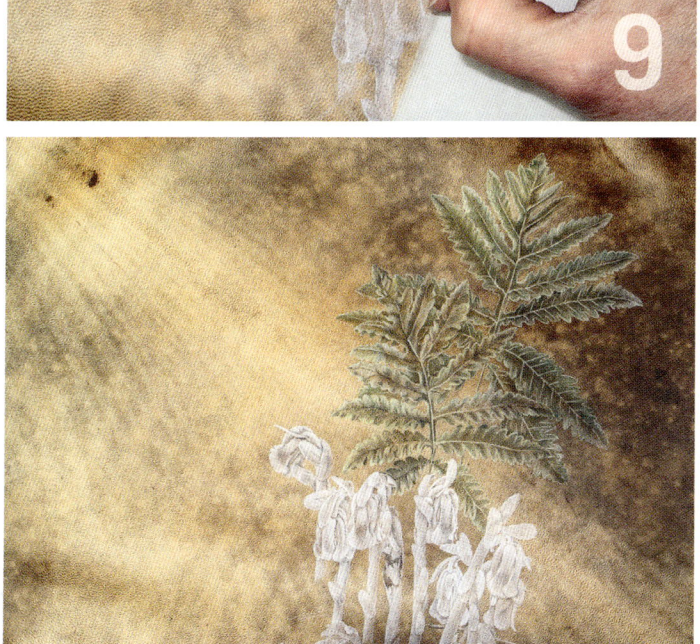

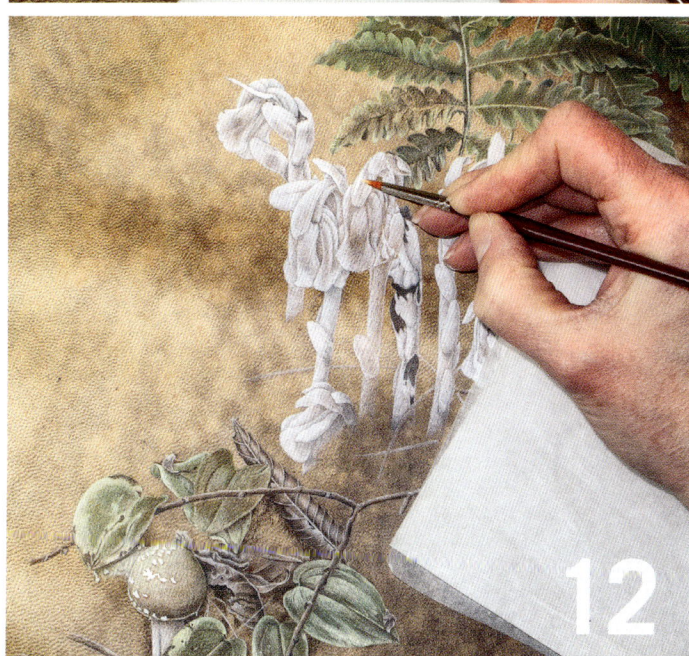

Use a mix of ultramarine blue and burnt sienna to develop the forms of the Indian pipes. Use a light touch with the tip of a no. 3 brush; when you are applying color over white paint, a little goes a long way.

Begin developing the foreground by defining the leaf shapes and veins, building up the twig forms, and adding an acorn to the left of the mushroom to further draw the viewer's eye around the painting. Some pine needles were part of the original design, and some were added along the way.

Apply a second layer of paint, and apply highlights and outlines in white throughout the painting on the major elements. Sketch in pine needles with pale white outlines. Lay in some shadows in leaves, mushroom, and the acorn.

Apply additional layers of white paint to the Indian pipes for highlights, and develop shadows and areas of discoloration further to convey the plant's aging process. Shading of form and depth in the foreground is also advanced.

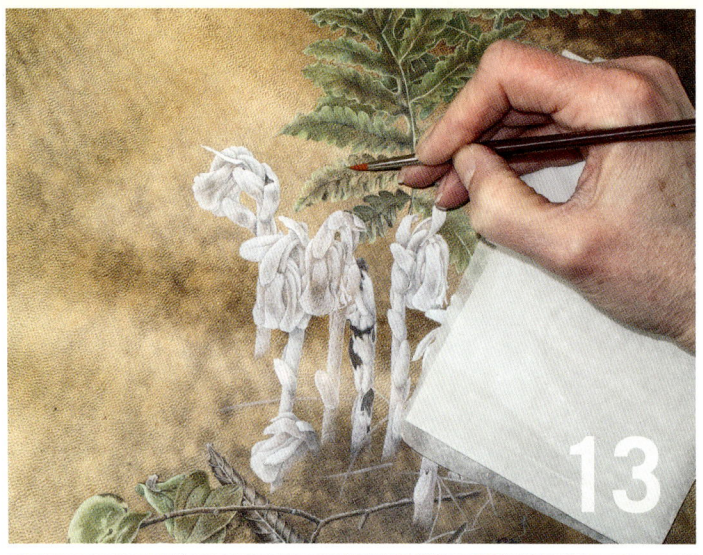

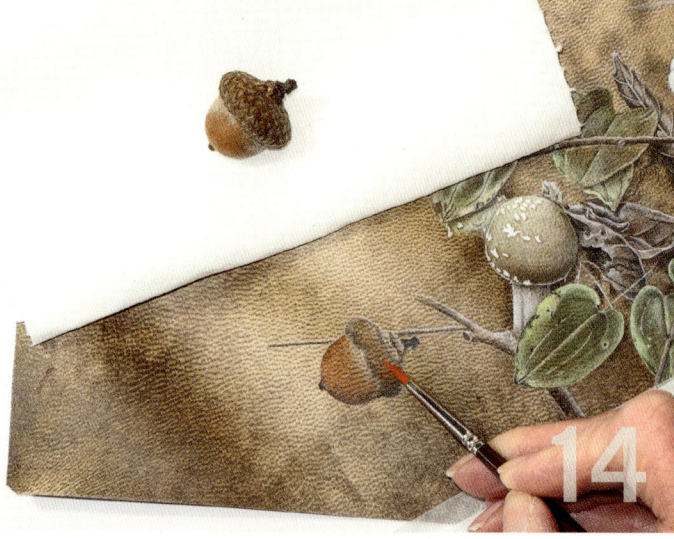

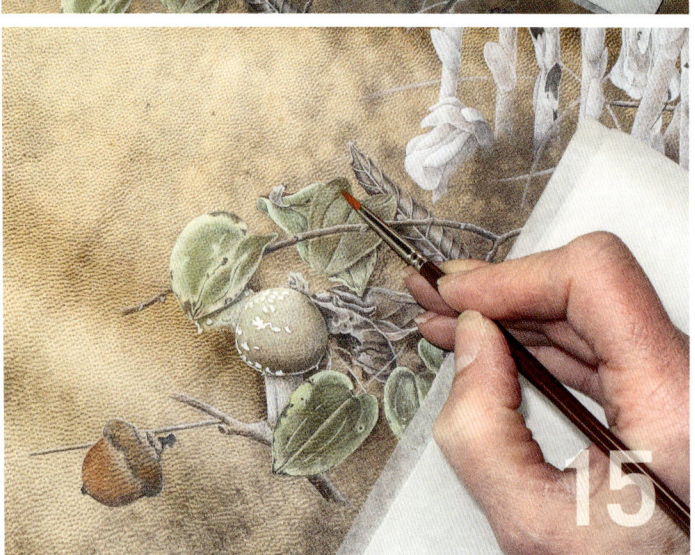

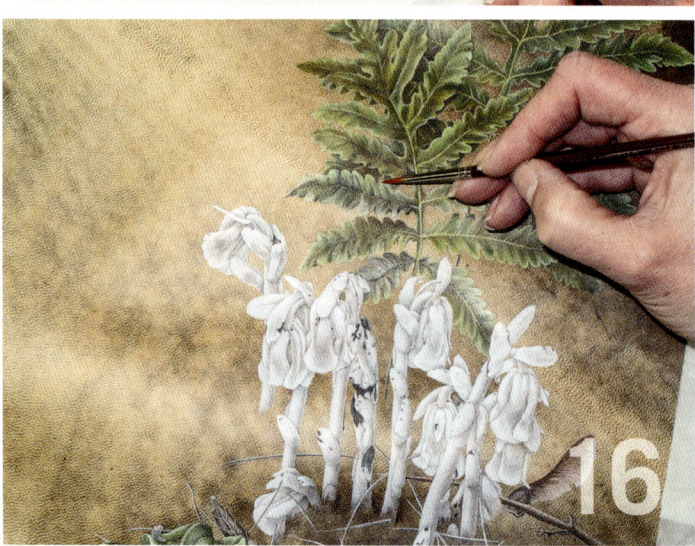

When glazing, a very thin, diluted layer of color is gently brushed over the previous layer: add just enough water to the pigment to allow the paint to be spread evenly without lifting previous layers. To unify the ferns' shading, a glaze of Hansa yellow light mixed with ultramarine green shade was applied over them.

Apply highlights and shadows to the painting over the glaze. Add more detail to the acorn. Pay attention to where the light source would hit the acorn and gradually build up the highlights.

The Canada mayflower leaves in the foreground were further defined with shadows and highlights. To connect the base of the Indian pipes to the foreground, add pine needles here and there. Begin with white strokes, emphasize some of the needles with subtle shadows, and add a final glaze of burnt sienna to add warmth.

Apply another glaze to the ferns, this time using transparent yellow. The glaze will add some warmth to suggest radiant light. A maple samara was added to the right of the Indian pipes.

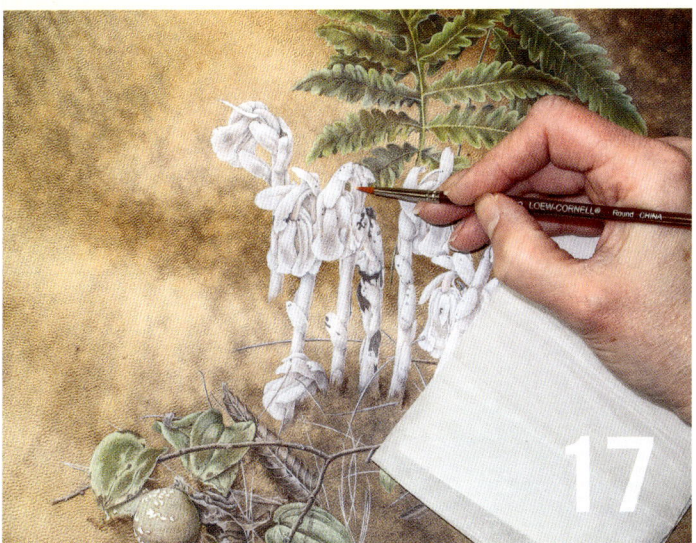

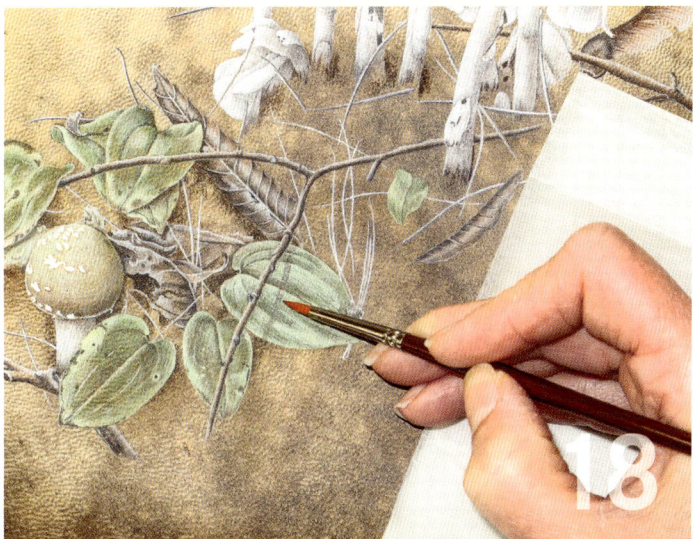

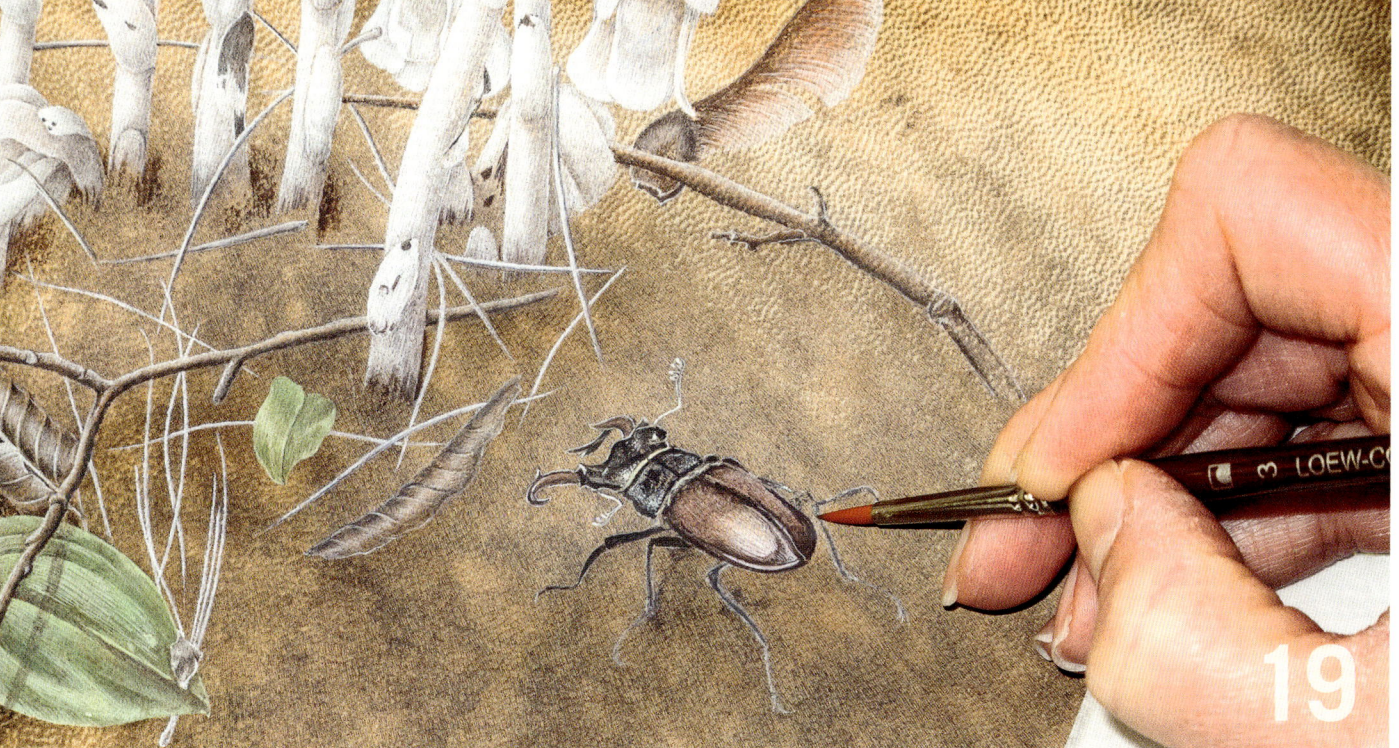

Indian pipes often have a slight warm blush color at the base of the flower, so apply a mix of Hansa yellow light with scarlet lake sparingly to this area of the flowers.

Apply some shadows to the leaves in the foreground. To convey a rich loam, apply a mix of ultramarine blue and burnt sienna (they create a deep brown color) at the base of the Indian Pipes. These areas need blending, because they were the first layers of paint applied.

Initially define the Stag beetle legs with a small amount of white paint, and follow that with a mix of dark brown applied on top. To prevent the beetle from looking outlined, careful softening of the white was needed. The highlight on the back of the beetle was eventually moved from the tail end to the higher, top edge of the beetle's back. As a final step, go through the entire painting carefully, adjusting highlights and shadows and tying the painting together.

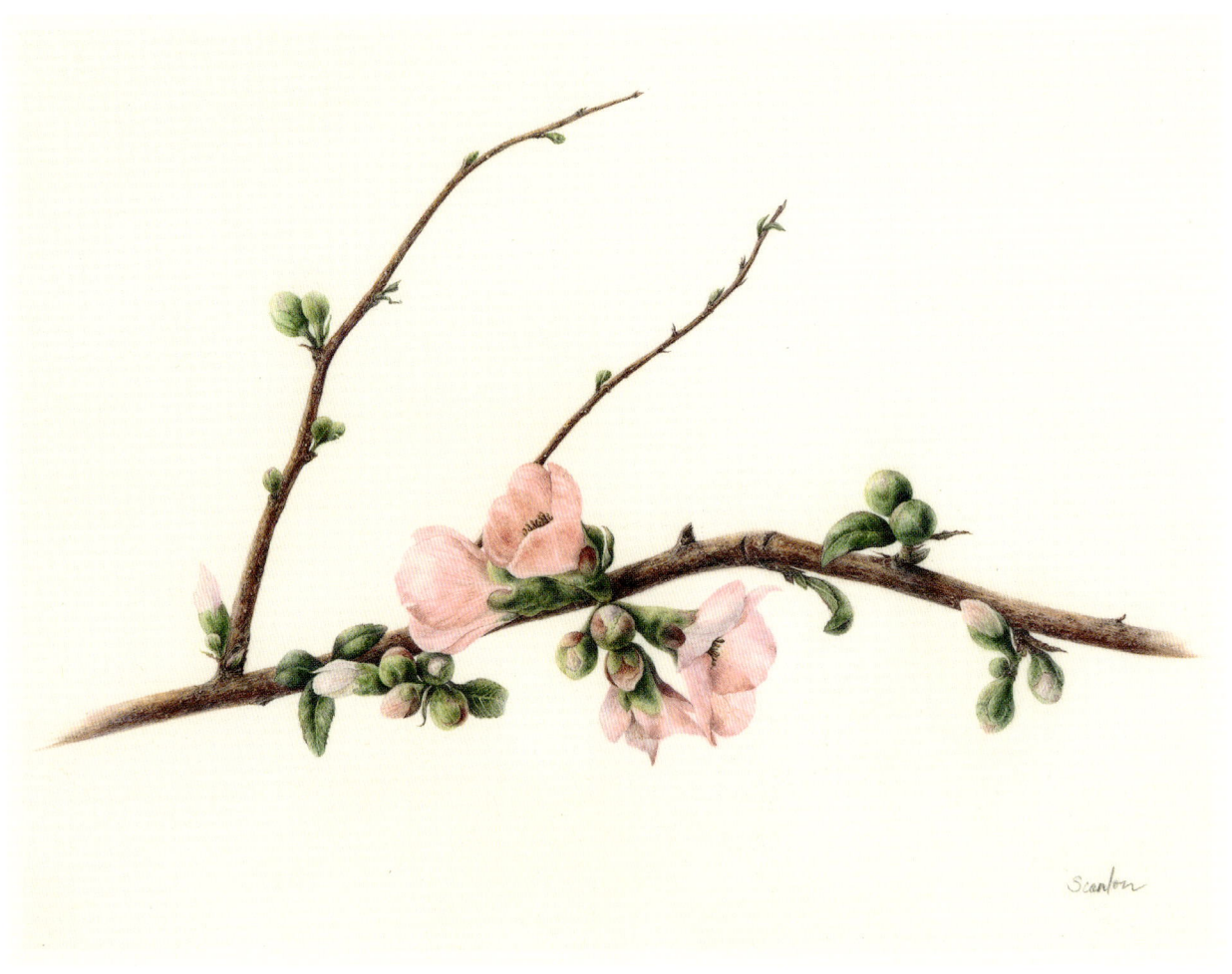

Buds and Branches on a Cherry Bough Watercolor on vellum 7 × 11 ½ inches [17.5 × 28.75 cm]
© Constance Scanlon HOURS TO COMPLETE: 60

MATERIALS: Magnifying glass; ruler; colorless art masking fluid; kneaded eraser; pointed cotton swabs; white porcelain plate for a palette of transparent watercolors; measuring compass; mechanical pencils with 2H and 4H leads; two Kolinsky brushes (no. 4); crow quill pen.

Washes on vellum are not like washes on paper—no water is laid down before placing color. It is more of a brushstroke that contains more dilute color than usual, spread broadly using the side of the brush. In Constance Scanlon's tutorial, this technique allows for mapping larger areas of color as a preliminary step to adding dry-brush layers. Also demonstrated are the use of masking fluid along with drybrush techniques, including scumbling, crosshatching, and color lifting.

Painting a Flowering Cherry Tree Bough

TUTOR: CONSTANCE SCANLON

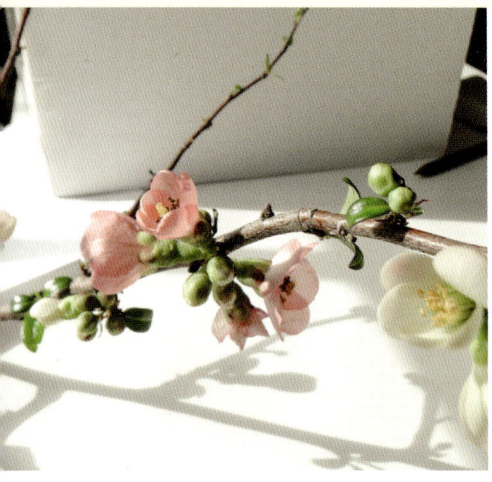

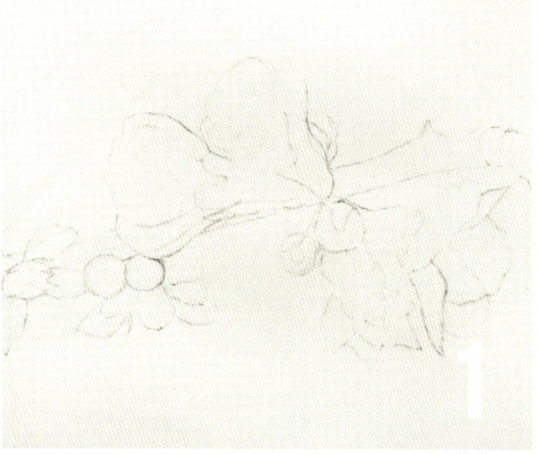

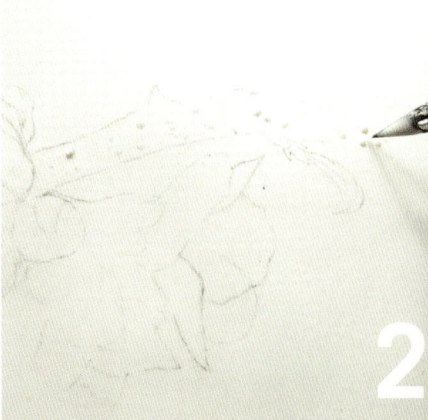

The peak of this cherry branch displays the details of the nuances on the bark. Additional photos focus on the buds and background branches; these will be used as reference once the flowers have wilted and changed.

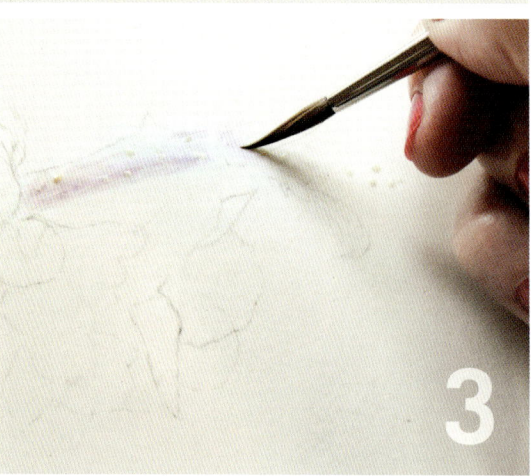

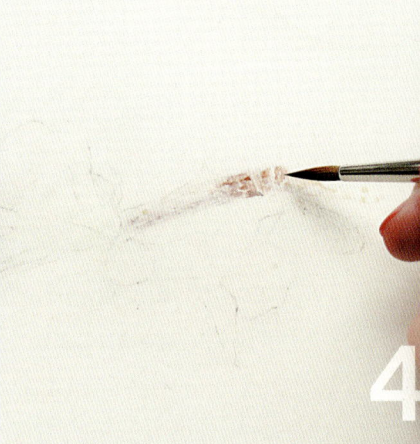

Transfer your drawing to vellum using graphite paper. Place the graphite side of the transfer paper onto the surface of the vellum, then place the drawing that was done on tracing paper on top of the graphite transfer paper. Using a sharp 4H pencil, trace over your drawing, pressing firmly to create adequate visual guidelines for painting.

Use a crow quill pen dipped in masking fluid to make small dots corresponding to the lenticels (pores) of the branch. If the masking fluid becomes too thick on the nib, dip the pen in water and wipe the nib on a paper towel to remove the excess water and masking fluid. Then dip into the masking fluid and begin again. Once all the dots are completed, let the masking fluid dry.

The reflected light on the under surface of the branch has a hint of purple hue, so the first layer of wash is a dioxazine violet. The masking fluid used for the lenticels will be more apparent after the first layer of color has been applied.

Painting on vellum is like ice skating—watercolor glides on a vellum surface. Errors can be corrected, but vellum is intolerant of too much water. Small strokes with minimal water on the pointed tip of the brush will keep the color skating on the vellum surface.

Use old brushes to add texture with scumbling. Dip the brush into the paint and blot the brush on a paper towel to release the excess moisture. Splay the bristles of the brush (the exact opposite of a pointy tip). Gently wiggle the brush across the vellum, creating textured surfaces of lines. Scumbling can also be used create final layers of color and texture.

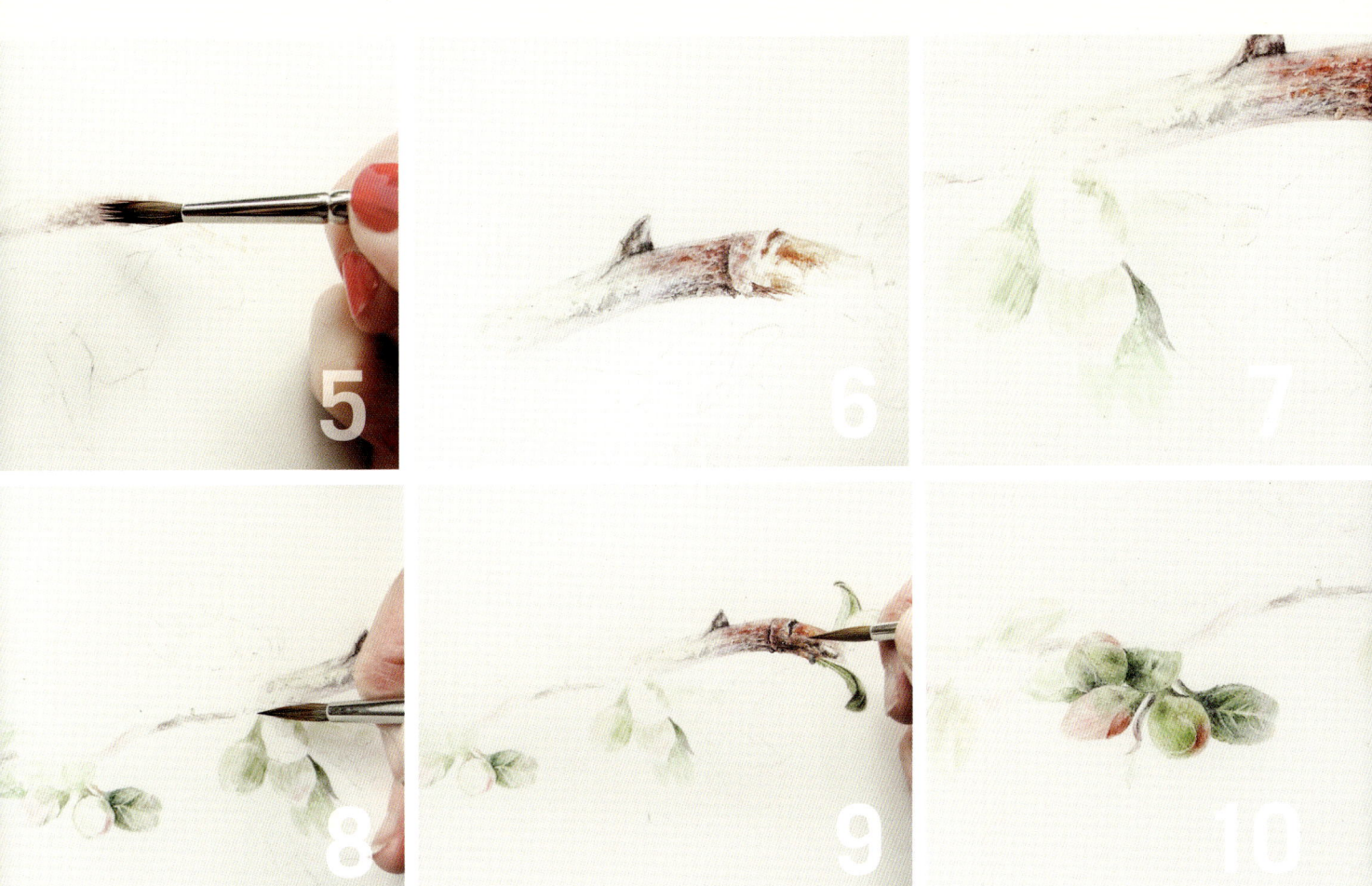

Begin working on one section of the branch until it is complete, thus building your confidence in achieving a satisfying end result. As often as possible, begin painting at the upper left, moving down and across the vellum to the bottom right (left-handed artists should begin from upper right).

The lower buds show initial drybrush hatching technique. A swath of initial color creates the base for future layers of color. Use the brush tip to pick up a film of paint color from the palette and apply in a delicate crosshatch motion. Layers of paint will build, interlocked by strokes of hatching, creating luminosity.

Use a mix of new gamboge and indigo to create greens for the leaves and buds. Hansa yellow light and ultramarine blue are also combined for a cooler green. These colors are used to begin laying out light, shadow, and form. Apply additional layers of paint only when the surface color has dried.

Remove the masking fluid from the lenticels by using the tip of a clean finger to wipe and tease it off the vellum. Add shadows to the undersides of the lenticels using shades of violet to give them depth and form.

Develop the bud color using quinacridone magenta, quinacridone coral, quinacridone rose, and permanent alizarin crimson. Simultaneously apply local colors, along with shading to show the roundness of the buds.

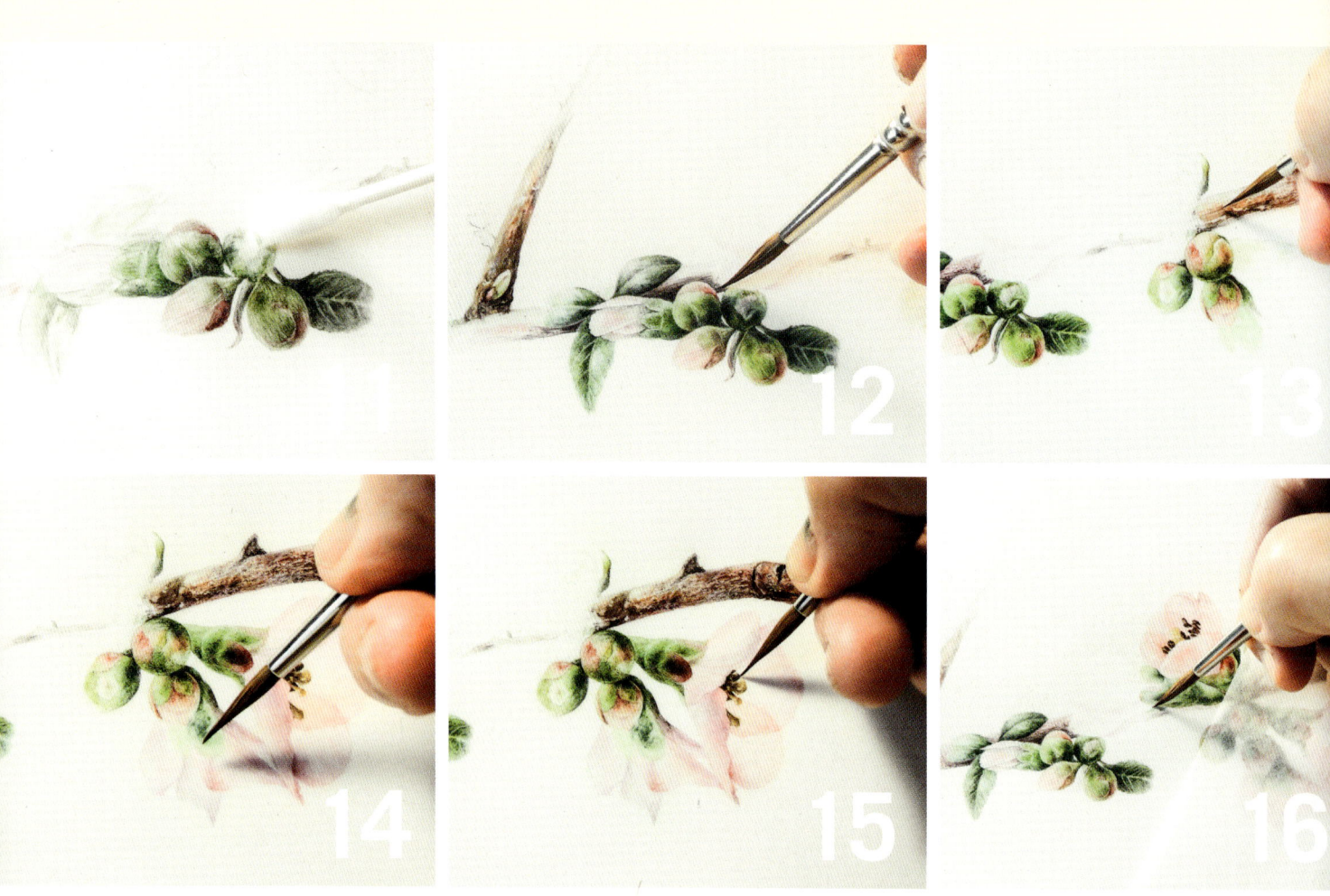

Last-minute space was made for a flower petal by removing watercolor from the vellum with a hint of water on a pointed cotton swab. The removed color is visible on the swab tip. You can also remove color by painting a small amount of water directly onto the area and dabbing it off with a clean paper towel.

The shape of the transparent flower petal is emphasized by layering color and texture on the underlying branch. Delicately layer soft pink onto the petals. Slowly develop the leaves and buds. The translucency of the petals contrasts with the opacity of the branch to create a sense of depth in the painting.

Striations of texture can be accomplished by using an almost-dry brush (without color) and gliding it across the painted vellum. This gently lifts color that is already on the vellum to enhance highlights. Create deep color striations in the branch by using a darker line of color. Indian red adds further detail and a natural hue to the cherry branch.

Rather than starting in the shadow and pulling the color outward, try painting into the shadows to create a natural depth. Here, a mixture of Payne's gray and Indian yellow is pulled into the shadow of the flower calyx. A complementary color (use red-purple shading with green leaves and buds) will also bring out depth in the painting.

Use a new no. 4 brush with a sharp point for the intricate detail of the anther and stigma of the flower.

Use a sheet of glassine paper to protect the painting from water drops and natural finger oils. Another method is to cut a square opening in a sheet of protective archival paper or in a portfolio sleeve, and lay it over the vellum, and paint through the opening.

Lenticels show depth through layers of color, shadows, and details. The lenticels will be lighter toward the branch top and have grayer hues as the branch turns into the shadow. Use sienna and browns to create the cast shadow of the bud onto the branch.

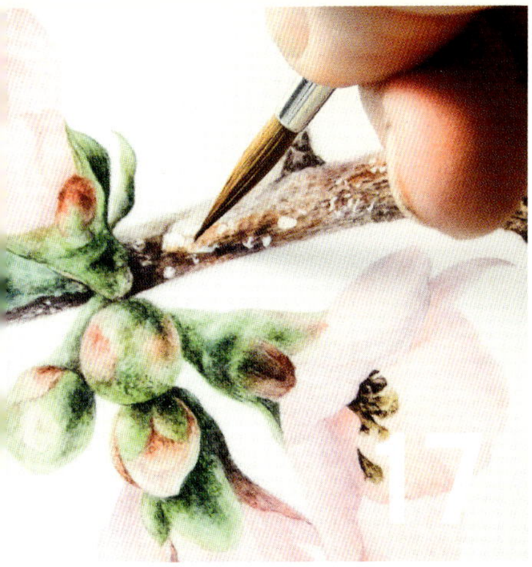

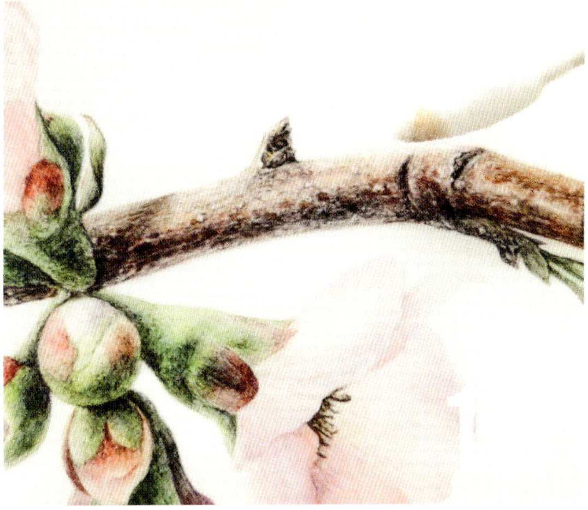

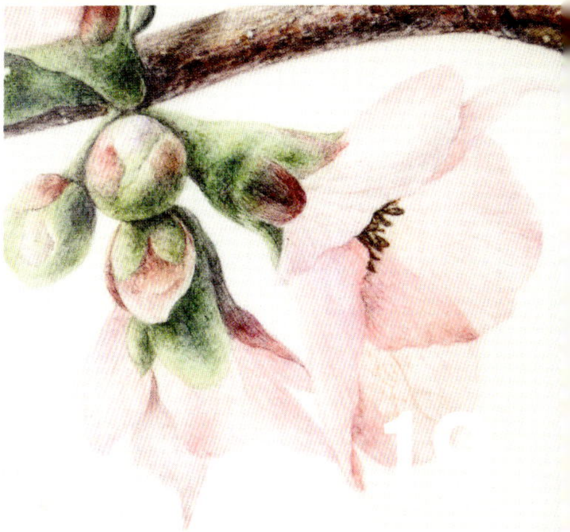

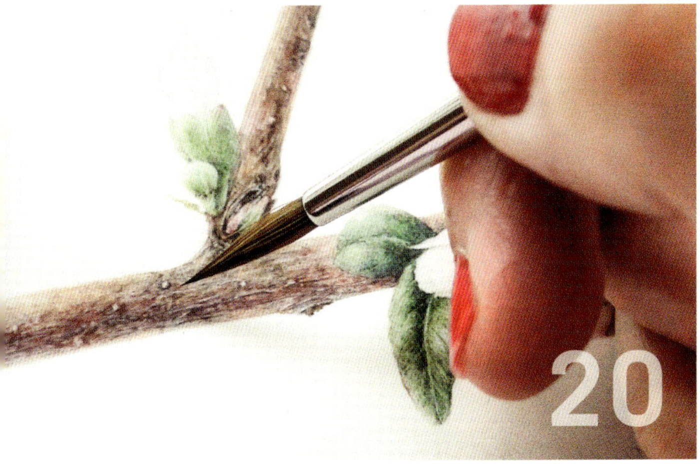

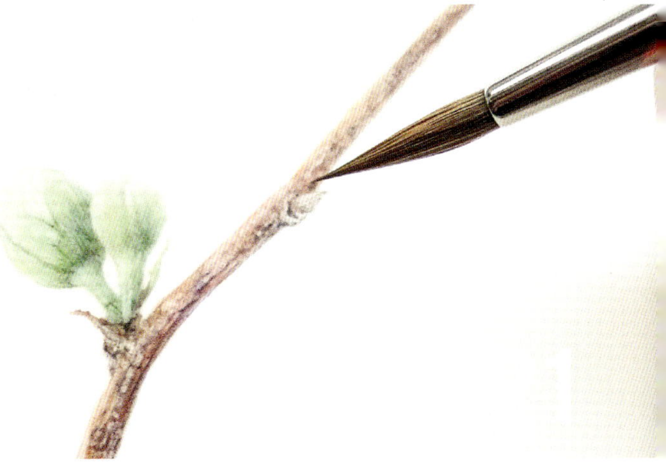

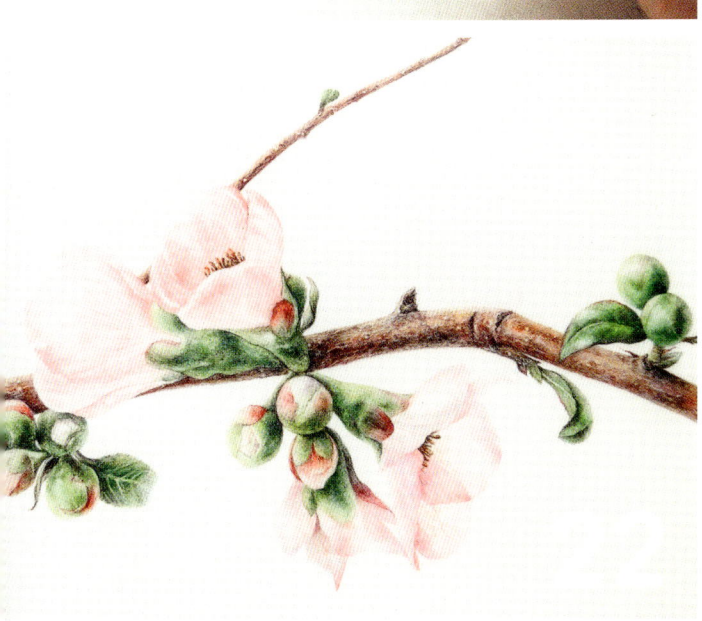

Use quinacridone gold for blending and the final petal veining. Occasionally, a small area of vellum might be resistant to watercolor. In those cases, paint can be stippled onto the vellum.

Give the upward branches some attention, and apply some final drybrush hatching to blend to the left side of the branch and slightly enhance the lenticel shadows. Depict additional texture by pulling gently across the branch to lift color with the tip of the paintbrush.

Give the smaller branches interest and form with drybrush hatching of layered detail and shadows. Darken the areas around emerging buds and the lower side of the branches.

Sharpen and adjust contrasts throughout to tie the painting together. Apply a final very light drybrush with Indian yellow to add an extra hint of warmth to the branch.

To create the effect of light shining on the branch, color was lifted from the top of the branch where it curves downward by rolling a cotton swab with a tiny bit of moisture on it over the area.

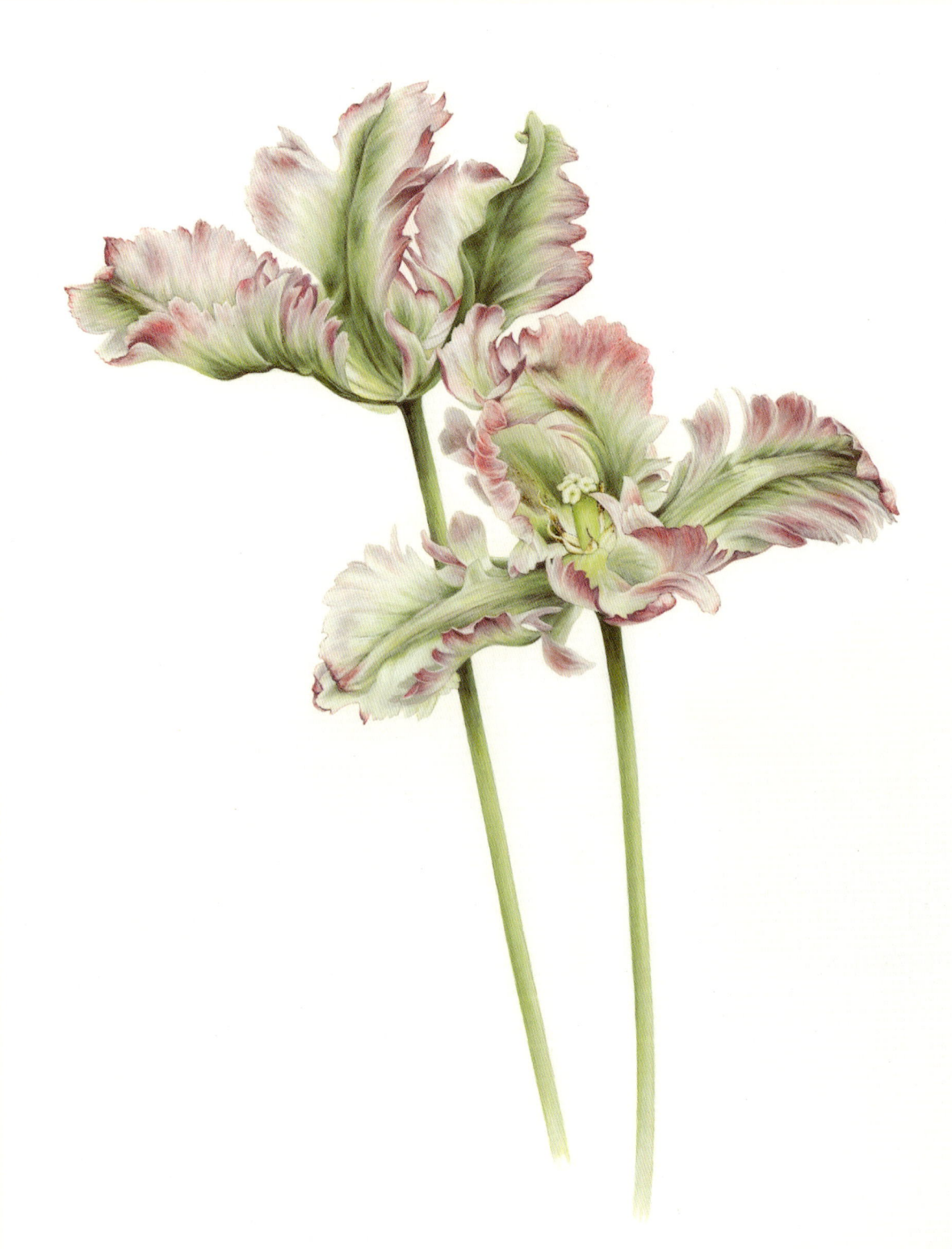

Green Wave Parrot Tulip *Tulipa* 'Green Wave' Oil on paper 19 × 15 ½ inches [48.26 × 38.75 cm] © Ingrid Finnan

PART 3

Specialized Techniques and Composition

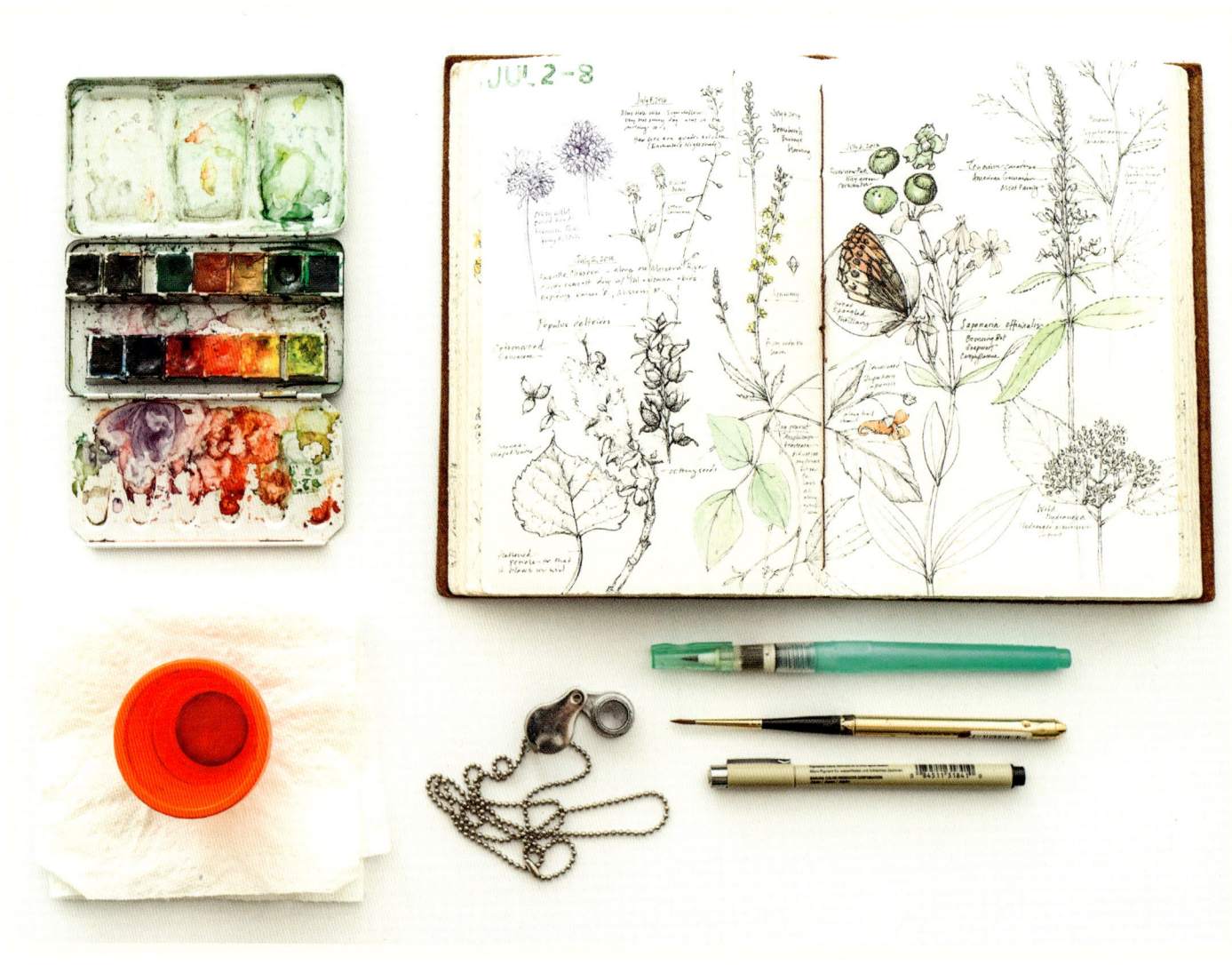

MATERIALS: (clockwise from top left): Portable watercolor set; handmade journal; water brush; portable paintbrush; pen; 10X hand lens; paper towel; portable cup for water.

Practicing sketching when you are not in your studio helps maintain strong drawing and observation skills. Field sketchbooks can serve as a starting point for more finished pieces later, and they can be considered valid works of art in their own right. For an annual perpetual journal like the one featured in this tutorial, use a sketchbook that lies flat, includes paper appropriate to the medium, and contains at least 52 page spreads.

Field Sketchbook and Journal

TUTOR: LAURA CALL GASTINGER

To set up a journal, begin by writing the date of the week of your first sketches in the top left corner. Continue through the journal, inscribing each spread with the dates of every week in the year. Draw within the spread of the current week. When you are starting a new entry, include information such as the date, location, and weather.

Making the first entry can be intimidating, but an interesting plant that presents itself will always lead to another discovery or question, which will help inspire you. With a pen, begin by lightly sketching the overall shape of the plant.

As your confidence in the layout increases, continue to add darker defined lines and more detail as necessary. Remember, this is a personal discovery for you—and every artist—and there is no right or wrong way to observe plants.

Finally, add text from field guides to plants. If you don't know the name of the plant you are drawing, write down observations that include the number and color of the petals, the leaf arrangement on the stem, what the leaf looks like, and the plant's height. This is also a good place to write questions or dissect small details of the plant.

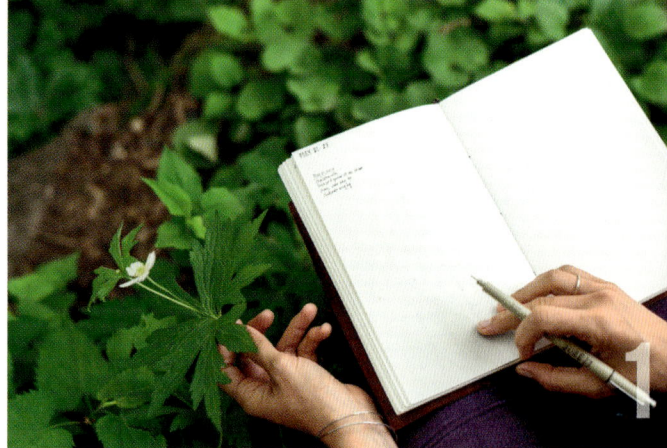

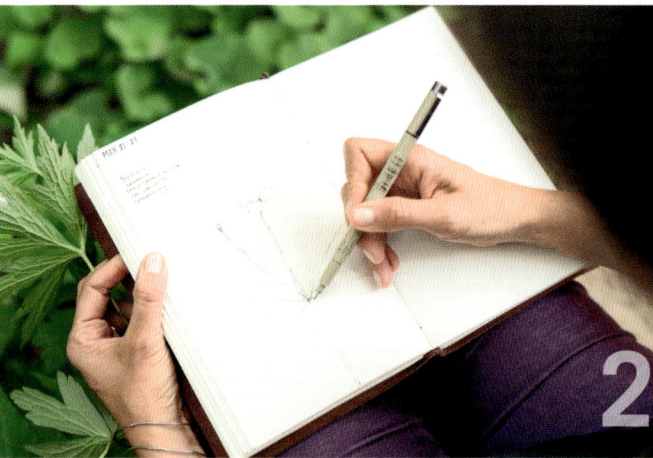

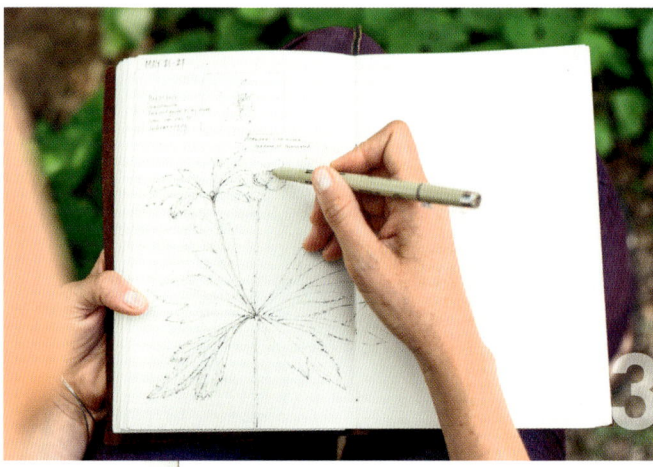

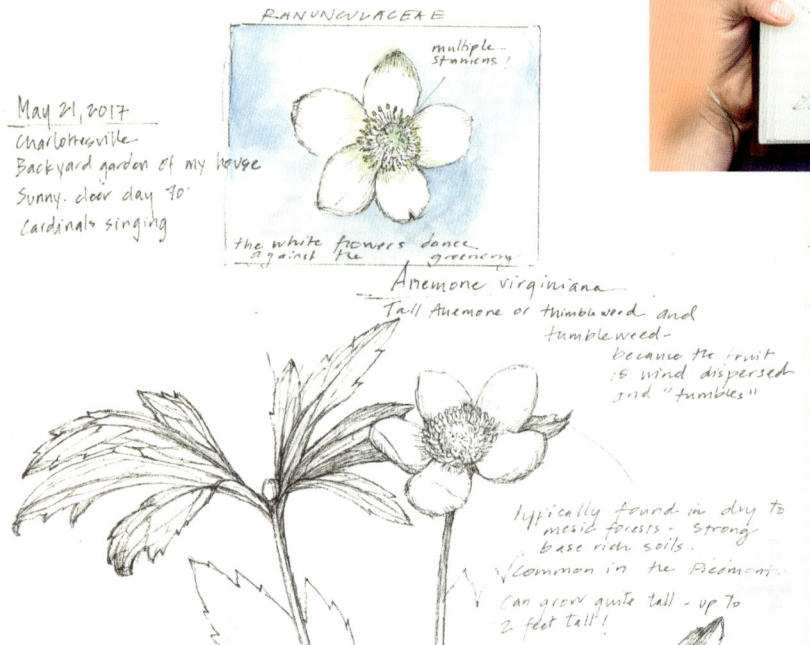

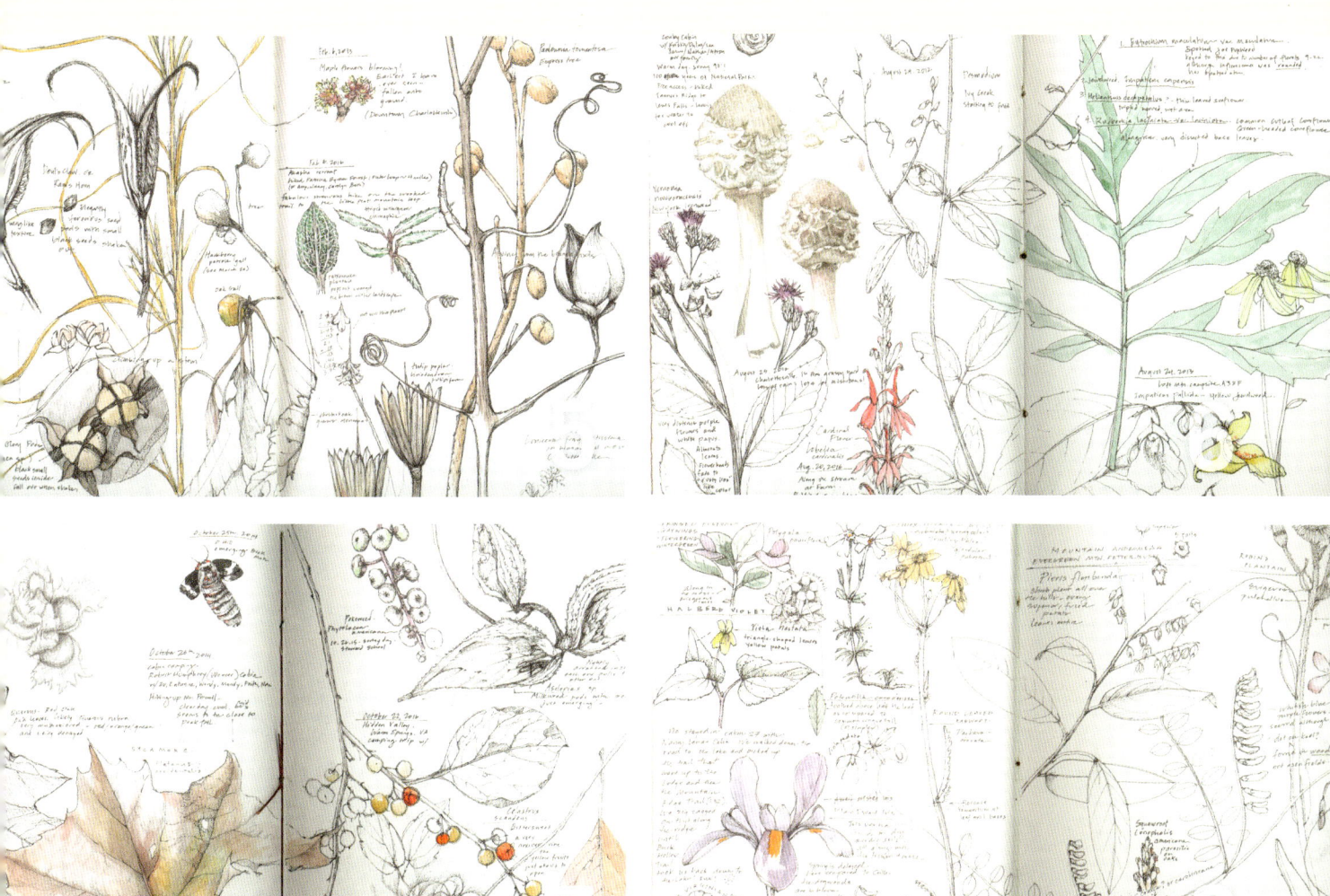

Another approach is to surround a detailed drawing with a circle or rectangle if it is disappearing into other drawings, as shown on the lower left of this page spread. This can also bring attention to a particular aspect of the plant that you have observed. Keep in mind that not every detail needs to be completed in a journal page. Use color and detailed rendering such as shading and stippling as needed but use it sparingly.

Here are examples of completed journal pages that were drawn over several years, with entries from 2012, 2013, and 2016 on this spread.

When you are composing a journal page, feel free to have your drawings cross the gutter in the middle of the page spread. Plants in the ground can come up from the bottom of the page, branches can come in from the sides, vines can climb down from the top of the page, and stand-alone specimens can float in the middle (sometimes in a box or rectangle).

During a trip where you are seeing new plants and you have time to draw them, combine your discoveries on a full page spread at the end of the journal, where there may be some undated blank pages. A perpetual journal should hold your attention, and your desire, to come back year after year. Seasonal patterns will become apparent, as will the development of your observational and documenting skills.

COMBINING GRAPHITE AND WATERCOLOR FOR VISUAL SEPARATIONS

Intrigued by the progression of flowering in a patch of *Chelone*, Gillian Harris gave some thought to how best to portray it. To capture the transition in color of the developing flowers, the central inflorescence is portrayed in watercolor. By adding graphite passages, information could be conveyed that didn't require color, while also emphasizing the featured watercolor elements. The graphite passages show how the structure of the inflorescences varies from plant to plant, especially as they pass from bud to flower (left) and from flower to fruit (right). The satisfying subtlety of graphite allowed portions to fade in and out to accentuate them or simply suggest them, balancing the composition and lending it depth. Harris enjoyed exploring the progression from line drawing to full-color rendering. Both graphite and watercolor passages include the bumblebees and spiders that are an essential part of the plant's story. The materials Harris used were watercolors, high-quality graphite pencils for continuous tone, and graphite in holders for line and detail.

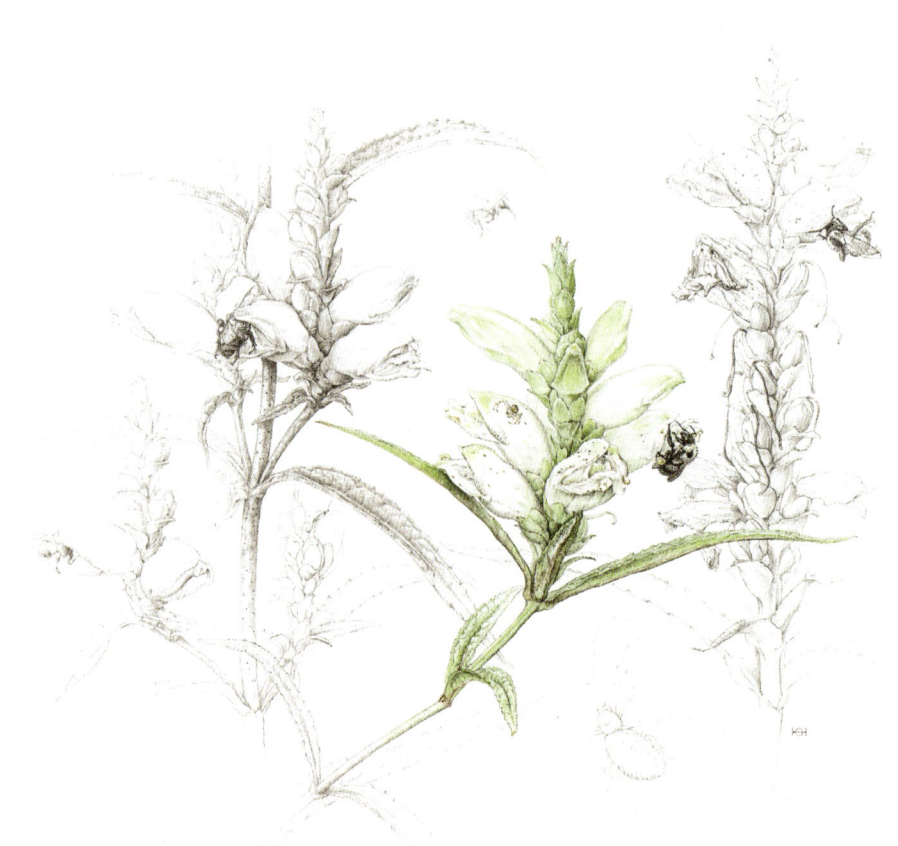

Chelone glabra
Watercolor and graphite on paper
13 × 12 inches [32.5 × 30 cm]
© Gillian Harris
HOURS TO COMPLETE: 30

The graphite techniques that work on paper also work wonderfully on vellum, with additional advantages. Lifting and corrections can be easier to do on vellum than on paper, and graphite can be moved around with a damp brush. Vellum surfaces can create interesting textures, and the various tonal values and patterns found in vellum can enhance composition.

Graphite and Watercolor on Vellum

TUTOR: DEBORAH B. SHAW

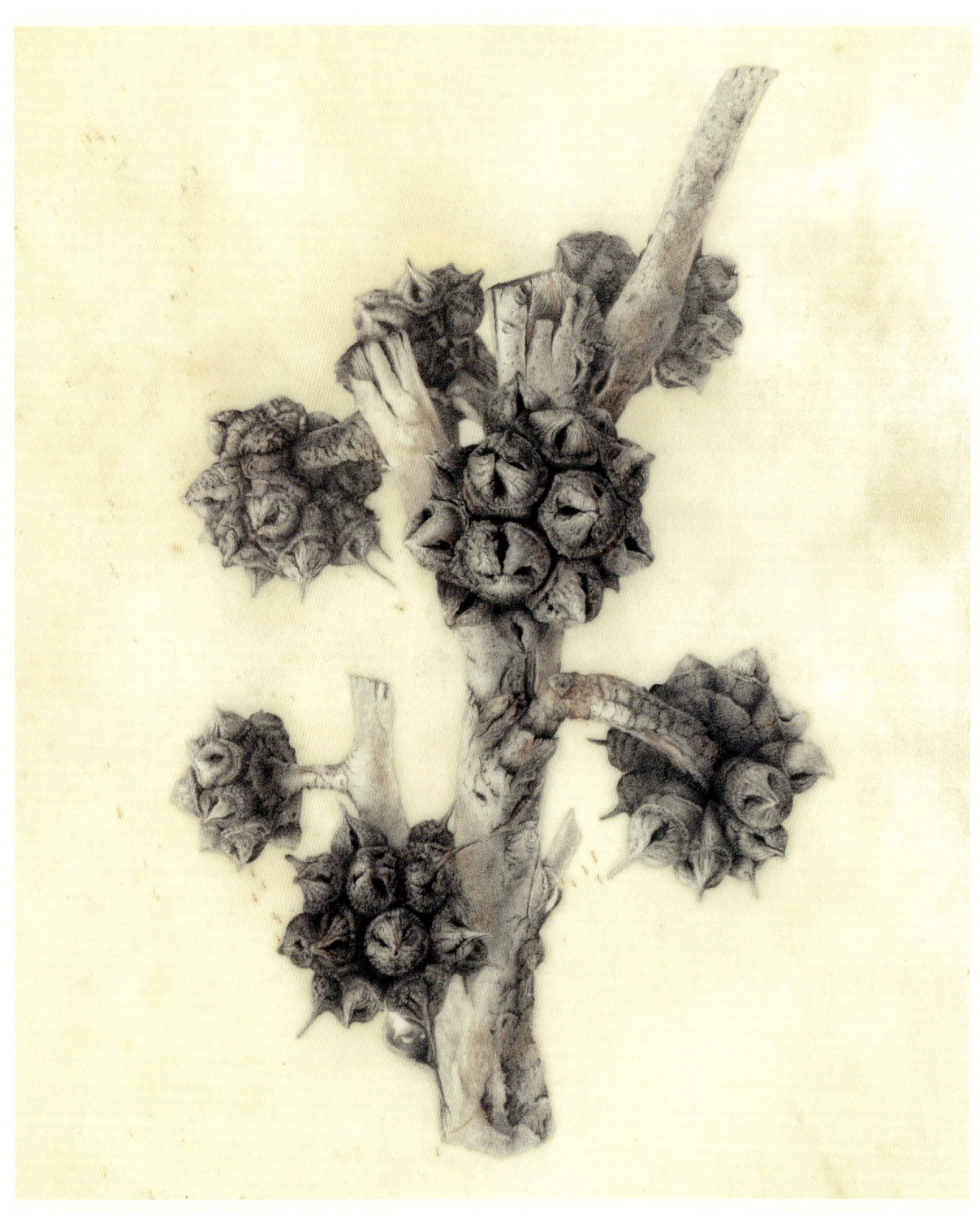

Bushy Yates Fruit *Eucalyptus lehmannii* Graphite and watercolor on vellum 13 × 8 inches [32.5 × 20 cm]
© Deborah B. Shaw HOURS TO COMPLETE: 13 (47 FOR THE FULL DRAWING)

MATERIALS: Sandpaper; handheld pencil sharpener; dry cleaning pad; scrap piece of vellum; wall putty; watercolor brush (no. 000); retractable erasers; graphite pencils; incising stylus.

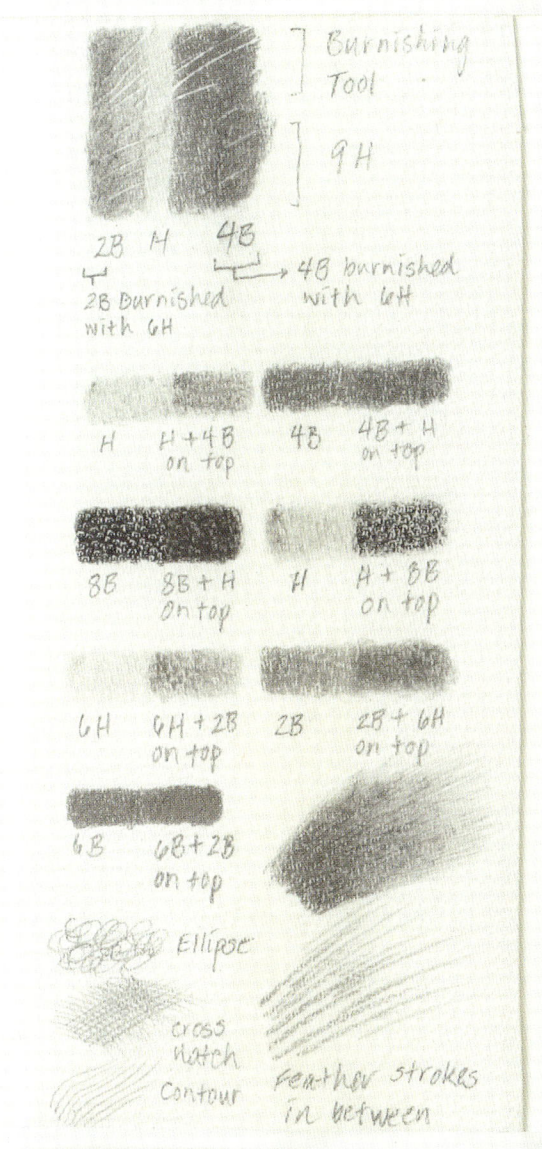

Graphite can be sharpened in different ways to provide a range of effects. Long, sharp points can be created by using knives or sanding blocks as sharpeners. For a chisel point, simply snap off the end, or rub one side of the lead on sandpaper. The flat side of a chisel point creates smooth tones, while the sharp side creates clean lines.

This sampler shows various graphite techniques on a highly textured piece of vellum.

- Incising tools, burnishing tools, and a 9H pencil can incise vellum. Create lines, veins, and texture patterns with an incising tool, then go over the marks, which may seem invisible, with layers of pencil; the lines, veins, and texture patterns will be revealed as white lines, because the graphite layers will not have penetrated them.

- Layer soft pencils first on vellum, then use harder pencils over the top to create a rich black. A harder pencil acts as a burnisher, filling in all the tiny gaps on the surface of paper or vellum.

- Using a hard pencil first keeps subsequent layers of softer graphite from getting as dark as they normally would. This is a great technique for protecting reflected-light areas from getting too dark.

- A few ways graphite can be applied (at bottom; greatly enlarged here for effect): small ellipses to create even tones; crosshatching; contour lines; and feathering.

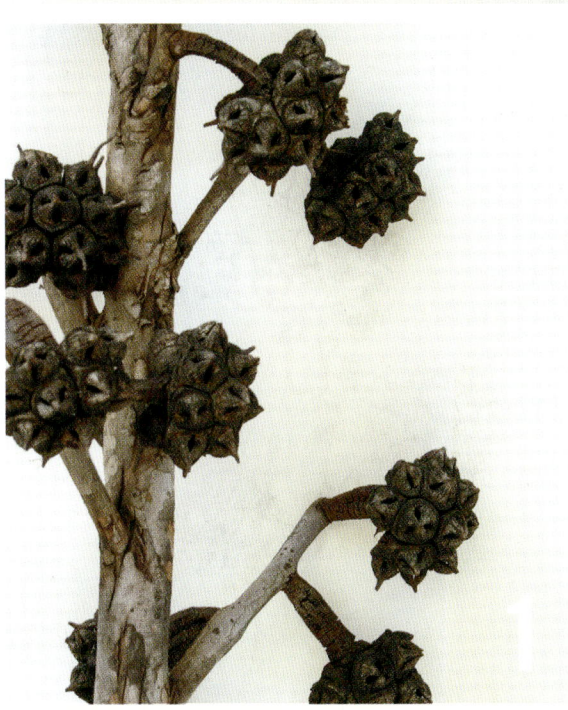

This tutorial will focus on a small part of a larger graphite drawing of this branch with fruits of *Eucalyptus lehmannii*. Before transferring a drawing, scrub the vellum with a dry cleaning pad to remove any oils. Do not use the cleaning pad after you have drawn on the vellum—it will erase the drawing. Irregular surfaces on the vellum can be sanded smooth with white extra-fine sandpaper (use P400 or finer).

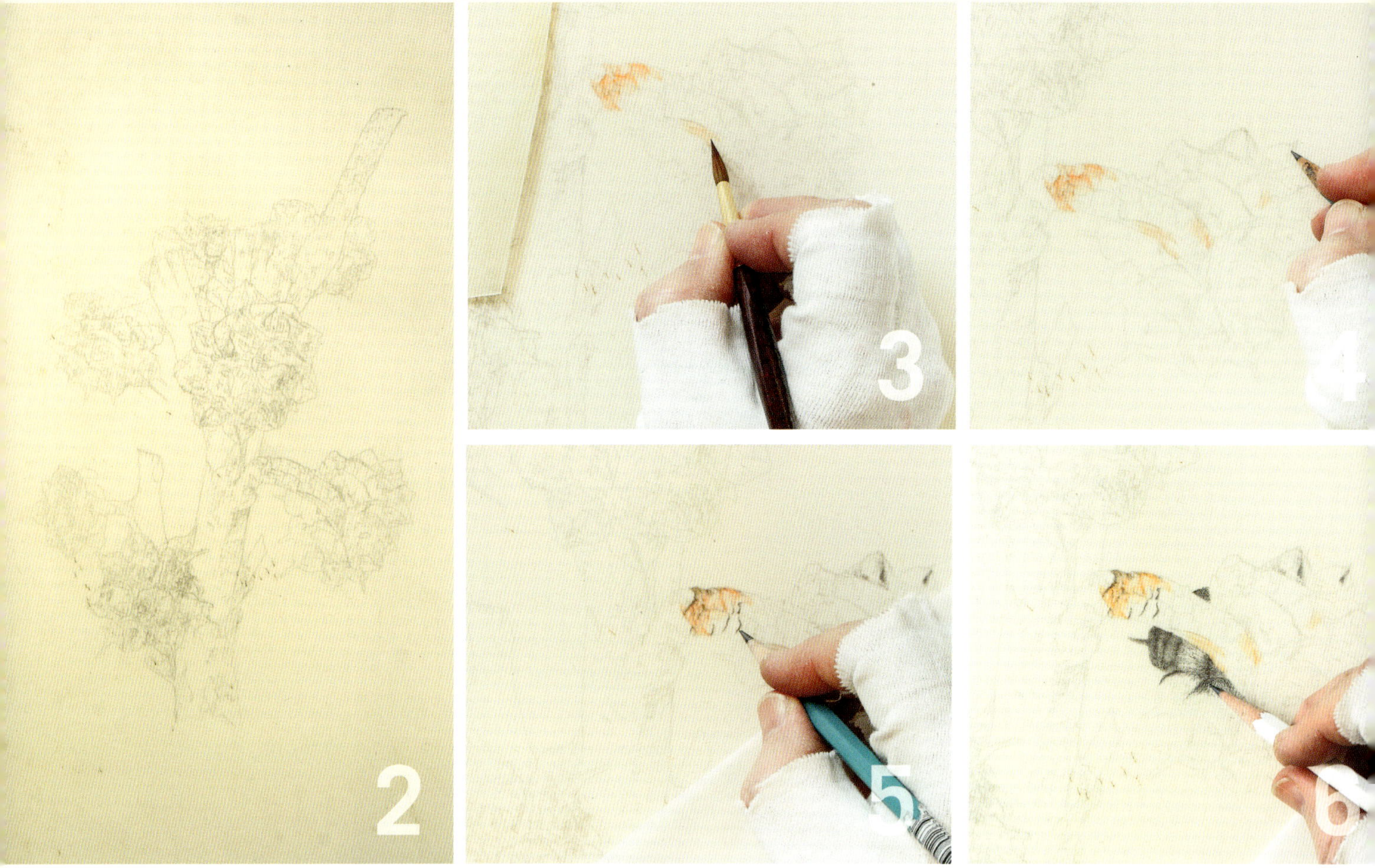

The entire drawing of the branch in graphite on the vellum, after it was transferred with tracing paper. Drawings can be transferred to vellum using graphite transfer techniques, or they can be drawn directly on the vellum. Tap the transferred graphite lines with a kneaded eraser or wall putty to remove excess graphite.

Although using only graphite on vellum can result in magnificent artwork, watercolor can be added underneath or on top of the graphite. Watercolor can be used underneath graphite to create interesting textures and effects. Experiment first on a scrap piece of vellum, using only a small amount of liquid. Let dry before applying graphite.

Start applying graphite to map out the subject. Very hard graphite can be applied next to highlight areas or areas of reflected light. This will preserve the reflected light and prevent softer pencils from darkening the area too much later. A 6H is being used here.

A few dark shadows in this subject were made using a 4B pencil, establishing the range of tonal values for the drawing. This fruit is toward the back, so the darkest shadows will stay in the 4B to 6B range. The shadows of fruits in the rest of the drawing in the front will be darker, in the 8B to 9B range.

Work back and forth between soft and hard pencils to start building form. Transitions between tonal values or interesting effects can be created by feathering strokes, leaving gaps between strokes that can be filled in using leads with differing degrees of hardness.

An incising tool is used to create veins, lines, ridges, and textures. Indenting the vellum with the tool retains the vellum background; and the indentations create lighter lines when soft pencil is laid over them. Here, the ridge around the funnel-shaped cap is being incised to keep it crisp and light in value.

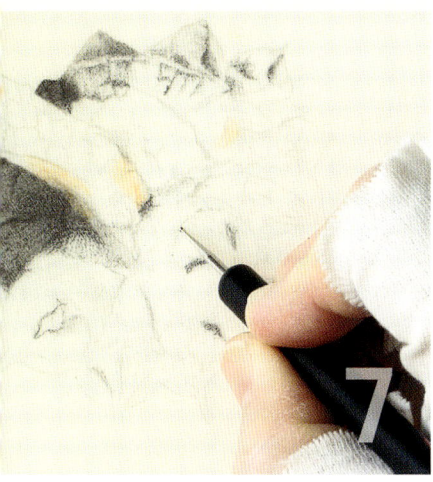
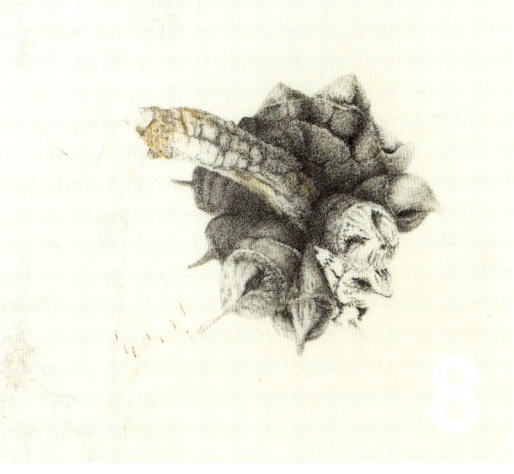
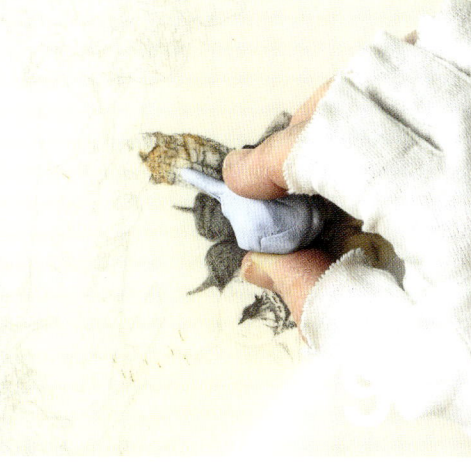

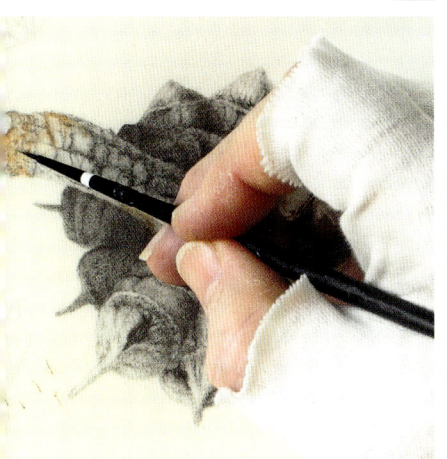
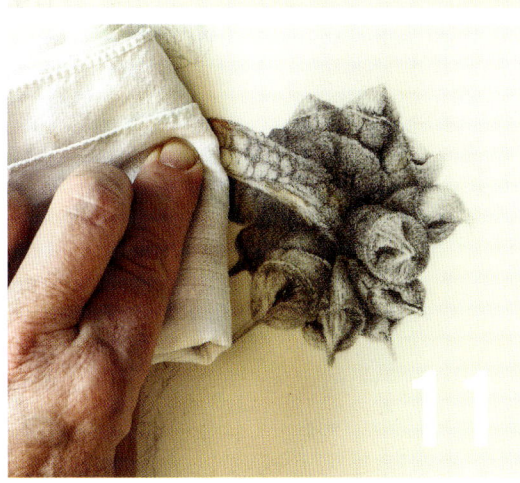
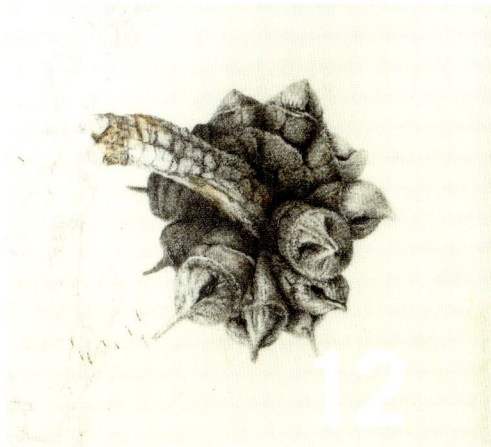

Continue to build form through tonal values. It's best to save burnishing and smoothing with the harder pencils until the last stages. Once an area is burnished, it is much more difficult to make changes by lifting and erasing, or trying to darken areas by adding more graphite.

Erasers and wall putty can be used to erase errors, but they can also be used as drawing tools in and of themselves. Wall putty can be shaped and erasers can be trimmed to lift graphite and create texture.

Use a damp brush to lift areas of graphite or paint, but do not use a lot of water. Dampen the area gently, and let the water soften the graphite or paint.

Once the water has softened the graphite or paint, blot the area with a clean, white cloth. Be careful not to scrub or move the cloth around—the graphite will smear. For smaller areas, use a small piece of paper or a cotton swab. Continue to apply sharply pointed 6B lead to the areas of darkest value.

Some tiny details or edges may need cleaning up. Use a damp brush to gently push the edge of the graphite where it should go. Use this technique to clean up any edges that would be too difficult (or dangerous) to clean up with an eraser.

Milk, eggs, and gum arabic are the binders in these versatile media: casein, egg tempera, and gouache. These three alternative and historic water-based media have some commonalities with transparent watercolor, allowing for the creation of the fine detail necessary for botanical art. They also possess individual unique qualities that make them well worth taking the time to explore.

Egg Tempera, Gouache, and Casein: A Comparison

TUTOR: KELLY RADDING

Egg Tempera

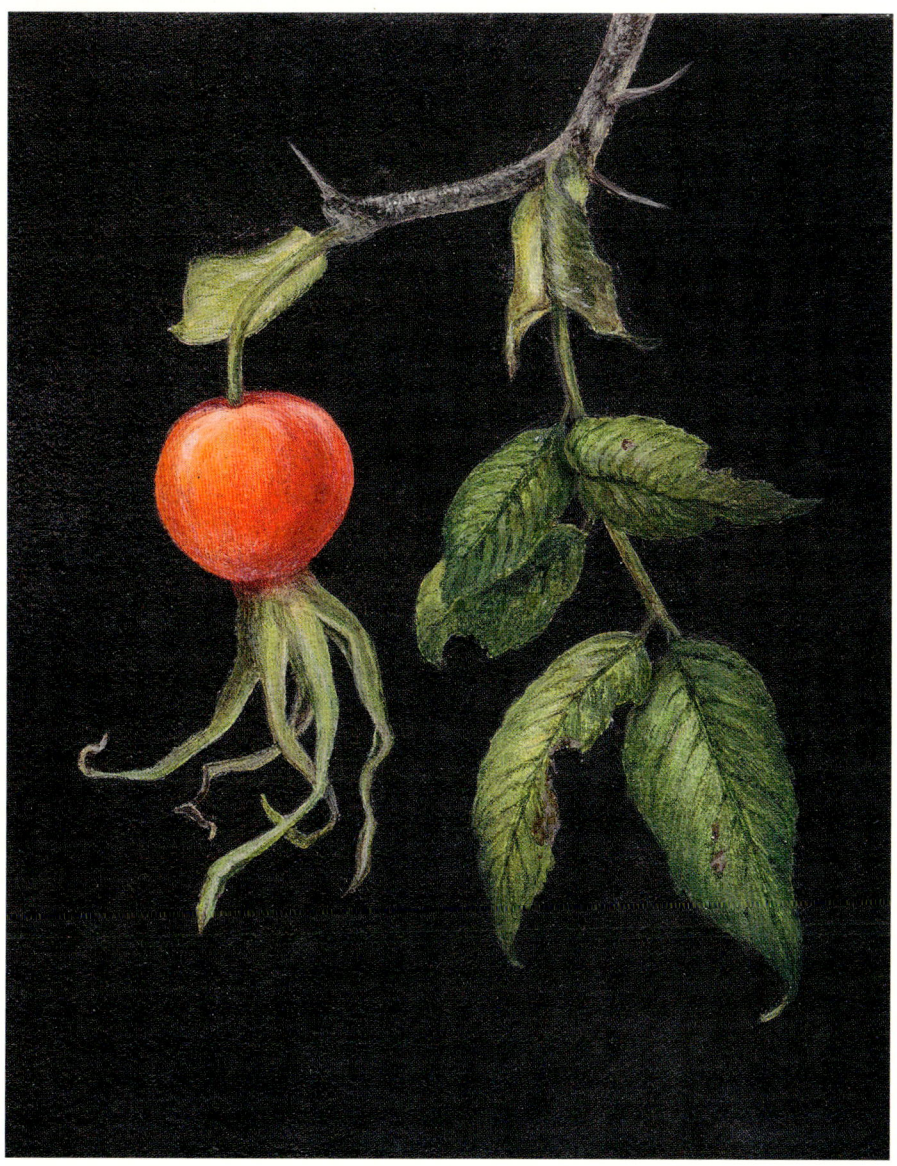

Rose Hip 1 Egg tempera on gessoed panel 5 × 3 inches [12.5 × 7.5 cm]
© Kelly Radding HOURS TO COMPLETE: 22

MATERIALS: Palette knives; eye dropper; jar with egg emulsion; egg; sponge; jars of
pigment; water in eye dropper bottle; container; spray bottle; paper towel; liquid frisket;
glass palette; plate; toothpicks; Kolinsky brushes (nos. 00, 2, and 0); synthetic brush
(no. 3); retractable eraser, white-plastic eraser.

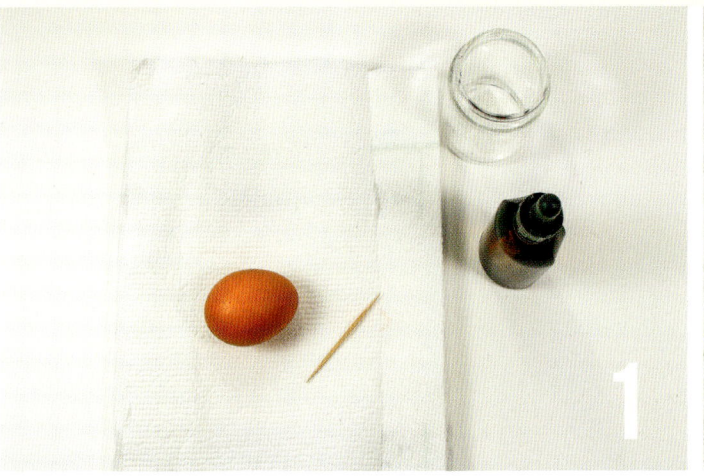

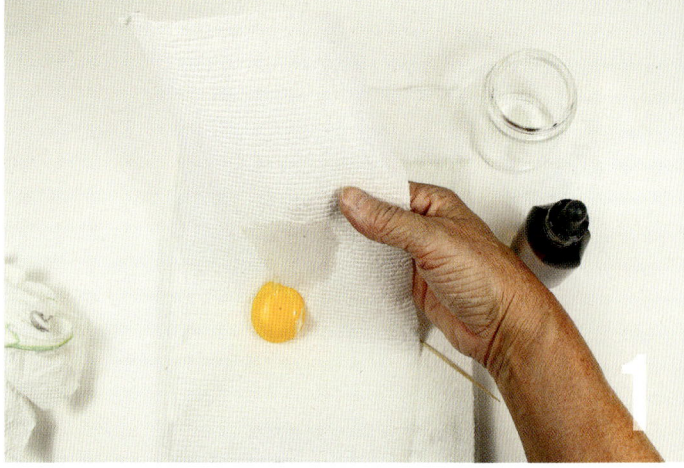

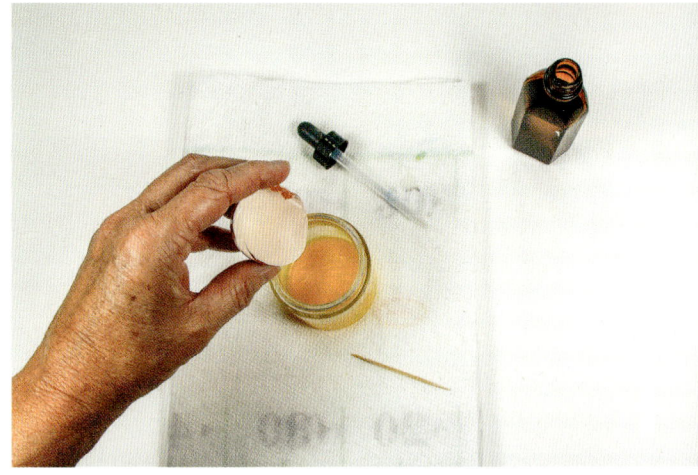

Made with an egg yolk as binder, egg tempera has been used as a medium for artists for hundreds of years, and is very durable. It does not yellow over time, and requires no toxic solvents. Clean-up can be accomplished with soap and water. Applied thinly in semi-opaque or transparent layers, egg tempera dries very quickly.

Egg tempera requires a rigid support, or substrate, because it becomes brittle as it ages and can crack on a flexible support. Typical supports are 300-pound [640 gsm] hot-pressed watercolor paper, heavy watercolor paper, illustration board, and mounted vellum.

Prepare the egg emulsion by separating the egg (save one of the shell halves), discarding the egg white and placing the egg yolk on a paper towel to clean off the whites. Lift up the paper towel with the yolk sac, hold it over a container, and use a toothpick to puncture the sac and release the yolk into a container. Discard the yolk sac. Add a one-to-one ratio of distilled water, using the reserved egg-shell half to estimate how much distilled water would equal the volume of the yolk. Mix well until the egg and water are emulsified. Add a few drops of vinegar to act as a preservative.

Using an approximately one-to-one ratio, mix the egg emulsion with pigment on a glass palette or in a separate jar. You'll know that the paint is tempered well when a dried layer curls up when scraped with a blade. If the paint cracks, there was not enough egg emulsion. If the dried paint is very shiny, then there was too much egg emulsion. If you get either of these results, you will have to start over.

After transferring the drawing, use a paper mask, paper frisket, or liquid frisket to keep color off the subject, then use a sponge to layer colors to create a luminous background. The combination of frisket and sponging is a quicker way to cover larger areas of color. If desired, use a paint brush and a hatching technique to refine the final layers.

Remove the frisket by rubbing it off with your fingers or a soft cloth. Clean the edges with a razor blade. Apply the beginning layers of egg tempera loosely. Refine the consecutive layers as the painting progresses using hatching and stippling to build up color. The more thin layers of transparent color you apply, the more luminous the painting will be. Shift from a larger brush to a smaller brush as the painting progresses.

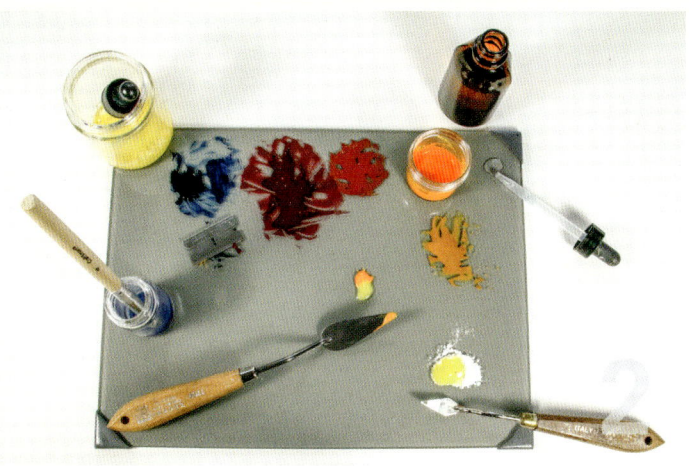

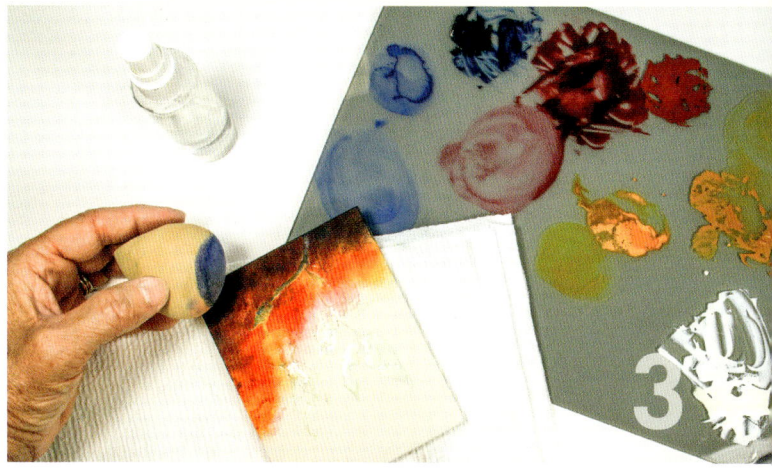

A thin layer of color applied semi-transparently with scrubbing strokes is called scumbling. White paint or white paint tinted with a little color applied by scumbling enhances the paint's luminosity. Scumbling of white or white lightly tinted will allow light to bounce back through consecutive transparent layers.

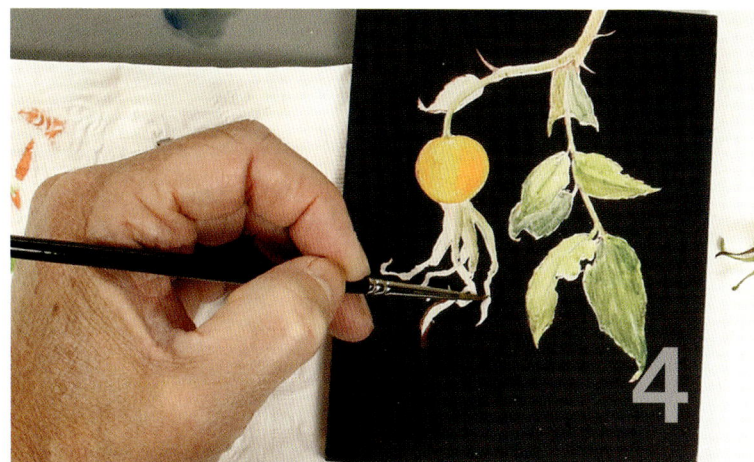

A glaze is a very thin, transparent layer of paint diluted with water laid over the top of other colors. It can be used to shift colors to either warm or cool. Egg tempera dries quickly, so many glaze layers can be applied in one session. However, if layers begin to lift, allow several hours for the paint to cure before adding more layers.

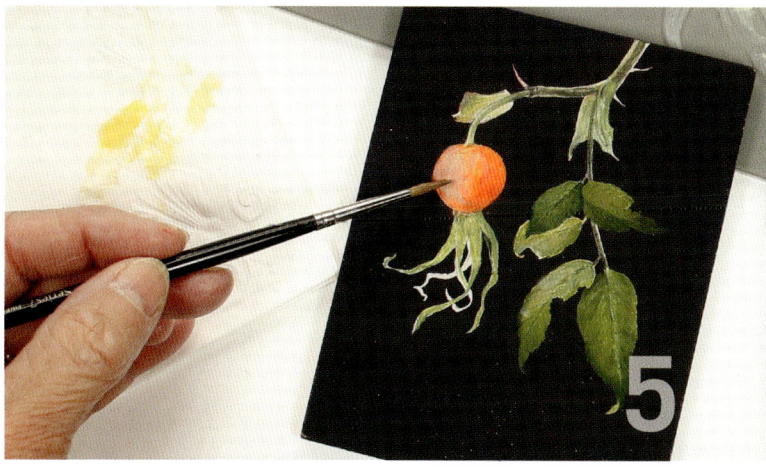

Egg tempera dries and fully cures in about six months to a soft eggshell finish. After six months, buff the painting with a soft cloth to enhance its characteristic eggshell finish. Once cured, egg tempera is impervious to moisture, and the finished painting can be framed without glass. It can also be varnished, like an oil painting, with a resin-based varnish such as damar varnish, or mineral-spirit acrylic varnish, to create a more glossy finish.

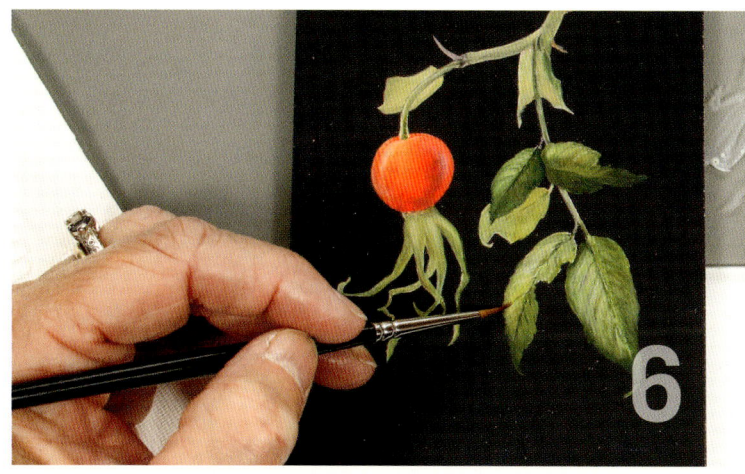

Gouache

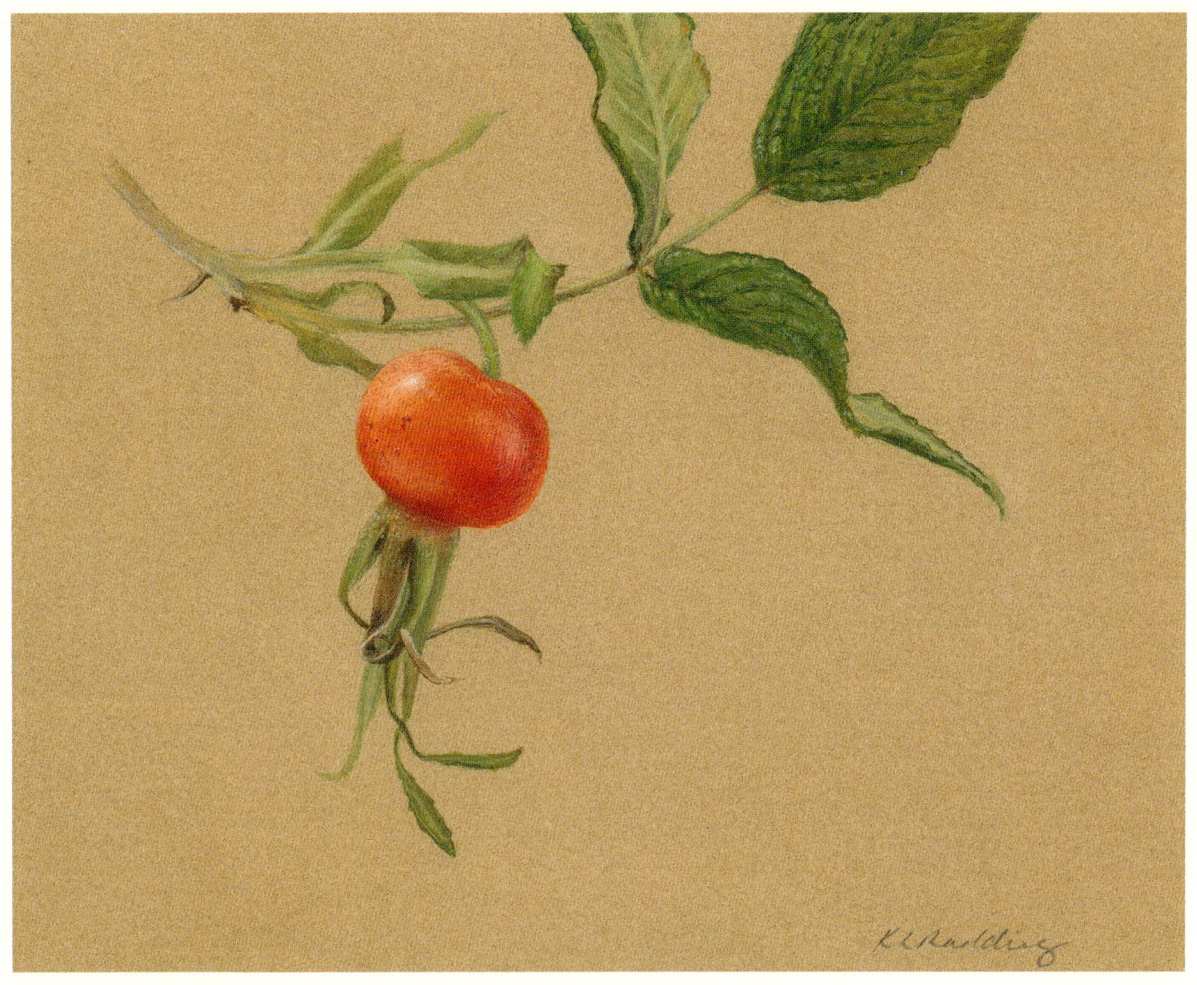

Rose Hip 2 Gouache on paper 4 × 5 inches [10 × 12.5 cm] © Kelly Radding

HOURS TO COMPLETE: 22

MATERIALS: White-plastic eraser; lead holder with lead; retractable eraser; Kolinsky brushes (nos. 000, 00, 0, 1, and 2); sharpener; graphite transfer paper; tube gouache; palette; tinted paper.

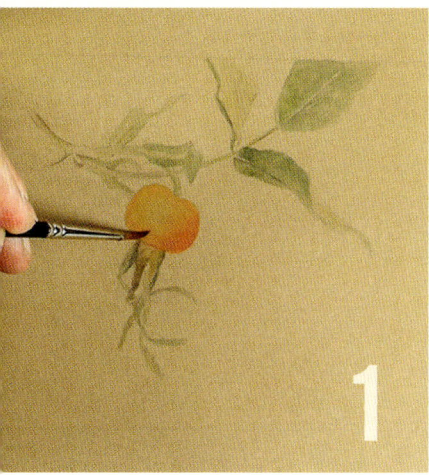 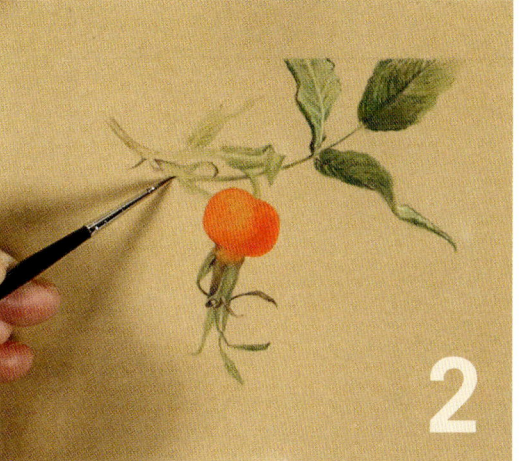 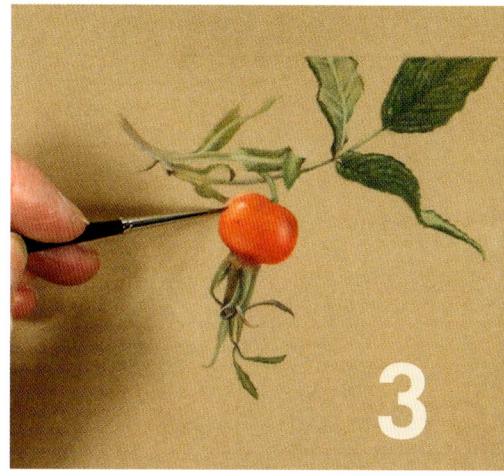

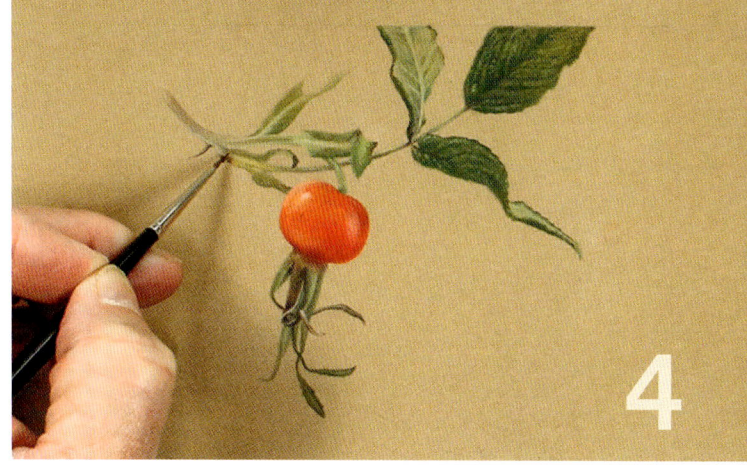

Gouache is a beautiful strong medium that dries to a uniform matte finish. Gouache colors are lightened by adding white pigments; they are not lightened by dilution to show more of the white paper, as is done with transparent watercolors. Colors can be watered down and used wet-on-wet like watercolor. However, because of the greater concentration of pigment and white filler in gouache, it will not flow or bloom like watercolor. Gouache can be used on any watercolor support. Hot-pressed surfaces are best for painting very fine detail in gouache. It is inherently an opaque medium, so it can be used on colored papers, boards, and vellums.

Gouache has a higher ratio of pigment to binder than watercolor, creating a continuous thick paint film. For this reason gouache pigment particles are not ground as fine as watercolor pigments, creating a paint with more tinting strength. Lighter colors tend to dry darker and dark colors tend to dry lighter. Gouache paintings need to be framed under glass for protection—like watercolor, their surface is not impermeable and can be damaged by moisture.

Gouache, when used in an undiluted mixture, can cover all the paint layers already on the painting, so it is a more direct method of painting—previous layers are unseen—unlike painting with transparent watercolors. A gouache painting can be built from light to dark, as in watercolor, or from dark to light by using white to lighten the color and make it more opaque. Start by diluting the paint with water and paint loose washes to establish form.

Begin by refining the painting using a drybrush technique. Because gouache can be reconstituted, consecutive layers require a ratio of less water to pigment to avoid picking up color from previous layers.

To paint light over dark, add white when mixing paint on the palette. Depending on the amount of white and water dilution, you can either fully cover the layers underneath or create an effect of luminosity, because the light will bounce down to the lighter layers and reflect back through a more semi-transparent layer. You can fix mistakes by painting tinted white layers over the previous layers.

Continue building up layers, alternating layers with and without white paint. As you build layers, use a dryer technique with smaller brushes for hatching and stippling techniques. To shift areas to warmer or cooler colors, glaze them with transparent colors. To get warmer highlights, add yellow ochre or another warm yellow.

Casein

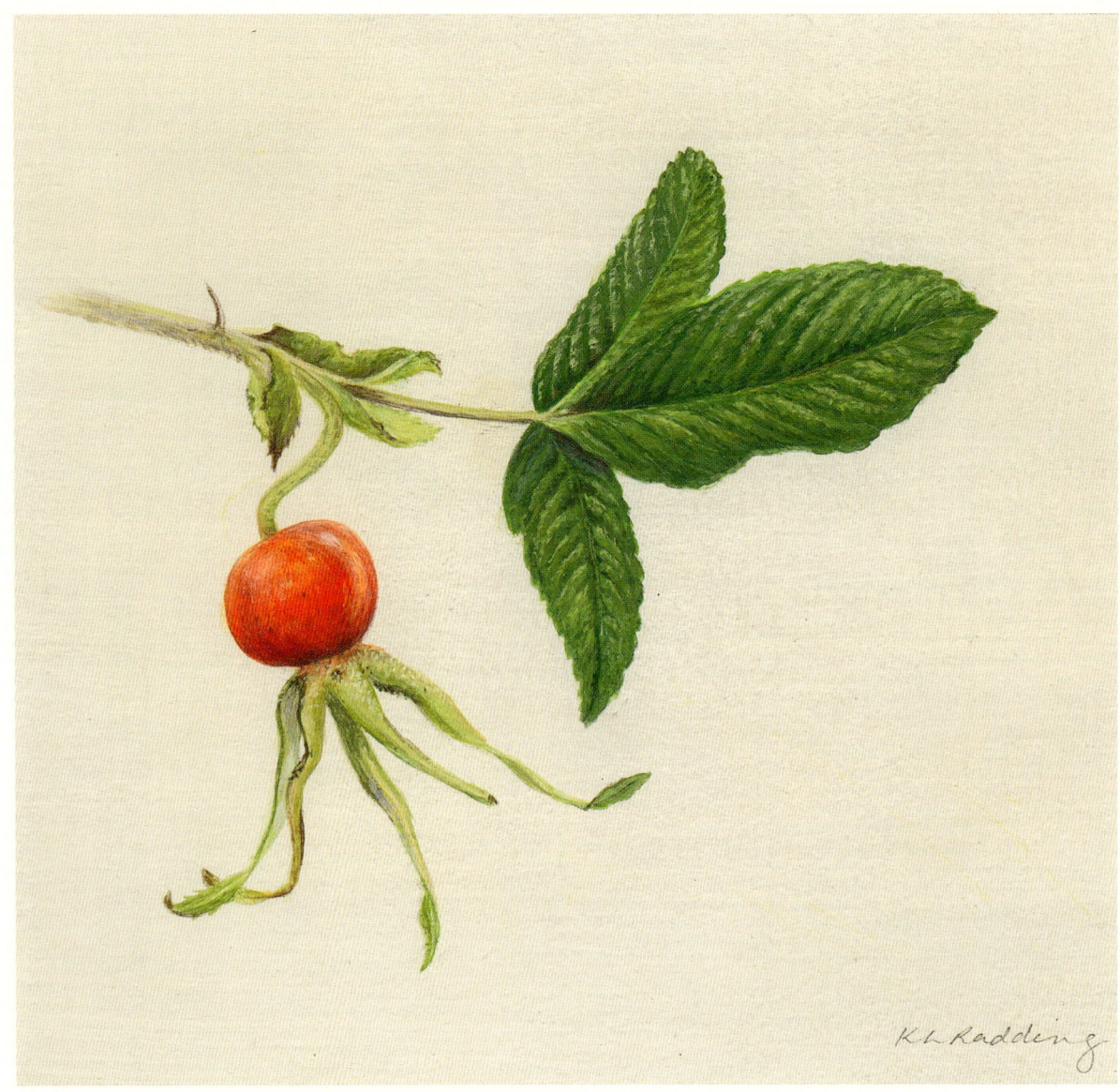

Rose Hip 3 Casein on prepared illustration board 4 × 5 inches [10 × 12.5 cm] © Kelly Radding

HOURS TO COMPLETE: 22

MATERIALS: Illustration board; white-plastic eraser; retractable eraser; water container; spray bottle; plastic palette; graphite transfer paper; waxed-paper palette; porcelain palette; Kolinsky brushes (nos. 0 and 00); synthetic brush (no. 2); synthetic ½-inch [1.25 cm] flat brush; casein paints in tubes; eyedropper; palette knife; paper towel.

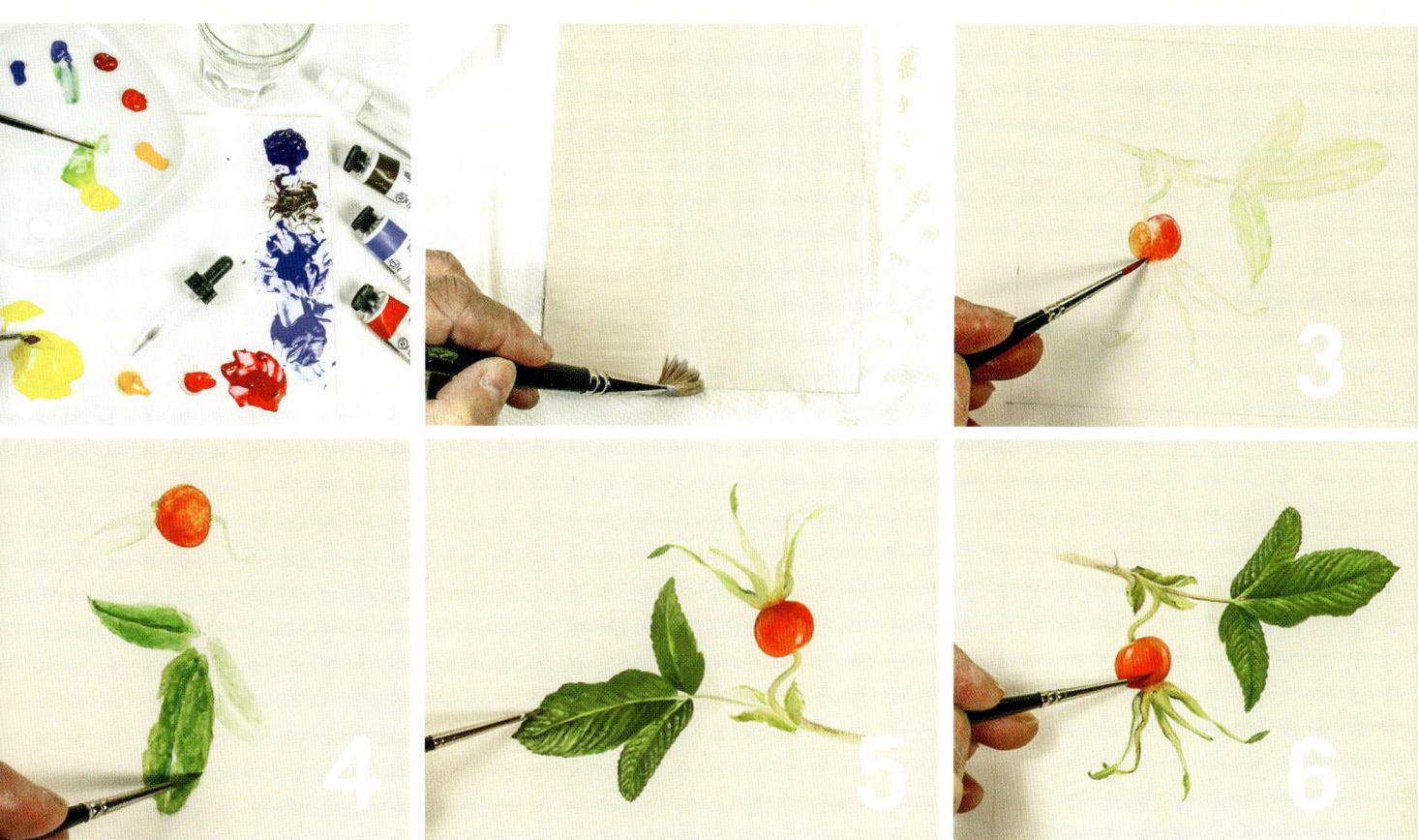

Casein is a phosphoprotein found in milk, long used as an adhesive and binder. Casein paint approaches the effects of oil paints, but it dries more quickly and with a matte finish. Casein becomes more brittle as it cures, so it requires a stiff support. Since it is opaque it can be used on colored backgrounds.

Casein is a versatile medium that responds to many different techniques. Casein paintings on panels can be buffed to an eggshell finish and left unframed. However, any painting on paper should be framed under glass.

Casein straight from the tube has a thick consistency. Prep casein for painting by using an eyedropper to add water to the paint and mixing it with a palette knife until its consistency is like thick cream. Casein can also be used straight from the tube diluted with water while you work. Mist casein to keep it moist; once it's dry, discard it. Casein can be cleaned up with soap and water.

Casein can be used to create a tinted background by adding a small amount of color to white casein. Dilute the mixture with water to a very thin consistency and use a large brush to cover the board. Let this layer cure for several days before beginning the painting.

Thin casein with water to apply beginning layers working from light to dark. Using a larger brush, begin to establish form. Let each layer dry and cure for at least 24 hours before adding more layers. Casein changes value as it dries, generally lightening.

Casein can be used in a way similar to oils by laying in colors and using a soft brush to blend them together. Because it dries fast you will need to work quickly. You can also dampen your brush if the colors are still semi-dry to blend a little.

Using less diluted color, begin using drier techniques such as hatching and stippling to continue building up form. Use white casein and casein pigments tinted with white to work lighter areas over darker ones and to fix mistakes. Continue layering with paint to build up the dark colors.

Because casein cures over time, a glazing technique for the final layers creates beautiful effects such as warming and cooling specific areas in the painting. Dilute the pigment with water, and use a larger brush to cover the intended area. Use smaller brushes with a drybrush technique to create finer details.

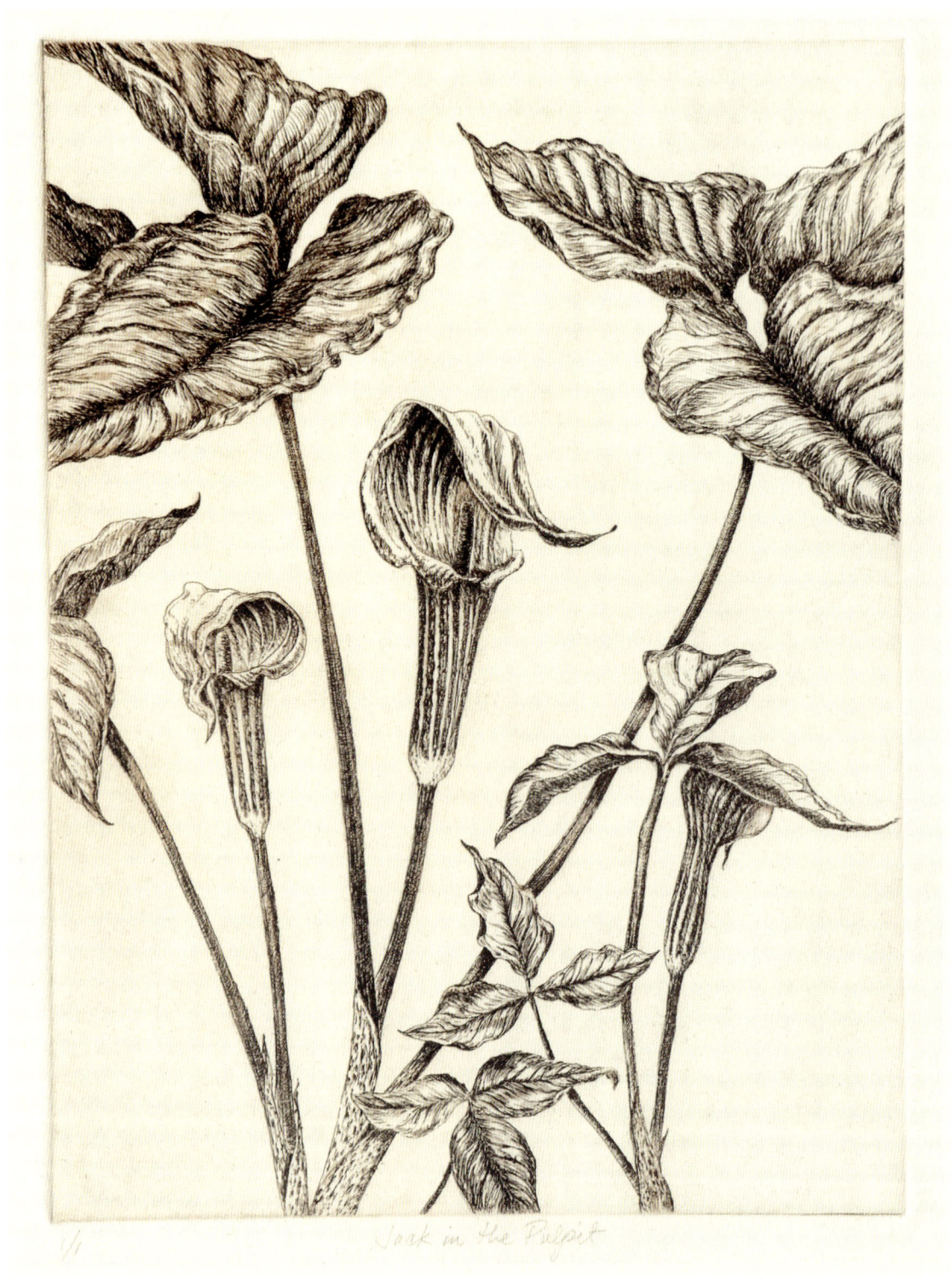

1/1 Jack in the Pulpit

Jack-in-the-Pulpit *Arisaema triphyllum* Etching 12 × 9 inches [30 × 22.5 cm] © Carol Till

HOURS TO COMPLETE: 54

MATERIALS: Etching paper; ink spatula; rag board tabs; phonebook pages (newsprint can be substituted for phonebook pages); tarlatan; polyethylene tray; nitrile gloves; nitric acid; enamel spraypaint; liquid hard ground; oil-based etching ink; soft brush; zinc etching plate; etching needle; scraper; burnisher; dot roulette; red ballpoint pen; metal file; 800-grit wet/dry sandpaper.

Etching is a time-honored technique for producing botanical illustrations. A metal plate is etched with an artist's design with the use of a resist (a coating) and a bath of acid, which cuts lines or textures into the metal. Those indentations hold ink, which is spread on the plate, pushed into the indentations and lifted off other areas. Then the plate is place through a press, pushing the plate and paper together, transferring ink to the paper.

Etching Techniques

TUTOR: CAROL TILL

First, make a graphite drawing of your subject. The subject here is *Arisaema triphyllum* (Jack-in-the-pulpit). Because the etching plate will print in reverse, make your drawing on tracing paper—it can then be turned over to transfer the drawing to the plate. Make a value study on a second sheet of paper to guide in creating tones on the plate.

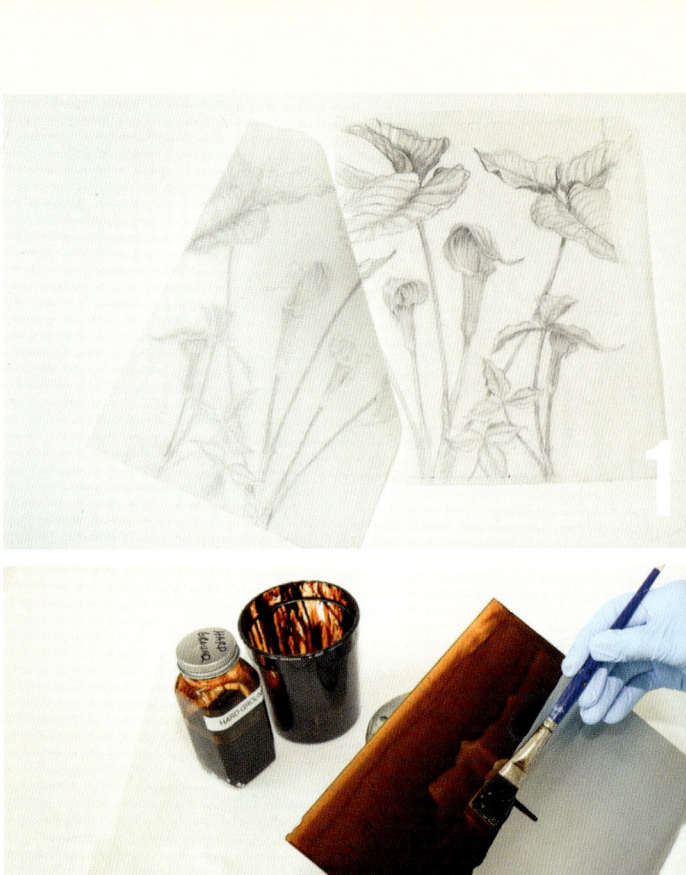

To prepare the etching plate for a line etch, brush a liquid hard ground onto the zinc plate with a wide, soft brush. Cover the entire surface of the plate evenly. Be sure to wear gloves for this step to protect your skin. This acid-resistant ground dries to a soft waxy surface that can be easily drawn through with a sharp point to expose the metal below. Let the ground dry. Handle the plate carefully after it has dried, because it is easily scratched.

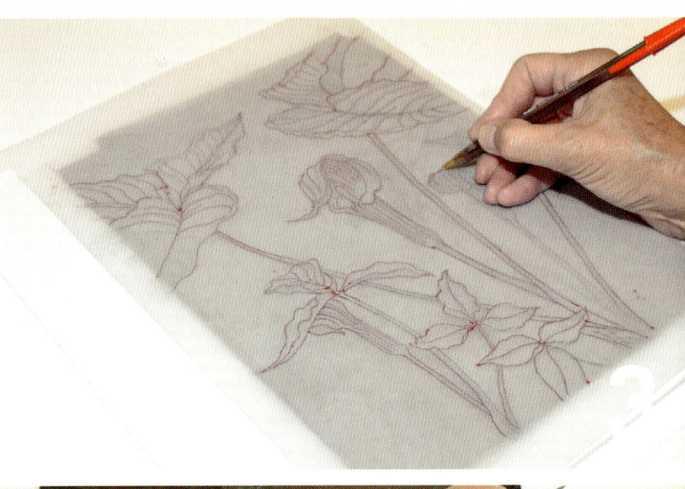

Transfer the drawing to the coated plate, leaving a reverse image on the plate. Place a sheet of carbon paper on the coated plate, place the drawing on the carbon paper, then place a sheet of tracing paper over the drawing. Use a colored ballpoint pen to carefully trace the contour lines of the drawing. Apply light pressure; the pen's rounded tip will transfer lines to the waxy ground without pressing through to the metal.

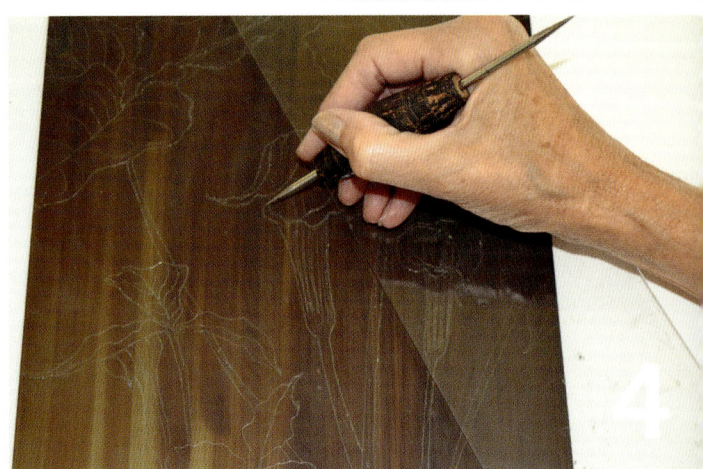

Inscribe fine lines by using a very sharp tool (needling) to draw over the contour lines of the transferred drawing just through the ground but not scratching into the metal. Only light pressure is required. The ground is waxy and soft, so use a bridge to prevent your hand from marring the surface of the ground.

The transferred lines are only a guideline for the composition. Add a variety of lines such as crosshatching and contour to build value and create dimension. You can work freely on the plate, using the value study as a guide.

Place the plate in a bath of dilute water and nitric acid (12 parts water to 1 part nitric acid) for about ten minutes. The shiny lines seen here show the acid biting into the metal. Use a brush to continually sweep over the plate to knock bubbles off the lines, keeping the etch even. The darker marks on the plate show where scratches were covered or corrections were made by brushing on more of the ground.

After removing the plate from the acid bath, rinse the plate with water. Clean the ground off the plate using mineral spirits and a paper towel. Use tabs of cotton-rag matboard to push oil-based etching ink onto the plate (cotton-rag matboard will not scratch the plate). Cover the plate completely with the ink, pushing it into the etched lines as you sweep the ink across the surface.

Use a pad of tarlatan, a stiff woven fabric, to both push ink into the etched lines and lift excess ink off the surface. Wipe thin paper such as newsprint flat across the plate to remove more ink. You can use a bare palm to wipe off the last traces of ink remaining on the plate surface.

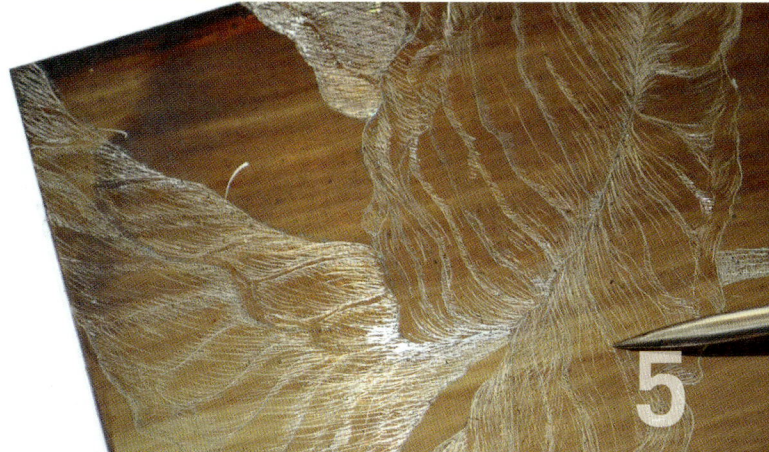

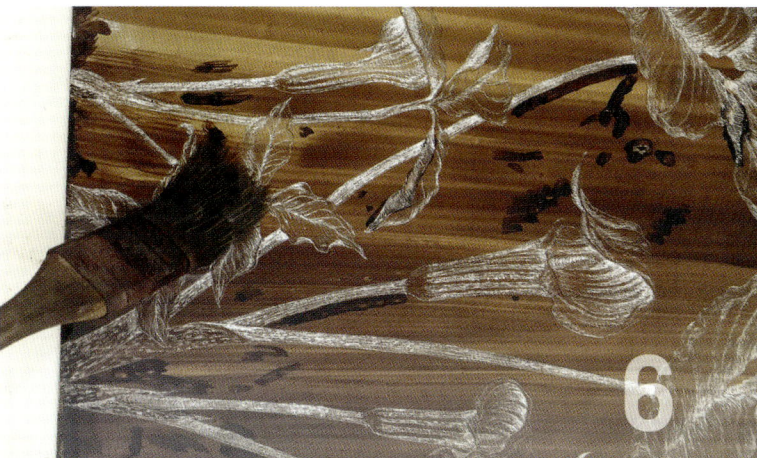

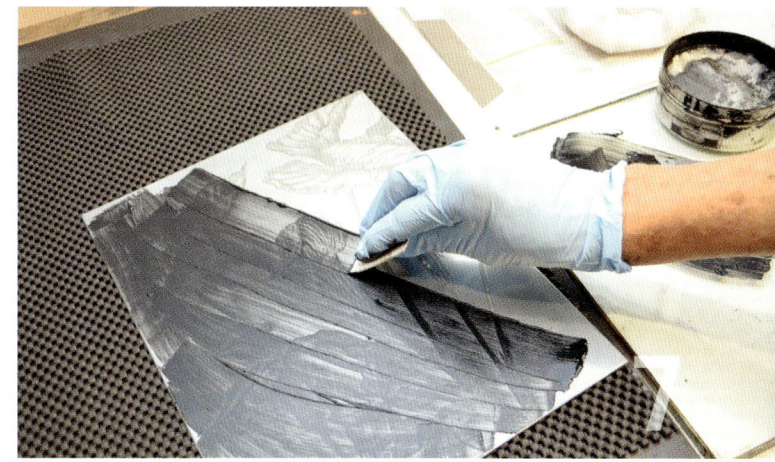

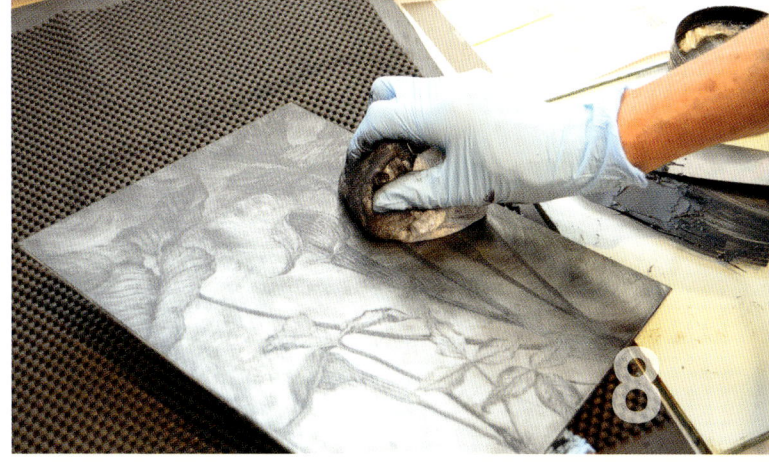

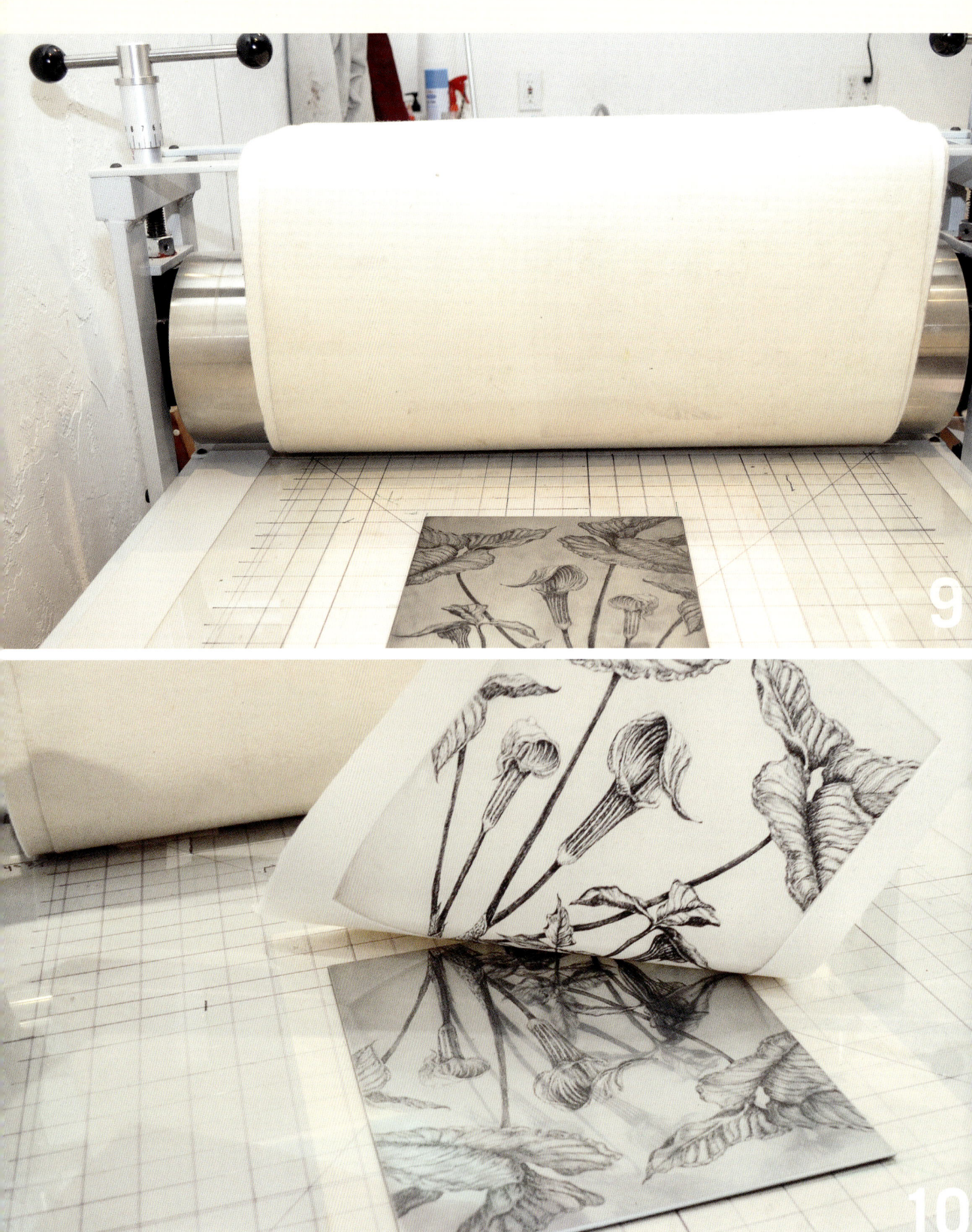

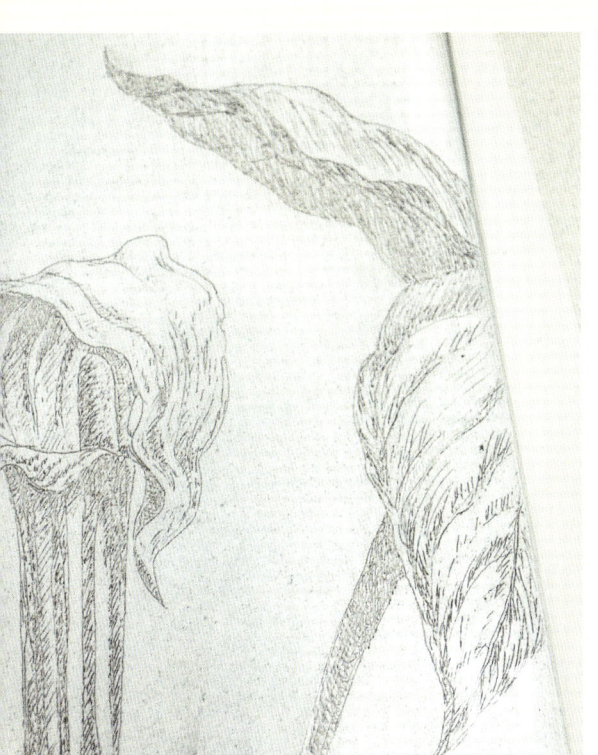

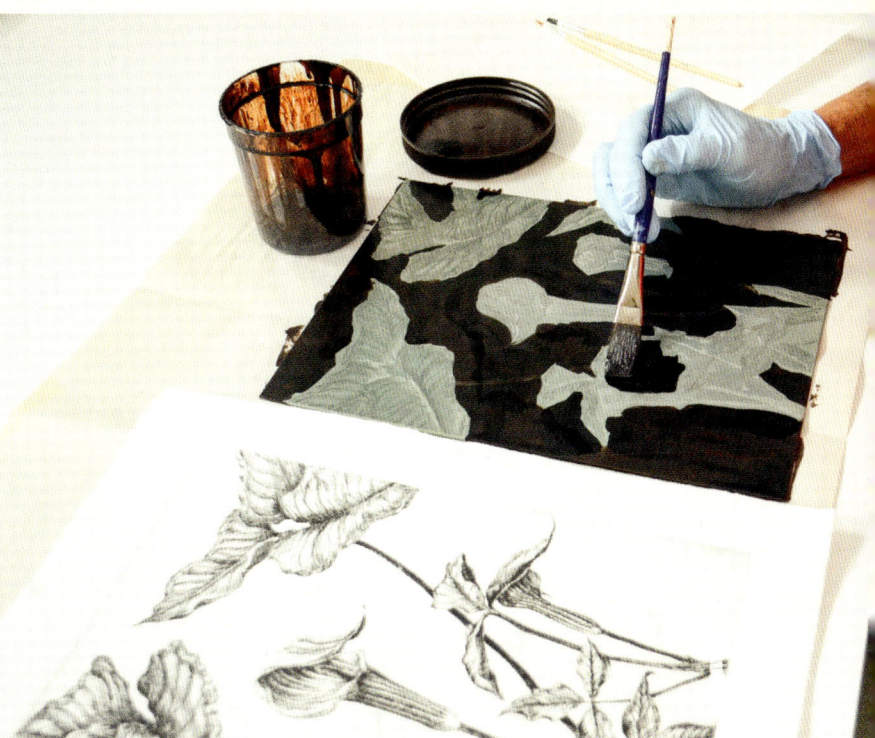

Place the inked plate on a template on the bed of the etching press. Place dampened paper over the plate, then place thick felt blankets on top of the paper, run them all through a rolling press under about 8,000 pounds [3,629 kg] of pressure. The press forces the paper against the inked grooves and picks up the ink from the etched lines.

Fold back the blankets and lift the completed print from the plate. The image is a reverse impression of the plate. The goal is to achieve a good strong line with a white background. Based on the quality of this proof, you can assess whether you would like to do additional work on the plate.

To add more shadow to the leaves in this print, an aquatint technique was used to create a continuous tone. Place the plate on clean, white scrap paper, then spray it with enamel paint to cover the plate at about a 50 percent grey. Since the amount of coverage on the plate is difficult to see, overspray onto the scrap paper. Use the spray pattern on the scrap paper to gauge the amount of coverage on the plate.

Paint liquid hard ground on the areas of the plate where no further etching is needed. Etch the plate in a bath of dilute water and nitric acid (12 parts water to 1 part nitric acid) for a few seconds; the enamel-paint resist will become a very light texture. After cleaning and re-inking the plate, the ink is held in this light, 50 percent texture to make a shadow on the leaves and spathes.

POLYMER PLATE ETCHINGS

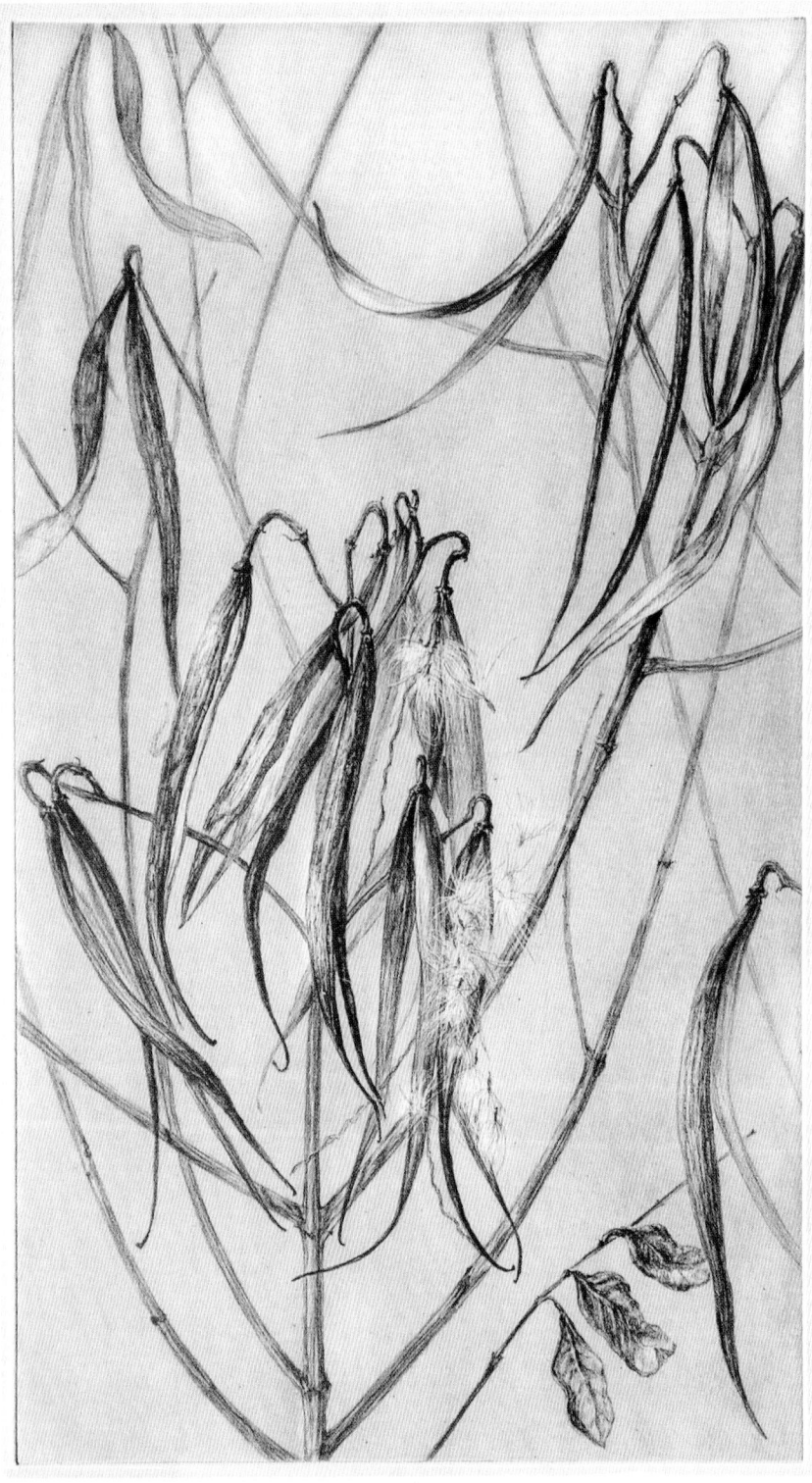

Indian Hemp
Apocynum cannabinum
Polymer plate etching
15 ½ × 8 ¾ inches [38.75 × 21.88 cm]
© Carol Till
HOURS TO COMPLETE: 34

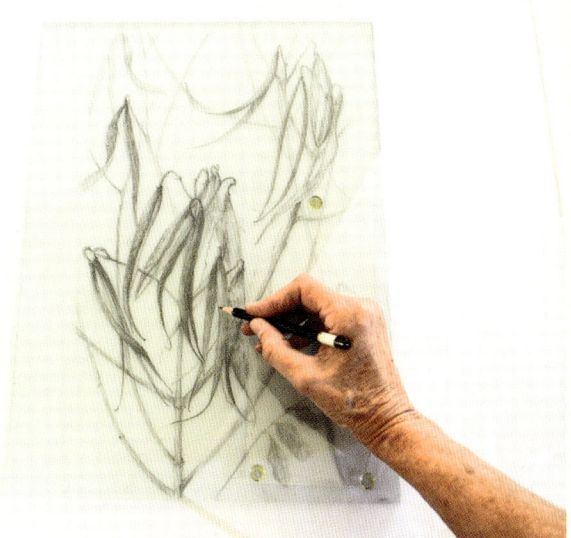

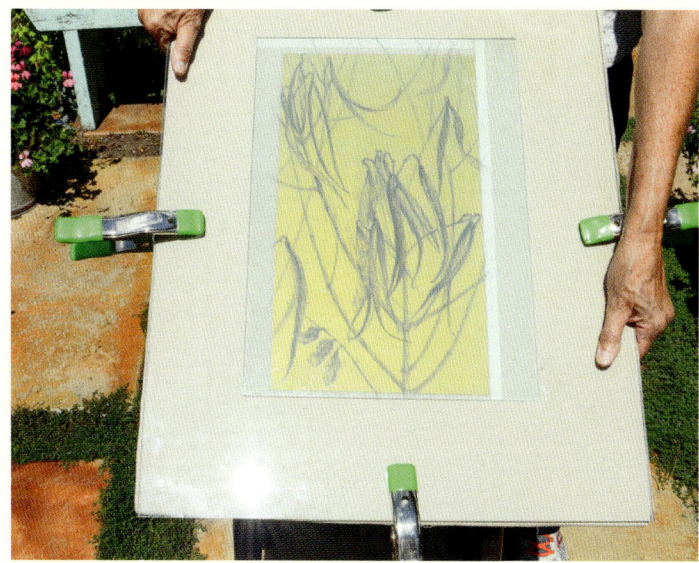

Polymer-plate etchings are made from a plate of light-sensitized polymer with a steel backing. The polymer is too soft to draw on directly, so the artwork is drawn with graphite pencils on a sheet of ¼-inch [0.6 cm] plate glass, coated on one side with carborundum. This creates a surface with enough texture to accept graphite for drawing.

The drawing on glass is placed in direct contact with the plate emulsion and clamped between a hard board and another sheet of clear glass. The unit is exposed to midday sunlight, glass side up, for one to two minutes. Immediately scrub the plate with water and a brush and the unexposed emulsion (shaded by the drawing) will wash away, in effect etching the plate with water.

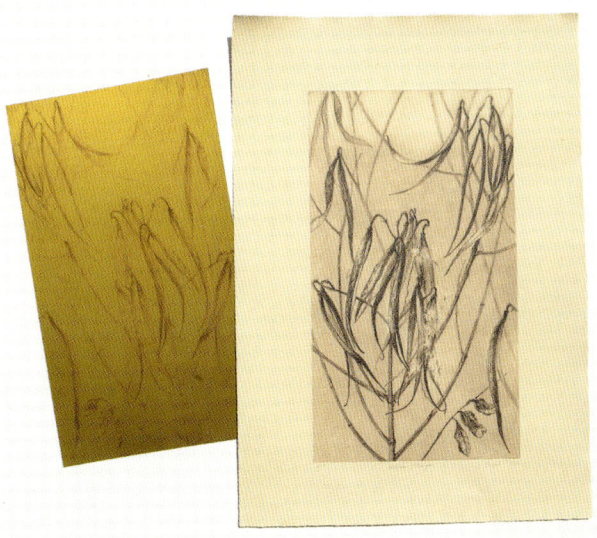

Quickly blot the plate dry with newsprint, then expose it to sunlight again for 10 minutes to harden the emulsion. Then ink the plate and make a print, inking as you would in making a traditional metal etching plate. The entire polymer-plate process is nontoxic and does not use acids or grounds. Unlike metal plates, polymer plates cannot be reworked so the drawing must be perfect before the plate is created.

CHINE COLLÉ
AND HAND-PAINTING
AN ETCHING

Chine collé is a printmaking technique used to enrich the tones and textures of a print. Literally meaning "glued Chinese paper," a reference to the fact that the paper for this technique was originally imported from China, chine collé involves adhering a thin piece of paper to a thicker support paper, such as a high-quality printing paper (usually a thick rag paper). The thin chine-collé papers are usually textured to varied degrees, and range from off-white to beige, with dyed papers available as well. The papers are made from a variety of plants, including rice, cotton, leaves, sedges, and papyrus, among others.

Monika de Vries Gohlke planned this etching to show off a red buckeye's profusion of bright scarlet flowers. Typically, to print the color, a second etched plate would have been needed, but de Vries Gohlke chose instead to hand-paint every blossom on each print.

She selected acrylic paint to color the buds and flowers, utilizing a commercial acrylic glazing liquid in a satin finish for tints. Colored pencil would also have worked, but not translucent watercolor, because it resists the fine film of oil left after the printing process.

To adhere chine-collé paper to the etching, the delicate paper was cut about one-sixteenth of an inch [0.02 mm] smaller than the size of the printing plate. This compensates for the its expansion as it absorbs water from the glue. The inked copper etching plate is placed on the etching press, the chine-collé paper is placed on the plate with its front side facing the plate, then methyl cellulose paste is brushed onto the back side of the chine-collé paper. The high-quality printing paper is laid on top of the glued chine collé, then all is run through the press; the chine-collé paper is now printed, glued to the printing paper, and is a permanent part of the artwork. By utilizing the techniques of hand-coloring and chine collé, each print from the plate offers unique qualities in color and texture.

Red Buckeye
Aesculus pavia
Etching, aquatint, hand-colored, chine collé
© Monika de Vries Gohlke
17 ½ × 12 inches [43.75 × 30 cm]
HOURS TO COMPLETE: 225

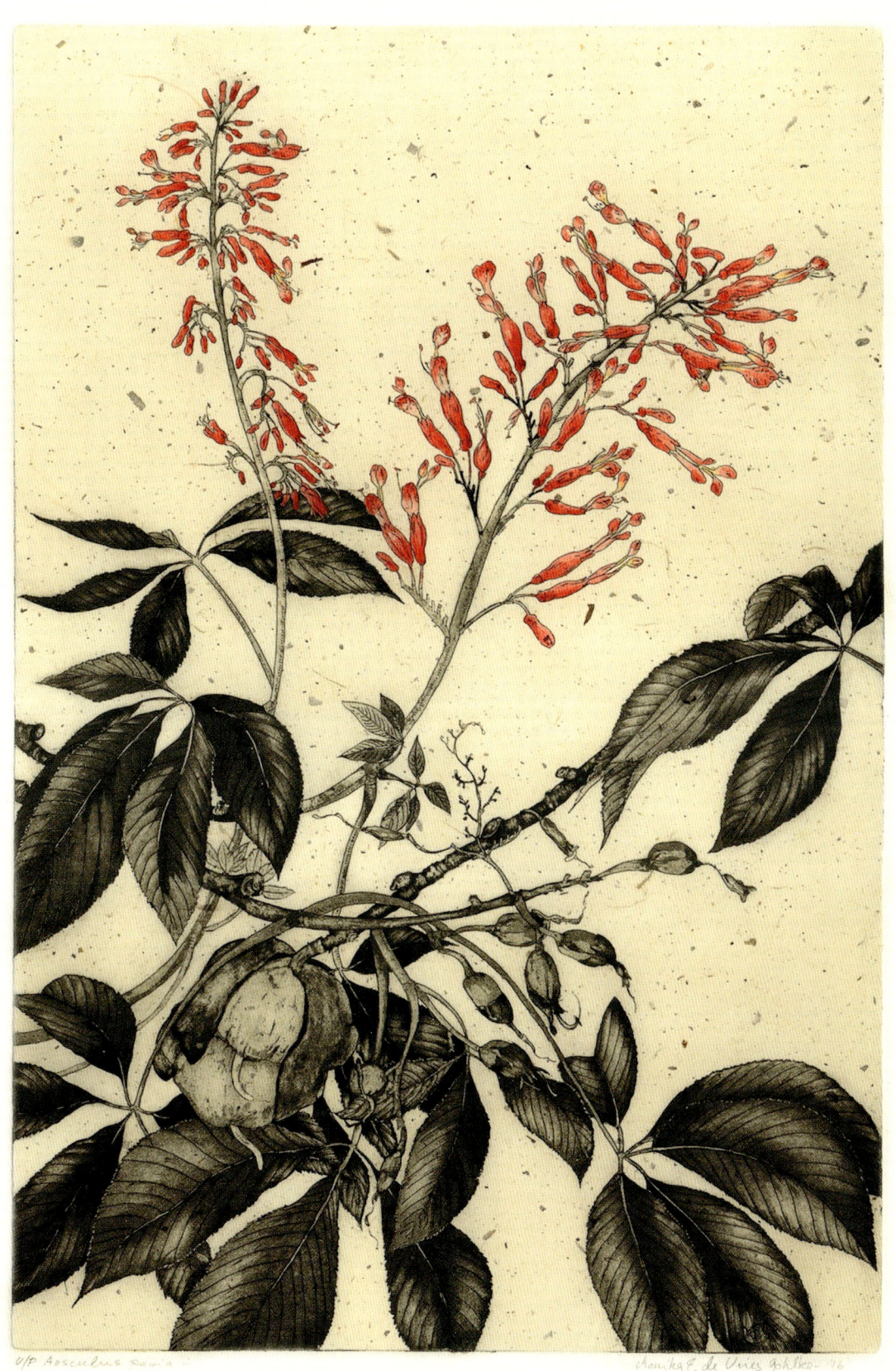

U/P Aesculus pavia

Monika E. de Vries Gohlke '96

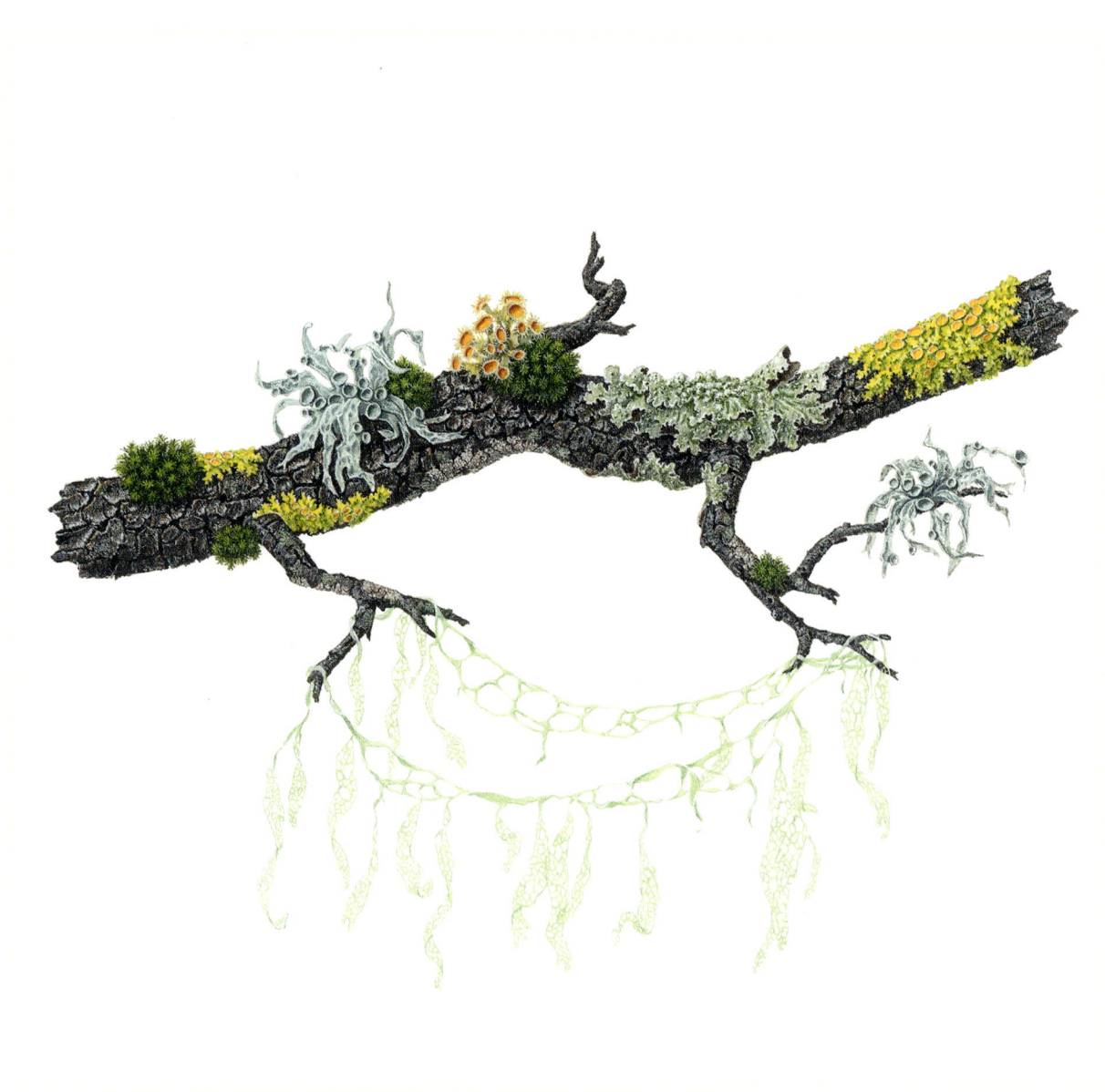

Small Oak Branch with Lichens *Xanthoria parietina, Ramalina leptocarpha, Teloschistes chrysophthalmus, Flavopunctelia flaventior, Ramalina menziesii* Gouache and watercolor on paper 8 × 10 inches [20 × 25 cm]
© Lucy Martin HOURS TO COMPLETE: 20

MATERIALS: Hot-pressed watercolor paper block; water; ox-gall liquid; linen cloth; lead holder with 0.3 mm H lead; white-plastic eraser; porcelain palettes; ⅛-inch synthetic filbert brush; synthetic round brushes (nos. 3, 1, 0, 2X0, and 5X0). Gouache colors: indigo; ivory black; permanent white; sap green; Hooker's green; yellow ochre. Watercolors: Van Dyke brown, ultramarine blue; Hansa yellow; brown madder; burnt sienna; perinone orange.

Gouache technique is opposite to watercolor technique, in that the artist usually works dark to light in its opaque colors, rather than the other way around. General areas of flat color are painted in, delineating outside edges of lichens and moss and providing an undercoat for the branch. Shading and highlights are used to paint the bark texture, then each lichen is painted using a variety of greens and golds. For the final steps, white paint is used either alone, or mixed in light tints to add form and highlights as needed.

Gouache and watercolor are used somewhat inter-changeably in this work; watercolor is used very undi-luted, so that it behaves more like gouache. One or the other was chosen based on the color, since the color in gouache or watercolor will be slightly different.

Painting a Branch with Lichens in Gouache and Watercolor

TUTOR: LUCY MARTIN

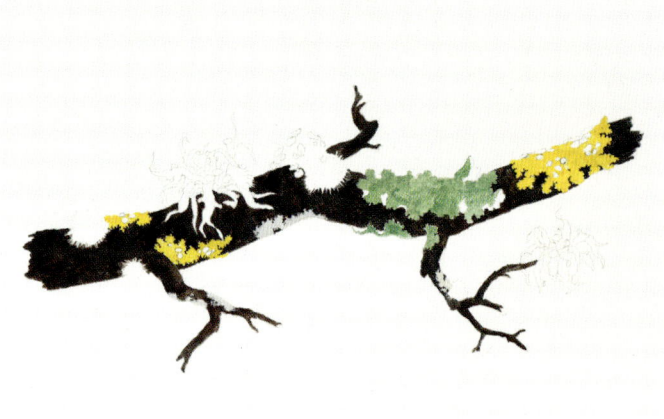
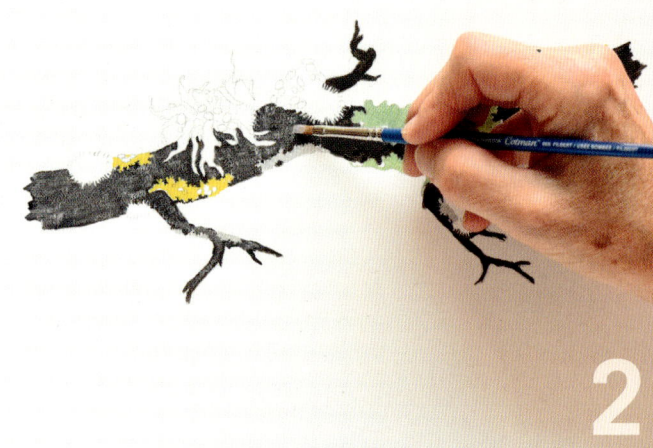

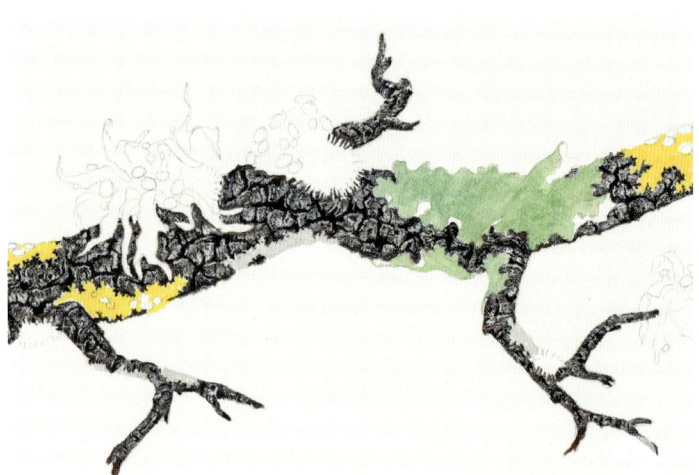
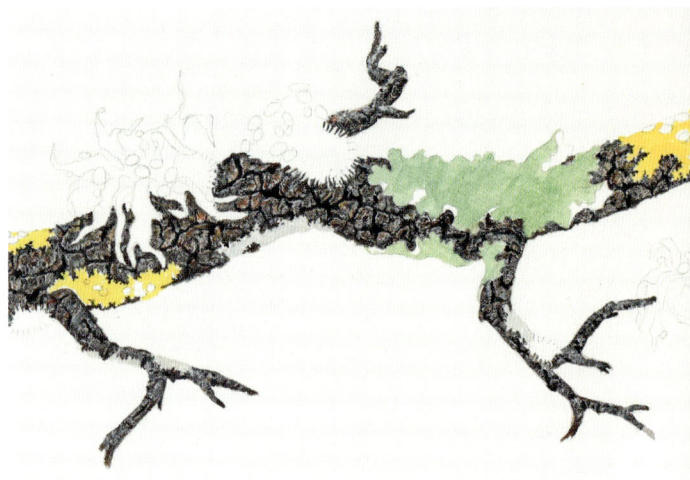

Transfer the graphite drawing of your subject onto the paper, then paint a layer of nearly flat color. Paint the bark with indigo and Van Dyke brown. Mix ultramarine blue, Hansa yellow, and white for the blue-green foliose (leafy) lichen. For the yellow foliose lichen, use a slightly greenish yellow. For the gray crustose lichen, use a mixture of tiny amounts of ultramarine blue and brown to white.

Apply drybrush texture to the bark. Brush a barely damp filbert brush on some dried white paint on your palette. This will draw out some of the liquid in the brush, making the white paint stickier and dryer. Then, holding the brush at an angle close to the paper, brush on the texture. It does not need to be perfectly even; the imperfections are part of the bark's texture.

Paint the darker cracks and the little holes in the bark with Van Dyke brown mixed with black. Paint very fine lines in white to highlight the lower, light-catching edges of the cracks, and slightly lighten the area of bark just above the crack. This area also catches the light because the flakes of bark curl up slightly.

This bark has subtle shades of burnt sienna, ochre, and reddish-brown. Create a wash for each color and then use very little on the brush. Apply color washes sparingly over the white texture and highlights on the bark. Go over each area only once, then let it dry. Using the color in dilute washes will allow the texture to still show through, preserving it. Repeat if the color needs to be deeper.

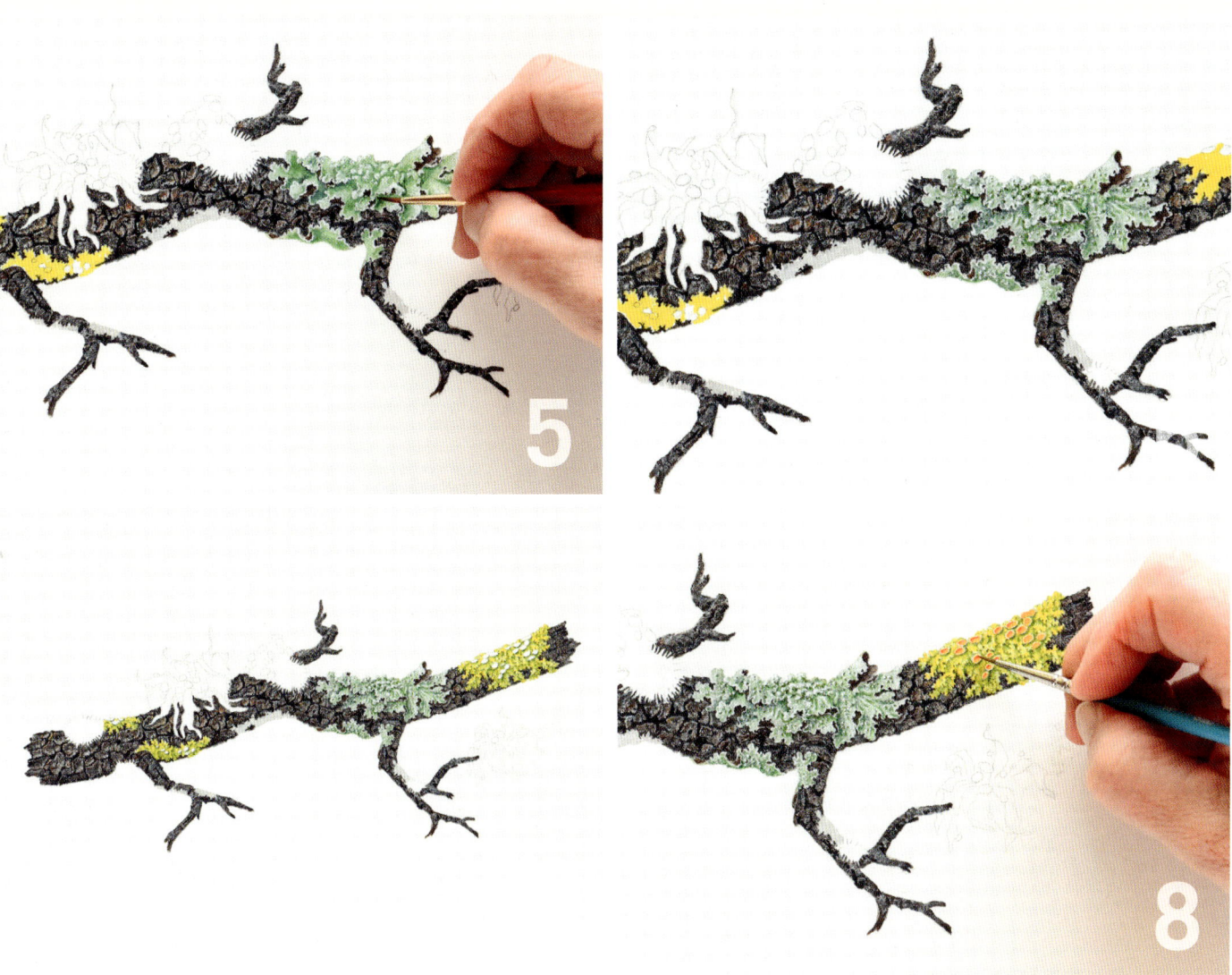

Outline the leaves of the blue-green foliose lichens with white and white mixed with a little green. Paint the undersides of the leaves with Van Dyke brown. Define the wavy shapes of the leaves using blue to create shadows and white, mixed with blue-green, for highlights. Lighten the very edges of the leaves with white. Darken the shaded areas to make the leaves lift from the ones beneath.

Use the drybrush technique described in step 2 to create a subtle texture on the surface of the green foliose lichen. Using white, paint the bumps, wrinkles, and dots characteristic of this species. Shade these areas, and continue to deepen the shadows and lighten the highlights.

For the yellow-green foliose lichen, follow a similar process: outline the leaves with green, then lay in shadows so that the leaves separate from one another. Use a little blue mixed with Hansa yellow to create the shading. Darken the areas toward the underside of the branch, place darker shadows under the lower edges of the white fruiting bodies.

Paint the cup-shaped fruiting bodies with Hansa yellow and a little perinone orange. Define the rims with yellow mixed with a little white. Add a little burnt sienna to Hansa yellow to shade the upper rims, creating the concave shape of the cups.

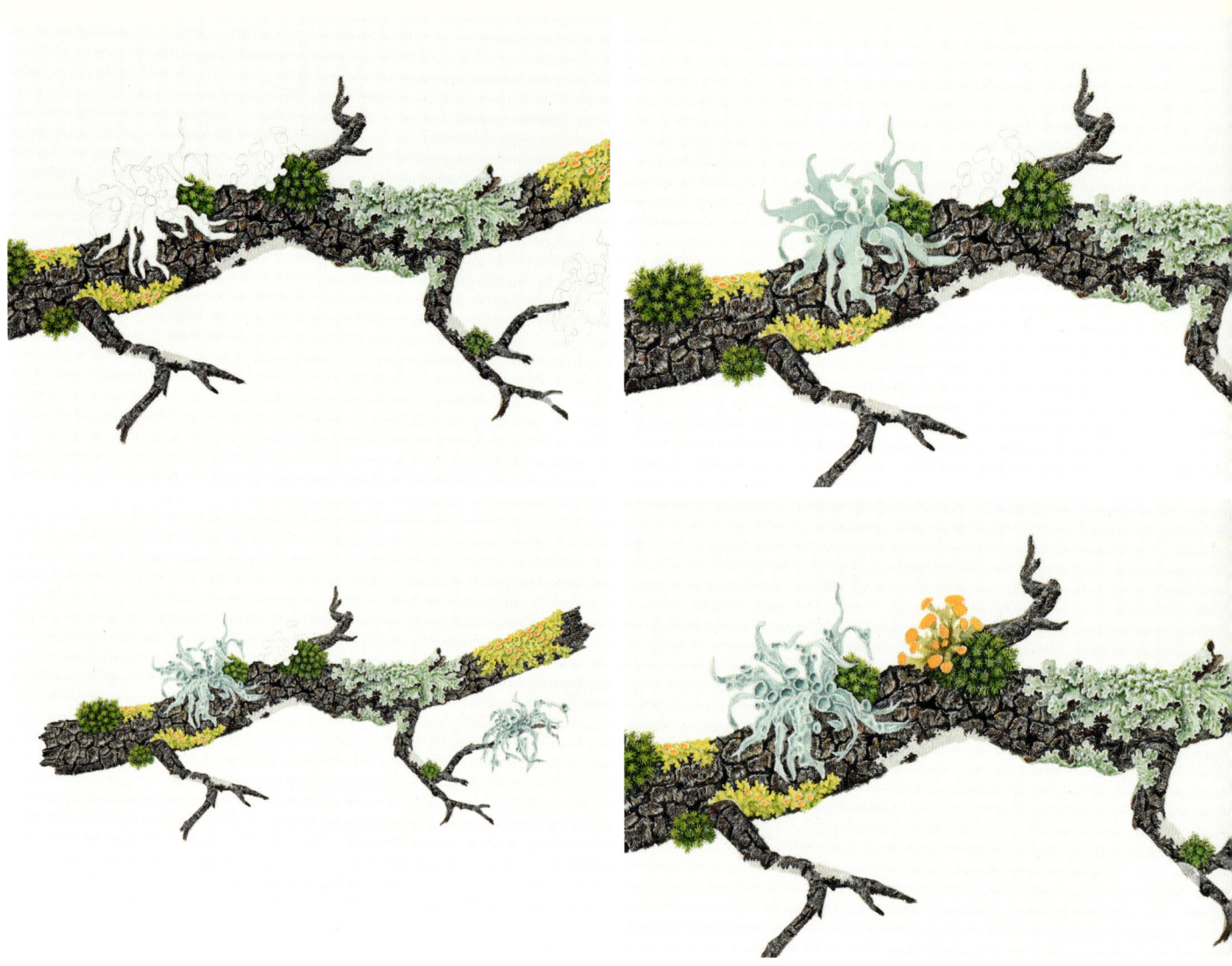

Paint the moss with a very dark color mixed with hooker's green, indigo and Van Dyke brown. Then paint the protruding leaves with a medium green. The leaves projecting forward will look star-shaped. Mix more yellow into the green and add more detail to each leaf. Repeat several times, each time making the color lighter and more yellow toward the end of the leaf.

The branched lichens are painted with a base color of indigo, sap green and white. Using a darker shade, define the edges where they overlap, and underneath the fruiting bodies. Paint the lichens and fruiting bodies toward the front with a mix including more white. Outline the cups of the fruiting bodies with white. Darken the bases of the branches closer to the bark.

Use a whiter mix to create the ridges on the lichen branches, and more blue for the depressions. Shade the cups of the fruiting bodies. Blend these colors to make smooth transitions. Darken the undersides of the branches.

For the lichen with fringed cups at the apex of the painting, begin by painting the cups in a reddish orange. Paint the stalks with a mix of ochre and sap green. Darken the stalks where they are closer to the bark. Define them by painting the shadows, adding blue and a little brown to the mix.

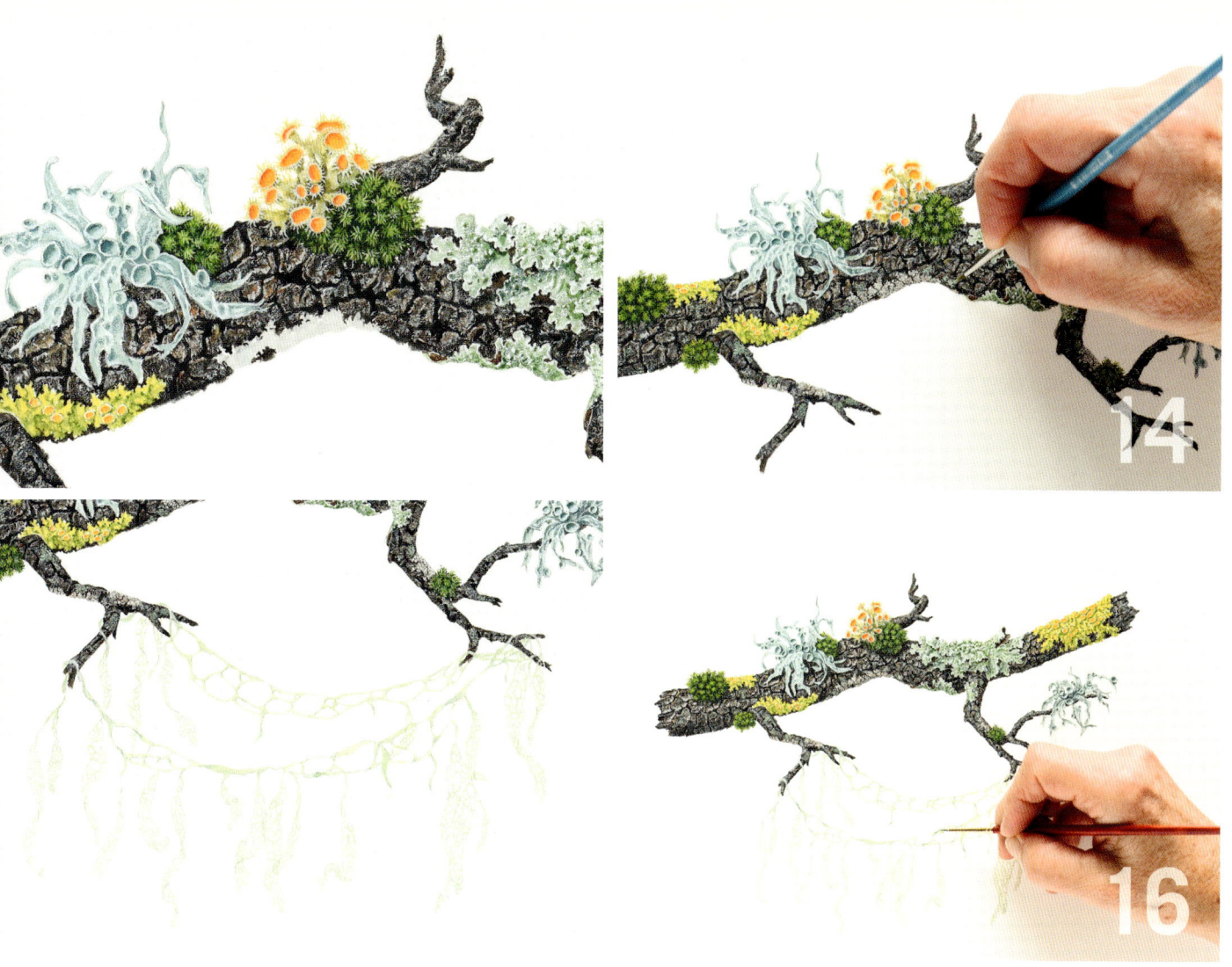

Paint the rims of the cups with a pale yellow. Paint the cilia with this yellow, paler where they show against the bark and a little darker where they show against the paper. There are cilia in some places on the stalks as well. Shade the upper interiors of the cups with red.

With the 5X0 brush paint the divisions in the crustose lichen with a dark color. Add subtle color with a little burnt sienna, ochre, and pale green. Continue painting the cracks in the bark through these areas of lichen. Using white with a little green and blue, paint the dots of the clusters of very fine-textured pale green lichen.

Paint the lace lichen with a mix of white, green, and blue. Use a magnifier if needed for the very fine parts of the nets. Thin the paint with ox-gall liquid instead of water, to help create a very fine, smooth line. Ox-gall improves the flow of the color. Add a few drops to a cup of water, then use it to thin the paint. Add more white where the strands of the lichen cross the twigs.

Finally, refine the whole painting. Shade the underside of the branch with a wash of indigo mixed with Van Dyke brown. Apply this wash over the existing painted areas lightly—only once, and allow the paint to dry—to preserve the details and texture. Add shading under each lichen. Deepen the shadows and brighten the highlights. Darken the lace lichen where the strands twist. Further define each lichen by sharpening the edges of each undulation and overlap.

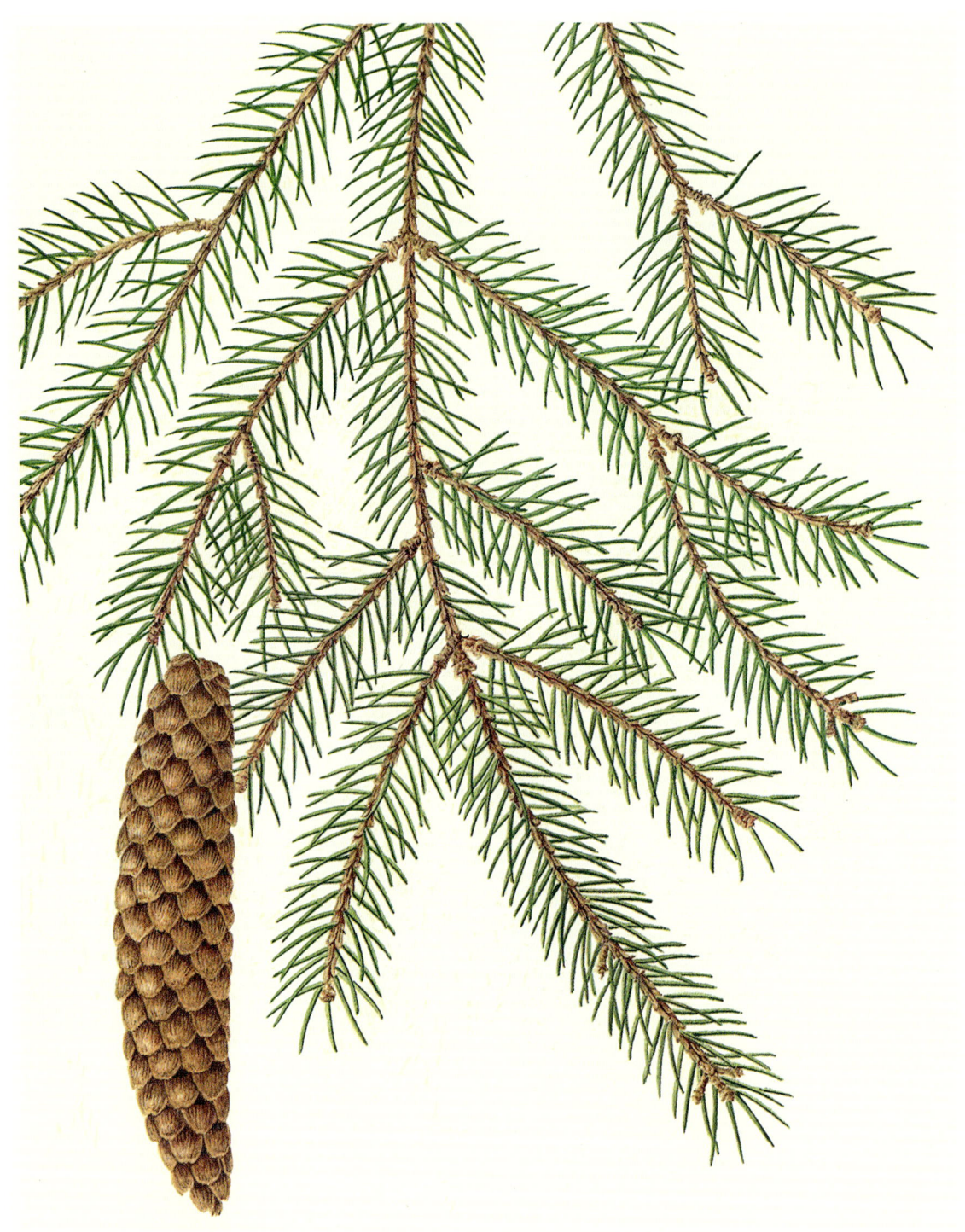

Norway Spruce *Picea abies* Gouache on paper 12 × 9 inches [30 × 22.5 cm] © Carrie Di Costanzo

HOURS TO COMPLETE: 40

MATERIALS: Tubes of gouache paint; kneaded eraser; container for water; small cloth; magnifying glass; plastic palette with wells; watercolor brushes (nos. 2, 1, 0, and 3X0); 3B and 2H pencils; scrap piece of watercolor paper. Colors: Titanium white, sap green; yellow ochre; burnt umber; ultramarine blue; alizarin crimson.

Depicting a conifer can be a daunting task, but taken in steps the process is demystified. In this gouache painting of a spruce branch, the first step of making a detailed drawing of the branch and cone, showing every needle and scale, has already been accomplished. Next, the paper is prepared with a pale yellow painted ground before the drawing is transferred to it. Then the painting is approached in a technique more associated with watercolor painting, working with lighter layers first, then finishing by adding contrast where shadows occur.

Gouache on Paper: Spruce Needles and Cone

TUTOR: CARRIE DI COSTANZO

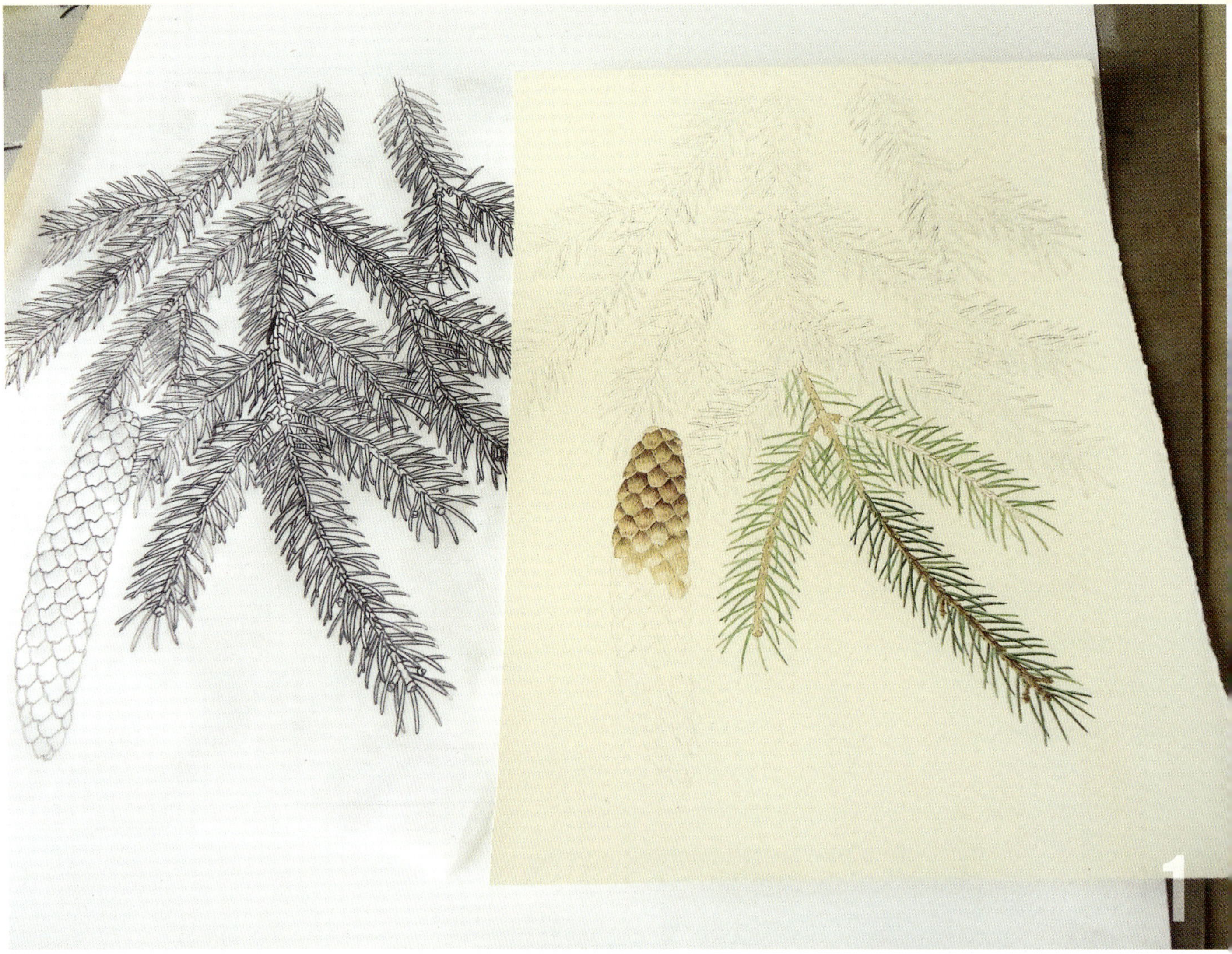

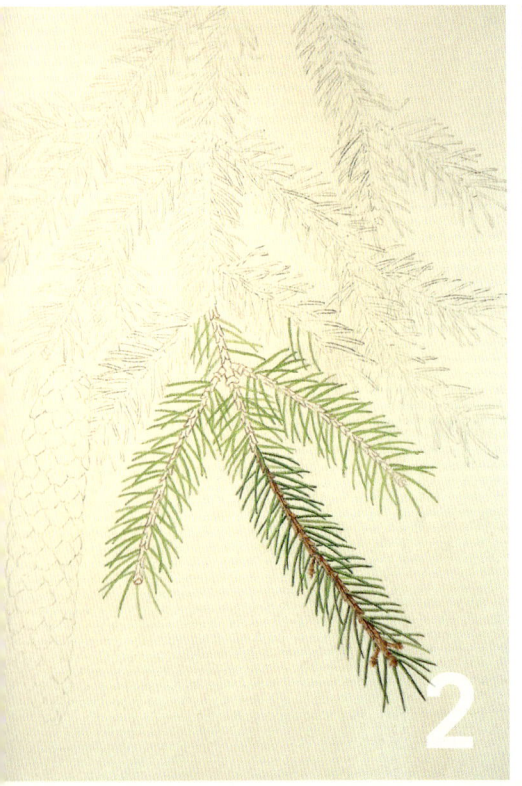

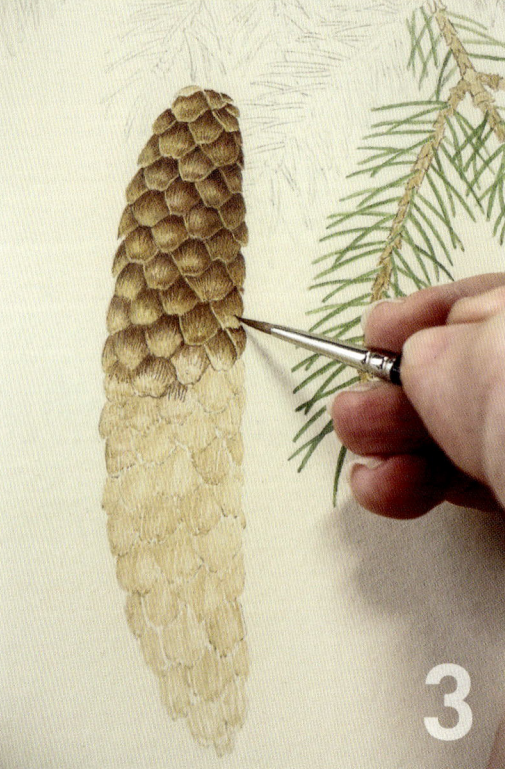

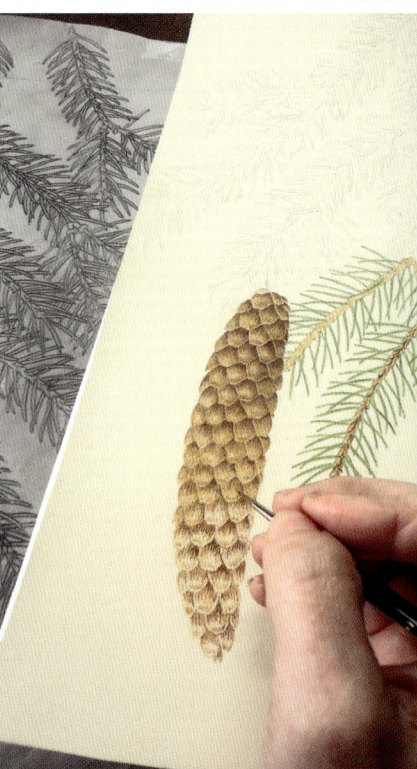

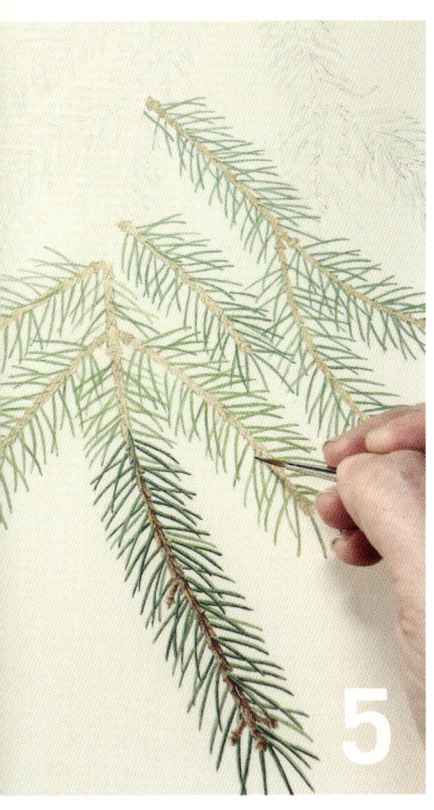
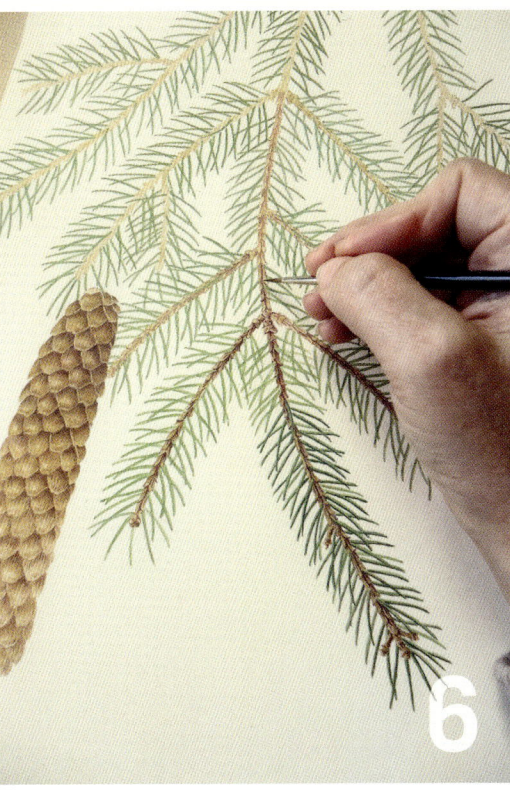
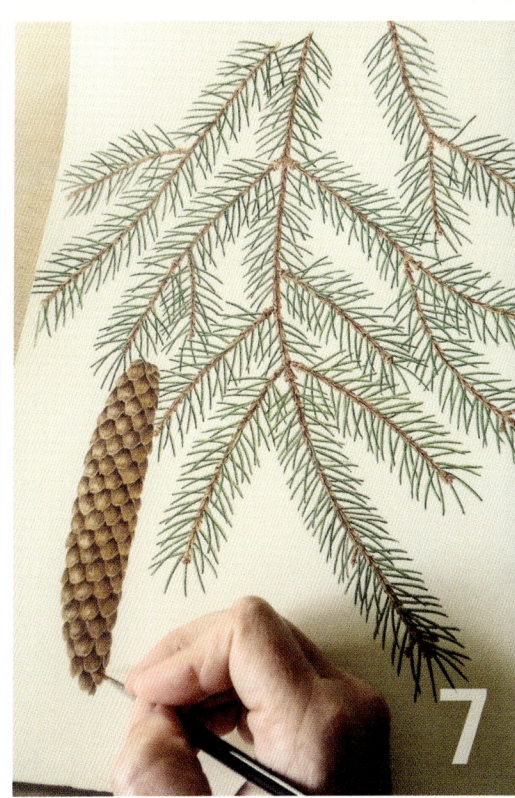

Complete a detailed line drawing of the subject on tracing paper. Prepare the hot-pressed watercolor paper with a ground color of titanium white and yellow ochre for a flat color with body. This mixture makes the paper look opaque and even throughout, and the white provides a smooth coverage. Transfer the line drawing to the paper with graphite.

Using a no. 2 brush, apply the first washes of local color for the needles, following the form of each element. The needles are a mixture of sap green, ultramarine blue, yellow ochre, and titanium white. White is added to give body to the paint, matching the weight of the ground color. Let each layer of paint dry before another one is added.

The cone and the branchlets are a mixture of yellow ochre, burnt umber, and a small amount of white. Paint the color in lightly, with each cone scale and branchlet scale defined in the first layer. As you add each successive layer of paint, use smaller brushes with less water and more pigment.

The next layer of paint for the cone should be darker in value—apply it to the areas where the scales overlap one another. Using burnt umber and yellow ochre, lay in lines of shading showing the undulations in each scale.

Use a single green tone for the first layer of each needle, then add a darker mixture of ultramarine blue and sap green to the needle undersides. Adding the darker mixture to the undersides gives depth to each needle so that they appear three-dimensional.

Apply a mix of alizarin crimson and burnt umber to the branchlets to add darker value and contrast and refine details and texture.

To unify all the colors, apply glazes of yellow ochre and burnt umber with drybrush to the cone and branchlets.

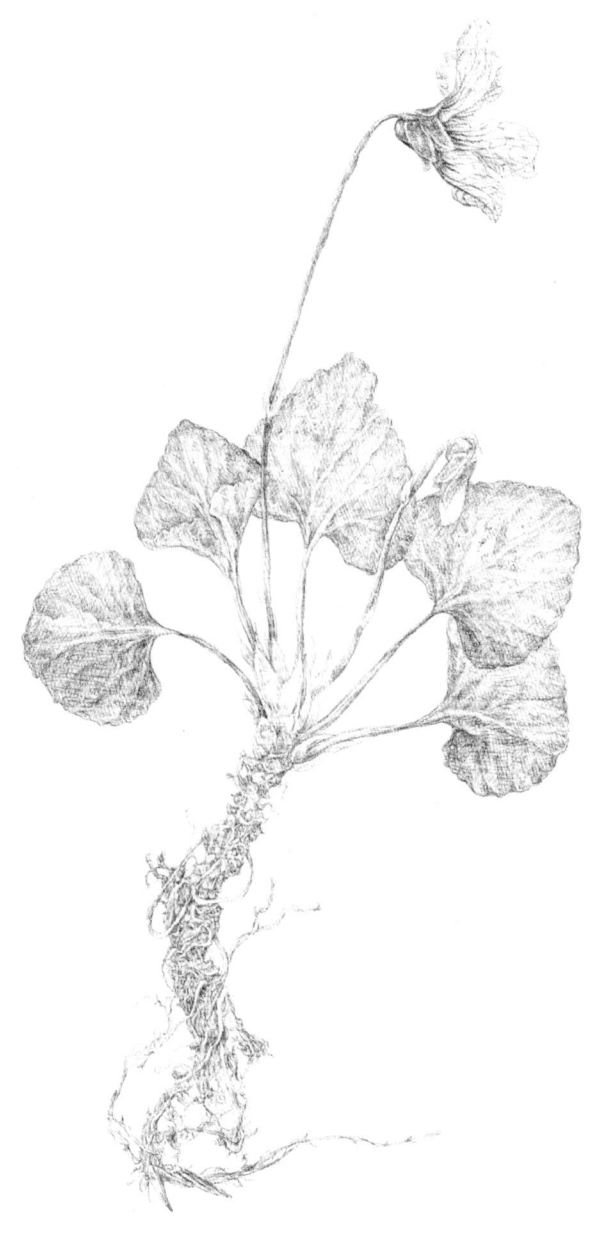

Viola sp. Silverpoint on traditional ground on paper 6 × 4 inches [15 × 10 cm] © Kandy Vermeer Phillips

HOURS TO COMPLETE: 25

MATERIALS: Copper wool pad; metalpoints in lead holders (copper, sterling silver, silver, and gold); scrap paper; bismuth metal; 800-grit sandpaper; triangular metal file; stylus with silver point; white gouache; brush (no. 000).

Metalpoint drawing is a Renaissance technique known for its delicate, high-key appearance. Its fine-line capabilities allow for delicate crosshatching, convincing texture, and extraordinary detail. A metalpoint artist uses a stylus, either a solid metal rod sharpened to a point or a piece of wire inserted into a lead holder, to draw their subject on paper that has been prepared with a ground. The ground may be tinted with color to provide a modulated mid-tone. While any metal, such as silver, copper, or gold, can be used, the most common metal used is silver.

All metalpoint lines initially appear as a warm or cool gray, but with the exception of lines made with a gold or platinum stylus, the gray will tarnish to some degree over time. Tarnishing is a chemical reaction between the metal, the ground, and the air quality. Each metal tarnishes to a different color: copper tarnishes to yellow (useful for underdrawing); sterling silver tarnishes to warm brown; and silver tarnishes to warm brown-black. Gold remains a cool gray. Contemporary artists remain captivated by the luminosity of metalpoint's silver and gold lines and the technique's extreme precision—the hallmarks of a metalpoint drawing.

Metalpoint

TUTOR: KANDY VERMEER PHILLIPS

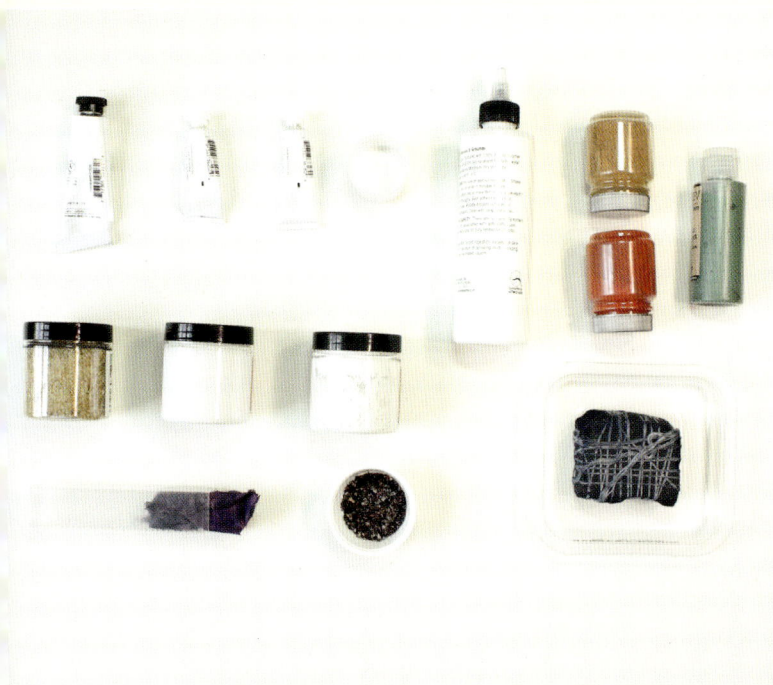

A variety of grounds are available for use in metalpoint. Gouache is the easiest ground to use, because it can be applied in any color, takes little preparation, and dries quickly. Traditional ground—a mixture of bone ash, rabbit skin glue, and marble dust—takes more time to prepare but adds the sparkle that marble dust creates. Acrylic's flexibility is ideal for sketchbook pages.

Grounds shown here (top row, left to right): Titanium white casein; zinc white gouache; titanium white gouache, bone ash (in cup); titanium white acrylic-based silverpoint ground; yellow ochre pigment; burnt sienna pigment; green earth pigment. Middle row (left to right): Rabbit skin glue granules; titanium white dry pigment; marble dust. Bottom row (left to right): Clothlet soaked in turnsole plant–based blue dye; dried cochineal (in cup); dried compressed indigo stone.

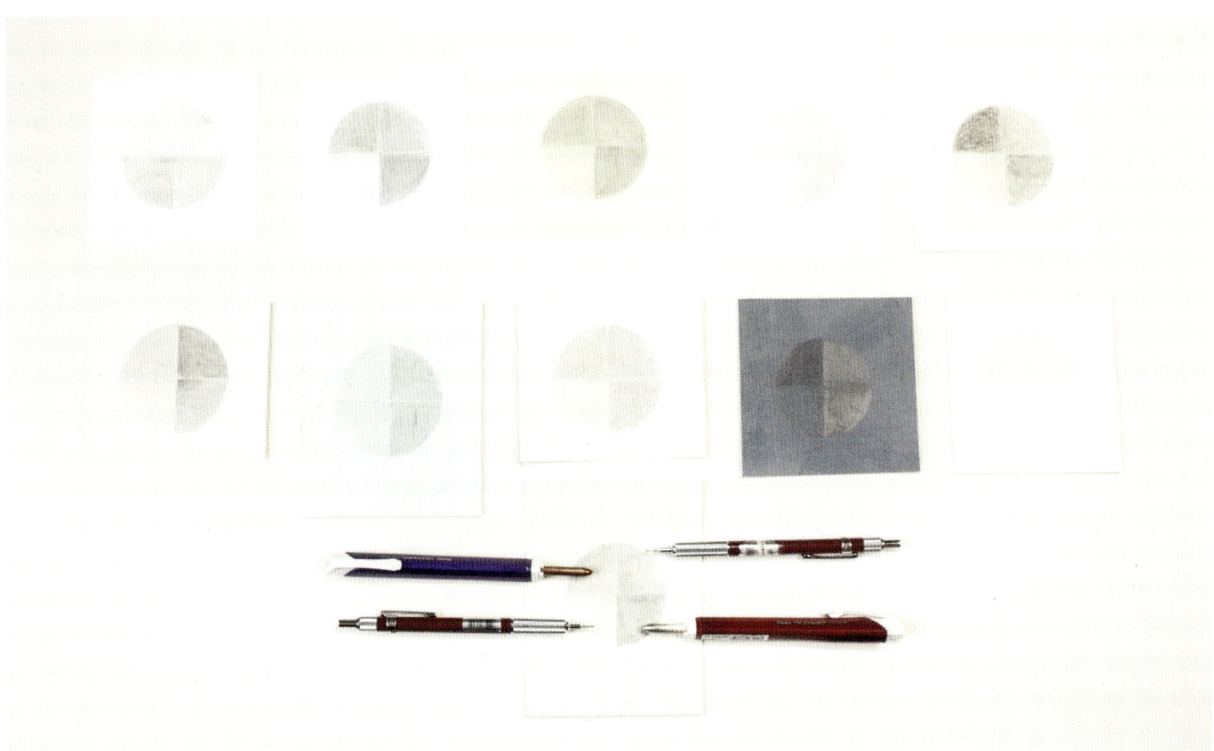

Test various paper, ground, and metal combinations to see how the metals react in your studio conditions. The examples here show the results of a variety of combinations.

Papers commercially prepared with grounds (top row, left to right): clay coated; white plastic-like; cream plastic-like; resin-based; acrylic-and-pigment coated.

Papers prepared by hand with grounds (middle row, left to right): white casein; tinted casein; gouache; traditional; and acrylic. These examples are on 300 lb. [640 gsm] hot-pressed watercolor paper.

At bottom are metals used in each of these examples: copper (top left); gold (bottom left); silver (top right); sterling (bottom right).

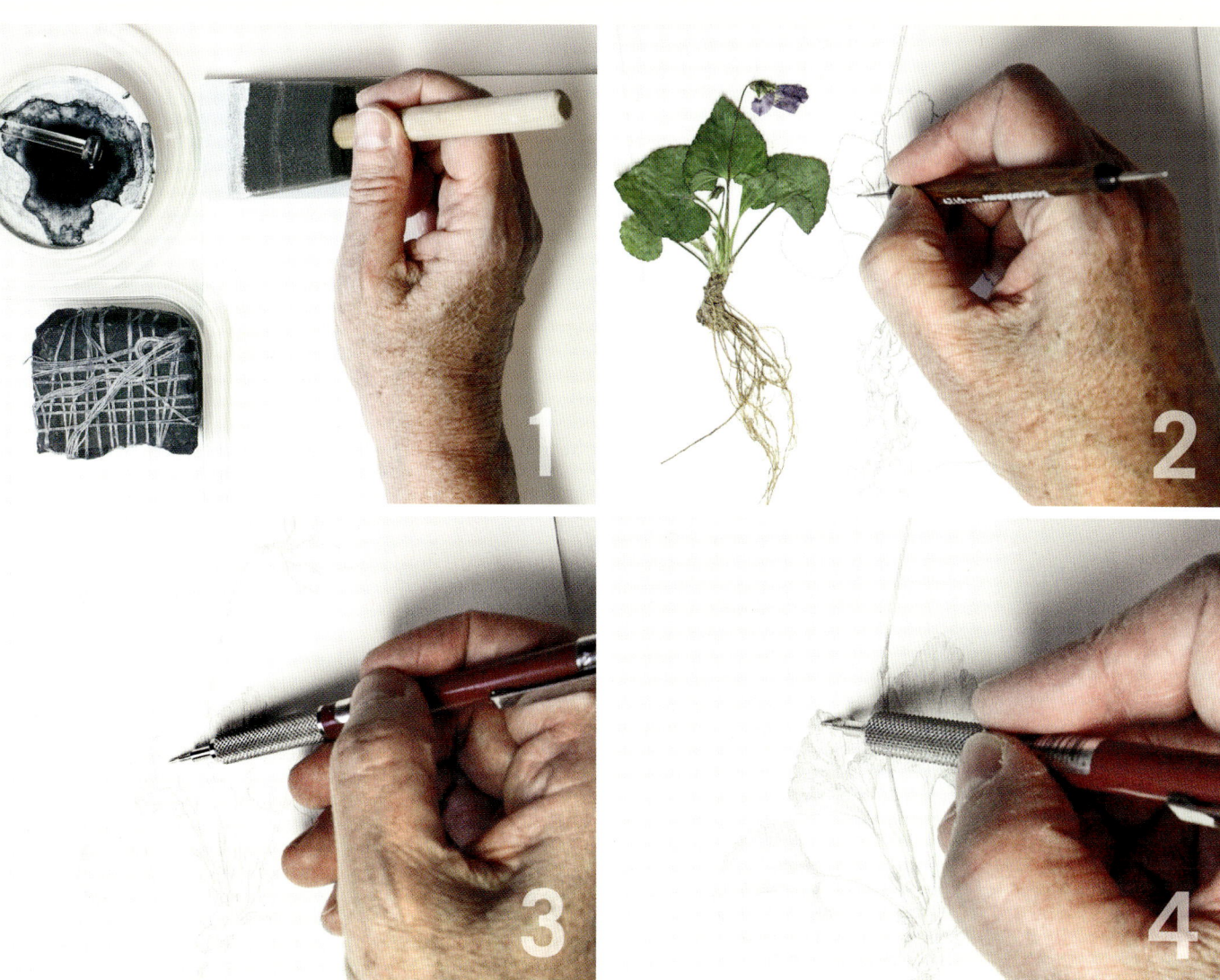

To apply a traditional ground to watercolor paper, tint the ground base of glue, bone ash, and marble dust with indigo pigment that has been mulled to a powder. Slowly mix in warm water, a little at a time, until the mixture reaches a creamlike consistency. With a foam or soft-haired brush, apply the ground using horizontal strokes; let dry, then apply another layer using vertical strokes. Let the ground cure for several days.

Next, transfer the subject to the prepared paper. This casein-prepared paper has cured for several weeks and has been lightly sanded with 800-grit sandpaper to remove imperfections. A traced drawing of a pressed violet was laid over the prepared paper and retraced using a blind stylus (a double-ended burnisher) and moderate pressure, which results in the image being lightly indented into the surface of the prepared paper. This method keeps the surface of the prepared paper clean.

Use an oblique light source to see the drawing's indentation, then lightly trace the indentation with a silverpoint. Lay down the first very faint layers of parallel lines to begin building tonal values (these lines are so small and close to one another they appear as a solid or tonal grey area). Gently hold the stylus at a near horizontal angle to ensure a feather touch. Values are slowly built up through multiple layers of parallel and diagonal crosshatched lines.

Continue to build value by adding more layers of cross-hatched silver lines. Hold the stylus closer to the point for greater control. Carefully apply more pressure on the point to slowly darken the lines. Too much pressure may chip and damage the ground, but you can repair the damage by sanding out the area using the side of a rolled-up piece of 800-grit sandpaper, then applying new ground.

When drawing the fine detail of the flower and roots, shape the point to a needle-like sharpness using a file and 800-grit sandpaper. The rich dark areas of the flower and leaves in this subject were developed by allowing the earlier layers to tarnish slightly prior to applying additional silver. This gives the drawing a translucent depth.

Permanent white gouache can be used to add highlights to a silverpoint drawing on a tinted ground. Dilute the gouache with water, a little at a time, until the mixture reaches a cream consistency. Using a 000 brush, dip the brush into the gouache and roll off the excess on a paper towel or white cloth to form a fine point. Hold the brush vertically and paint delicate lines to indicate light.

The variety of grounds, papers, and metals, along with each metal's specific patina and tarnishing characteristics, allow you to achieve a diverse range of effects in metalpoint drawing, as seen in these completed studies. Left to right: sterling silver on stone paper; silver on ochre-tinted bone-ash ground; silver on white casein; gold on terre verte–tinted traditional ground; copper on stone paper.

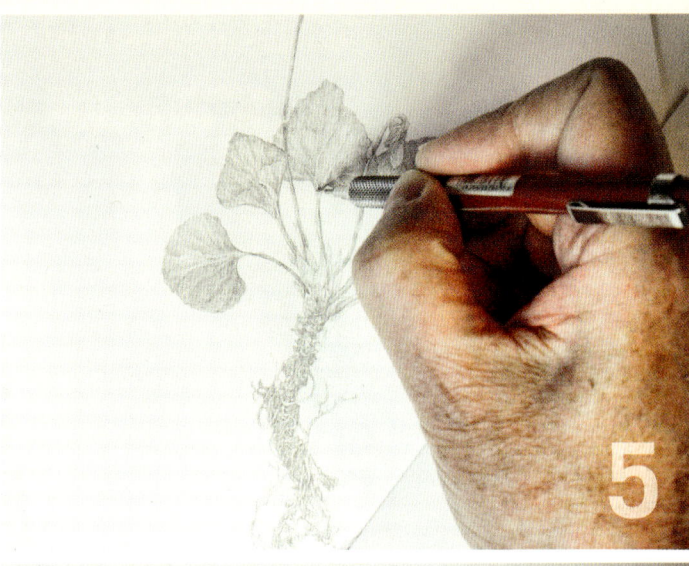

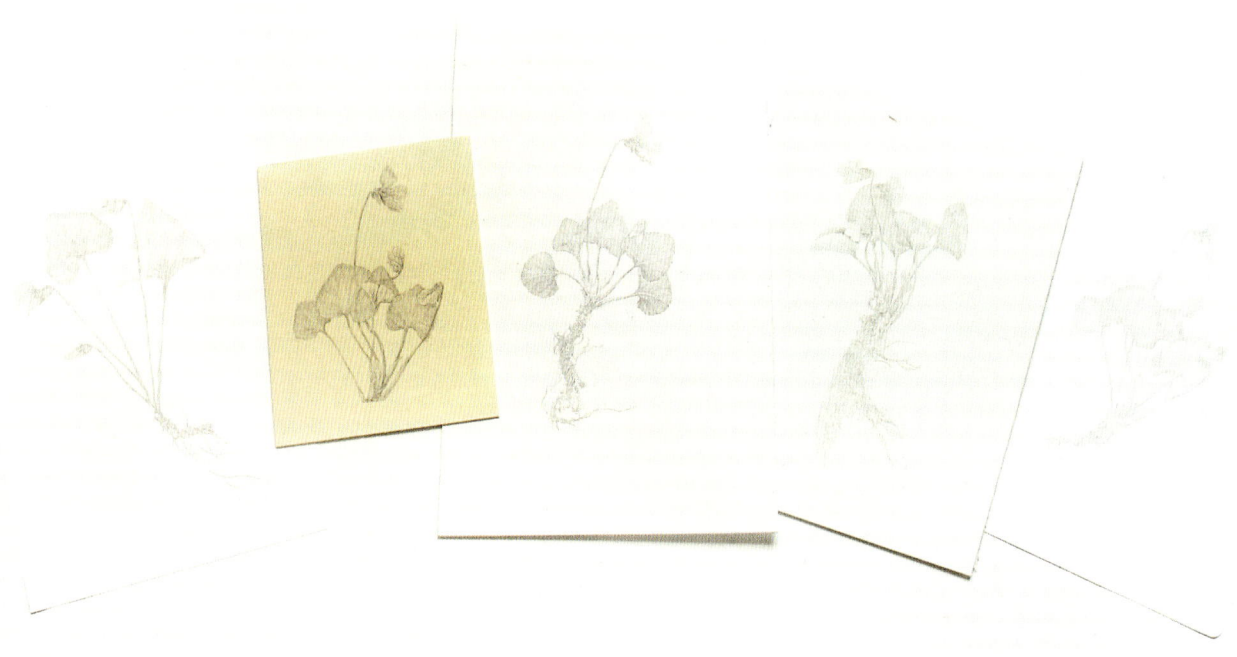

SILVERPOINT

For this silverpoint drawing, artist Linda Nemergut first prepared one side of a 140 lb. [300 gsm] hot-pressed watercolor paper with two thin, even coats of a silverpoint primer. Nemergut doesn't plan the composition with a sketch; the drawing develops organically as she works. She used a silver wire held in a lead holder for both crosshatching and several layers of light toning, with heavier pressure used in the darkest areas. With silverpoint, a flexible-composition eraser can be used very gently to make small corrections, but it's preferable to work mistakes into the drawing. Tarnishing happens gradually or quickly depending on environmental conditions.

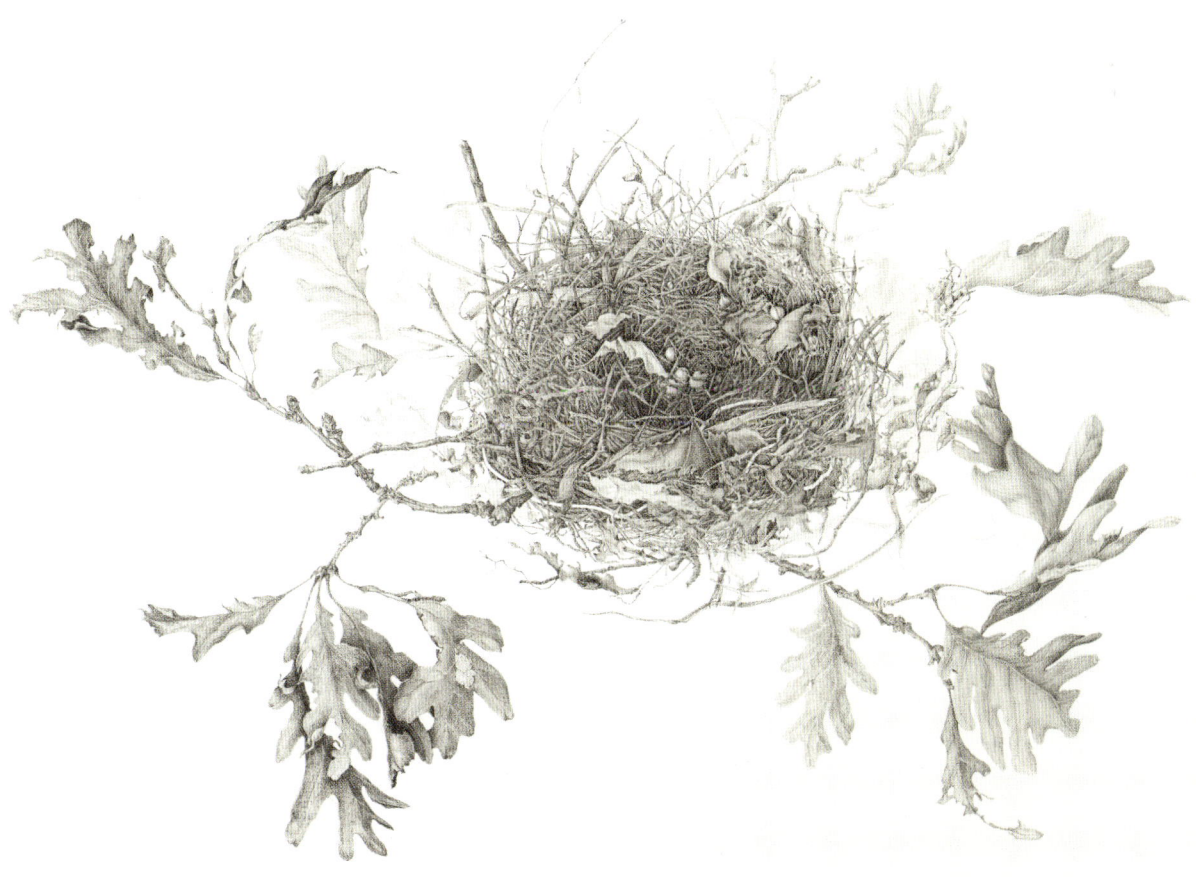

Bird's Nest
Silverpoint on coated watercolor paper
13 ½ × 18 ½ inches [33.75 × 46.25 cm]
© Linda Nemergut
HOURS TO COMPLETE: 30

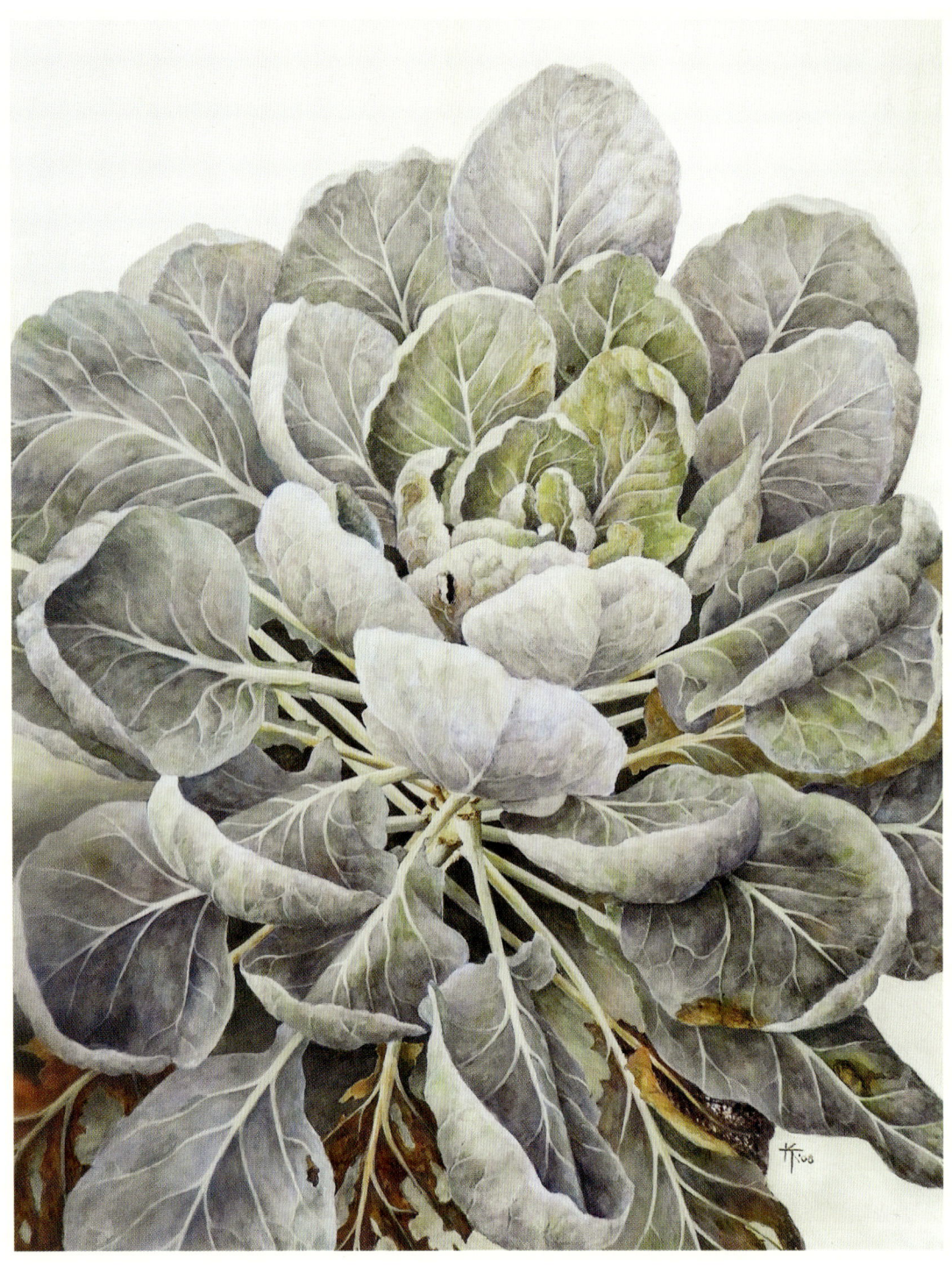

Brussels Sprouts Acrylic on gesso board 14 × 11 inches [35 × 27.5 cm] © Katie Lee

HOURS TO COMPLETE: 24

MATERIALS: Gesso board (¾ inch) [1.88 cm]; tracing paper; wet palette (a wet piece of palette paper on a sponge in an airtight container with a lid); palette knife; acrylic pigments: azo yellow, cadmium yellow, quinacridone rose, cadmium red light, ultramarine blue; container for water; gesso and matte medium; removable tape; white-plastic retractable eraser; 9H, HB, 0.3 mm HB, and 0.2 mm HB pencils; round synthetic brushes (for subject; nos. 2 and 4); 1-inch [2.5 cm] and 3-inch [7.5 cm] synthetic brushes (for background).

Acrylic paints aren't often used in botanical artwork, but they can yield compelling depictions. A modern medium, acrylics are made with a polymer binder and should contain at least 60 percent pigment to 40 percent binder. Depending upon how they are used, they can resemble anything from a watercolor painting to an oil painting. Acrylics become impermeable once dry, so, unlike watercolors, acrylic paintings can be framed with no glass.

Painting in Acrylics

TUTOR: KATIE LEE

Gesso is an important ingredient when painting in acrylics. Gesso is used to prime the painting surface, making a solid foundation for all the subsequent layers. It can also be used as a medium, as well as a lightener when mixing color. Artists should look for a gesso made in the traditional manner, using just enough acrylic polymer to bind the dry solids. If you purchase preprimed boards, be sure to find a maker that produces boards that won't warp and that contain sufficient layers of high-quality gesso.

A gessoed board and painted dried acrylics do not have an absorbent surface. Because the board surface is not absorbent, acrylic paint, when dry, remains on the surface—so the most dominant color is the last one applied; each successive layer blocks or minimizes the one before. Once complete, the painting should be sealed with a matte medium to ensure that the final thin glazes will not lift when the surface is wiped.

How to lighten values:

Adding gesso will lighten a pigment, according to how much gesso is added. Gesso will keep the paint opaque enough to cover previously painted layers and will not lift when dry, but it will make the paint look less translucent.

Adding water to pigment is a very effective way to lighten a value, as long as the dilution is no more than 35 percent to 40 percent water. If too much water is added, the pigment will sit on the surface and bead, creating a thin area with hard edges when dry. This layer will lift when more paint is applied.

This painting was worked in thin layers to create depth of color and rich complexity. To keep the colors clear and not muddy, a limited palette was used. Layers progressed from dark to light, from mixed colors to pure single pigments. Large areas were worked in first, gradually progressing to fine details. A slightly damp brush should be used to add initial glazes. A dry brush, with pigment only on the tip, should be used for the final details. Sometimes a final, dilute glaze of pure paint is needed to brighten or shift color.

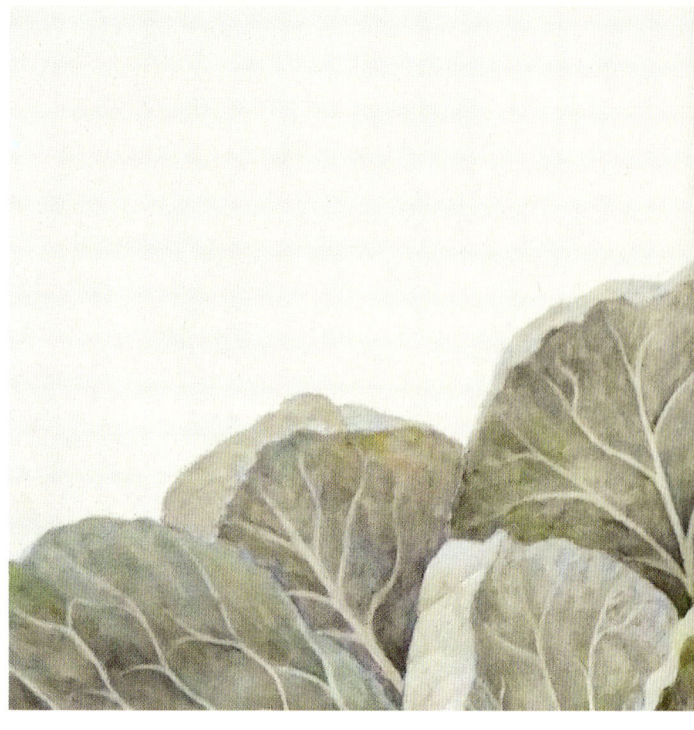

For the background, the board was simply toned with little or no detail. It can be as light or dark as is needed. This background is lighter at the top and darker toward the bottom. It was toned using a mix of ultramarine blue, cadmium red light, and cadmium yellow, with gesso, and was allowed to dry completely before any further painting.

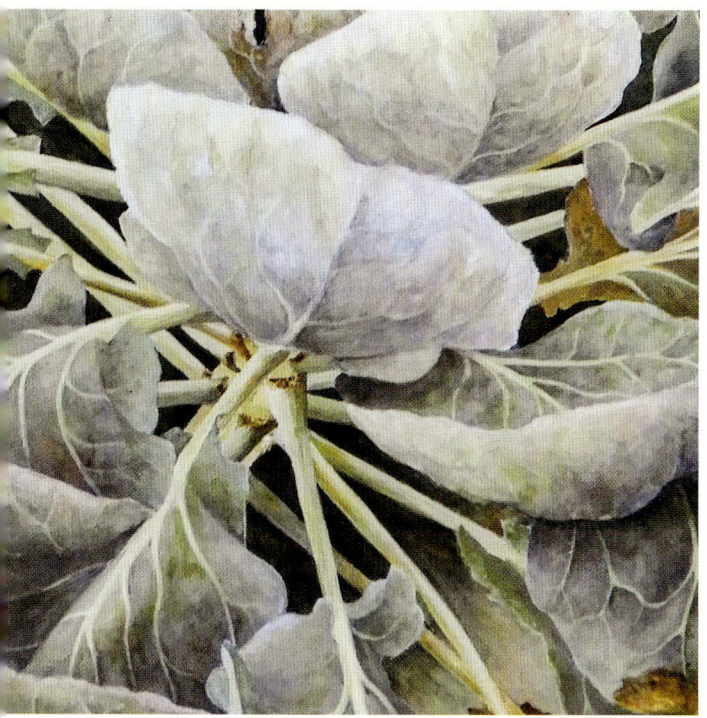

The stem and leaf petioles have been painted in. This layer creates the anatomical foundation of the plant. Even though most of this work will be hidden by subsequent layers of leaves, the foundation is critical for accuracy. Leaf center-lines can then be connected to the petioles. Next, the leaves are added, from those farthest away from the viewer to the closest. Some of the surfaces of the first leaf layers painted will be covered by additional layers, but this is how this plant grows, layer on top of overlapping layer.

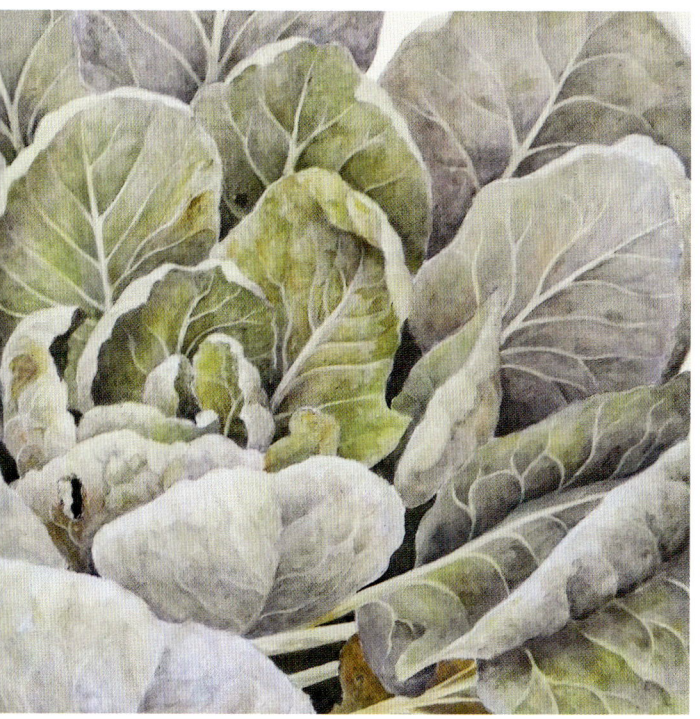

A variety of greens, blues, and violets have been used, and several brownish leaves at the base impart a fresh-from-the-garden aspect to the painting. The newest leaves were painted in a warmer, yellow green. The leaves are cupped inwardly, and this shape is modeled by adding shading to leaf bases and by showing a curled edge rolling over in highlight. Once all leaves were painted in, a single light source was defined by clarifying highlights and shadows. Dark shading behind the petioles provides depth, and cool highlights on leaf edges contrast with deeper shadows on leaf tops. Leaf undersides are lighter in value.

Oil painting is a technically challenging medium. To create fine details, like those found in botanical art, a variety of media are needed to improve its fluidity. Unlike watercolor, which dries almost immediately, oil paint dries slowly. However, when oil paint dries it is impermeable, so it can be painted over again and again. You can obtain a vibrancy, luminosity, and subtlety in the color with oil paint, and a variety of brushstrokes can create different textures. Both help to convey the richness and nuances of botanical subjects.

Painting in Oils

TUTOR: KERRI WELLER

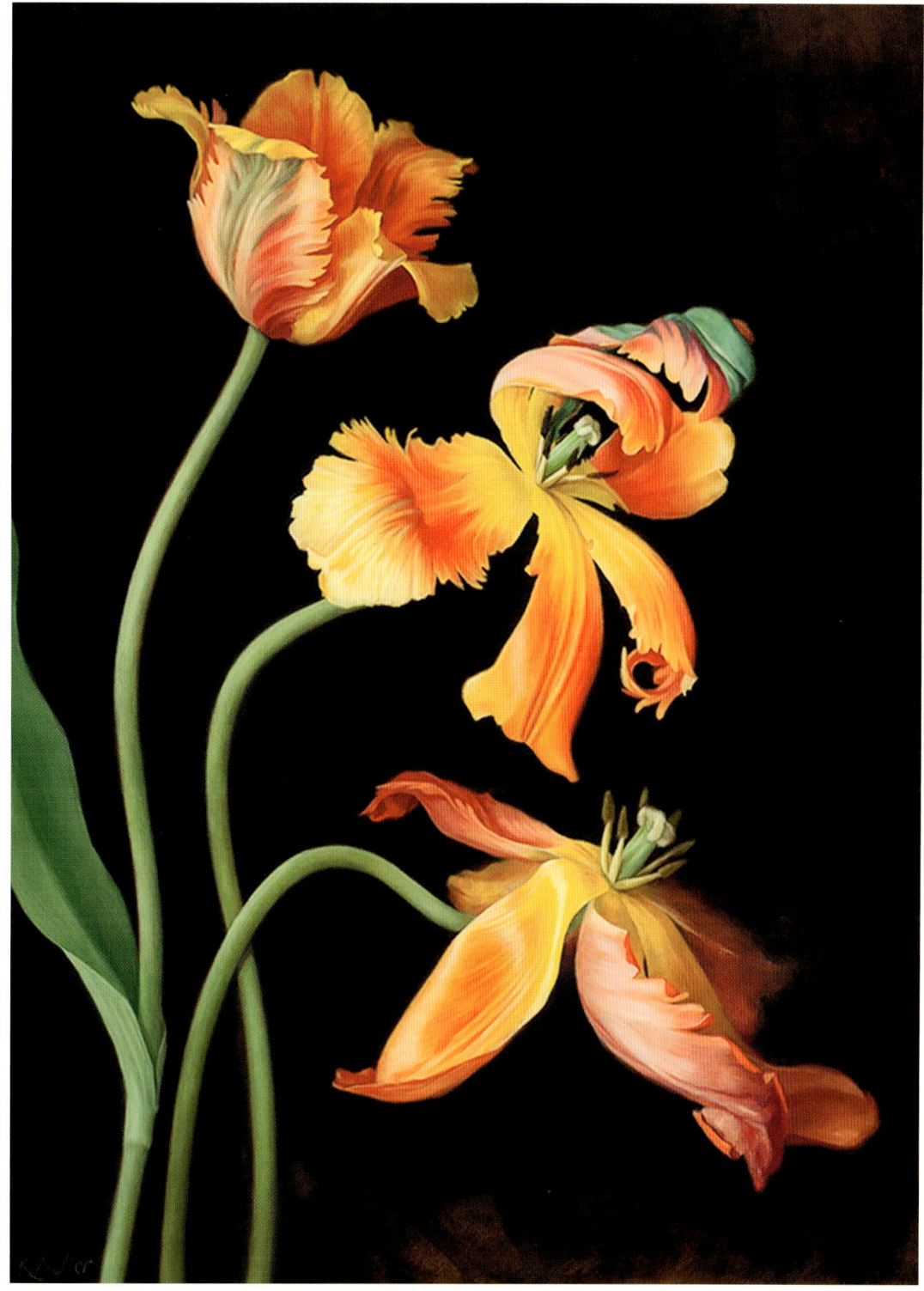

Parrot Tulips *Tulipa ×hybrida* Oil on panel 18 × 13 inches [45 × 32.5 cm]© Kerri Weller

HOURS TO COMPLETE: 120 HOURS

MATERIALS: Container for odorless mineral spirits; lint-free paint rag; palette knife; small round brush for details; four flat synthetic brushes in various sizes; filbert brush; bristle brush; mahl stick; wooden palette; oil paints; cool and warm versions of yellow, red, and blue; an earth color; metal cup clipped to palette for odorless mineral spirits.

Types of brushes and their uses for oil painting:

- Small brushes are for details and intricate passages of paint.
- Filbert brushes are used for soft edges and blending.
- Flat brushes are used to lay in areas of flat color.
- Bristle brushes are used to lay in composition and for drawing with a brush in dilute color, to guide the artist through the early stages of a painting (later covered up).

When you are working on the design of a composition, shapes are of prime consideration in describing the form and defining the subject. For this tulip painting, both the positive shapes of the flowers and the negative shapes of the background were considered. The goal in this painting was to show the tulips past their prime, but aging with grace and beauty.

Lighting for your subject: The quality and quantity of light reveals three-dimensional form and color. Natural, northern daylight provides light from one direction. Light from one direction can capture the nuances of color, texture, and form that give each flower its character. It provides light, mid and dark tonal values to create form, and gentle transitions between light and shadow.

Matching color: Mixing the exact color can be tricky. Use a neutral grey card with a small hole paper-punched in the center. Hold it up to the specific color on the subject to help identify hue, value, and chroma precisely. This isolates the color from all other surrounding colors.

A. Color

The colors are vivid yellow, orange, and saturated reds, but they become much more muted in the shadows and aging petals. To achieve these brilliant colors, yellows are first painted opaquely with little medium (odorless mineral spirits) in the paint. Then the reds are diluted with a small amount of medium and glazed thinly over yellow, giving vibrancy and the brightest chroma. In shadow areas, colors are dulled by mixing with complements. For example, yellow is mixed with purple, either on the palette or mixed directly on the painting. Because oils stay wet for an extended period of time, much color work can be done directly on the canvas, mixing into previous color applications to achieve further nuances.

B. Creating Depth

A range of tonal values from light to dark were used to create three-dimensional form. The petals are lighter in the foreground and darker as they recede. Contrast between light and dark is greater in the foreground and lesser in the background. And chroma is employed to create depth as well, ranging from bright to dull.

C. Using Edges

Edges describe texture and create depth. Sharp, detailed, and descriptive edges advance elements forward, whereas vague and soft edges make parts recede. Sharp edges in the foreground were clarified with small brushes, and soft edges in the tulip at bottom right were made with filberts and blended into the background color.

D. Using Highlights

Highlights help define textures, such as those in a silky smooth or dull, papery petal. A more abrupt end to a highlight makes a glossier sheen, and a more gradual highlight tapering into the petal color conveys a more velvety or dull petal. In oil paint, these highlights can be added over layers of other colors, using pale tints, whereas in some other media, highlight areas need to be isolated and worked around.

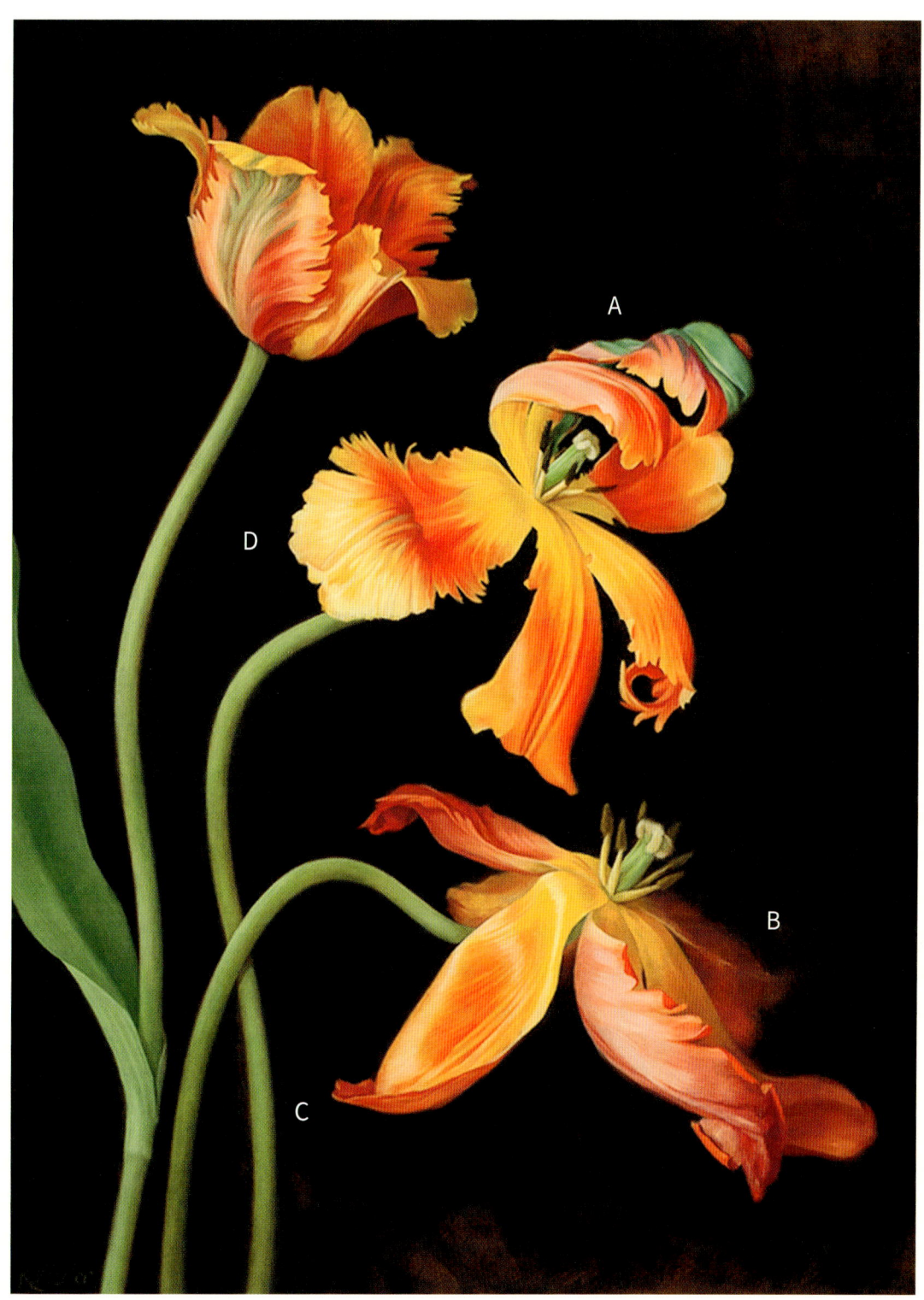

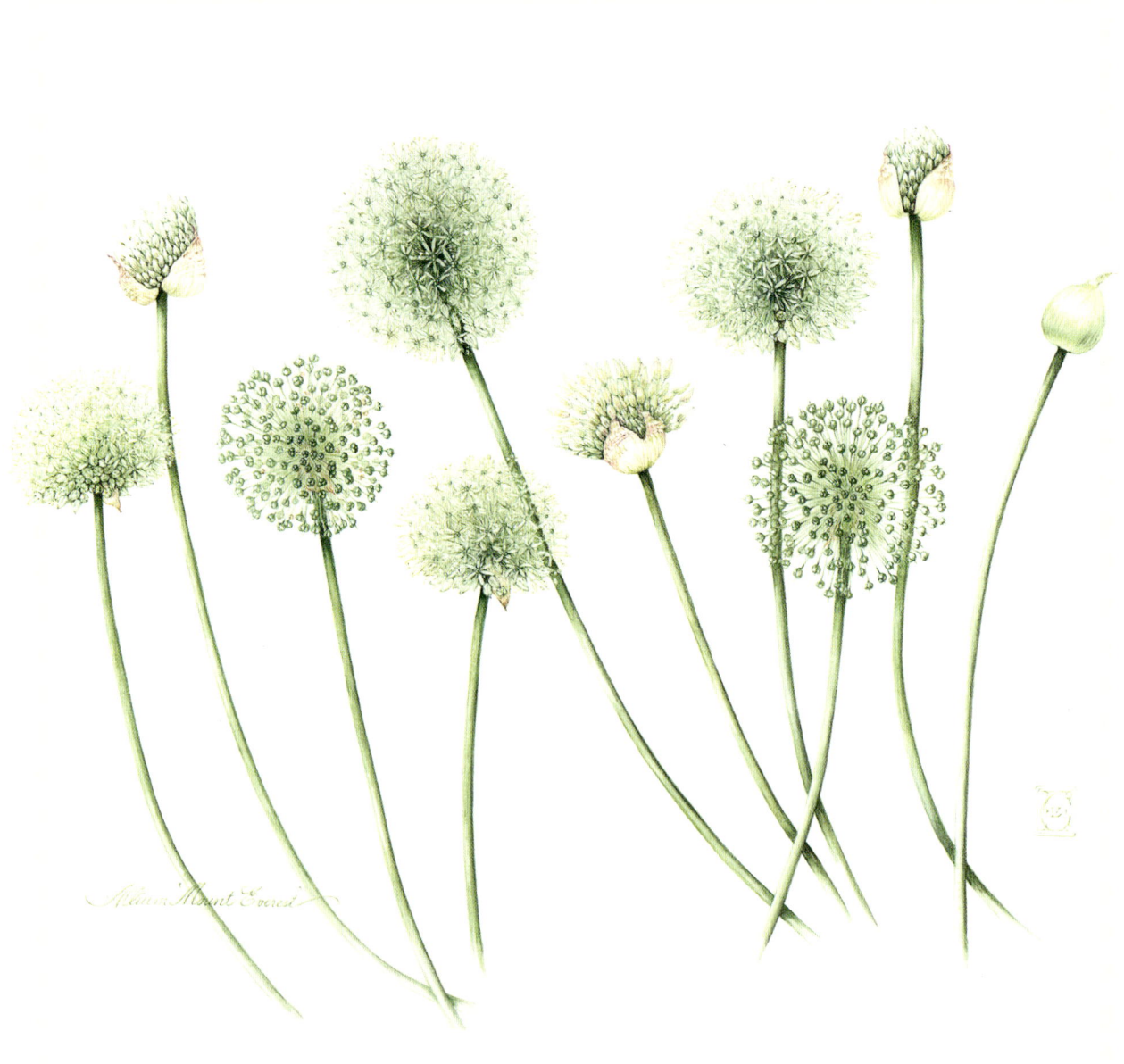

Allium 'Mount Everest' Watercolor on paper 19 ½ × 26 inches [48.75 × 65 cm] © Carol E. Hamilton

All artists develop their own approach to designing compositions, but nature itself is the best designer. Many artists make detailed compositional drawings and transfer them to the final work surface to begin. Others draw directly on the final surface, or even paint directly without drawing. A common practice is to make studies and preliminary drawings from life and use them as a starting point. These life studies provide the basis of a composition, but often further information is gathered from the same or similar specimens at the onset or as the work progresses. In these examples, design choices are made at a variety of stages to arrive at a final composition.

COMPOSITION

Principles and Approaches

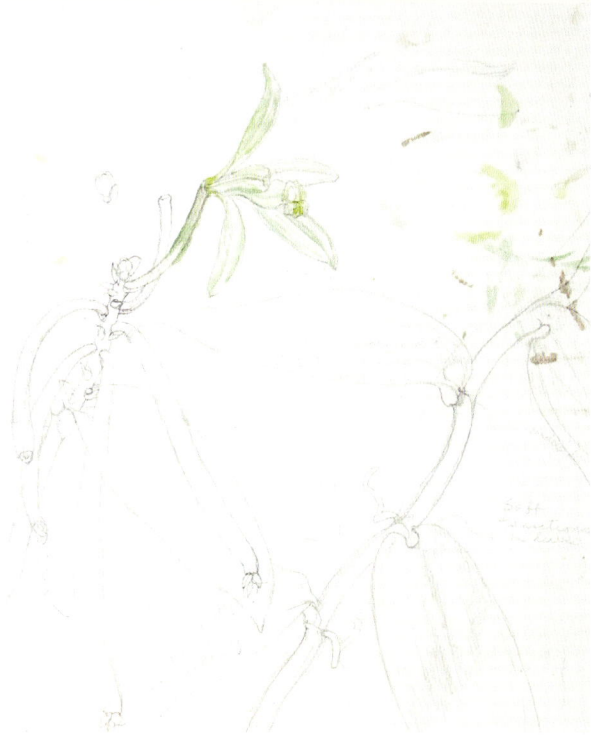

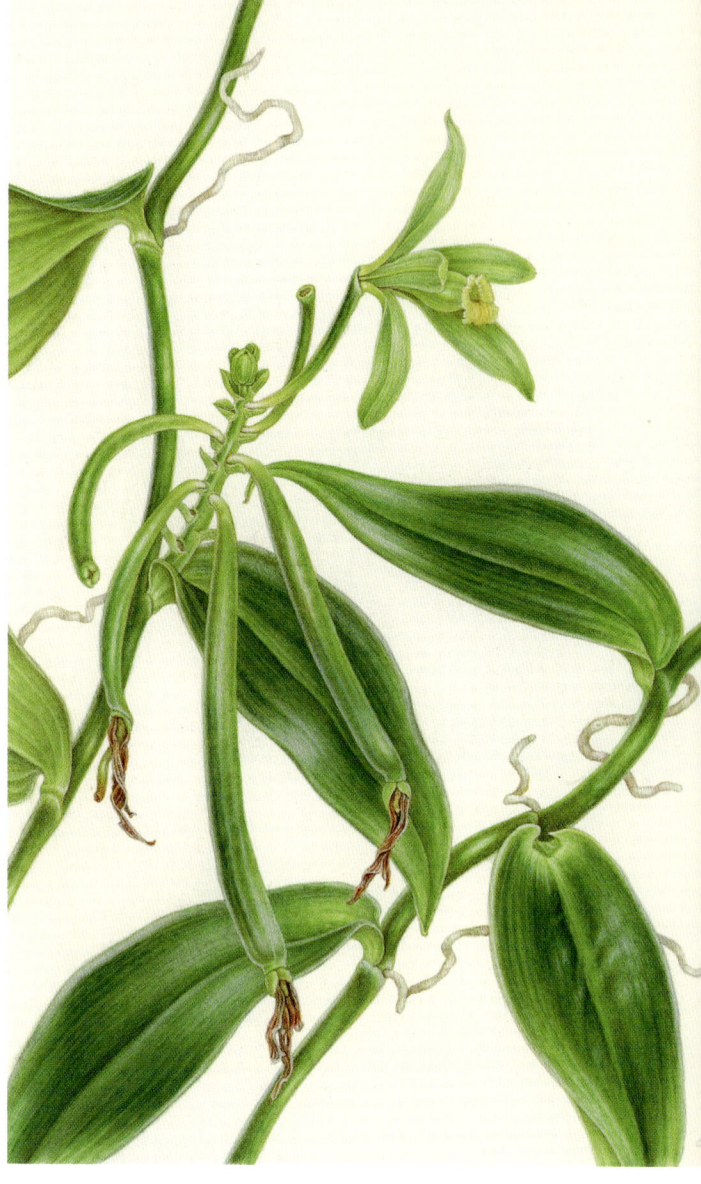

Composition in Practice

TUTOR: CAROL WOODIN

Vanilla planifolia is the species that is cultivated for its vanilla pods, and it makes a very interesting subject. The goal with this painting was to make a composition similar in format to a botanical book plate, but larger. Studies were done on one sheet carried from the east coast, where the leaves of the plant were studied, to the west coast, where the flowers and developing pods were found. This study was nearly complete as a composition, but changes were called for, and were drawn on an intermediary sheet of paper, then transferred. Lines were drawn around the image as intended edges for the composition and were adjusted while working when needed. Further additions were made as the painting advanced.

The upper right leaf segment on the right vine was reversed and moved to the bottom of the left vine. Pods were slightly repositioned and the entire left stem was moved upward. The composition was expanded at the bottom, extending the lower leaves on the right vine, which was also tilted at a sharper angle. The two stems in the study were almost parallel, so care was taken to make sure they were not parallel in the final. As the painting developed, it became apparent that some anchoring of the left stem would be needed, so a few different positions of an extended

Vanilla planifolia
Watercolor on vellum
14 × 9 ⅜ inches [35 × 23.75 cm]
© Carol Woodin

vine were tried, until a satisfactory position was achieved. When further information on leaves, vines, and roots was needed, the vanilla was visited in the conservatory. The two main directional lines made by the vines form a modified V, opening to reveal the flower, which is the primary focus.

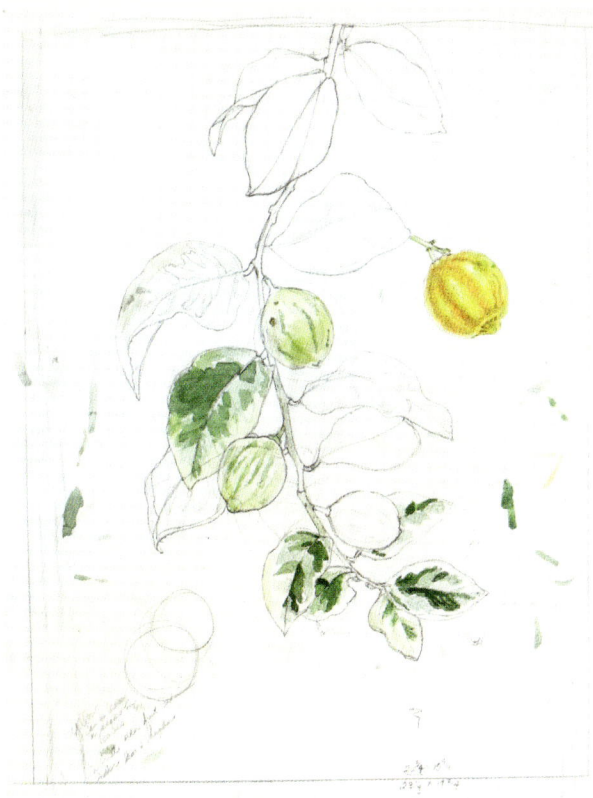

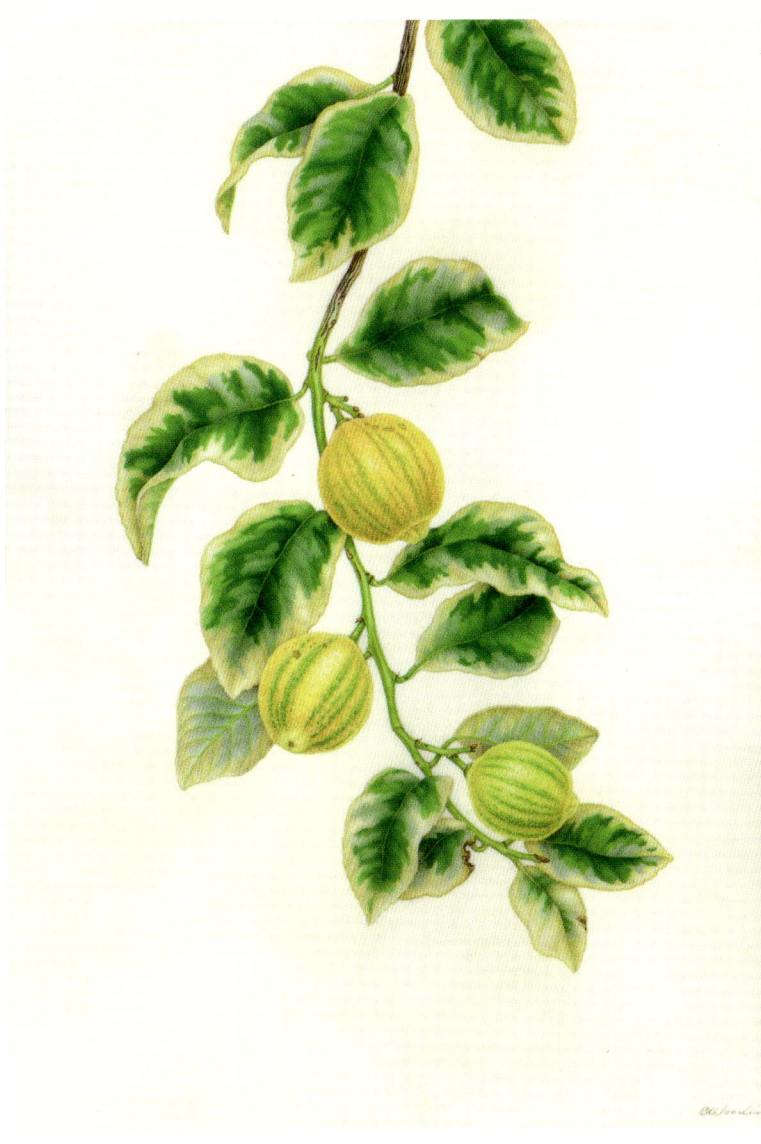

Ideally, one finds compositional direction in the living plant subject. Capturing its inherent dynamism imparts some of the life of the plant as well as its response to its environment. In the case of this variegated lemon, much of the composition was worked out while graphite and watercolor studies were made in a botanical garden conservatory. The composition began with the irregularly curving branch which provided an axis for the painting. Careful outline drawings were made of the leaves. Lemons at three stages of development were studied in color, and three were placed on the branch. An idea of placing a sectional slice of the lemon at lower left was considered but jettisoned, as can be seen by the sketched circles. The exact size of the picture plane was decided upon before tracing and transferring the compositional drawing. This is a necessity when painting on a panel. There can be more flexibility when not working on a panel, as long as there is sufficient substrate around the image area.

The evolution of study to final painting involved several alterations. To add weight to the top of the painting and anchor it more firmly, the upper right leaf was moved upward, adding its width to the upper edge of the painting. The main branch arches leftward, then to the right, and the asymmetrical composition is slightly closer to the left side of the picture plane, giving more breathing space around the lower, right end tip. The upper lemon in the sketch

Camouflaged
Citrus limon 'Eureka'
Watercolor on vellum over panel
20 3/4 × 15 3/4 inches [51.88 × 39.38 cm]
© Carol Woodin

was replaced with an intermediary between the two upper sketched lemons, but placed in almost the same position, as was the middle lemon. However, the bottom lemon was moved downward to add lower weight, and to make sure the spacing wasn't equal between all three lemons. Finally, some of the leaves were turned to their undersides to add interest and make them recede into the background. The lemon tree was visited several times to check details as painting progressed. A lemon of the same cultivar was on hand during most of the painting to provide reference for surface coloration and texture.

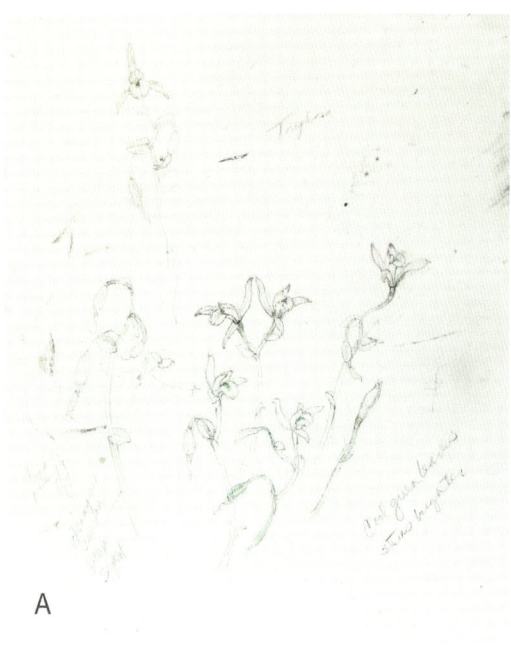

A

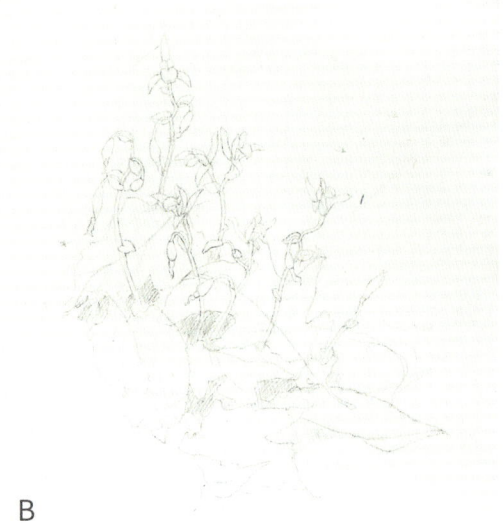

B

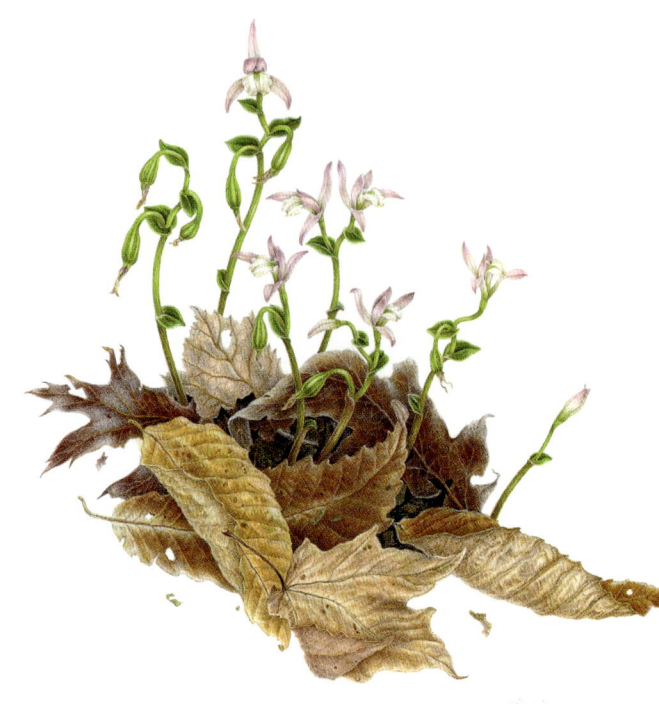

Three-birds Orchids, Catskills
Triphora trianthaphora
Watercolor on vellum
12 ¾ × 13 inches [31.88 × 32.5 cm]
© Carol Woodin

The flowers of this orchid only last a day, so when studying them in the field one has to make the most of it. Field studies (A) are a way to understand and memorize your subject. The process of drawing and painting makes a physical record on paper as well as a record in one's internal memory. Enough plants and positions were studied to create interest and a full composition. Only the subject itself was studied in the field, but notes were made recording the types of leaves in the leaf litter.

In the compositional drawing (B), the flowers and stems were organized visually to make an elliptical arrangement, sweeping downward from the upper left. Dried leaves were gathered, groupings of leaf litter were tried out, and a composition was designed with dark shadows under leaf layers noted. Then the drawing was traced and transferred.

First the orchids were begun, laying in basic shapes and colors. These were not changed from the original compositional drawing. Leaf litter was started, but a slightly stronger diagonal was sought, so a different beech leaf was found to extend the composition on the right. The dried leaf at far left didn't work, so it was replaced with the red oak leaf to extend the diagonal line through the forest floor elements. A large chestnut oak leaf was placed under the foreground maple leaf to provide a middle ground. The curled-under oak leaf at the back of the composition was positioned in a darker shadow to become a foil for the plants in front of it and to add depth to the overall composition. Three areas of very dark shadow were emphasized in the ground litter to add contrast and weight. These tiny, delicate orchids manage to push themselves up and through gaps in layers of dried leaves and it was hoped that impression would be captured.

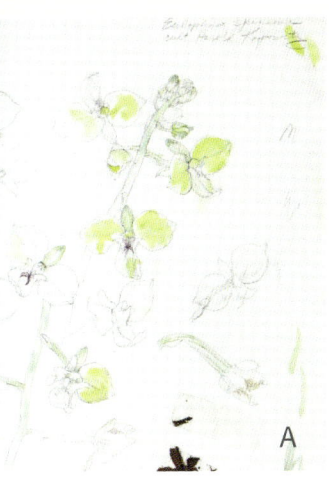

A

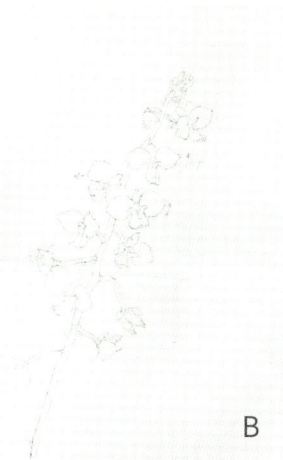

B

C

This statuesque South African orchid was studied while traveling, so it was studied in pieces on small sheets and assembled later (A). From the moment this plant was seen, the idea was to produce a tall, narrow composition echoing the robust and lush inflorescence. Flowers were studied from many different angles, as was the way the ovaries join to both the inflorescence and individual flowers. All details of the plant were drawn precisely and colors understood since the plant would not be available while the painting progressed.

Later in the studio a compositional drawing was made (B). Leaves were kept exactly as drawn in the study, but slightly more cropped on the left. Individual flowers were traced from the studies and the flowers on the forward side of the stem were placed into this intermediate drawing. Then the drawing was transferred to the final vellum stretched over a board to size. Some alterations were made once the painting was in progress.

An additional forward-facing flower was placed near the lower flowers to fill a gap in the composition, after removing a portion of the partially painted stem. Positioning was tested out with the flower drawn on tracing paper (C).

Leaves and plant base were cropped to anchor the lower part of the composition and counterbalance the tall stately inflorescence. The most difficult part of the painting was placing the individual flowers on the inflorescence. Flowers were begun as placed on the compositional drawing, as well as stem and leaves. Once color and shape began to clarify, the positions of the flowers on the back of the stem were drawn in graphite, then painted in. The flowers must be attached realistically—ovaries cannot be overly lengthy or too short. Consideration was given to ensure the flowers didn't line up perfectly along the outside edges of the inflorescence. The wilted flower at the bottom right was moved outward and

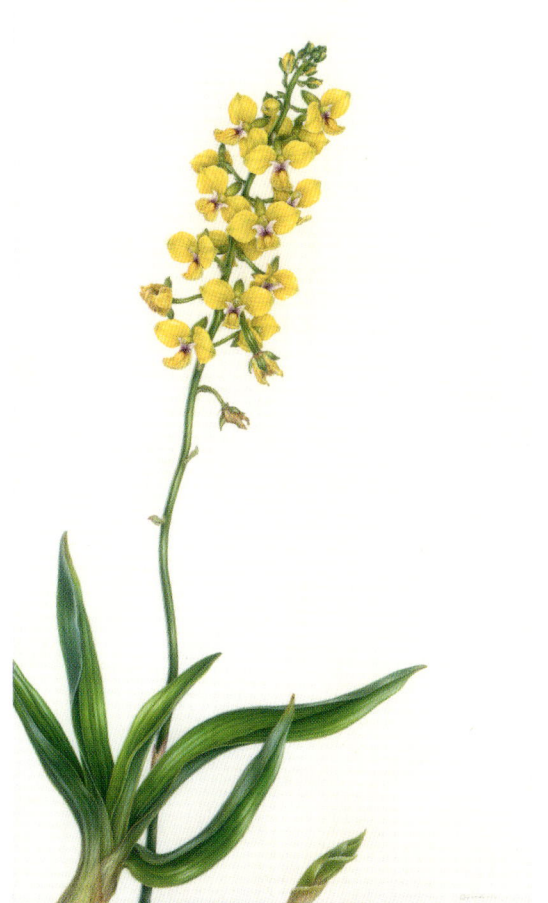

Eulophia speciosa
Watercolor on vellum over panel
27 × 15 inches [67.5 × 37.5 cm]
© Carol Woodin

downward and the possible addition of one at lower left was jettisoned. Once all other design decisions had been made, the new emerging leaf growth was traced and tested in various positions, then drawn in and painted.

Elements and Principles of Composition in Botanical Art

Composition is one of the most challenging aspects of botanical art. Formality has long been associated with botanical art and illustration, but, as with all art forms, contemporary artists are innovating and changing many conventions that have been viewed as traditional in botanical art.

Composition can be defined as the organization, or grouping, of the different parts of a work of art into a unified whole. This gives the artwork a structure and helps convey the artist's intent. The artist's visual tools in composing a work are its elements, and how those elements are used are considered its principles.

Although composition is challenging, it is essential to a successful work of botanical art. A great deal of time is spent on executing a work from start to finish, so considering and understanding some of the aspects of composition will help you avoid conceptual shortcomings. Below are some of the formal concepts of composition for visual arts in general, followed by the application of these concepts to botanical art. Finally, a number of widely differing composition types will be examined and discussed in terms of these elements, each illustrated by completed works by various artists.

Elements

Line All two-dimensional artwork begins with line. Line can be composed into simple or complex shapes, and it defines the edges of a form. Line can be thick or thin, horizontal or vertical, curved or oblique. Line creates a path moving through space that can also be used to drive a viewer's eye around the artwork.

Shape This is the overall outline of an object on the page. Some examples are round, cylindrical, triangular, or irregular.

Form Form defines an object in space in three dimensions: width, length, and depth. Form may have a geometric basis or it may be more irregular and organic.

Space In general, space applies to the area within the picture plane. The open area of substrate or flat background around the objects in a composition is considered negative space. The area that is occupied by the image is positive space.

Color All elements of color are included here, including chroma, value, hue, and tint. These elements of color can help create a sense of verisimilitude, or convey atmospheric perspective, among other things.

Texture This refers to the surfaces of three-dimensional objects and the ability to portray the surfaces convincingly in a two-dimensional work. Surfaces may be glossy, velvety, waxy, fuzzy or hairy, or they may exhibit a pattern or a bloom. Depicting texture well adds believability to works of art.

Principles

Focus is the star of the show, the most dominant emphasis in an artwork. In a botanical artwork, a single form might be depicted, or many objects, with one main resting point. Focus is not the same as focal distance, wherein artists sometimes choose a close-up focal distance, and at other times a farther-out view.

Contrast relates to value and refers to the extremes of change between dark and light. Botanical artworks can have differing levels of contrast between light and dark. Some artists fade out background elements, lessening contrast in the artwork, and others place background elements in shadow, adding to contrast. Varying light and dark can emphasize one element over others and convey the three-dimensionality of objects.

Movement is a sense of action or dynamism created in an artwork through the arrangement of its elements and the use of line. The viewer's eye is directed around the artwork, resting at places chosen by the artist.

Rhythm concerns repeated motifs, shapes, colors, patterns, or other elements adding punctuation to the movement in a work of art.

Proportion/Scale is the comparison between elements in scale and size. Often botanical artists use differing scales among elements in the work, enlarging some parts to make detail more apparent. This can also refer to objects rendered at larger-than-life size.

Balance is the placement of the elements of design in such a manner as to produce an aesthetically pleasing or harmoniously integrated whole. Balance can be achieved whether a composition is symmetrical or asymmetrical.

Unity is a state of harmony and completion in a work of art. No matter how many details need to be attended to, they should all serve the overarching intent of the work of art.

Asymmetry is a composition that cannot be divided into equal parts. This allows the artist more freedom to devise a balanced composition and adds action and dynamism. **Symmetry** is the division of a whole into two or more parts equal in size and shape.

The Three Pillars of Botanical Art and Illustration

There are essentially three indispensable pillars of a successful botanical artwork:

Scientific accuracy All parts of the plant that are shown must be botanically accurate. Its proportion should be correct, regardless of the scale used, and botanical details should not be generalized.

Aesthetic quality The illustration or artwork should have a strong composition, and the plant's three-dimensionality should be believably conveyed. Perspective should be proficiently depicted, and color should be accurate and lifelike. All the elements of the work should exhibit a consistent standard.

Artistic proficiency The artwork should demonstrate a superior control of and comfort with the chosen medium. The piece should exhibit a high standard of practical and technical application of the medium. Technical proficiency results in the successful execution of botanical accuracy and aesthetic quality.

Botanical art runs the gamut from traditionally composed works to works that are influenced by more contemporary concepts of composition. Compositions are often dependent upon the end use of the work, whether for scientific illustration, commercial application, or strictly as a fine-art piece. Regardless of the end use, the three pillars described above apply.

In scientific illustration, the requirements to be met are more numerous. The plant's habit is shown—either the entire plant, often at a reduced size, or a branch including leaves, conveying diagnostic characteristics. A floral dissection is given including the corolla (petals), calyx (sepals),

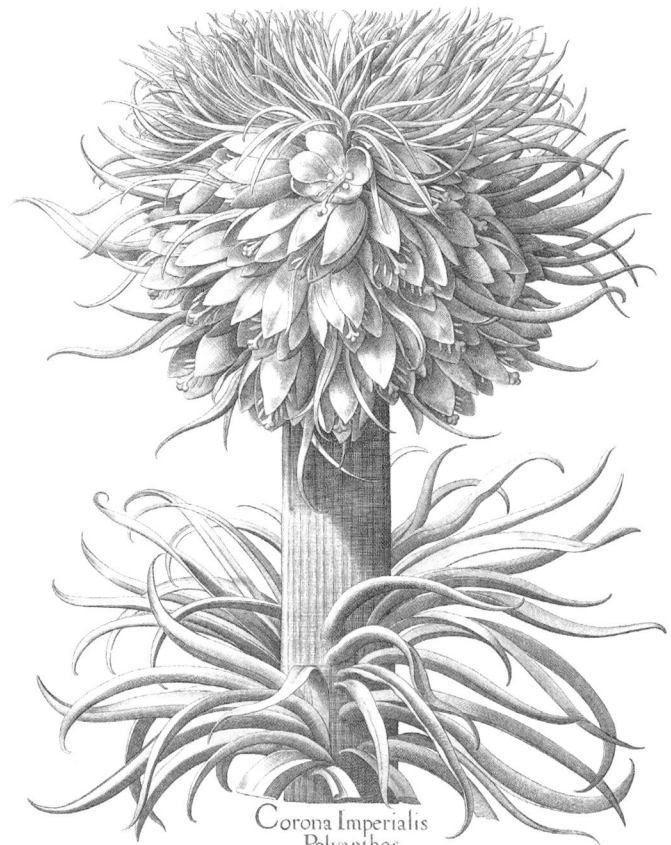

Corona Imperialis (*Fritillaria imperialis*) Engraving from Basilius Besler *Hortus Eystettensis* Eichstatt: J. G. Sthenander, 1713 Courtesy the LuEsther T. Mertz Library, The New York Botanical Garden

This engraving is an early example of a symmetrical composition in botanical art.

stamens, pistil, ovary, fruit, and seeds. All aspects of the plant's reproductive parts must be shown, and they are often shown in a magnified size for viewing. All the parts must fit in a pleasing way on a predetermined sheet size for reproduction.

A commercial project or commissioned artwork contains varying levels of requirements, which can include subject matter, plate size, medium, or even style. These must be considered when you are composing single or multiple works.

When the end goal is a fine artwork, these requirements do not apply; artists can choose to depict as much or as little of a plant as desired, in any stage of its growth, from seedling to wilted autumnal leaf or flower. A fine artwork leads to great freedom in composition.

Regardless of the composition you are devising, some basics are important. Many artists begin by making thumbnail sketches to try out different page layouts and see which is the most satisfying. These sketches can help prevent flaws that may become apparent as the artwork progresses. Some challenges to consider when you are composing an artwork include:

- Planning the negative space around the objects depicted
- Designing the subject elements to prevent a static composition
- Mindfully placing the objects in relation to one another to avoid aligning the artwork's components horizontally or vertically, unless that alignment is intentional
- Gauging in advance the size of sheet needed for the final artwork to avoid having to squeeze the subject's components onto a sheet size that is too small
- Providing variety in the positioning and gesture of repetitive shapes

This watercolor by Rose Pellicano is an example of excellent handling of repetitive shapes. With a single, central stem, simple entire leaves and many similar flowers in a raceme topping the stem, the possibility of a repetitive, formulaic approach was high. However, the artist used subtle undulations in the stem to add motion and grace and placed the leaves in multiple positions and carriages around the stem. Flowers are placed organically rather than mechanically, and they are shown fully open at the bottom and in rich coloration. As they progress up the stem toward the tip, flowers fade in color and gradually reduce in size to small buds at the tip.

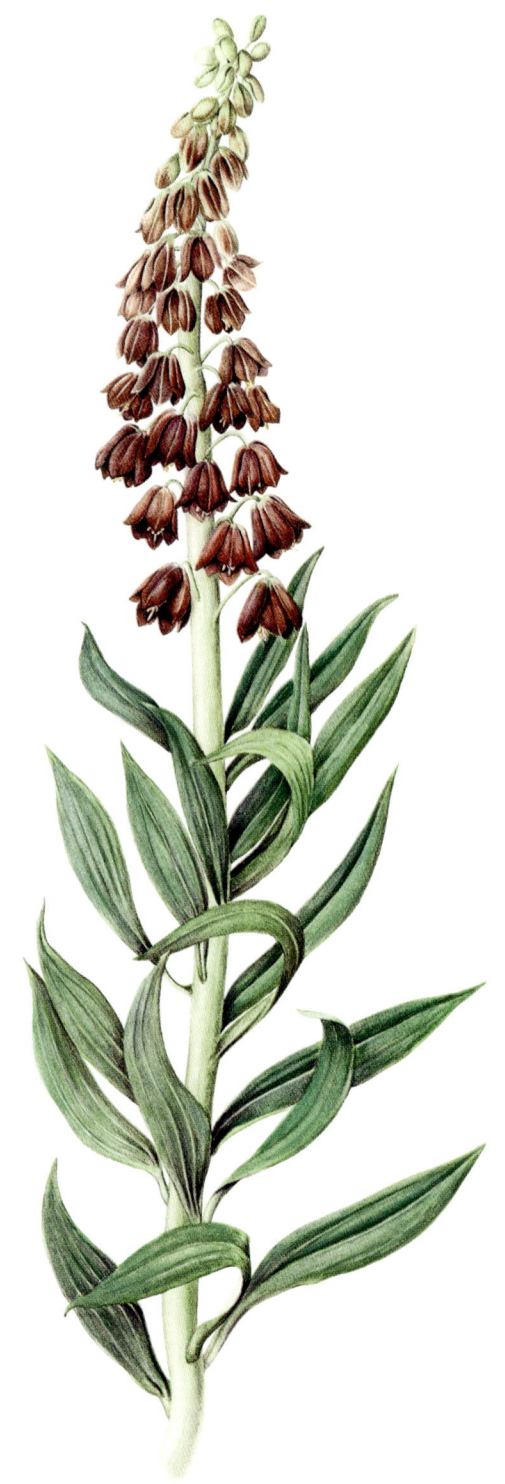

Persian Lily
Fritillaria persica
Watercolor on paper
18 × 14 ½ inches [45 × 36.25 cm]
© Rose Pellicano

Akiko Enokido has depicted this *Tacca* in an advanced composition, showing buds, fully open flowers, and flowers progressing into seed pods. She has used contrasting values to depict shadow and to lay objects in front of others (as in the main upper flower cluster brought forward by deep shading between it and the two large bracts behind). The eye is moved through the painting, first observing its two main flower clusters, then noticing the tiny newly developing cluster at lower right as a counterpoint. Leaves show a range of values from bright highlights through the dark shadows that place the back leaf behind the two more forward leaves. Because of the skillful use of highlights and shadows, even the little whiskers cascading downward don't get lost, whether passing through white space or passing before leaf surface of varying values. The placement of the entire composition on the page is perfectly balanced.

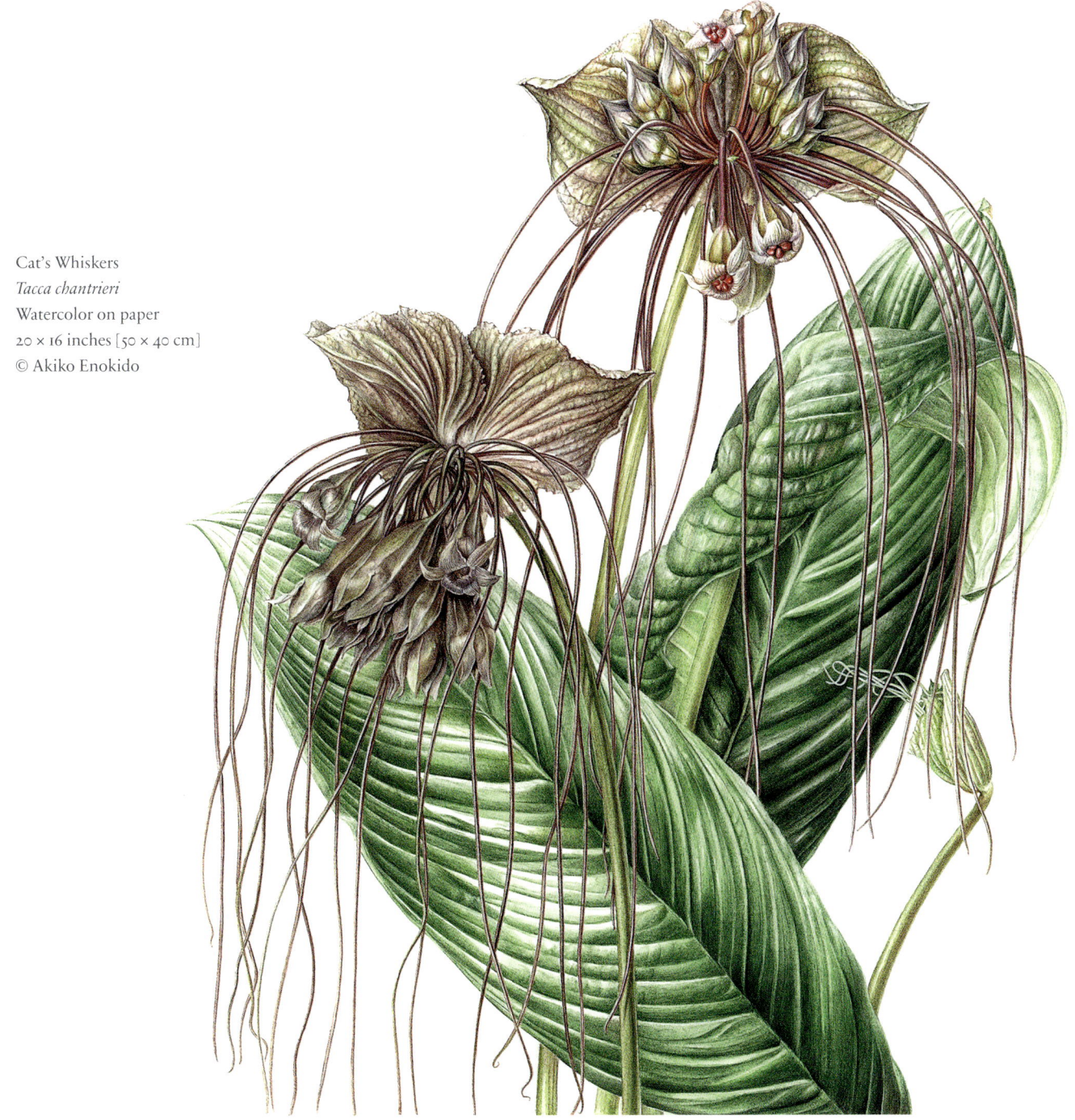

Cat's Whiskers
Tacca chantrieri
Watercolor on paper
20 × 16 inches [50 × 40 cm]
© Akiko Enokido

Different Approaches to Botanical Composition

TUTORS: CAROL WOODIN AND ROBIN A. JESS

Although a baseline standard of botanical accuracy is required, there is still a great deal of freedom within the art form. Artists find that the discipline in achieving this standard of clarity and detail is one of its most enjoyable aspects. Each artist over time develops an individually recognizable style and has great latitude in content and design. We can examine composition through a wide range of approaches used by various artists. Each of these instructive examples serves to illustrate some of the principles of composition.

1. **One plant in space** at one specific stage can be shown, surrounded by negative space. This type of botanical composition has long been practiced, from seventeenth- and eighteenth-century works by artists such as Nicolas Robert and Georg Dionysius Ehret, to today, where this is the most frequently used compositional type. A common impulse among botanical artists is to be captivated by how a plant looks at one particularly moment, and to want to pass that vision on to others.

Carrie Di Costanzo is known for her powerful images of plants, and for her versatility. She works in gouache, acrylic, watercolor, and egg tempura creating images with great impact. This painting of an iris is a perfect representation of a snapshot of a plant as it appears on a single day. The composition includes strong verticals, and a central V opening between the leaves to give space to a perfectly flowering iris. By cropping the leaves at the edge of the picture plane, Carrie anchors the substantial weight of the large flower, and she shows two flower buds to add interest to the composition. Her depictions of a variety of textures, including waxy leaves, velvety falls, frilly standards, and tissue-like bracts, add interest to every inch of the painting.

2. **Life cycle** can be depicted to show, for example, how flowering progresses or how a seedling matures to fruit. This is generally a more traditional style of composition, and it may include close-up details of some aspects of the plant.

This complex watercolor of a mahogany tree in fruit (PAGE 384) might be considered a more traditional composition, but Jessica Tcherepnine imparts a contemporary freshness to the subject through her approach to watercolor. Unlike most botanical artists, she does not draw out her composition in advance, but rather works directly on the page, beginning with an initial gesture and composing as she goes along. The entire sheet can be seen here, displaying how ideally the elements of design are placed on the page. The naturalistic gesture of the branches adds dynamism, and diverse forms are placed in a rhythmic way, so one's eye is drawn through the painting. This painting shows four different stages of the developing seed pods still on the branch, and three further stages punctuate the bottom of the painting.

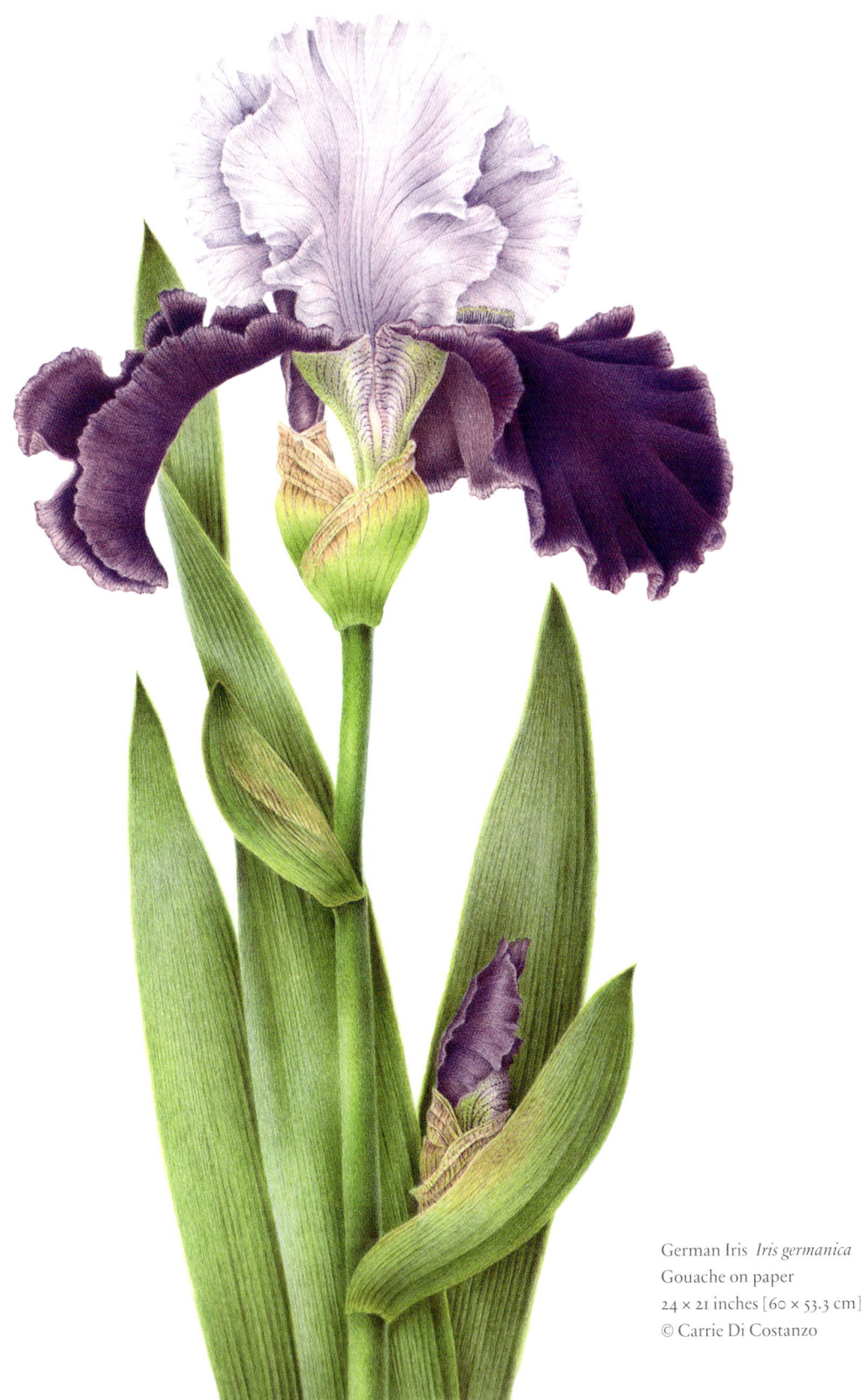

German Iris *Iris germanica*
Gouache on paper
24 × 21 inches [60 × 53.3 cm]
© Carrie Di Costanzo

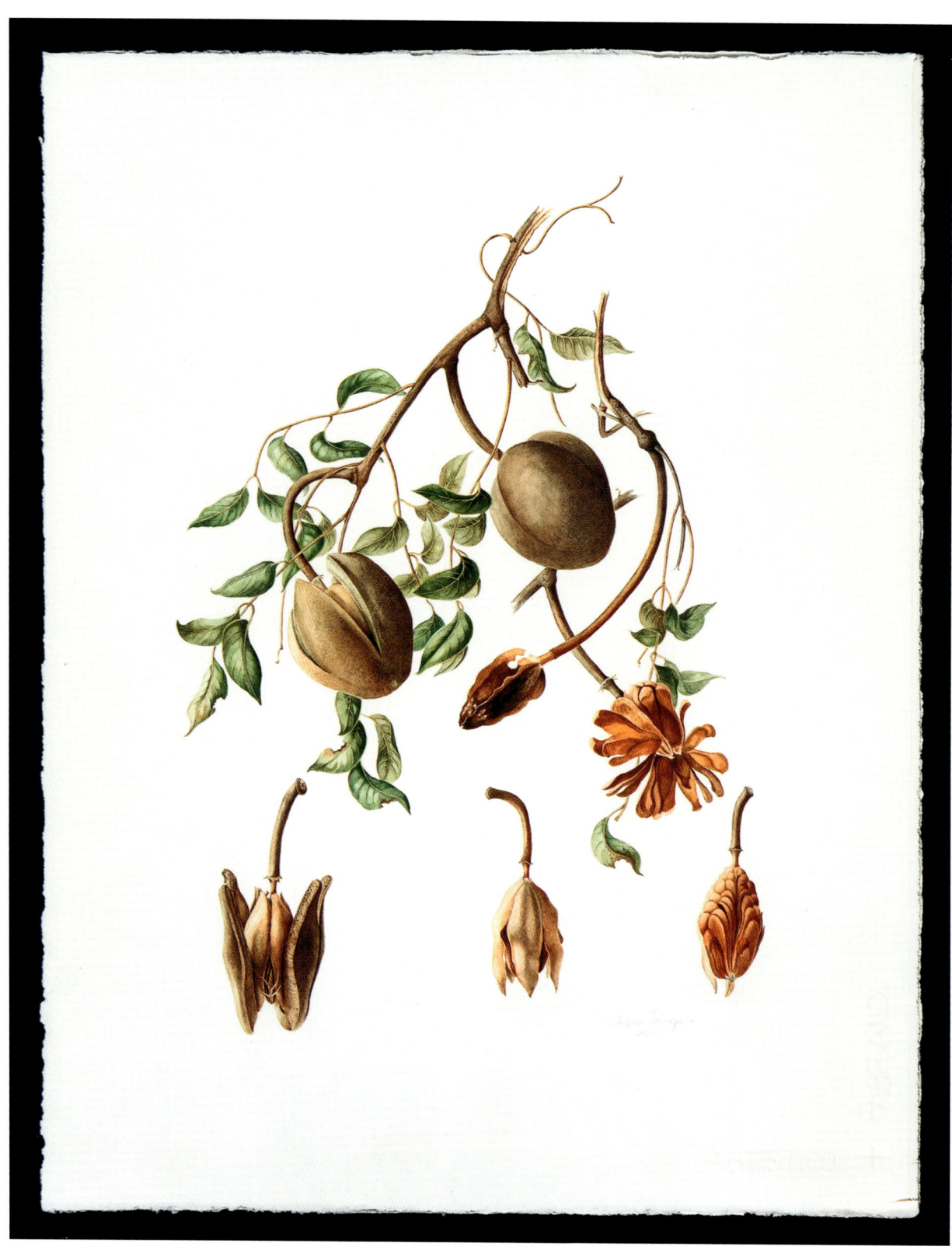

Mahogany Seed Pods *Swietenia mahagoni*
Watercolor on paper 26 ¼ × 21 ⅛ inches [65.62 × 52.8 cm]
© Jessica Tcherepnine

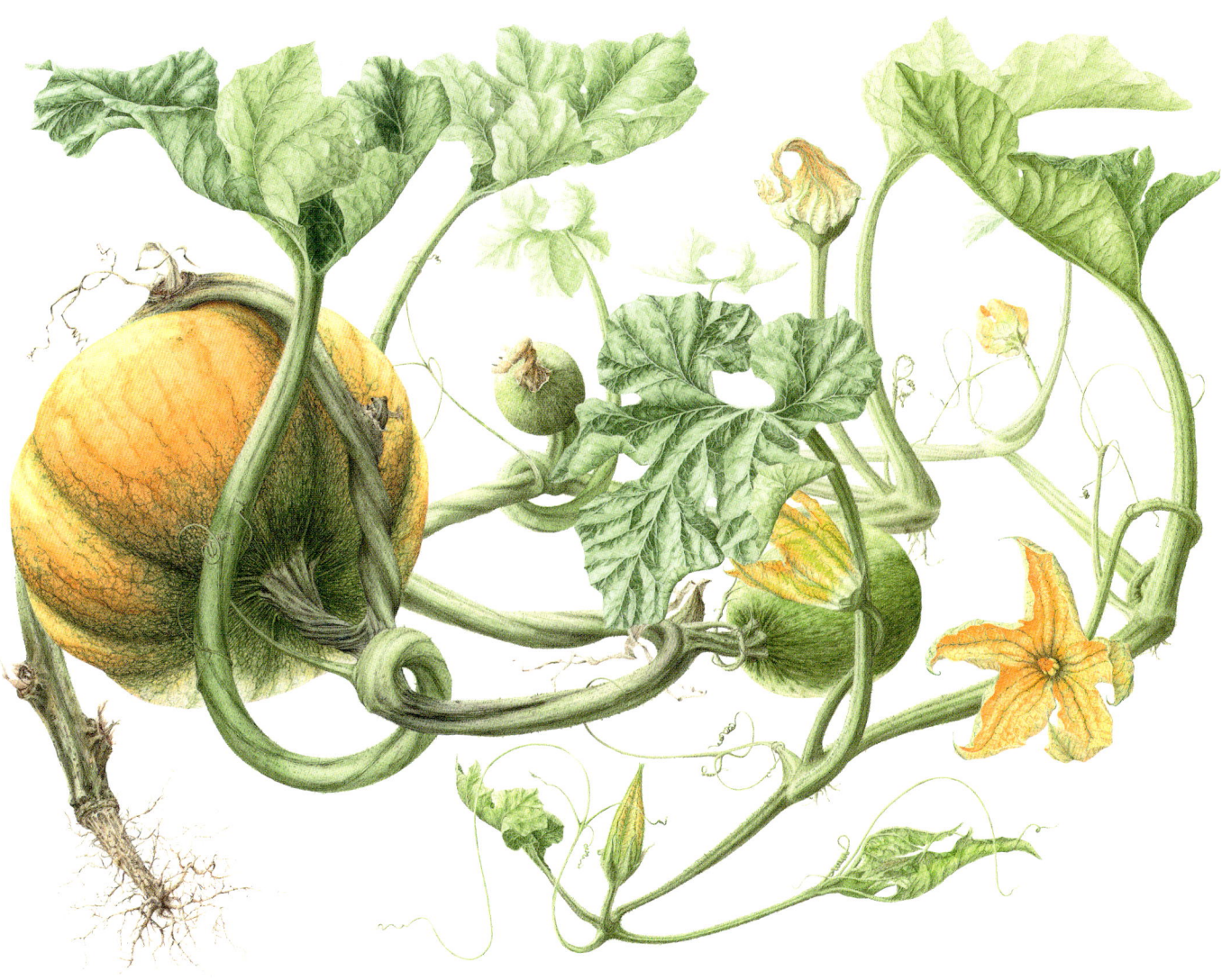

Pumpkin Vine *Cucurbita pepo*
Watercolor on paper 22 × 30 inches [55 × 75 cm]
© Hillary Parker The Alisa and Isaac M. Sutton Collection

In this example of a naturalistic life-cycle painting, Hillary Parker directs the viewer around her composition from bud to mature pumpkin. The heavy leaves on top create one side of a classic triangular arrangement; the other sides begin in the top corners and culminate in the lower center at a tiny bud. That bud is the focus of this whirlwind, providing a starting point to trace the development of the fruit. Balance is achieved by color; the glowing orange hues are strategically placed amongst the green vines and leaves.

The interesting negative spaces on the right are filled with buds, flowers and tendrils which visually match the heavy pumpkin on the left. From the bud, the vine meanders to the right, then across behind the plant, almost disappearing. It is cleverly brought, robust and sinewy, into the center. Looping to the left, it holds the pumpkin, then in its last appearance, reveals the uprooted end, showing that this pumpkin's time on the mortal coil is complete.

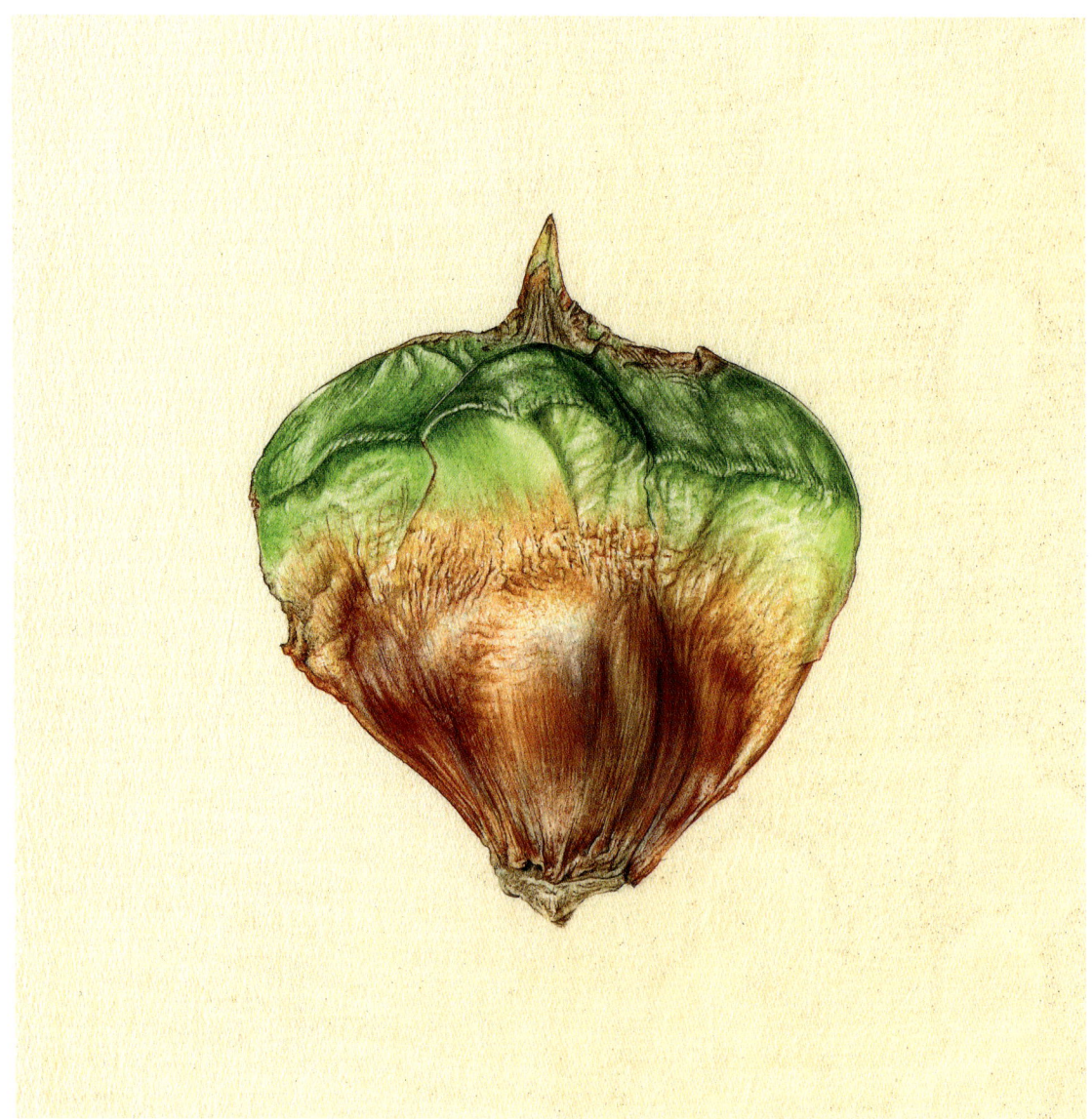

Ovuliferous Scale
Bunya Pine *Araucaria bidwillii*
Watercolor on vellum 6 ¼ × 5 ½
inches [15.62 ×13.75 cm]
© Mali Moir

3. **The icon** of a plant or plant part suspended in space is a newly developed stylistic choice. Often this icon is shown at an enlarged scale to display fine details or textures.

Mali Moir (ABOVE) has chosen to focus on a single scale from the cone of a Bunya pine, allowing a close look at one of between 50 and 100 scales that a cone typically contains. This surprising choice yields great rewards for the viewer. The scale floats in space and contains a range of hues from siennas to golds and greens in varying values, as they move over the three-dimensional surface of the scale. Strongly lit from the left, deep shadows on the right side of the bulging seed contrast with the highlights on its golden upper edges. Ridges formed by the press of the now missing scale that would have lain on top of this one, create a topography that Moir has skillfully used to advantage, to create visual interest throughout the scale.

4. **The collection** is a composition of many plant parts, not necessarily from the same plant.

Asuka Hishiki has an original take on the collection approach to composition (BELOW). Using color, pattern, and size she creates visual interest with eight kinds of beans and four kinds of beetles. Larger beans and beetles form a central cross, while concentric rings alternate between light tones of yellow and green, and dark tones of burgundy and sienna. Everything is lit from the right, unifying all elements. Starting with a 2 ½-inch-square [6.25 cm] grid used for her series of collections paintings (RIGHT), circles have been laid over the grid to retain its geometric underpinning. The four corners of the overall rectangle are marked by small upended beans, like megaliths seen from far above, an unexpected viewpoint that changes one's relation to the composition: suddenly the viewer is standing above instead of in front of the painting. The series includes paintings of beans in double circles, which you can also see on the grid layout, as well as beans laid out in horizontal rows.

Grid layout for collections series,
Asuka Hishiki (BELOW)

B & B, Multiple Circles Watercolor on paper
9 ½ × 12 ½ inches [23.75 × 31.25 cm]
© Asuka Hishiki (BOTTOM)

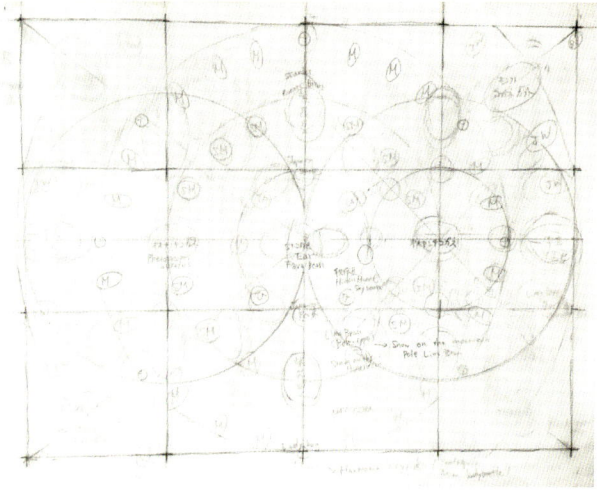

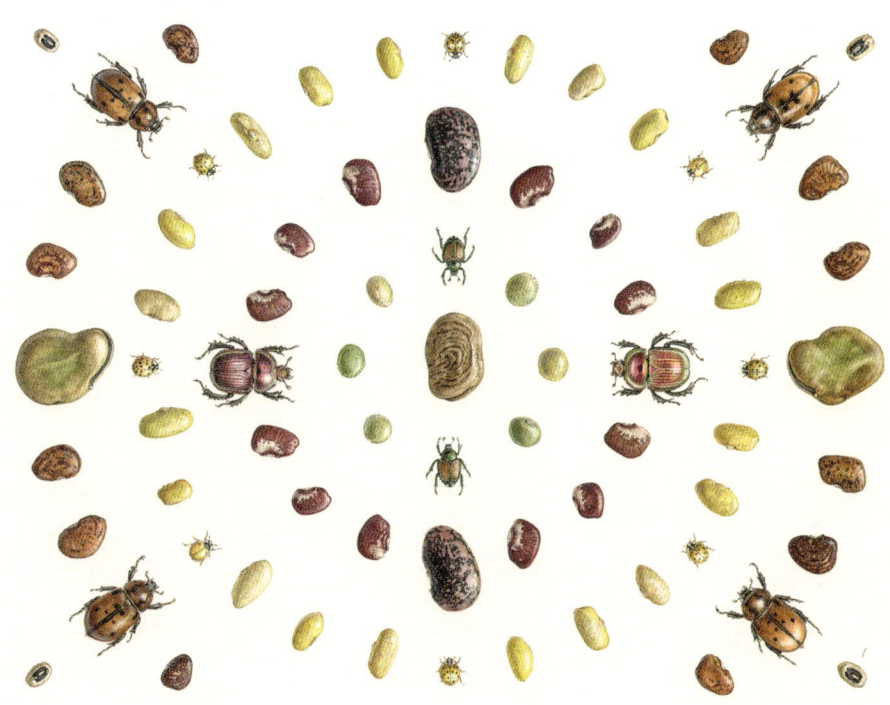

5. **The bouquet** has long been a way of grouping together a variety of flowers or plants in an aesthetically-focused composition.

This arrangement in whites and blues (BELOW) is a great example of why the bouquet represents a high level of achievement in botanical art. Composing a group of different sizes and types of flowers in a tight cluster, with seamless flow and graceful positioning, is not an easy task. Karen Kluglein has handled this commissioned assignment with great aplomb – three large round forms of hydrangea flowers are dispersed through the arrangement, along with a single lily and a ranunculus in its center. Less weighty flowers such as Queen Anne's lace and lisianthus add some lightness and allow greens to surround the center of the bouquet. The stems are bunched together, and partially hidden by leaves with blue highlights. These highlights and other blue-green elements echo the color of the smaller blue flowers that are sprinkled around lending a unity to the piece. Positioning the bouquet horizontally provides a completely different dynamic than the typical upright position.

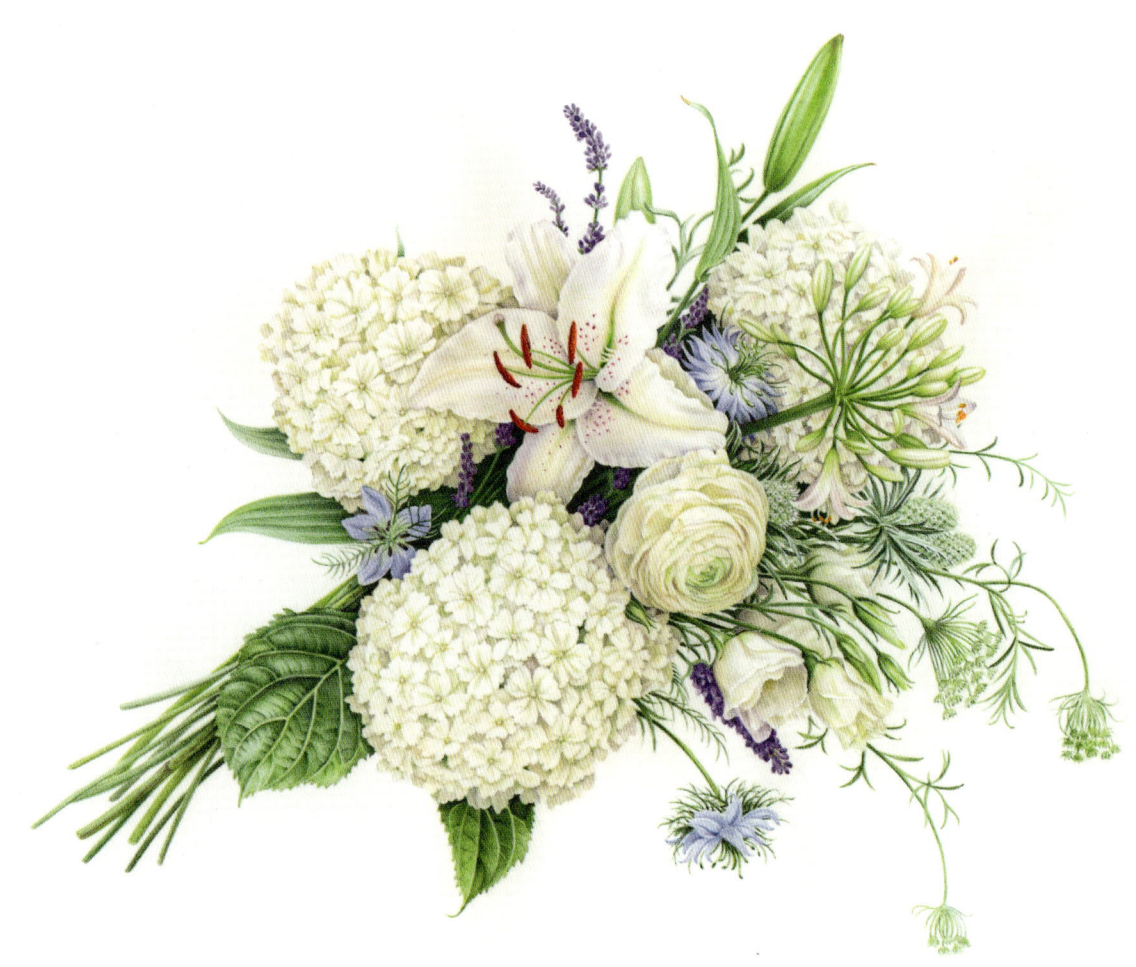

Something Blue (bouquet) Watercolor on vellum
9 × 12 inches [22.5 × 30 cm]
© Karen Kluglein

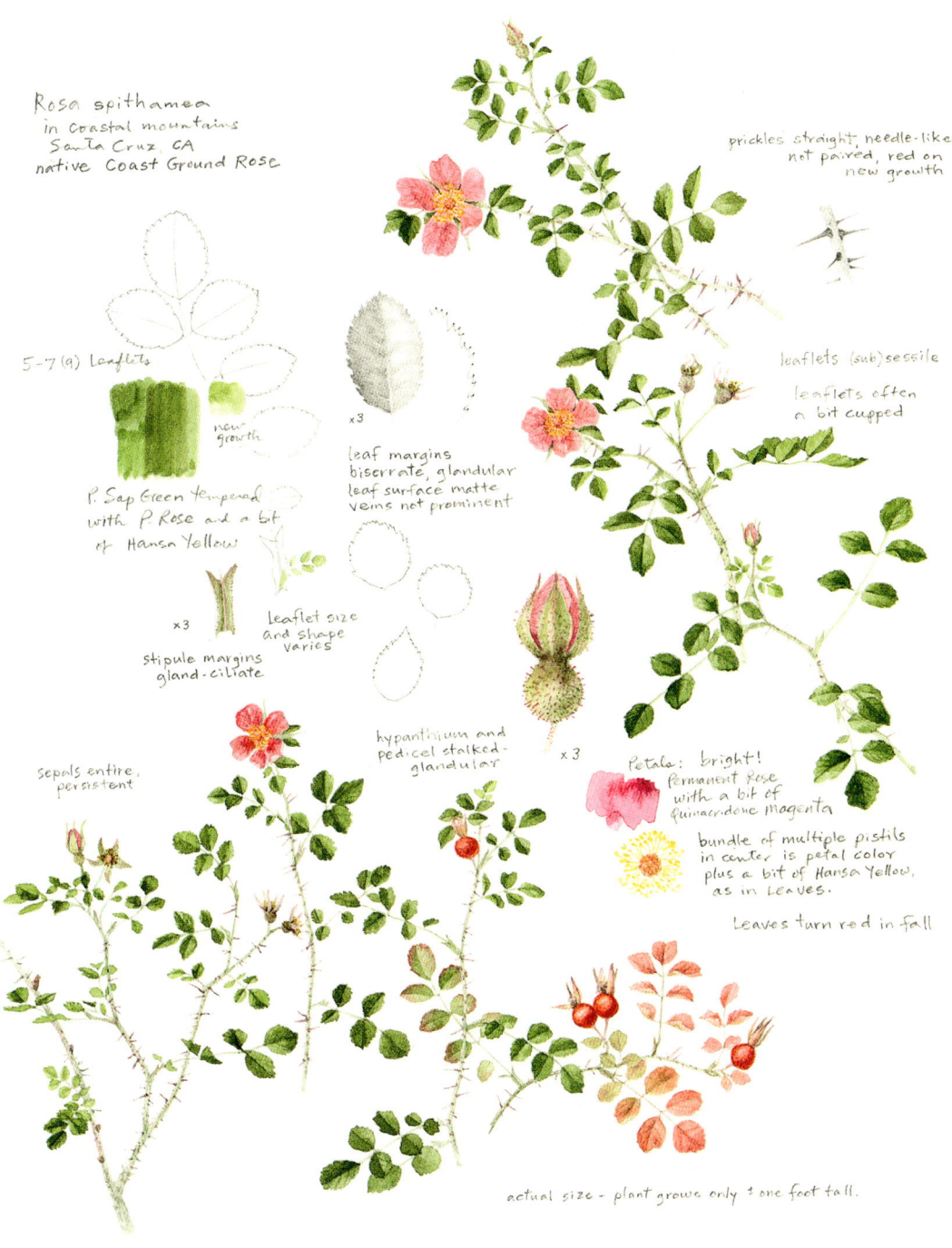

Rosa spithamea
in Coastal mountains
Santa Cruz, CA
native Coast Ground Rose

prickles straight, needle-like
not paired, red on
new growth

5-7 (9) leaflets

new
growth

P. Sap Green tempered
with P Rose and a bit
of Hansa Yellow

x3

stipule margins
gland-ciliate

x3

leaflet size
and shape
varies

x3

leaf margins
biserrate, glandular
leaf surface matte
veins not prominent

leaflets (sub)sessile

leaflets often
a bit cupped

sepals entire,
persistent

hypanthium and
pedicel stalked-
glandular

x3

Petals: bright!
Permanent Rose
with a bit of
Quinacridone Magenta

bundle of multiple pistils
in center is petal color
plus a bit of Hansa Yellow,
as in Leaves.

Leaves turn red in fall

actual size - plant grows only ± one foot tall.

Coast Ground Rose *Rosa spithamea*
Watercolor and graphite on paper 14 × 11 ½ inches [35 × 28.75 cm]
© Maria Cecilia Freeman

6. The study page is often research and documentation used exclusively as the artist's background materials for a separate, finished work. At other times, it can be considered a completed work in its own right.

This composition (OVERLEAF) documents the distinctive characteristics of a small wild rose that grows in the Santa Cruz mountains and is identified as the California native fire-adapted species *Rosa spithamea*. Maria Cecilia Freeman planted a 3-inch [7.5 cm] rhizome and watched it grow, bloom and set hips for two years, making drawings and color samples along the way. The artist began with the watercolor habit study in the lower portion of the page. To balance color and movement around the page a bud and blooming canes were placed in the upper right, adding color swatches to record the rose's palette. Detail studies in graphite, and annotations as a deliberate part of the composition, sit in a logical but balanced distribution around the page. The result is a fresh and lively spontaneous composition that seems to share the artist's process with the viewer. The time spent on this study page span the two years included observing, making informal preliminary drawings, selecting and arranging drawings into a composition, transferring them to watercolor paper, and finishing in graphite and watercolor.

7. Overall sheet format can influence the impact of an artwork. The most frequently seen format is found in standard sheet sizes, roughly in a ratio of 3:4, whether 9 × 12 or 22 × 30. However, more extreme ratios that are strongly vertical or horizontal can be used to great effect.

By using a sheet that is long and narrow, Denise Walser-Kolar (RIGHT) conveys something about this hyacinth that might have been lost in a more standard format. Parts of the plant normally unseen occupy nearly half of the image length in this linear composition. Leaves are held upright and close to the stem, adding to the energetic quality of the raceme of buds ready to burst. The second raceme on the right makes the composition slightly asymmetrical and is balanced by longer roots on the left side. Blues and violets in the flowers are repeated in the lower end of the painting in the bulb and roots unifying the whole image. Deep contrast between leaves, small touches of shadow behind flowers, and rich browns in the bulb lend a full range of tones, providing volume and depth in the painting from top to bottom.

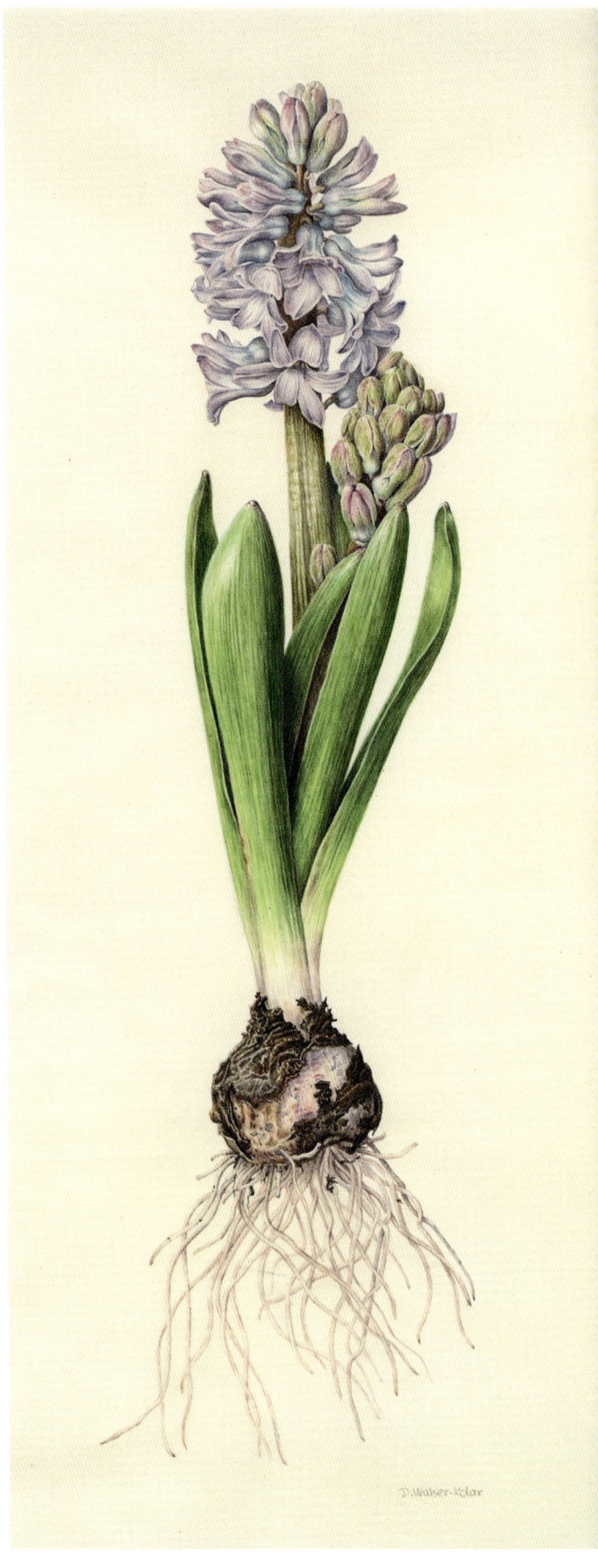

8. **Expanded sheet size** can be used to create either very large images, joined images, or diptychs or triptychs of any size. When the limits of a single sheet have been reached, multiple sheets or rolled paper can be used to allow impressively large depictions.

This species of bamboo is very tall, so this view of a horizontal section of stems, branches, and leaves by Beverly Allen (BELOW) is an original take on the subject. Striated stems provide strong verticals, and are clustered into three groups, opening up negative space between the groupings. White space on the painting's right edge amplifies the asymmetry of the composition and is sliced through above center by two twigs. Intertwined leaf clusters hold the composition together and create diagonals through the composition. The viewer, being drawn into this large and beautifully rendered depiction, gains a sense of standing in the middle of a bamboo forest.

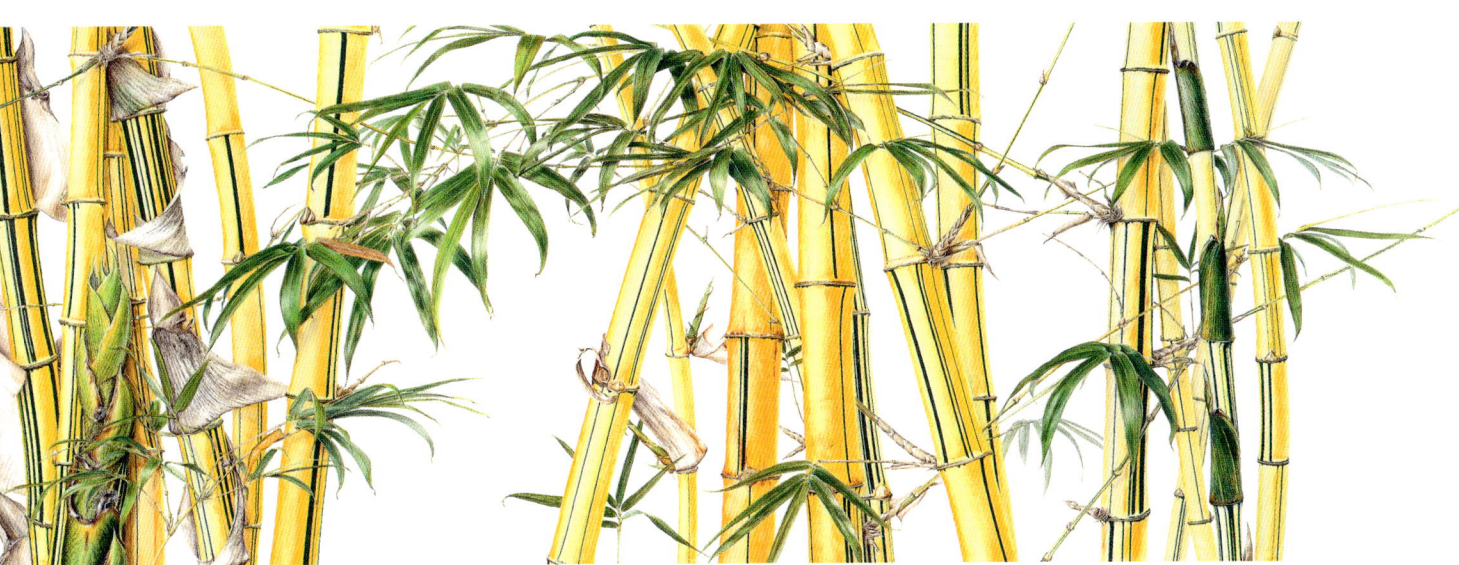

Bambusa vulgaris 'Striata'
Watercolor on paper
26 × 61 ½ inches [65 × 154 cm]
© Beverly Allen
(ABOVE)

Hyacinth *Hyacinthus orientalis*
Watercolor on vellum
17 × 7 inches [42.5 × 17.5 cm]
© Denise Walser-Kolar
(OPPOSITE)

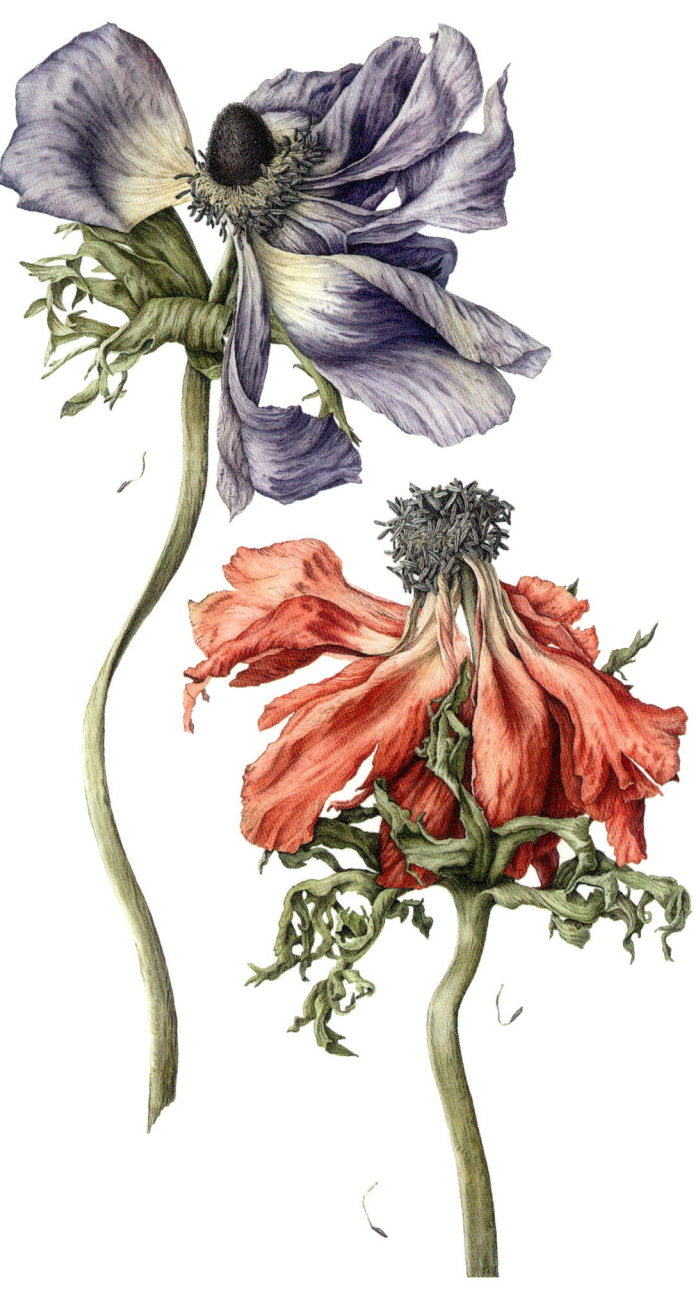

9. **Focal distance** can be used to create entirely different readings of subjects. Close-ups allow the artist to draw the viewer into the detail they find compelling. A focus that is further out allows a greater proportion of the subject to be depicted and provides more negative space around the image.

Leaves and flowers past their prime are a favored subject of Julia Trickey, who slowly air dries the subjects herself. A comparison of these two paintings of anemones provides instruction about the value of focal distance as a tool. The two anemones (LEFT) display movement through undulating stems and petals. As petals have dried, venation becomes more prominent, and contrast helps create depth between petals in the foreground and those behind. Negative space is well distributed and holds the image area together. The single anemone cropped in tightly (BELOW) gives the viewer a close-in study of veins and stamens, and its petals become the dynamic actors of the composition. The focal point, the flower's central axis, is placed in the upper third of the image area and slightly left of center, causing an energetic motion. More white space enters the upper part of the painting, lending weight to the bottom and balancing the composition. Each image leads to different readings of similar flowers, each asymmetrical, energetic, and well-balanced, one with a light, airy sense, and the other dramatically filling the picture plane.

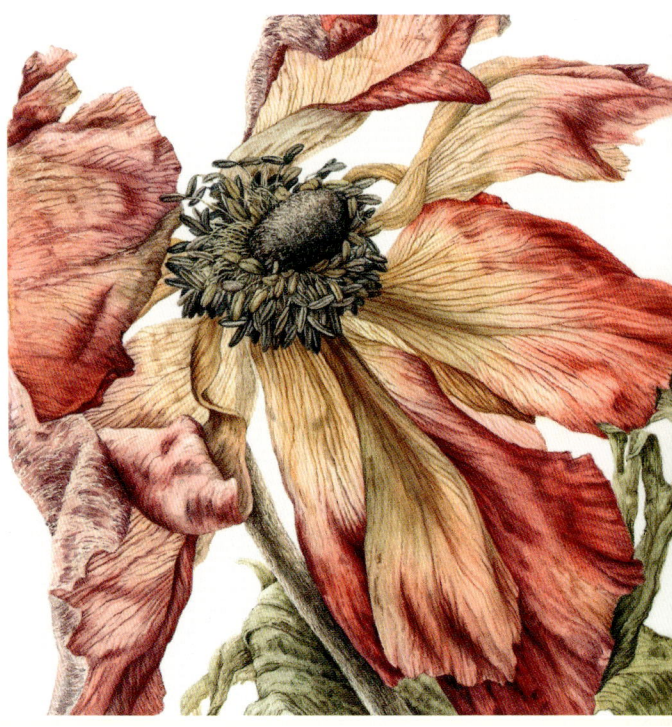

Larger Than Life—Two
Fading Anemones
Anemone coronaria
Watercolor on paper
29 × 20 ½ inches
[72.5 × 51.25 cm]
© Julia Trickey
(ABOVE)

Enduring Elegance—Fading
Red Anemone Flower
Anemone coronaria
Watercolor on paper
8 ½ × 8 inches [21.25 × 20 cm]
© Julia Trickey
(RIGHT)

10. **Cropping** can be used to bring details closer to the viewer, to reduce white space around the plant, or to anchor the image in space. Sometimes cropping is used to fit a very large plant into a small area.

Elaine Searle has used several important compositional devices to give this painting of rhubarb (BELOW) the impact it has, including strategic cropping. The whole plant is shown, from roots to flowering tips, with the weight most apparent in the lower part of the picture plane. Contrast is skillfully used to focus attention, with the deepest values in the root bundle, a fresh reminder of how tough and firmly rooted a plant this is. A deep understanding of how it grows is exhibited with leaves at all stages, from those just poking out of the soil to very large leaves perched atop rosy stems. The flower spike becomes a focal point by the greater contrast in the spike and around it, as well as in the foreground leaves. Its positioning toward the left side of the painting allows for a dynamic movement up the stem and around the darker leaves in front, and white space is reduced by the addition of two large leaves in atmospheric perspective in the background. Searle further pushes the focus into the center of the plant and fills the picture plane by cropping off the ends of leaves and roots. The cropped root on the left angles into the picture and is crucial to the dynamism of the composition.

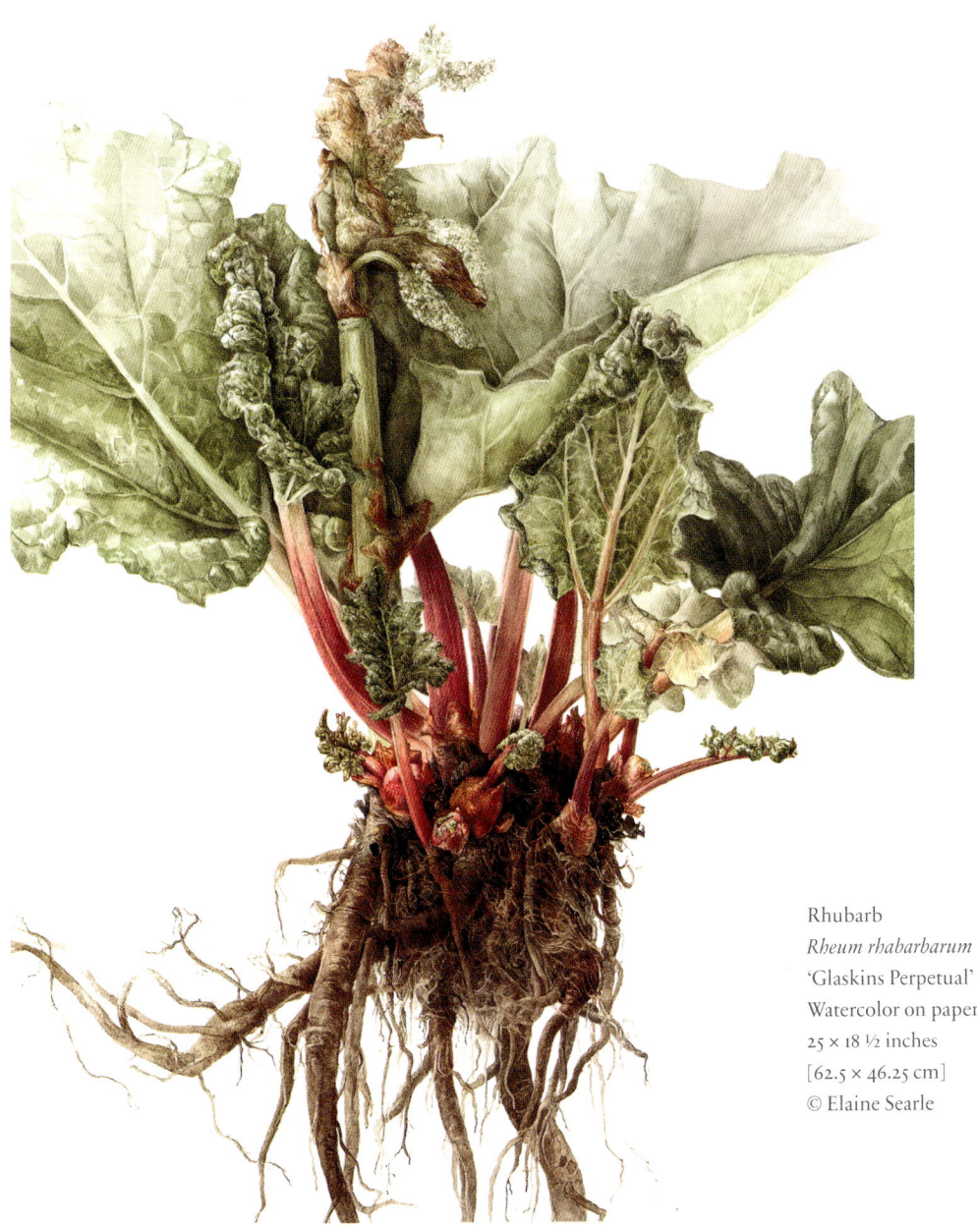

Rhubarb
Rheum rhabarbarum
'Glaskins Perpetual'
Watercolor on paper
25 × 18 ½ inches
[62.5 × 46.25 cm]
© Elaine Searle

11. Scale can be used to add impact by enlarging the subject. Artworks with greatly enlarged subjects can also help the viewer to see details more clearly.

This composition featuring closely placed nectarines (below) is drawn at three times life size. High chroma circular shapes exhibit a luminous surface texture and glossy highlights. This lifelike vibrancy of color is achieved partly by using liquid paraffin to facilitate smooth coverage. Two of the fruits have patterned skins, adding further eye appeal. Ann Swan sets up rhythm in the drawing by creating intersections where one fruit meets another. Each intersection is worthy of attention, with some fruits placed in shadow behind others, some lightly touching and creating a small area of deepened value where they meet. Nectarines are rolled into differing positions, some shown top-down, some sidelong, and others bottom-up. This allows the eye to dwell on stem details or on the undulation caused by the fruit's lobes. Bold cropping causes negative spaces to take on triangular shapes, each unique, but smaller than the fruits. This moves the eye throughout, via the cropped circular shapes that occupy the positive space, and the triangular wedges occupying the negative spaces.

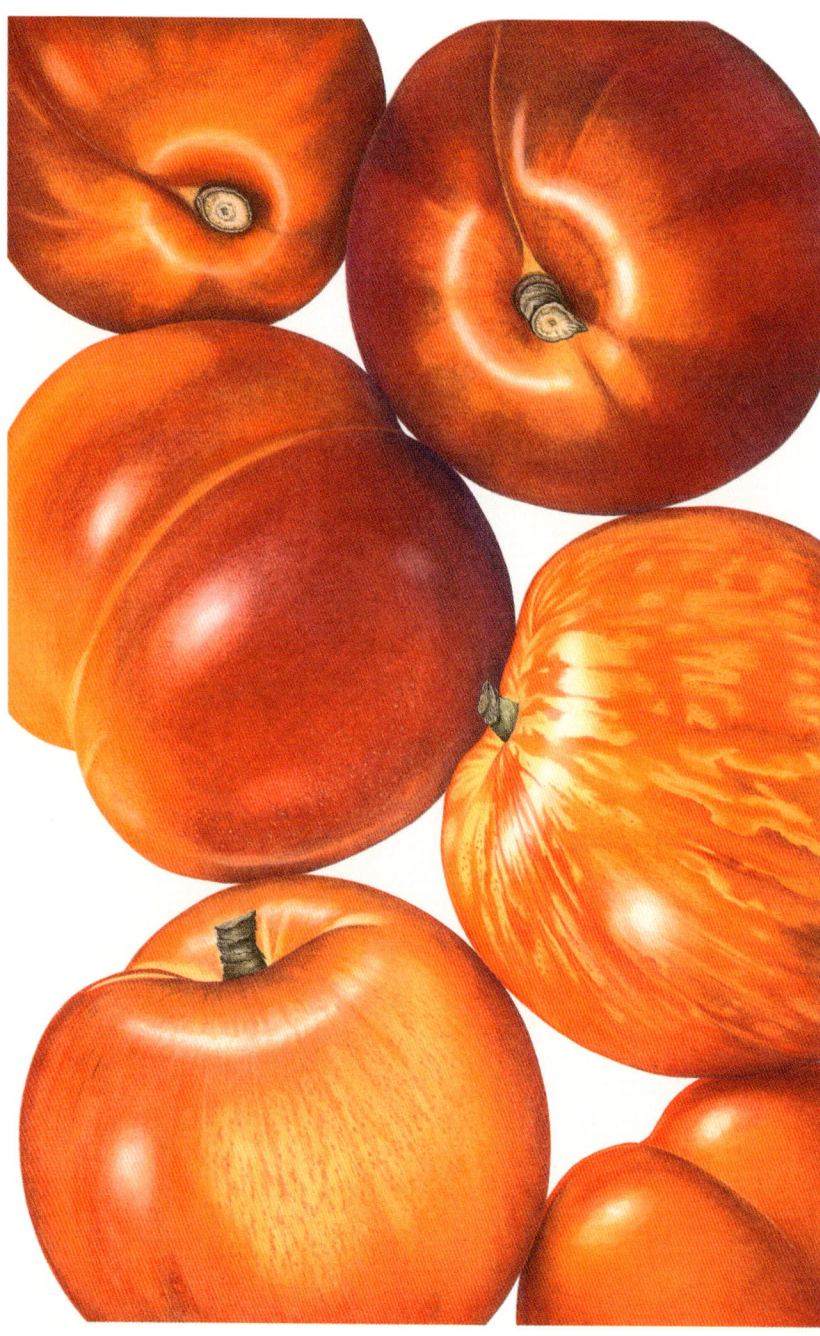

Nectarines
Colored pencil and
liquid paraffin wax on
hot-pressed paper
17 ½ × 11 ½ inches
[43.75 × 28.75 cm]
© Ann Swan

12. Contextualization. A habitat vignette is one with central subject(s) complemented by plants that might occur naturally in the same habitat. A similar composition is an **assemblage** of plants to illustrate a habitat type or a plant group. This type of grouping is contrived rather than naturalistic, as it combines plants that wouldn't necessarily all grow near one another. Both of these types of composition deliver supplemental ecological information to the viewer.

The habitat vignette is Betsy Rogers-Knox's forté, and this earth-toned watercolor of milkweed in situ (BELOW) is part of a series of six illustrating the plant throughout its growing season. The main subject of the painting is shown against a white background so details can be clearly seen. However, the ethereal milkweeds are held together and given weight by the inclusion of part of the ground where they have grown. The asymmetrical, irregular edge of the cluster of oak leaves is a counterpoint to the verticals of the milkweed stems. Movement is generated through the placement of the pods, bursting seeds with pappi, and pale dried goldenrods. A stem cuts into the picture plane from the bottom left edge, establishing a foreground and setting the entire vignette into a middle ground.

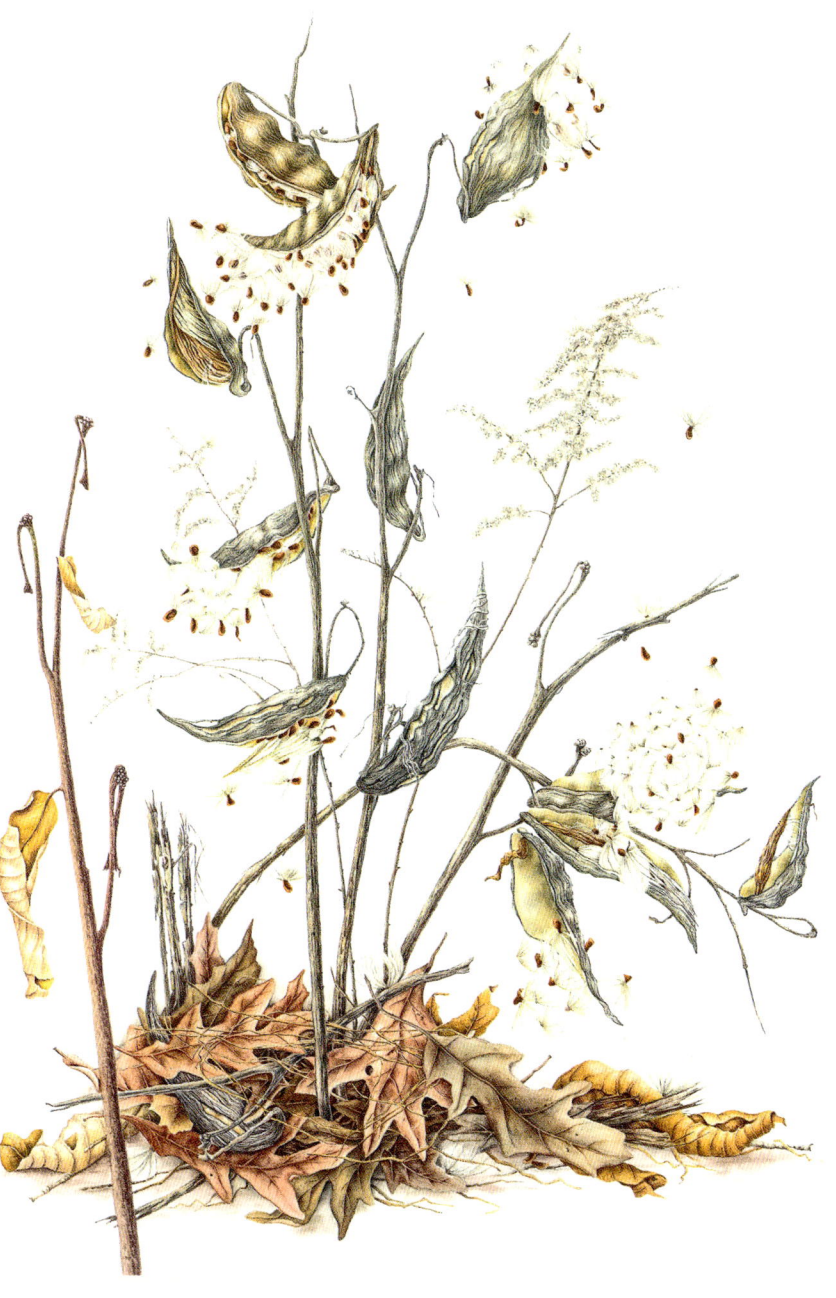

Seedburst Finale
Asclepias syriaca
Watercolor on paper
20 × 15 inches [50 × 37.5 cm]
© Betsy Rogers-Knox

A **ground view** is a direct depiction of what is seen when looking downward to the ground. Plants may fill the picture plane in a top-down view.

Specializing in plants of the southwestern United States, Joan McGann often depicts her subjects from a top-down vantage point. She has used contrast here to draw attention to the focal subject, *Mammillaria grahamii*, with the darkest values ink stippled in the shadows between and around the cacti (BELOW). Their cranial shapes are garlanded with flowers. By intentional placement of each cactus, a dynamic movement through the cactus cluster is generated, following the rings of high-chroma flowers. The ground that occupies the rest of the picture plane shows a softer range of values: earthy, gently modulating tones of sand, rock, and dry vegetation exemplify the desert habitat. Three dried twigs cut into the picture plane from the bottom, leading the eye to the cactus cluster from two different directions.

The **landscape view** depicts the central subject in its immediate habitat and in its broader landscape. By illustrating the landscape in which a plant grows as well as its botanical features, this type of composition conveys a great deal of information.

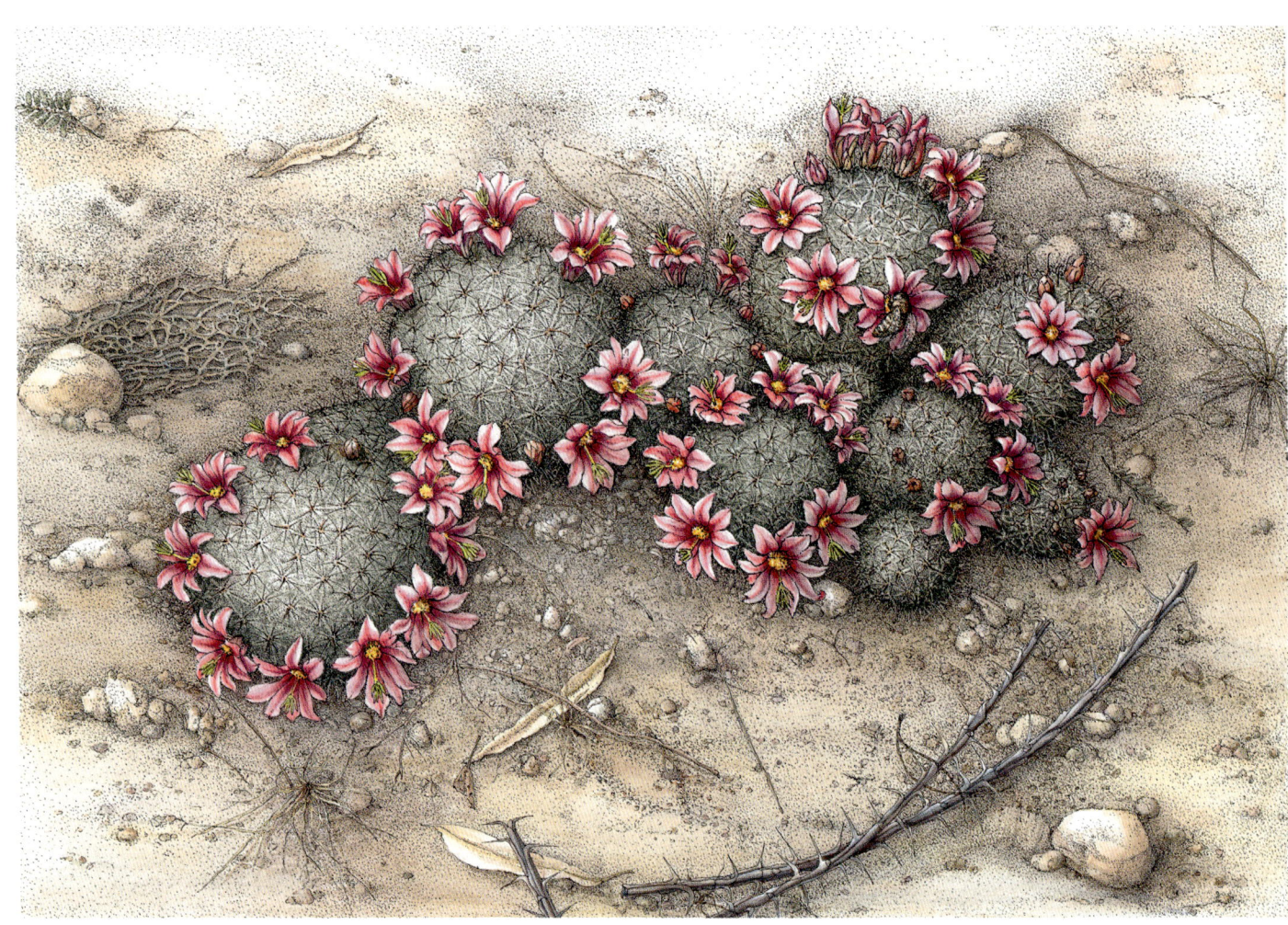

Mammillaria grahamii
Ink and watercolor on board
11 × 17 inches [27.5 × 42.5 cm]
© Joan McGann

This fascinating depiction of a carrion flower (BELOW) carries with it a deep story about the plant and how it grows in the South African highveld grasslands. Jenny Hyde-Johnson shows the succulent at a larger than life size, so it is clearly the central focus. She uses atmospheric perspective here—the central plant subject is shown in richer hues and in greater contrast than the background, which is softened so it recedes to the distant hills. One sees the plant's dry habitat and understands what it must do to survive in this harsh situation. A portion of the plant in flower has been lifted out of the ground and placed over a nearly white background to focus attention on it. Long roots to anchor and feed the plant are revealed, leading the eye to its succulent, water-storing leaves. Carrion-mimicking flowers stand out vividly, richly painted in a deep burgundy, with a banded blowfly perched on the flower's edge. Where trees had been blackened by the habitat's fire ecology, the artist painted them in white to introduce veins of light in the composition.

As illustrated by these examples, compositional possibilities in botanical art today are only limited by the artist's imagination. New ways of working are often improvised in response to challenges. Each completed artwork contains a unique aesthetic that attempts to engage the viewer's consciousness. Each also contains elements of a more intellectual sort, describing details and telling stories about the plant and its place in our contemporary world. Technical facility with the media used, ability for visual representation, along with a strong composition, are the vehicles used to bring unity to these two aspects of botanical art. They allow artists to achieve their goals for each completed artwork, and to effectively reach out to their audience.

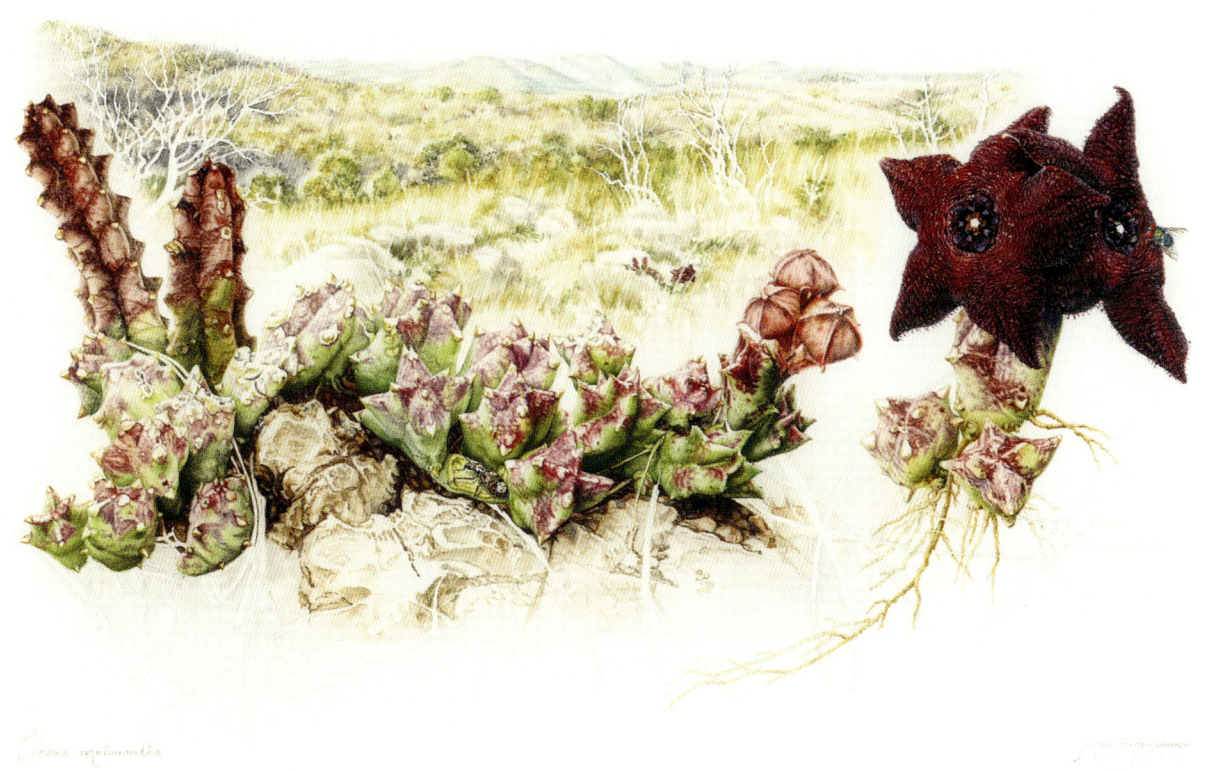

Orbea melanantha
Watercolor on paper
15 × 20 ½ inches [37.5 × 51.25 cm]
© Jenny Hyde-Johnson

Additional Reading

Blunt, Wilfrid and Stearn, William T., *The Art of Botanical Illustration*, Suffolk, UK: Antique Collectors Club Ltd., 2015

Brodie, Christina, *Drawing and Painting Plants*, Portland, OR: Timber Press, 2007

Brooks, Charlotte, *RHS Botanical Illustration: The Gold Medal Winners*, Suffolk, UK: ACC Art Books, 2019

Evans, Anne-Marie and Donn, *An Approach to Botanical Painting*, UK: Hannaford and Evans, 1993

Fraser, Susan, and Sellers, Vanessa Bezemer, *Flora Illustrata: Great Works from the LuEsther T. Mertz Library of the New York Botanical Garden*, New Haven, CT: Yale University Press, 2014

Glimn-Lacy, Janice, *Botany Illustrated: Introduction to Plants, Major Groups, Flowering Plant Families*, New York, NY: Springer, 2006

Hollender, Wendy, *Botanical Drawing in Color: A Basic Guide to Mastering Realistic Form and Naturalistic Color*, New York, NY,: Watson-Guptill, 2010

King, Christabel *The Kew Book of Botanical Illustration*, Kent, UK, Search Press: 2015

Lee, Katie, *Fundamental Graphite Techniques*, Hilton Head, SC, Lydia Inglett Publishing: 2010

Lighthipe, Mindy, *The Art of Botanical and Bird Illustration*, Lake Forest, CA; Walter Foster Publishing, 2017

Lupo Rogerio, *Graphite and its Possibilities Applied to Scientific Illustration*, digital download, https://pt.slideshare.net/bioartes/graphite-for-scientific-illustrations

Mee, Margaret, *In Search of Flowers of the Amazon Forest*, Suffolk, UK: Nonesuch Editions, 1988

Pell, Susan K. and Angell, Bobbi, *The Botanist's Vocabulary*, Portland, OR: Timber Press, 2016

Ravet-Haevermans, Agathe, *The Art of Botanical Drawing*, Portland, OR: Timber Press, 2009

Scott, Mary Ann, and Stevens, Margaret, *Botanical Sketchbook*, London, UK: Batsford, 2015

Sherwood, Shirley, *A New Flowering, 1000 Years of Botanical Art*, Oxford, UK: Ashmolean Museum, 2014

Sherwood, Shirley, *The Sherwood Collection: Modern Masterpieces of Botanical Art*, Surrey, UK: Kew Publishing, 2019

Sherwood, Shirley, and Kress, John, *The Art of Plant Evolution*, Surrey, UK: Kew Publishing, 2009

Sherwood, Shirley and Rix, Martin, *Treasures of Botanical Art*, Surrey, UK: Kew Publishing, 2019

Showell, Billy, *Botanical Painting in Watercolor*, Kent, UK: Search Press, 2016

Simblet, Sarah, *Botany for the Artist, An Inspirational Guide to Drawing Plants*, London, UK: DK Publishing, 2010

Stevens, Margaret, *The Art of Botanical Painting*, London, UK: Collins, 2015

Swan, Ann, *Botanical Portraits with Colored Pencils*, Hauppauge, NY: B.E.S. Publishing, 2010

Tomasi, Lucia Tongiorgi, Tosi, Allesandro, and Sherwood, Shirley, *Botanical Art into the Third Millennium*, Pisa, Italy: Edizioni ETS, 2013

Trickey, Julia, *Botanical Artistry, Plants Projects and Processes*, Reading, UK: Two Rivers Press, 2019

West, Keith, *Painting Plant Portraits: A Step-by-step Guide*, Portland, OR: Timber Press, 1991

Wunderlich, Eleanor B., *Botanical Illustration in Watercolor*, New York, NY: Watson-Guptill, 1991

Zomlefer, Wendy B., *Guide to Flowering Plant Families*, Chapel Hill, NC: The University of North Carolina Press, 1995

Acknowledgments

The richness, variety, and value of this handbook is predicated on the artists who unselfishly shared their talent, expertise, and knowledge so that others might gain insight into the creative processes and technical skills that inform botanical art. Special gratitude is given to the over 70 artists and contributors without whom there would be no book. We are indebted to each of them.

We extend our thanks to the editors, designers, and staff at Timber Press, including Andrew Beckman, Tom Fischer, Sara Milhollin, Mike Dempsey, and Lesley Bruynesteyn, for their insight, creativity, patience, and cooperation. We recognize their consummate abilities.

Since the inception of this project in 2016, the members of the American Society of Botanical Artists' Board of Directors have supported its goals and purpose. We acknowledge Rick Darke and Hélène Lesger for initial advice and Patricia Jonas for ongoing editorial assistance.

As always, we express our sincere gratitude to The New York Botanical Garden for providing ASBA's headquarters. We also extend special appreciation to Sara Hobel of the Horticultural Society of New York, who first connected ASBA and Timber Press with the idea of this handbook.

Contributors

Beverly Allen's (Australia) paintings are held in The Florilegium: Royal Botanic Gardens Sydney, the Shirley Sherwood Collection, The Highgrove Florilegium, The Transylvania Florilegium, the Royal Horticultural Society Lindley Library, the Royal Botanic Gardens Kew Library, and the Hunt Institute for Botanical Documentation. She holds gold medals from the Royal Horticultural Society and The New York Botanic Garden and is the recipient of the 2016 ASBA Diane Bouchier Artist Award.

Margaret Best (Canada) is an internationally renowned botanical artist and teacher. Her professional qualifications as an art instructor have positioned her to be effective in both group studio workshops as well as in individual, bespoke mentoring. She teaches on a regular basis in locations across Canada, has taught in more than ten countries. She resides in Chester, Nova Scotia.

Dr. Diane Bouchier (United States) received her doctorate from Harvard University and was Professor of Sociology at SUNY-Stony Brook from 1977 to 2016. Dr. Bouchier also held visiting appointments at Boston College, Cambridge University, and Essex University. While studying for her certificate in botanical illustration, she founded the American Society of Botanical Artists. Since her retirement, she has mounted a touring exhibition of native plant drawings and taught botanical drawing and nature art.

Lara Call Gastinger (United States) was the chief illustrator for the Flora of Virginia after receiving a master's degree in plant ecology. She has been awarded two gold medals (2007, 2018) at the Royal Horticultural Society show in London and has shown her work in numerous American Society of Botanical Artists exhibitions and at the Hunt Institute for Botanical Documentation.

Karen Coleman's (United States) art and her passion pivoted to the world of plants and traditional botanical art several years ago. Reflecting a variety of media, her works include colored pencil, watercolor, graphite, and pen and ink. One of her favorites is colored pencil, which she finds allows a great deal of flexibility and depth of color while producing wonderful visual results.

Dorothy DePaulo (United States) works primarily in colored pencil and has shown her work in many local, national, and international shows. She has also co-authored and illustrated a book about the flora and fauna of parks and open spaces. She is an active member of the American Society of Botanical Artists and is a past president of the Rocky Mountain Society of Botanical Artists.

Monika de Vries Gohlke (United States), an artist who paints and prints botanical subjects, graduated from Parsons School of Design and New York University with a BFA. After many years working in the commercial world of textile and home-furnishings design, she now works exclusively making her own art. Her work has been exhibited nationally and internationally and can be found in many public and private collections.

Carrie Di Costanzo (United States) worked as a fashion illustrator before shifting her focus to botanical art. She has exhibited extensively with the American Society of Botanical Artists and in other group exhibitions throughout the United States. Her work is held in the botanical collections at The Huntington Library, Art Collections, and Botanical Gardens; the Hunt Institute for Botanical Documentation; and private collections.

Trained in color and abstraction, Jean Emmons (United States) came to botanical art through a love of gardening. Plants provide the perfect subject for studying light on form, and their reflective and iridescent qualities present a challenge. Among many awards, Jean has won two gold medals and "Best Painting of Show" from the Royal Horticultural Society and the 2005 ASBA Diane Bouchier Artist Award.

Akiko Enokido's (Japan) work has been shown in various exhibitions, including the American Society of Botanical Artists *Annual Internationals*, Hunt Institute for Botanical Documentation Internationals, and The New York Botanical Garden's Triennial. In 2016, she was awarded a gold medal by the Royal Horticultural Society. Her work is in the botanical collections at The Huntington Library, Art Collections, and Botanical Gardens; the Royal Botanic Gardens, Kew; and the National Tropical Botanical Garden in Hawaii.

Ingrid Finnan (United States) began painting botanicals in oil after a long career designing for the decorative textile market. Since 2006, she has been represented in all American Society of Botanical Artists *Annual International* exhibitions, The New York Botanical Garden Triennials, and Filoli's *Annual Botanical Art Exhibitions*. She is represented in the Shirley Sherwood Collection.

Susan T. Fisher (United States) is the former coordinator for the Botanical Art and Illustration Program at Denver Botanic Gardens and the former director of the Art Institute at Arizona-Sonora Desert Museum, where she created the Nature Illustration Certificate Program. She is a past president of the American Society of Botanical Artists' board, and her work appears in numerous publications and private collections including that of the Hunt Institute for Botanical Documentation.

Maria Cecilia Freeman (United States) lives, paints, and teaches in Santa Cruz, California. Her work includes scientific illustration and botanically accurate fine art, often combining the two in graphite and watercolor studies. She takes a special interest in portraying native plant species with a view to their preservation, and particularly loves drawing and painting heritage and species roses.

Marilyn Garber (United States) is a botanical artist and founder of the Minnesota School of Botanical Art in Minneapolis in 2001. A longtime member of the American Society of Botanical Artists, she served as its president from 2007 through 2009. Her work has been included in international exhibitions including Royal Botanic Gardens, Kew, and the Queen Sirikit Botanical Garden, Thailand.

A retired architect, Howard Goltz (United States) redirected his architectural rendering skills through classes at the Minnesota School of Botanical Art. His botanical artwork is in the Eloise Butler

Wildflower Garden Florilegium, and has been shown at the Bakken Museum, Minneapolis Central Library, Hopkins Center for the Arts, Ames Art Center, American Society of Botanical Artists Small Works, North American Mycological Association, and the University of Minnesota Arboretum.

Carol E. Hamilton (United States) is driven by lyrical subject matter, finding satisfaction in creating large works or series that have a more complex story to tell. Her paintings have been exhibited throughout the United States, in the Shirley Sherwood Collection and at the Royal Botanic Gardens, Kew. She served as president of the board of the American Society of Botanical Artists and received its 2005 James White Award for Service to Botanical Art.

Gillian Harris (United States) is a naturalist and artist working in southern Indiana. Her botanical art, illustrations, and writing are centered around native plants and their faunal associates, including pollinators, caterpillars and other wildlife. Her illustrations have appeared in garden books, field guides, exhibit signage, and most recently a children's book about spring wildflowers.

Having grown up with nature books and frequent visits to gardens in Kyoto, Asuka Hishiki's (Japan) curiosity about nature grew tremendously. Naturally, she was drawn to portray its subjects. After completing her degree, she spent ten years in New York City delving further into her work. Her paintings have been shown in numerous exhibitions around the world. Now, she lives and works in Hyogo, Japan.

Ann S. Hoffenberg (United States) is a freelance biological illustrator/artist and former teacher of the biological sciences. Botanical art has enabled her to combine a fascination with natural science and an appreciation for plant form and color. Ann works in watercolor, colored pencil, graphite, gouache, and pen and ink. Her work has been exhibited in numerous venues within the United States.

Wendy Hollender (United States) is a botanical artist, author, and instructor and leads workshops throughout the world. Hollender's illustrations have been published extensively. She has exhibited in natural history museums and botanical institutes, including a solo exhibit at the US Botanic Garden. Wendy has four books on botanical drawing. Her newest, *The Joy of Botanical Drawing*, was released in 2020.

After a career in graphic design, Jenny Hyde-Johnson (South Africa) began painting full time in 2006. Her botanical paintings received gold medals at Kirstenbosch Biennales in 2006, 2008, and 2013, and at the 21st International Orchid Congress in 2014. Her work is included in collections of the South African National Biodiversity Institute, Woodson Art Museum, Hunt Institute for Botanical Documentation, and the Shirley Sherwood Collection.

Paintings by Mieko Ishikawa (Japan) can be found in the collections of the Hunt Institute for Botanical Documentation; the Shirley Sherwood Collection; the Royal Horticultural Society Lindley Library; the Royal Botanic Gardens, Kew; and The Highgrove Florilegium of HRH Prince Charles. In 2006 she was awarded a gold medal by the Royal Horticultural Society and in 2017 received the ASBA Diane Bouchier Artist Award. She specializes in carnivorous plants and other rare species.

Rose Marie James (United States) holds a master's degree in art education, and a certificate in botanical art and illustration from The New York Botanical Garden, where she currently teaches classes. Her work is in the permanent collection of the Hunt Institute for Botanical Documentation. She is an active member of the American Society of Botanical Artists and served on its board from 2014 to 2016.

Vincent Jeannerot (France) studied at France's National School of Fine Arts and is a member of La Maison des Artistes, Société Française d'Illustration Botanique, and the American Society of Botanical Artists. Owner of a gallery in Lyon, France, he has published several books, the most recent being *Regards*. He has had exhibitions in Paris, London, Melbourne, Moscow, and Seoul, and has taught workshops around the world.

A self-taught artist, Martha G. Kemp (United States) specializes in using graphite pencil to depict botanical specimens. She's the recipient of the 1999 ASBA Diane Bouchier Artist Award, five gold medals from the Royal Horticultural Society, and numerous other awards. Her drawings are held in private and public collections. She served for twelve years on the American Society of Botanical Artists' board of directors.

Known as a wildflower painter, Heeyoung Kim (United States) documents native plants of prairies and woods of the midwestern United States. She has received numerous awards including a Royal Horticultural Society gold medal (2012), Best of Show (American Society of Botanical Artists/HSNY, 2012), and the 2012 ASBA Diane Bouchier Artist Award. She is the founder of the botanical art program at Brushwood Center (Ryerson Woods). Her works are included in The Transylvania Florilegium.

Esther Klahne (United States) is a botanical and naturalist painter living outside Boston, Massachusetts. She graduated from Rhode Island School of Design with a BA in Apparel Design, and studied botanical art at Wellesley College through the Friends of Horticulture Certificate Program. Esther captures the beauty of the natural world by choosing compelling subjects that are featured in watercolor paintings on vellum.

Karen Kluglein (United States) was an illustrator before concentrating on botanical art. She exhibits in the American Society of Botanical Artists *Annual Internationals* and received the 2010 ASBA Diane Bouchier Artist Award. Her work is in The New York Botanical Garden's LuEsther T. Mertz Library and many private collections. She is represented by Susan Frei Nathan Fine Works on Paper, and her work is licensed with HG Caspari.

Jee-Yeon Koo (South Korea) was born in Seoul. She holds a BA from Dongduk Women's University, an MA from Chung-Ang University, and she holds a certificate in botanical art and illustration from The New York Botanical Garden. Jee-Yeon is a principal art director for a national project for illustrating Korean plants sponsored by the Korea National Arboretum, and she teaches at the Dongduk Women's University.

An award-winning artist, Libby Kyer (United States) has taught colored-pencil arts for more than 20 years as a faculty member at the Denver Botanic Gardens School of Botanical Art and Illustration and at workshops for nature-based art nationally and internationally. A happy control freak, she finds that humans are hardwired to make order out of chaos. Finding and painting that order is her passion.

Katie Lee (United States), a graduate of The New York Botanical Garden's Botanical Art and Illustration program, was an instructor there for 23 years and now teaches at the Coastal Maine Botanical Garden and conducts online art courses. Her work is in private art collections worldwide. Katie wrote and illustrated *Fundamental Graphite Techniques*, which has become a standard reference book for developing drawing skills.

Rogério Lupo (Brazil) graduated as a biologist from the University of São Paulo and studied at the Classical School of Art of São Paulo. A freelancer since 1997, he is a biological illustrator and teaches the subject in Brazil and internationally. Among his awards are the Margaret Mee National Contest of Botanical Illustration (2002 and 2003), and the Margaret Flockton Award (2010 and 2013).

For Katy Lyness (United States), a lifetime of drawing and nearly two decades of gardening have happily converged in the realm of botanical art. Since discovering the community of botanical artists, she has been represented in the 18th ASBA *Annual International* exhibition and is active in the Tri-State Botanical Artists Group. Katy lives, gardens, and draws in Jersey City, New Jersey.

Lucy Martin's (United States) paintings reflect her lifelong connection with nature and her love for the life of forests. She paints in gouache and watercolor, focusing on the mysterious beauty of fungi and lichens. She lives in Sonoma County, California, and exhibits in local galleries as well as in international exhibitions of the American Society of Botanical Artists.

Tammy S. McEntee (United States) has had a lifelong love affair with drawing and gardening, and her work marries these two passions. She received a degree in painting with a minor in art history from Montclair State College and went on to a career in floral design. She is a 2017 graduate of The New York Botanical Garden's Botanical Art and Illustration program.

Joan McGann's (United States) botanical illustrations focus on plants native to the Sonoran Desert, including protected and endangered species. Joan works on paper with graphite pencil, colored pencil, pen and ink, and watercolor. She has exhibited throughout the United States and has work in the permanent collections of the Hunt Institute for Botanical Documentation, the Arizona-Sonora Desert Museum, and the Shirley Sherwood Collection.

Mali Moir (Australia) began her career as a botanical artist at Australia's National Herbarium of Victoria, contributing pen-and-ink drawings to many scientific publications. Mali's interest in conservation and species documentation contributes to her dedication to combine a fascination for the natural sciences with an active desire to render works of art with beauty, character, and scientific integrity.

Bill Moye (United States) produced drawings for botanists as illustrious as Arthur J. Cronquist, Rupert C. Barneby, Sir Ghillean Prance, and others. Moye currently works to conserve the South Mountain region of North Carolina, where he discovered a new species of *Yucca* and another of *Stenanthium*. He also maintains a highly organized presentation of his art and photography on Flickr.

Born and raised in the United Kingdom, Derek Norman (United States) is a longtime designer, creative director, television producer, and educator. He is represented in the collections of the Hunt Institute for Botanical Documentation, the Library of Congress, and The British Museum, and he is the recipient of Royal Horticultural Society gold and silver-gilt medals. He is a past

president of the American Society of Botanical Artists (2013–2015) and a fellow of The Linnean Society of London.

Eunike Nugroho (Indonesia) is an artist who fell in love with botanical art through her encounters with botanical societies in the United Kingdom. Her work is in the Hunt Institute for Botanical Documentation. She adores watercolor and finds that the perfect balance between the freshness of the medium and a portrayal of realistic form is a perpetual challenge. She is founder of the Indonesian Society of Botanical Artists.

Hillary Parker (United States) is an international award-winning botanical watercolor artist with a thirty-year career of painting, teaching workshops, and private instruction, along with accepting public and corporate commissions. Her work has been published in magazines and books and exhibited in juried international exhibitions, and her paintings hang in eleven countries in prominent collections, including the Shirley Sherwood Collection.

John Pastoriza-Piñol (Australia) is a contemporary botanical artist based in Melbourne. His many awards, including the 2013 ASBA Diane Bouchier Artist Award, have afforded him international recognition as one of the foremost contemporary botanical artists. His work is held in many prominent collections including The Highgrove Florilegium and Transylvania Florilegium. John is represented by Scott Livesey Galleries, Melbourne.

Rose Pellicano's (United States) interest in botanical painting began in 1993, and since then she has exhibited in many American Society of Botanical Artists juried exhibitions in the United States and in Europe. A botanical art instructor, her paintings are in the collection of the Hunt Institute for Botanical Documentation, and her illustrations have been included in magazines, books, advertising campaigns, and branding logos.

Kandy Vermeer Phillips (United States) has been drawing with silverpoint since the 1970s. She is currently working on a series of silverpoints based on Emily Dickinson's poetry and herbarium. Kandy's silverpoint drawings are included in the collections of the Hunt Institute for Botanical Documentation, the National Gallery of Art, and the Botany Department of the Smithsonian's National Museum of Natural History.

Kelly Leahy Radding (United States) is inspired by all things in nature and considers herself a painter of contemporary naturalism, interpreting experiences and observations in the field into paintings and drawings. A love of traveling to wild places provides ideas for her work, but she also finds inspiration closer to home—a farm tucked into her beloved New England woods.

Dick Rauh (United States) came to botanical art late in life, but has made the most of it. With a PhD in plant sciences (2001) and a Royal Horticultural Society gold medal (2006), he has been teaching at The New York Botanical Garden for more than 35 years. His artwork is in the Shirley Sherwood Collection, the Royal Horticultural Society Lindley Library, and the Hunt Institute for Botanical Documentation.

Jeanne Reiner (United States) is a nationally recognized botanical artist who holds a certificate in botanical art and illustration from and teaches at The New York Botanical Garden. She is cofounder of the Tri-State Botanical Artists, an artists' circle of more than 70 members of the American Society of Botanical

Artists. She exhibits frequently in New York, Connecticut, Florida, and California.

Sarah Roche (United States) moved to the United States from the United Kingdom in 1993, where in her early career she exhibited at and illustrated for the Royal Horticultural Society, as well as for many publications. Her work is included in many collections in Europe and the United States. She is Education Director of the botanical art program at Wellesley College Botanic Garden, where she enjoys teaching botanical watercolor.

Inspired by her English grandfather, Betsy Rogers-Knox (United States) has been painting and drawing since childhood. She received a certificate in botanical art and illustration from The New York Botanical Garden, and she enjoys illustrating plants in their habitats. Her work has been shown widely in the United States in the 11th through 21st American Society of Botanical Artists *Annual Internationals* and in London in the Royal Horticultural Society exhibition.

Lizzie Sanders (United Kingdom) lives close to the Royal Botanic Garden Edinburgh, Scotland. She has been producing botanical paintings for some thirty years, aiming to produce contemporary graphic images where neither art nor science is compromised. She is the recipient of numerous awards, including three Royal Horticultural Society gold medals, and her work is included in the Shirley Sherwood Collection, the Royal Horticultural Society Lindley Library, and The Highgrove Florilegium.

Constance Sayas (United States) used a degree in fine arts for a career in science education. An exhibition designer for several major museums, then scientific illustrator for *Encyclopedia Britannica*, she currently teaches at the Denver Botanic Gardens' School of Botanical Art and Illustration. Her award-winning watercolors appear in numerous publications and collections including the collection of the Hunt Institute of Botanical Documentation.

Constance Scanlon's (United States) critical skills of observation as a former cardiac intensive-care nurse are invaluable in her creation of contemporary botanical art. Her work has been included in the 17th through 21st American Society of Botanical Artists *Annual International* juried exhibitions, the 2016 Hunt Institute for Botanical Documentation's *International Exhibition*, and the 2013 Royal Horticultural Society Exhibition. She lives and paints in Saint Paul, Minnesota.

A design career informs Elaine Searle's (United Kingdom) botanical artworks. Her work is included in the collections of The Prince of Wales's Highgrove Florilegium and Transylvania Florilegium, The Hunt Institute, The Huntington Library, and those of many private collectors. Elaine instructs courses and masterclasses at UK, European, and US venues. She is a Fellow of the Linnean Society and the Society of Botanical Artists (UK).

Deborah B. Shaw (United States) has a degree in fine art from Pomona College, The Claremont Colleges, in California. Her work has been in juried and non-juried exhibitions internationally and is in the collection of the Hunt Institute for Botanical Documentation; the Botanical Collections at The Huntington Library, Art Collections, and Botanical Gardens; and in private collections. She has received numerous awards for art, illustration, and design.

After careers in education and law Heidi Snyder (United States) turned to scientific illustration. Heidi prefers colored pencils for her detail-driven art focusing on wild species and strives to depict them in their native habitat. With Dorothy DePaulo, she co-authored *Wild in the City: Fauna and Flora of Colorado Urban Spaces* (2015) and uses art to raise environmental awareness.

Scott Stapleton (United States) did not discover botanical art until his retirement from the ministry. He had also been an art librarian and, before that, a BFA and MFA student specializing in printmaking and graphic design. Nothing clicked, however, until he took his first course at the Minnesota School of Botanical Art in 2014—Marilyn Garber's Color Theory class.

Ann Swan (United Kingdom) is one of the leading botanical artists and tutors in the UK. Her mission is to spread the joy of working with pencil and colored pencils to depict botanical subjects. She has won four Royal Horticultural Society gold medals for *Lycaste* orchids and has had three works purchased by the Royal Horticultural Society Lindley Library. Her best-selling book, *Plant Portraits with Coloured* Pencils, was published in 2010.

As a staff illustrator for the Botany Department, National Museum of Natural History, Smithsonian Institution, Alice Tangerini (United States) has specialized in drawing plants since 1972 in pen and ink, graphite, and, recently, digital color. Her artwork has appeared in scientific periodicals, floras, and books, and she teaches, presents lectures, and juries exhibitions. Alice manages and curates an extensive collection of botanical illustrations at the Smithsonian.

Jessica Tcherepnine (United States, 1938–2018) was a botanical artist for about fifty years, one of the first whose work brought a contemporary sensibility to the art form. She is the recipient of two Royal Horticultural Society gold medals, the 2003 ASBA Diane Bouchier Artist Award, and her work is held in the Shirley Sherwood Collection, The Highgrove Florilegium, and The British Museum, among others.

A full-time artist residing in Colorado's Front Range, Carol Till (United States) specializes in making contemporary intaglio prints. Inspired by natural subjects, she translates her finely detailed drawings into etchings. Creative printing techniques allow Carol to expand the possibilities of the image using colored inks and paints, unique papers, and layered prints.

Melissa Toberer (United States) received a BFA from the University of Nebraska at Omaha. She has exhibited at Omaha's Lauritzen Gardens and in the American Society of Botanical Artists' *Following in the Bartrams' Footsteps*, the Horticultural Society of New York's *18th Annual International*, and the *21st Annual International* at Wave Hill. In 2015 she received the Brooklyn Botanic Garden Award for Print or Drawing.

Julia Trickey (United Kingdom) has been a botanical artist for twenty years and is an experienced tutor. Her botanical watercolors have been exhibited, and she has taught worldwide. Julia has received four gold medals from the Royal Horticultural Society, among many other awards. She has written books and produced educational resources for students of botanical art.

Alexander "Sasha" Viazmensky (Russia) resides in St. Petersburg. He is a graduate of the Graphic Design School, Leningrad (1984), and Leningrad Academy of Arts (1991). Sasha has artwork in museums and private collections around the globe. Since 2004, he has been teaching botanical art classes in the United States, and in

2012 he organized the first botanical art classes in Russia. He specializes in illustrating mushrooms in his native Russia, where he says mushrooms are considered national treasures.

Denise Walser-Kolar (United States) began her journey into botanical art after receiving a botanical art class from her parents as a birthday gift. She received the 2015 ASBA Diane Bouchier Artist Award and received a silver-gilt medal from the Royal Horticultural Society in 2011. Her work is held in the permanent collection of the Hunt Institute for Botanical Documentation.

Educated at the Royal Academy of Fine Arts in The Hague, Anita Walsmit Sachs (Netherlands) worked at the National Herbarium, Leiden University, as a scientific illustrator and head of the art department. She received a Royal Horticultural Society gold medal, second-prize winner of the Margaret Flockton Award, and a Royal Award. She participated in The Highgrove Florilegium and Transylvania Florilegium.

Catherine Watters (United States) teaches at Filoli in Woodside, California; University of California Botanical Garden at Berkeley; Wellesley College; and in France. Her work is exhibited in the United States, England, France, Italy, and Australia. She is cofounder of the Alcatraz Florilegium and the Château de Brécy Florilegium in France, and her illustrations are included in several international florilegia, books, and magazines. She received a BA in French and art from University of California, Davis.

Kerri Weller (Canada) lives in Ottawa. Oil paint is her favorite medium in which to express the beauty of the plant world. Her work has been published in *Fine Art Connoisseur* magazine, juried into international art exhibitions, and is in the collection of the Hunt Institute for Botanical Documentation. Kerri's design graces the 2018 gold coin, the *Armistice Poppy*, by the Royal Canadian Mint.

A scientific illustrator at Naturalis Biodiversity Center, Esmée Winkel (Netherlands) also paints unique plants she comes across in her spare time. A recipient of three gold medals from the Royal Horticultural Society (2013, 2016, and 2018), she also received the Jill Smythies Award from the Linnean Society of London and the 2016 ASBA Botanical Illustrator Award for Excellence.

Index

A

Acer saccharinum, 213
achene, 29–30
acrylics, 365–367
Aesculus pavia, 346
Alcea rosea, 84
Algerian ivy, 285
Alismataceae, 12
Allen, Beverly
  artwork, 252, 391
  composition style, 391
  studio, 25
  tutorial, 251–257
Allium cepa var. *aggregatum*, 165–166
Allium 'Mount Everest', 372
Alstroemeria stramonia, 34
American Society for Testing and Materials (ASTM), 188
androecium, 26–27
Anemone coronaria, 392
anemones, 392
anther, 26, 27, 176, 316
anther cap, 114, 120
anthuriums, 15
Apocynum cannabinum, 344
apple
  clipping branches, 15–16
  drybrush techniques, 199–204
  Gala, 204
  Granny Smith, 64–65
  graphite skills, 64–65
  tonal patterns, 65
  watercolor on paper, 199–204
aquatint technique, 343
Araucaria bidwillii, 386
Arisaema triphyllum, 338
artichoke, 82–83
artists
  botanical vs. floral, 10
  community of, 12
  composition styles, 382, 385–388, 390–397
  historical botanical, 191
  motivations of, 11–12
  palette philosophies, 189–191
  studios / work areas, 22–25, 126–128
art supplies field kit, 18
ASBA Code of Ethics, 17
Asiatic lily, 15
asymmetry, 375, 379, 391–392
azaleas, 16

B

balance, 378, 381, 385, 390, 392
bamboo, 391
Bambusa vulgaris 'Striata', 391
Bauer, Ferdinand, 191
bearded iris, 208–209
Besbicus conspicuus, 290
Best, Margaret
  artwork, 213, 216
  tutorial, 212–218
binders, 160, 186, 365
bird's nest, 363
bloom, depicting on fruit, 235–239, 294–298
Boletus edulis II, 30
botanical art and illustration
  defined, 10–11
  misconceptions about, 12
  renaissance in, 11–12
  three pillars of, 379
bouquet, 388
bract, 27, 109, 147–148, 247
branches
  cherry, 312–317
  colored pencil on film, 178–181
  cylindrical forms, 74–75
  forced spring, 15–16
  gouache, 354–357
  gouache and watercolor, 349–353
  magnolia, 74–75
  oak with lichens, 348–352
  preparing as subjects, 15–16
  spruce, 354–357
  watercolor on vellum, 312–317
brussels sprouts, 364
buds, 312
Bulbophyllum sp. aff. *ankylodon*, 114, 116–122
bunya pine, 386
bushy yates fruit, 326
butterfly, 260

C

California poppies, 134
calyx, 26–27, 297, 316
camellia, 78–79
Capsicum annuum and *chinense* varieties, 76
carnations, 14
carpel, 26, 27, 29, 30
carrot, 66–67

casein, 336–337

cat's whiskers, 381

cattails, 138

Celosia cristata, 147–148

chayote squash, 70–72

Chelone glabra, 318

cherry branch, 312–317

chine-collé, 346

chrysanthemum, 49–51, 151–152

cirsium, 109

Cirsium pitcheri, 106

Citrus limon 'Eureka', 375

classification, 31

coast ground rose, 389

cockscomb, 147–148

Coleman, Karen

  artwork, 154, 156, 158

  tutorial, 153–159

color. *See also* contrast; tone; value

  brightness, 137

  chroma, 137, 370

  color wheels, 137, 189

  complementary colors, 136

  defined, 189–190

  elements of, 378

  flocculating, 186

  grammar of, 136

  hue, 136–137

  implying with graphite, 76

  lifting, 215, 273–275, 293

  local, 137, 144, 145

  matching, 370

  metal tarnishing effects on, 359

  primary, secondary, and tertiary, defined, 136

  saturation, 137

  sepiatone, 227–229

  shade, 136–137

  tint, 136–137

  use in scientific illustration, 126

color, mixing and blending

  adding gesso, 366

  casein, 337

  charging, 195, 198

  color bias, 190

  drybrush, 241–247

  layering, 144

  in mixing tray wells, 212, 214, 217

  oils, 370

  from a six-color palette, 190

colored pencils

  basic skills, 140–145

  burnishing, 144, 159, 177, 329

  color mixing and blending, 144–145

  embossing, 145, 155, 169, 170, 176–177

  ergonomics, 141

  on film, 156–157, 180–181

  grisaille, 148, 152, 162, 166, 167, 169–171

  layering, 143–145, 175–177

  materials, 140

  oil-based, 160

  pastel dust, 146–150

  pen and ink comparison to, 172–173

  point, position, pressure (three "Ps"), 141–143

  resist effect, 145, 169, 170, 177

  solvents, 145, 149–150

  stipple / stippling, 112, 172

  textures, 143, 146–150, 153–159

  whites, 145

  workhorse strokes, 143

color palettes, 189–191

common crabapple, 178

common mullein, 61

common polypody, 31

composite flowers, 15, 49–51

composition. *See also* focus; negative space; shapes

  asymmetry / symmetry, 375, 378, 379, 391, 392

  balance, 378, 381, 385, 390, 392

  basics, 380

  considering shapes, 370

  diagonal patterns, 376, 391

  elements and principles of, 378–380

  form, 378

  incomplete areas, 109

  landscape view, 396–397

  life studies as basis of, 373–377

  mid-project alterations, 374–377

  most frequently used style, 382

  picture plane, 19, 375, 378, 393, 395–396

  positive space, 378, 394

  relationship to artwork end use, 379

  sheet format, 390–391

  sketches, preparatory, 380

  unity, 379, 388, 397

composition, approaches to

  bouquet groupings, 388

  collections, 387

  contextualization, 395–397

  cropping, 393–394

  focal distance, 392

  icon suspended in space, 386

  life cycle, 174–177, 382, 384–385

  one plant in space, 382

  study page, 389–390

compositional layout, transferring, 192–194

conifers and cones, 33, 80–81, 354–357

continuous tone

  aquatint technique, 343

  colored pencil skills, 142

continuous tone (*cont.*)
    graphite skills, 60, 62
    pen and ink skills, 126
    stipple / stippling, 132
contrast
    defined, 378
    lessening with pen and ink, 42
    uses, 258, 393, 396, 397
corolla, 26, 27, 150, 379
corymb, 27, 28
Coryphantha robustispina, 172–173
crabapple branch, 15–16, 178–181
Cronquist, Arthur, artwork, 132
crosshatching. *See* hatching / crosshatching
Cucurbitaceae, 29
Cucurbita pepo, 161, 385
cylindrical forms
    branches, 74–75
    carrot, 66–67
    cylinders, 46, 220
    roots, 30, 226
    stems, 221–225
    twigs, 46, 73, 225
cyme, 27

D

daffodils, 14–15
Dahlia 'Groovy', 276, 278
daisy, 28
daisy-type flowers, 14, 15, 28
daylilies, 14–15
DePaulo, Dorothy
    artwork, 178
    studio, 23
    tutorial, 179–181
depth, establishing. *See also* three-dimensionality
    atmospheric perspective, 258–259, 393, 397
    fore, mid, and background elements, 305–311
    stipple / stippling, 112, 172
    tonal values, 247, 263, 357, 370
    using edges, 370
    watercolor techniques, 316
detritus, 17
diagonal patterns, 79, 83, 376, 391
Di Costanzo, Carrie
    artwork, 354, 383
    composition style, 382
    studio, 22
    tutorial, 355–357
disk flowers, 27, 28, 50, 51, 152
dividers, 50, 57–58, 60–61, 81
drawing. *See also* field sketching
    dissection drawings, 11

gestural, 19, 86, 92, 382
metalpoint, 359
transferring drawings, 192–194
working with geometric shapes, 49–51, 52–53, 63–65
drybrush techniques
    color mixing and blending, 241–247
    detailing, 203–204, 350–351
    glazing, 202, 281
    layering, 200–201, 272
    lines, 278–279

E

Echinacea stem, 14
Echinocactus grusonii, 110
ecological awareness, 11
edges, 370
eggplant, 163–164
egg tempera, 330–333
Emmons, Jean
    artwork, 266, 276
    studio, 24
    tutorial, 277–281
    watercolor palette, 190
Enokido, Akiko
    artwork, 283, 285, 287, 381
    tutorial, 282–288
ergonomics, 141
Eschscholzia californica, 134
etching
    chine-collé and hand-painting, 346
    ink plate technique, 340–343
    polymer plate technique, 345
Eucalyptus lehmannii, 326
Eulophia speciosa, 377

F

ferns, 31
fiddleheads, 31
field photography, 19
field sketching
    backcountry locations, 20
    drawing from, 107–110
    gathering specimens, 19
    materials and supplies, 18, 320
    sketchbooks / journals, 321–323
    studies, 19
    visual separations, 324
    wild plants, 16–20
filament, 26, 27, 176
Finnan, Ingrid, artwork, 318
Fisher, Susan T., tutorial, 183–189
Flavopunctelia flaventior, 348

Flora Graeca, 191

floribunda rose, 184, 210–211

flowering plants, botanical form and function, 26–27

flowering quince, 16

focal distance, 378, 392

focal points, 258, 259, 393

focus

    defined, 378

    of specific artworks, 301, 307, 385, 392, 393, 397

form, 378. *See also* shapes

forsythia, 16

Fragaria 'Lipstick', 90, 92

Freeman, Maria Cecilia

    artwork, 389

    composition style, 390

Fritillaria persica, 377, 380

fruit

    botanical form and function, 29–30

    depicting bloom, 235–237, 294–298

    scale in composition, 394

fruits and vegetables as subjects, 13

fungi, 30

G

Garber, Marilyn, tutorials, 136–137, 189–191

Gastinger, Lara Call

    artwork, 228

    tutorials, 227–229, 321–323

Gerberas, 14

German iris, 383

gesso, 366–367

gestural drawing, 19, 86, 92, 382

gladiolus / *Gladiolus*, 15, 28

glazing, 202, 310, 333, 337

glossy highlights, 59, 265, 284, 394

Gohlke, Monika de Vries

    artwork, 346–347

    hand-painting an etching, 346

Goltz, Howard, artwork, 76

gouache

    painting techniques, 335, 357

    properties, 335

    use with metalpoint, 360, 362

    use with watercolor, 349–353

gourd / gourd family, 29, 161–162

grapes, 76, 234–239

graphite

    cleaning up edges, 329

    continuous tone, 60, 62

    details in scientific illustrations, 128

    hatching / crosshatching, 87, 327, 363

    implying color with, 76

    layering, 76, 85–88, 327

    leaves, 56–62

    light and shadow on basic shapes, 44–47

    line control, 37–38, 38–39

    line weight techniques, 41–42

    making corrections, 103, 325

    pencil carriage, 37–38

    sharpening, 327

    stipple / stippling, 87

    techniques on vellum, 327–329

    textures, 87–88, 94

    tools, 36

    values, 43, 65–67

green wave parrot tulip, 318

grisaille, 148, 152, 162, 166, 167, 169–171

ground

    papers prepared with, 360

    use in etching, 340, 341, 343

    use in metalpoint, 360–362

ground litter, 249–250

ground view, 396

gynoecium, 26–27

H

habit, 28

habitat vignette, 395

Hamilton, Carol E., artwork, 372

Harris, Gillian, artwork, 324

hatching / crosshatching

    egg tempera, 332

    graphite, 87, 327, 363

    pen and ink, 102, 113

    watercolor on paper, 229, 263–264

    watercolor on vellum, 280, 315, 317

head (pseudanthium), 27, 28, 147, 148

Hedera canariensis, 285

Helleborus 'Penny's Pink', 258–259

highlights

    about, 370

    glossy, 59, 265, 284, 394

Hishiki, Asuka

    artwork, 260, 387

    composition style, 387

    tutorial, 261–265

Hoffenberg, Ann

    artwork, 57, 59, 61

    tutorial, 56–62

Hollender, Wendy

    artwork, 168

    tutorial, 167–171

hollyhock, 84, 86–90

hue, 136–137

hyacinth, 391

Hyacinthus orientalis, 391

Hyde-Johnson, Jenny
  artwork, 397
  composition style, 397
Hydrangea quercifolia, 287

I

Ilex opaca, 59
incising tool, 327, 328
Indian hemp, 344
Indian pipes, 306–311
inflorescences
  botanical form and function, 27–28
  colored pencil skills, 147–148, 151–152
  flat-headed bloomers, 28
  graphite skills, 85–89, 324
  parts (diagram), 27
  realistic depictions of, 377
in situ subjects, 10, 18–19, 20, 249–250, 395
invasive plants, 17
involucre, 27
irises, 14–15, 208–209, 383
Iris germanica, 383
Ishikawa, Mieko
  artwork, 21
  working in a backcountry location, 20

J

jack-in-the-pulpit, 338
James, Rose Marie, tutorial, 195–198
Japanese lilac tree sucker, 73
Jeannerot, Vincent, artwork, 31
Jess, Robin A.,
  artwork, 64, 66, 68, 70, 73, 74
  tutorial, 63–75
  working in a backcountry location, 20

K

Kalmia, 16
Kemp, Martha G.
  artwork, 90
  tutorial, 91–95
Kim, Heeyoung
  artwork, 40, 49, 52, 54
  tutorials, 36–47, 48–55
kiwi, 174–177
Klahne, Esther
  artwork, 306
  tutorial, 305–311
Kluglein, Karen
  artwork, 234, 388
  composition style, 388

  tutorial, 235–239
Koo, Jee-Yeon, artwork, 182
Kyer, Libby, tutorial, 139–145
  working in a backcountry location, 20

L

lamb's ear, 154–155
Latin binomial, 31
layered components, 258–259
layering
  colored pencils, 143–145, 175–177
  drybrush techniques, 200–201, 272
  graphite, 76, 85–88, 327
  watercolor on paper, 200–201, 215–218, 261–265
  watercolor on vellum, 272, 277–281, 294–298, 299–304, 315–316
leaves
  arrangement on stem, 28–29
  botanical form, 28–29
  colored pencils, 153–159
  dried, 289–293
  graphite, 56–62
  lobed, 28–29, 57–58, 213–217, 287–288
  sepiatone, 227–229
  simple lobed (palmate), 29, 57
  stripping from cut flowers, 14
  textures, 56–62, 153–159
  watercolor on vellum, 282–288, 289–293
leaves, specific types
  black gum, 156
  bur oak, 216–218
  camellia, 283
  chrysanthemum, 14
  elm, 228–229
  holly, 59
  hydrangea, 287–288
  ivy, 285–286
  lamb's ear, 154–155
  magnolia, 158–159
  oak hydrangea, 287–288
  silver maple, 213–215
  southern magnolia, 158–159
  sweet gum, 57
Lee, Katie
  artwork, 364
  tutorial, 365–367
Lepisanthes rubiginosa, 96
lichens, 30–31, 256, 348–353
life cycle composition, 174–177, 382, 384–385
life studies
  as basis of composition, 373–377
  Citrus limon 'Eureka', 375
  Eulophia speciosa, 477
  mid-project alterations, 374–377

three-birds orchids (*Triphora trianthaphora*), 376
    Vanilla planifolia, 374
lifting color, 215, 273–275, 293
light
    depicting reflected, 237, 265, 327
    effect on watercolor paints, 188, 189
light and dark contrasts, 378, 386
light and shadow
    cast shadows, 44, 65, 171, 207, 211, 255, 316
    on a cone and cup, 47
    conveying three-dimensionality, 46, 102, 120, 122
    on a cylinder, 46
    on a sphere, 44–45
light box, 23, 92, 120, 145, 213–218, 308
lightfastness ratings, 188
lilacs, 15
lilac tree sucker, 15, 73
Lilium philadelphicum, 16
Limnocharis sp., 124, 126–128, 131
line, defined, 378
Liquidambar styraciflua, 57
Lupo, Rogerio, artwork, 34
Lyness, Katy, artwork, 76

M

magnolia, 74–75, 158–159, 251–257
Magnolia grandiflora, 158–159
Magnolia ×soulangeana, 74–75, 252–258
mahogany seedpods, 382, 384
Malus domestica 'Gala', 204
Malus sylvestris, 178
Mammillaria grahamii, 396
Martin, Lucy
    artwork, 348
    tutorial, 349–353
masking fluid, 231–233, 253–254, 256, 261–265, 313–315
McEntee, Tammy
    artwork, 161, 163, 165
    tutorial, 160–166
McGann, Joan
    artwork, 110, 172–173, 396
    composition style, 396
    tutorial, 111–113
measuring
    relative dimensions, 56–58, 60–61, 65–66, 69
    scaling images, 123
    specimens, 86, 118, 165
    using dividers, 50, 57–58, 60–61, 81
    working with geometric shapes, 49–50, 52, 54–55, 81
meristems, 28
metalpoint, 359–362
milkweed, 395
milkweed seedpod, 40

milky sap, 15
Moir, Mali
    artwork, 386
    composition style, 386
Monotropa uniflora, 306, 307
Moses Harris Color Wheel, 137
mountain laurel, 16
movement
    in composition, 86, 392, 393, 395, 396
    defined, 378
    undulation, 147, 177, 218, 303, 357, 380, 394
mushrooms, 30–31, 266, 307, 309

N

nectarines, 394
negative space
    creating, 175–177, 382, 391–392, 394
    defined, 378
    effects, 75, 109, 385
Nemergut, Linda, artwork, 363
Nepenthes, 20
Nepenthes rajah, 21, 57
Newton, Isaac, on color, 189–190
Norman, Derek
    artwork, 106
    tutorials, 104–106, 107–110
Norway spruce, 354
Nugroho, Eunike, artwork, 134
Nymphaea odorata, 132
Nyssa sylvatica, 156–157

O

oak branch with lichens, 348
oak gall, 290–293
oils, 368–371
Orbea melanantha, 397
orchids
    composition, 376–377
    graphite skills, 54–55
    holding in place, 15
    pen and ink skills, 116–122
    Phalaenopsis orchid, 54
    roots, 30
    slipper orchid, 231–233
    South African orchid, 377
    species illustration, 114, 116–122
    three-birds orchids, 376
    vanilla orchid, 240, 242–247
ornamental strawberry, 90–95
ovary, 26, 27, 28, 29
ovuliferous scale, 386

P

Pacific Northwest mushrooms, 266
Paeonia suffruticosa, 182
Paphiopedilum ×sanderianum 'Screaming Eagles', 230
Parker, Hillary
  artwork, 385
  composition style, 385
pastel dust, 146–150
Pastoriza-Piñol, John
  artwork, 230
  tutorial, 231–233
  watercolor palette, 191
peach branches, 15–16
pedicel, 27, 132, 247
peduncle, 27, 40, 65, 88
Pellicano, Rose, artwork, 380
pen and ink
  basic inking techniques, 101–103
  colored pencil comparison to, 172–173
  continuous tone, 126
  dip pens, 104–105
  hatching / crosshatching, 102, 113
  inking paper, 98
  inks, 99
  line characteristics, 104–105
  shading, 102
  stipple / stippling, 101–102, 109, 111–113, 121–122,
    132, 172
  technical pens, 98
Persian lily, 380
persimmon, 295–298
perspective
  aerial, 112
  atmospheric perspective, 258, 393, 397
  in scientific illustration, 119
petals. *See also* corolla
  botanical form and function, 26–27
  drawing using geometric shapes, 49–55
  graphite skills, 42, 49–55, 86–88, 93
  painting approaches, 205–211
  plants with waxy, 15
  spiral patterns, 79
  textures, 208–209, 370
  using highlights, 370
  watercolor on paper, 205–211
  wet-on-wet color blending, 206–210
petunia, 149–150
Phalaenopsis orchid, 54
Phillips, Kandy Vermeer
  artwork, 358
  tutorial, 359–362
photographs
  compositional, 242, 245

field photography, 19
  supplemental, 13, 131
Picea abies, 354
Picea mariana, 32
picture plane, 19, 375, 378, 393, 395–396
Pima pineapple cactus, 172–173
pistil, 26, 27, 30, 379
Pitcher's thistle, 106
plant family, 31
plant parts, 26–31. *See also specific names of parts*
  botanical form and function, 26–30
  diagrams, 26, 27
  reproductive parts, 10, 379
plum branches, 15–16
Polypodium vulgare, 31
potato, 68–69, 300–304
printmaking technique, 346
proportion and scale
  enlarging subjects, 394
  scale, defined, 378
  scientific accuracy, 379
  scientific illustration, 123, 132
pseudanthium, 27, 28
pumpkin vine, 385
purple potato, 300–304
pussy willows, 16

Q

Quercus lobata, 290
Quercus macrocarpa, 216
quinacridones, 190, 191

R

raceme, 27, 380, 390
Radding, Kelly Leahy
  artwork, 78, 80, 82, 331, 334, 336
  tutorials, 77–84, 330–337
Rafflesia, 20
Ramalina leptocarpha, 348
Ramalina menziesii, 348
Rauh, Dick
  artwork, 32
  tutorial, 26–31
ray flowers, 27, 50, 151
receptacle, 27, 148
red buckeye, 346
Reiner, Jeanne
  artwork, 147, 149, 151
  tutorial, 146–152
resist effect, 145, 169, 170, 177
Rheum rhabarbarum 'Glaskins Perpetual', 393
rhododendrons, 16

rhubarb, 393

rhythm, 394, 398

Roche, Sarah, tutorial, 219–226

Rogers-Knox, Betsy
    artwork, 248, 395
    composition style, 395
    tutorial, 249–250

roots
    botanical form, 30
    colored pencil skills, 166
    in composition, 226, 247, 301, 390, 393, 397
    as cylindrical shapes
    metalpoint, 361–362
    watercolor on paper, 226, 247
    watercolor on vellum, 301–304

Rosa spithamea, 389

rose hips, 168, 331–337

roses
    cutting and holding in position, 16
    floribunda rose, 184, 210–211
    Rugosa, 223
    stems, 223
    watercolor on paper, 210–211, 223
    wet-on-wet techniques, 210–211

S

Sachs, Anita Walsmit, artwork, 96

samara, 30, 310

Sanders, Lizzie
    artwork, 240
    tutorial, 241–247

sap, milky, 15

Sayas, Constance
    artwork, 184, 206, 208, 210
    tutorial, 205–211

scale. *See* proportion and scale

Scanlon, Constance
    artwork, 312
    tutorial, 313–317

scientific accuracy, 379

scientific illustration
    artistic requirements, 379
    dissection drawings, 11, 118–119, 379
    drawing, 119–120
    fine art vs., 379
    fragment packet, 127
    goal of, 115
    graphite details, 128
    herbarium specimens, 125–127
    inking tools and technique, 121–122, 129–131
    new species description, 126
    pen and ink skills, 115–122
    perspective, 119

as representation of species characteristics, 116
    scaling images, 123
    size, 117
    study procedure, 116–119
    tools / materials, 116, 126–129
    work area, 126–128

scumbling, 143, 314, 333

Searle, Elaine
    artwork, 258–259, 393
    composition style, 393
    use of layered components, 258–259

seed dispersal, 395

seedpods, 40, 86, 382–384

sepal
    botanical form and function, 26, 27
    colored pencil skills, 164, 170
    graphite skills, 52–54, 93
    pen and ink skills, 121–122, 128
    synsepals, 232
    watercolor on paper, 223, 225, 245–246, 262, 264
    waxy, 15

sequoia cone, 80–81

shadow. *See* light and shadow

shallot, 165–166

shapes
    in composition, 378
    cone, 47
    cup, 47, 52–53
    cup-shaped fruiting bodies, 351–353
    cylindrical, 46, 66–67, 73–75, 219–226
    ellipses, 49–50, 94, 327
    geometric shapes in drawing, 49–51, 52–53, 64–65
    grid layout, 387
    light and shadow on, 44–47
    ovoid, 70–72
    rectangle, 49, 52, 54, 61, 323
    repetitive, 380
    sphere, 44–45, 64–65
    tonal values, 65–67, 69
    triangle, 52
    unusual, 68–69

Shaw, Deborah
    artwork, 290, 326
    tutorials, 289–293, 325–329

sheets
    expanded, 391
    gauging in advance, 380
    herbarium, 125
    strongly vertical, 390

silverpoint, 358, 363

Sir Isaac Newton's Color Wheel, 189

skunk cabbage, 19

snapdragons, 14

Snyder, Heidi, artwork, 138

Solanum melongena var. *esculentum* 'Ichiban', 163–164

Solanum tuberosum, 300

southern magnolia, 158–159

space, defined, 378. *See also* negative space

spathes, 15

specimens

  gathering wild, 19

  herbarium, 125–127

  types, 117

spiderwort, 104

spike, 27

spines and thorns, 111–113, 222–223

spiral patterns, 79, 81, 83

spruce branch, 32, 354–357

spruce cone, 354–357

squash, 70–72

Stachys byzantina, 154

stamens

  botanical form and function, 26, 27

  close-in view, 392

  colored pencil skills, 150

  graphite skills, 93

  removing, 15

stems

  adding motion, 380

  botanical form and function, 28

  colored pencil skills, 155, 157, 159, 170, 177

  in composition, 374, 377, 380, 390–395

  cutting, 14–16

  cylindrical forms, 46, 73, 221–225

  graphite skills, 49, 50, 85–86, 88, 93–94

  hairy, 224, 232

  leaf arrangement on, 28–29, 322, 367

  texture, 153–159, 224

  thorny, 222–223

  watercolor on paper, 202–203, 214, 215, 218, 219–225, 243–244

  watercolor on vellum, 287, 303

  woody, 15–16, 225

stereomicroscope, 127

stigma, 26, 27, 150, 316

stipple / stippling

  building up form, 337

  establishing depth, 112, 172

  graphite skills, 87

  pen and ink skills, 101–102, 109, 111–113, 121–122, 132, 172

  process, 132

  role in botanical illustration, 132

  textures, 101, 243

  watercolor on paper, 224, 243, 245, 246, 247

  watercolor on vellum, 293, 297, 317

strawberry, 90–95

style (plant part), 26, 27, 28, 152

subjects

  light sources for, 64, 370

selecting, 11

in situ, 10, 18–19, 20, 249–250, 395

sunflowers, 14, 15, 104

Swan, Ann

  artwork, 174, 394

  composition style, 394

  tutorial, 175–177

Swietenia mahagoni, 384

symmetry, 36, 48, 54, 61, 379

Symplocarpus foetidus, 19

T

Tacca chantrieri, 381

Tangerini, Alice

  artwork, 124

  tutorial, 125–131

tarnishing effects on color, 359

Tcherepnine, Jessica

  artwork, 384

  composition style, 382

Teloschistes chrysophthalmus, 348

textures

  colored pencil skills, 143, 146–150, 153–159

  defined, 378

  enriching with chine-collé, 346

  fuzzy, 88, 148, 256

  graphite skills, 87–88, 94

  hairy, 62, 94, 154–156, 176–177, 224

  hatching / crosshatching, 113

  leaf, 261–265

  scumbling, 314

  stipple / stippling, 56–62, 101, 153–159, 243

  of vellum surfaces, 327

  velvety, 149–150, 208–209

  watercolor on paper, 207, 224, 261–265

  watercolor on vellum, 282–288, 316

thorns and spines, 111–113, 222–223

three-birds orchids, 376

three-dimensionality. *See also* depth, establishing

  in composition, 258–259

  contrast, 378

  drybrush detailing, 203

  graphite skills, 46

  light and shadow, 46, 102, 120, 122

  pen and ink skills, 102, 120, 122

  watercolor on paper, 203, 222, 243

three pillars of botanical art / illustration, 379

Till, Carol

  artwork, 338, 344

  tutorials, 339–343

tint, defined, 136

Toberer, Melissa

  artwork, 84

tutorial, 85–89
tomato, 260–265
tone
    continuous, 60, 62, 126, 132, 142, 343
    defined, 137
    tonal values, 247, 328, 361, 370
toned drawing paper, 80
transferring drawings, 192–194
Trickey, Julia
    artwork, 392
    composition style, 392
tropicals as subjects, 15
tulip
    adding texture, 207
tulips
    graphite skills, 52–53
    Greigii tulip, 206–207
    parrot tulips, 318, 369
    preparing as subject, 14
    watercolor on paper, 206–207
    wet-on-wet color blending, 206–207
twig, 73

U

Ulmus sp., 228
umbel, 27, 28
undulation, 147, 177, 218, 303, 357, 380, 394
unity, 379, 388, 397
US Department of Agriculture plant database, 17

V

valley oak, 290
value
    creating three-dimensional form, 370
    diagramming, 65–67
    graphite skills, 43, 65–67, 88, 328–329
    lightening acrylics, 366
    stipple / stippling, 132, 172
    tonal, 328–329, 370
Vanilla imperialis, 240, 242–247
vanilla orchid, 240, 242–247
Vanilla planifolia, 374
vegetables and fruits as subjects, 13
vellum. *See also* watercolor on vellum
    cleaning, 270, 291, 327
    colors and surfaces, 268–269, 299
    defined, 269–270
    Kelmscott, 268, 299
    opportunities of colors and markings, 307
    painting on, 314
    response to atmospheric conditions, 291
Verbascum thapsus, 61

Viazmensky, Alexander, artwork, 30
Viburnum carlesii, 225
Viola sp., 358
volume, 101, 102, 121, 122, 172, 390

W

Walser-Kolar, Denise
    artwork, 295, 391
    composition style, 390
    tutorial, 294–298
washes
    charging, 198
    flat, 198
    graded, 197
    on paper, 195–198, 212–218, 231–233, 251–257
    on vellum, 279–280, 313–314
watercolor on paper
    drybrush techniques, 197, 200–204, 261–265
    hatching / crosshatching, 229, 263–264
    layering, 200–201, 215–218, 261–265
    sepiatone, 227–229
    stipple / stippling, 224, 243, 245, 246, 247
    textures, 207, 224, 261–265
    use with gouache, 349–353
    using masking fluid, 231–233, 253–254, 256, 261–265
    washes, 195–198, 212–218, 231–233, 251–257
    wet-on-wet techniques, 206–210
watercolor on vellum. *See also* vellum
    achieving deep color, 299–304
    basic techniques, 270–275
    brushstrokes, 271
    with graphite, 325–329
    hatching / crosshatching, 280, 315, 317
    layering, 272, 277–281, 294–298, 299–304, 315–316
    materials, 270
    opaque on dark vellum, 305–311
    stipple / stippling, 293, 297, 317
    textures, 282–288, 316
    using masking fluid, 313–315
    washes, 279–280, 313–314
watercolor palettes, 189–191
watercolor pencils, 145, 153, 155, 167–170, 186
watercolors
    changes in ingredients, 187
    flocculating color, 187
    labeling, 187, 188
    light, effect on, 188, 189
    lightfastness ratings, 188
    materials, 185
    as a medium, 183
    opacity and transparency, 186–187
    palette philosophies, 189–191
    pigment, 186

watercolors (*cont.*)

    pigment identification system, 187

    properties of, 184–189

    quinacridones, 190, 191

    techniques on vellum, 270–275

    toxicity, 188

water lily, 132

Watters, Catherine,

    artwork, 204

    tutorial, 199–204

Weller, Kerri

    artwork, 369

    tutorial, 368–371

wet-on-wet techniques, 206–211

Wilcox Split Primary Palette, 191

wildflowers, 248–250

wild plants

    alternative sources, 17–18

    backcountry locations, 20

    capturing in the field, 16–19

    conservation status, 17

    ethics of interaction with, 17

    field kits, 18

    guidelines for gathering, 17

    information-collecting methods, 18–19

    location status, 17

Winkel, Esmée

    artwork, 114

    tutorials, 97–105, 115–122

wisteria, 15

witch hazels, 15–16

Woodin, Carol

    artwork, 300, 374, 375, 377

    tutorials, 16–19, 192–194, 267–275, 299–304, 373–377

wood lily, 16

woody plants, 28

woody stems, 15–16, 225

X

Xanthoria parietina, 348

About the Editors

CAROL WOODIN has been a botanical artist for 30 years, and her work has been exhibited around the world. She is recipient of the 2018 ASBA James White Service Award, the 1998 ASBA Diane Bouchier Artist Award, the Orchid Digest Medal of Honor, and a Royal Horticultural Society gold medal. A past board member of the American Society of Botanical Artists, Carol has served as its director of exhibitions since 2004. In this role, she organizes and curates exhibitions that travel around the country. Her work has appeared in six of Dr. Shirley Sherwood's books, in *Curtis's Botanical Magazine*, in three Kew monographs, and in many other publications.

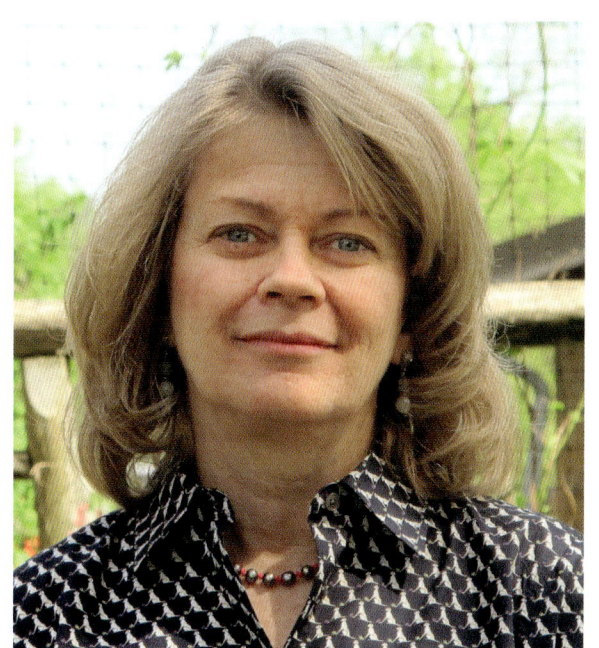

ROBIN A. JESS is coordinator of the Botanical Art and Illustration Certificate program at The New York Botanical Garden, where she began her career as an illustrator for Dr. Arthur Cronquist. She recently retired as the executive director of the American Society of Botanical Artists. Robin developed her love for art and botany at the University of Delaware and subsequently earned an MA from Pratt Institute. In 1990, the New Jersey State Council on the Arts awarded her a Distinguished Artist Fellowship. She began painting New Jersey's Pinelands flora, culminating in the traveling exhibition, *Protecting the Pinelands through Art*, funded by the Geraldine R. Dodge Foundation.

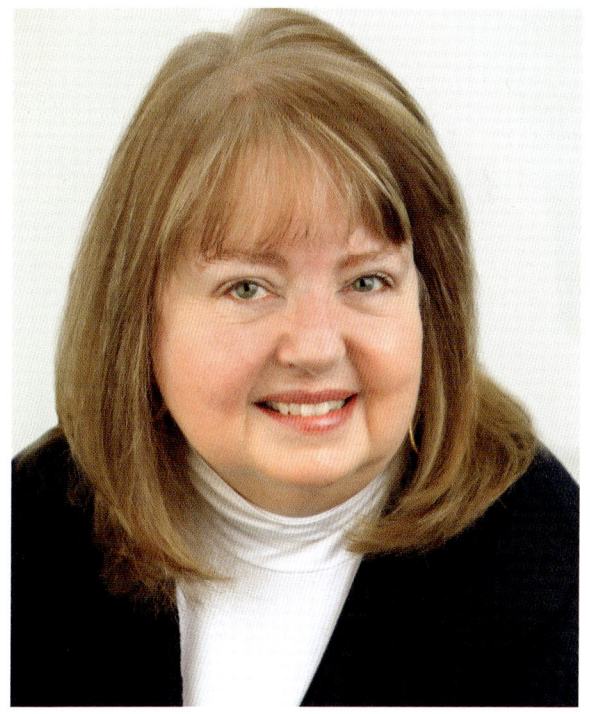